Truths We Confess

Truths We Confess

A SYSTEMATIC EXPOSITION

of the

WESTMINSTER CONFESSION OF FAITH

Revised Edition

●

R.C. Sproul

 LIGONIER MINISTRIES

Truths We Confess: A Systematic Exposition of the Westminster Confession of Faith; Revised Edition

© 2019 by R.C. Sproul

Published by Ligonier Ministries
421 Ligonier Court, Sanford, FL 32771
Ligonier.org

Printed in China
RR Donnelley
0000324
First edition, seventh printing

ISBN 978-1-64289-162-1 (Hardcover)
ISBN 978-1-64289-163-8 (ePub)

Cover design: Ligonier Creative
Interior design and typeset: Katherine Lloyd, The DESK

Unless otherwise noted, Scripture quotations are from the ESV® Bible (The Holy Bible, English Standard Version®), copyright © 2001 by Crossway, a publishing ministry of Good News Publishers. Used by permission. All rights reserved.

Scripture quotations marked KJV are from the King James Version. Public domain.

The Westminster Confession of Faith, Westminster Shorter Catechism, and Westminster Larger Catechism are from *The Confession of Faith and Catechisms: The Westminster Confession of Faith and Catechisms as Adopted by the Orthodox Presbyterian Church; with Proof Texts* (Willow Grove, Pa.: Committee on Christian Education of the Orthodox Presbyterian Church, 2005). Used by permission.

The Library of Congress has cataloged the Reformation Trust edition as follows:

Names: Sproul, R. C. (Robert Charles), 1939-2017, author.

Title: Truths we confess : a systematic exposition of the Westminster Confession of faith / by R.C. Sproul.

Description: Revised edition. | Orlando : Reformation Trust, 2019. | Includes index.

Identifiers: LCCN 2018055747| ISBN 9781642891621 (hardcover) | ISBN 9781642891645 (kindle) | ISBN 9781642891638 (e-Pub)

Subjects: LCSH: Westminster Confession of Faith.

Classification: LCC BX9183.W473 S67 2019 | DDC 238/.5--dc23

CONTENTS

FOREWORD

It is a privilege indeed to sound a fanfare for Dr. R.C. Sproul's *Truths We Confess*. Although it is a large volume written by a learned theologian, and although it expounds a document that is now almost four hundred years old—in the words of the angel, "Fear not!" For here you will find "good news of great joy . . . for all the people." In these pages you will find a treasure trove of rich biblical instruction written in a style that is as accessible as it is pastoral.

There is a simple reason for this—it was written by R.C. Sproul.

Some four decades ago, a friend, recently returned from the United States, asked me if I had ever heard of R.C. Sproul, and he immediately added, "He is said to be the greatest communicator of Reformed theology in the world." You do not easily forget a statement like that.

Not long afterward, on first meeting and hearing R.C., and then during the decades that followed, I was frequently to experience the key words in my friend's simple statement: "theology," "Reformed," "communicator." All three were present in R.C.'s life and ministry to a very high degree and in an unusual unity.

Some individuals are marked by one or perhaps two of these characteristics; to be marked by all three is rare. But R.C.'s passion for the Holy One was expressed in his whole-souled commitment to and his remarkable ability to communicate the truth, power, and life-transforming wisdom of the theology that the Reformers and Puritans had mined from the pages of Scripture. He had sat at the feet of the master theologians for long hours and learned from them. But even more important than what he learned from Martin Luther, John Calvin, and Jonathan Edwards was his own encounter with the God of the Bible, who was their God, too. So, theology was never an armchair hobby for him. Instead, it was an essential ingredient in the flatten-you-on-your-face, life-changing, personal knowledge of the Lord who had revealed Himself to Moses and Isaiah, to Daniel and John.

In this sense, R.C. Sproul would not have been out of place in the gathering of ministers and others who assembled in Westminster Abbey in London in the early summer of 1643 in order to produce materials that would bring a greater sense of unity and cohesion to the Reformed churches in Europe. They began by revising the Church of England's Thirty-Nine Articles. They ended by producing a quite different series of documents altogether: two catechisms (which are conveniently printed as appendices to this volume), directories for church government and public worship, and their pièce de résistance, the Westminster Confession of Faith.

I rather suspect R.C. would have loved to have been part of the hard thinking, the vigorous debating, and the creating of bonds of fellowship after defending one's theological convictions that marked this several-years-long gathering. But more than that—as the labor that lies behind this volume indicates—he loved the product of their hard work. For these became for him, and for the ministry (Ligonier) and the church (Saint Andrew's Chapel) of which he was founder, the very stuff of life and ministry. Whether he was in the classroom as a professor of theology, in the pulpit as pastor of a large church, at conferences for ministers and laypeople, in front of the camera and behind the microphone, or writing books and creating a massive library of biblical and theological instruction, the Westminster Confession was the anatomy of everything he preached and taught. For that reason, few things will do you more good or set you on a safer path than to sit now at R.C.'s feet and read through his exposition of the great doctrines of the Christian faith.

I use the phrase "sit at his feet" deliberately, because you will soon realize that this is exactly what you feel you are doing. Indeed, if you ever had the privilege of hearing R.C. speak, I suspect that you, like me, will hear his voice virtually reading his own book to you. One of its characteristics is the sense it gives of having been written for just one person alone—for you. It may well be the next best thing to sitting on your own with R.C. and listening to him talk to you about the great doctrines of the Christian faith.

Truths We Confess is not an academic, technical discussion of an ancient document. Such works have their place and value. However, the

Westminster Confession of Faith was written not to be dissected by academics but to guide the church and to instruct Christians and help them grasp the structure of the gospel. It does for us what, sadly, is no longer done as a matter of course either in the church or in the educational system: it teaches us first principles, and it shows us how to think through everything in light of them. And the inclusion here of the two catechisms helps us see how these first principles are to be worked out in the context of a world that throws up all kinds of challenges to the Christian. Insofar as that is true, this is a book for every Christian home and family and one that will be especially valuable for younger Christians setting out on the way.

Two anecdotes will, I hope, underscore the worthwhileness of the commitment of time and energy you are making as you begin to read through these pages.

After a weekend away enjoyed by the young people in our church, I heard the following. On one of the evenings, when all the activities of the day were over, the youngsters were "chilling out" with one or two of the mothers who had accompanied them. They began to ask question after question—worldview questions, ethical questions, theological questions, Bible questions. One of the mothers patiently, succinctly, and impressively answered them all. Later, the second mother said to her: "That was amazing what you did there with the youngsters tonight! How did you know all these answers?" The first mother simply smiled and said, "Oh, they're all basically in the Shorter Catechism." She had grasped the doctrinal first principles and had learned to think about everything in light of them.

I feel confident that if you sit at R.C.'s feet in *Truths We Confess*, you will discover that you, too, understand the gospel more fully and are better equipped to live an intelligent and wise Christian life. Not only so, but whether you are a parent, a student, a neighbor, or a colleague at work, you will be all the more able to "make a defense to anyone who asks you for a reason for the hope that is in you" and to "do it with gentleness and respect" (1 Peter 3:15).

The second story may well make you smile—at least, it has that effect on me! Dr. Derek Thomas and I have enjoyed the privilege not only of being Ligonier Teaching Fellows together but of serving as ministers in the same congregation. One weekend, R.C. honored us by coming to teach and preach in our church. At the Sunday morning services, he preached on the person of Christ. As the members of the congregation left through the various exit doors, one of them greeted Dr. Thomas with the words, "About time somebody was teaching some theology in this church!"

The comment might have hurt—after all, we were both professors of systematic theology as well as pastors in the congregation! What had we been doing? But instead, we laughed together. Truth to tell, we had been teaching doctrine to the congregation—but apparently, we did not have the R.C. touch. In the world of popular communication of the great truths of the faith, he was the undoubted master. Thousands of people around the world—indeed, hundreds of thousands—have been introduced to thoughtful Christianity through him and have come to appreciate the Godness of God the Holy One through his ministry.

As you will discover in these pages, like all systematic theologians, R.C. loved little Latin phrases. Older writers used to distinguish between what they called *theologia viatorum* and *theologia gloriae*—the theology we understand as pilgrims on the way, and the theology we will understand only when we are in glory. R.C. went to be with the Lord on December 14, 2017, and now enjoys the *theologia gloriae*. But thankfully, he has left behind for our benefit and blessing this marvelous compendium of the *theologia viatorum*. And since we are still pilgrims on the way, it is exactly what we need. So, in words once famously heard by Augustine of Hippo, a theologian R.C. ranked among the greatest, *Tolle lege*—Take up this book, and read it!

—Dr. Sinclair B. Ferguson
Ligonier Ministries Teaching Fellow
Carnoustie, Scotland

PREFACE

For centuries, the church of Jesus Christ has found it necessary to confess its faith before the watching world. Confessions of our faith have come in the forms of brief creedal statements and larger, more comprehensive confessional documents. From the early days of the Apostles' Creed—which includes the opening statement "I believe," from the Latin *credo*—the church has shown its obedience to the command of our Lord not only to believe in our hearts but also to profess with our lips what we believe. Christianity is a religion with content. Its truths are central to the life and practice of the church.

It is necessary in every generation for the church to clarify its beliefs against constant attacks and distortions of her body of truth. Christianity is sometimes called a faith, the "Christian faith." In using the term *faith*, what is in view is the body of truths that the church affirms and puts her trust in and by which the content of Christianity is defined.

One of the most important confessions of faith ever penned, particularly in the English-speaking world, is the Westminster Confession of Faith. By the confession's own statements, no confession written by uninspired authors is to be taken as having supreme authority over the believer. Confessions cannot bind the conscience in the manner that the Word of God can and does. At the same time, though human confessions and creeds are penned by fallible people without the benefit of the inspiration of the Holy Spirit, the profound level of theological and biblical precision manifest in the Westminster Confession of Faith is awe-inspiring.

The Westminster Confession is the most precise and accurate summary of the content of biblical Christianity ever set forth in a creedal form. Creeds such as the Belgic Confession, the Heidelberg Catechism, and the Scots Confession should be highly regarded, but no historic confession surpasses in eloquence, grandeur, and theological accuracy the Westminster Confession of Faith.

Though by no means a political document, the confession was forged in the midst of political turmoil in England in the seventeenth century. England's Reformation did not have the most auspicious beginning, perhaps sparked less by theological conviction and more by Henry VIII's desire for a male heir and thus his split with the Roman Catholic Church over his freedom to divorce. From there, things only got worse, as a series of monarchs saw England flip from Protestant to Catholic and back again. Eventually, this gave rise to an unhappy medium, which in turn sparked the rise of the Puritan movement. The Puritans were committed Protestants who wanted to see the church purged of any influence from the Roman Catholic Church.

During the English Civil War, as King Charles I's tenuous grip on the English throne slipped, he called the Long Parliament, which in turn called the Westminster Assembly. Originally charged with revising the Thirty-Nine Articles, the confession of the Church of England, the assembly soon shifted focus to put together a whole new confession.

The end result was a well-balanced consensus document. There were heated debates on sundry issues, most notably church government. There was, however, a level of clarity and precision that the pastors and theologians who composed the document—known as divines—could be thankful for.

This exposition of the Westminster Confession of Faith is not written in a technical, academic way but is designed to be accessible to the lay reader. It is my hope that as people study the articles set forth in this confession, they will come to a deeper understanding of and greater love for the doctrines of grace so ably set forth by the Westminster divines. It is my prayer that the confession will drive us constantly to the Scriptures themselves for the confirmation of what is hereby professed.

Of the Holy Scripture

1. Although the light of nature, and the works of creation and providence do so far manifest the goodness, wisdom, and power of God, as to leave men unexcusable; yet are they not sufficient to give that knowledge of God, and of his will, which is necessary unto salvation. Therefore it pleased the Lord, at sundry times, and in divers manners, to reveal himself, and to declare that his will unto his church; and afterwards, for the better preserving and propagating of the truth, and for the more sure establishment and comfort of the church against the corruption of the flesh, and the malice of Satan and of the world, to commit the same wholly unto writing: which maketh the Holy Scripture to be most necessary; those former ways of God's revealing his will unto his people being now ceased.

2. Under the name of Holy Scripture, or the Word of God written, are now contained all the books of the Old and New Testaments, which are these:

Of the Old Testament:

Genesis	II Chronicles	Daniel
Exodus	Ezra	Hosea
Leviticus	Nehemiah	Joel
Numbers	Esther	Amos
Deuteronomy	Job	Obadiah
Joshua	Psalms	Jonah
Judges	Proverbs	Micah

Ruth	Ecclesiastes	Nahum
I Samuel	The Song of Songs	Habakkuk
II Samuel	Isaiah	Zephaniah
I Kings	Jeremiah	Haggai
II Kings	Lamentations	Zechariah
I Chronicles	Ezekiel	Malachi

Of the New Testament:

The Gospels	Galatians	The Epistle
according to	Ephesians	of James
Matthew	Philippians	The first and
Mark	Colossians	second Epistles
Luke	Thessalonians I	of Peter
John	Thessalonians II	The first, second,
The Acts of the	to Timothy I	and third Epistles
Apostles	to Timothy II	of John
Paul's Epistles	to Titus	The Epistle
to the Romans	to Philemon	of Jude
Corinthians I	The Epistle to	The Revelation
Corinthians II	the Hebrews	of John

All which are given by inspiration of God to be the rule of faith and life.

3. The books commonly called Apocrypha, not being of divine inspiration, are no part of the canon of the Scripture, and therefore are of no authority in the church of God, nor to be any otherwise approved, or made use of, than other human writings.

4. The authority of the Holy Scripture, for which it ought to be believed, and obeyed, dependeth not upon the testimony of any man, or church; but wholly upon God (who is truth itself) the author thereof: and therefore it is to be received, because it is the Word of God.

5. We may be moved and induced by the testimony of the church to an high and reverent esteem of the Holy Scripture. And the heavenliness of the matter, the efficacy of the doctrine, the majesty of the style, the

consent of all the parts, the scope of the whole (which is, to give all glory to God), the full discovery it makes of the only way of man's salvation, the many other incomparable excellencies, and the entire perfection thereof, are arguments whereby it doth abundantly evidence itself to be the Word of God: yet notwithstanding, our full persuasion and assurance of the infallible truth and divine authority thereof, is from the inward work of the Holy Spirit bearing witness by and with the Word in our hearts.

6. The whole counsel of God concerning all things necessary for his own glory, man's salvation, faith and life, is either expressly set down in Scripture, or by good and necessary consequence may be deduced from Scripture: unto which nothing at any time is to be added, whether by new revelations of the Spirit, or traditions of men. Nevertheless, we acknowledge the inward illumination of the Spirit of God to be necessary for the saving understanding of such things as are revealed in the Word: and that there are some circumstances concerning the worship of God, and government of the church, common to human actions and societies, which are to be ordered by the light of nature, and Christian prudence, according to the general rules of the Word, which are always to be observed.

7. All things in Scripture are not alike plain in themselves, nor alike clear unto all: yet those things which are necessary to be known, believed, and observed for salvation, are so clearly propounded, and opened in some place of Scripture or other, that not only the learned, but the unlearned, in a due use of the ordinary means, may attain unto a sufficient understanding of them.

8. The Old Testament in Hebrew (which was the native language of the people of God of old), and the New Testament in Greek (which, at the time of the writing of it, was most generally known to the nations), being immediately inspired by God, and, by his singular care and providence, kept pure in all ages, are therefore authentical; so as, in all controversies of religion, the church is finally to appeal unto them. But, because these original tongues are not known to all the people of God, who have right unto, and interest in the Scriptures, and are commanded, in the fear of God, to read and search them, therefore they are to be translated into the vulgar language of every nation unto which they come, that,

the Word of God dwelling plentifully in all, they may worship him in an acceptable manner; and, through patience and comfort of the Scriptures, may have hope.

9. The infallible rule of interpretation of Scripture is the Scripture itself: and therefore, when there is a question about the true and full sense of any Scripture (which is not manifold, but one), it must be searched and known by other places that speak more clearly.

10. The supreme judge by which all controversies of religion are to be determined, and all decrees of councils, opinions of ancient writers, doctrines of men, and private spirits, are to be examined, and in whose sentence we are to rest, can be no other but the Holy Spirit speaking in the Scripture.

The Westminster Confession of Faith is one of the most important Protestant confessions, for it gave substantial definition to Reformed theology in the seventeenth century. It is often compared to similar confessions of faith, such as the Belgic Confession, the Heidelberg Catechism, the Scots Confession, and the Thirty-Nine Articles.

There was an internal debate as to where to begin a study of Reformed theology: with the doctrine of God or with the doctrine of Scripture. It is significant that the Westminster divines began their confessional statement with sacred Scripture. They were concerned about two principles. One, which is at the very heart of Christianity, is the concept of divine revelation. Christianity is a revealed religion, constructed not on the basis of speculative philosophy but in response to what God Himself has made manifest. Second is the principle of *sola Scriptura*, developed by the Reformers. It acknowledges that the final authority in all matters of theology and in all controversies of faith and life is not the decrees or traditions of the church but sacred Scripture itself. The Westminster Confession affirms the central importance and sufficiency of Scripture—a Reformational concept.

1. Although the light of nature, and the works of creation and providence do so far manifest the goodness, wisdom, and power of God, as to leave men unexcusable; yet are they not sufficient to

give that knowledge of God, and of his will, which is necessary unto salvation. Therefore it pleased the Lord, at sundry times, and in divers manners, to reveal himself, and to declare that his will unto his church; and afterwards, for the better preserving and propagating of the truth, and for the more sure establishment and comfort of the church against the corruption of the flesh, and the malice of Satan and of the world, to commit the same wholly unto writing: which maketh the Holy Scripture to be most necessary; those former ways of God's revealing his will unto his people being now ceased.

The first sentence distinguishes between the divine revelation that is sufficient for salvation and the divine revelation that is not sufficient for salvation. **The light of nature** refers to Paul's teaching about general revelation (Rom. 1). Classic Reformed theology distinguishes between general (or natural) revelation and special revelation.

God's general revelation is His revelation of Himself principally through nature and also through history, through the ministry of His providence to His people, and through His works of creation. "The heavens declare the glory of God, and the sky above proclaims his handiwork" (Ps. 19:1). Paul teaches that all men, by nature, know something of the existence, character, power, and deity of God, because God so clearly manifests Himself in general revelation (Rom. 1:18–20).

God's general revelation can be either "immediate" or "mediate." *Immediate* means "direct, without any medium or intervening agency." Paul talks about God's revealing His law inwardly through the human heart, so that every person is born with a conscience (Rom. 2:14–15). God plants a sense of Himself immediately in the soul of His creatures. John Calvin calls this the *sensus divinitatis*, "the sense of the divine." As fallen creatures, we suppress the knowledge of right and wrong that God plants within us. But try as we may, we can never extinguish it. It is still present in the soul. That is immediate general revelation.

Mediate general revelation has to do with the way in which God manifests Himself through creation itself. Nature points beyond itself to its Maker and Creator. Paul speaks of mediate revelation when he says that the invisible things of God, even His eternal power and divine nature, are understood through the created order. That knowledge also is squelched, repressed, and unacknowledged by fallen creatures. The indictment of the whole human race is that while we know God by virtue of general revelation, we refuse to honor Him as God and are not grateful to Him (Rom. 1:20–21).

It is no wonder that the Westminster divines wrestled over whether to begin the confession with the doctrine of revelation or with the doctrine of God—the two are intimately tied together. God is not only a God who exists but also a God who speaks. Communication is essential to His being. This is why, in turn, natural revelation quickly turns to natural theology. God has revealed through nature not only His law, by placing that law in our hearts, but also His nature. Natural theology encompasses all that is knowable about God apart from special revelation. Paul describes this as "his eternal power and divine nature" (Rom. 1:20). We not only can but do know that the creation requires a Creator and that the Creator must be sovereign over His creation, both in terms of His authority and His power.

General revelation, unlike special revelation, comes to us through nature and is called general for two reasons. First, the audience is general; God gives knowledge of Himself universally, so that every human has this revelation, which is built into nature. Second, the content of general revelation gives us a knowledge of God in general. It reveals that He is eternal; it reveals His power, deity, and holiness. General revelation, however, does not disclose God's way of salvation. The stars do not reveal the ministry of Christ. In fact, general revelation reveals just enough knowledge of God to damn us, to render us without excuse. Christ came into a world that was already under the judgment of God because we had already rejected the Father. Revelation is general, then, in terms of both audience and content. Paul in Romans 1 explains that through creation we know enough about God and about ourselves to stand condemned before God. The word *general* here means that all men know this. The *revelation* includes the revelation of the wrath of God against us. Because of the depth of our sin, our response to the revelation of God is not gratitude and repentance but rebellion and suppression.

The term *special revelation* refers to the revelation of God inscripturated in the Bible. It is special in the same ways that general revelation is general: with respect to audience and content. There have been and still are many people who have never heard the stories of Abraham, Isaac, Jacob, Moses, David, or even Jesus. The Word of God has not yet gone everywhere. People are exposed to special revelation when someone tells it to them or when they read it in Scripture. The term *special* also describes the content of the revelation, for it opens up to us God's plan of salvation, specifically concerning the person and work of Christ.

Clearly in view in chapter 1 of the confession is the distinction between general and special revelation and between sufficiency and insufficiency in revelation. General revelation is not sufficient to give us the knowledge necessary for salvation; special revelation is sufficient for that purpose.

Some people attack the doctrine of the sufficiency of Scripture by pointing out that Scripture does not teach all that we need to know about everything. For example, we know nothing about the body's circulatory system from the Bible. But that is not what the doctrine of the sufficiency of Scripture means. This doctrine means that Scripture reveals what is necessary to know for salvation. It is not necessary to know about the circulatory system in order to understand what is needed to be saved, but we do need to know the gospel that is revealed in Scripture.

Therefore it pleased the Lord, at sundry times, and in divers manners, to reveal himself, and to declare that his will unto his church; and afterwards, for the better preserving and propagating of the truth, and for the more sure establishment and comfort of the church against the corruption of the flesh, and the malice of Satan and of the world, to commit the same wholly unto writing. God, who "at many times and in many ways" revealed Himself "long ago," has now in these last days given us the culmination of His revelation in the person of His Son, Jesus Christ (Heb. 1:1–2). The confession echoes the teaching of Scripture that God has, in various ways, revealed Himself in the past. But now, for the better preserving and propagating of the truth, and for the more sure establishment and comfort of the church against the corruption of the flesh, and the malice of Satan and of the world, God has committed His revelation wholly unto writing. In the early days of the Apostolic church, the life and teachings of Christ had not yet been set down in writing. This information was transmitted orally from person to person. But it pleased God, in His providence, to have that special revelation inscripturated, or put into written form. For this redemptive purpose we have the Bible.

Which maketh the Holy Scripture to be most necessary; those former ways of God's revealing his will unto his people being now ceased. Scripture is necessary for our comfort and strength. Having been written in final form, it supersedes the various ways in which God revealed Himself in former days. God formerly revealed Himself through the Urim and Thummim, through the prophets, through dreams, and in other ways. The confession points out that the culmination of revelation has been preserved for us in Holy Scripture, and that God's special revelation, having been inscripturated, no longer continues.

2. Under the name of Holy Scripture, or the Word of God written, are now contained all the books of the Old and New Testaments, which are these:

Of the Old Testament:

Genesis	II Chronicles	Daniel
Exodus	Ezra	Hosea
Leviticus	Nehemiah	Joel
Numbers	Esther	Amos
Deuteronomy	Job	Obadiah
Joshua	Psalms	Jonah
Judges	Proverbs	Micah
Ruth	Ecclesiastes	Nahum
I Samuel	The Song of Songs	Habakkuk
II Samuel	Isaiah	Zephaniah
I Kings	Jeremiah	Haggai
II Kings	Lamentations	Zechariah
I Chronicles	Ezekiel	Malachi

Of the New Testament:

The Gospels	Galatians	The Epistle
according to	Ephesians	of James
Matthew	Philippians	The first and
Mark	Colossians	second Epistles
Luke	Thessalonians I	of Peter
John	Thessalonians II	The first, second,
The Acts of the	to Timothy I	and third Epistles
Apostles	to Timothy II	of John
Paul's Epistles	to Titus	The Epistle
to the Romans	to Philemon	of Jude
Corinthians I	The Epistle to	The Revelation
Corinthians II	the Hebrews	of John

All which are given by inspiration of God to be the rule of faith and life.

An ongoing controversy exists concerning which books should be included in the canon of Scripture, especially the books known as the Apocrypha. The apocryphal books were written primarily during the intertestamental period, between the end of the Old Testament canon (the book of Malachi) and the opening of the New Testament. The Roman Catholic Church holds to the canonical status of the Apocrypha, while for the most part Protestant bodies do not. These books are recognized as interesting historical sources of a secondary level but lacking the authority of Scripture itself.

There is also debate over the extent of the Jewish canon. The New Testament refers back to the Old Testament. Paul wrote to Timothy, for example, that "all Scripture is breathed out by God" (2 Tim. 3:16). Paul was referring to a body of literature that was well known to Timothy and every pious Jew. What were the sacred Scriptures of the Jews?

The great library of Alexandria, where Philo and others worked, was a cultural center for Hellenistic (Greek-speaking) Jews. The canon of the Alexandrian Jews included the Apocrypha. Historical evidence indicates that the Palestinian canon, used by the Jews in Israel, did not contain the

Apocrypha. From the Reformers' perspective, the original Jewish canon was the Palestinian canon, not the Alexandrian canon. Interestingly enough, in the later twentieth century, some evidence emerged to indicate that even among the Alexandrian Jews the Apocrypha was accorded only deuterocanonical (secondary-level) status. More and more, the evidence seems to confirm the Protestant conclusion that the original books of sacred Scripture were the sixty-six books currently in the Protestant Bible. Section 2 ends with this comprehensive statement: **All which are given by inspiration of God to be the rule of faith and life.**

> 3. The books commonly called Apocrypha, not being of divine inspiration, are no part of the canon of the Scripture, and therefore are of no authority in the church of God, nor to be any otherwise approved, or made use of, than other human writings.

Although the Apocrypha are not part of the canon of the Scripture, these books need not be completely ignored or discarded. We do not throw away the letters of Clement, Ignatius, or other church fathers, which are of historical interest. The confession makes the point only that the books of the Apocrypha are not inspired and therefore do not belong in the canon.

The idea of inspiration finds its root in the teaching of the Apostle Paul, who wrote, "All Scripture is breathed out by God and profitable for teaching, for reproof, for correction, and for training in righteousness" (2 Tim. 3:16). The King James and other versions of the Bible say the Bible is "given by inspiration," which translates the Greek word *theopneustos*—a combination of *theos*, meaning "God," and *pneō*, meaning "to breathe, blow"—which literally means "God-breathed." Paul is saying that sacred Scripture is God-breathed.

In both Roman Catholic and Protestant circles, the theory of inspiration is that, though the documents of sacred Scripture were written by human authors, they were not merely recording their own opinions or recollections. They were performing their task as agents of revelation under the superintendence of the Holy Spirit. The human authors were given the ability to write just what God wanted to be written. The authority of their words was not their own but God's authority. We do not know how the Holy Spirit inspired them. We do know that the writers were not reduced to automatons, with God moving their hands. The books of the Bible are clearly written in different styles, with different vocabularies and grammatical structures. When we contrast the writings of Paul with those of John or Peter or Jeremiah, we see their different styles. God obviously worked through their individual styles and mannerisms. The doctrine of inspiration, as mysterious as it is, declares that while humans were writing, God the Holy Spirit ensured that what they wrote was without error and was actually *verbum Dei*, the Word of God itself.

When Paul says that all Scripture is inspired, or God-breathed, he is technically saying that Scripture is breathed out of the mouth of God, where it originates. The term *breathing in* refers to the secret operation of the Holy Spirit by which He produces the Word of God from the word of men, yet without human invention. The accent is on its origin and consequently its authority. All Scripture, Paul says, is breathed out by God, and is nothing less than the Word of God, which has binding authority upon us.

> 4. The authority of the Holy Scripture, for which it ought to be believed, and obeyed, dependeth not upon the testimony of any man, or church; but wholly upon God (who is truth itself) the author thereof: and therefore it is to be received, because it is the Word of God.

Here we read a phrase that is important to Protestantism: the authority of the Holy Scripture, for which it ought to be believed. The confession asserts that the Bible's authority is so strong, so supreme, that it imposes on us a moral obligation to believe it. If we do not believe it, we have sinned. It is not so much an intellectual as a moral issue.

If the Lord God Almighty opens His mouth, there is no room for debate and no excuse for unbelief. It is the Word of God, and everyone is duty-bound to submit to its authority.

Satan beguiled Eve with the question, "Did God actually say . . . ?" (Gen. 3:1), calling God's authority into question. When Satan tempted Jesus in the wilderness, all three temptations centered on whether Christ would trust and live by every word that proceeds from the mouth of God (Matt. 4:1–11). Throughout church history, the supreme attack of the world, the flesh, and the devil against godliness has been an attack on the authority of God's Word. Fierce assaults on the authority of Scripture, which came out of the Enlightenment, made their way into the universities and seminaries. They also came from within the church, in the name of biblical criticism or higher criticism.

At the end of the nineteenth century and the beginning of the twentieth, Abraham Kuyper, prime minister of the Netherlands and founder of the Free University of Amsterdam, observed that biblical criticism had become biblical vandalism. No treasure has been more subject to malicious attack than Scripture itself.

Section 4 is a concise and theologically precise statement. The Westminster divines used the word received purposely. In the controversy with the Roman Catholic Church, then and now, the question is this: Does final authority reside in the church or in the Bible? This is what *sola Scriptura* was all about in the sixteenth century. Rome strongly contended that the Bible gets its authority from the church. Martin Luther, Calvin, and the other Reformers debated this regularly in the sixteenth century. The Westminster divines studied the early centuries of church history to arrive at the word received.

When the early church settled on the books of the canon, it spoke of receiving these books as canonical. They did not declare the books of the Bible to be the books of the Bible, as if the Bible's authority were dependent on them. They said *recipimus*, Latin for "we receive." The church fathers were humbly recognizing the authority of these books, not presuming to give them authority, when they stated, "We receive these Apostolic writings as the sacred Scriptures, as the authoritative Word of God." The church did not need to declare this truth in order for it to be so. The church no more gave the Bible its authority than the individual gives Christ His authority by embracing Him as Lord. He is Lord—we are simply called to recognize it. The authority of Scripture does not depend on the testimony of any man or of the church; its authority depends and rests wholly on God, the supreme author of the Bible. Scripture should be received, not so that it can become the Word of God, but because it already is the Word of God.

This wording and principle proved to be prophetic with the rise of Neoorthodoxy in the twentieth century. Neoorthodox theology argues not that the Bible is the Word of God (accusing the historical view of "bibliolatry") but that as we encounter the Bible, it "becomes" the Word of God. It is only in this existential encounter that God speaks, according to this view. The Bible is not itself revelation but is only a witness to revelation. The divines affirmed the very opposite—that the Bible is God's Word from beginning to end, whatever we may do with it.

5. We may be moved and induced by the testimony of the church to an high and reverent esteem of the Holy Scripture. And the heavenliness of the matter, the efficacy of the doctrine, the majesty of the style, the consent of all the parts, the scope of the whole (which is, to give all glory to God), the full discovery it makes of the only way of man's salvation, the many other incomparable excellencies, and the entire perfection thereof, are arguments whereby it doth abundantly evidence itself to be the Word of God: yet notwithstanding, our full persuasion and assurance of the infallible truth and divine authority thereof, is from the inward work of the Holy Spirit bearing witness by and with the Word in our hearts.

This section introduces a concept that was central to the teaching of John Calvin. The ideas in his famous *Institutes of the Christian Religion* are brought almost verbatim into the Westminster Confession at this point. This concept is what we call the internal testimony of the Holy Spirit.

Previously, the confession stated that Scripture's authority comes from God, not from any man or from the church. Section 5 now acknowledges that, though Scripture does not receive its authority from the church, we are to respect the testimony and teaching of the church. The Reformers, though denying tradition as a source of truth equal to the Scriptures, nevertheless esteemed the teaching office of the church through the ages. Apart from the Bible, the source most quoted by Calvin was Augustine. Luther also quoted Augustine frequently, as well as other church fathers. Church councils and gifted teachers have had great insight and are to be taken seriously.

We may be moved and induced by the testimony of the church to an high and reverent esteem of the Holy Scripture. In our day and age, even within the church, we often find anything but a high view of sacred

Scripture. Throughout church history, however, virtually every confession of faith, whether Roman Catholic, Lutheran, Presbyterian, or something else, has strongly affirmed Scripture's divine authority. The confession says that the testimony of the church may influence us to hold Scripture in high esteem.

In his *Institutes*, Calvin wrote of the internal indicators or evidence that the Bible is the word of God, sometimes called the *autopistae*, "the self-authentication of Scripture." When one immerses oneself in sacred Scripture, one encounters certain ideas that are most impressive and that bear witness to its divine source. Calvin called this the *indicia*, "the evidences." They ought to be sufficient to prove to every human being that the Bible is the Word of God. Human reason is such, however, that these indicators or internal evidences do not give people a full measure of confidence that the Bible is the Word of God.

Calvin then distinguished between proof and persuasion. The proof is objective; the evidence leaves no room for reasonable doubt. But people may refuse to accept that evidence because they have a strong bias against what it affirms. Scripture's portrait of the fallen character of the human race reveals that, by nature, we do not want God in our thinking, preferring darkness to light. Paul explains in Romans 1 that because we have rejected His revelation, God has given us over to reprobate minds, darkened by unbelief.

The fall is so deep, and its impact on the mind is so strong, that the best reasoning one human can offer for the Bible's truth will not convince another, no matter how sound, valid, and compelling it may be. The confession lists various aspects of the internal evidence of Scripture.

And the heavenliness of the matter. C.S. Lewis, who immersed himself in the great literature of Western civilization, once observed that he could not read Scripture without recognizing a transcendent quality missing from all other literature. I was trained in philosophy to take nothing for granted and to analyze critically the affirmations and assertions in every document. But I found when reading Scripture that in a very real sense I, rather than the text, was the object of criticism. The Bible was criticizing me more than I was able to criticize it. One is confronted with the heavenliness of the matter.

Thomas Watson gets at the divine quality of the Bible in His *Body of Divinity*, where he writes:

> The Scripture appears to be the Word of God, by the matter contained in it. The mystery of Scripture is so abstruse and profound that no man or angel could have known it, had it not been divinely revealed. That eternity should be born; that He who thunders in the heavens should cry in the cradle; that He who rules the stars should suck the breasts; that the Prince of Life should die; that the Lord of Glory should be put to shame; that sin should be punished to the full, yet pardoned to the full; who could ever have conceived of such a mystery, had not the Scripture revealed it to us? So, for the doctrine of the resurrection; that the same body which is crumbled into a thousand pieces, should rise *idem numero*, the same individual body, else it were a creation, not a resurrection. How could such a sacred riddle, above all human disquisition, be known, had not the Scripture made a discovery of it? As the matter of Scripture is so full of goodness, justice and sanctity, that it could be breathed from none but God; so the holiness of it shows it to be of God.

The efficacy of the doctrine. This phrase reminds us of Paul's statement to Timothy that "all Scripture is breathed out by God and profitable for teaching, for reproof, for correction, and for training in righteousness, that the man of God may be complete, equipped for every good work" (2 Tim. 3:16–17). The doctrine found in Scripture is effective and powerful. The Apostle Paul further writes that the power is of God for salvation (Rom. 1:16) and is not found in the eloquence or knowledge of the preacher. The power of God for salvation is in the message. The doctrine of the gospel has impact and is efficient and effective; thus, we speak of the efficacy of the doctrine.

The majesty of the style, the consent of all the parts. Is that not an interesting affirmation to make in the seventeenth century? When the Enlightenment philosophers laid an ax to the root of the tree of biblical authority, they intended to chop down all the alleged inconsistencies and contradictions. Even in light of the higher criticism to which I was exposed in my academic background, I have been most impressed by

Scripture's incredible symmetry. The most infinitesimal details in Jeremiah and Ezekiel fit together so perfectly with what was proclaimed centuries later by James, John, and Paul. This harmony of Scripture is a beautiful melding and merging together in a unified proclamation of truth. This confession, like other Protestant and Roman Catholic confessions, cites the unity and coherence of Scripture (the consent of all the parts) as a testimony to its divine origin.

The scope of the whole (which is, to give all glory to God), the full discovery it makes of the only way of man's salvation, the many other incomparable excellencies, and the entire perfection thereof, are arguments whereby it doth abundantly evidence itself to be the Word of God. The arguments (indicators, internal evidences) do not just hint at the divine origin of Scripture but abundantly affirm it. Calvin would say that the *indicia*, the evidence, is so abundant that it should stop the mouth of every skeptic. But this phrase from the confession ends with a colon.

Yet notwithstanding, our full persuasion and assurance of the infallible truth and divine authority thereof, is from the inward work of the Holy Spirit bearing witness by and with the Word in our hearts. This is the doctrine of the internal testimony. A person will not be fully persuaded or assured that the Bible is the Word of God unless and until God the Holy Spirit does a work in his heart, which is called the internal testimony of the Spirit.

This could sound like a defense of Scripture that is sheer subjectivism. If an appeal for truth is based on some inner light such as "The Holy Spirit spoke to me" or "I had this intense feeling," this cannot be tested objectively and either verified or falsified. The unspoken argument for flight into subjectivism is "It's true because I believe it." This formula assumes that anything I believe must, in fact, be the truth. It is in effect a claim of personal infallibility. This is not what the doctrine of internal testimony teaches.

The Spirit's internal testimony does not give the believer private, esoteric knowledge or information that is unavailable to anyone else. In fact, this testimony communicates no new content. Rather, the Holy Spirit works on our obstinate will to overcome our natural antipathy toward the Word of God. In simple terms, the Spirit melts our hearts so that we are willing to surrender to the objective truth that is there. Calvin used the word *acquiesce*, "to submit or surrender to." Calvin said that the Spirit causes us to acquiesce in the *indicia*.

In a watershed sermon early in his ministry called "A Divine and Supernatural Light," Jonathan Edwards preached about the Spirit's work of changing the obstinate, recalcitrant hearts of sinners by inwardly changing the disposition of their souls. That is what the confession is talking about here: God melts our hearts and makes us fully persuaded and assured of Scripture's infallible truth and divine authority.

Is from the inward work of the Holy Spirit bearing witness by and with the Word in our hearts. The Reformers strongly believed in the importance of the ministry and operation of God the Holy Spirit. Calvin was called the theologian of the Holy Spirit. Yet the Reformers were clearly distinct from the radical spiritualists, who sought private revelations from God beyond the content of sacred Scripture. Around us today are people claiming new revelation, which may or may not conform to the Word of God. I have encountered people who took actions that were clearly opposed to the teaching of Scripture. They claimed that when they prayed about it, the Lord told them it was fine. The Holy Spirit does not speak with a forked tongue. He never grants us the right to disobey what His inspired Scriptures instruct us regarding our duty. The Spirit works with and through the Word, never apart from or against it.

6. The whole counsel of God concerning all things necessary for his own glory, man's salvation, faith and life, is either expressly set down in Scripture, or by good and necessary consequence may be deduced from Scripture: unto which nothing at any time is to be added, whether by new revelations of the Spirit, or traditions of men. Nevertheless, we acknowledge the inward illumination of the Spirit of God to be necessary for the saving understanding of such things as are revealed in the Word: and that there are some circumstances concerning the worship of God, and government of the church, common to human actions and societies, which are to be ordered by the light of nature, and Christian prudence, according to the general rules of the Word, which are always to be observed.

We see here an affirmation of the sufficiency of Scripture with respect to the whole counsel of God, a phrase that is sometimes used in the church in a cavalier manner. Pastors are enjoined to preach the whole counsel of God—not just the part they like, not just what is comfortable or what the people in the pew want to hear, but the whole counsel of God. In preaching through a book of the Bible, staying with the text, a pastor has to preach whatever comes next. Sometimes I look at what's next and think, "Oh, my, this is a church-emptier."

One text in John, for example, unavoidably, plainly, and clearly teaches the doctrine of definite atonement, which is probably the single most unpopular concept of historic Reformed theology. This text teaches that Christ died specifically for the elect and only for the elect. From all eternity, God had a plan to save some, and to accomplish that plan He sent His Son into the world. God gave to His Son a certain number of people, and Christ laid down His life for them. The atonement is efficacious only for those whom the Father gives to the Son. That text (John 6:35–40) is very unpopular because contemporary evangelicalism assumes that Christ died for everyone's sins. The text teaches that Christ died only for believers, and the only ones who believe are the elect. Atonement was not made for the sins of unbelievers. Had their sins been atoned for, God would be unjust to punish them. This is a very difficult doctrine, one over which people often stumble. A preacher's mandate, however, is to be faithful to the text and to the whole counsel of God. Since this text is part of the whole counsel of God, there is no choice but to proclaim it.

Concerning all things necessary for his own glory. That is the *soli Deo gloria* of the Reformation. What we do will be measured by how faithfully we have manifested the glory of God and exalted him.

The whole counsel of God concerning all things necessary for his own glory, man's salvation, faith and life, is either expressly set down in Scripture, or by good and necessary consequence may be deduced from Scripture. Some believe that logic is the enemy of Christianity, an intrusion into spiritual things derived from Aristotle and Greek thinking. In my experience, however, the vast majority of errors in biblical interpretation occur because a person is not using logic properly, not deducing by good and necessary consequence. The whole counsel of God is known not only by what Scripture teaches explicitly but also by what it teaches implicitly, which can be learned by clear and necessary deduction. If God calls us to honor our fathers and mothers, does He not also call us, by good and necessary consequence, not to dishonor them? When the law prohibits something, it implicitly, by good and necessary consequence, commands the opposite.

The divines were careful to affirm not that we are free to add whatever we think *might* be a consequence of what the Scripture says but only that which is necessary. Every truth brings with it implications that may follow, and inferences that must follow. It is vital that we remember that distinction and only hold one another to that which *must* follow.

The Reformers knew that once the church's authority as the supreme interpreter of the Bible was set aside in favor of the individual's right to "private interpretation," a floodgate would be opened. It is not enough simply to agree that the Bible is the supreme authority. One must determine what that authority teaches and requires. In its fourth session, the Council of Trent decided that no man has the right to distort the Scriptures by private interpretation. With the right and privilege of private interpretation always comes the burden of responsibility for correct interpretation. For this reason, the Westminster Confession says that all deductions are to be by good and necessary consequence. Interpretations can be tested objectively to determine whether they comply with what the Bible actually teaches.

Unto which nothing at any time is to be added, whether by new revelations of the Spirit, or traditions of men. The canon of Scripture is closed in the sense that it cannot be amplified or added to by church tradition or private revelation. We have inscripturated divine revelation to govern the life of the Christian and the church.

Nevertheless, we acknowledge the inward illumination of the Spirit of God to be necessary for the saving understanding of such things as are revealed in the Word. Some charismatics believe that they receive new revelation—revelation not found in Scripture. Reformed theology declares that there is no new revelation. This is not to deny new activity by the Holy Spirit, for there is a sharp distinction between revelation and illumination. In revelation, the Spirit works to reveal divine content as is found in the Bible. Therefore, when Paul wrote Romans, it was inscripturated divine revelation.

How do we penetrate the meaning of Scripture? Paul wrote:

> But, as it is written, "What no eye has seen, nor ear heard, nor the heart of man imagined, what God has prepared for those who love him"—these things God has revealed to us through the Spirit. For the Spirit searches everything, even the depths of God. For who knows a person's thoughts except the spirit of that person, which is in him? So also no one comprehends the thoughts of God except the Spirit of God. (1 Cor. 2:9–11)

Paul is speaking here not only of revelation but also of illumination. The Holy Spirit is not a seeker. When Paul uses the metaphor of the Spirit's searching, he means not that the Spirit is searching the truth of God for Himself but that the Spirit is putting a searchlight on the Word of God for us.

As we read and study Scripture, the Spirit opens our eyes, not to add anything to what is already there, but to clarify what is there and to apply it to our lives. Reformed theology does not deny the importance of divine illumination, in which the Spirit casts light on the content that He revealed through Apostles and prophets. He helps our infirmities, counteracts our biases and fallenness, and convinces us of the truth through His work of illumination. We acknowledge the illumination of the Spirit to be necessary for the saving understanding of such things as are revealed in the Word.

Nevertheless, we acknowledge the inward illumination of the Spirit of God to be necessary for the saving understanding of such things as are revealed in the Word: and that there are some circumstances concerning the worship of God, and government of the church, common to human actions and societies, which are to be ordered by the light of nature, and Christian prudence, according to the general rules of the Word, which are always to be observed. This qualifying section elucidates the previous sentence. The confession acknowledges another source of revelation, which we touched on in section 1: general revelation, God's revelation of Himself in and through nature.

Is general revelation infallible? Some reply that infallibility belongs only to special revelation, the Bible, because it is revelation from God, who cannot fail or err. If His special revelation is infallible because He is infallible, however, would it not follow that His general revelation is also infallible? The church of all ages has answered yes. We tend to think that, while special revelation is infallible, general revelation in nature is not, so science and intellectual inquiry may be mistaken. Scientists may err when they interpret the data of nature, but their imperfect interpretations do not vitiate general revelation itself. Just as theologians can distort biblical revelation, so scientists can distort general revelation. We sometimes assume that the theologian is right and the scientist is wrong, or the converse. The confession acknowledges that the church learns things not only from the Bible but also from nature: **there are some circumstances concerning the worship of God, and government of the church, common to human actions and societies, which are to be ordered by the light of nature, and Christian prudence.**

Christian prudence refers to wisdom. For example, in some denominations, when deliberations take place at the session, presbytery, or general assembly, they follow Robert's Rules of Order. These rules for discussion, debate, and hearings are not found in the Bible, but they are broadly used in church life because they have stood the test of time. This is an example of general, natural law that has emerged. We talk about the *jus gentium*, the "law of nations." Virtually every nation in the world follows certain bedrock principles of ethics, to which the church also pays attention. We call this the *lex naturalis*, the "natural law," which, though not specifically spelled out in Scripture, may be examined and known from a study of the church's corporate activity throughout history. This may benefit church life because it reflects Christian prudence. We might subsume this idea under the concept of tradition. From a biblical perspective, human tradition must never be elevated to a position above the law of God, supplanting that law or binding the consciences of people. But tradition can be a valuable purveyor of the church's cumulative wisdom. Even though tradition is not infallible, we would be foolish to ignore this corporate wisdom. Paul enjoined the Thessalonians not to forget the apostolic tradition they had received (2 Thess. 2:15). The "traditions" we have received are not the same as the Bible. But they can be, and in fact are, important while subsidiary. Whether it is the Westminster Confession or the Apostles' Creed, we need to be slow to jettison that which has been handed down to us. Is it possible the Apostles' Creed disagrees with the Bible? Yes. Is it likely? No.

> 7. All things in Scripture are not alike plain in themselves, nor alike clear unto all: yet those things which are necessary to be known, believed, and observed for salvation, are so clearly propounded, and opened in some place of Scripture or other, that not only the learned, but the unlearned, in a due use of the ordinary means, may attain unto a sufficient understanding of them.

The propriety of private interpretation was hotly debated during the sixteenth century. The Roman Catholic Church had taken the position (and reinforced it in the fourth session of the Council of Trent) that scriptural interpretation belongs to the teaching office of the church, and that no one has the right to interpret Scripture in a way contrary to the interpretation of Holy Mother Church. Luther, however, argued for the right and responsibility of Christians to read the Scriptures for themselves and for the right of private interpretation.

Luther also warned against reading into Scripture things that are not there. He affirmed the doctrine of the perspicuity (or clarity) of Scripture. This doctrine does not mean that every part of the Bible is equally clear. Luther acknowledged that biblical doctrine can be exceedingly complex and difficult, confounding the minds of the church's best scholars. Interpreting the book of Revelation has been difficult for the church throughout the ages, and to this day we have no consensus on the proper interpretation of it. What Luther affirmed was that Scripture is clear in its basic message, that is, in communicating what is necessary for salvation. The gospel does not require a Ph.D. in theology or New Testament studies in order to be grasped. To Luther, the importance of getting the message of salvation to every person in the world far outweighs the dangers of corruption from private interpretations.

The Roman Catholic hierarchy feared that if people were left to interpret the Bible for themselves, sects, denominations, and splinter groups would arise, and that is exactly what happened. Luther thought that if the Bible were in the hands of the common people, their misinterpretations would be dwarfed by the gospel knowledge they would gain. We take for granted that we can purchase a Bible in our language and read it without being arrested or tortured. But that was not the case for much of church history, during which the Bible was literally chained to the church lectern and only the priests were allowed to read it. At the heart of the concept of the private interpretation of Scripture is the concept of its clarity or perspicuity.

Embedded in this discussion is an important principle of hermeneutics, which refers to the proper rules of interpreting the Bible. One basic principle is that the implicit is always to be interpreted in light of the explicit, not vice versa.

John 3:16 gives us an example of this: "For God so loved the world, that he gave his only Son, that whoever believes in him should not perish but have eternal life." This text teaches explicitly that all who "believe" will not "perish" and will have "eternal life." The text does not say who has the moral power or ability to believe, yet many people assume that everyone has this natural ability. But that is only implicit in the text, if there at all. Three chapters later, John quotes Jesus as saying, "This is why I told you that no one can come to me unless it is granted him by the Father" (John 6:65). This is an explicit statement about our natural inability to come to Christ. But when people embrace the implicit idea from 3:16 that anyone is able to come to Christ, they have to bury the explicit teaching of 6:65 under it.

The framers of the Westminster Confession spelled out the same principle when they wrote: **Those things which are necessary to be known, believed, and observed for salvation, are so clearly propounded, and opened in some place of Scripture or other, that not only the learned, but the unlearned, in a due use of the ordinary means, may attain unto a sufficient understanding of them.** Here the principle in view is that the obscure must be interpreted in light of the plain, which is similar to interpreting the implicit in light of the explicit. If the Bible clearly teaches something in one passage, while another passage on the same topic uses arcane and mysterious symbols, we interpret the symbols in light of the clear and plain teaching. If we use unclear or difficult passages to formulate our teaching and then distort the meaning of plain passages accordingly, we go astray. Always interpret the implicit in light of the explicit, the obscure in light of the clear. These underlying principles in the Reformed doctrine of hermeneutics presuppose that the Bible is the Word of God. The Holy Spirit is not an author of confusion; nor does God speak with lies or contradictions. Therefore, God is not going to say one thing in one place and a contradictory thing in another. Coherence and unity are present everywhere and are necessary in the revelation that comes from God. If we find what we think is a contradiction, the problem is with our sight, not with the Word of God. Contradiction is the hallmark of error.

8. The Old Testament in Hebrew (which was the native language of the people of God of old), and the New Testament in Greek (which, at the time of the writing of it, was most generally known to the nations), being immediately inspired by God, and, by his singular care and providence, kept pure in all ages, are therefore authentic; so as, in all controversies of religion, the church is finally to appeal unto them. But, because these original tongues are not known to all the people of God, who have right unto, and interest in the Scriptures, and are commanded, in the fear of God, to read and search them, therefore they are to be translated into the vulgar language of every nation unto which they come, that, the Word of God dwelling plentifully in all, they may worship him in an acceptable manner; and, through patience and comfort of the Scriptures, may have hope.

The Reformation affirmed, in addition to the clarity of the Scriptures and the right of private interpretation, the right to translate the Bible into the vernacular, the language of the people. The fact that today we can read the Scriptures in English came with a price tag. The original translators of the Bible into English and other languages often paid for it with their lives. One of the first things that Luther undertook after the Diet of Worms in 1521, after fleeing to Wartburg Castle, was to translate the Bible into German. God has preserved His original message intact, and the confession affirms that it is proper and appropriate to translate the Bible into various human languages.

Reformed theology teaches the infallibility and inerrancy of Scripture. That affirmation applies only to the autographs—the original manuscripts created by those who wrote the Bible. The process of copying these manuscripts and of translating them into other languages is not inspired by God, as was the process of writing the original documents. Some people believe that the only viable English translation is the King James Version, but the church does not hold to the infallibility of translations. Different English translations sometimes translate the same verse in incompatible ways, and so at least one must be in error. We acknowledge errors in copying and translating, but the original message that came from God Himself is infallible. The confession affirms in section 8 the right to translate the Bible into the languages of the people, because the truth to be learned from those translations far exceeds the occasional error.

> 9. The infallible rule of interpretation of Scripture is the Scripture itself: and therefore, when there is a question about the true and full sense of any Scripture (which is not manifold, but one), it must be searched and known by other places that speak more clearly.

In section 9 the authors come to the Reformed principle of hermeneutics known as *analogia fide* (the analogy of faith). This means that the primary rule of biblical interpretation is that Scripture is its own interpreter. The supreme interpreter of Holy Writ is the Holy Spirit, who inspired the text and who illumines and guides the believer in interpreting it. Serious dangers mark this process of interpretation. Throughout church history, there have been instances of so-called pneumatic exegesis or "spiritual interpretation" of the Bible. People claiming to have direct illumination from the Spirit have propounded bizarre interpretations of Scripture that cannot be objectively discerned in the text itself. They claim that the Holy Spirit has revealed to them the text's "real meaning." Others do what we call "lucky dipping." When a problem arises in their life, they say a prayer, open the Bible at random, and put their finger on the open page. The verse so identified is presumed to be their Spirit-given answer, even though the text may have absolutely nothing to do with the problem at hand. All such "spiritual interpretation" is unsupported by the confession. What the Holy Spirit inspired in one passage helps us understand what He inspired in another. We must interpret Scripture by Scripture.

A different kind of biblical interpretation has emerged in our day and worked its way deeply into the evangelical world: atomistic exegesis. In both philosophy and theology, an antipathy to any philosophical or theological system has arisen. Much of the scholarship in the last two centuries has been influenced, knowingly or unknowingly, by an existential approach to truth that abhors any systematic approach. What I feel at the moment is what matters, and everything else must adjust to it. Existential philosophy uses its opposition to systematics like a Procrustean bed. The Greek myth recounts that in order to fit travelers into his bed, Procrustes either stretched their bodies or cut off their legs. In this case, where the Bible does not fit the preferred philosophy, it is trimmed and forced to conform to it. With an existential approach, we can cut this text one day and stretch it the next. Or we can stretch this text to get it to fit with how we cut that other text. This faulty way of interpreting Scripture is a subtle step away from rejecting the system of doctrine contained in it.

Theological education has historically revolved around biblical studies, historical studies, and systematic theology. Systematic theology examines related passages of Scripture and comes to a unified knowledge of the whole. For example, classical systematic theologians study what Paul wrote on the subject of justification in Romans, Galatians, Ephesians, and Colossians in order to determine the various aspects of his teaching. They assume that Paul's doctrine of justification does not change from Galatians to Ephesians, since God is the author of it. But today, there is so little confidence in Scripture's inspiration that some prefer to approach the Bible atomistically, studying specific bits of data in isolation without comparing them to each other. These scholars are so preoccupied with the particulars that they feel no obligation to see how the particulars stand with the universal.

This atomistic approach violates the principle of interpreting Scripture by Scripture. In the Reformed analogy of faith, we trust the Word of God. We trust that what Paul teaches the church in Ephesus and what he teaches the churches in Galatia are coherent, unified, and consistent. If there seem to be two alternative interpretations of a given passage, one of which is compatible and consistent with everything else the author says and one of which seems to be contradictory, common courtesy dictates that the author be allowed to speak coherently through the whole of his writings. It is bad hermeneutics to violate this standard with any author, but particularly so when the author is God Himself.

The full sense of any Scripture, according to section 9, is not manifold, but one. A professor once assigned his students one verse of Scripture, asking them to write down fifty things they had learned from it and turn in the assignment the next day. The students groaned, stayed up late that night, compared notes, and came dragging in the next day with their lists of fifty. The assignment for the next day was to prepare a list of fifty more. What the professor was endeavoring to inculcate in his students was that a single text of Scripture may have a thousand possible applications, but only one correct meaning. Discerning the original, intended meaning is called grammatico-historical exegesis. We do not have any right to look at a biblical text from the perspective of the twenty-first century and change its meaning. If the perspective of the twenty-first century doesn't fit with the Bible, it is the perspective that is wrong, not the Bible.

10. The supreme judge by which all controversies of religion are to be determined, and all decrees of councils, opinions of ancient writers, doctrines of men, and private spirits, are to be examined, and in whose sentence we are to rest, can be no other but the Holy Spirit speaking in the Scripture.

Recapitulated in this final section of chapter 1 is the principle of *sola Scriptura*, which means that Scripture alone is the final, supreme arbiter of all theological controversies, all disputes and debates among Christians. It alone is the infallible rule of faith and life.

With the rise of Neoorthodox theology in the first half of the twentieth century came a strong rejection of propositional revelation. The advocates of Neoorthodoxy contended that the Bible is not an objective body of propositional truth but instead a witness to truth. Karl Barth, for example, popularized the idea that the Bible becomes the Word of God if and when the Spirit speaks through it—although in and of itself the Bible is not the Word of God. Barth claimed that the Bible's words somehow become transformed into the Word of God when the Spirit uses that text to speak to us. This was a radical form of existentializing the biblical record, and it has caused far-reaching consequences in the life of the church.

Others today are departing from the confession's teaching that the Bible is the only infallible rule of faith and practice. They claim that the Bible is infallible only when it speaks on matters of faith and practice, not when it talks about history, science, or anything else not directly related to religious faith or practice. But section 10 affirms that the Holy Spirit speaking in the Scriptures is infallible in the whole of our lives—in everything He teaches and everything He touches. He is supreme. There is not one body of truth found in Scripture and a distinct body found in the world. The Bible never steps outside its area of expertise, because the ultimate Author is not just an expert on everything, but He knows all things and made all things.

Of God, and
of the Holy Trinity

1. There is but one only, living, and true God, who is infinite in being and perfection, a most pure spirit, invisible, without body, parts, or passions; immutable, immense, eternal, incomprehensible, almighty, most wise, most holy, most free, most absolute; working all things according to the counsel of his own immutable and most righteous will, for his own glory; most loving, gracious, merciful, long-suffering, abundant in goodness and truth, forgiving iniquity, transgression, and sin; the rewarder of them that diligently seek him; and withal, most just, and terrible in his judgments, hating all sin, and who will by no means clear the guilty.

2. God hath all life, glory, goodness, blessedness, in and of himself; and is alone in and unto himself all-sufficient, not standing in need of any creatures which he hath made, nor deriving any glory from them, but only manifesting his own glory in, by, unto, and upon them. He is the alone fountain of all being, of whom, through whom, and to whom are all things; and hath most sovereign dominion over them, to do by them, for them, or upon them whatsoever himself pleaseth. In his sight all things are open and manifest, his knowledge is infinite, infallible, and independent upon the creature, so as nothing is to him contingent, or uncertain. He is most holy in all his counsels, in all his works, and in all his commands. To him is due from angels and men, and every other creature, whatsoever worship, service, or obedience he is pleased to require of them.

3. In the unity of the Godhead there be three persons, of one substance, power, and eternity: God the Father, God the Son, and God the Holy Ghost: the Father is of none, neither begotten, nor proceeding; the Son

is eternally begotten of the Father; the Holy Ghost eternally proceeding from the Father and the Son.

C hapter 2 of the Westminster Confession deals with the subject called "theology proper." All study of the things of God is theology, but within the science of theology there are subdivisions such as Christology, pneumatology, soteriology, and eschatology. The "proper" study of theology is the study of God Himself. The doctrine of God as set forth in historic Reformed theology is not particularly distinctive. Statements and affirmations in Reformed confessions are similar to those in Anglican, Roman Catholic, Lutheran, Methodist, and Baptist confessions. Paradoxically, then, the most distinctive characteristic of Reformed theology is its doctrine of God. This is so because Reformed theology, more than any other theology, consistently applies its understanding of God to every other doctrine in its theological system, making it altogether theocentric (God-centered) from start to finish.

1. There is but one only, living, and true God, who is infinite in being and perfection, a most pure spirit, invisible, without body, parts, or passions; immutable, immense, eternal, incomprehensible, almighty, most wise, most holy, most free, most absolute; working all things according to the counsel of his own immutable and most righteous will, for his own glory; most loving, gracious, merciful, long-suffering, abundant in goodness and truth, forgiving iniquity, transgression, and sin; the rewarder of them that diligently seek him; and withal, most just, and terrible in his judgments, hating all sin, and who will by no means clear the guilty.

This section begins with a string of attributes, or characteristics, of God. At the very beginning it affirms monotheism, the view that there is one and only one God.

In nineteenth-century scholarship, the redemptive-historical school argued that monotheism (belief in only one God) was a late development within Judaism. Religion, this school argued, normally develops from animism (which sees spirits dwelling in objects like stones and rivers) to polytheism (in which there are many gods, matched up with basic human concerns: a god for war, one for love, one for fertility, etc.) to henotheism (worship of one god without denying the existence of others) to monotheism. In the henotheistic stage, the Philistines had Dagon, the Canaanites Baal, and the Jews Yahweh. Each nation has its own god to take care of its needs. Evolutionary theorists of the nineteenth century argued that Judaism evolved from henotheism to monotheism under Moses or the eighth-century prophets. These theorists made this claim despite the fact that the Bible, from the very first page onward, affirms monotheism. Nothing is more central to Jewish theology than the *Shema*: "Hear, O Israel: The LORD our God, the LORD is one. You shall love the LORD your God with all your heart and with all your soul and with all your might" (Deut. 6:4–5). In Judaism and then in Christianity, there is one Most High God, who alone creates, sustains, and rules over all things.

The confession then qualifies it further: There is but one only, living, and true God, which points to His singularity. The God professed here is neither an abstract, impersonal force nor a philosophical concept, but a personal, living being. He is not imagined or invented but is real, alive, and the source of life itself.

The confession, at the beginning of its statement of theology proper, distinguishes between the true God and false gods. The conflict between godliness and evil ultimately focuses on idolatry. The most basic, fundamental sin, the most wicked propensity of fallen humanity, is to exchange the true God for one that we have made and can control. Whether God is replaced by crass, brutish idols fashioned out of stone and metal or redefined by philosophical concepts, He is stripped of His attributes. As the Apostle Paul tells us in Romans, there is an evil tendency in the human heart to exchange the truth of God for a lie, and serve and worship the creature rather than the Creator (Rom. 1:25). At the very outset, the confession clearly affirms that God is one, that He is alive, and that there is only one true God.

This idea is often negotiated in our pluralistic society. Nothing is more repugnant to the politically correct atmosphere of our day than a claim to exclusivity. However, that is precisely what the confession claims: there is only one true God. All other gods are false pretenders and idols, and to worship another god incurs God's wrath.

When speaking of God as infinite in being, we mean that His being has no ontological boundaries. There is no place, zone, or venue that His being does not permeate. His being is everywhere, and that incorporates another attribute: God's omnipresence. We believe that He is omnipresent because He is infinite in being.

One way to describe God is called the *via negationis*, the way of negation. This method describes what God is not. For example, God is not finite. To describe God in this way gives us a human frame of reference, for finitude defines our very existence. There are temporal beginning and ending points to our lives. We have spatial boundaries. But God is without bounds and boundaries, everywhere and eternally in His being. His very essence is everywhere. That may raise the question of pantheism: "If God's being is infinite, is everything God?" The Bible makes a clear distinction between God the Creator and His creatures. The creatures live and move and have their being in God. Our being is limited, finite, contingent, derived, and dependent on the infinite being of God, who is perfect in His infinity.

We should never consider the character of God to be too deep to think about. The more we reflect on His greatness, the more our souls are moved to adore Him and worship Him for His magnificence.

The universe has no room for more than one infinite being. If there were a second infinite being, then the first one would have a boundary to His essence, in which case His essence would not be infinite. The confession says that there can be only one God because philosophically there can be only one infinite being. God is that being.

God is infinite in . . . perfection. Anselm of Canterbury described God as the *ens perfectissimum*, the most perfect being. This idea of God has enjoyed a long life in the church and in theology, but "most perfect" seems redundant. Absolute perfection does not admit to degrees. An altogether perfect being cannot become more perfect or most perfect. Perfection is perfection, and if God is perfect in His entire being, then He cannot become more perfect or less perfect.

God's perfection in His being must be understood in its ultimate sense: He is perfect in every respect. His holiness and wisdom are infinitely perfect. There are no failures, no lapses; nothing is lacking in His excellence.

There is not the slightest shadow in His being. In the twentieth century, some people suggested that within God there is a certain ambivalence—a good side, but also a dark side, forcing Him to struggle within His own character. This is blasphemy. In the biblical God, there is no hint of imperfection of any kind. If we project onto God the imperfections that we find in ourselves or our fellow human beings, we begin to limit His authority, knowledge, wisdom, and eternality.

God is **a most pure spirit, invisible, without body, parts, or passions.** God is here affirmed to be a most pure spirit. Later in the list of characteristics, God will be described as **most holy.** Let us go to the term *holy.* When the Bible speaks of holiness, without which we cannot see God (Heb. 12:14), the concept is one of moral perfection or purity. The term holy also speaks of God's transcendence—his supreme greatness compared to all created things. So to say that He is holy is to say that He is transcendent above and beyond all creatures.

God is also **pure.** Note the dimension of His purity: He is a most pure spirit. The confession affirms that, as Jesus Himself taught (John 4:24), God is a **spirit.** That is, God is immaterial in His being. He has no extension that can be measured with a ruler or weighed on a scale. Because His being is unextended, immaterial, and spiritual, God is invisible. We cannot see Him unless He manifests Himself through some physical medium. For this reason, Paul says that the invisible things of God are clearly seen through the things that are made (Rom. 1:20). A vision of God that comes through physical things is mediated, but God Himself, a spirit with no physical body, is invisible.

God is also **without . . . parts.** This is one way to affirm what is called the simplicity of God. God is a simple being, rather than a complex being who can be divided into parts. A human being is a complex being with a head, ears, eyes, a nose, arms, feet, and various organs—parts. When we seek to understand God, we tend to project our human complexity onto His being. We list His attributes—immutability, eternality, omniscience, omnipresence, holiness, and all the others. We sometimes tend to think that God is made up of one part holiness, one part immutability, one part omnipotence, and several other parts, but all of God is all of His attributes in their entirety. God's holiness is immutable, omnipotent, eternal, and omnipresent. In like manner, His immutability is holy, omniscient, and eternal. His omnipotence is not arbitrary or capricious but holy and immutable. God's power will never weaken, for it is unchangeable. Every attribute we ascribe to Him applies to the whole of God. His attributes all exist mutually in a kind of reciprocity of attributes. For further study, I strongly commend the excellent work done by James Dolezal on the doctrine of God's simplicity in his book *All That Is in God.*

God is **without . . . passions.** There is often confusion on this subject. Heresies have resulted from attributing emotional disturbances and upheavals to God. For example, the tranquility and felicity that God enjoys in and of Himself is eternal and immutable. **Without . . . passions** means that He does not experience mood swings or become depressed, not that He has no cares. Yet Scripture plainly teaches that God has an emotive side: He takes delight in things, He loves, He regards us with affection. God is not an abstract force but a personal being.

The phrase **without . . . passions** means that God is not subject to human passions. The Bible states that He is a jealous God, but that does not mean that He is jealous of us. He is jealous for us and for His holiness—that is, He cares strongly about us. Even His wrath manifests His grave concern for the behavior of His creatures.

God is **immutable, immense, eternal, incomprehensible, almighty, most wise, most holy, most free, most absolute.** God's immutability is something we never want to negotiate. **Immutable,** "without change," means not that God is immobile, inert, or incapable of motion, but that His being never suffers mutations. He is omniscient, ubiquitous, and immense, and His attributes never cease or change.

The kenotic heresy of the nineteenth century argued that to become incarnate, the Son of God gave up certain divine attributes. This heresy was reassessed in the twentieth century by advocates of the "death of God," who categorically denied God's immutability. Modern versions of "open theism" have God changing in His knowledge as He gains new information from our decisions. This theology would destroy His immutability, because what He was yesterday is not what He is today after gaining this new information by observing His creation. In addition, were God to change, He would of necessity become a creature. He would "become." He would be what He once was not. To worship a creature, any creature, is idolatry (see Rev. 19:10).

God, however, knows all things. He knows all things because all things have their being in Him. Aristotle is helpful here with his categories of being and becoming. He points out that change itself requires both continuity and difference. When "I" change, there is both a part of me that stays the same (the "I") and a part of me that changes. We are a combination of both being and becoming. God, however, is pure being. He does not change because He cannot change. He is pure actuality, no potentiality.

In his sermon on why we are enemies of God by nature, Jonathan Edwards asks what it is about God that makes us hate Him. Edwards answers that we hate God first because He is holy and we are not. He is omniscient and we cannot fool Him. We may hide our iniquities from other prying eyes, but we cannot escape the gaze of God, who has complete knowledge of what is in our minds and lives. He is omnipotent, and our power can never overthrow Him.

Edwards answers, second, that we hate God because He is immutable or changeless. We know that God is holy, immutably so. Even as time passes, God cannot become corrupt. There will never be gaps in His knowledge, nor will He lose any of His omniscience. His strength will never dissipate, nor will He ever be less omnipotent. Edwards observes not only that God is holy, omniscient, and omnipotent but that He is unchangeably so. There is no possibility that He will ever stop being these things, and that troubles us.

When we read in the confession that God is immense, we may think of immensity as largeness. A person who is more than just big is immense. But the immensity of God means not that He is big in size but that He is everywhere at all times, or omnipresent. God is present in San Francisco at the same time he's present in New York or Chicago. Moreover, wherever He is, God is present in His fullness, eternality, immutability, simplicity, omniscience, and omnipotence; all of God is present. Because He is one, it is not the case that part of Him is in one place and part in another, as if He were spread thin. Wherever He is, which is everywhere, He is all there.

The Apostle Paul perhaps had this in view when discussing the incarnation. In Colossians he writes that the fullness of the Godhead dwelt bodily in Christ (Col. 2:9). The being of God is not restricted to the geographical boundaries of Jesus' human body. Nevertheless, the incarnate Word—the second person of the Trinity—has all that God is in Him.

God is eternal. Eternality goes in both directions, backward in time and forward. Because of philosophical concerns, some argue that God is outside of time, that time is a corollary of space, and that at no time was there no physical creation. That is an interesting point for speculation. However, everything that God has revealed to us has been revealed in temporal terms. Even though He communicates to us in temporal language, He Himself is higher than time. At no point did God not exist.

People may argue that if every effect has a cause, then God must have a cause. They may therefore ask, What was there before God? But the eternal God is not an effect. There never was a time when He was not. God's being is derived from nothing outside of Himself, nor is He dependent on anything outside of Himself. Nothing differentiates God from the creature more dramatically than this, because the creature, by definition, is dependent, contingent, and derived and lacks the power of being in and of himself. God requires nothing; He exists from all eternity.

Eternality goes in the other direction as well. There will never be a time in the future when God will cease to be. His being remains self-existent for all eternity. If anything exists, then something has always existed. If there ever was absolutely nothing, then nothing could possibly be now, because you cannot get something out of nothing. Conversely, if there is something now, then that in itself demonstrates that there always was something. And that which always is exists in and of itself. That is the One who has the power of being within Himself, the living God. So His eternality is another attribute that should incite our souls to adoration and praise: we are made by One who has the very power of being in Himself eternally. Imagine the greatness of a being like that.

His eternality, perhaps more than anything else, sets God apart from us. His holiness refers not only to His purity but also to His otherness or transcendence—the sense in which He is different from us. One thing we human beings have in common is that we are creatures, who by nature are temporal. At the end of a person's life, when he is buried, his grave is marked by a tombstone on which are inscribed his name and the dates of his birth and death. We live on this earth between those two dates: birth and death. There are no such dates for God. He is infinite not only with respect to space but also with respect to time. There never was a time when God was not. He is from everlasting to everlasting.

God's eternality is inseparably related to His self-existence, His aseity. Yet the word *aseity* is virtually absent from the average Christian's vocabulary. Aseity means "to have being or existence within oneself." The mathematician and philosopher Bertrand Russell, in *Why I Am Not a Christian*, spelled out the reasons for his unbelief. Until he was a teenager, Russell had been convinced that there had to be a God to explain the universe. Then he read John Stuart Mill, who disputed the traditional cosmological argument for God's existence, which reasons from the presence of things that are now in existence back to a first cause. This reasoning is based on the law of causality, which says that every effect must have an antecedent cause. Mill asserted that if everything must have an antecedent cause, then God Himself must have one as well. But if God has an antecedent cause, then He is a creature like everyone else. When he read this in his late teens, Russell decided that the classical argument for God's existence is fallacious. Russell maintained that position until his death, failing to realize that it was built on a faulty definition of the law of causality.

The law of causality teaches that every effect must have a cause, not that every thing must have a cause. Effects, by definition, are caused by something outside of themselves. However, we need not assume that everything is an effect—temporal, finite, dependent, and derived. There is nothing irrational about the idea of a self-existent, eternal being who has the power of being within Himself. In fact, such a concept is not only logically possible but (as Thomas Aquinas demonstrated) logically necessary. For anything to exist, something somewhere, somehow, must have the power of being, for without the power of being, nothing could possibly be. That which has the power of being in and of itself, and is not dependent on anything outside of itself, must have the power of being from all eternity. This is what distinguishes God from us. We recall the first sentence of the Old Testament: "In the beginning, God created the heavens and the earth" (Gen. 1:1). Everything in the cosmos, apart from God, is creaturely. Everything in creation—in the universe—has a beginning in time. God alone is from everlasting to everlasting and possesses the attribute of eternality. That majestic aspect of God's nature so far transcends anything that we have ever conceived of in this world that it alone should be enough to move our souls to praise and adore Him. He alone has the power of being in and of Himself. We do not think about these things often enough. If we reflect on a being who is eternal, who generates the power for everything else that exists, including ourselves, we should be moved to worship Him.

Next the confession says that God is incomprehensible. When teaching theology proper, I always start with God's incomprehensibility, because humility demands that we understand at the outset that we are like infants struggling to understand a genius who is speaking to us in our own terms. Our tiny minds cannot begin to grasp in its fullness the concept of God. John Calvin used the formula *finitum non capax infinitum*, "the finite cannot contain (or grasp) the infinite." A finite mind cannot attain an exhaustive, comprehensive understanding of the infinite, for we lack any reference by which to grasp it. When we die and go to heaven, we will experience a huge leap in our understanding and apprehension of God, when so much of the mist will be removed from the dim and dark mirror through which we now look. Yet even in heaven we will still be finite creatures. However glorified we will be, we will still be incapable of comprehending God completely.

When we say that God is incomprehensible, we do not mean that He is so obscure that we can know nothing of significance about Him. Luther said that God is not only *Deus absconditus*, the hidden God, but also *Deus revelatus*, the revealed God, who has been pleased to unveil things about Himself to us. To whatever degree it is possible for His creatures to apprehend Him, God has made Himself known. Moses tells us that "the secret things belong to the LORD our God, but the things that are revealed belong to us and to our children forever" (Deut. 29:29). We end up in utter skepticism if we say that God is totally unknowable.

When we say that He is incomprehensible, we mean that no one can completely grasp what or who God is in the fullness of His being; our knowledge of God can never be exhaustive.

Theology distinguishes between a comprehensive (exhaustive) knowledge of God, which we cannot have, and an apprehensive knowledge, which is the limited, finite, human, creaturely knowledge that we can have. Apprehensive knowledge admits to degrees, so we can know God, more or less, in this human framework. Even if we master every iota of information given by Scripture and nature about the character of God and fully understand all that has been revealed, our knowledge will still be far from comprehensive. In this world, because of the weakness of our flesh, our slothfulness, and our slowness of mind, we do not even begin to master what He has revealed. Thus, our apprehensive knowledge is weak and frequently attended by error.

One thing we do know in our study of God is that comparisons and contrasts can help. In a sermon on Isaiah 6, focusing on Isaiah's reaction to the heavenly vision—"Woe is me! For I am lost; for I am a man of unclean lips" (Isa. 6:5)—Edwards states that people lack a proper sense of who they are until they behold the majesty of God. Isaiah was devastated by a heightened awareness of who God is. He became aware not simply of the contrast between God's holiness and our filthiness but also of the contrast between God's knowledge and our ignorance. When Isaiah saw God on the throne, he became aware of how little he had understood of God's nature. Edwards makes the application that there is nothing like seeing what God is to make men sensible of what they are. Of course, no man ever comes to know who God is comprehensively or comes to know and understand all the mysteries of His nature. God teaches us that we do not and can never know fully what He is:

> Who has ascended to heaven and come down?
> Who has gathered the wind in his fists?
> Who has wrapped up the waters in a garment?
> Who has established all the ends of the earth?
> What is his name, and what is his son's name?
> Surely you know! (Prov. 30:4)

Notice the image: "Who has gathered the wind in his fists?" This is the Wisdom Literature of the Old Testament. The wind blows. A person feels its pressure against his face, but he cannot reach out and take hold of it and grip it in a tight fist. Edwards says that Scripture uses comparisons like this to instill humility and teach us how little we know of God.

Edwards uses another illustration about things that are illumined in the dark, which I will restate in twenty-first-century terms. Many people have a watch or a bedroom clock with a luminous dial. Upon awakening in the middle of the night, they can read their clock because the dial shines. It stands out as the only thing they can see in the otherwise dark room. That power of illumination seems significant in the dark, but under the noonday sun you can detect no illumination. The illumination that shows in the dark is completely vitiated by sunlight; the light of the clock is insignificant when compared to the light of the sun. This analogy helps us understand the incomprehensibility of God. Whatever light we have and whatever we have mastered of the things of God pale into insignificance when we step into the fullness of His light.

Edwards then talks about the biblical image of God as dwelling in inapproachable light. Light as a metaphor for the glory of God is found throughout Scripture. His transcendent majesty, the *shekinah*, is always expressed in terms of light—the light that blazed the sky outside Bethlehem on the night Jesus was born, the light that burst through the garments of Christ on the Mount of Transfiguration. God's glory is communicated over and over in terms of a blinding, dazzling brilliance. Using biblical language, Edwards calls it the light inapproachable.

What light is so intense that you dare not approach it? In a small way, it is what Moses experienced in the Midianite wilderness when the bush began to burn and shine. Moses was terrified to come near because the small light of God shining out of that bush was enough to paralyze him. Again, after Moses saw the glory of God on Mount Sinai and came down from the mountain, his countenance shone so brightly that people were terrified, and that was just a reflection of this inapproachable light.

We live in an egalitarian culture in which everyone is to be equally accessible to, and approachable by, everyone else. To be aloof is to commit a social sin. We are casual and familiar, not formal. We then project that onto God, as if we can come into His presence in a cavalier spirit of familiarity, the kind of familiarity that breeds contempt. It is true that we are given access to God by virtue of the work that Christ has accomplished for us, but our justification does not change God's character. The fact that He has saved us and adopted us into His family does not mean that He has stopped being holy or eternal, or that He has stopped dwelling in light inapproachable. If anyone should understand the glorious majesty of God, it is the believer. We should not be cavalier or casual when we come to him. When we see the inapproachable light, we should react as Isaiah did.

Thomas Aquinas is generally considered, even by Protestant scholars, to be one of the greatest Christian intellectuals ever. The prodigious power of his intellect has never been surpassed in the church. Few people realize that, along with his brilliant intellect, Thomas had a mystical side. The story is told that once, as he was writing, he had a mystical apprehension of the greatness of God, and he put aside his pen. When asked why he had stopped writing, he explained that he had had an ineffable experience of God that he could not articulate. This man, who possessed prodigious theological acumen, once he had a deeper glimpse of God's nature, gave up trying to communicate to people about the majesty of God. We recall that Paul the Apostle was caught up in the third heaven and could not speak of the things he had experienced (2 Cor. 12:2).

Next, God is almighty, an attribute usually called omnipotence. To be truly omnipotent is to have all power. I have been asked, "If God is omnipotent, can He create a rock so big that He can't move it?" If I say yes, He is not omnipotent because He cannot move the rock. If I say no, He is not omnipotent because He cannot create such a rock. The correct answer, however, is no, because if God created a rock so big that He could not move it, He would no longer be omnipotent. Someone may then point out that I have already denied His omnipotence by saying that He cannot do something. Indeed, there are many things that God cannot do: He cannot die, He cannot lie, He cannot be God and not be God at the same time and in the same relationship. Being immutable, He cannot stop being omnipotent. The omnipotent God has all power over creation, so nothing in creation can overpower him, including any rock He decides to move. When we say that God is all-powerful, almighty, omnipotent, we mean that His power surpasses everything in the universe. Nothing can resist His power or overpower Him.

Throughout our lives, we experience various manifestations of power. In some sense, we are power-hungry. In spite of the awe-inspiring power we see in creation—the ocean, volcanic eruptions, and so on—we must understand that it is nothing compared to the power of God. He can simply speak and the worlds come into existence.

As we read in Numbers 11, the children of Israel complained because they were tired of manna—manna for breakfast, manna for lunch, manna for dinner. And if they wanted a midnight snack, it was manna. Despite the great work of redemption that God had done for them, their souls were not fixed on the wonders of God. Their bellies became their god, and they griped and complained that it had been better for them in Egypt. They preferred to return to Egypt and make bricks without straw because there they had leeks and garlic and onions.

They were ready to trade their salvation for onions and leeks and garlic. Moses angrily told God that if He loved him at all, He would kill him, because he could not bear the people alone. He reminded God that these were His people and that He should take care of them. God declared that if the Israelites wanted meat to eat, He would give them meat—not for one day or seven days but for thirty days, until that meat came out their nostrils and became loathsome to them. Moses was frightened and wondered how God would accomplish this. Where would God secure enough meat to feed this multitude for so many days? He feared that God would take all their herds and completely consume them for this short-term feast. In other words, Moses was saying that God could not do what He said He would do. God replied, "Is the LORD's hand shortened? Now you shall see whether my word will come true for you or not" (Num. 11:23). Even Moses, with his intimate knowledge of God, was overwhelmed by God's power.

The concept of God's almighty power is a theme of the book of Job. The name *El Shaddai* appears more frequently in this book than in any other in the Bible. This name has been given different meanings, but one of the most popular is "the One who is the overpowerer, the almighty

One." In the midst of his suffering, Job asked God to speak to him and to be merciful to him. Job began to interrogate God, subjecting Him to cross-examination.

When God appeared, He said to Job:

> Who is this that darkens counsel by words without knowledge?
> Dress for action like a man;
> I will question you, and you make it known to me. (Job 38:2–3)

God's question for Job was: "Where were you when I laid the foundation of the earth?" (38:4). He also asked Job where he had been when He made the seas. He asked Job if he had drawn out the Leviathan with a fishhook or set the courses of the Pleiades. God never answered Job's theological questions. He simply revealed Himself to Job in His power, greatness, and majesty. This manifestation was enough for Job. His questions meant nothing because God revealed Himself in unspeakable power. He is the One who overpowers.

These are examples of what Edwards was talking about with respect to Isaiah's vision of God. There is nothing like seeing what God is to make us realize what we are. Our weakness is revealed in God's strength. In our sinful unbelief, we stagger at the promises that God makes to His people. We impute to God, or project upon Him, the same inadequacies, the same powerlessness, that we experience in our finite lives. We stagger like Moses. "How are You going to do it?" The power of the Lord will bring it to pass. Whatever God says He will do, He can do. He is able to do what He says He is going to do because He is almighty. Because of His perfect moral character, He will keep His word. Nothing in the universe can prevent God from doing what He promises to do for His people. That is the testimony of redemptive history. God brings something out of nothing. He easily frees a nation of slaves from the clutches of Pharaoh, the most powerful ruler on earth. We fear the devil and the power of death. We fear a host of things around us, forgetting that God promises to redeem us fully and finally and that He has the power and determination to do it.

God is also most wise, most holy, most free, most absolute. He is *ens perfectissimum*, the most perfect being. Perfection does not admit to degrees, but the Westminster divines use the term most to emphasize the superlative quality of the attributes manifested by God. **Most wise** describes not only God's omniscience, His knowledge of all things past, present, and future, but also His wisdom—and the Bible differentiates between knowledge and wisdom.

Scripture says that "the fear of the LORD is the beginning of wisdom" (Prov. 9:10) and that "the fool says in his heart, 'There is no God'" (Ps. 14:1). Denying the existence of God is not simply wicked but foolish. There is no wisdom in it. So Proverbs tells us to get knowledge, but even more to get wisdom (Prov. 4:5–7). There is a difference. You can have knowledge without wisdom.

Some think you can have wisdom without knowledge, but you cannot. That is why we must study God's Word diligently. We need to know the things of God, remembering that even if we get the knowledge, we can still lack the wisdom. We cannot get the wisdom without the knowledge. Knowledge is a necessary condition for wisdom but not a sufficient condition. God not only knows all things, but He also knows what to do with them. He knows how to exercise His government over them. He has never made a foolish decision or conceived a bad plan. He is completely enveloped in pure wisdom, knowing the right thing to do.

Wisdom is not an abstract philosophical concept. It has to do with practical actions. It compels us to live righteously—to know and do the right thing. At times, we lack this wisdom, but God, the source of supreme wisdom, promises to give it to us liberally. Who is this God whom we worship? We keep coming back to who He is. If we considered only His wisdom, that would be enough to keep us worshiping Him forever.

God is **most holy.** In the book of Isaiah, the seraphim sing, "Holy, holy, holy" (Isa. 6:3). This threefold repetition is a literary device that calls attention to the highest degree. In this case, the angels elevate God's holiness to the highest possible degree—the superlative degree—referring to His majesty or greatness. The term *holy* is used biblically in two distinct ways: to refer to God's otherness, the way in which He is different from us and transcends all created things, and to refer to His moral perfection. A simple table grace says, "God is great, God is good, let us thank Him for this food." That attribution of greatness and goodness to God can be summed up as "He is holy," because holiness incorporates both greatness and goodness.

God is **most free**; that is, His freedom is unlimited. He is sovereign. The most frequent objection to His sovereignty is that if God is truly sovereign, then man cannot be free. Scripture uses the term *freedom* to describe our human condition in two distinct ways: freedom from coercion, whereby man is free to make choices without coercion, and moral freedom, which we lost in the fall, leaving us slaves to the evil impulses of our flesh. Humanists believe that man can make choices not only without coercion but also without any natural inclination toward evil. We Christians must be on guard against this humanist or pagan view of human freedom.

The Christian view is that God creates us with wills, with a capacity to choose. We are volitional beings. But the freedom given in creation is limited. What ultimately limits our freedom is God's freedom. This is where we run into the conflict between divine sovereignty and human freedom. Some say that God's sovereignty is limited by human freedom. If that is the case, then man is sovereign, not God. The Reformed faith teaches that human freedom is real but limited by God's sovereignty. We cannot overrule the sovereign decisions of God with our freedom, because God's freedom is greater than ours.

Human family relationships provide an analogy. Parents exercise authority over the child. The child has freedom, but the parents have more. The child's freedom does not limit the parents' freedom in the way that the parents' freedom limits the child's. When we come to the attributes of God, we must understand that God is most free.

When we say that God is sovereign, we are saying something about His freedom, although we tend to think that sovereignty means something quite different from freedom. God is a volitional being; He has a will and makes decisions. When making decisions and exercising His will, He does so sovereignly as the ultimate authority. His freedom is most free. He alone has supreme autonomy; He is a law unto Himself.

Humans seek autonomy, unlimited freedom, desiring to be accountable to no one. In a real sense, that is what happened in the fall. Satan enticed Adam and Eve to reach for autonomy, to become like God, to do whatever they wanted with impunity. Satan was introducing a liberation movement in the garden to free human beings from culpability, from accountability to God. But He alone has autonomy.

This provokes the question of whether God operates arbitrarily. In the Middle Ages, some argued that God is *ex lex*, "outside of the law." They reasoned that if God were bound by some external standard or law, then He would be judged by that external law. In that case, the ultimate authority would not be God but would be some cosmic law. But others said that God cannot act in an arbitrary or capricious manner and so is *sublego*, "under law."

Both theories raise problems. *Ex lex* suggests that God is arbitrary; *sublego*, that God is subordinate to some greater principle outside of Himself. The church condemned both ideas and acknowledged God to be a law unto Himself. In doing so, the church distinguished between God's external righteousness and His internal righteousness. External righteousness refers to His behavior, His actions—what He does. It always flows out of and is in accord with His internal character. God's behavior is contingent on no external law or force imposed on Him from without. It is determined by His own character. God acts according to what He is. In His nature, He is righteous, sovereign, and free. These concepts combine as the idea that God is **most absolute.**

At the heart of postmodernism today is the rejection of any absolute, and therefore our society is sliding into paganism and barbarism. An attack on absolutes is an attack on the ultimate absolute, God Himself. There is nothing relative about Him; in His being, He is objective, eternal, and absolute.

Working all things according to the counsel of his own immutable and most righteous will. This point will be elaborated on in chapters 3 (Of God's Eternal Decree) and 5 (Of Providence). Here we have a summary statement about the working out of God's will. God works all things according to the counsel of His own will. He does not work things out according to my will or your will or popular opinion. He does not rule by referendum. The Ten Commandments (not suggestions) express God's own will. What He wants determines how He works. That is fundamental to our understanding of God. Even Jesus, in His agony in Gethsemane, prayed, "Nevertheless, not my will, but yours, be done" (Luke 22:42), because He understood that God does what is best and righteous. God's choices and actions are determined by His omniscience, righteousness, holiness, and the rest of His attributes. He will act not according to a lesser being's desire, opinion, or counsel but according to His own counsel.

Scripture asks the rhetorical question, "Who has measured the Spirit of the LORD, or what man shows him his counsel?" (Isa. 40:13). Some people ask, If God works out His own counsel all the time, why should anyone even bother to pray? Does prayer change God's mind? To ask such a question like that is to answer it.

Suppose for a second that prayer could change God's mind. What in my prayer could cause Him to change His mind? Before I pray, does He purpose to do something for which He lacks some information or wisdom that I could supply? As I pray, can I give Him information, instruction, or advice that will cause Him to change His mind? That is absurd. Surely, no one would think that. God knows what we are going to pray before we say it. We have no wisdom that is lacking in His own counsel. God does not need our counsel or advice. We will not change His mind.

Do we now jump to this conclusion that, if we can't change God's mind, we shouldn't bother to pray? The purpose of prayer is not to change God's mind but to change ours, to bring us into communion with Him, to come to our heavenly Father and tell Him what is on our hearts. He invites us—no, He commands and encourages us—to do that. He asks us to come into His presence and recount our afflictions and stories, but not for His information or guidance. God uses a person's prayers as He was determined to do before the person ever prayed. God uses our prayers as a means to accomplish His plan. So when we are praying to God, we are part of His plan. God is being gracious to make use of our prayers. Yet Scripture tells us that "the prayer of a righteous person has great power as it is working" (James 5:16). When we are praying, we should consider two things: who we are and who God is. Remembering who He is, we acknowledge that God orders all things according to His will. Some people are critical of ending prayers with "Your will be done," thinking it shows a lack of faith. No, it shows a lack of pride and arrogance. With it we affirm that God's will will be done and that we want it no other way.

For God's people, there has never been an unanswered prayer. People claim they have a crisis of faith when God does not answer their prayers. What does that mean? When we make a particular request of God and He does not grant it, we declare that prayer unanswered. We are like the child who asks his parents, "May I go to Billy's house and play this afternoon?" When the parent replies, "No, I'm sorry, but you have to stay home," the child complains, "My mother didn't hear my request." Actually, the request was heard and denied. So it is with our prayers. God hears our prayers and sometimes answers yes, but at other times He answers no. Either way, we receive an answer. We should rejoice in His response, for He answers our prayers according to His own counsel, righteousness, and omniscience. We should always pray with the assumption that God knows best.

God works all things according to the counsel of his own immutable and most righteous will. There is a difference between *according to His will* and *willy-nilly*. Willy-nilly has no purpose or principle and is chaotic or irrational. God's will, on the other hand, is immutable because it is eternal and is based on His most wise and righteous counsel. What would cause God to change His plan?

We now have a movement in the church that considers God a kind of cosmic errand boy or a celestial Santa Claus to whom we send up our petitions and who must respond to our requests. It is as though His will changes according to the decisions or requests made by human beings. One theologian has said that this view should be called not *open theism* but *limited godism*. *Open* is a good word; openness is a virtue. Open theism teaches that God adjusts His plans according to what we do because He does not know in advance what our decisions will be. This theory is popular because it exalts human decision-making. But the price is the death of the biblical God. The confession, however, declares God's sovereign will to be immutable because it is indefectible; it is perfect. God does not have to guess what is going to happen fifteen minutes from now. He does not work on the basis of computerized probability quotients. He knows with absolute certainty what will happen, and so His most wise counsel remains unchanging and unchangeable.

The biblical teaching of God's sovereignty, particularly with respect to predestination, is set forth throughout Scripture, but nowhere more clearly than in Ephesians and Romans. When the Apostle Paul speaks about predestination, he is referring to God's election, His choosing of people according to the good pleasure of His will. People complain about this and accuse God of being arbitrary. If God chooses a person without considering anything within that person, then God is flipping coins or playing a lottery, they claim. Scripture says that the basis of God's election is the good pleasure of His will; that is, it pleases Him to do what He does, and His pleasure is good. God takes no delight in evil. He bases His decisions with respect to salvation on what pleases Him, and that is always good. The Apostle Paul tells us that God makes His decisions on the basis of the good pleasure of His will, and that is what the framers of the confession emphasize when they say that He works all things according to the counsel of His will, His own unchangeable and most righteous will.

When something calamitous happens in our world or in our lives, we shrink back and declare, "That can't be the will of God, because God is righteous and what happened was terrible." But, amazingly, God works His will through both righteous and wicked activities. The Bible says, "And we know that for those who love God all things work together for good, for those who are called according to his purpose" (Rom. 8:28). This verse does not say that all things are good in and of themselves. They may indeed be calamitous, but God works calamity for His righteous purpose.

A clear example of this is the story of Joseph and his brothers. The brothers, terrified because of their sinful decisions and actions toward Joseph, fear that he will exact revenge against them. Joseph, however, says, "You meant evil against me, but God meant it for good" (Gen. 50:20). Judas intended evil when he betrayed Jesus, but God was working out His will through the wicked will of Judas. God's will is righteous. Do not misunderstand: evil is evil, and it is a sin to call evil good. Evil is not good. But if God exists, then evil is real; and if God is omnipotent and sovereign, then it must be good that there is evil. That is not the same as saying that evil is good. God cannot will even permissibly that which is not good according to His most righteous will. Obviously God could, if He wished, stop all the evil in the world. The fact that He allows evil to continue implies that there must be good reason for it, because He only allows things to happen that are in accordance with His most righteous will.

We see a further qualification in the confession: for His own glory. God works all things according to the counsel of His immutable, righteous will, but to what end? What is the teleology (the goal or purpose) here? He does this for His glory. If an ordinary person said that he did everything for his own glory, what would you think of him? You would consider him sinful and self-centered. But we must never level the same charge against God. If a sinful creature works everything for his personal glory, that is bad. But if the righteous, good, and holy God works everything for His glory, that is only the way it should be. There is never a reason for God to undermine the absolute character of His own glory. It is for our good that God is jealous of His own glory. He will not share that glory with us, for that would diminish it and He would lose the radiance of His own majesty. Nothing is more proper than for a perfect being to work all things for the exaltation of His perfection and righteousness.

Most loving, gracious, merciful, long-suffering, abundant in goodness and truth, forgiving iniquity, transgression, and sin; the rewarder of them that diligently seek him; and withal, most just, and terrible in his judgments, hating all sin, and who will by no means clear the guilty. God is most loving, and this superlative love manifests itself in His grace and patience. The love of God has three aspects. First is His love of benevolence. *Bene* means "good," and *volence* is related to volition. God's benevolent love has to do with His good will toward His creation. Everyone experiences the benefits of that benevolence. Second is God's love of beneficence, shown in His good deeds. He gives rain that falls on the just and the unjust. This love is manifested in the good gifts He gives to both good and bad people. And third is God's love of complacency, the supreme love reserved for His redeemed. Those who are redeemed in Christ are loved by Christ in a special way, for the redeemed receive the final measure, the ultimate level, of God's grace.

God's love is seen in His graciousness. He is gracious. To be gracious is to treat people better than they deserve. We define grace as unmerited favor. If God treated us strictly according to the canons of justice, He would punish us for eternity. But instead, He is gracious, tender, and merciful. He reserves the right to extend that mercy and grace to those He sovereignly chooses. God said, "I will have mercy on whom I have mercy, and I will have compassion on whom I have compassion" (Rom. 9:15). One of the greatest misconceptions about biblical truth is the idea that God is somehow obligated to be equally merciful to everyone. If He were obligated to be merciful, then it would be justice, not mercy; it would be what He must do if He is righteous. The whole point of mercy is that it is free and voluntary. God is so loving that He gives mercy far beyond anything we could ever hope or imagine.

God is merciful, long-suffering, abundant in goodness and truth, forgiving iniquity, transgression, and sin. We find the deepest manifestation of God's grace and love in His forgiveness. This is at the heart of the gospel. Our sins have been remitted by Christ, and because of His ministry we are forgiven. It is not that we are forgiven because God is required to forgive us or because we can earn His forgiveness. We are unprofitable servants who cannot possibly pay our debts, but God forgives our sins and transgressions. "He rewards those who seek him" (Heb. 11:6).

We must be careful here. God promises in the Bible, as part of His grace, to increase grace to those who diligently seek Him. At the same time, the Bible teaches us that only believers seek Him. In our culture, the idea prevails that we should distinguish between "believers" and "seekers." Seekers are thought to be unbelievers—unsaved people—who are searching for God. But the Bible says that no one (in his natural state) seeks after God. Instead, people seek God's benefits, the things that only He can give them, while they are fleeing from God Himself. Genuine seeking after God begins only at conversion and is (as Jonathan Edwards wrote) the main business of the Christian life. Jesus said to believers, "Seek first the kingdom of God and his righteousness, and all these things will be added to you" (Matt. 6:33). We are running from God until we are converted. Once converted, we begin our pursuit of God. We pursue Him, knowing that He has promised to reward those who seek Him diligently.

We are also warned that God is most just, and terrible in his judgments. This does not say that He is most just, *but* terrible in His judgments. We have the mind-set today that if God judges and punishes sin, His character must be defective. The defect is in our reasoning. If we had judges in our criminal courts who never found anyone guilty or never punished sin, would we describe them as just or good? Of course not. God is the judge of all the earth. He does what is right, and His punishments are awesome. They are as terrible as they are most just. No punishment from God could be so terrible that it would reveal an injustice in Him. In fact, the punishment that the most wicked people receive from God is always less than that which they ultimately deserve.

Hating all sin, God will by no means clear the guilty. Even among Christians who know their doctrine well, such as pastors, this can be a tricky point. Some believe that the only way God ever clears the guilty is through the atonement of Jesus Christ. But the confession says otherwise. The confession says that God **will by no means** (which includes the cross) **clear the guilty.** He redeems and saves the guilty, but He does not clear them. They are still guilty. It is only because of His grace, His most loving mercy, and His imputation of Christ's righteousness that God justifies us while we are still sinners.

> 2. God hath all life, glory, goodness, blessedness, in and of himself; and is alone in and unto himself all-sufficient, not standing in need of any creatures which he hath made, nor deriving any glory from them, but only manifesting his own glory in, by, unto, and upon them. He is the alone fountain of all being, of whom, through whom, and to whom are all things; and hath most sovereign dominion over them, to do by them, for them, or upon them whatsoever himself pleaseth. In his sight all things are open and manifest, his knowledge is infinite, infallible, and independent upon the creature, so as nothing is to him contingent, or uncertain. He is most holy in all his counsels, in all his works, and in all his commands. To him is due from angels and men, and every other creature, whatsoever worship, service, or obedience he is pleased to require of them.

The precision of the confession's language is amazing. It expresses truth biblically and exactly. At the same time, its language has a lyrical quality, a richness to the way it flows.

In section 2 of chapter 2, we see this richness and precision again. This section begins, **God hath all life, glory, goodness, blessedness, in and of himself.** This is what makes God utterly transcendent. **Life** is something that God possesses in and of Himself. Most precious to us, of course, are our own lives, for we understand our mortality. Scripture tells us that life is like the grass; it withers and then dies. We are always dependent on support systems—food, oxygen, water, and human fellowship—to continue living, because we do not have life in ourselves. At Mars Hill, Paul said, "In him we live and move and have our being" (Acts 17:28). God has all life in and of Himself. As we probe reality, we discover that nothing is more mysterious than life itself. We find reality ultimately in God; without Him there is no plant life, animal life, or human life, because all power to live comes from Him, who alone has all life in and of Himself.

God also has **glory . . . in and of Himself.** A burning issue today is that of self-worth, self-esteem, and human dignity. From a biblical perspective we see that dignity, worth, or esteem, when attributed to human beings, is a gift. We prefer to think that our dignity is intrinsic to our humanity, but dirt has little inherent dignity. We were created out of dust, and we return to dust. We cannot find in ourselves any basis for exalting humanity, because our dignity, according to Scripture, is not intrinsic. It is extrinsic, an assigned dignity. We have worth because God says so, because He assigns value and importance to human beings, and because He has made us in His image. God puts a premium on the sanctity of human life.

We may contrast our dignity, which is derived from God, to God's dignity, His glory, His gravitas. His dignity is in and of Himself, by the sheer nature of His being, and this glory is eternal. In one sense, God can set within His creation different levels of derived glory. As Paul tells us, the sun, the moon, and the stars have a certain glory (1 Cor. 15:40–41), but it does not compare with the eternal glory of God, which He shares with no creature. A creature can reflect God's glory, but that glory is inherent only in God Himself.

One of the most provocative statements in the New Testament appears in Hebrews 1:2–3, where Christ is introduced in all His magnificence.

The author calls Christ "the radiance of the glory of God" (Heb. 1:3). The Bible usually expresses God's glory in terms of a blinding, dazzling light. Yet the author here asserts that the very brilliance of divine glory is found in the second person of the Trinity.

God is the source not only of life but also of **goodness**. He is the standard for everything that is good. He is the power and definition of goodness. Speaking somewhat philosophically, we can say that the Bible describes God's goodness in ontological categories. Goodness is not just a quality of His behavior but an attribute of His essence or being. This captivated the imagination of Augustine as he wrestled with the problem of evil. He (and later Thomas Aquinas) pointed to evil's parasitical nature. As a parasite, evil has no ontological status, no independent being. Only that which is in the first instance good can manifest evil, because evil reflects a lack, privation, or negation of the good. To Augustine, God alone has the being of good in and of Himself. He can assign goodness to humans, but our goodness is always associated with a certain lack or negation. We do not have a perfect, eternal, immutably good nature. God's behavior flows out of His good nature. His external righteousness reflects His internal goodness, which He has eternally in and of Himself. He is the source of life, value, and all goodness.

To goodness is added God's **blessedness, in and of Himself.** Blessedness comes to us humans from the outside. We recall Abraham's encounter with Melchizedek, when the king of Salem gave Abraham the blessing of God Most High (Gen. 14:18–19). Blessedness, a condition of personal joy, fulfillment, and wonder, is bestowed on us by God, who has an interior, inherent blessedness. The Christian can hope for nothing higher or more blessed than to see behind the veil, to see God as He is. We cannot see Him now, nor enjoy that permanent state of blessedness, because we are sinful. Who are promised that they shall see God? The pure in heart (Matt. 5:8).

If Jesus was sinless and lived His entire life with a pure heart, would it not follow (as some ancient theologians suggested) that even during His earthly incarnation Jesus never lost His state of blessedness with the Father? Jesus laid aside His glory and reputation, but did He lay aside His state of blessedness? If Jesus never lost the beatific vision and if throughout His life He had that uninterrupted vision of God's glory (something we will experience only in heaven), then while He was on earth Jesus had that blessed condition that flows from perfect communication with God. If this speculation is true, then the impact of the cross becomes all the more horrible. When God turned His back on sin on the cross, the pure state of blessedness that Jesus had enjoyed throughout His incarnate state was lost. Darkness came upon Him, not because of His sin—He was sinless—but because of the imputation of our sin to Him.

Such speculation, rooted and grounded in the biblical concept of blessedness, has merit. But God's blessedness, enjoyed in and of Himself, does not depend on what you and I do. No one gives God a blessing. Though we say, "We bless you, O God," we cannot add to His blessedness. He was as blessed before the world was created as He is now, and all our prayers, worship, and songs can add nothing to the perfection of blessedness and felicity that He enjoys.

God is alone in and unto himself all-sufficient. God is all-sufficient not only in Himself, but also for Himself, in the absolute sense, needing nothing from any creature. Christians often use expressions that are well meaning but that, if analyzed carefully, approach blasphemy. For example, "I'm so glad that so-and-so allowed God to work through him," or "Thank you for letting God work through you." Does this mean that God cannot work through me unless I allow Him? God does not need our permission to do anything, any more than He needed Paul's permission to appear to him on the Damascus road, or Judas' to use him for His greater glory, or that of Balaam's ass to speak prophetically. God is self-sufficient, both in Himself and for Himself.

We should be delighted to have God work through us. We should pray that He will work through us and give us the unspeakable privilege of being used by Him in His kingdom. But that does not involve giving our permission to God. We should listen to how we talk and make certain that we are biblically correct.

God is not standing in need of any creatures which he hath made, nor deriving any glory from them. A great painter, musician, or other artist learns from others and depends on his medium to make his creations. The artist gets a certain glory from the fruit of his labor, but God receives none of His glory from the creation. The creation manifests, or bears witness to, His glory. However, the creature does not add to or subtract from the eternal glory of God. We need to understand this, lest we boast and think that somehow we are adding something to God's inherent glory by our obedience or worship.

God is only manifesting his own glory in, by, unto, and upon them. The creature can reflect, mirror, or be the image of the glory that belongs to God only if He is pleased to manifest Himself in us, by us, and through us.

God is the alone fountain of all being. We discussed His self-existence or aseity earlier, and this is the weightiest philosophical assertion of the Christian faith: God alone is a pure, eternal, self-existent being, and nothing can exist apart from Him. "In him we live and move and have our being" (Acts 17:28). He is the fountain, the source of the stream from which we assuage our thirst. He and He alone is pure being, and all other beings, including human beings, are dependent, contingent, and derived from Him.

Of whom, through whom, and to whom are all things. God is the One in whom, by whom, and for whom all things exist. That may be bad news to us. Alas, we are not the ultimate goal or purpose of the universe, and the world does not revolve around us. The most crowded places for indispensable people are the cemeteries of the world. We must understand that everything exists for God, for His glory and majesty. From this comes the purpose of our being.

God hath most sovereign dominion over them. Many people step aside from classical theology when trying to grasp the phrase "most sovereign dominion." God is not just sovereign, but sovereign to a superlative degree. He is most sovereign, and that sovereignty means dominion. We can distinguish different areas in which He is sovereign: nature, the stars in their courses, the boundaries of the universe, and so on. He created the external world and upholds it moment to moment by His sovereign power. Not a single molecule runs loose in the universe outside the scope of God's control. He rules over all things in nature. If God is sovereign over all, then He is the source of all authority. His Word imposes on us absolute obligations. God alone can bind the human conscience with ethical mandates because His will is sovereign. If the Lord God omnipotent says, "You shall," or, "You shall not," there is no room for debate. He has the sovereign authority to rule what He creates, including us. Most Christians claim to believe that God has the right to rule over us, yet we belie that confession by committing sin. We try to impose our will as if it were higher than His.

At the next level comes the real crisis: the sovereignty of God's redeeming grace. Many people have a hard time accepting that God's mercy is part of His sovereignty. But God did say to Moses, "I will have mercy on whom I have mercy" (Rom. 9:15, quoting Ex. 33:19). Most professing Christians try to claim some sort of partnership with God. But listen to the confession: God **hath most sovereign dominion over them, to do by them, for them, or upon them whatsoever himself pleaseth.** God has every right to do with us whatever He deems good, whatever pleases Him.

Do we really believe that? Think of Job, in His hellish misery, declaring, "Though he slay me, I will hope in him" (Job 13:15), and "The Lord gave, and the Lord has taken away; blessed be the name of the Lord" (Job 1:21). God has the right to do whatever He wants to do with us. Perhaps you have heard someone say, "God saves as many people as He can." God could save every person, because He has the ability and the authority to do so. But when we start talking about what God can and cannot do with His grace, we have undermined the biblical concept of His most sovereign dominion over everything He has created. Then we fail the real test of whether we believe in the sovereignty of His grace and mercy.

In his sight all things are open and manifest, his knowledge is infinite, infallible, and independent upon the creature. Against this doctrine we have seen the heresy called open theism. It states that God does not know the future decisions of volitional creatures such as ourselves. Therefore, God's omniscience is not really "omni," but rather is limited by the future decisions of mortal free agents. God is ever learning. He is open to future possibilities that He does not currently know and about which He will not know until they happen.

Over against that ghastly view of God, we have the confession's affirmation that in His sight all things are open and manifest. All knowledge is in His mind already, an infinite knowledge of the past, present, and future. Furthermore, God never learns anything from us. Before we say a word, before it is on our tongue, He knows it. He knows what we are going to do before we do it, and it is not a last-minute knowledge. He knows all things from before time began.

So as nothing is to him contingent, or uncertain. When we say things are contingent, we mean that they are not logically necessary and are dependent on things outside themselves. For example, at a fork in the road, we can go either left or right. Which way we go is contingent on what decision we make.

When we play chess, our opponent has certain moves open to him. We must figure out a response to those contingencies. If he makes a certain move, we can choose from among an array of moves in response. If he makes move B, then we choose from among a different set of responses. The master chess player must consider all possibilities, or contingencies.

The confession says that God knows not only all the realities but also all the possibilities. He knows all the contingencies. His knowledge is infinite, infallible, and independent of the creature, so nothing is to Him contingent. He knows all the contingencies, but the contingencies are not contingent to Him. God never has to wait for the possibilities to become actualities before He knows what will happen.

There is another perspective that has attempted to deal with the challenge of human freedom and God's sovereignty. This approach speaks of a kind of knowledge in God called middle knowledge. It was first proposed by a Spanish Jesuit priest named Luis de Molina (and is thus called Molinism) in the sixteenth century, and it argues that God not only knows all that is, but all that could be. He is able to imagine every conceivable potential universe and to know what choices we would each make in any given circumstance. He then chooses to create that universe wherein the outcomes He desired come to pass freely. This attempt, instead of working through the challenges of our understanding of the sovereignty of God and human freedom, actually runs headlong into the same challenges. On the one hand, our choices are no more "free" since

God determined what He wanted and brought to pass. On the other hand, God is no more disconnected from our failures because, again, He chose that universe in which we "freely" choose to sin.

The confession, on the other hand, affirms that God not only knows all things but controls all things. In addition, it safeguards against any accusation against His character based on our sins by affirming in the next clause that God is utterly holy in all that He does.

God is most holy in all his counsels, in all his works, and in all his commands. The holiness of God in the superlative degree is found in His holy counsel, His holy plan. No diabolical scheme is hatched against us, for the purposes of His counsel are only good. This is a very difficult concept because we see real evil around us, and it is a sin to call evil good. Evil is evil, but God is sovereign over evil. This means that in His counsel God has, for His own reasons, determined that evil should be, and that does not make His counsel wicked. By God's holy counsel, the earth is fallen. By His holy will, we have fallen into corruption. This does not mean that we are thereby excused or that our corruption is lessened; but His sovereign will covers all that now is and all that happens. His counsel and plan are without blemish. He is most holy, not only in His plan, but also in the execution of His plan in all His works. He is most holy in everything He does and commands. God does not command His creatures to sin. He commands us to be holy, just as He is holy (Lev. 11:45).

To God is due from angels and men, and every other creature, whatsoever worship, service, or obedience he is pleased to require of them. Mortimer Adler set forth the hundred most basic concepts in Western philosophy and civilization, concepts such as justice, freedom, and value. We speak of these concepts regularly, yet when we analyze them carefully, we find them exceedingly difficult to define.

Take the concept of justice. While we often struggle to define it with precision, Aristotle thought about justice a great deal and provided a helpful definition. He defined it as giving to every person their due, that which is owed them—in some cases reward, in some cases punishment. The something that is due often comes by virtue of a covenant or agreement, and justice requires that the terms of the covenant be fulfilled.

From this we get the principle of something's being "due." A person is not due any money from someone else inherently, but once they enter into a financial agreement to trade goods or services for an agreed-upon fee, then the buyer is obligated to pay that fee to the seller. The buyer would be acting unjustly if he failed to give the seller his due. This concept of "due-ness" is tied historically, in Western thought, to the principle of justice. It is fascinating that, in light of God's goodness and holiness, the confession uses the concept of due-ness: **To him is due from angels and men, and every other creature, whatsoever worship, service, or obedience he is pleased to require of them.** God does not have to enter into a voluntary covenant with us, in which we agree to certain terms, before we are obligated to give Him His due. By the nature of His perfection and holiness, I already owe Him everything. I have an inherent obligation to obey, worship, honor, and glorify God because exultation from the lips of the creature is His due.

Paul arraigns the whole world before the tribunal of God for their foundational sin: "Although they knew God, they did not honor him as God or give thanks to him" (Rom. 1:21). The most fundamental sin of the human race is withholding from God the honor that is His due. To be sure, worship is a privilege, but it is also a duty. It is troubling when people say, "We don't worship God because it's a duty; we worship Him to fulfill ourselves." True, worship does fulfill us, but most importantly, it is His due by His very nature as God. He has the right to impose absolute obligations on us, to bind our consciences, so that justice demands that we give Him whatever He requires and commands. We have no escape from total obedience to Him.

We believe that we do not really owe God obedience, but that He really does owe us mercy and forgiveness. But mercy is not our due. Whenever we receive mercy, it is because of grace, not justice. Justice requires that we obey God. Justice does not require God to forgive and show mercy to us. That is grace.

3. In the unity of the Godhead there be three persons, of one substance, power, and eternity: God the Father, God the Son, and God the Holy Ghost: the Father is of none, neither begotten, nor proceeding; the Son

is eternally begotten of the Father; the Holy Ghost eternally proceeding from the Father and the Son.

This section provides a brief statement of the doctrine of the Trinity, a formula that is not self-contradictory but that does not penetrate the depths of the mystery of God's nature. We have here the ancient formula that God is one in essence and three in person.

To understand this, we begin with the concept of "person." We say that there are three persons in the Trinity—one essence or substance, but three persons. But when we speak of Christ, we meet one person with two natures (or essences), and that complicates matters. When we use the formula "one in nature, three in person," we tend to stumble over this word *person* because we bring to it the common understanding of personhood and our own everyday use of the term. *Person* comes from the Latin *persona*, and originally it did not have exactly the same connotation as our word *person* has today.

The first to use this distinction between essence and person (*persona*) was Tertullian, an early church father and a lawyer. *Persona* had a specific meaning in the law courts, as well as the theater. Perhaps you have seen, in the modern theater, the symbol of the two masks, one for comedy and one for tragedy.

Some time ago I saw the long-running Broadway play *J.B.* Though the play was written in the modern vernacular, the character J.B. represents the Old Testament character Job. The book of Job begins with a dialogue between God and Satan. The actor Basil Rathbone appeared on stage with two masks. One depicted God, the other Satan. When Rathbone assumed the role of God, he held that mask in front of his face and spoke through it. When changing to the role of Satan, Rathbone put down the first mask, picked up the second, and spoke through it. As incongruous as it seems to us, the J.B. production recaptured some of the ancient theatrical practice of casting roles, wherein a single actor would play multiple parts and would represent each part through the use of masks.

What does this have to do with the Trinity? The Latin word used for those masks was *personae*—the plural form of *persona*. An individual mask was a *persona*, and multiple masks were *personae*. In courts of law, *persona* carried the idea of personal property, so your estate or personal possessions could be called *personae*—those things that belonged to you. Tertullian adapted the word *persona* from these two contexts when formulating the essence-person distinction—God is one essence and three *personae*.

But Greek theologians used a Greek term to designate the three persons of the Trinity: *hypostasis*. They did not understand the three persons as three distinct existences or persons (in our common use of the term *person*). That would indicate three separate beings and would engage us in tritheism, a form of polytheism, which would contradict our commitment to monotheism. The theological concept represented by *hypostasis* was that of "subsistence." The word *subsistence* has something in common with our everyday word *existence*. We need to understand that in a certain sense God does not *exist*, at least in terms of the original meaning of *existence*. To exist comes from the Latin *existere*. *Ex* means "from" or "out of." *Sistere* means "to stand." So the literal meaning of *existere* (exist) in antiquity was "to stand out of."

What is it, then, that we are standing out of? In the old Latin language, the answer was essence or being. So to the ancient philosophers, to exist meant "to stand out of essence or being." If you follow modern existential philosophy, this might make more sense to you. Imagine a circle on the chalkboard representing being or essence. A stick figure has one foot inside the circle and the other foot outside—one foot in being, the other in nonbeing. "To stand out of" was thought to mean "to stand out of being," but not totally outside it, because that would make us pure nonbeing. Philosophers had the idea that things of a creaturely nature—such as trees, rocks, fish, plants, and people—exist by virtue of having one foot in being and one in nonbeing. They were attempting to capture the idea that we do not have our being in and of ourselves. Unlike God, we are not perfect, eternal, immutable beings.

God alone has pure being, but we creatures cannot exist except by virtue of the power of God, in whom "we live and move and have our being" (Acts 17:28). We creatures have existence, while the Creator has pure essence. That is why I said we do not want to affirm God's *existence*. We do want to affirm His reality, His being, but we do not want to reduce

Him to the level of existence in the sense just explained. But in today's language, when we say that God exists, we mean that He really is, that He is not a figment of someone's imagination.

The term *to exist* described finite creatures to the ancients. *Essence* referred to eternal, self-existing being—pure being. When we say that God is one in essence and three in person, we confront another term used by the Westminster divines: God is one in essence and three in subsistence. We use the term *subsistence* to describe the condition of people who live in poverty, barely eking out an existence. We say that they live at the subsistence level. The prefix *sub* means "under"; *subsistence*, "to stand under." The theologians were saying that the personal distinctions of the Godhead are to be understood not as three distinct existences, but as three subsistences; so the distinction in the Godhead of the three persons is *real*, but not *essential*.

To say that something is not essential seems to imply that it is not vitally important. However, that is not what we mean. The term *essential* is being used in its technical, metaphysical sense. In saying that the distinctions between the three persons in the Godhead are not essential, we mean that there are no differences of essence, because they are all one essence. But within that one essence, there are three distinct subsistences—three things not outside the essence, but within the very being of God—and we distinguish them as the Father, the Son, and the Holy Spirit.

This technical discussion of the Trinity can be confusing, but here is what we should come away with: the Westminster divines, following the historic formulas of the church, are being extremely careful to affirm the full deity of the Father, the Son, and the Holy Spirit, and at the same time to steer clear of tritheism or polytheism. In simple terms, the Westminster divines are saying that in an absolute, ultimate sense, God is one—one being—yet within the Godhead are three distinct persons or subsistences that must be recognized if we want to be faithful to Scripture.

The subsistences, or persons, are more than offices, more than modes, more than activities, more than masks, and more than ways of appearing. The church historically has said that we do not understand how God is three in one. But we do understand that He is not three gods, and that the Father, the Son, and the Holy Spirit are all divine.

In the unity of the Godhead there be three persons, of one substance, power, and eternity. The Council of Nicaea in 325 said that Christ is consubstantial and coeternal with the Father. John records: "In the beginning was the Word, and the Word was with God, and the Word was God" (John 1:1). The council affirmed that the Word (the Logos), the second person of the Trinity, is not only of one essence with the Father, but also coeternal, and therefore not a creature.

At that time, the great threat to the church was the Arian heresy. Arius taught that Christ, the Logos, was the most exalted being ever created by God, the firstborn of creation, but nevertheless created and not eternal. By denying the deity of Christ, Arius also denied the Trinity. He appealed to Colossians 1:15, which calls Christ "the firstborn of all creation," and to John 1:14, which calls Him "the only begotten (*monogenēs*) of the Father"—that is, "the uniquely begotten one of the Father." Arias argued that if Christ was born, even as the firstborn, then there was a time before He was born. But if Christ is a creature, even the most exalted creature, then to worship Him is to violate the first and second commandments and to engage in idolatry. The struggle over Arianism led to the Council of Nicaea. Although rejected by that ecumenical council, Arianism remained powerful for much of the fourth century. Today, the Jehovah's Witnesses and others deny the deity of Christ and make the same arguments that the Arians made.

The Arians used a method common in their day to circulate their ideas. They composed rousing songs that promoted their views and insulted the Trinitarians. The Trinitarians responded by writing their own song, and historians tell us that at the height of the controversy the Arians stood on one side of the river and sang, while the Trinitarians stood on the other side and sang. The Trinitarians' song was the *Gloria Patri*: "Glory be to the Father and to the Son and to the Holy Ghost, as it was in the beginning, is now and ever shall be, world without end, amen." Today we tend to sing this song in somber reverence, whereas it was originally composed as a fight song.

The word used at Nicaea to define the relationship between Christ and the Father was *homoousios*, which means "of the same being." This was the most important theological formula of the fourth century, if not the church's first thousand years. It affirms that Christ, in His divine nature, is of the same essence as the Father. Thus, He is (as the Council of Chalcedon later affirmed) *vere homo, vere Deus,* "truly man and truly God."

Another important phrase in the Nicene Creed says that Christ is "begotten, not made"—He is "the only begotten." When people and other creatures are begotten (propagated), they are made, but Christ was begotten in eternity in a unique way that did not involve being made. The force of the term *monogenēs,* "only begotten," is that Christ is uniquely begotten of the Father, that He is the one and only, the once for all. As the *monogenēs,* Christ is uniquely begotten, not in time as a creature, but eternally as the Son of God. John indicates this by saying that the Logos "was with God" and "was God" at the beginning (John 1:1).

If the Logos, the second person of the Trinity, is eternally begotten by the Father, then there never was a time when Christ was not begotten of the Father. The second person of the Trinity has an eternal relationship of sonship with the Father.

There are two special relationships in the Trinity. First, the Son is eternally begotten from the Father (and not vice versa). Second, the Holy Spirit proceeds eternally from the Father and the Son (not vice versa). These relationships define the ontological relationships among the three persons of the Trinity.

The Father is of none, neither begotten, nor proceeding. The Father is that personal subsistence in the Godhead from whom the Son is begotten and from whom (with the Son) the Holy Spirit proceeds. There are relations of origin within the Godhead that describe the personal properties that differentiate the three persons from one another, not descriptions of ontological (pertaining to being or essence) superiority or inferiority. The Father is eternally unbegotten, the Son is eternally begotten of the Father, and the Holy Spirit proceeds eternally from the Father and the Son. At the same time, the Father, Son, and Holy Spirit are *homoousios,* one with the other, having equal value, power, eternity, dignity, and authority.

The processions within the Trinity are reflected in the redemptive missions of the Son and Holy Spirit, but when we read about the sending of the Son and the Spirit in Scripture, we must be on guard against reading any kind of subordination into the very being of the Trinity itself because that being is one. The Son assumes a human body and soul in the incarnation, a true human nature. In His state of humiliation, therefore, the Son submits to the Father according to His humanity, but this submission does not reflect or entail any kind of subordination within the Godhead. Such would be impossible given that the Son is *homoousios* with the Father according to His divine nature.

Of God's Eternal Decree

1. God, from all eternity, did, by the most wise and holy counsel of his own will, freely, and unchangeably ordain whatsoever comes to pass: yet so, as thereby neither is God the author of sin, nor is violence offered to the will of the creatures; nor is the liberty or contingency of second causes taken away, but rather established.

2. Although God knows whatsoever may or can come to pass upon all supposed conditions, yet hath he not decreed anything because he foresaw it as future, or as that which would come to pass upon such conditions.

3. By the decree of God, for the manifestation of his glory, some men and angels are predestinated unto everlasting life; and others foreordained to everlasting death.

4. These angels and men, thus predestinated, and foreordained, are particularly and unchangeably designed, and their number so certain and definite, that it cannot be either increased or diminished.

5. Those of mankind that are predestinated unto life, God, before the foundation of the world was laid, according to his eternal and immutable purpose, and the secret counsel and good pleasure of his will, hath chosen, in Christ, unto everlasting glory, out of his mere free grace and love, without any foresight of faith, or good works, or perseverance in either of them, or any other thing in the creature, as conditions, or causes moving him thereunto; and all to the praise of his glorious grace.

6. As God hath appointed the elect unto glory, so hath he, by the eternal and most free purpose of his will, foreordained all the means thereunto. Wherefore, they who are elected, being fallen in Adam, are redeemed by Christ, are effectually called unto faith in Christ by his Spirit working in due season, are justified, adopted, sanctified, and kept by his power,

through faith, unto salvation. Neither are any other redeemed by Christ, effectually called, justified, adopted, sanctified, and saved, but the elect only.

7. The rest of mankind God was pleased, according to the unsearchable counsel of his own will, whereby he extendeth or withholdeth mercy, as he pleaseth, for the glory of his sovereign power over his creatures, to pass by; and to ordain them to dishonor and wrath for their sin, to the praise of his glorious justice.

8. The doctrine of this high mystery of predestination is to be handled with special prudence and care, that men, attending the will of God revealed in his Word, and yielding obedience thereunto, may, from the certainty of their effectual vocation, be assured of their eternal election. So shall this doctrine afford matter of praise, reverence, and admiration of God; and of humility, diligence, and abundant consolation to all that sincerely obey the gospel.

---

1. God, from all eternity, did, by the most wise and holy counsel of his own will, freely, and unchangeably ordain whatsoever comes to pass: yet so, as thereby neither is God the author of sin, nor is violence offered to the will of the creatures; nor is the liberty or contingency of second causes taken away, but rather established.

Section 1 affirms something—that God ordains whatsoever comes to pass from all eternity—that is not unique to Reformed theology. Rather, it is a doctrine that expresses classical Jewish orthodoxy, Muslim orthodoxy, and Christian orthodoxy with respect to the nature of God. All this does is affirm theism. It affirms that God is sovereign. If in some sense God does not ordain everything that comes to pass, then He is not really sovereign; and if He is not sovereign, He cannot be God. If we self-consciously reject the sovereignty of God, we are rejecting the very nature of God and are not entitled to the term *theist*.

Why is eternal ordination so essential to sovereignty, and why is sovereignty so essential to our understanding of God? We might think that God concerns Himself only with the big things—important people, weighty events. He might be unconcerned with the small details. There might be a molecule out there in space—a maverick molecule—over which God has no control. We might think that wouldn't matter. But some apparently insignificant detail, like a maverick molecule going in a particular direction, can have radical consequences.

One historian contended that the history of Western civilization was changed by a grain of sand in Oliver Cromwell's kidney, which caused his demise. A bug bit Alexander the Great and changed the course of history. Some say the devil is in the details, but Christians should say that God is in the details. As our Lord Himself said, not a single bird lands on the ground apart from the Father's knowledge. Even the hairs of our head are numbered (Matt. 6:25–34). God knows everything there is to know about everything there is. He knows us comprehensively. He knows all contingent things—things that we say could have happened.

God not only knows all contingencies, but knows nothing contingently Himself. That is, God does not need to wait for things to happen in order for Him to know what is going to happen. He knows every word that we are going to speak. Before the word is even formed on our lips, He knows what it will be.

Now some simple questions: Does God have power over our lives? Could He take our lives at any second? Does He have the authority or right to do so? Would He be violating any principle of justice if He took them this second? If God knew what we were going to say and did not approve of it, could He keep us from saying it?

Of course He could. If He could have stopped us from saying it, but chose not to, then in a sense He ordained that we would say it. Without necessarily forcing you to say it, He knows what you are going to say. He can keep you from saying it, and insofar as He refrains from stopping you from saying it, in a sense He chooses that you say it. If what you are about to say or what you want to say would completely destroy His eternal plan of redemption for this planet, do you suppose He would let you say it?

Does God say anything about future events in Scripture? Did the Old Testament, divinely inspired, predict the cross of Christ? Was there any sense in which Christ needed to die on the cross, or was that a complete accident? Was it possible for Jesus to escape this death if God had decreed that He would be crucified?

On the judgment day, can Judas stand up before God and claim: "I should be recognized as a hero here. If I had not betrayed Jesus and delivered Him into Pilate's hands, the most important act of redemption would not have happened"? Does that excuse Judas? Not at all. He might try to say, "God, You owe it to me that this came to pass." But even Judas' sin was part of God's sovereign plan, which does not excuse Judas because God did not force him to do it. The same can be said of us and our sin.

Here is the real problem: if in a certain sense God ordains everything that comes to pass, then in a certain sense He even ordains my sin. Does He know that I am going to sin from all eternity? Yes. Could He stop me from all eternity? Yes. Does He choose not to stop me? Yes. So in the sense that He permits me to sin, I am still the sinner; I am doing the bad thing. But I cannot even sin apart from the permissive will of a sovereign God. He is not forcing me to sin and then holding me accountable for what I was forced to do. He can stop me from doing anything I do at any time. But I cannot excuse myself by saying to God, "You let me do it."

One of Scripture's most difficult concepts is that God can bring good out of evil. We remember that Joseph's brothers betrayed him and, upon being reunited with him in Egypt, feared his revenge. But Joseph said to them, "You meant evil against me, but God meant it for good" (Gen. 50:20). That was God's intention. He used the brothers' treacherous activity in order to save lives, sanctify Joseph, and bring His plan to pass.

One of the most comforting passages in the New Testament is Paul's statement that "for those who love God all things work together for good, for those who are called according to his purpose" (Rom. 8:28). We must be careful here. Paul does not say that everything that happens, considered in and of itself, is good. Nor is our theme song "Que Sera, Sera," "Whatever will be, will be." We do have the astonishing promise, however, that everything will work together for good for those who love God and are called according to His purpose. This means that even from the bad things that happen to us, God is bringing about good. This glorious concept means that we should trust God—even in the midst of tragedy, pain, disease, and suffering of all kinds. God assures us that He is working all things together for our good.

God can work all things together for good only if He is sovereign. If God is not sovereign over the details, He cannot guarantee His promise to work all things together for good, because one thing keeps lurking in the background: the maverick molecule. This molecule may set off a collision with other molecules that can end up disrupting the best plans of God.

Yet so, as thereby neither is God the author of sin, nor is violence offered to the will of the creatures; nor is the liberty or contingency of second causes taken away, but rather established. These are important qualifying words, each one carefully chosen. The confession says that God ordained whatever comes to pass. He ordained not only the ends, but also the means. He ordained not only that Christ be crucified, but also the human instruments through whom that crucifixion would come to pass, including Caiaphas, Judas, and Pontius Pilate. Joseph was correct when he said, "You meant evil against me, but God meant it for good." The end that God had in view when ordaining the betrayal of Joseph was the rescue of all Israel. The means by which God brought to pass that holy and righteous end were the wicked actions of Joseph's brothers.

To help clarify this, theologians for centuries have distinguished between primary and secondary causality. In a football game, when the quarterback throws the ball to a wide receiver, in one very real sense the quarterback is the cause of that ball's flying through the air, having exercised the strength of his arm. The quarterback is the outside force that acts on the ball by throwing it to the receiver.

Paul teaches that it is in God that "in him we live and move and have our being" (Acts 17:28). God is the ultimate source of all power in the universe. The creature is in every respect dependent on the Creator for its very being and for its continuing existence. So the quarterback is the secondary cause of the ball's flying through the air to the receiver, and God is the primary cause.

Deism, a religious movement that developed out of the Enlightenment, was popular for only a short period, but it had a strong impact on some of America's founding fathers, such as Thomas Paine. Deists taught that God was the first cause of the universe, and He created it to run on its own. Since then, God has remained remote and aloof from the world and has been uninvolved in its activities. God was the great watchmaker, who built the watch, wound it up, and then left it alone to run by itself.

Almost no one today calls himself a deist. As popular as deism was in the eighteenth century, it has virtually disappeared as a conscious system of belief. However, it is likely that the overwhelming majority of modern Americans, including most professing evangelicals, are in their thinking fundamentally deistic. The fundamental concept behind deism is that the universe is like a machine. It may owe its origin to a divine act of creation, but it works by its own inherent forces. All our instruction in science assumes the independent causal power of natural things. But that assumption is on a collision course with biblical Christianity, which at the very beginning makes a radical distinction between the Creator and the creature. God not only creates things but He also sustains them. We are as dependent on Him for our continued existence as we were for the beginning of our existence. If God were to cease to exist tonight, what would happen to us? If the world's very existence is dependent on God, then we and the whole world would collapse.

What does this have to do with primary and secondary causes? Christianity allows for the existence of real causal power in this world. The quarterback really does exercise power when he throws the football; God does not throw it for him. But he could not throw it were it not for his moment-by-moment dependence on the being and power of God. Whatever power is exhibited in this world is not due to an independent machine with its own source of power and energy. What scientists call the laws of nature we call the normal operations of the sovereign God. They are His laws; they are not independent in nature. They simply describe the regular, normal way in which God manages or governs His universe. He is the primary cause of everything that comes to pass, the power supply for all force; secondary causes are always dependent for their power on the primary source of power.

This concept of primary and secondary causality might sound strange. Nearly everyone has uncritically accepted the basic assumption of the secular worldview—that the world operates independently, by its own power. We can see the negative reaction to the idea of God as primary cause when someone suggests that events, especially tragic events, are governed by the sovereignty of God. When Pat Robertson told Floridians that hurricanes may be part of God's plan, it created a media backlash. People were upset with the idea that God has anything to do with hurricanes.

God is not the only worker in the universe, however. We are also workers. We are actively involved in making choices and exercising real power. Energy is really transferred from one thing to another. But these things do not happen independently of God. He exercises His power and sovereignty over all created things.

The more we reflect on this and work through some of the apparent difficulties, the more we realize that our lives are not exposed to the blind forces of chance or fate. This is our Father's world, and our lives are in His hands. His purpose and will are being brought to pass. For this reason, no consistently Reformed person can be a pessimist, and least in the long run. We can see and understand that God is in control and He is working out all things for our ultimate good. If we believe that God is sovereign over all things, that should affect our whole way of thinking. To think theistically, to have a Christian worldview, is to see ourselves, the world, life, and history under the guidance, direction, and will of God.

2. Although God knows whatsoever may or can come to pass upon all supposed conditions, yet hath he not decreed anything because he foresaw it as future, or as that which would come to pass upon such conditions.

One concern of Reformed theology is the eternal perspective of God's plan of salvation, a plan involving sovereign decisions that we call decrees. When He orders that something should come to pass, He is expressing His decretive will. We distinguish between God's preceptive will, by which He commands our obedience through laws, commandments, and precepts, and His decretive will, by which He brings to pass whatever He decrees shall come to pass.

One example of God's decretive will is creation. God brings the world into existence, not by using preexisting matter, but by fiat. According to the biblical record, God created the world by issuing sovereign commands such as "Let there be light" (Gen. 1:3). By virtue of His sovereign decree, God brought the universe into being. From the perspective of the Westminster divines, God's sovereign decrees do not apply merely to the creation, but also to the work of redemption. His plan of redemption is rooted and grounded in His eternal, sovereign decree.

In section 1, we spoke of God's holy counsel, whereby everything comes to pass through His divine ordination. We explained the relationship between God's ordaining of all things (the primary cause) and the decisions of human beings (secondary causes). The confession elaborates on this concept in section 2. Here we see reiterated what we read in chapter 2 with respect to God's omniscience and His other attributes. That chapter affirmed that God knows all things past, present, and future, and that He knows not only everything that is, but everything that could possibly be. He knows all contingencies, yet at the same time He knows nothing contingently Himself—that is, He does not need to wait for certain conditions to be met before He knows what will take place.

The writers of the confession, when dealing with God's eternal decrees, introduce this aspect of God's knowledge of the future for a simple reason. Historically, every major Christian tradition has had some doctrine of election or predestination. The idea of predestination was not invented by Augustine, Luther, Calvin, or Edwards; it is a biblical concept. The word *predestination* appears in the New Testament, so Christians recognize that the Bible teaches some kind of predestination.

But how do we understand predestination biblically? What shape or form does this doctrine take? The most popular form is the prescient view. Prescience is synonymous with foreknowledge. For example, in Romans we read: "Those whom he foreknew he also predestined. . . . And those whom he predestined he also called, and those whom he called he also justified, and those whom he justified he also glorified" (Rom. 8:29–30). This is called the golden chain of salvation; it shows an unbreakable sequence from foreknowledge to glorification. According to the prescient view, God bases predestination on His prior knowledge of human decisions. That is, He looks down the corridors of time and observes that certain people will respond positively to the gospel, while others will reject it. Then He issues

His decree of election to match those future human decisions. So election is ultimately based on what the creature does, rather than on what God decrees beforehand. We call this conditional election, because election is based on condition, that is, faith. Anyone who meets the condition of faith is chosen by God on the basis of that foreseen faith.

This view of predestination is not biblical. It denies the biblical view because there is no real predestinating involved in the prescient view, only foreknowing. God does not determine in advance who can and will believe. The Reformed doctrine of predestination, by contrast, is called unconditional election. It teaches that election is based not on people's meeting conditions but on the eternal decree of God Himself.

Although God knows what will happen, yet hath he not decreed anything because he foresaw it as future, or as that which would come to pass upon such conditions. Lurking beneath the surface is the question of God's foreknowledge. How does He foreknow what will take place? He does not decree anything on the basis of His knowledge of future events or possibilities; instead, He knows things in advance because He has decreed them in advance. He knows what will happen tomorrow because He has decreed what will happen tomorrow. Some people respond to the gospel and some do not because God has chosen to bring some to Himself. In Romans 9:11–13, Paul says of Jacob and Esau, "Though they were not yet born and had done nothing either good or bad—in order that God's purpose of election might continue, not because of works but because of him who calls—she was told, 'The older will serve the younger.' As it is written, 'Jacob I loved, but Esau I hated.'" Paul goes on to say, "So then it depends not on human will or exertion, but on God, who has mercy" (v. 16). In Ephesians, Paul presses the point that the ground of our election is not in us, but in the sovereign good pleasure of God (Eph. 1:5).

> 3. By the decree of God, for the manifestation of his glory, some men and angels are predestinated unto everlasting life; and others foreordained to everlasting death.

Notice the shift in the language here from *predestinating* to *foreordaining*. That could be merely stylistic, designed to mix up the synonyms that are used, but I think instead that there is a theological reason for it.

The decree in the first instance is to manifest God's glory. The reason for any salvation, for any election, is to manifest the glory of God. People may say: "I see how God's glory is manifested in saving fallen human beings who are incapable of redeeming themselves. This is a marvelous display of His mercy and grace that redounds to His glory. But what about the rest of mankind, those who perish in their sins, who receive no benefits of this supreme act of divine mercy? How can people who perish in hell add to the glory of God?" This is one of the most difficult concepts for Christians to accept: that God is glorified by bringing judgment on sin and sinners. From a biblical perspective, it is safe to say (though it may be difficult for us to grasp emotionally) that God is glorified by the judgment of the wicked in hell just as much as He is glorified by the rescue of the saints in heaven. On the one hand, God's mercy is made manifest. On the other, His justice is made manifest. When God's justice is demonstrated, He is glorified because it shows His goodness.

This is precisely the point in dispute, however. The biggest argument against the Augustinian and Reformation doctrine of predestination is that it does not, in fact, manifest the goodness of God. Critics say that the Reformed doctrine makes God unrighteous. It is unfair of Him, they say, to give saving grace to one person and to withhold it from another. Both are equally guilty before Him, so how can a righteous God treat them differently? Isn't that unfair? Isn't God obligated to extend His mercy to all equally?

In Romans 9, the Apostle Paul gives his most extensive explanation of the doctrine of election. In the process, he anticipates objections that will be raised. In the middle of his discussion of election, he raises a question before his readers can: "What shall we say then? Is there injustice on God's part?" (v. 14). That is the first objection the Apostle expects to hear from his readers, so he deals with it up front.

Paul responds emphatically: "By no means!" He reminds his readers that God, speaking through Moses, has said, "I will have mercy on whom I have mercy" (vv. 14–15). God makes it clear that He has the sovereign prerogative to give mercy and bestow grace on whomever He wants to. He can give an executive order of unmerited clemency to those whom He pleases. That is why it is mercy. That is why it is grace.

The framers of the confession had something theological in mind when they changed the terminology from **predestined unto everlasting life** to **foreordained to everlasting death**. One area of confusion is the question of so-called double predestination. Some Christians believe that the Bible teaches predestination, but only single predestination: God elects some to salvation, but does not predetermine the reprobate to damnation. They think that God's decree is only positive; it has no negative dimension to it.

The Reformed view is called double predestination because it includes both election (the positive side) and reprobation (the negative side). We who hold this view need to be cautious in how we articulate it. If everyone except for one person were eternally foreordained or predestinated to salvation, and only one were not, the problem would still remain. We must deal with the reality that at least one person falls outside the category of the elect. So there are the elect and the nonelect. We can escape that problem only if everyone is elect. As long as the distinction between particularism (not everyone is elect) and universalism (everyone is elect) exists, we must face the problem of the flip side of election, or double predestination.

To be consistent with the biblical doctrine of predestination, we must affirm double predestination. It is not enough, however, just to make that assertion. We should also distinguish between different views of double predestination. In his book *On the Bondage of the Will*, Martin Luther labors this distinction in responding to Erasmus' semi-Pelagian *Diatribe*.

One kind of double predestination, advocates of which are usually called hyper-Calvinists, argues that the decrees of election and reprobation are symmetrical. This means that both election and reprobation are equally ordained and enforced by divine intervention. With respect to the elect, God intervenes in their lives to create faith in their souls and bring them to a state of salvation. In like manner, God intervenes in the lives of the reprobate to create a hardness of heart, or a fresh evil in their heart, which becomes the grounds of their justifiable damnation and reprobation.

The Bible teaches, for example, that God hardened Pharaoh's heart (Rom. 9:17–19; cf. Ex. 7:3–4). According to Luther, the act of God's judgment called hardening involves two important concepts. Through-out Scripture God's judgment is often manifested or explained in terms of a kind of poetic justice, in which He gives people over to their already evil inclinations. In the final judgment, John writes, "Let the evildoer still do evil" (Rev. 22:11). In His judgment on the nonelect, God gives them over to their sinful desires, a common theme found throughout Scripture. God did not need to create fresh evil in Pharaoh's heart to redeem His chosen people. There was already enough evil in Pharaoh's heart to last forever. God needed only to withhold from Pharaoh whatever grace was restraining his wickedness and to allow him his way. By doing this, God hardened Pharaoh's heart. Such is the natural consequence of our own sinfulness.

Reformed theology rejects this form of double predestination, which is often called equal ultimacy. According to this idea, God works posi-tively in the elect to bring about faith and also works positively in the reprobate to prevent faith. If this were so, the charge of unfairness would be understandable. Pharaoh was only doing what God was forcing him to do.

The Reformation view of double predestination is not this symmet-rical, positive-positive view, but rather a positive-negative view. When God made His eternal decrees of salvation and reprobation in light of the (still future) fall, His decision to elect some people was based on His knowledge that people would need salvation. God's decree of salvation was based on His knowledge of a world that is fallen. Contemplating the whole of humanity, God knew that every last one of them would be dead in sin and trespasses, fallen, corrupt, hostile to him, having no inclination toward divine things. Every one of them would be a slave to sin, refusing to have God in their thinking, walking according to the course of this world and the power of Satan. That is the condition of fallen, corrupt humanity that God saw when decreeing election. Out of this group of rebels, God, in His mercy, elected to save some and to visit them with His special grace of redemption. He positively intervenes in their lives to quicken them from spiritual death and to work faith in their hearts, thereby meeting the condition for salvation. The others He passes over, leaving them in their sin. He does not force them into unbelief. But He knows that unless He intervenes, they will indeed persist in unbelief and end up in damnation. On the mercy side of the ledger, God intervenes in people's lives and brings their salvation to pass; on the other side, He does not intervene, leaving people to their own devices.

Some might ask, If God has the right and the power to intervene in people's lives and to bring them to a state of saving faith, then why doesn't He do it for everyone? The Bible does not answer this question. We know that the answer does not reside in the individual. Some people believe that God does bestow His saving grace on everyone, so that everyone is saved whether they believe or not. Others believe that He bestows a kind of grace called prevenient grace (meaning that it comes before) that allows people to exercise faith and meet the conditions of salvation. They think that God has thus done His part, and the final decision depends on what each individual does with that grace. This is a semi-Pelagian position, and it still leaves the question of why some people cooperate with grace while others reject it.

Someone who takes the position that the final decision remains with the individual faces a new kind of problem. Such a person has to wrestle with the fact that he has believed while others, perhaps a friend or family member, have not. Is it because he is somehow better or smarter than his friend who has not believed? Is that why he has faith and his friend does not? He would likely not say this. But he should. After all, he gave the right response to God's grace, and his friend gave the wrong one. In the end, the semi-Pelagian is in the kingdom and his friend is not because the semi-Pelagian did the righteous thing and his friend did the unrighteous thing. Whether the semi-Pelagian wants to say it out loud or not, he has something to boast about.

Even if the Bible never used the words *predestination* or *election*, what it teaches about our natural, fallen condition would force us to devise a doctrine of predestination to account for salvation. As Christ said, "No one can come to me unless it is granted him by the Father" (John 6:65), and, "All that the Father gives me will come to me" (v. 37).

In our fallen condition, we do not have the moral power to embrace the gospel. That is why God does more than offer Himself to people. He must do a work not only for us, but also in us. Paul wrote that while we were still in a state of spiritual death, God redeemed us (Eph. 2:5). Jesus said, "Unless one is born again he cannot see the kingdom of God" (John 3:3), and, "Unless one is born of water and the Spirit, he cannot enter the kingdom of God" (John 3:5). Semi-Pelagianism teaches that masses of people—people who cannot see the kingdom of God or enter it, because they are not yet regenerated—embrace the kingdom. This turns the biblical order of things upside down. Two factors drive the semi-Pelagian view: a misguided effort to exalt the power for good that resides in the human heart, causing an exaggerated view of mankind or a diminished view of our fallenness, and a desire to absolve God from any charge of being arbitrary, unfair, or unrighteous.

The sweetness of divine grace is shown more clearly in the Reformed view than in any semi-Pelagian view. In the semi-Pelagian view, God's grace makes salvation possible for everyone but certain for no one. If He gives only prevenient grace and if it is up to us to cooperate with it or not, then it is theoretically possible that not a single human being will ever reach a state of salvation. In the biblical view, people who are elected by divine grace to believe and be saved will believe and be saved. God's redemptive work accomplishes what His sovereign decree of election determined to accomplish, namely, the salvation of the elect, whom He has chosen for His own good pleasure.

The change in language in section 3 from **predestinated** (for the elect) to **foreordained** (for the reprobate) cautions against a positive-positive view of double predestination. It signals that we should not understand both clauses in an equally ultimate way.

> 4. These angels and men, thus predestinated, and foreordained, are particularly and unchangeably designed, and their number so certain and definite, that it cannot be either increased or diminished.

The Lord knows from all eternity who are His. From all eternity, He has chosen certain vessels for salvation, and these are so predestined and foreordained that they are particularly and unchangeably designed. God's decrees are final, the confession says. This causes much grief among people who say, "That means that those who aren't predestined don't have a chance. So why should we be involved in evangelism? Why pray for the salvation of the lost?"

We evangelize because God commands us to, and we understand that through our preaching God brings His elect to salvation. The gospel is the power of God for salvation (Rom. 1:16). Rather than despising what our sovereign God commands us to do, we should be zealously engaged in doing it.

Christians are called to proclaim the gospel as widely, plainly, and accurately as we can and then to realize that only God can bring the increase and that He has promised to bring the increase. That is why Jesus prays in the upper room, "I am not praying for the world but for those whom you have given me, for they are yours" (John 17:9). He is praying for the elect. That principle appears throughout Scripture: the number of elect men and angels is a particular, not a universal, number. It is an unchangeable number by divine design. The number of the elect is so certain and definite that it can be neither increased nor diminished.

A group of Christian leaders, in the midst of a serious theological controversy, met to resolve a conflict so as to maintain their unity in Christ. After a measure of resolution occurred, one leader said to another, "If we hadn't had this meeting today, millions of people would have been lost." To that, we can say this: "If they hadn't met, not one person would have been lost. The number of the saved is decreed by almighty God from all eternity, and it does not depend on the machinations of Christian leaders." We need to understand that. How comforting it is to know that the final state of the church is in God's hands, not ours. All Christians have a responsibility to proclaim the gospel, but we do not have the power to bring spiritual life out of spiritual death. Only God can do that.

> 5. Those of mankind that are predestinated unto life, God, before the foundation of the world was laid, according to his eternal and immutable purpose, and the secret counsel and good pleasure of his will, hath chosen, in Christ, unto everlasting glory, out of his mere free grace and love, without any foresight of faith, or good works, or perseverance in either of them, or any other thing in the creature, as conditions, or causes moving him thereunto; and all to the praise of his glorious grace.

In a sense, this section summarizes everything the confession teaches about the doctrine of election. Many aspects of that doctrine are expressed here that receive greater attention later in the confession. In some cases, entire chapters are devoted to truths that are merely mentioned in this section. Let us look at the string of specific assertions that we find here.

First, these decrees were made by God **before the foundation of the world was laid**. That is, election and predestination took place in eternity, "before" creation. But what is the logical order of the decrees themselves? In particular, which decree came first: the creation (and fall into sin) or salvation? This question has become significant in modern times because Karl Barth, one of the most famous theologians of the twentieth century, adopted a position that he called a purified supralapsarianism: creation and the fall were decreed by God as the necessary means to carry out His eternal plan of redemption.

Normally, Reformed theology sees the decrees of creation and the fall coming first, followed by the decree of the plan of salvation (infralapsarianism). In some ways, the order of the decrees does not make much difference, as long as we understand whose decrees they are. The point Barth made so zealously is that God's plan, from the very beginning, was a positive one—a plan of redemption, a plan of bringing to Himself a redeemed people in the love of the Beloved, in Christ Himself. That is why Barth placed the decree of salvation before the decree of creation.

In any case, section 5 says that God's decrees originated **before the foundation of the world was laid**, according to God's **eternal and immutable purpose**. When God decrees something, He does so for a reason. God's decrees are never capricious, flippant, or in any way quixotic. They are teleological—that is, there is a purpose behind them. Redemption is grounded in eternity and in God's counsel, His intent for redemption, and that purpose is both eternal and immutable.

God has no alternative plan because His counsel is always rooted in His infallibility, His omniscience, and His perfect righteousness. Nothing could ever come up in nature's contingencies that would incline God to change His eternal purpose. He knows the end from the beginning. Because He knows all contingencies, His plan is fixed, and that is what the confession affirms here again—that God's will is immutable.

What are some practical considerations at this point? People ask, "Can we pray for people when they may not be numbered among the elect?" A similar question is, "Can our prayers persuade God to change His eternal decrees and add someone to the number of the elect who was not there originally?" Section 4 clearly states that the number of the elect cannot be either increased or diminished. If someone is not numbered among the elect, all the intercessory prayers that the people of God bring in his behalf will not cause him to be added to that number. If that is so, why should we bother to pray for anyone's salvation?

We cannot know in this life who are not elect. We can know, after conversion, that we are numbered among the elect; we can have assurance of our salvation. But we can never be sure that we are not numbered among the elect. That can only be known posthumously, because we may not be converted until we are on our deathbed. Since we cannot penetrate the secret counsel of the Most High God, we have no idea who is numbered among the elect and who is not. For this reason, we might presume the election of every person we meet.

How would this affect our prayers? Not knowing a person's destiny in terms of God's decrees, we might ask that, if this person is elect, God would bring His election to fulfillment and realization in his life at this time. We can pray constantly for people who are not yet Christians, remembering (as we will see later) that God works through means to bring about His ends. One of the means is the prayers of His people. That the elect are rooted and grounded in an immutable decree in eternity is no reason for us to cease witnessing to, preaching to, or praying for people who are not yet converted.

Predestination is according to his eternal and immutable purpose, and the secret counsel and good pleasure of his will. Here are some important qualifiers. First, we hear about the secret counsel of God. Luther made an important distinction between what he called the *Deus absconditus* and the *Deus revelatus*. When we come before the living God of the Christian faith, we deal with a God who, on the one hand, is hidden (*absconditus*). That God is in some sense hidden doesn't mean that He does not reveal things about Himself or His plan. It merely affirms that He has not revealed everything there is in Himself or His plan. Thus, we do not know who the elect are, though He surely does.

God is also revealed (*revelatus*). He has been pleased to reveal many vital things about Himself, but He has not revealed everything that He could possibly reveal to us at this time. "The secret things belong to the LORD our God, but the things that are revealed belong to us and to our children forever" (Deut. 29:29). We should be concerned to master the material that God has been pleased to reveal and should not worry about what He has not been pleased to reveal—that which remains hidden from us and is a part of His secret counsel.

One of the most common questions that Christians ask is, "How can I know the will of God for my life?" They want to know what God's will is especially when it comes to their career and whom they should marry. If we say that we want to know the will of God, we must specify which will of God we are talking about: His revealed will or His hidden will. If we mean the former, then we must pour ourselves into a study of God's Word. There, we learn that His will for our lives is our sanctification (1 Thess. 4:3), and how to get there is set forth for us throughout sacred Scripture. He has told us that we have been redeemed "unto good works" (see Eph. 2; Titus 2). Jesus is about the business of removing from us every blot and blemish (Eph. 5). We are being remade into the image of the Son. It may not be flashy. It may not be prophetic. But we can know His revealed will for us, whereby He tells what pleases Him, and that should be more than enough to direct our steps.

If we are asking instead to know God's secret will, the answer is that we cannot. God has chosen not to reveal it, and one reason for that is that His secret counsel is none of our business. Trying to probe the secret counsel of God is an exercise not of piety and spirituality but of impiety. We should not pursue matters that God has not been pleased to reveal.

So, then, how do we make decisions? How do we know what the right thing to do is? We must look at God's revealed will. That gives us manifold principles on which to make ethical decisions and judgments. The Bible reveals that we are to act according to the gifts that God has bestowed on us, and we are to seek the counsel of others to help us understand our gifts.

For this reason, in most churches you cannot become a minister just by deciding you want to be one. The church must confirm that you have the necessary gifts and talents. The New Testament sets forth the qualifications for deacons and elders, revealing God's principles for the church to operate by. If you lack those qualities, then you do not need a special message from heaven revealing the secret counsel of God to you. His will revealed in Scripture will show you that.

Sometimes Christians face difficult situations and wonder what God would have them do. For instance, a Christian woman might be married to a non-Christian man. She might feel lonely, sharing a marriage with a man who didn't participate in what she loved most. But based on God's revealed will, she would not have warrant to divorce him if he wanted to remain married to her (1 Cor. 7:13). If he decides to leave, she can let him go, but biblically, she is not allowed to leave him.

Christians might say that they have prayed and God has given them peace in pursuing a sinful course of action. We dare not say such things, because in such cases, it is not the Lord who is giving them peace, because they are acting in complete contradiction to God's express law and commandment, which reveal His will.

Calvin agreed with Luther on the distinction between God's hidden and revealed wills. Calvin commented, "Where God closes His holy mouth, I will desist from inquiry." The Reformer saw speculation about God's secret counsel as irreligious and forbidden.

Some of the strongest prohibitions in the Old Testament outlaw sorcery, fortune-telling, and necromancy, all of which are an abomination to God. I suspect they are such because they are an attempt to peek behind the curtain, to discover God's own secrets. That temptation has not changed with the passing of time. People today go to tarot card readers, palm readers, and fortune-tellers. They are trying to look into God's secret counsel, and that is an abomination to Him.

Section 5 tells us that the decrees of election—the hidden decrees—are part of the hidden counsel of God and the good pleasure of His will. The Apostle Paul says that God predestinates according to the good pleasure of His will (Eph. 1:5). He bases His election on His good pleasure. This statement can provoke the objection that God is arbitrary or capricious. Both the Bible and the confession, when referring to God's election according to His pleasure, clearly mean His good pleasure. It is not even remotely possible that God could take pleasure in doing something wicked. The only thing that God is pleased to do is a good thing. Therefore, when God acts according to what pleases Him—in His will, according to His purpose—you may rest assured that He has made a good decision.

When our fallen nature takes over, we try to second-guess the eternal plan of God. Why does He not save everyone? He may appear from heaven to convert Saul, who was breathing out fire against the church, but hide Himself from Pontius Pilate. He may reveal Himself to Abraham in the midst of His Mesopotamian paganism and hide Himself from Hammurabi. We do not like that. But God has a purpose in doing this, and He does it according to His will, not ours, and that which pleases Him is always good. To believe God, to have faith in Him, is to trust Him to do what He says He will do and to trust in His goodness. We know that He does all things well.

We jump to the conclusion that God is arbitrary as soon as we say that there is no reason in us why He should select us. But that does not make the selection arbitrary. To be arbitrary is to have no reason. The reason is in God's counsel, His purpose, that the purposes of election may stand in the honoring of His Son. Just because it is not in us does not mean that God has no reason. Section 5 says that God's decrees come from His eternal purpose, and that purpose is good and not arbitrary.

Hath chosen, in Christ. That is important. Election in the Bible is always "in Christ." The ultimate object of divine election is Christ. In eternity, the Father chooses the Son for glory; but, desiring to glorify His Son, the Father gives gifts to His Beloved. He gives Him people who belong to the world, whom the Father takes out of the world and gives to His Son. Jesus speaks that way frequently in the gospel of John, about those whom the Father has given Him. He prays for them specifically: "I am not praying for the world but for those whom you have given me, for they are yours" (John 17:9). Those who are given to Christ are elected in Him, the Beloved. So the only reason we can give for our election is Christ. The only reason for election at all is the exaltation of the Son, that He may see the travail of His soul and be satisfied (see Isa. 53:11).

God has chosen the elect in Christ **unto everlasting glory.** This citation in section 5 is from Ephesians:

> He chose us in him before the foundation of the world, that we should be holy and blameless before him. . . . making known to us the mystery of his will, according to his purpose. . . . In him we have obtained an inheritance, having been predestined according to the purpose of him who works all things according to the counsel of his will. (Eph. 1:4, 9, 11)

Again: "For God has not destined us for wrath, but to obtain salvation through our Lord Jesus Christ" (1 Thess. 5:9). Nothing in this affirmation was not first in the Apostolic teaching. It summarizes almost verbatim Paul's teaching in Ephesians.

Out of his mere free grace and love. Here is *sola gratia*, the overlooked *sola* of the Reformation. This *sola* was first coined by the one who was called the "doctor of grace," Augustine of Hippo, chief tutor of both Luther and Calvin. We think of Luther as being the champion merely of *sola fide* and *sola Scriptura*, but in the debate over salvation, Luther was challenged by a former friend, Desiderius Erasmus. Erasmus wrote a diatribe against Luther's doctrine of election. In response, Luther said that *sola fide* is only the tip of the iceberg. *Sola fide* is front and center, but what underlies it is *sola gratia*. Anyone who does not understand *sola gratia*, Luther said, does not grasp *sola fide*. Conversely, he who does not properly understand *sola fide* does not understand *sola gratia*, because "faith alone," the means by which we are saved, is based on "grace alone." It is not a cooperative venture of works and grace, or merit and grace, whereby those who cooperate receive enough grace for salvation. No, faith itself is a gift, given freely by God on the basis of His grace, not because of foreseen actions or responses in the believer. Thus, *sola gratia* and *sola fide* are inseparably connected.

Later generations separated *sola gratia* from *sola fide*, so that in evangelical Christianity the majority of people, whether they know it or not, still affirm *sola fide* but deny *sola gratia*. They take a synergistic approach, with both God and man involved in our salvation. Luther could not tolerate this split. Nothing in Calvin's doctrine of election was not first in Luther's, as can be seen in Luther's book *On the Bondage of the Will.*

Without any foresight of faith, or good works, or perseverance in either of them, or any other thing in the creature, as conditions, or causes moving him thereunto; and all to the praise of his glorious grace. The other *sola* in view here is *soli Deo gloria*, "to God alone be the glory." All of this redounds to the praise of God for His glorious grace. His glorious grace is not mixed with human response, activity, willing, running, choosing, or doing. Our salvation is based entirely on the grace of God.

> 6. As God hath appointed the elect unto glory, so hath he, by the eternal and most free purpose of his will, foreordained all the means thereunto. Wherefore, they who are elected, being fallen in Adam, are redeemed by Christ, are effectually called unto faith in Christ by his Spirit working in due season, are justified, adopted, sanctified, and kept by his power, through faith, unto salvation. Neither are any other redeemed by Christ, effectually called, justified, adopted, sanctified, and saved, but the elect only.

There is a difference between means and ends. The Bible frequently speaks about a plan of salvation. At no point does the Bible provide a complete list of all the steps in this plan, or what theologians call the *ordo salutis*, the order or plan of salvation. When talking about the order of salvation, we refer mostly to logical rather than temporal order. What does logical priority mean? In the statement "We are justified by faith," we discern a relationship, connection, or link between faith and justification. But what is that link or connection? Are we justified and then, as a result, have faith, or is justification a consequence of our faith? How long must a person have faith before God lowers the gavel and declares this person just in His sight? For five minutes, perhaps? No, faith and justification happen simultaneously with respect to time. The very second someone has authentic faith, God justifies him. When we say that faith precedes justification, we mean that it precedes logically, because justification depends on faith. Faith does not logically depend on justification.

In the book of Romans, Paul gives us an outline of the plan of salvation: those whom God foreknew, He also predestined; those whom He predestined, He also called; those whom He called, He justified;

those whom He justified, He glorified (Rom. 8:29–30). This text mentions elements of the *ordo salutis*: foreknowledge, predestination, calling, justification, glorification. But faith is not mentioned here, nor is sanctification. We wrestle with where faith fits in, where regeneration and repentance fit in, where sanctification fits in. All these elements in the process of our salvation fit into a logical sequence. Section 6 says that God does not decree in eternity that certain people are elect and then forget the rest of the plan. The plan is conceived eternally but realized temporally. Although someone could be elect the moment he is born, he is not justified at that time. He has no faith then. Many aspects of the way of salvation have not yet been realized in his life. That takes place in space and time, and the end of the plan is glorification.

To bring to pass the goal of His plan for salvation, God uses means. In His eternal purposes, God has appointed not just the final result but the means by which that result is achieved.

In his final sermon, speaking about the power of the gospel, Luther talked about the propensity of people to seek out relics: a hair from the beard of John the Baptist or a vial of milk from the breasts of Mary. Luther called these alleged relics "the pope's junk."

Why did people do that? What were they seeking? Christians look for the same thing today. We look for power because we sense a lack of it in our spiritual lives. So we go to a healer's charismatic service to get slain in the Spirit and to see manifestations of power. But the power is right in front of us. The power is in the Word and the sacraments. Luther said we have this glorious gospel, which God says is the divine power for salvation (Rom. 1:16). Instead of attending to the sermon on Sunday morning, we run off to look for some other way, an easier, quicker method than God's way.

God has chosen to save the world through the foolishness of preaching the gospel. Paul tells us that the gospel is the power of God for salvation—not rhetoric, gifts, persuasive power, or the number of verses of a hymn sung after the sermon. The power is in the gospel, and the gospel has a certain required, specific content. It has to do with the person and work of Christ, who came as our Redeemer. He bore our sins on the cross, was raised for our justification, and promises that all who put their trust in Him will participate completely in the inheritance that the Father gives to Him, which is by faith. That is what we should be preaching. That is where the power is.

The preaching of the gospel has been at the forefront of every revival in church history that has had an impact on the world. John Wesley, who did not embrace the doctrines of grace, was nonetheless committed to the doctrine of justification by faith alone. That doctrine inflamed his heart. Justification by faith alone, preached by Jonathan Edwards and George Whitefield, brought about the First Great Awakening in America. The Reformation occurred because God used the power of the gospel to revive His church. He works through the Word, the sacraments, and prayer: these are the means of grace.

God uses the means of grace to bring about His saving purposes in our lives. When we join a church, we have to vow that we will diligently use the means of grace. We should not miss the Lord's Supper or Sunday morning services. Corporate worship is a means of grace. We should always attend to the preached Word. This is not a casual thing. It is not about being religious. It is about being diligent in pursuing the means that God has ordained for bringing people to faith. God's appointed means are not our marketing techniques. There is nothing in them that is ostentatious or peculiar; they are simply the tools that God Himself has ordained to allow us to grow us in grace.

> 7. The rest of mankind God was pleased, according to the unsearchable counsel of his own will, whereby he extendeth or withholdeth mercy, as he pleaseth, for the glory of his sovereign power over his creatures, to pass by; and to ordain them to dishonor and wrath for their sin, to the praise of his glorious justice.

Those who hold to single predestination characteristically believe that not everyone is saved and that God has, from all eternity, sovereignly decreed to save some. However, even among those who are not predestined to salvation, some may still be saved if they make the appropriate response to the gospel. The driving force behind single predestination is the rejection of reprobation, the flip side of election. Election is the positive side of predestination, whereby God elects to Himself certain people in Christ Jesus to be saved. Reprobation has to do with those whom God has not elected or positively chosen to be saved. Advocates of single predestination sometimes call double predestination a *decretum horribile*, a "horrible decree." Double predestination suggests that from all eternity God has not only chosen the specific part of humanity to be saved but also eternally decreed that the rest of humanity will be damned. That raises questions for many. We have just finished studying section 6, where we read strong statements that God foreordains not only that certain people will be saved but also how they will be saved. That section also says that only those who receive this gracious divine intervention will be saved. Section 7, dealing with reprobation, spells this out.

As he pleaseth, for the glory of his sovereign power over his creatures, to pass by. Reformed scholars have historically maintained that, if someone's doctrine of election is not in some sense universal, then he must have a doctrine of reprobation. He might ignore it and, as some do, refuse to say anything about the other side of the decree. But if God ordains to save some people and not all, then obviously there exists another group of people who are not elect. That means there must be a flip side to election. If we embrace predestination at all, and are not universalists, we must embrace some form of double predestination.

The rest of mankind God was pleased, according to the unsearchable counsel of his own will, whereby he extendeth or withholdeth mercy. In the case of the elect, God extends mercy. In the case of the reprobate, He withholds it. "I will have mercy on whom I have mercy, and I will have compassion on whom I have compassion" (Rom. 9:15). There is no equal ultimacy in the distribution of God's mercy and grace. He extends His mercy and withholds it as He pleases. We all enter this world as fallen, sinful creatures. God exercises His saving grace on the elect, and the rest He leaves in their fallen, sinful state.

Let us take predestination out of the mix altogether and discuss the broader question of particularism and universalism. If we are particularists—meaning that we believe that not everyone is saved, that there is a hell and some people go there—must we not conclude that in some sense God ordains that people go to hell? Who sends people to hell? Does the devil sentence them to hell? Do people sentence themselves to hell? Some would argue that because people go to hell as a result of their own sin, they are, in effect, sentencing themselves to hell. However, their sin only exposes them to a just sentence; they do not actually judge themselves on the judgment day. The judge is God, and He determines who goes to hell and who does not. Now, God has ordained whatever happens (section 1). So if God sends someone to hell, He must have ordained that person to go there. If God redeems some people from this prison of sin, He must have ordained that He would do so; if He chooses not to redeem other people, He must have ordained not to do so.

And to ordain them to dishonor and wrath for their sin, to the praise of his glorious justice. Is God just? Is He a good judge? If a judge never punishes sin, he has little regard for goodness or justice. When God exercises His justice, it is, as the confession says, a glorious justice that redounds to His own glory.

We do not like that. We prefer to hear the good news about God's mercy and grace, but good news is good only against the backdrop of bad news. And the bad news is that God is holy and we are not. He has appointed a day on which He will judge the world in righteousness and condemn some people to hell. He does not condemn innocent people. If He did, He would not be just. One group gets mercy; the other gets justice.

The grace of God redounds to His glory. We understand that God is wonderful because He is so kind, merciful, and gracious, and we see how grace displays the glory of God. But do we see how His justice also displays His glory? To rescue a sinner from His damnation is a wonderful thing, but to punish unrighteousness justly is also good. So in God's way and plan of salvation, He determines from the beginning to manifest both grace and justice—never injustice—by rescuing some (grace) and passing over the others (justice). No one gets injustice.

8. The doctrine of this high mystery of predestination is to be handled with special prudence and care, that men, attending the will of God revealed in his Word, and yielding obedience thereunto, may, from the certainty of their effectual vocation, be assured of their eternal election. So shall this doctrine afford matter of praise, reverence, and admiration of God; and of humility, diligence, and abundant consolation to all that sincerely obey the gospel.

Many people struggle with whether they are among the elect. We all tend to vacillate, to have various degrees of confidence as to our standing before God, particularly when troubled by a guilty conscience. We ask ourselves, "How could God save a wretch like me?" The more acutely conscious we are of our wretchedness, the more that tends to militate against any assurance that we are in the family of God.

The doctrine of election can actually be very helpful for our assurance of salvation. Our assurance rests not in our self-examination but in our confidence in God's promise to bring His people safely through to the final state of our salvation. A chief benefit of understanding the biblical doctrine of election is a greater sense of assurance of our standing before God. The authors of the confession are not interested only in our personal assurance. There are other repercussions or ramifications: **So shall this doctrine afford matter of praise, reverence, and admiration of God.**

Besides Paul's teaching on election in Romans 9, an extremely helpful treatment of this doctrine is found in Jonathan Edwards' *The Freedom of the Will*. When Edwards finally became convicted of this doctrine, he had a strong psychological response. First came the intellectual conviction that the doctrine is biblically inescapable. It took some time, however, for him to see the doctrine's sweetness and excellence. It draws our attention away from ourselves and our petty concerns and directs our gaze to God, who is truly sovereign and purposive in His determination to bring about the salvation of His people. He does not simply make salvation possible and then sit like a spectator, leaving our final destiny in our own hands. The biblical doctrine of sin makes it clear that if God left our future in our hands, we most assuredly would not end up in heaven.

When we see the lengths to which God goes to bring His people to the fullness of salvation, we stand in awe before His grace. Is there anything more amazing than that we should be called children of God? The Apostle John writes to his flock: "See what kind of love the Father has given to us, that we should be called children of God" (1 John 3:1). This helps us see the excellence and sweetness of grace, and it moves us to praise, reverence, and admiration.

Historically, nearly all Christian communions have held similar views on the nature and character of God. Reformed theology, however, consistently applies this doctrine of God to every other doctrine. The contemplation of God in this great and high mystery results in an overwhelming sense of reverence. Although assured of their salvation and delighting in their acceptance in the Beloved, the people of God should nevertheless have a sense of holy fear before the majesty of God. This sense of reverence is largely missing in the modern American church.

We Americans have tried to level everything and turn the kingdom of God into a democracy, ruled by referendum. We rugged individualists are repulsed by the idea that we should be obliged to bow down before anyone, including God. But we should come together on the Sabbath day, not simply to hear a sermon or be entertained by music, but chiefly to worship God in a spirit of adoration. Where there is no reverence, there is no worship. God wants people to worship Him in spirit and in truth, and the proper spirit is a reverent one.

As we contemplate the high and holy mystery of predestination, we should be moved to reverence by it, even though our initial reaction to that doctrine may have been negative and even hostile.

Many churches sing the Doxology at some point during their services, often after the offering. When we sing, "Praise Him above, ye heav'nly host," we are calling on the myriads of angels that surround the throne of God to join in this celebration of praise, worship, and adoration. "Praise Father, Son, and Holy Ghost." How easy it is for us to sing this and not think about its meaning. The Doxology has survived through the centuries and been integrated into the worship services of a vast number of denominations for a good reason: it ascribes praise, honor, and dignity to God.

It has been said that all true theology begins and ends with doxology. In other words, the fear of the Lord is the beginning of wisdom. It is not, of course, a servile fear but a reverential posture before God, and that is the beginning of wisdom. We begin with a feeble, childlike sense of praise and doxology before God, but the more we learn of Him, the more resounding the doxology becomes.

The Apostle Paul was the greatest theologian that God has given to the church. Writing under the inspiration of the Holy Spirit, Paul sometimes rambled or broke off in the middle of a thought to digress to other subjects. Sometimes, in the middle of a deep exposition of difficult doctrine, he breaks out in a doxology like this one: "Oh, the depth of the riches and wisdom and knowledge of God! How unsearchable are his judgments and how inscrutable his ways!" (Rom. 11:33). Paul understood that theological reflection should move our souls to worship and reverence. That is what section 8 is saying.

And of humility, diligence, and abundant consolation to all that sincerely obey the gospel. Many Christians struggle with a kind of implicit pride in being a believer. They tend to think that it was their own doing that they placed their faith in Christ, and that therefore they are somehow superior, more righteous, than those who have not. The truth is that believers believe because God Almighty in His grace changed the disposition of our hearts, and by His effectual grace He brought us to Christ. So we have nothing of which to boast and all the more for which to praise, adore, and love the God who has been so merciful to us. This should eliminate all boasting—all of it—and leave us with a proper sense of humility.

Karl Barth once said that the three most basic sins of the human heart are dishonesty, pride, and sloth. That is just one theologian's opinion, but look through Scripture and see how much it speaks about pride—the pride that goes before . . . what? "Pride goes before destruction, and a haughty spirit before a fall" (Prov. 16:18). We usually telescope those two lines and say, "Pride goes before a fall." Pride does go before a fall, but the text says, "Pride goes before destruction." Pride is our built-in resistance to God. It raises its ugly head no place more viciously than when we wrestle with this inner resistance. One of the most humiliating experiences for any creature is to come to the place to which Isaiah came—"Woe is me! For I am lost; . . . for my eyes have seen the King, the LORD of hosts!" (Isa. 6:5)—and realize that there is nothing within him to commend him to God as worthy of any favor.

How humiliating it is to believe that the only way we can be saved is by grace. It may be less humiliating to admit that we all need the assistance or help of grace: "I certainly don't believe that I can live a perfect life without assistance from grace. I need some help. But God is the partner. He is the Helper; He may be even the senior partner. There's got to be something I can do, so that salvation is a cooperative, joint venture. That leaves me some island of pride."

The Bible, however, takes away this pride and causes us to say: "If God were to count on us to cooperate in this joint venture, our contribution would be just enough to put us in hell forever. We need grace totally to come to Christ. We need as much from God to be saved as Lazarus did to be raised from the tomb. That wasn't a joint venture between Lazarus and Jesus. Lazarus was dead, and we are spiritually dead. Unless God makes us alive, we're going to stay dead. We may be biologically alive, but we are spiritually dead."

That is difficult to swallow. But if election is true, salvation is all of grace. And all of us—rich and poor, mighty and weak, famous and obscure—stand before God on a level playing field, all totally dependent on His grace.

Of Creation

1. It pleased God the Father, Son, and Holy Ghost, for the manifestation of the glory of his eternal power, wisdom, and goodness, in the beginning, to create, or make of nothing, the world, and all things therein whether visible or invisible, in the space of six days; and all very good.

2. After God had made all other creatures, he created man, male and female, with reasonable and immortal souls, endued with knowledge, righteousness, and true holiness, after his own image; having the law of God written in their hearts, and power to fulfill it: and yet under a possibility of transgressing, being left to the liberty of their own will, which was subject unto change. Beside this law written in their hearts, they received a command, not to eat of the tree of the knowledge of good and evil; which while they kept, they were happy in their communion with God, and had dominion over the creatures.

---

1. It pleased God the Father, Son, and Holy Ghost, for the manifestation of the glory of his eternal power, wisdom, and goodness, in the beginning, to create, or make of nothing, the world, and all things therein whether visible or invisible, in the space of six days; and all very good.

There are those who reject the Christian view of creation and argue instead for a kind of self-creation, a spontaneous generation, in which things just pop into being. When the Hubble telescope was launched, a scientist spoke in terms of the Big Bang theory of the origin of the cosmos. He said that fifteen to eighteen billion years ago, the universe exploded into being. It is one thing if he meant that the universe came into being as a result of an explosion caused by something other than the universe, but it is another thing if he meant that the universe, by its own power, exploded into being. It is nonsense to say that the universe exploded into being, because it could move into being only from nonbeing. If it exploded from nonbeing into being, it created itself. A Nobel Prize–winning physicist from California wrote in an essay some years ago that modern science can no longer give any credence to the doctrine of spontaneous generation. "The idea of spontaneous generation, where something suddenly, by itself, emerges out of nothing, is scientifically untenable," he said. "We now must speak of gradual spontaneous generation." In other words, something cannot come from nothing suddenly, but it can do so if given enough time.

Until the Enlightenment, the most firmly established article of Christian faith in the secular world was that of creation. It had been established not only by revelation but also by reason, not only by religion but also by science. To medieval philosophers, the idea of something coming from nothing was absurd, unscientific, and illogical. If something exists, it must either have the power of being in itself or it must come from something that has the power of being in itself. Otherwise, nothing at all could exist. This point is important because atheists and secularists in recent centuries have focused their attention on creation. If they can undermine our certainty that we live in a created universe, they can undermine any argument for the existence of God. If you do away with creation, you do away with the Creator.

The classic Christian doctrine of creation is creation *ex nihilo* (out of nothing). The writer who most thoroughly developed this concept was Augustine. He said God spoke the universe into being out of nothing. God did not take eternally preexisting matter or substance and reshape or reconfigure it into the present world. His creative activity is not like that of human artists.

Think of Michelangelo, who sculpted magnificent statues from stone. Michelangelo believed that he did not create a statue but released the figure from its stone prison. It is inconceivable that his statues could have created themselves without the work of a master sculptor. Michelangelo's genius was his unique ability to reshape a block of stone into a magnificent figure. But he had to start with some substance or material. Similarly, Rembrandt had to begin with his canvas and paints. His inventive brilliance was in working with materials already at his disposal. We call this creativity, but no one in this world has the power or ability to create something out of nothing. Only God can do that.

When we assert creation *ex nihilo*, the obvious question is, How could God possibly do such a thing? It almost sounds like magic, where God is the magician who pulls a rabbit out of a hat. But in the act of creation, there were no trick mirrors, no rabbits, no hats, and not even a magic wand. Every effect must have a cause. There are different kinds of causes. Aristotle, for example, differentiated between several kinds, using the example of a sculpture: its *material* cause (out of which something comes) is the block of stone; its *instrumental* cause (the means by which the effect is brought to pass) is the chisel and hammer, instruments the sculptor uses to bring about the effect; its *formal* cause (the idea to which the effect must correspond) is the sketch used as the image is shaped; its *final* cause (the purpose for which it is made) is to beautify a building, fulfill a commission, or some other reason. Aristotle also distinguished between *efficient* and *sufficient* causes: the efficient cause is the sculptor, who actually brings about the sculpture; the sufficient cause is the power needed to bring the effect into being.

Creation had neither a material nor an instrumental cause. There was a formal cause, a final cause, an efficient cause, and a sufficient cause. The formal cause was God's idea and plan to create the world, not out of necessity or His own need, but according to His own purpose. The final cause was God's purpose, a plan He executed initially by the actual work of creation. The final cause was God's ultimate glory and our well-being (which also redounds to His glory). God was both the efficient cause and the sufficient cause because He alone had the power to bring something out of nothing.

By what means did God accomplish the feat of creation *ex nihilo*? By His speech. Augustine called this the divine imperative or fiat. God spoke the words "Let there be" (Gen. 1:3, 6, 14)—meaning "There must be"—and things appeared. In the film *The Ten Commandments*, Pharaoh Rameses II frequently says, "So let it be written; so let it be done." That is an imperial command that cannot be countermanded. In creation, there was no block of stone or mass of unstructured matter, but only the command of God, who alone had the power to make things happen simply by uttering a command. It was the power of His word that created.

By the power of His word and His sovereign, efficacious will, God can make things happen simply by decree. We see this demonstrated to some degree when at Jesus' command the Sea of Galilee stopped raging and the wind ceased blowing. Jesus said: "Peace! Be still!" (Mark 4:39), and it was still. In response, the disciples' fear increased rather than decreased. Terrified of Jesus, they cried out, "Who then is this?" (Mark 4:41). They had never met someone with an authority so transcendent, holy, and majestic that even the winds and the sea obeyed him.

Jesus also displayed this power when raising Lazarus from the dead. After being dead for four days, Lazarus, in the language of the King James Version, "stinketh" (John 11:39). That description underscored the fact that Lazarus was indeed dead, and that his body had begun to decay. When raising Lazarus from the dead, Jesus stood outside the tomb and cried out, "Lazarus, come out" (John 11:43). At the verbal command of the incarnate Christ, Lazarus' heart immediately began to pulsate and to pump blood throughout his vessels, oxygen began to flow, brain waves were initiated, and Lazarus woke up and came out of the tomb a living man.

In the book of Romans, Paul speaks of the uniqueness of God, who alone can bring something out of nothing and life out of death (Rom. 4:17). Paul tells us that the energizing power of God's Word is that which raises us from spiritual death and translates us from the kingdom of darkness into the kingdom of light. God can assure His church that His Word will not return to Him void because it contains His power (Isa. 55:11). We stand in awe that our Creator formed the entire vast universe out of nothing by the sheer command of His voice.

Some profound philosophical questions flow from the concept of creation *ex nihilo*. Although there was no preexistent material out of which God ordered the universe, it is not as if there was absolutely nothing. *Ex nihilo* means that there was no substantive or physical reality, but obviously there was always God Himself and His spiritual reality. We learn in Scripture never to identify the universe or any part of it with God Himself. To confuse the Creator and the creature is to fall into pantheism, which obscures the clear distinction between creature and Creator. Yet we hear from the Apostle Paul, citing Greek poets, that "in him we live and move and have our being" (Acts 17:28). For our very existence we are utterly dependent on the sustaining power of God. That which He creates, God holds in existence. We depend on Him not only for the original act of creation but also for existence from moment to moment. There is no life apart from Him.

When we say that our being is in God, we raise the question of whether the stuff of the universe is an extension of God's being, somehow a part of Him. This gives rise to forms of pantheism. It is difficult to understand how God, who is infinite in His being, can permeate everything and yet allow something to exist that is completely distinct from His own being. We do, in some sense, owe our existence to His very being, but that does not deify us in any way. There is a distinction between self-existence and creaturely existence, and we are never to think of ourselves as little gods or sparks of the infinite. We do not exist on our own power but depend every second on the being of God for our existence. We are not God, and how we exist under the influence of His creative power is something that no one can explain. Of this we can be certain: unless that power of being is over us and prior to us, nothing could possibly be.

Scientists have proposed various views of cosmology (the study of the nature of the cosmos) and cosmogony (the study of the origin of the cosmos). For example, there is the steady-state theory, according to which the universe is a closed, mechanistic, self-sustaining system that goes on forever in equilibrium.

The steady-state theory, which was once widely held, has been replaced by the expanding universe theory, which is closely related to the Big Bang theory. According to this view, the universe is continually expanding. It follows that long ago the universe was smaller and more compact. If we go back far enough, all the matter and energy in the universe was compacted in one infinitesimal, highly condensed point of singularity.

When atoms are compacted in one tiny point until there is no space left, leaving just mass and energy, it is called a singularity. The Big Bang theory teaches that a compact singularity for some unknown reason, billions of years ago, blew up. From that initial explosion, the entire universe was formed, and the effects of that explosion are still being felt as the flying bits continue on their outward course. As a result of that explosion, everything is going out from the center.

But why did that singularity explode? The law of inertia teaches that bodies at rest remain at rest unless acted on by an outside force; bodies in motion remain in motion unless acted on by an outside force. What was that immensely powerful force that set off the Big Bang? It must have transcended the singularity itself.

The current model of cosmogony screams for a self-existent, eternal being who brought about the act of creation. Apart from the *if* and *how* of creation, a controversial issue in Christian circles is the *when* of creation. Did it take place billions of years ago or several thousand years ago? Was it something that God accomplished over billions of years, or did He do it in six twenty-four-hour days?

In the beginning, to create, or make of nothing, the world, and all things therein whether visible or invisible, in the space of six days; and all very good. In the Genesis account of creation, we read, "There was evening and there was morning, the first day" (Gen. 1:5). This narrative proceeds from the first day to the sixth, each time referring to evening and morning and numbering the day. On the seventh day, God rested (2:2). In the modern age, a considerable number of theories have arisen denying that the creation as we know it took place in six twenty-four-hour days. Common to these theories is the acceptance of the dominant scientific view that the earth and life on it are very old. Many consider the biblical account to be primitive, mythological, and untenable in light of modern scientific knowledge. This crisis has resulted in several attempts to reinterpret the Genesis account of creation.

In the sixteenth century, Copernicus and his followers repudiated the old Ptolemaic view of astronomy. They argued that the center of the solar system is not the earth (geocentricity) but the sun (heliocentricity). It was a sad chapter in the history of the church, which had believed for more than fifteen hundred years that the Bible teaches geocentricity, when it condemned Galileo for believing and teaching heliocentricity. Both Luther and Calvin opposed Copernicus' views, believing them to undermine Scripture's authority.

The Bible does not explicitly teach geocentricity anywhere. Scripture describes the movements of the heavens from the perspective of someone standing on earth: the sun moves across the sky, rising in the east and setting in the west. We use that same language today. The church thought that because the Bible uses this kind of descriptive language, it therefore teaches something about the relationship between the sun and the earth. This is a clear case of scientific knowledge correcting the church's misinterpretation of the Bible.

There are two spheres of revelation: the Bible (special revelation) and nature (general revelation). In the latter, God manifests Himself through the created order. What God reveals in nature can never contradict what He reveals in Scripture, and what He reveals in Scripture can never contradict what He reveals in nature. He is the author of both forms of revelation, and God does not contradict Himself.

The church has always taken the position that all truth meets at the top, and that science should never contradict Scripture. Scientific discoveries, however, can correct the theologian's faulty understanding of Scripture, just as biblical revelation can correct faulty speculations drawn from the natural order. When the scientific consensus on a particular point collides with the unmistakable teaching of Scripture, I trust Scripture before I trust the speculations and inferences of scientists. That is consistent with the history of the church and Christianity. We believe that sacred Scripture is nothing less than the Creator's truth revealed.

We have a problem not only with a six-day creation but also with the age of the earth. Is the earth a few thousand years old or billions of years old (as scientists today insist)? Although the Bible clearly says that the world was created in six days, it gives no date for the beginning of that work. It would be a mistake to become embroiled in too much controversy about the date of creation.

In the seventeenth century, an archbishop named James Ussher made some calculations based on the genealogies in Genesis 5 and 11 and other chronological clues in the Old Testament. He concluded that the world was created in 4004 BC. He even pinned down the day of the week and the time of day when creation occurred. But we must be very careful to distinguish between the text of Scripture and additions to the text. In defending biblical authority, we are not obligated to defend a theory based on the speculations of a bishop in times past.

Even so, if we take the genealogies that go back to Adam, and if we make allowances for certain gaps in them (which could certainly be there), it is a big stretch to go from 4004 BC to 13.8 billion years ago (the current scientific estimate for the age of the universe). We also have the problem of the antiquity of the human race. It seems as if every time a new skeleton or skull is discovered, scientists push back the date of man's origin another million years.

Scholars have proposed four basic theories to explain the time frame of Genesis 1–2: (1) the gap theory, (2) the day-age theory, (3) the framework hypothesis, and (4) six-day creation.

The gap theory was made popular by the *Scofield Reference Bible* (1909), which informed the theology of an entire generation of evangelicals and more than any other single edition of Scripture is responsible for propagating dispensational theology throughout America. In this Bible, Genesis 1:1 reads, "In the beginning, God created the heavens and the earth," and verse 2 reads, "And the earth *became* without form, and void; and darkness was upon the face of the deep." Other Bibles read, "The earth *was* without form and void, and darkness was upon the face of the deep." Verse 2 describes what most scholars consider to be the as-yet-unordered, basic structure of the universe—darkness, emptiness. Then the Holy Spirit hovers over the waters (v. 2) and God says, "Let there be light" (v. 3). Thus came the light and then the creation of the heavens, fish, birds, animals, and so on.

The Hebrew word in verse 2 translated "was" is the common verb *hayah*, which ordinarily means "to be." *Hayah* means "to become" only in special circumstances, which are not present here. The *Scofield Reference Bible* translates verse 2 as "became" instead of "was" in order to facilitate the gap theory. As a result, only verse 1 refers to the original creation. Verse 2 then refers to a cosmic catastrophe in which the originally good and properly ordered creation became chaotic, dark, and fallen. After this period of darkness (the gap), God re-created the universe in the six days beginning in verse 3. Thus, the universe could have been created billions of years ago, followed by a gap of billions of years, after which God returned to His distorted creation and renovated or reconstituted it relatively recently. The gap theory has also been called the restitution hypothesis, meaning that the creation narrative in Genesis is not about the original creation but about the restitution of a fallen creation.

An entire generation was taught this theory through the *Scofield Reference Bible*. However, Scripture nowhere explicitly teaches that the original creation was marred and then after many years reconstituted. The broader context of the whole of Scripture militates against the gap theory.

According to the second approach, the day-age theory, each "day" of Genesis 1 may be an age. After all, one day in the Lord's sight is like a thousand years (2 Peter 3:8). Also, expressions like "in the days of Noah" and "in Abraham's day" can refer to open-ended periods. The Hebrew word *yom*, translated "day" in Genesis 1, can mean something other than a twenty-four-hour period, as it must in Genesis 2:4, which refers to "the day that the LORD God made the earth and the heavens." Accordingly, each "day" in Genesis 1 may refer to a thousand years, and perhaps even to millions of years. This will at least ameliorate some of the difficulties we have with those who argue for a gradual evolution of life-forms on this earth.

However, the day-age theory, like the gap theory, ignores the immediate context as well as the larger biblical context. It ignores the fact that each of the six days of creation consists of an evening and a morning. If *yom* here means something like ten million years, then we need to give the words *evening* and *morning* the same kind of metaphorical meaning. From a literary, exegetical, and linguistic perspective, the day-age theory is weak.

The day-age theory tends to accommodate a theory of biological macroevolution that is incompatible with the Bible and purposive creation—the creation of all living things by the immediate agency of the sovereign God. Macroevolution teaches that all life has developed from a single, original cell, and that this happened through a chance collision of atoms, without an intelligent planner or Creator orchestrating the emergence of these species. Those who favor the day-age theory often link themselves with a position called theistic evolution, which grants the basic premises of biological evolution but says that God, not chance, guided the process of evolution.

Macroevolution differs from microevolution. While the former teaches that all living things have developed from one original cell, the latter teaches that, over periods of time, species undergo slight changes in order to adapt to their environment. Microevolution is not in dispute, either biblically or scientifically. Macroevolution has never been substantiated by observation or experiment, and it places its faith in an endless string of extremely improbable yet beneficial chance mutations.

A frequent argument for macroevolution is the principle of common structure. All forms of life are made up of the same basic substances: amino acids, proteins, DNA, and that sort of thing. Because all living things have similar constituent parts, the argument goes, they must have developed from common ancestors. A common substance or structure, however, does not necessarily imply a common source. The fact that all forms of life are made of the same basic building blocks neither negates the possibility of evolution nor substantiates it. One would expect an intelligent Creator to have made all life-forms with a similar design—one that works on this earth.

Macroevolution is not a question of biology or natural science, which rely upon experimental verification, but of history, which tries to interpret evidence left from the past in a coherent fashion. The discipline of paleontology, which studies the fossil record, claims to put evolution on a scientific footing, but it performs no experiments to substantiate evolutionary processes. It simply lines up similar fossils and infers that one creature must be related to another by common descent.

In the recent past in Russia, leading international scholars who favor macroevolution met. While comparing notes, they found that the weakest evidence for their theories is the fossil record. I remember reading the royal society's bulletin at that time and thinking, "What other source matters?"

The fossil record is often put forward as the evidence for macroevolution, and yet it militates against that theory. Scientists argue for an old earth on the ground that stratifications in the rocks contain fossils, which indicates a uniformitarian process that took millions of years to produce the whole formation. They then determine the age of each stratum by determining the kinds of fossils contained in each. This is a blatant example of what logicians call begging the question. It is circular reasoning to date the fossils by the rocks and then date the rocks by the fossils.

We now have good evidence that stratification of rocks proves the antiquity of nothing. Within days after the Mount St. Helens explosion had subsided, scientists discovered that the cataclysmic upheaval of that volcanic explosion had laid down the same rock stratification that had been assumed would take millions of years to develop. In other words, Mount St. Helens proved that catastrophic upheavals can produce the same empirical data as twenty million years of gradual deposition.

The third approach, called the framework hypothesis, was originally developed by the Dutch scholar Nicolaas Ridderbos. He argued that the literary form of the first few chapters of Genesis differs from that of its later chapters. Certain basic characteristics found in poetry are missing from historical narrative, and certain characteristics found in historical narrative are missing from poetry. For example, the book of Exodus, with its account of the Jewish captivity in Egypt, has genealogies, family names, real historical places, and an unmetered literary style (i.e., lacking a particular rhythm), making it clearly prose and historical narrative. After the account of the exodus, the book's author inserts the song of Miriam, which is in metered rhythm and is therefore clearly poetry. The literary structure before the song manifests all the characteristics of historical narrative, as does the structure after the poem.

Therefore, it is usually not difficult to distinguish between poetry and historical narrative in the Old Testament. But the opening chapters of Genesis, according to Ridderbos, exhibit a strange combination of literary forms. On the one hand is a discussion of the creation of a man and a woman who are given names that thereafter appear in genealogical accounts. In Hebrew literature, this clearly signals historicity. The garden of Eden is said to be set among four rivers, two of which we know were real rivers: the Tigris and the Euphrates. The style of writing is not metered or rhythmic, as Hebrew poetry normally is. All this indicates that the opening chapters of Genesis are historical narrative.

There are some anomalies, however. We find trees in this garden with strange names: "the tree of the knowledge of good and evil" and "the tree of life" (Gen. 2:9). Had they been apple or pear trees, there would be no problem. But what does a tree of life look like? Is the author of Genesis telling us that a real tree was off limits, giving it a metaphorical meaning as the tree of life? We are also introduced to a serpent who speaks (3:1). Because of these two features, some have argued that the literary structure of the opening chapters of Genesis was self-consciously and intentionally mythological, or at least filled with legend and saga.

Ridderbos contended that the beginning chapters of Genesis are a mixture of historical narrative and poetry, with part of the poetic structure being the repeated refrain, "There was evening and there was morning" (Gen. 1:5). Ridderbos concluded that Genesis gives us not a historical narrative of the when or the how of divine creation but a drama in seven acts. The first act ends with the statement, "There was evening and there was morning, the first day." The author of Genesis, then, is trying to show that God's work of creation took place in seven distinct stages, which incidentally fit remarkably well into the stages identified by the modern theories of cosmic evolution.

Therefore, the framework hypothesis allows one to step into a Big Bang cosmology while maintaining the credibility and inspiration of Genesis 1–2. This is not history but drama. The days are simply artistic literary devices to create a framework for a lengthy period of development.

In America, Ridderbos' work was widely disseminated by Meredith Kline, who for many years taught Old Testament at Westminster Theological Seminary, then at Gordon-Conwell Theological Seminary, and then at Westminster Seminary California. Because Kline endorsed the framework hypothesis, many people, particularly in the Reformed community, have embraced it, provoking a serious crisis in some circles. Some Reformed pastors today hold to a literal six-day creation, while others hold to the framework hypothesis, and yet they otherwise hold to the same system of orthodox theology.

The fourth alternative, that of a literal six-day creation, is the traditional view and the one that best accounts for the biblical data. Genesis says that God created the universe and everything in it in six twenty-four-hour periods. According to the Reformation hermeneutic, the first option is to follow the plain sense of the text. One must do a great deal of hermeneutical gymnastics to escape the plain meaning of Genesis 1–2. The confession makes it a point of faith that God created the world in the space of six days.

And all very good. Here the confession echoes the sentiment of Scripture with respect to God's work of creation. At various points in Genesis 1, we read statements like, "And God saw everything that he had made, and behold, it was very good" (Gen. 1:31). That is, He pronounced a positive assessment on His own creative work. In fact, the very first time we hear a negative assessment is when God declared, "It is not good that the man should be alone" (2:18).

That may seem elementary and simple, but God's positive assessment of His created universe collides with other philosophies and worldviews, many of which have distorted the thinking of Christians, both past and present. According to these worldviews, anything that is physical or material is inherently bad. Plato's philosophy of idealism distinguished between ideas (or spiritual entities) and the physical realm. He said that all physical objects are receptacles, imperfect copies of the spiritual or archetypal ideal.

We see different kinds of objects in this world, and we identify them. Take, for example, chairs. There are rocking chairs, lounge chairs, wingback chairs, and desk chairs. But a piano bench is not a chair, even though you sit on it. Plato said that in the ideal realm, there is the perfect idea of a chair, perfect "chairness." The idea of perfect chairness is not just a mental construct but a reality. According to Plato, a perfect chair exists in its pure, idealized form in the supratemporal world of ideas. He argued that we can identify one object over there and another over here as chairs because our souls are eternal. They come into this world, into our bodies, with a knowledge of the perfect chair, and whenever we see something that approximates that perfect, eternal idea, we identify it through this built-in knowledge.

Each chair is a receptacle. That is, it receives its pattern from the eternal idea, but no chair in this world perfectly recapitulates or incarnates the absolute, ideal chair. Every chair is at best an imperfect copy of the original. To Plato, everything in the physical world is at best an imperfect copy of an idea and therefore inherently imperfect. Plato's idea of the tension or disparity between the spiritual and physical realms has had an enormous impact on the history of Western civilization. And Eastern religions generally teach that there is an eternal struggle between the physical and the spiritual and that every evil thing is related to the physical.

In the New Testament, Paul speaks of the ongoing warfare in the Christian's life between the Spirit and the flesh (Rom. 7:14–20; Gal. 5:17). When reading such passages, we tend, as a result of cultural history, to think that Paul is speaking of a conflict between our souls and our bodies. He is talking instead about a conflict between the things of God and the things of our fallen humanity. "The flesh" refers not exclusively to the body but to the fallen nature. For centuries, the church, influenced by Plato and Neoplatonic philosophy, was caught up in the idea that anything physical is imperfect and a carrier of evil. That was a motivating force behind the monastic movement in the early Christian church. People sought to withdraw from the physical world as much as possible. They thought that to eat too much food or to drink wine is wicked because it indulges the body. They saw sexual relationships as inherently evil. No less a saint than Augustine taught that although the Bible permits marriage and allows sexual relationships within that bond, these relationships are at best a necessary evil to propagate the species.

The vow of celibacy for the clergy and the concept of Mary's perpetual virginity, taught in Roman Catholicism, are based on the idea that even sexual relations within marriage taint the soul. This doctrine required the church to maintain Mary's perpetual virginity even after the virgin birth, forcing it at the same time to deny what the Bible clearly teaches: that Jesus had brothers and sisters.

On the other hand, the Bible speaks on many occasions about the sin of misusing physical things. Overindulgence in eating food is the sin of gluttony; drinking too much wine can lead to the sin of drunkenness. Laws that circumscribe the propriety of sexual relationships within marriage are very clear in Scripture. The Bible prohibits the abuse and misuse of sexual relationships, but it is speaking about the misuse of the physical dimension of life, not the inherent wickedness of physical things.

A major distinction between Platonism and Christianity is that Plato describes the body as the soul's prison house. He was influenced by the Pythagorean doctrine of the transmigration of the soul, a form of reincarnation. According to this view, the soul migrates from body to body until it achieves in this world the level of virtue necessary to escape the reincarnation cycle and be released to a level of pure spiritual existence. For Plato, the soul is redeemed when it is liberated or released from its prison and has no more contact with the flesh.

This idea stands in stark contrast to the biblical view, which looks forward to the resurrection of the body. When we say with the Apostles' Creed that we believe in the resurrection of the body, we are talking not about the resurrection of Christ's body but the resurrection of our own bodies. Christians see that as the ultimate redeemed state of human beings. We will not be disembodied spirits but will have our physical bodies glorified and patterned after Christ's resurrection body. Christianity does not demean the body or the physical dimension of life. Many of God's Old Testament promises to His people included their physical well-being: they would have land, one that would flow with milk and honey; He would provide food and the fruit of the vine, as well as everything else that is integral to man's physical fulfillment and happiness. The biblical promise of redemption entails the renovation of this fallen world—a new heaven and a new earth—not its annihilation.

The Bible does speak at times of this world and this present age as being evil. It does so, however, not because this world is physical but because it is fallen and infected by sin. The biggest stumbling block in the New Testament message of faith and hope is the doctrine of the resurrection. If we know anything from natural science, we know that when people die, they stay dead. What is most difficult to embrace is the story that Jesus died, was held captive by death, and then was raised from the dead. This is an astonishing truth that we proclaim as Christians.

In first-century Greek culture, when the early church proclaimed the gospel, the biggest stumbling block was not the resurrection but the incarnation. That the Word could become flesh and dwell among us was more than the thinking Greek could handle. For God to take upon Himself a body would be, to the Greek mind, for God to become imperfect and evil. One of the earliest heresies the church encountered was Docetism, a subdivision of the Gnostic heresy. Docetism—from the Greek word *dokeō*, meaning "to seem, to appear, to think"—taught that Jesus only appeared to have a physical body, while in reality He was a kind of apparition, a ghostly figure who manifested Himself as if He were physical.

In his letters, the Apostle John taught that any spirit that fails to confess that Jesus Christ has come in the flesh is not of God but is the spirit of the Antichrist (1 John 4:3). Docetism was rooted and grounded in the idea that the physical world is evil. If Jesus is our perfect Redeemer, Docetists said, He could not have a physical body. That shows how far this thinking penetrated the ancient world.

Many Christians still suffer from a mentality that denigrates the physical world. We think that the real sins are the physical ones, not the spiritual ones. There are indeed physical sins, but physicality, in and of itself, is not evil. The material world is the creation of a perfectly good and righteous God, who declared His approval of the work of His hands, the physical world, and said it was good.

Christians today are still influenced by the Augustinian notion that sexual relations, even in marriage, are at best a necessary evil, rather than a blessing that God has given to man and woman. Because of the sanctity of marriage, God carefully regulated the bounds in which sexuality is to be expressed. This should happen in the context of trust—trust based on solemn, sacred oaths taken publicly before friends, family, church authorities, the authority of the state, and, most importantly, God Himself. Marriage is to be a safe place to be naked spiritually, psychologically, and physically in the context of permanent commitment. Militating against this blessedness is the fallenness of the flesh and cultural distortions that still exercise an amazing influence on human joy and fulfillment in the sight of God.

This goes back to the idea that if it is physical, it must be bad. God made the physical world and pronounced it good. His first command to His creatures was to be fruitful and multiply (Gen. 1:22). It was God who created the body, marriage, and sex as the means through which the world would be populated and the binding union of two humans would be enhanced. Marriage is just one area where a distortion of the biblical understanding of the physical world becomes a plague to our whole lives and experience.

2. After God had made all other creatures, he created man, male and female, with reasonable and immortal souls, endued with knowledge, righteousness, and true holiness, after his own image; having the law of God written in their hearts, and power to fulfill it: and yet under a possibility of transgressing, being left to the liberty of their own will, which was subject unto change. Beside this law written in their hearts, they received a command, not to eat of the tree of the knowledge of good and evil; which while they kept, they were happy in their communion with God, and had dominion over the creatures.

After God had made all other creatures, he created man, male and female. Here we have the generic language for the human race that has been so widely attacked in our day. When God created human beings, He called humanity "man." God created humanity both male and female. After creating plants, birds, fish, and animals, God created man, His crowning act of creation. We read in the Bible that God scooped up clay from the ground, molded and shaped it into the figure of a human person, and breathed into this lump of clay the breath of life. Man became a living soul, the origin of the human species. God named the creature Adam, which means "mankind," and then declared, "It is not good that the man should be alone" (Gen. 2:18). God brought the animals before Adam, but none was comparable to him. So God created woman, a perfect partner for Adam. When Adam looked at her, he said, "This at last is bone of my bones and flesh of my flesh" (v. 23), and the two became one flesh.

We are living in a time of unprecedented hostility between the genders, which is a tragic distortion of creation. It is true that God made Eve to be a helpmate to Adam (as both Paul and Peter reiterate in the New Testament), not Adam to be a helpmate to Eve. There is an economy, a division of labor, in which the wife is subordinate to her husband. According to the Apostles, that was the order of creation, an order that has been violently attacked in our day, to the detriment of both men and women. Helping to fuel this controversy has been the false assumption of many men—readily communicated to women—that the subordination of women means that they are inferior people.

God made humans male and female. Both the man and the woman are fully in the image of God and have equal value and dignity. That the husband is called to lead in the relationship does not mean that he is of greater value. That a private in the army receives order from a sergeant doesn't mean the sergeant is a better soldier, much less a better man. It is simply the nature of the relationship.

Another distortion of the creation account implies that God created Eve to be Adam's slave. That was not the case. God assigned to both man and woman the task of ruling over nature (Gen. 1:28). God made Adam a king, whose dominion was the earth, and Eve a queen, with both king and queen fully manifesting and displaying the image of God.

With reasonable and immortal souls, endued with knowledge, righteousness, and true holiness. The Westminster Confession of Faith is the most precise summary of Reformed theology ever written, but it is not infallible. This is one of those rare moments when the giants of the faith stumbled, for there is a word in this section that is problematic. The word is immortal.

Were we created with immortal souls? That which is immortal cannot die. The concept of immortal souls is rooted in Greek philosophy. The Greeks believed that the soul is both eternal (not having a beginning) and immortal (not having an end). Christian theology denies the soul's eternality, saying that every human soul is a work of divine creation, and that there was a time when our souls did not exist. Orthodox Christianity teaches that, though there was a time when each soul did not exist, after its creation there will never be a time when it no longer exists. Christianity denies any doctrine of the soul's annihilation, either at death or afterward. God has created us with the capacity to live forever. In fact, we will all live forever in our souls—including the damned. Perhaps that is what the Westminster divines had in mind when using the term immortal to describe the created souls of human beings. Although the souls of all people will continue to live forever after being created, they will continue to exist only because God sustains life in the soul, not because the soul itself is incapable of dying. If God were to stop sustaining them, our souls would perish in an instant.

The confession's framers would likely agree. If we asked them, they would probably retreat from the word immortal because it means "incapable of mortality." Or they might say that the soul is incapable of dying because God, having sovereignly decreed to preserve our souls forever, will not allow that to happen.

He created man . . . after His own image. Man is used here generically, referring to *mankind*. In Genesis we read: "Then God said, 'Let us make man in our image, after our likeness. And let them have dominion over the fish of the sea and over the birds of the heavens and over the livestock and over all the earth and over every creeping thing that creeps on the earth.' So God created man in his own image, in the image of God he created him; male and female he created them" (Gen. 1:26–27).

Here we encounter the concept of the *imago Dei*, the image of God. This is a striking assertion in the first chapter of sacred Scripture: of all the creatures He made, God endowed (or stamped) only one with His own image. This text gives rise to two questions: What does it mean that we are created in the image of God? And do we still have the image of God after the fall? These answers are important to our understanding of the whole work of redemption.

When analyzing what it means to be made in God's image, we encounter a problem immediately. The biblical text, "Then God said, 'Let us make man in our image, after our likeness'" (Gen. 1:26), employs the words *image* and *likeness*. Are God's image and His likeness two distinct things?

The Roman Catholic Church for centuries has said yes, we are made not only in God's image but also after His likeness. Rome takes the position that the words refer to distinct aspects of our humanity: *image* to our rational capacity as reasonable creatures, and *likeness* to a particular virtue that is a special, added gift of original holiness. God implanted this additional gift of righteousness, called the *donum superadditum* or superadded gift, in Adam and Eve, so it was not something they achieved.

The classic Protestant interpretation of Genesis 1:26 regards the words *image* and *likeness* as synonyms, both referring to the same thing.

The two synonyms reinforce each other and emphasize different aspects of the situation. A similar example of this literary technique is found in Romans 1:18, where Paul says that God has revealed His wrath "against all ungodliness and unrighteousness of men." *Ungodliness* and *unrighteousness* refer not to two separate categories of behavior but to the same thing. They describe the wickedness of men in two slightly different ways. Traditional Protestantism contends that *image* and *likeness* refer to the same thing; they are not two distinct concepts, but redundancies. But to what one thing do the two words refer?

Analogia is the Latin word from which comes the English word *analogy*; *entis* is Latin for "being." The *analogia entis* means that some similitude exists between God and His human creatures, that in some way we are like God. We must be careful how we say that, for it does not mean that we are God. There is no identity between human creatures and God, but there is a point of likeness between them.

Some theologians in our day describe God as being "wholly other," meaning that He is utterly different from us. But if God were absolutely and categorically different from us in every respect, we could know nothing about Him; there would be no common ground. Anything He spoke to us about Himself would be meaningless because there would be no analogy or point of reference. He would be incapable of giving us meaningful revelation if He were utterly dissimilar to us. We have problems communicating among ourselves because of our differences. For us to receive and understand God's Word, we must be like Him in some sense. When He communicates to us, He uses our language, not His. He stoops, as it were, to lisp in order to communicate to us. He describes Himself in human terms, yet warns us that He is not a man. We, of course, do the same thing when we speak in analogies. We are trying to explain one thing through a point of contact with another. Because the two things we speak of are not identical, it is true that all analogies break down eventually. There is, however, a point of contact, a realm of overlap, not absolute equivalence nor absolute difference.

In what sense are we like God? For one thing, we have **reasonable . . . souls**. That is, we have the capacity to think rationally, to make deductions. We are not limited to responding to external stimuli, but can work through syllogisms and think in a cognitive, logical manner. God has a mind; we have minds. God is a volitional being, having a will and making decisions; we are volitional beings and make decisions. We also are capable of affection in a degree that is governed by our mind. Thus, our constituent makeup as human beings points to these aspects of our humanity that in a way are similar to the nature of God.

An image represents or reflects something else. We humans have been given a unique ability and responsibility to mirror and reflect the character of God. He says, "Be holy, for I am holy" (Lev. 11:44). God created Adam and Eve with all the necessary equipment and ability to reflect the righteousness and true holiness of God to the rest of the created realm. With that capacity and responsibility, men and women have been granted dominion over all the earth as His vice-regents.

We should be concerned with our environment because God placed man in His garden and made Him responsible to dress, fill, keep, and replenish it. Adam and Eve were not given the right to exploit or abuse the created world. They were, however, made superordinate, not subordinate, to the animals. Animals are here for our well-being. We do not exist to serve them; they exist to serve us, and we are to rule them benevolently. Today, naturalism has replaced God with Mother Earth, and we do more to protect fish eggs than human fetuses. Our priorities are out of order.

After the fall, we still have the image of God, but it is broken or marred. In our fallen state, we fail to faithfully reflect and mirror His character to the world. In effect, fallen humanity is a walking, talking, breathing lie to creation because we misrepresent and distort the character of God. Paul talks about the shame of believers and says that the gentiles blaspheme because of us (Rom. 2:23–24). One could say that the deer and the antelope blaspheme because of us. Animals have a natural fear of us, which would not be the case if our dominion over them truly reflected the Creator.

The prophets in particular negatively compare human beings to animals. The ox knows his master's crib, but we do not even know our Creator. The eagle obeys God's laws and the swallows fly to Capistrano when God tells them to. But when He told Jonah to go to Nineveh,

Jonah headed for Tarshish. We disobey God instinctively, whereas dumb animals obey Him instinctively. Disobedience is part of our fallen nature.

Genesis 9 addresses the remaining image of God in man. Here we read about the institution of capital punishment: "Every moving thing that lives shall be food for you. And as I gave you the green plants, I give you everything. But you shall not eat flesh with its life, that is, its blood. And for your lifeblood I will require a reckoning: from every beast I will require it and from man. From his fellow man I will require a reckoning for the life of man" (Gen. 9:3–5). Then God adds, "Whoever sheds the blood of man, by man shall his blood be shed, for God made man in his own image" (v. 6). This verse is not a prophecy that those who live by the sword will die by the sword. Instead, it is an imperative, a command: whoever sheds man's blood, by man shall his blood be shed. The reason for capital punishment is the sanctity of human life: "for God made man in his own image."

Some people reject capital punishment and cite biblical grounds to do so. "You shall not murder," the Bible says (Ex. 20:13). Similarly, some people say it is inconsistent to oppose abortion but support capital punishment. Such people do not understand that the reason for supporting capital punishment and the reason for opposing abortion are the same: the sanctity of human life.

God says that a human life is so sacred that if any person willfully, with malice aforethought, takes the life of a human being, that person is to be executed. To unjustly assault or violate a human being is in effect to attack God Himself. The victim, no matter how sinful he is, represents his Creator. However, God does appoint the state to carry out capital punishment. When He says, "By man shall his blood be shed," He means, "By the civil magistrate shall his blood be shed," as Paul makes clear in Romans 13:1–5.

Throughout the Bible, we see that what makes humanity so sacred is not the inherent dignity of human creatures but the value and dignity that God assigns to them. That is why we are not allowed to murder people. In Genesis 9, the text presupposes that the creature is still, to some degree, in the image of God, despite the fall. All the dignity, love, justice, and righteousness that we are called to give to our neighbor was not abrogated at the fall; we are called to love all people because people are, in some sense, still in the image of God.

To be consistent with Scripture, we must understand that in some sense the image of God remains in us even after our fall into corruption, and that in another sense the image of God is not there anymore—until and unless we are renewed by the Holy Spirit, after the image of Christ, who is the perfect image of God. Therefore, we distinguish between the *material* image, the image of God in the wider sense, and the *formal* image, the image of God in the narrower sense.

When speaking of the image of God in the material or wider sense, we mean that even after the fall we are still human beings. The fall did not destroy our humanity. We still have the faculty of thinking, though our thinking is corrupted; we are still volitional creatures, though our choices are imprisoned by sin. But in the formal or narrower sense, we have lost the ability to obey God and thereby reflect His image. With the Spirit's regeneration, we have been changed, and this formal or narrower sense of the image of God in us is renewed, so that now we do have a capacity, to some degree, to mirror and reflect the character of God.

A fascinating thing in the creation account is what happens on each day. The work begins simply and progresses to the creation on the sixth day of man as male and female, the crowning act of creation. That ought to be a warning to us. We are by nature humanists, man-centered rather than God-centered, and we like to think that man is the reason why God created the universe. But the sixth day is not the ultimate day but only the penultimate day. The ultimate day is the seventh day when God rested. He did not hallow the sixth day; He hallowed the seventh.

Throughout Scripture, the Sabbath functions not just as a time to rest from our labor and to gather for worship. It is God's promise, symbol, and guarantee of the future fulfillment and consummation of His kingdom. There still remains a Sabbath for the people of God, when we enter heaven and enjoy the glory of God. In a sense, the Sabbath points to our destiny and purpose. Our purpose is Sabbath holiness; we were made to be holy. We were made to mirror and reflect the character of God Himself, a mandate fulfilled in the life of Christ, who is the new Adam, the perfect humanity. He reveals to us what it means to be the brightness of His glory and the express image of His perfection.

Of Providence

1. God the great Creator of all things doth uphold, direct, dispose, and govern all creatures, actions, and things, from the greatest even to the least, by his most wise and holy providence, according to his infallible foreknowledge, and the free and immutable counsel of his own will, to the praise of the glory of his wisdom, power, justice, goodness, and mercy.

2. Although, in relation to the foreknowledge and decree of God, the first Cause, all things come to pass immutably, and infallibly; yet, by the same providence, he ordereth them to fall out, according to the nature of second causes, either necessarily, freely, or contingently.

3. God, in his ordinary providence, maketh use of means, yet is free to work without, above, and against them, at his pleasure.

4. The almighty power, unsearchable wisdom, and infinite goodness of God so far manifest themselves in his providence, that it extendeth itself even to the first fall, and all other sins of angels and men; and that not by a bare permission, but such as hath joined with it a most wise and powerful bounding, and otherwise ordering, and governing of them, in a manifold dispensation, to his own holy ends; yet so, as the sinfulness thereof proceedeth only from the creature, and not from God, who, being most holy and righteous, neither is nor can be the author or approver of sin.

5. The most wise, righteous, and gracious God doth oftentimes leave, for a season, his own children to manifold temptations, and the corruption of their own hearts, to chastise them for their former sins, or to discover unto them the hidden strength of corruption and deceitfulness of their hearts, that they may be humbled; and, to raise them to a more close and constant dependence for their support upon himself, and to make

them more watchful against all future occasions of sin, and for sundry other just and holy ends.

6. As for those wicked and ungodly men whom God, as a righteous Judge, for former sins, doth blind and harden, from them he not only withholdeth his grace whereby they might have been enlightened in their understandings, and wrought upon in their hearts; but sometimes also withdraweth the gifts which they had, and exposeth them to such objects as their corruption makes occasions of sin; and, withal, gives them over to their own lusts, the temptations of the world, and the power of Satan, whereby it comes to pass that they harden themselves, even under those means which God useth for the softening of others.

7. As the providence of God doth, in general, reach to all creatures; so, after a most special manner, it taketh care of his church, and disposeth all things to the good thereof.

The doctrine of providence, one of the most important Christian doctrines, has for many reasons become eclipsed and obscured. In earlier generations, Christians were constantly aware of divine providence. They were so immersed in providence that Providence became a name for God.

Some years ago, during a television special on the Civil War, one of the more dramatic moments was the reading of letters written by soldiers, on the eve of battle, to their wives, sweethearts, or parents regarding the uncertainty ahead. Those letters frequently referred to Providence. The soldier would write: "My beloved wife, Providence has brought me to this point in my life, and I know not what Providence has in store for me tomorrow. And if it should be according to Providence that I not survive the morrow, I will entrust the care of you and of the children to that same benevolent Providence." Over and over, these letters referred to Providence. Many of these soldiers died in battle. There was such a keen sense of God's providence that this word was a normal part of Christian vocabulary. General Stonewall Jackson would say to his troops on the eve of battle: "The battle is ours. The outcome belongs to Providence. It is of God." A town established in the early days of our country was even named Providence.

Since then, the concept of providence has diminished in significance because of our culture's dominant worldview. It assumes that we live in a closed, mechanistic universe, in which everything happens according to the direct causality of physical things, by the fixed laws of nature, which operate independently of God. Nothing is more repugnant to the biblical view of God than the idea that the world exists independently of Him, functioning and operating on its own power, obeying its own built-in, inherent laws.

From a Christian standpoint, the laws of nature describe the normal ways in which God operates His universe. Natural law should not be conceived of as functioning independently of God. This would work against the idea of our being alert to God's hand in history and our lives. When Adam Smith wrote his monumental work *The Wealth of Nations*, he tried to discern the normal laws governing economic affairs, such as the law of supply and demand. He said that he was attempting to detect, in the history of economic action and reaction, "the invisible hand of God." Smith concluded that the affairs of men and the world are ultimately ordered and governed by God, whose rule is invisible. To Isaac Newton, the task of science is to think God's thoughts after Him. In their investigation of the behavioral patterns of natural things, these earlier scientists sought to understand the normal ways in which God governs His world.

Because we live in a time when the divine aspect is ignored or set aside, we have lost the sense of God's providence. Through the study of providence, we may all become more alert to that invisible hand on our lives. We can look to the past and see how God has worked in our lives. We can think of the critical turning points, which often took place in ways we were unaware of at the time. Think of decisions that have been made that have changed the course of history forever. According to Christian theology, there are no accidents or chance meetings of people; all our footsteps are guided by the Lord.

The word *providence* consists of a prefix, *pro*, meaning "in front of" or "before," and the Latin root *videre*, "to see." Based on its etymology, *providence* means "to see beforehand." In theology, however, providence is not mere foreknowledge. It is not limited to God's ability to see into the future. Providence refers specifically to God's care of the world and

His ultimate supervision of it. Providence has to do not only with God's supervision of the universe but also (and more importantly for us) with His provision.

In His providence and foresight, God takes steps in advance to provide for His people. We think of this far less in terms of some kind of sight and more as a kind of action. Paul says that the husband or father who fails to provide for his own family is worse than an unbeliever (1 Tim. 5:8). This man has not made sure that his family will be cared for in the event of a famine or other emergency. If we hear of a hurricane that might hit us, we exercise foresight and stock up on provisions. We become agents of providence when engaged in providing for our families. This is the sense of seeing into the future that is involved in God's providence. He ensures a future for His people by making the necessary provisions for them.

The concept of providence first appears in Scripture in Genesis. When offering Isaac on the altar, Abraham refers to God as *Jehovah Jireh*, "The LORD will provide" (Gen. 22:14). Before being placed on the altar of sacrifice, Isaac asks his father, "Behold, the fire and the wood, but where is the lamb for a burnt offering?" Abraham answers, "God will provide" (Gen. 22:7–8). And that is exactly what God did. He stayed Abraham's hand and provided the sacrifice, a ram caught by its horns in the thicket. This event anticipates the substitute that God provided for us in the Lamb without blemish, who was offered on the cross to satisfy God's justice. In His providence, God arranged for that ram to be caught in the bush at that particular moment. It was not a fortuitous event or cosmic accident. Throughout Scripture, we see God governing and managing His universe.

> 1. God the great Creator of all things doth uphold, direct, dispose, and govern all creatures, actions, and things, from the greatest even to the least, by his most wise and holy providence, according to his infallible foreknowledge, and the free and immutable counsel of his own will, to the praise of the glory of his wisdom, power, justice, goodness, and mercy.

This unequaled summary of Reformed theology first refers to God as **the great Creator of all things** who **doth uphold . . . all creatures, actions,** and things. The Hebrew concept of creation is not that of a momentary action but that of an action that is kept going. The first aspect of providence we encounter in the confession refers to God's work of sustenance. What He creates, He sustains; He upholds the world by His own power.

This differs sharply from views of creation that were on the rise when the confession was written. Deists saw God as the great clockmaker in the sky. He designs the clock, builds it, winds it up, and then lets it operate on its own internal power. Although the religion of Deism is long gone, its philosophy has captured modern culture. For the Christian and the Hebrew, however, God created the world, and the world remains dependent on Him for its continued existence.

In Athens, Paul declared that it is in God that "we live and move and have our being" (Acts 17:28). This does not mean that God merely set the universe in motion or created the first life-forms. Nor does it mean that He is simply the primary being from whom other beings are derived. It means that all present life, all present motion, and all present being are as dependent on the being of God for the continuance of their existence as they are for the origin of their existence.

When the New Testament speaks about creation, Jesus, the second person of the Trinity, is specifically mentioned as the originator of the created world. It is in Him that all things are made, Him by whom all things are made, and Him for whom all things are made (Col. 1:16). He is "the founder and perfecter" not only of our faith (Heb. 12:2) but of creation itself, the *Logos* introduced to us by John (John 1:1). "In him all things hold together" (Col. 1:17).

Nothing could have come into existence except by the power of God, and nothing can be held in existence except by His power. We depend on God's creative power for our origin and on His sustaining power for our continued existence.

A difference between God and His creatures is that He is eternal. He is self-existent and independent; we are temporal, dependent, and fragile. We need to be sustained by air, water, and food. God, on the other hand, needs nothing outside of Himself for His continued being. Through God's providence, we make important decisions in our lives by which our paths are directed according to His will. By His providence, we do whatever we do, for we cannot even breathe without Him. At no point are we free of His providence and sustaining power.

The confession continues after the word uphold with the word direct. God doth uphold, direct, dispose, and govern. So the second aspect of providence has to do with divine government. God not only sustains what He makes but also governs everything He makes. This refers to His absolute sovereignty, His eternal and inalienable right to govern and rule what He owns, and to dispose of those things according to the good pleasure of His will. By His providence, He upholds, directs, disposes, and governs all things. He governs the rulers of this world. We are all under His authority and control.

In the book of Daniel, we see an example of this. King Belshazzar had no concerns. Enough provisions had been stored to care for everyone in Babylon for years, and Babylon's defenses were impregnable. The king made a great feast for a thousand of his lords, and a drunken orgy ensued for days. He commanded that the gold and silver vessels captured from the Jewish temple be brought and used in the festal celebration. As they drank their wine and praised the gods of gold, silver, bronze, iron, wood, and stone, a disembodied hand appeared and began to write on the wall. Belshazzar was frightened. The hand wrote, "MENE, MENE, TEKEL, and PARSIN" (Dan. 5:25). Daniel translated, "You have been weighed in the balances and found wanting" (v. 27). Daniel then told Belshazzar that God was going to remove him. "That very night Belshazzar the Chaldean king was killed" (v. 30).

Ancient historians tell us that the Persians knew that water flowed into Babylon through a conduit under the walls. The army dammed up the rivers, dried the riverbeds, and in the middle of the night marched into the city unmolested through those water pipes. They easily conquered the Babylonians and founded the Persian Empire. King Belshazzar thought he was safe, but in the providence of God he was defeated. Similar events occur many times over in Scripture. No one gains any office, power, or authority except by God's disposition. He disposes, directs, and governs all things.

God directs, disposes, upholds, and governs all things by his most wise and holy providence. It is never arbitrary, frivolous, or capricious. He governs not according to polls or political expediency but by His most wise and holy counsel.

A particular application of this truth has to do with suffering. For the Christian, there ought to be nothing more comforting than the doctrine of divine providence. If we are suffering from an illness, we can look at it as a result of a chance invasion of microorganisms in our body, or we can say that even microorganisms are ultimately upheld, directed, and disposed by the wise and holy providence of God. If tragedy should befall us, it would exacerbate our pain to see all our pain, suffering, loneliness, and grief as a cosmic accident. However, if we see these painful things as coming to us from the hand of a good, holy, and kind God who is working all things together for our good, we will have reason to endure it. That will not erase our pain, but it can help us to endure it without bitterness.

We have looked, by way of introduction, at the doctrine of providence, its meaning and extent. God sustains, upholds, and orders all things by his most wise and holy providence, according to his infallible foreknowledge, and the free and immutable counsel of his own will. In selecting the particular attributes named here, the Westminster divines did not mean to exclude other attributes that are integral to God's being and character. God governs His universe and exercises His providence in accordance with His nature and character. That is why, at the beginning of the confession, we dealt with God's attributes. We saw at that time that the biggest difference between Reformed theology and other theologies has to do with the doctrine of God, because this doctrine controls all others. After starting with the doctrine of God, we do not then forget about it when moving on to other doctrines. All doctrines of the faith must be understood in light of the nature and character of God. He does not sustain and govern all things apart from His nature and character.

This should be obvious, but we sometimes forget it when we are facing pain or tragedy. When big things assail us or smaller things annoy us, do we rest in the knowledge and assurance that they have come to us through the providence of a God who is supremely wise and holy? We question His wisdom as well as His goodness when we murmur and complain about our lot in this world. The confession teaches us that God governs all creatures, actions, and things . . . by his most wise and holy providence.

We can memorize that truth but never understand it. We confess our faith in the sovereignty of God, who orders all things, and we confess that God is good and righteous. That should be the end of our asking why things happen to us. He does these things, the confession says, **to the praise of the glory of his wisdom, power, justice, goodness, and mercy.** His providence evokes our praise because it manifests His glorious majesty. His wisdom and power transcend any conception of wisdom and power that we have experienced in this world. In God's providence, we see a mixture of His justice and His mercy, both of which manifest His goodness.

This affirmation sets forth the contrast between justice and mercy. In 1 Samuel 3:2–18, we read that the boy Samuel, while under the care of Eli, a judge of Israel, was awakened at night by a voice calling his name. He arose, went to Eli, and said, "Here I am, for you called me." But Eli replied, "I did not call; lie down again." Samuel went back to sleep, and again someone called him, "Samuel!" He got up and went to Eli again, but Eli had not called him. The third time someone called Samuel, Eli realized that the one calling him was the Lord. Eli instructed Samuel, "If he calls you, you shall say, 'Speak, LORD, for your servant hears.'" Samuel obeyed Eli's instructions and God spoke to Samuel, telling him that He was bringing judgment on Eli and his family. In the morning, Eli asked what God had said. When Samuel told him, Eli responded: "It is the LORD. Let him do what seems good to him." If we heard that, what would our natural response be? In spite of Eli's weaknesses, particularly as a father, he remained a man of God. He knew that if God, in His providence, manifested His judgment on him, it would be just. He did not cry out, "That's not fair!" He said, "Yes, that is the Lord." Eli recognized that the sentence coming down on him and his house manifested God's justice. Eli understood repentance.

In Psalm 51, penned by David after Nathan rebuked him for his sin with Bathsheba, we have the greatest expression of repentance anywhere in Scripture. Paul later quotes Psalm 51:4: "That you may be justified in your words, and prevail when you are judged" (Rom. 3:4). David is acknowledging that God has every right to judge him. Not attempting to minimize or rationalize his guilt, David recognizes the justness in what

God had done to him. It is important to understand this because we live our lives in two dimensions: the horizontal dimension of life, in which we relate to other people in this world, and the vertical, in which we relate to God.

Each of us, at some point, has suffered from an injustice imposed by another person. We have had broken relationships. We have been slandered, libeled, or hurt by other people. And we struggle with all of that. There also have been times when we have treated people in an unjust manner. On the horizontal plane, we have become masters of inflicting unjust pain on others, and we have also been the object of such pain. We must remember, however, that the worst possible injustice inflicted on us in this world has happened through the providence of God. He makes provision for us to rectify these injustices on the horizontal level. He established a court system in Israel. Having established courts in the church and a civil magistrate to be the minister of righteousness and justice in this world, God allows us to seek redress. Though wounded unjustly by our fellow man, we can never say to God, "You have been unjust to allow this to happen to me." Any true injustice received at the hands of men we also receive through the hand of God, justly. Why is it just for God to allow men to inflict injustice on us? Because in terms of our vertical relationship to Him, we deserve it.

We are debtors who cannot pay our debts. We are sinners who cannot atone for our sin. If God is pleased to visit His justice on us through the means of unjust people, it is not unjust of Him to do so, even though, in terms of the horizontal relationship, the action is unjust. The Jewish people in the Old Testament struggled with this, as witnessed in the books of Job and Habakkuk and many other places.

Throughout the Old Testament, murmuring and complaining were common. When reading these accounts, we have the perspective of the omniscient writer, who tells us what is going on in the hearts and minds of people as the story unfolds. It is as if we were eavesdropping on David, Samuel, Eli, and others as we read how they react to life's circumstances and see that their earthly reactions against God are improper. Lacking the omniscient perspective, they responded with grumbling, murmuring, and complaining. They could not see the invisible hand of providence as it was directing their lives. To walk by faith means to trust the character of God.

In the midst of his tremendous agony, Job exclaimed, "Though he slay me, I will hope in him" (Job 13:15). God's providence is wise and holy, and it should move us to praise the glory of his wisdom, power, justice, goodness, and mercy.

> 2. Although, in relation to the foreknowledge and decree of God, the first Cause, all things come to pass immutably, and infallibly; yet, by the same providence, he ordereth them to fall out, according to the nature of second causes, either necessarily, freely, or contingently.

People tend to feel uncomfortable when reading that God from all eternity, immutably and freely, ordains whatsoever comes to pass. This means, after all, that everything that happens in this world, including the evil things that others do to us and, astonishingly enough, our own sins against others, is immutably foreordained by almighty God. If we have been eternally ordained to commit sin, why does God find fault? We may as well sin with abandon, knowing that we are being directed by the providence of God. This is the mystery of providence. Doing no violence to the will of His creatures, God achieves His purposes through His chosen means.

One view has it that, as we hurtle through space, centrifugal force, gravity, and centripetal force keep us from collapsing and falling out of existence. These forces and powers are real. Gravity exists, but its power is not inherent. Even the power of gravity rests on the primary power of God. Gravity is not an independent primary cause. The only primary cause is the one by whom all things are made and in whom all things hold together. Ultimately, what keeps us from falling off the edge of the earth is the hand of God. But He exercises His power through the real power of secondary causes, such as gravity.

In terms of human relationships, we are secondary causes, and the powers we exert are real, not illusory. We are not puppets with no volition, freedom, or power, but we have no volition, freedom, or power beyond that given to us by God. He remains sovereign over all these things, bringing His sovereign will to pass.

When discussing God's decrees, we speak of the concurrence of the human and divine wills. *Concurrence* is also called *confluence*. Both words mean "a flowing together."

A biblical example of concurrence is the story of Joseph. After enduring unspeakable suffering and injustice at the hand of his brothers, Joseph wound up in solitary confinement in a foreign land. After a time, he was released from prison and elevated to the office of prime minister in the world's most powerful empire, Egypt. Then famine came, and Joseph's father, Jacob, sent his sons to Egypt to appeal for food. The brothers encountered Joseph but did not recognize him until he revealed his identity. Because they had mistreated him and they knew that Joseph had the power to take revenge on them, they were terrified and confessed their sins. Joseph said about their actions, "You meant evil against me, but God meant it for good" (Gen. 50:20).

In this drama there is a concurrence between God's intention and men's intention. One intention is motivated by pure holiness, the other by sheer wickedness. Joseph's brothers meant his suffering for evil, and insofar as this was their motivation, they were culpable before God. But God had ordained that through the brothers' choices, He would bring Joseph to Egypt. Working above and through secondary causes, God would save the people of Israel. God used the work of Joseph's brothers for redemptive purposes. That does not, however, excuse the brothers. Through the great mystery of providence, the transcendent Governor of all things brings good out of evil. Instead of overruling the wicked desires of Joseph's brothers, God transcended them and by His power brought good out of evil.

How can God bring good out of evil? That great mystery is the most comforting promise in the New Testament: "For those who love God all things work together for good, for those who are called according to his purpose" (Rom. 8:28). This does not mean that everything that happens is good in and of itself; but due to Providence everything that happens is working toward our good. Without the concept of providence, we would miss the comfort, consolation, and joy of knowing that God stands above and beyond all things. He is not an isolated spectator who roots for us. A common view in the evangelical world today is that God is powerless to stop all these bad things: He is standing on the sidelines, hoping that the ball bounces the right way so that His eternal purposes are not thwarted. But His purposes cannot be thwarted, because He will work through even bad bounces to bring about victory.

God does not direct injustice toward His people. In fact, every tragedy becomes a blessing. There are no ultimate blessings for unbelievers, however, because every blessing they receive for which they remain ungrateful only redounds to their greater guilt. In the final judgment, every blessing unbelievers have received at the hands of a benevolent God becomes the foundation of their curse. So for believers, there are no tragedies, and for unbelievers, there are ultimately no blessings.

3. God, in his ordinary providence, maketh use of means, yet is free to work without, above, and against them, at his pleasure.

We have already seen that God is the primary or first cause of everything that comes to pass, and we have distinguished between primary and secondary causality. In like manner, we see that when God purposes to accomplish something by His will, He often does so by using means. When speaking of the means by which He works, we are thinking of the ways or instruments He uses to bring to pass whatever He wills.

For example, if someone's goal is to reach San Francisco, he has several possible means to accomplish that end: he could make the journey by car, bus, train, or airplane. Any of these options could become the means by which he arrives at the end. God may ordain that he reach San Francisco, and He may further ordain that he do so by plane. At the same time, He does not pick the person up and place him in a seat on an airplane. There are other means to that end, means in which the person is directly involved. For example, he needs to make a reservation, purchase his tickets, and use some means of transportation to get to the airport.

Just as we use means to reach various ends or purposes, so does God. When God has ordained that certain ends will be achieved, He works through means in order to accomplish them. Some of the means He uses to bring His people to salvation are the preaching of the gospel and the prayers of His people. God ordains both the preaching and the prayers to achieve His ends.

The confession is careful to say that God ordinarily makes use of means. For example, God ordinarily answers prayer for the restoration of someone's health by using the means of physicians, medicine, and perhaps surgery. At the same time, He remains free to work without means, above means, and against means. That is, He can bring someone to a state of health inexplicably without using medicine or doctors. He can exercise His power over and above the ordinary power that He imparts through medical skills, or He can even work against that power, according to His pleasure.

Section 3 states that God ordinarily uses secondary causes to achieve His ends, but at other times He acts directly and immediately brings His ends about. When Israel crossed the Red Sea, God used a great wind to separate the waters (Ex. 14:21). The wind was the means by which the end, Israel's escape from Egypt, was effected. When Jesus raised Lazarus from the dead, however, He employed no means except His direct command to Lazarus to come forth (John 11:43). Lazarus was raised immediately, without the application of intervening means. God has the power to work in either manner.

> 4. The almighty power, unsearchable wisdom, and infinite goodness of God so far manifest themselves in his providence, that it extendeth itself even to the first fall, and all other sins of angels and men; and that not by a bare permission, but such as hath joined with it a most wise and powerful bounding, and otherwise ordering, and governing of them, in a manifold dispensation, to his own holy ends; yet so, as the sinfulness thereof proceedeth only from the creature, and not from God, who, being most holy and righteous, neither is nor can be the author or approver of sin.

When we ponder God's providence, the most vexing question is this: How do God's sovereign authority and providence relate to the origin of evil? Some people, feeling the pressure of this difficulty, have considered this the Achilles' heel of Christianity, that which makes Christianity inexplicable and indeed unbelievable. We will study this issue in detail in chapter 6. When discussing the origin of evil with respect to providence, we face what theologians call the mystery of iniquity. But we notice in this segment of the confession that even the very presence of evil and sin in the world do not cancel out God's power, wisdom, or goodness. We read that God's power is almighty, His wisdom unsearchable, and His goodness infinite. His power, wisdom, and goodness manifest themselves completely in everything He ordains, including the fall of the human race and all other sins of angels and men.

Let us stop for a moment. When reading that God's providence includes the fall of man and all other sins of angels and men, many want not only to pause but to gasp in disbelief. But that is indeed what the confession asserts. Everything that comes to pass is in some way ordained by God's sovereign will, and that includes even the fall of the human race and the sins we commit daily.

Many are willing to say, "Yes, God permits such things to take place, even though it is contrary to His will." They contend that to safeguard the creature's free agency, God steps out of the picture and allows things to happen that He would never ordain but that chooses to allow for His own good reasons. Many would say that is what the confession means by bare permission. This seems to be an easy way to avoid the difficulties of this vexing problem. But such an answer to the puzzle of evil is simplistic. For God to allow it to happen, He must choose to allow it. If He chooses to allow something to happen that He has the power to prevent, then in some sense He has ordained that it come to pass; its coming to pass is within the context of His wisdom, power, and goodness, and it manifests His own holy ends. Yet, says the confession, sinfulness comes only from the creature, not from God, who neither is nor can be the author or approver of sin.

We must avoid the trap of saying that good is evil or that evil is good. Nor can we blame our wickedness on the will of God, as if He coerced us to sin, and thus excuse ourselves from culpability in such transgressions against His holiness. At the same time, we must acknowledge that if a fall occurred in the past, even the fall of the human race, it was in some sense ordained by God. If He had not ordained it, the fall would not and could not have occurred. Here we pause with trepidation before declaring that, though the fall and our abiding sin are in and of themselves evil things for which Adam and we are culpable, from the perspective of the mystery of divine purpose and providence, it is ultimately good that there is evil. Again we pause, making sure that we distinguish between saying, "Evil is good," and, "It is good that there is evil." Evil is real, and it is real evil. Yet, the fact that evil exists in a universe governed by a perfectly holy God must mean that He has good purposes in mind. We see this in God's answer to the wickedness of Joseph's brothers: the brothers meant their deed for evil, and it was terribly evil, but God meant it for good and brought much good out of it.

We assume that God is not the author (or doer) of sin, as is also stated in chapter 3, section 1. We have a clear revelation, in both nature and Scripture, of God's righteousness and holiness, and we understand intuitively or rationally that sin is incompatible with moral perfection. Since God is indeed righteous and holy, it is unthinkable that He Himself would commit sin or do something wicked or evil.

If God is eternally righteous, then it is unthinkable that He would ever sin. If it is unthinkable for God to sin, and if He created all things, how can there be evil in the world? Why, within His universe and under His sovereignty, are creatures like us running loose and doing evil? The confession says that God not only permits us to sin, but in His sovereignty He ordains that we sin. Paul anticipates this objection from the creature: "You will say to me then, 'Why does he still find fault? For who can resist his will?' But who are you, O man, to answer back to God? Will what is molded say to its molder, 'Why have you made me like this?'" (Rom. 9:19–20).

As we have argued above, it is good that there is evil. If it were not good, then God would be sinful in even allowing for its possible existence. God always had the authority and power to prevent evil in the first place. He could have stopped Adam and Eve from transgressing against Him. He knew before they sinned that they would do so. Knowing that, He could have decided not to create them in the first place. Even though He knew what they would do, He still created them, according to the good pleasure of His will, which is perfect in its exercise. Knowing what they would do, He chose to allow them to do it. He actually ordained that they would do it; without His ordination they could not have done it. This does not mean that He made them do it and then blamed them for it but that He gave them the capacity to do it and ordered the events around them so that they would do it.

If Adam and Eve could not sin apart from divine providence, and if they did sin under that providence, we must conclude that in some sense it is good that they sinned. The sin itself was not good, of course, but allowing and ordaining it was part of God's will, and He wills only that which serves His good purposes. That is a tough concept. We are not saying that Adam's fall was really a wonderful event. It was terribly evil. Nevertheless, it worked out in history according to God's eternal plan.

The fall of Adam and Eve is another example of concurrence. Adam and Eve meant their sin for evil, but God meant it for good. We could apply this principle also to Judas' betrayal of Jesus. Judas, who betrayed an innocent man for his own personal gain, intended something altogether wicked, selfish, and abhorrent. He had bloody hands. Yet through his act of perfidy, atonement is made by which we are redeemed. Judas' wickedness redounds to the greatest good that has ever occurred—not by his design but by the secret design of God.

> 5. The most wise, righteous, and gracious God doth oftentimes leave, for a season, his own children to manifold temptations, and the corruption of their own hearts, to chastise them for their former sins, or to discover unto them the hidden strength of corruption and deceitfulness of their hearts, that they may be humbled; and, to raise them to a more close and constant dependence for their support upon himself, and to make them more watchful against all future occasions of sin, and for sundry other just and holy ends.

This section has an important practical and spiritual application to our own Christian pilgrimage. Every earnest Christian has experienced what the saints called "the dark night of the soul." This refers to a period in our personal relationship with God when it seems that He has left us alone. Listen to the painful, anguished cries of Luther in the midst of his experiences. Or listen to David as he cries: "Answer me quickly, O Lord! My spirit fails! Hide not your face from me, lest I be like those who go down to the pit" (Ps. 143:7).

We could give a facile answer to this plea: "God promises never to leave us or forsake us. If we feel that He has removed Himself from our presence, this is simply a matter of our sensuous unbelief. Because we do not feel His presence, we deny the promise of His presence, relying too much on our own feelings instead of His Word." That is the easy solution to the problem, and in many cases it is accurate. We rest too much of our confidence on some kind of spiritual tingling up and down our spine instead of on the Word of God. We become sensuous Christians, whose testimony and faith are only as strong as our feelings at the moment. But beyond that, the Westminster divines say, God does on occasion leave us—not totally and completely, but for a season. In a sense, He exposes us to temptation and further corruption, but not in the same way He treats the unbeliever.

According to Scripture, God ultimately judges the unrepentant by giving them over to their sins. In the final judgment God will say to them, "Let the evildoer still do evil, and the filthy still be filthy" (Rev. 22:11). In the New Testament, to be excommunicated from the church is to be turned over to Satan and delivered out of the realm where are concentrated the means of grace that protect our souls from the enemy's assault. That is the dreadful thing about excommunication: we are sent "outside the camp" to the lonely place where we are vulnerable to enemy attacks. Jeremiah warned the Jewish people that unless they turned from their sin, God would give them up, surrender them, and give them over to the enemy.

It is difficult to think of any greater horror than to be abandoned by God and given up or turned over to sin. That is what God does to the reprobate in hell. The confession speaks here not of what God does to the wicked, but of what He does to His own children. For a season, He will withdraw Himself from His own people as a form of chastening.

If we have been justified by faith alone, the ground for our eternal salvation is secure—not because of our obedience or disobedience, not because of our righteousness or lack of it, but because of the perfect righteousness of Jesus, which God counts as ours when we receive Christ by faith. Christ's perfect righteousness can never be augmented or diminished. Even though His righteousness secures our eternal salvation, in our daily walk with God we are either pleasing Him or displeasing Him. He is now our Father and has adopted us into His family. We need not fear being sent to eternal perdition. Nevertheless, we begin a relationship with God at the moment of justification and it progresses through sanctification. During this time we are either pleasing or displeasing God with the manner of our lives. In that pilgrimage, we may do such violence to the Holy Spirit and to God the Father that He will chasten us.

Scripture reminds us that as the father chastens a child out of his love for the child, so God chastens His own children, not as their final Judge but as the tender Father who exercises discipline: "For the Lord disciplines the one he loves, and chastises every son whom he receives" (Heb. 12:6). When the Lord sees us drifting away, wandering into disobedience, He may at times keep us on a long leash, letting us wander to a place where we feel far removed from Him and where we are exposed to trials and temptations.

In the Lord's Prayer, Jesus told His disciples how to pray: "Pray then like this: 'Our Father in heaven, hallowed be your name'" (Matt. 6:9). One petition of this prayer is, "And lead us not into temptation, but deliver us from evil" (v. 13). Delivering us from evil involves delivering us also from the evil one, Satan; it means protecting us from demonic assaults. When Jesus was sent by the Spirit into the wilderness to be tempted for forty days, He had to quench the fiery darts of the devil and withstand his attack. When we pray, we ask that we will never need to go through such an experience. We pray that we will be delivered from the enemy. We ask God not to put us in that place of exposure. But we must realize that He may do so if He thinks it is required for our further sanctification. Part of His providential care is to expose us from time to time.

The most wise, righteous, and gracious God doth oftentimes leave, for a season. For how long? The critical phrase is for a season—not a long duration, but perhaps a brief interval. He may leave his own children to manifold temptations, and the corruption of their own hearts. After encountering a man who had been born blind, the disciples came to Jesus with a question: "Rabbi, who sinned, this man or his parents, that he was born blind?" (John 9:2). Jesus might have replied that the disciples committed a logical fallacy called the fallacy of the false dilemma or the either-or fallacy. They had reduced the options to two, when in fact there was a third option. Jesus then gave them the third option: "It was not that this man sinned, or his parents, but that the works of God might be displayed in him" (v. 3). God had a holy, redemptive purpose for having this man born blind that had nothing to do with his parents' sin or his sin. God's eternal purpose was to be glorified; for this purpose He gave this man over to blindness for a season.

The disciples were wrong to reduce the options to two, but their thinking was not that far off. They understood that the presence in this world of suffering and pain is ultimately related to sin. Had there been no fall, there would be no blindness. The friends who visited Job had concluded that he must have been the worst sinner in the world because of the magnitude of his suffering. The book of Job teaches that it is wrong to conclude that people suffer in this world in proportion to the extent of their sin. At the same time, we must not leap to the conclusion that our suffering is never related to our sin. There are many times when God's hand is heavy on us because He is chastening us for our sins. We must be very careful, however. If we go through a particularly dark time in our lives, we cannot jump to the conclusion that God is punishing us, but neither can we be certain that He is not punishing us. He may very well be correcting us.

Being unable to read the divine mind, what do we do, practically speaking, when going through a dark night of the soul? First, we trust God's providence and goodness. Second, we ask, "Lord, what do You have in mind?" Third, we examine ourselves.

The fact that Christ has taken our punitive wrath does not prevent us from experiencing God's corrective wrath. Section 5 talks about this when it says to chastise them for their former sins, or to discover unto them the hidden strength of corruption and deceitfulness of their hearts, that they may be humbled. The heart is deceitfully wicked above all things (Jer. 17:9). Not one of us has begun to grasp the full extent and gravity of our own transgressions. We tend to give ourselves the highest possible approval rating and our enemies the lowest. We see every peccadillo they commit as evidence of their despicable corruption. Remember how the speck in our brother's eye commands our attention and how the plank in our own eye is difficult to see because we do not want to see it (Matt. 7:3–5). Sometimes God makes clear the weight of our sins by removing His blessings. Sometimes we will not and cannot see it until God's chastening reduces us to this broken state. "Work out your own salvation with fear and trembling, for it is God who works in you, both to will and to work for his good pleasure" (Phil. 2:12–13). God is assisting us in His providence: "For those who love God all things work together for good, for those who are called according to his purpose" (Rom. 8:28). Even our chastisement, our sense of abandonment for a season, and our temporary exile from the comforting presence of God are for our benefit.

That they may be humbled; and, to raise them to a more close and constant dependence for their support upon himself, and to make them more watchful against all future occasions of sin, and for sundry other just and holy ends. This is a simple expression of God the Father's benevolent care for His children. His principal will for our lives is our sanctification. Would you like to know what God wants from us? He wants us to be holy, conformed to the image of His Son. That should be our chief concern in life.

6. As for those wicked and ungodly men whom God, as a righteous Judge, for former sins, doth blind and harden, from them he not only withholdeth his grace whereby they might have been enlightened in their understandings, and wrought upon in their hearts; but sometimes also withdraweth the gifts which they had, and exposeth them to such objects as their corruption makes occasions of sin; and, withal, gives them over to their own lusts, the temptations of the world, and the power of Satan, whereby it comes to pass that they harden themselves, even under those means which God useth for the softening of others.

God gives people over to Satan to be exposed to His manifold temptations. God does not just allow these things but positively ordains them. This may be the hardest and most controversial section in the confession.

Section 6 expands on the manner in which God imposes His just punishment on corrupt people. He not only subjects them to further temptations but also works to harden their hearts and blind them.

Wrestling with this dimension of providence is difficult. At times, Scripture itself says that God blinds people, stops up their hearing, or (as in Pharaoh's case) hardens their hearts. After imposing these punishments, God further punishes them for their godlessness.

In calling Isaiah, God asks, "Whom shall I send, and who will go for us?" Isaiah said: "Here I am! Send me" (Isa. 6:8). God gave the prophet these instructions:

> Go, and say to this people:
> "Keep on hearing, but do not understand;
> keep on seeing, but do not perceive.'
> Make the heart of this people dull,
>   and their ears heavy,
>   and blind their eyes;
> lest they see with their eyes,
>   and hear with their ears,
> and understand with their hearts,
>   and turn and be healed." (vv. 9–10)

Isaiah's mission was one of hardening the people. God declared that He would make the eyes of the people blind, their ears deaf, and their hearts fat, "lest they see with their eyes, and hear with their ears, and understand with their hearts, and turn and be healed" (v. 10). God took an active role in preventing these people from repenting and being restored.

That is hard for us to understand. Jesus explained to the disciples why He taught in parables. These stories are a double-edged sword: they not only give clarity to the teaching of Jesus for those who fundamentally understand what He is saying but also hide His teaching from the reprobate (Matt. 13:11–15). God does this as an act of judgment.

It is one thing to hear, and another thing to heed. We can hear an order from a policeman, a teacher, a boss, or even God, and fail to heed it. Obedience comes when the message we hear grabs hold of our will and we respond with obedience.

The people of Israel heard God's commands but did not obey them. They heard but did not heed. God's punishment for sin tends to be a kind of poetic justice, giving people over to their sinful desires. In the final judgment, God will say to the wicked, "Let the evildoer still do evil, and the filthy still be filthy" (Rev. 22:11). When abandoning people, God abandons them to themselves. Far from taking away their free will, He delivers them over to their free will, by which they choose to do the evil desires of their hearts.

In our natural state, we have hearts of stone (Ezek. 36:26). A heart of stone does not pulsate with affection. It is not alive but calcified. At the core of our natural state is a heart that is insensitive with respect to the things of God. We do not want to hear or see Him, and we do not want to respond to Him affectionately and positively. As part of His judgment, God gives the reprobate what they want.

This blinding and hardening manifests God's righteous judgment. He withholds His grace from people, grace that may have enlightened their understanding and worked upon their hearts. Sometimes He also gives them over to their lusts, the world's temptations, and Satan's power, whereby they harden themselves, even under the means that God uses to soften others.

The New Testament describes the gospel as the light and grace of God for those who are being saved (2 Cor. 4:4). At the same time, the gospel is the judgment of God for those who are perishing. Every time a person hears the gospel, there are two outcomes. If he responds positively to the gospel, that abounds to his blessedness; if he rejects it, his guilt before God increases. Every time someone says no to God, he is, as Paul puts it, "storing up wrath for [himself] on the day of wrath" (Rom. 2:5).

People are in one of two states: saved or unsaved. An individual goes either to heaven or to hell. More than twenty-five New Testament texts tell us that in heaven God distributes to His people rewards that are unequal. Some receive a greater reward than others. Similarly, there are degrees of punishment in hell. As John Gerstner used to say, "The sinner in hell would do anything that he could and give everything that he had to make the number of his sins during his lifetime one less." Every time an unbeliever commits a sin and continues in that sin without repentance, that person heaps up wrath against himself on the day of wrath.

We can also harden ourselves. The prophet Jeremiah admonished Israel for having "the forehead of a whore" (Jer. 3:3), which means that, through repeated acts of disobedience, the Jewish nation had lost its capacity to blush. The whore can be involved in degrading activity without any sense of shame. This happens not only to whores but to everyone. We constantly sear our consciences and harden our hearts as we become more and more accustomed to sin. We do not start out as innocent people with a righteous nature only to become corrupted by civilization at some point during adolescence. It does not work this way. We are born with a corrupt nature, and the older we get, the more we manifest this corruption.

Fallen man naturally lowers the standard to where he is. Which of us takes seriously the fact that we will be judged on the last day against the standard of perfection, which is measured by the holiness of God? The law given to every creature is this: "Be holy, for I am holy" (Lev. 11:44). Having become so unholy, we are unconcerned. We assume that God cannot hold us accountable to such a high standard when no one reaches it. Surely, He will adjust the standard downward, as we have done in our own minds. Part of God's judgment is that He allows us to quiet our consciences. Part of His judgment is to give us over to the very things we desire.

As Luther said of Pharaoh, it was not that God intervened in the life of a just, righteous, and innocent man, planting an evil desire or disposition in his heart and thereby creating fresh evil in him. God withdrew His restraint and Pharaoh's heart became hard. The hardening was itself a judgment, and Pharaoh could not then say to God, "I sinned because You hardened my heart and I could do nothing else."

When interceding for Sodom and Gomorrah, Abraham manifested a lack of confidence in God's goodness. He asked God if He would destroy everyone in the area because of the sinners in it: "Will you indeed sweep away the righteous with the wicked?" (Gen. 18:23). He added, "Far be it from you to do such a thing, to put the righteous to death with the wicked" (v. 25). Abraham did not seem to understand that God would not punish an innocent person (except Jesus, for a redemptive purpose). Abraham asked the rhetorical question, "Shall not the Judge of all the earth do what is just?" (v. 25). The answer is obvious. Of course God will do only what is just.

When people's hearts are hardened, their eyes are blinded, and their ears are deafened to the things of God, it is not because He is acting tyrannically, arbitrarily, or capriciously. The Judge of all the earth inflicts these things on His creatures as judgments for sin. Section 6 makes the point that God punishes the wicked justly for their sins when their hearts are hardened. And the very things that God uses to soften the hearts of His people may harden the hearts of the wicked. We hear the gospel and it softens. But our neighbor, who hates the gospel, hears it and responds with more enmity and animosity than before. God owes grace to no one, and the common grace He gives to everyone becomes an exercise of His judgment, because the wicked resist even that.

> 7. As the providence of God doth, in general, reach to all creatures;
>   so, after a most special manner, it taketh care of his church, and
>   disposeth all things to the good thereof.

In this brief statement referring specifically to God's care for the church, we notice first that it distinguishes between God's general providence and His special providence.

Reformed theology includes a third category, called miracle. Theologians use this term in a more narrow or precise way than is usual in the church. The Bible has no single word for miracle. Some of the more recent translations of the Bible, like the New International Version, use the word *miracle*, but the Greek language of the New Testament has more specific words, usually translated "signs," "powers," and "wonders." The Apostle John's favorite is the word translated "sign": "This, the first of his signs, Jesus did at Cana in Galilee, and manifested his glory" (John 2:11). "This was now the second sign that Jesus did when he had come from Judea to Galilee" (John 4:54).

Theologians take these supernatural signs and wonders and extrapolate from them the general idea of miracle. They define *miracle* narrowly as a manifestation of the power of God in the visible world, whereby He acts *contra naturam*, against the normal laws of nature, immediately and supernaturally. A miracle is something that only God can perform, such as raising someone from the dead or bringing something out of nothing. God's acts of *general providence* are things that happen generally, all the time. In *special providence*, God works through the ordinary means of nature, but in an extraordinary manner. For example, when we pray for someone who is ill or injured, with little hope of recovery, and yet the person recovers, it is extraordinary, but not necessarily a miracle in the narrow sense. A miracle occurs when God does something that goes against the normal laws of nature.

This section discusses special providence, not miracle. The confession says that God cares for His church not only as part of His normal, day-to-day government of the universe, but with a special providence.

As an example of God's special providence, consider the books of the Bible. How do we know that the right books are in the Bible? In the early church, there was debate over which books to include. How do we know that the right books ended up in our Bible?

The Roman Catholic Church claims that the canon was established by the church, which had been empowered by God with infallible authority to make that decision. Therefore, the church must have made the right decision when deciding in the third and fourth centuries which books would be in the canon. But the Reformers, rejecting the infallibility of the church, said that the authority of the church rests on the authority of Scripture and the Apostles. They pointed out that the fourth-century church councils only claimed to have "received" (*recipemus*) these books as canonical, not to have created the canon. They granted the remote or theoretical possibility that the church had made a mistake, for example, in including Hebrews and excluding the *Shepherd of Hermas*.

We can know that the church made the right decision in every case because the church's confidence in the canon it has received has historically been so firm and strong. Many Protestants have concluded that, although God has not empowered His church with infallibility, there are in history special matters in which God has taken special pains to guide His church. We believe that He exercised a special providential care during the history of the church's decisions with respect to the canon. There is nothing in the Bible to suggest that the Holy Spirit guided the church to the right books. It is an article of faith. We look backward and say that we believe the invisible hand of providence took great care to preserve the books of Scripture for the benefit of the church.

If we broaden this idea of special providence, we can apply it to the crisis today in the church. Historians indicate that we are living in the post-Christian era. In Western Europe, church membership and church attendance have fallen dramatically. The great cathedrals of France, Germany, and other nations have been turned into museums, which remain valuable as tourist attractions but lack much other usefulness in today's secular civilization.

The state of the church in the world and particularly in America is worrisome. Nineteenth-century liberal theology sought to reduce Christianity to a naturalized religion, stripped of everything supernatural. The Christian message was reduced to matters of ethics and values; the gospel was recast as a kind of humanitarianism that attempts to alleviate pain and suffering in this world. Everything supernatural in Scripture was denied, including the deity of Christ. His substitutionary atonement, resurrection, and ascension were all rejected. Modern theology took hold of churches and educational institutions.

The second half of the twentieth century saw mainline churches in America lose members at the rate of a hundred thousand per year. People have left the liberal churches in droves because there is little substance in liberalism. Yet liberalism has influenced evangelical churches, and evangelicalism has been seriously diluted during the last quarter-century. This should motivate us to take steps to protect the church.

Individual congregations and denominations come and go. They appear with great vitality and devotion, then lose their enthusiasm, become reprobate, and die out. In the eighteenth century, Methodism swept through this country, but it is largely liberal today. The First Great Awakening in New England came about through the impact of Congregational churches, but Congregationalists are now virtually held captive by liberalism.

When we see these things take place, we may succumb to the Elijah syndrome. The prophet Elijah courageously stood up against hundreds of the prophets of Baal, King Ahab, Jezebel, and King Ahaziah, all of whom wanted him killed. Finally, Elijah cried to God, "Lord, they have killed your prophets, they have demolished your altars, and I alone am left" (Rom. 11:3). That is the Elijah syndrome. But God heard the prophet's complaint and responded, "I have kept for myself seven thousand men who have not bowed the knee to Baal" (v. 4).

That is what the confession means when it speaks of the special providence and care that God gives to His church. It guarantees that He will preserve not a particular local church or denomination but a remnant. Isaiah also asked the Lord how long he had to preach to people who would not see or hear. God answered, "Until cities lie waste without inhabitant" (Isa. 6:11). But God assured Isaiah that He had reserved for Himself a tenth of the people as a remnant (v. 13).

The Old Testament records the history of the apostasy and corruption of the visible church. It is the story of people rejecting their covenant agreement with God and substituting idol worship and other pagan practices in place of the purity of the covenant that God had made with them. But throughout this drama is an undercurrent of God's preserving His people. He preserved Noah, Abraham, Isaac, and Jacob. Those few, a remnant, remained faithful, so that the covenant did not die out.

Between first-century Jerusalem and the church in America today, many parallels exist. The church of Israel was decadent when Jesus was born. The Pharisees (the religious class) were corrupt, as were the Sadducees and priests. There was little piety or devotion, and little commitment to the Word of God. People were following tradition rather than Scripture.

The voice of prophecy had been quiet for four hundred years before John the Baptist emerged from the wilderness. In Luke's narrative of Christ's infancy, the first person we meet is Zacharias, apparently one of only a few priests who were still believers. God announced to him that he and his godly wife, Elizabeth, would have a child, John the Baptist. After the angel's announcement to Mary of Jesus' birth, she responded with a song of praise known as the *Magnificat*: "My soul magnifies the Lord" (Luke 1:46). Mary continued to praise God because He had remembered His promise to Abraham (v. 55). In his *Benedictus*, Zacharias also spoke of God's having remembered His ancient promise to Abraham (vv. 72–73). Simeon, a just and devout man who had faithfully waited for the Messiah, was in the temple when Mary and Joseph brought the infant Jesus to be presented to God. When he saw the child, Simeon sang the *Nunc Dimittis*: "Lord, now you are letting your servant depart in peace, according to your word; for my eyes have seen your salvation" (2:29–30). Anna the prophetess, who was also present in the temple at that time, gave thanks to the Lord for sending the Redeemer (2:38).

Zacharias, Elizabeth, Mary, Joseph, Simeon, and Anna were faithful to a centuries-old promise that others had forgotten. They did not succumb to the spirit of the age. They were faithful, just as Elijah and Jeremiah had been. God had preserved His remnant. In His special providence, He preserved this small group of people. And from Abel to this day, there has always been a church. That church is the only institution with an absolute guarantee of its perennial survival.

The church is the most important institution in the world, and because of that it is also the most corrupt. Hell will hurl everything it has against the church. Christ said, "On this rock I will build my church, and the gates of hell shall not prevail against it" (Matt. 16:18). "The gates of hell" does not refer to the attack on the church by satanic forces. In Scripture, the church is on the offensive, called to knock down the battlements of hell. God will not protect the citadels of Satan from us. At the same time, we enjoy Christ's special care of those who belong to him. That is the original meaning of the term *church*, *kyriakos*, "those who are the possession of or who belong to the *kyrios* or Lord." Through His special providence, God preserves the church, and that is encouraging in an age when the church seems to have less influence, credibility, and significance. We can be optimists if we believe in God's providence and Christ's lordship over His church. The church cannot be destroyed because God will preserve His people now and forever.

Of the Fall of Man, of Sin, and of the Punishment Thereof

1. Our first parents, being seduced by the subtlety and temptation of Satan, sinned, in eating the forbidden fruit. This their sin, God was pleased, according to his wise and holy counsel, to permit, having purposed to order it to his own glory.

2. By this sin they fell from their original righteousness and communion with God, and so became dead in sin, and wholly defiled in all the parts and faculties of soul and body.

3. They being the root of all mankind, the guilt of this sin was imputed; and the same death in sin, and corrupted nature, conveyed to all their posterity descending from them by ordinary generation.

4. From this original corruption, whereby we are utterly indisposed, disabled, and made opposite to all good, and wholly inclined to all evil, do proceed all actual transgressions.

5. This corruption of nature, during this life, doth remain in those that are regenerated; and although it be, through Christ, pardoned, and mortified; yet both itself, and all the motions thereof, are truly and properly sin.

6. Every sin, both original and actual, being a transgression of the righteous law of God, and contrary thereunto, doth, in its own nature, bring guilt upon the sinner, whereby he is bound over to the wrath of God, and curse of the law, and so made subject to death, with all miseries spiritual, temporal, and eternal.

We all love life and cling to it, yet we know there is something systemically wrong with our bodies and souls. All is not right with the world.

In his masterful study of original sin, Jonathan Edwards observes that if the Bible did not explicitly teach a historical fall of the human race, the sheer universality of human sin, throughout history and the world, would force us to postulate a historical fall. Evidence for the fall is everywhere and overwhelming. The things we would do, we do not do, as the Apostle Paul lamented, and the things we would not do are the very things we do (Rom. 7:15). We understand that sin, far from being a foreign problem, is one we struggle with in our own lives and in our own souls. Sometimes we are tempted to think that if we had been the architects of the human race, we would have created ourselves differently.

Humanity, Blaise Pascal observed, is the supreme paradox. We are at the same time the creatures of the highest grandeur and the worst misery, able to reflect on our existence in a way that other creatures cannot, but also able to contemplate a better life, one we cannot achieve. We can contemplate life without disease, death, pain, sorrow, and sin, but so far we have been unable to achieve such an existence—though Christians look forward to it in the new heaven and the new earth. The Bible declares that man was created not in the state of fallenness as we experience it today but in a pristine state of original righteousness, where there was no sin, death, or pain.

Secular anthropologists look at the development of the human race in terms of evolutionary theory. In this scheme of things, history and the human race itself are marching inexorably on an upward, progressive path. History, however, would seem to gainsay such optimism. Scripture depicts the history of mankind in terms of devolution, not evolution. Man was created on a far higher plane of existence than any of us presently occupies. When we imagine our first parents, Adam and Eve, enjoying a life without the ravages of sin in their bodies and minds, we must conceive of them as being almost superhuman in their powers. Imagine a human being with a mind that is not hampered by the effects of sin, whose reason is not clouded or biased, whose thinking is so precise that he makes only correct inferences from data he observes. With this understanding of our first parents in their created state, we can only be that much more perplexed by their fall from that state of total innocence into the corruption with which we are all too familiar.

The entrance of sin into the world of human beings is one of the most difficult theological questions we face. We cannot explain how it happened. We can only retreat to what theologians call the mystery of iniquity. We are beginning to study that as we begin chapter 6.

1. Our first parents, being seduced by the subtlety and temptation of Satan, sinned, in eating the forbidden fruit. This their sin, God was pleased, according to his wise and holy counsel, to permit, having purposed to order it to his own glory.

The fall is recorded for us in Genesis: "Now the serpent was more crafty than any other beast of the field that the LORD God had made. He said to the woman, 'Did God actually say, "You shall not eat of any tree in the garden"?'" (Gen. 3:1).

Edward J. Young, in a monograph on Genesis 3, pointed out that the opening sentence of this chapter, "Now the serpent was more crafty than any other beast of the field," is somewhat jarring. It suddenly introduces into the biblical record of creation an ominous and foreboding note, creating an expectation that something bad will soon take place. Of course, what does take place sets the stage for the drama of redemption outlined in the rest of Scripture. From Genesis 4 to the end of the book of Revelation, Scripture deals with God's response to, and remedy for, the events recorded in Genesis 3.

The crafty serpent came to Eve with a question: "Did God actually say, 'You shall not eat of any tree in the garden'?" (Gen. 3:1). The serpent's question may have planted a seed of doubt about God's integrity and His goodness, perhaps suggesting that God's making restrictions was somehow unjust, unfair, or tyrannical.

Jean-Paul Sartre, who developed atheistic existentialism and a nihilistic view of man, concluded that man is a "useless passion." In existential categories, the uniqueness of humans is their subjectivity, and the essential element of subjectivity is volition or freedom. Sartre argued that a human being can be completely morally free only when autonomous.

The prefix *auto* means "self" and *nomos* means "law," so autonomy refers to that which is a law unto itself and is therefore accountable to no one. Sartre was saying that unless a person is morally autonomous, he is not really free. We have become so restricted by rules and regulations imposed by all kinds of authorities—civil, religious, and social—that we have lost our freedom. Sartre held that anything short of absolute autonomy is simply the illusion of freedom. If we must answer to anyone other than ourselves, we are not truly free.

When the serpent asked about God's restrictions, his unspoken, seductive hint was this: God might as well have said that you can eat from none of the trees because, by restricting you at all, He has taken away your freedom. God has imposed His will on you and taken away your dignity. The serpent's seduction, then, was his pretense of autonomy.

Eve's answer showed that she did indeed understand what God had commanded: God allowed them to eat the fruit of every tree in the garden except one in the middle of the garden. And she understood the stated sanction for disobedience: "We may eat of the fruit of the trees in the garden, but God said, 'You shall not eat of the fruit of the tree that is in the midst of the garden, neither shall you touch it, lest you die'" (Gen. 3:2–3).

Satan immediately challenged her understanding of the situation: "You will not surely die. For God knows that when you eat of it your eyes will be opened, and you will be like God, knowing good and evil" (vv. 4–5). There, set before mankind in the garden, is the temptation: to become like God and achieve autonomy.

In simple language, it was the question of obedience. Will you obey God or will you do what is right in your own eyes? Doing what you want to do rather than what God requires you to do is sin. If our only desire were to please and honor God, we would never sin, but there are conflicts between God's law and our desires, and therein lies the problem.

Subtle similarities exist between the serpent's temptation of Adam and Eve and Satan's temptation of Jesus for forty days in the wilderness—the temptations of the first and last Adam. For example, in both cases there is a probation. Our first parents were placed on probation and exposed to the test; the last Adam was driven into the wilderness by the Holy Spirit also to be exposed to a probationary period of testing.

The settings for their temptations differed, however. The first Adam was tested in an immaculate garden, a paradise filled with magnificent trees whose fruit was good to eat. Adam and Eve could satisfy their physical needs completely. Jesus was tempted in the Judean wilderness, where there was little to eat. Adam and Eve had each other for strength, encouragement, and comfort; Christ was exposed to the forces of hell alone.

Satan did not say to Jesus, "Since You are the Son of God. . . ." Instead, he said, "The devil said to him, "*If* you are the Son of God, command this stone to become bread" (Luke 4:3, emphasis added). The last words Jesus heard before entering the wilderness were God's declaration, "This is my beloved Son, with whom I am well pleased" (Matt. 3:17). All three times in the New Testament when God speaks audibly, He declares the sonship of Christ: "This is my beloved Son, with whom I am well pleased; listen to him" (Matt. 17:5).

As soon as God announced that Jesus was His beloved Son, the Spirit drove Jesus into the wilderness, where for forty days He remained in isolation. Satan subtly suggested to Jesus, "How could the Son of God possibly be subjected to such treatment?"

Satan took the same approach with Eve: "Did God actually say . . . ?" Today, the Bible's authority as the written Word of God has come under such severe attack that the church is tempted not to submit to it. The satanic suggestion continues for us: "This is the Word of God? How can this be the Word of God? Did God really say . . . ?" In the context of the temptation to turn stones into bread, Jesus responded, "It is written, 'Man shall not live by bread alone, but by every word that comes from the mouth of God'" (Matt. 4:4).

Adam was satisfied to live by some words that come from the mouth of God, but not by every word. Jesus, in the same kind of confrontation, did not negotiate His Father's will but lived by every word that God had spoken.

Adam and Eve saw that the Tree of Knowledge of Good and Evil was good and pleasing to the eye, and they ate its fruit. They made an evil choice. Here is the philosophical problem: How can a creature who has no sinful disposition, no evil desire, and no evil inclination whatsoever make a wicked choice? If we choose something freely, we choose what we want. Saying that they had free will does not answer the question. Free will means that they were not coerced into sinning, but that does help us understand how they sinned.

Assume for a moment that Adam and Eve were coerced into eating the forbidden fruit. If they were truly forced to eat it by the serpent, they would not be morally accountable. The only evil would be what the serpent did, not what Adam and Eve did. The biblical record indicates that they were not coerced but seduced, and there is a difference.

What if Adam and Eve had been forced to eat the fruit by God? If He had forced them to sin and punished them for it, then God would be the sinner, not Adam and Eve. God held them accountable and responsible, which presupposes that they had the moral ability to refuse the temptation. Instead, they succumbed to it. To make a moral choice, we must have a conscious mind. There are voluntary and involuntary actions. We do not decide to have our heart beat. But to do something that is moral or immoral, we must voluntarily choose to do it. If we do something for no reason whatever, we have not made a moral choice, but a physical response. Desire or inclination or disposition is a necessary condition for making a decision in the first place.

If Adam and Eve chose according to their desires, and if they chose an evil action, then they must first have had an evil desire. Where did it come from? Were they born with evil desires? Did God make them with evil desires? If so, then God is the author of evil. If an evil desire rises spontaneously within the soul of a righteous creature, we have an inexplicable event, what Karl Barth called *die unmögliche Möglichkeit* (the impossible possibility). We do not know what motivated Adam and Eve. Somehow, a good desire got twisted into a bad result.

We get a clue from Jesus' temptation involving hunger. He had a physical desire for food. Nothing is sinful about a hungry person's wanting to eat. The desire is perfectly righteous. But if He had acted on that desire in response to Satan's temptation, He would have failed the test. This does not mean that Jesus' desire to eat was a sinful one. No matter how great His physical desire for food was, He desired even more to obey His Father at every point. A desire for something, in and of itself, can be morally neutral, but in certain circumstances a desire can become wicked.

Perhaps something like this took place with Adam and Eve, but the Bible does not tell us how it was possible for them to sin. We do know, beyond any shadow of a doubt, that they did sin. How sin got here we do not know, but it is here. The good news of Scripture is that there is redemption from sin.

> 2. By this sin they fell from their original righteousness and communion with God, and so became dead in sin, and wholly defiled in all the parts and faculties of soul and body.

Since later statements elaborate on this, let us move on to section 3.

> 3. They being the root of all mankind, the guilt of this sin was imputed; and the same death in sin, and corrupted nature, conveyed to all their posterity descending from them by ordinary generation.

The idea that Adam's guilt and sin were imputed to his posterity is found frequently in the New Testament, particularly in Romans and 1 Corinthians. Paul writes that through one man's trespass, death came into the world, and that through his disobedience, all have died (Rom. 5:12; 1 Cor. 15:21–22). This doctrine immediately raises the question of God's justice: Is it just for Him to punish the whole human race for the transgression of one person?

What is the relationship of Adam to his descendants? Historically, the two most popular theories have been realism and federalism. Although there are varieties of these theories, we will look at them generally, beginning with realism. The fundamental principle behind this theory is that God can justly hold us accountable for Adam's sin only if we were really there. Otherwise, we are born in a state of sin and spiritual death for which we are punished by God and may justly complain, "That is not fair. God can punish someone only for his own personal crimes."

In Ezekiel, the people complain that God is unfair: "The fathers have eaten sour grapes, and the children's teeth are set on edge" (Ezek. 18:2). God answered by reminding the people that they were being punished for their own sins, not the sins of their fathers. Although the Decalogue says that God visits the iniquity of people on the third and fourth generations

(Deut. 5:9), this does not mean that the third and fourth generations are immediately punished for their ancestors' sins. It means that the consequences of our sin will have an impact on our descendants to the third and fourth generations. The principle in Ezekiel is that God holds us accountable for the sins that we commit, not for the sins that someone else commits.

But that principle only exacerbates the question of the human race's ruination as a result of Adam's sin. Realism seeks to solve that problem by suggesting that we can be held accountable for the sin of Adam because we really sinned with Adam. In this view, Adam constituted the whole of humanity (besides Eve, of course), and each of his descendants, coming from his body, has been an individuation of that human nature. Just as "one might even say that Levi himself, who receives tithes, paid tithes through Abraham" (Heb. 7:9), so all the descendants of Adam sinned through Adam, for they were in the loins of Adam when he was in the garden of Eden. In this sense, all of Adam's descendants sinned in Adam. However, the words "one might even say" imply that Levi was not really in the loins of Abraham. Also, the notion that people are individuations of a single unit of human nature has no biblical support. That is the simple, more crude form of realism, based on a weak exegesis of Hebrews 7:9.

Federalism, the opposite of realism, emphasizes Adam's representative character. Adam is the federal head of the human race, like elected representatives in a federal republic. Jesus also fills a representative function by entering a role of corporate solidarity with Israel. He becomes Israel. He represents that nation. In terms of His work on the cross, He is our substitute, standing in our place. God counts us as righteous because He transfers to us the righteousness of Jesus. Likewise, He transfers our guilt to Christ. Our salvation involves that double transfer, our sin to Jesus and His righteousness to us. Salvation rests on the validity of some kind of representation. If we object in principle to representation before God, we would negate the representative redemption won for us by Christ.

Adam is a single individual, yet in Eden he was the federal head of the human race, representing himself and all his seed. The probation Adam underwent was not just for himself but for the human race. When he fell, so did all whom he represented. People complain, "Why am I held accountable for what another person did?" Federalism answers, "Because that person represented you." We may complain further: "I did not select him as my representative." It is true that we did not choose Adam to represent us. We usually do not trust someone else to appoint our representatives. However, we can be confident that God selected him as the one who would represent us perfectly. We therefore cannot say that Adam misrepresented us. As God's perfectly selected representative, Adam represented us flawlessly.

> 4. From this original corruption, whereby we are utterly indisposed, disabled, and made opposite to all good, and wholly inclined to all evil, do proceed all actual transgressions.

If I were to choose one statement in the entire confession that crystallizes the distinctive characteristics of historic Reformation theology, it would be this one. Here lies the focus of the historic debates between Reformed theology and other theologies concerning the degree to which we human beings have fallen from our original righteousness. That is, it states the scope and extent of original sin.

Nearly every church affirms some doctrine of original sin. One cannot read Scripture without concluding that the human race is fallen, that we are by nature in a state of corruption. Christian bodies dispute, however, the extent or degree of that corruption. One word in section 4 deserves our close examination: inclined. It has to do with the moral disposition or bent of fallen humanity. An inclination denotes a condition of the heart, out of which behavior flows.

Section 4 also teaches that out of our inclination flow all actual transgressions. Theologians distinguish between original sin and actual sin. Original sin refers to our moral condition, from which our actual behavior flows. The Bible calls us sinners, not merely because we commit sins, but because we are by nature sinful—inclined or disposed toward sin.

In *The Freedom of the Will*, Jonathan Edwards argues that we always choose according to our strongest inclination at the moment. Suppose a man is accosted by a robber who points a gun at him and says, "Your money or your life!" The robber has reduced the victim's options to two, but he still has a choice. He can surrender his money or lose his life. He will weigh his options and act according to his strongest inclination at the moment.

Where does this "strongest inclination" come into play in section 4? Why exactly do we sin? The simple answer is this: we sin because we want to sin. We are strongly inclined to sin. We are disposed to sin. In our fallen nature, we have a desire for sin. At the moment of sinning, we want to sin more than we want to please Christ and obey God. Otherwise, we would not do it.

Jesus, our Savior, is the only One who has ever been sinless. The reason is that He was utterly disinclined and indisposed toward sin. He had a consuming passion to please His Father. He desired obedience alone. His meat and drink were to do the Father's will. By comparison, in our most advanced degree of sanctification, our disposition and inclination for good are at best an appetizer. None of us has such a consuming zeal for obedience that it can be described as our meat and drink. On the contrary, as section 4 expresses, we possess a consuming passion for sin that marks our fallen state.

Part of the reason for this passion is that sin is attractive to us. We find our highest pleasure in sin. The goal of hedonism is to attain the greatest possible pleasure while avoiding the most pain, and we are by nature pleasure-seekers and pain-avoiders. We seek the pleasures of sin because we think they will bring happiness. Scripture says that Satan, the father of all lies, was a liar from the beginning. His greatest lie, starting with Eve in the garden, is that we can be happy only by disobeying God. We assume that if we deny ourselves any allurement, we will in effect deny our happiness.

The first question in the Westminster Shorter Catechism is "What is the chief end of man?" The answer: "Man's chief end is to glorify God, and to enjoy Him forever." We often fail to understand that to glorify God means to obey Him. We do not see the joy in obedience; we think that obeying God will deprive us of the joys we desire. This is Satan's great lie and deception. As Augustine said, "Oh, Lord, Thou hast made us for Thyself, and our hearts are restless until they find their rest in Thee." Nothing can possibly satisfy the deepest desires and needs of the human soul as can fellowship with God.

We may think that the confession is exaggerating when it says that the fall has left us utterly disinclined toward good. Is it our nature as human beings to be utterly disinclined toward righteousness? Perhaps you know some examples where even unbelievers seemed to manifest a genuine inclination or disposition to the good. But Paul, quoting the psalmist, says: "None is righteous, no, not one; no one understands; no one seeks for God. All have turned aside; together they have become worthless; no one does good, not even one" (Rom. 3:10–12; see Ps. 14:1–3).

This is difficult to understand. John Calvin taught that fallen creatures still have a capacity for what he calls civic virtue—keeping certain laws, rules, and regulations of society, or acting and interacting with others in ways that are not vicious or evil. These are behavioral patterns involving other people. In terms of our earthly relationships, we may be good, charitable, honest, compassionate, and industrious. Indeed, non-Christian people sometimes put Christians to shame with their sacrificial giving and good attitudes toward their fellow man.

Given this kind of human behavior, why does the Bible take such a dim view of man's moral condition? The answer is that what fallen man can do on the horizontal plane in his behavior toward other people he cannot do on the vertical plane in his behavior toward God. When the Scripture records, "No one does good, not even one," good is more narrowly defined than it usually is.

The rich young ruler who came to Jesus was clearly a man of high standing in the community, though unregenerate. He asked Jesus in flattering terms, "Good Teacher, what must I do to inherit eternal life?" Jesus responded: "Why do you call me good? No one is good except God alone" (Luke 18:18–19). To understand this exchange, we must pay close attention to Jesus' first response, which in a sense framed the entire discussion: "Why do you call me good?"

Some critics say that Jesus here denied His own deity and perfection. But Jesus did not say, "Why do you call Me good? I am not good." Nor did He say, "Why do you call Me good? I am not God." Jesus knew that the man had no idea who He was.

The ruler had a superficial, defective understanding of goodness that was inadequate for his concerns. To reveal this to him, Jesus employed the Socratic method. It is one thing to tell a person that he is not as good as he thinks he is, but it is another to lead him to discover it on his own. Rather than give the young man a direct answer, Jesus simply said, "You know the commandments: 'Do not commit adultery, Do not murder, Do not steal, Do not bear false witness, Honor your father and mother'" (Luke 18:20).

When repeating the Ten Commandments, Jesus did not start with the first commandment. Instead, He started with what some theologians call the second table of the law, the commandments dealing specifically with our behavior toward other people. The first table deals with our behavior toward God.

After Jesus cited the commandments dealing with our behavior toward other people, the young man responded: "All these I have kept from my youth" (Luke 18:21).

Jesus could have said: "Where were you when I preached the Sermon on the Mount? If you had been there, you would not respond so hastily. I explained that if you hate someone, are angry at someone unjustly, or even call someone a 'fool' without just cause, you have violated the broader content of the law against murder. If you have ever lusted after a woman in your thoughts, you have broken the law against adultery" (see Matt. 5:21–22, 27–28).

Jesus taught in the Sermon on the Mount that the application of God's law is far broader than the narrow view of the Pharisees. Had the rich young ruler never slandered another person? Had he never had a lustful thought or been angry without just cause? Instead of wagging His finger in the man's face and saying, "Don't tell Me you have kept the commandments all your life," Jesus counseled: "Sell all that you have and distribute to the poor, . . . and come, follow me" (Luke 18:22).

Some say that Jesus was promoting the renunciation of all earthly possessions as the path to heaven. But that was not His point. This young man had just looked at Jesus and said, "All these I have kept from my youth." Instead of arguing with him, Jesus juxtaposed the unspoken first commandment—"You shall have no other gods before me" (Deut. 5:7)—with the ruler's obvious preoccupation with riches, wealth, and possessions. Jesus offered him the opportunity to demonstrate how he kept the law by telling him to sell all he had, give it to the poor, and follow Jesus. Luke says that the young man "became very sad, for he was extremely rich" (18:23). He evidently had not been present when Jesus said, "No servant can serve two masters. . . . You cannot serve God and money" (Luke 16:13). Jesus did not say that it is wrong to own things. He said that if we love our possessions more than we love God, we violate the first commandment. Goodness has both a horizontal and a vertical dimension.

Scripture says that when God judges us for our actions and behavior, He considers two things: the outward acts and the inward motivation. He considers the acts to see if they conform to His law. Consider the unregenerate person who exercises civil virtue and refrains from stealing. He passes the first half of the test—external conformity to the law—but what about the second half—his motivation? A good deed is one that is objectively good, but it must also be motivated by a good inclination or a desire to please God. Most of us understand that it is in our best interests to behave well toward others. But for God to deem such behavior good, it must be motivated by a love for God and a genuine desire to please Him.

God looks at the heart. He delights in obedience from a heart that genuinely loves Him. It is easy to deceive ourselves, however, about the degree to which our obedience arises out of a genuine delight in Him. That is why the Bible says that none is righteous and no one does good. Augustine said that our greatest virtues are at best splendid vices, because a pound of flesh attaches to everything we do.

Reformed theology teaches that the fall is so serious and profound that, if left to ourselves, to our own inclinations and natural dispositions, we would never come to Christ. No one would pursue the things of God, no one would choose Him, because nothing in our flesh is inclined to God. Only when God, in His grace and mercy, changes our heart's disposition do we incline toward Him. That is what happens when we are reborn. A person who is not reborn can never take the slightest step in a vertical relationship, because that person is spiritually dead. We are in bondage to a will that is inclined only to evil; the desires of our heart are only wicked continually in our basic fallen nature (Gen. 6:5). In our flesh, we can do no good thing; "The flesh is no help at all" (John 6:63).

That is why, if the vertical relationship to God is to begin, our hearts must be changed, and that change has to penetrate to our deepest inclinations, desires, and disposition. Only the Holy Spirit can change our natural disposition and inclination and create in our souls a genuine love for God. Unless He moves to change us, the only good we will ever do is on the horizontal plane, and that will not satisfy the law of God.

> 5. This corruption of nature, during this life, doth remain in those that are regenerated; and although it be, through Christ, pardoned, and mortified; yet both itself, and all the motions thereof, are truly and properly sin.

After considering the reality of original sin and our corrupt nature, the confession explains that regeneration does not instantly and automatically eliminate the consequences of our fallen nature. Although we are justified in an instant, we are not instantly sanctified. We remain tainted by sin's power until we are completely glorified in heaven after death. Regeneration frees us from total bondage to sin, from moral inability. When He justifies us, God pardons our original sin and places it in a dying condition. Nevertheless, the corruption remains throughout our lives, and its remains yield actions that may truly and properly be called sin. Section 5 denies any notion that the Christian is perfected in this life, either initially by regeneration or later in a special work of sanctification. The effect of the grace of sanctification is taken up in greater detail in chapter 13.

> 6. Every sin, both original and actual, being a transgression of the righteous law of God, and contrary thereunto, doth, in its own nature, bring guilt upon the sinner, whereby he is bound over to the wrath of God, and curse of the law, and so made subject to death, with all miseries spiritual, temporal, and eternal.

Both actual sin and original sin bring guilt on the sinner. Guilt is defined biblically as something objective, not just a subjective feeling. Something as basic and fundamental as this should require little explanation, and throughout most of church history it has required little. Yet this has changed in the recent past, as the last several decades have brought on a new cultural order that has seen widespread upheaval in our customs, values, and way of living.

In the 1960s and early 1970s, we saw a revolution in sexual mores, the emergence of the drug culture, the breakdown in authority systems, the nationwide enshrinement of a legal right to abortion, and the rise of popular movements based on existential philosophy, which separated personal ethics from social ethics. In the sixties, many interesting buzzwords or slogans were used, one of which was this: "Everyone is entitled to do his own thing." When embracing subjectivism, we contradict objective truth and authority. Everyone is then entitled to do his own thing, as though no moral absolutes or objective truth existed. Another buzzword, a cry against the older generation and the establishment, was this: "Tell it like it is."

There is a dichotomy or tension between people's doing their own thing—subjectivity—and telling it like it is—objectivity. We probably have not yet fully grasped the tremendous impact of that cultural revolution on the church or the broader society. At the heart of the problem is the question of guilt and its objectivity. This generation of people determines truth and reality by their feelings. If it feels good, it is good. How can something be wrong when it feels so right? Even when asked what they think, people say, "I feel this," and, "I feel that." To say what one thinks about something is to give one's analysis of it, one's cognitive understanding of it, not one's emotional reaction to it. In our speech, however, we blur the distinction between thought and feeling.

Nowhere is this blurring more pervasive than in the case of guilt, where we distinguish between guilt and guilty feelings. It is possible to incur guilt and not feel guilty. We know from Scripture that we can so sear our consciences, become so recalcitrant in our hearts, that we can stifle the voice of conscience, stopping our ears and hearts from feeling any remorse for our sins. Some people see guilty feelings as the test of guilt: "If I don't feel guilty, I'm not guilty." One place where that kind of thinking does not work well is the criminal courts. If someone is accused of first-degree murder and offers as a defense, "I don't feel guilty, therefore I'm not guilty," he will not get very far. As to the question of whether the crime was committed and the law violated, one's feelings have nothing to do with it.

The confession affirms that every sin we commit brings objective guilt, and guilt measures the degree to which we have transgressed an objective law. If we break the law, we are guilty. If we feel guilty, as we should, that is good. The Bible's only cure for objective guilt is objective forgiveness. The reality of guilt can be dealt with only by real forgiveness. Again our feelings can come into play: "If I don't feel forgiven, I must not be forgiven." The test, however, is not our feelings. If God says He will forgive us in certain circumstances and on certain conditions, then we can rely on the objective truthfulness of that declaration and know that we are forgiven. The other reality that connects real guilt and real forgiveness is real repentance, which we will look at later.

The first consequence of transgressing God's law is guilt, and this guilt is real. The rich young ruler blithely went through life assuming he had kept God's law perfectly, when in fact he had become a master of lawbreaking by the time he met the Savior. One of the sweet things about God's mercy and grace is His tenderness. He does not reveal to us all at once the full measure of our guilt. If Isaiah came apart on seeing the holiness of God, what do you think would happen to us if we had a comprehensive view of our sin? It would destroy us, and we would collapse under the burden of it. But the Holy Spirit gently convicts us of our sin and moves us to the proper state of repentance and contrition in the gradual process of our sanctification. Sin brings guilt, and we are guilty people. Scripture teaches that those who are indicted by God at the last judgment, the supreme tribunal, will respond only with silence. Every mouth will be stopped because when God reveals to us the full extent of our transgressions, there will be nothing left to say. Who will deny the Almighty's assessment of our innocence or guilt? Our mouths will be shut because of the objective reality of our guilt. After the last judgment, there will be no court of appeals.

The second consequence of violating the law of God and doing violence to His righteousness is exposure to His wrath. This is a difficult subject to communicate to twenty-first-century Americans. One of the theological revolutions that began in the nineteenth century was a denial of the reality of God's wrath. During the First Great Awakening in the eighteenth century, the three preachers most used of God were George

Whitefield, John Wesley, and Jonathan Edwards. The message of these preachers has been characterized—and sometimes caricatured—as one of hellfire and damnation. In simple terms, they preached that man is very bad and God is very mad. Some have called the theology of Edwards and Whitefield in particular a "scare theology."

Edwards based his famous sermon "Sinners in the Hands of an Angry God" on the text "Their foot shall slide in due time" (Deut. 32:35, KJV). Edwards offered three major images from Scripture to illustrate the guilty person's precarious position before the face of an angry God. The first was that of a rope bridge with wooden planks, suspended over a huge chasm. The boards have rotted and are covered with algae and slime. Edwards said that as we make your way across that unstable bridge, sooner or later our feet will slip and we will fall into the abyss.

The second image, borrowed from the Psalms, comes from archery. Edwards said that God has bent His bow and is aiming the arrow at our hearts. The bow has been drawn back so far that all God needs to do is release it and the arrow will pierce our hearts. The only thing that keeps the arrow from penetrating our hearts is God's hand, which holds it back.

The third and most famous image is that of a spider hanging by a slender thread over a burning fire. We are likewise suspended over the flames of divine wrath, which beat and thrash about our single thread, burning it and finally dropping us into the fire. Then Edwards said: "O sinner, God loathes you even more than a righteous prince abhors the rebels in His kingdom, and you can give no reason why you haven't fallen into the pit of hell since you arose from your bed this morning other than that God's hand has held you up." The point of the sermon was God's grace. Edwards emphasized that God's hand holds us and preserves us from falling into the flames of unmitigated wrath.

What would happen today if we heard sermons like that on a consistent basis? We are unwilling to think of ourselves as sinners in the hands of an angry God. Reaction to this eighteenth-century preaching came in the next century, when European liberalism denied the supernatural, the atonement, the doctrine of original sin, and God's wrath.

A summary of the basic message of the nineteenth century could be this: man is not so bad, and God is not so mad. Because wrath is, in and of itself, a bad thing, it would be beneath God's dignity for Him to be wrathful. If He ever became angry, He could not be God. The objectivity of God's wrath is routinely denied even in our churches today. Salvation is of the Lord. But if God is our Savior, from what are we saved? If Christ performs the work of reconciliation, to whom are we reconciled? According to the New Testament, we are saved "from the wrath to come" (1 Thess. 1:10). God saves us, in Christ, from His own judgment and wrath. Jesus of Nazareth taught that a day is coming when every human being will be brought before God's tribunal, and each of us will be held accountable for everything we have ever done, said, or thought (Matt. 12:36–37).

In the nineteenth century, Friedrich Nietzsche declared that God is dead. The liberal movement of that day rejoiced. We have seen the death-of-God movement revived in our time, and its advocates exhibit a certain glee in announcing His death, as well as a new optimism based on nineteenth-century positivistic philosophy.

They were optimistic because, with "the death of God," the church no longer had a stranglehold on science, economics, or world civilization. With more education, technology, and expertise, a new world order would bring peace among nations. War would be no more. Disease and poverty would be conquered. With God dead, there was no more accountability, and that produced a spirit of delight.

Then, after the War to End All Wars (World War I) did not end all wars, the advances in education did not cure humanity's ills, and the World War II death camps were revealed, pessimistic humanists arose under the guise of modern existentialism. They said that man is a useless passion, that life is meaningless, and that no one is "home" out there. Philosophers such as Albert Camus and Jean-Paul Sartre looked at the price tag on the cloak of liberation that naive nineteenth-century humanists had celebrated. The price tag was this: if there is no God, then we are a cosmic accident that has emerged from the slime. We have come from *das Nichtigkeit* (the nothingness), and we are destined inexorably for the abyss of nothingness. Our origin and destiny are meaningless, as is everything in between.

Sartre and his colleagues understood that if we are not ultimately accountable, then ultimately we do not count. To this day, some claim that there is no judgment—that when we are dead, we are dead. At death, we will not have to appear in the courtroom of the Lord God. But if by some chance He does judge, His mercy and love will cancel out any wrath.

The truth is that if we do not believe in God's wrath, we cannot be considered Christians. It is that simple. Divine wrath is integral to the classic biblical concept of faith. We cannot be Christians if we do not believe in the cross, which is the purest demonstration of the reality of God's wrath. If God's manner is simply to forgive us, overlook our sin, and exact no payment for our guilt, then the cross was unnecessary. The significance of the cross, the reason we run to it and cling to it, is that there Christ bore the objective wrath of God in and of Himself for His people. Knowing the reality of it, Jesus saved us from the wrath to come.

In addition to the objectivity of the guilt and the wrath, section 6 speaks of the curse. The idea of the curse comes from man's fall and God's judgment on man. In the Christmas carol "Joy to the World," how far does that joy extend? "Far as the curse is found." How far is that? Throughout the entire creation. "For we know that the whole creation has been groaning together in the pains of childbirth until now," waiting "for the revealing of the sons of God" (Rom. 8:22, 19). God has pronounced judgment on the whole world because of sin.

According to Scripture, apart from the fall and sin, there would be no disease, pain, or death. We remain under this curse, and we will not escape from it until we step across the vale and into our Father's house. Only there is one totally free from the curse. Meanwhile, we live in a cursed world.

The origin of that curse is recorded in Genesis:

> But the LORD God called to the man and said to him, "Where are you?" And he said, "I heard the sound of you in the garden, and I was afraid, because I was naked, and I hid myself." He said, "Who told you that you were naked? Have you eaten of the tree of which I commanded you not to eat?" The man said, "The woman whom you gave to be with me, she gave me fruit of the tree, and I ate." Then the LORD God said to the woman, "What is this that you have done?" The woman said, "The serpent deceived me, and I ate." (Gen. 3:9–13)

The first time God confronted guilty people, they tried to shift the blame to someone else and deny their guilt. This was no isolated episode unique to the garden of Eden. It is you and me; it is how we are. God said to the serpent, "Because you have done this, cursed are you above all livestock and above all beasts of the field; on your belly you shall go, and dust you shall eat all the days of your life" (v. 14). Classic art depicting the temptation of Eve and Adam in the garden always represents the serpent as a snake, slithering around on its belly. But that is not how this serpent approached Eve and Adam. Only after God's curse fell on him was the serpent forced to eat dust for the rest of his days.

Here is the rest of the curse: "I will put enmity between you and the woman, and between your offspring and her offspring; he shall bruise your head, and you shall bruise his heel" (v. 15). This is the first announcement in sacred Scripture of the gospel. So the first proclamation of the gospel of Jesus Christ, which is good news, was, in context, a proclamation of unspeakably bad news for Satan. God said that Eve's seed would bruise Satan's head, and that Satan would bruise His heel. Christ, the seed of the woman, was crucified, hurt, and bruised. He was broken when He crushed the head of Satan on the cross.

God goes on to assign responsibilities in marriage, and the partner with the heaviest burden is the husband, because he must imitate Christ and is inadequate for the task. The married woman must live with a man who is not prepared to give himself totally to her or to love her as Christ loves the church, a man who will exploit and neglect her. This will multiply her sorrows. She is the vulnerable one in this relationship, because her husband will be selfish, and that is the curse (v. 16).

And the man? God said to Adam: "Because you have listened to the voice of your wife and have eaten of the tree of which I commanded you, 'You shall not eat of it,' cursed is the ground because of you; in pain you shall eat of it all the days of your life" (v. 17). Some people think that work is part of this curse. But God worked for six days creating the world, and after creating Adam and Eve, God put them to work dressing, keeping, and tilling the garden. Adam's labor was fulfilling and a joy to him, for he was not estranged from the work of his hands. Before the fall, Adam cultivated the garden, which had no weeds, parasites, or blights.

He did not have to weed, fertilize, or spray insecticides. He could walk through the garden and pick at his leisure the magnificent fruit that grew so abundantly in paradise. After Adam sinned, God put a curse on his work, telling him that the earth would resist him. When he planted seeds, the result would be briars, thistles, and weeds. Adam would be forced to eke out his existence by the sweat of his brow while experiencing stress and fatigue. "By the sweat of your face you shall eat bread, till you return to the ground, for out of it you were taken; for you are dust, and to dust you shall return" (v. 19).

Some people think that the Genesis account of the fall is a myth, but no one thinks that sorrow, stress, and toil are myths. The curse under which we live is real, and it is inseparably related to sin. Think of the pain that you and I experience in this world—pain from illness, the loss of loved ones, broken relationships, being the victim of a gossip or a thief. What pain have you ever known that is not directly associated with sin? This world is cursed because it is sinful. The guilt is objective, the wrath is objective, and the curse is objective, which means they correspond to reality.

Shall we go home and give up? Or shall we anticipate that out of this law and this indictment comes the gospel, which gives objective forgiveness, objective peace with God, and the objective, eternal removal of God's curse? That is why the best thing that ever happened in this world is the cross. If a single pill were discovered that could cure cancer, everyone would hail it as the greatest discovery of all time. But the greatest discovery ever was made by the women who went to Christ's tomb, could not find His body, and left saying, "He is risen!" That takes care of it all. We still live in a fallen world where there is pain and guilt. Even if a cure for cancer is discovered, we will still die of something else. But the gospel removes our guilt and the curse, and that is the hope and assurance shed abroad in our hearts. We have tasted the heavenly gift and know the future promise. In Christ, we find the remedy for all that is wrong with the world and all that is wrong with us.

Of God's Covenant
with Man

1. The distance between God and the creature is so great, that although reasonable creatures do owe obedience unto him as their Creator, yet they could never have any fruition of him as their blessedness and reward, but by some voluntary condescension on God's part, which he hath been pleased to express by way of covenant.

2. The first covenant made with man was a covenant of works, wherein life was promised to Adam; and in him to his posterity, upon condition of perfect and personal obedience.

3. Man, by his fall, having made himself incapable of life by that covenant, the Lord was pleased to make a second, commonly called the covenant of grace; wherein he freely offereth unto sinners life and salvation by Jesus Christ; requiring of them faith in him, that they may be saved, and promising to give unto all those that are ordained unto eternal life his Holy Spirit, to make them willing, and able to believe.

4. This covenant of grace is frequently set forth in Scripture by the name of a testament, in reference to the death of Jesus Christ the Testator, and to the everlasting inheritance, with all things belonging to it, therein bequeathed.

5. This covenant was differently administered in the time of the law, and in the time of the gospel: under the law, it was administered by promises, prophecies, sacrifices, circumcision, the paschal lamb, and other types and ordinances delivered to the people of the Jews, all foresignifying Christ to come; which were, for that time, sufficient and efficacious,

through the operation of the Spirit, to instruct and build up the elect in faith in the promised Messiah, by whom they had full remission of sins, and eternal salvation; and is called the old testament.

6. Under the gospel, when Christ, the substance, was exhibited, the ordinances in which this covenant is dispensed are the preaching of the Word, and the administration of the sacraments of baptism and the Lord's Supper: which, though fewer in number, and administered with more simplicity, and less outward glory, yet, in them, it is held forth in more fullness, evidence and spiritual efficacy, to all nations, both Jews and Gentiles; and is called the new testament. There are not therefore two covenants of grace, differing in substance, but one and the same, under various dispensations.

---

1. The distance between God and the creature is so great, that although reasonable creatures do owe obedience unto him as their Creator, yet they could never have any fruition of him as their blessedness and reward, but by some voluntary condescension on God's part, which he hath been pleased to express by way of covenant.

Chapter 7 introduces the concept of **covenant**. It assumes that the Creator has authority over His creatures. Since we are dependent on the Creator for our very existence, it follows that we are morally obligated to render obedience to Him, the author of our very lives. His authorship gives Him authority to command whatever He will from that which He made.

God's willingness to enter into a covenant (that is, an agreement, contract, or pact) with us is itself a matter of grace. Although section 2 will spell out the covenant of works and distinguish it from the covenant of grace, section 1 reminds us that any covenant into which God enters with us is an act of condescension. Because He is not obligated to be in a covenant relationship with us, even the covenant of works is founded on God's grace.

Reformed theology is often called "covenant theology." The concept of covenant, which provides the structure or framework of redemptive history and of the whole scope of theology, is vitally important. It provides the context within which God reveals Himself to us, ministers to us, and acts to redeem us. The Bible speaks frequently about covenants of all sorts—for example, the covenant with Noah, the covenant with Abraham, and the covenant with Moses. In Jeremiah's prophecies, God promised to establish a new covenant. Jesus announced this new covenant to His disciples in the upper room as He celebrated the Passover with them on the night before His death. The language and idea of covenant pervade redemptive history and the Bible.

A covenant, in the simplest terms, is a formal agreement between two or more parties. That covenant, pact, or contract has definite content. We are familiar with the covenant concept at many levels in contemporary society, probably the most obvious being the covenant of marriage. This relationship is based on a formal agreement between two people that involves promises, stipulations, witnesses, vows, and oaths. We also understand the idea of covenant in business relationships. There is, for example, an agreement between employer and employee, in which certain promises, agreements, and stipulations are made between two parties. Vendors and buyers also enter into contractual agreements.

To broaden our understanding of a covenant, let's look at some important research done in the 1950s by George Mendenhall. His monograph *Law and Covenant in the Ancient Near East*, which analyzed ancient Hittite treaties, sent shock waves throughout the scholarly world and precipitated further research on this subject, including Meredith Kline's *By Oath Consigned*, the title of which referred to the basic structure of the biblical relationship between God and His people. In his analysis of treaties entered into by Hittite kings with their vassals, Mendenhall showed that the particular format, legal structure, or framework of these treaties was not unique to the Hittites but was common to treaties throughout the ancient Near East, including Israel.

The first part of an ancient Near Eastern covenantal arrangement was the preamble, which identified the suzerain (the overlord of a vassal state). Hittite treaties have sometimes been called suzerain treaties because they were initiated by the dominant party, the king. The king identified himself in the preamble something like this: "I, Hammurabi, king of all the Hittites, the one who reigns supreme over all vassals in this realm. . . ." He specified that he was the author of the agreement and had the authority to initiate it.

Israelite treaties in the Old Testament begin similarly. The Ten Commandments, for example, are introduced by: "I am the LORD your God" (Ex. 20:2). God, like the Hittite kings, identifies Himself in the preamble by name: "I am Yahweh, your sovereign." This covenant is not with Mother Nature but with a God who is personal, who has a name. That may seem insignificant, but it makes the point that we are entering into a legal relationship defined not only by abstract rules and regulations but also by a personal relationship with the Lawgiver. This is not simply rule by law, but rule by God, who is personal. He creates persons, and He gives His law to define our relationship with Him and with each other.

The second part of Hittite suzerain treaties was the historical prologue, in which the king briefly summarized the history of his relationship with his vassals: "I, Hammurabi, king of all the Hittites, am the king who defended your borders from the invasion of the Amalekites. I am the king who filled your coffers with surpluses of grain. I am the king who shared the treasuries with you in times of famine." The ruler reminded his vassals of his track record. When the covenant or treaty was renewed, the historical prologue was brought up to date to answer the question, "What have you done for me lately?"

We also find a historical prologue in the Mosaic covenant: "I am the LORD your God, who brought you out of the land of Egypt, out of the house of slavery" (Ex. 20:2). In this brief prologue, God brings up to date the history of His relationship with His subjects. Throughout the Old Testament, there is this abiding sense of continuity. The God of Jacob was not a new God who replaced the God of Abraham. The God of Moses was not a new God who superseded or supplanted the God of Isaac or of Noah or of Adam. The entire Old Testament, in one sense, functions as historical preamble or prologue to the coming of Christ, because the same Sovereign creates the world, relates to Adam, renews the world with Noah, calls Abraham out of Ur of the Chaldeans, relates to Isaac, Jacob, and the tribes of Israel, and is the Father of our Lord Jesus Christ.

When Old Testament covenants are renewed, as in Joshua 24, the historical prologue is brought up to date. Joshua speaks to the people, not just about Abraham, Isaac, Jacob, and the exodus, but also about crossing the Jordan River, driving out the Canaanites, and being established in the promised land. The God of the Bible is the God of history. He is a personal God, and His track record is important to New Testament faith.

The third part of Hittite suzerain treaties consisted of promises and stipulations. A present-day example of this section appears in the workplace. An employee agrees to fulfill the terms of his job description, and the employer promises to pay him certain wages and benefits. In this covenant, we have the terms, promises, and conditions.

The Hittite suzerain said to his vassal: "If you pay a head tax of so many shekels, I will guarantee your water wells and protect them against all thieves, marauders, and invaders." God makes promises to us in every covenant, as when He said, "You shall be my people, and I will be your God" (Jer. 30:22). But every covenant also contains stipulations. It is dangerous to think that the law is found only in the old covenant and not in the new covenant. Christ says that if we love Him, we will keep His commandments (John 14:23). The New Testament is filled with commandments.

How many times have we heard it said, "Christianity is not a bunch of rules and regulations; it is about a personal relationship"? That is a false dichotomy. Christianity is certainly not rules and regulations alone. At its heart, it is a personal relationship. But that relationship, because it is a covenant relationship, is defined by rules and regulations. It is based on promises and conditions: "If you love me, you will keep my commandments" (John 14:15).

In the Old Testament, the law had a covenantal framework. That God entered into this covenant at all is a matter of grace. Grace provided a foundation for the law. Though rooted in God's graciousness, the law defined how we are to relate to God and each other. God expressed His sovereign will for His people: "I am the LORD your God, who brought you out of the land of Egypt, out of the house of slavery. You shall have no other gods before me" (Ex. 20:2–3). The sovereign is setting forth a stipulation for the subordinates who are entering into this gracious contract with Him.

Although God promised Abraham a blessing, He also imposed obligations on him. "Go from your country and your kindred and your father's house to the land that I will show you" (Gen. 12:1). In entering into this relationship with God, Abraham had to meet certain requirements.

One of the requirements for Christians is to belong to the visible body of believers. When Christ saves us, He puts us into a body, the church, which is invisible in its spiritual dimension. But Christ established not only an invisible church but also a visible church. He commands and expects all His people to be in a valid church, where they will be under the spiritual care of the elders. People should not join a church to avoid feeling guilty. They need to understand that Christ established the church and wants each of us and our families to be part of the visible body. Church membership is part of our covenant relationship with Christ and with God. In other words, it is the law, the New Testament law.

There is an antinomian attitude in our culture. A lot of Christians like to believe that we have no laws in the new covenant. However, there cannot be a covenant without stipulations, conditions, and requirements. As part of the formal stipulations, law is part of God's covenant.

The fourth part of Hittite suzerain treaties consisted of sanctions. These were double sanctions: benefits or blessings and punishments or cursings. The king promised his vassals that he would do certain good things for them on certain conditions, but that if they did not meet those conditions, they would experience his wrath. The vassals would be in trouble for every broken promise and stipulation. If they kept the stipulations, they would receive benefits; if not, they would be penalized.

In Deuteronomy, when the law was given again by Moses, God promised the people that if they diligently took heed to themselves and kept His commandments, they would be blessed, but if they broke the law, they would be cursed. This concept of blessing and curse was not first introduced by Moses; it was already present in the sanctions delivered to Adam and Eve. God promised them the tree of life if they were obedient to His law in the garden of Eden; if they were disobedient, a curse would come on them and the land. Due to these sanctions, the whole creation fell under the curse of God.

The fifth part of Hittite suzerain treaties was an oath, a sacred vow that established the covenant. The same thing was true of biblical covenants. God swore by Himself, by His very deity. The Westminster Confession takes oaths and vows so seriously that it devotes an entire chapter to the subject. A covenant is contracted by a sacred oath with witnesses. People swear by God or in His name because they are appealing to Him as the supreme witness to the oath they are taking.

Young couples today, on this side of the cultural revolution, ask: "Why do we have to get married? What is significant about a piece of paper? Why can't we just live together and have a private agreement?" They misunderstand the sacred nature of the marriage covenant. The couple stands publicly in front of friends, family, the church, the government, and ultimately God, and they vow that, no matter what comes their way, they are committed to each other. They will love and cherish each other as long as they both shall live, and they make this promise in the presence of witnesses and of God Himself. When someone breaks the marriage vow, committing adultery or deserting his spouse, he violates that sacred oath and the contract is destroyed. There are witnesses and stipulations. Oaths and vows are taken to swear loyalty, to swear allegiance to the terms of the covenant.

God is a covenant-keeper and we are covenant-breakers. No one, apart from Jesus, has ever kept the covenant that God made with His people. One reason we lack faith, have crises of faith, and are assailed by doubts about our future is that we project on God our own cavalier attitude toward vows, oaths, and promises. We forget that God has never once broken a promise. When He swears a covenant, He keeps it forever. His promise will not fail.

There are two more points. In the ancient Near East, when a covenant was made, invariably it was ratified by some kind of cutting rite, usually a blood rite. To ratify the covenant with Abraham, God required him to cut off the foreskin of his flesh (Gen. 17:9–14). Meredith Kline writes that this rite symbolized the dual sanctions. God was saying to Abraham, "I am cutting you off from this fallen world, consecrating you, separating you to Myself. I am giving you a mark in your body that says you belong to Me and I belong to you and that says we are in a covenant agreement together." Like other dual sanctions, circumcision was also a negative sign. Abraham was saying, "O God, if I do not keep the terms of this covenant, may I be cut off from Your presence, cut off from all of Your benefits, cut off from Your love and grace, just as I have cut off the foreskin of my flesh."

The parallel of circumcision is baptism, which signifies our participation in Christ's death and resurrection. Baptism is the sign of all the blessings, all the benefits God promises us in the new covenant in Jesus Christ. In a sense, God is saying, "This is a sign by which I am cleansing you. I am setting you apart to receive all the things I have for you in Christ if you have faith in Him. If you do not have faith, this is a sign that you are being inundated in the flood of God's wrath and are being cut off from My blessings."

The new covenant was ratified with a blood rite, and it took place on the cross. The significance of Christ's blood is twofold. First, it is the outward sign of His death, of His life being offered for us. Second, it is covenantal. By this blood rite, Christ signs and seals God's pledge in the new covenant with His own blood. Christ is cursed, cut off; He is circumcised on the cross.

Finally, when ancient Hittite treaties were entered into, duplicate copies were made, one for the king and one for the vassals. The copies were displayed in a public place for safekeeping, to be examined in case of a dispute and to be read publicly from time to time for the purpose of renewal. In the case of weddings, a marriage license is required. After the minister and witnesses sign this document, it is sent to a government office where it is held in safekeeping as a record.

The terms and stipulations of the Sinai covenant were recorded on two tablets of stone. But why were there two tablets? The first tablet, Luther said, contained the requirements that define our relationship to God (commandments one through four); the second tablet contained the requirements that define our relationship to other people (commandments five through ten). Kline argues persuasively, however, that each tablet contained all ten commandments—one tablet for God and one for the people. Both were stored in the ark of the covenant, under the mercy seat (the most sacred depository in Israel), in the Holy of Holies (the most sacred place).

> 2. The first covenant made with man was a covenant of works, wherein life was promised to Adam; and in him to his posterity, upon condition of perfect and personal obedience.

The Westminster divines, in articulating the structure of the covenant, distinguished between the covenant of works and the covenant of grace, an important distinction on which we must spend some time to understand properly.

It is no accident that chapter 7 of the Westminster Confession, on God's covenant with man, was placed between chapter 6, on the fall of man, and chapter 8, on Christ the Mediator. The framers of the confession understood these things as Scripture does. After describing the ruin into which Adam plunged the human race (chapter 6), they want to turn their attention to Christ, who came to restore our relationship with God (chapter 8). But to understand Jesus and His redeeming work, we must first understand the covenantal structure in which God provided a Savior for a lost and fallen race (chapter 7).

Section 2 recalls the garden of Eden—the lush, magnificent place where God placed our primordial parents and offered them the tree of life if they remained obedient. He prohibited them from eating fruit from the tree of the knowledge of good and evil; their response to this commandment would determine their destiny. If theirs was a righteous work, a work of obedience, then they and their posterity would receive the tree of life. But if theirs was a rebellious work, a work of disobedience, then they would leave for their posterity an inheritance of death and judgment.

God promised life to Adam and Eve on the basis of their works. How good did their works have to be? The confession says that their works had to be **perfect**, without even a shadow or hint of sin. As people who live by referendums and compromise, who are accustomed to being graded on a curve, we must understand that God judges His people by the standard of His own perfection. When He legislates the responsibilities to which He calls us, He requires perfect obedience: "You shall be holy, for I am holy" (1 Peter 1:16). God says to us, in effect: "If you are holy, and if the obedience you render to Me is perfect, My eternal life is yours. But mar it with the slightest imperfection, commit the slightest peccadillo, and you will die." As God said to His people through the prophet, "The soul who sins shall die" (Ezek. 18:20).

The controversial Roman Catholic theologian Hans Küng, in his book *Justification*, answers the objection that the God who manifests Himself in the Old Testament is too ferocious. This God, who destroyed the world with a flood, seems capricious and arbitrary and has an explosive temper. When the ark of the covenant was about to tumble into the mud and Uzzah reached out to steady it, God executed him instantly (2 Sam. 6:5–8). Nadab and Abihu, sons of Aaron, offered strange fire on the altar and died instantly (Lev. 10). God commanded Israel to conquer Canaan completely, even requiring them to eliminate every person in the land—man, woman, and child (Deut. 2:34; 3:6).

From the viewpoint of this century, we ask, "How can we believe in such a barbaric and bloodthirsty God?" Küng says we tend to react to the God of the Old Testament because the punishments meted out against sin in the New Testament seem to be much less severe. The only sin in the New Testament requiring the death penalty is arguably first-degree murder, whereas the capital offenses in the Old Testament—children being unruly and disobedient to parents, homosexual activity, adultery, and public blasphemy—do not seem to be capital offenses any longer.

Küng reminds us that from God's creation of man to His delivery of the stone tablets to Moses, the number of capital crimes declined far more than it did between the time of Moses and the New Testament. We forget, Küng says, that in creation all sin was a capital offense. God said that the person who sins will die. In His original covenant with His creatures, God imposed obligations that flow out of His character, obligations that mirror and reflect Him. He exercised His right as Creator to impose His will on His creatures. He only made one prohibition: that they not eat from one particular tree. And that is what they did.

Do we realize, Küng asks, the evil inherent in the slightest, tiniest transgression? If we seek to obey God in all things but disobey Him in the tiniest point, we are saying to Him that our will and our judgment surpass

His and that He has no right to tell us what to do. Think about the level of defiance implicit in the slightest transgression. We become traitors to the ruler of heaven and earth, trying to pull Him down from His place of authority and replace His authority with ours. It is no wonder that Satan couched the temptation as he did: "You will be like God" (Gen. 3:5). That is exactly what we choose. Every time we sin, we choose ourselves to be God rather than God to be God, which is why sin is so serious.

We are left with a problem. The only way anyone can be saved is by works—by perfect obedience. As evangelical Christians, we proclaim the gospel of justification by faith alone. This is shorthand for what chapter 7 is getting at: justification is actually by works alone because the only way anyone will ever stand justified in God's presence is if the covenant of works is perfectly fulfilled. Notice in section 2 that the requirement is **perfect and personal obedience**.

The distinction between the covenant of works and the covenant of grace can be a little misleading because it is not absolute. That God enters into a covenant relationship with us in the first place and that He condescends to promise us life, which He does not owe us, is already a work of grace. That is, the covenant of works has its roots in God's grace. Any relationship we have with Him that involves a promise is gracious.

We point this out because sin is so deceiving that we could go through life assuming that God owes us blessing and life. The more God gives us out of His grace, the more we expect and then the more we demand. We fail to understand that it is only by grace that He promises us anything at all. It is all grace. We must be careful when distinguishing between the covenant of works and the covenant of grace. The terms of the first covenant are based on God's command that we do good works, in perfect, personal obedience, in order to receive life. The covenant of grace comes into play because the covenant of works was broken. After the fall, we were left exposed only to judgment.

3. Man, by his fall, having made himself incapable of life by that covenant, the Lord was pleased to make a second, commonly called the covenant of grace; wherein he freely offereth unto sinners life and salvation by Jesus Christ; requiring of them faith in him, that they may be saved, and promising to give unto all those

that are ordained unto eternal life his Holy Spirit, to make them willing, and able to believe.

The **covenant of grace** is not so called because God no longer requires obedience and now negotiates His holiness and righteousness. God does not repudiate the covenant of works or His own righteousness. He does not change the standards. In the covenant of grace, it pleased the Lord to provide a substitute, a champion to obey His law perfectly and personally for us. God loved the world enough to send His only begotten Son and to place Him under the law, having Him do for us what Adam failed to do. The Son performed the terms of the covenant of works perfectly. God will accept us on the basis of what His Son has done, on the condition that now, in the covenant of grace, we put our faith in Him.

We are obstinate people. We ask, "Why do I need to believe in Jesus? Why can't I have my own religion?" The reason is that no one has kept the covenant of works perfectly. Throughout Scripture, God reveals that we may receive eternal life on the basis, not of our perfect and personal obedience, but of the obedience of His Son. God requires that we put our trust in His Son and in Him alone. Through the power of the Holy Spirit in our hearts, God will perform in our souls a supernatural work that enables us to meet this condition. Salvation is of the Lord from beginning to end; it is completely by His grace.

The covenant of grace does not annul the covenant of works. The covenant of grace is what God does to ensure that, under the covenant of works, we do not perish, but are redeemed by Jesus Christ's fulfillment of this covenant.

We are justified by the works of Christ. When the New Testament distinguishes between justification by faith and justification by works, it means that we can be justified only by putting our faith in Christ. In the final judgment, we will be judged by the law of God, and we will stand there on the grounds of either our works or Christ's works. He had to spend His earthly life in perfect obedience because God required that for His death to be acceptable. He had to be the mediator of a new covenant, and He had to do what we cannot do. That is why, as Christians, we flee to Him and cling to Him. We know that if God looks at our iniquity, we cannot stand. Christ alone covers our sin. He alone is perfect. This is the good news of the gospel.

God made not only the covenant of works but also the covenant of grace. Christ fulfilled the covenant of works for you and for me.

4. This covenant of grace is frequently set forth in Scripture by the name of a testament, in reference to the death of Jesus Christ the Testator, and to the everlasting inheritance, with all things belonging to it, therein bequeathed.

Here the confession's framers shift from the concept of covenant as a promissory agreement, containing stipulations, sanctions, oaths, and vows, to the concept of covenant as a testament. We speak of the old covenant or the Old Testament; we talk of the new covenant but more frequently of the New Testament.

Today we talk about testaments most frequently when settling the estates of the deceased. The person who leaves a last will and testament intends to bequeath certain things to his heirs. The document listing these things comes into effect only when the testator dies.

In His last discourse with His disciples before His trial and execution, our Lord emphasized His last will and testament. Jesus says to His disciples, "Let not your hearts be troubled. Believe in God; believe also in me." He then makes this promise to His disciples: "In my Father's house are many rooms. If it were not so, would I have told you that I go to prepare a place for you? And if I go and prepare a place for you, I will come again and will take you to myself, that where I am you may be also" (John 14:1–3). In the midst of this discourse, Jesus gives His legacy, His last will and testament: "Peace I leave with you; my peace I give to you. Not as the world gives do I give to you. Let not your hearts be troubled, neither let them be afraid" (John 14:27). Jesus focuses on the transcendent, supernatural, singular peace that He is bequeathing to His followers.

In the book of Romans, Paul concludes His discussion of the gospel and the doctrine of justification by saying that, being justified, we have peace with God and access to His presence (Rom. 5:1–2). When summarizing the benefits that Christ achieved for us through His person and work, Paul homes in on this concept of peace. At Christ's birth, angels announced that there would be "on earth peace" (Luke 2:14). Christ is called the "Prince of Peace" (Isa. 9:6). This peace concludes a war.

When Jesus gives us peace, He is talking not about the end of a conflict between world powers but about a peace that transcends such conflicts. He is talking about the end of warfare between God and us. People do not get excited about this because our culture assumes that no one is at war with God or estranged from Him. Scripture clearly tells us, however, that we are by nature the enemies of God, and that His wrath is directed against those who are in rebellion against Him (Eph. 2:1–3). The healing of this estrangement is what the gospel is about. It is about reconciliation, repairing a broken relationship, ending a war. The chief aspect of Jesus' legacy is *shalom*, the transcendent peace that obtains when the warfare between us and God is over.

Peace in this world is always temporary, awaiting the next outbreak of hostilities. But the legacy of Christ is a permanent peace, one that passes understanding and that can never be disturbed. Through Him, we have been reconciled to God and justified in His sight. God has pronounced us pardoned and forgiven, and He has adopted us into His family, never again to rise up in warfare against us. This peace is everlasting.

5. This covenant was differently administered in the time of the law, and in the time of the gospel: under the law, it was administered by promises, prophecies, sacrifices, circumcision, the paschal lamb, and other types and ordinances delivered to the people of the Jews, all foresignifying Christ to come; which were, for that time, sufficient and efficacious, through the operation of the Spirit, to instruct and build up the elect in faith in the promised Messiah, by whom they had full remission of sins, and eternal salvation; and is called the old testament.

Part of our problem in understanding this legacy is the problem of Old Testament people looking for peace before the birth of Christ. Did they have any hope of a permanent peace with God, or was that something far in the future?

According to a widely held view, people were saved under the old covenant quite differently from the way they are saved under the new. In American evangelicalism, the most popular theology is dispensationalism. The original *Scofield Reference Bible*, more than anything else, disseminated this theology throughout the nation. A dispensation, according to this view, is a particular testing period in which God relates to people in a particular way. This view has been altered in modern dispensationalism, but earlier versions envisioned seven or so distinct testing periods or dispensations in redemptive history, ending with the dispensation of grace. The problem is that this designation gave people the idea that law is restricted to the Old Testament and grace to the New. We have already seen in the New Testament that the new covenant is filled with commandments. Jesus said, "If you love me, you will keep my commandments" (John 14:15). So law is not only in the Old Testament, nor is grace only in the New.

More significant was the idea that people in the Old Testament were saved in a different manner than we are saved today. Some people concluded that in Old Testament times, people were saved by keeping the law of Moses—in other words, by their works—whereas in the New Testament era, people are saved by faith and grace. This is a serious misunderstanding of biblical faith and introduces a radical discontinuity between the old and new covenants.

When writing to Christians in Rome, Paul explained the gospel, the significance of the work of Christ, and the doctrine of justification. He raised this question: "What then shall we say was gained by Abraham, our forefather according to the flesh? For if Abraham was justified by works, he has something to boast about, but not before God. For what does the Scripture say? 'Abraham believed God, and it was counted to him as righteousness.' Now to the one who works, his wages are not counted as a gift but as his due" (Rom. 4:1–4). In other words, Abraham was not justified by works, the law, or merit. Paul shows that neither Christians nor Jews are saved by their own merit. The whole point of the law was to show that a person cannot be saved by good works. Paul drives home the point in Romans 4 that the manner of justification and salvation is part of the continuity between the two covenants—that Old Testament saints were also saved by faith, by grace, by Christ.

Paul's prime example is Abraham, who is called the father of the faithful. In almost astonishing terms, Paul says that the way of salvation in the Old Testament was exactly the same as it is today. If that is true, then why do we not have burnt offerings, a temple, the Day of Atonement, and the Old Testament ceremonies? The New Testament says that those things were types and shadows, rituals and practices that dramatized how salvation would come through the atonement of the One whose sacrifice is perfect and sufficient for all time. The author of Hebrews writes that people who trusted in the ceremonies trusted in vain. Old Testament believers trusted in what the ceremonies signified: they were vivid, concrete illustrations of salvation through the work of the coming Redeemer. That is why Jesus could say, "Your father Abraham rejoiced that he would see my day" (John 8:56).

The big difference between the old and new covenants is the difference between promise and fulfillment. Abraham and the other people of the Old Testament lived before Jesus came into the world, before there was a cross. Nonetheless, the ground of Abraham's salvation was Christ's righteousness. Since creation, the only way anyone has been justified in God's sight is by works—not our works, but Christ's.

The covenant of grace, rather than annihilating the covenant of works, makes provision for someone else to fulfill the covenant of works for us. When we say that we are justified by faith, that is theological shorthand for saying that we are justified by the perfect work of Christ. When we put our faith in the perfect work of Christ, God accounts us just in His sight. We are still justified by works—the works of Jesus, not our own.

Our faith today looks back in time to the person of Christ and the work He accomplished once for all. He lived a life of perfect obedience and fulfilled all the law's requirements. He suffered the consequences of all our sin by offering Himself as a perfect sacrifice for us. We hear the gospel, which announces what Christ has done and calls us to faith in what He has done, the finished work of One who lived nearly two thousand years ago. So we are trusting in a work that has been perfectly accomplished in the past.

Abraham lived before the incarnation, before the perfect work of Jesus was wrought. Paul says that Abraham is the model for justification: "Abraham believed God, and it was counted to him as righteousness" (Rom. 4:3, quoting Gen. 15:6). What did Abraham believe? He trusted in the promise of God. He did not understand all the details that would be worked out in the actual life of Jesus. Not much information was given to Abraham. Through the centuries that followed, God gave more information about the gospel, the person and work of God's Anointed, the Redeemer of Israel, and the Suffering Servant. Abraham believed God, and it was accounted to him for righteousness. The meritorious ground of Abraham's salvation was Christ. His link to Christ was the same as mine—faith. Christ is the Savior of Abraham, Moses, David, and all the other Old Testament saints. The merit of Christ is transferred to them by faith, as Paul writes in Romans 4. We are saved the same way Adam was saved. The only difference is that people then trusted divine promises that had yet to be fulfilled. Looking ahead to a better country, whose builder and maker was God, they trusted in promises that had not yet been realized. We, on the other hand, trust in promises that have been fulfilled. The new covenant is far richer and more effective because we live on this side of the cross and of the fulfillment of those promises, but the way of salvation is the same.

The confession says that the covenant of grace was made manifest in different ways in the old covenant than in the new. That is, the covenant of grace was **administered** in the time of the law differently than in the time of the gospel. Under the Old Testament principle of the law, the covenant of grace was demonstrated through promise rather than fulfillment, through prophecies of things to come, through sacrifices and rites such as circumcision, the slaying of the Passover lamb, and other things that were shadows or types of things that would come in their fullest reality and final measure in and through the ministry of Jesus. All these things, according to the confession, were **foresignifying Christ to come.** They pointed beyond themselves to the final fulfillment in the promised Redeemer. The Holy Spirit used them to instruct and edify people in the faith of the promise. In the Old Testament, that faith in the promise was the instrument that linked people to the benefits of the Redeemer, who was to come. They were saved just as much by the work of Jesus, which from their perspective had not yet been accomplished, as we are by that work, which from our perspective has been accomplished.

6. Under the gospel, when Christ, the substance, was exhibited, the ordinances in which this covenant is dispensed are the preaching of the Word, and the administration of the sacraments of baptism and the Lord's Supper: which, though fewer in number, and administered with more simplicity, and less outward glory, yet, in them, it is held forth in more fullness, evidence and spiritual efficacy, to all nations, both Jews and Gentiles; and is called the new testament. There are not therefore two covenants of grace, differing in substance, but one and the same, under various dispensations.

Section 6 speaks of the covenant's administration under the gospel, where Christ, the substance of that gospel, is made plain. The ordinances in this new situation include the preaching of the Word, and the administration of the sacraments of baptism and the Lord's Supper. Lacking the detailed ritualistic manifestation present in the sacrificial system of the Old Testament, these sacraments are therefore exhibited with more simplicity. Yet they manifest greater fullness and spiritual efficacy—not only to the nation of Israel but also to the gentiles. There are not two covenants of grace that differ in substance. They are the same in substance, though their forms differ from the Old Testament economy to the New. Section 6 makes the striking point that though the forms change in the administration of the covenant of grace, the substance remains the same.

Of Christ the Mediator

1. It pleased God, in his eternal purpose, to choose and ordain the Lord Jesus, his only begotten Son, to be the Mediator between God and man, the Prophet, Priest, and King, the Head and Savior of his church, the Heir of all things, and Judge of the world: unto whom he did from all eternity give a people, to be his seed, and to be by him in time redeemed, called, justified, sanctified, and glorified.

2. The Son of God, the second person in the Trinity, being very and eternal God, of one substance and equal with the Father, did, when the fullness of time was come, take upon him man's nature, with all the essential properties, and common infirmities thereof, yet without sin; being conceived by the power of the Holy Ghost, in the womb of the virgin Mary, of her substance. So that two whole, perfect, and distinct natures, the Godhead and the manhood, were inseparably joined together in one person, without conversion, composition, or confusion. Which person is very God, and very man, yet one Christ, the only Mediator between God and man.

3. The Lord Jesus, in his human nature thus united to the divine, was sanctified, and anointed with the Holy Spirit, above measure, having in him all the treasures of wisdom and knowledge; in whom it pleased the Father that all fullness should dwell; to the end that, being holy, harmless, undefiled, and full of grace and truth, he might be thoroughly furnished to execute the office of a mediator, and surety. Which office he took not unto himself, but was thereunto called by his Father, who put all power and judgment into his hand, and gave him commandment to execute the same.

4. This office the Lord Jesus did most willingly undertake; which that he might discharge, he was made under the law, and did perfectly fulfill it; endured most grievous torments immediately in his soul, and most painful sufferings in his body; was crucified, and died, was buried, and remained under the power of death, yet saw no corruption. On the third day he arose from the dead, with the same body in which he suffered, with which also he ascended into heaven, and there sitteth at the right hand of his Father, making intercession, and shall return, to judge men and angels, at the end of the world.

5. The Lord Jesus, by his perfect obedience, and sacrifice of himself, which he, through the eternal Spirit, once offered up unto God, hath fully satisfied the justice of his Father; and purchased, not only reconciliation, but an everlasting inheritance in the kingdom of heaven, for all those whom the Father hath given unto him.

6. Although the work of redemption was not actually wrought by Christ till after his incarnation, yet the virtue, efficacy, and benefits thereof were communicated unto the elect, in all ages successively from the beginning of the world, in and by those promises, types, and sacrifices, wherein he was revealed, and signified to be the seed of the woman which should bruise the serpent's head; and the Lamb slain from the beginning of the world; being yesterday and today the same, and forever.

7. Christ, in the work of mediation, acts according to both natures, by each nature doing that which is proper to itself; yet, by reason of the unity of the person, that which is proper to one nature is sometimes in Scripture attributed to the person denominated by the other nature.

8. To all those for whom Christ hath purchased redemption, he doth certainly and effectually apply and communicate the same; making intercession for them, and revealing unto them, in and by the Word, the mysteries of salvation; effectually persuading them by his Spirit to believe and obey, and governing their hearts by his Word and Spirit; overcoming all their enemies by his almighty power and wisdom, in such manner, and ways, as are most consonant to his wonderful and unsearchable dispensation.

1. It pleased God, in his eternal purpose, to choose and ordain the Lord Jesus, his only begotten Son, to be the Mediator between God and man, the Prophet, Priest, and King, the Head and Savior of his church, the Heir of all things, and Judge of the world: unto whom he did from all eternity give a people, to be his seed, and to be by him in time redeemed, called, justified, sanctified, and glorified.

It pleased God. According to these opening words of section 1, the work of redemption comes from the good pleasure of God Himself.

In his eternal purpose. As we think about Christ as the Mediator, it is important to understand that His work of mediation was ordained from all eternity by the One from whom we were estranged because of our sin.

Mediators are often used in disputes. Mediation presupposes an estrangement, a falling-out between two or more parties who now oppose each other. For example, in labor-management conflicts, when unions go on strike and work is suspended or the company is threatened, the courts will often intervene and appoint a mediator, who will try to bring both sides together in some sort of agreement.

The Bible says that by nature we are at enmity with God (Rom. 8:7), estranged from Him. To grasp the importance of this, we must cut through the assumption often made today that God is not estranged from us but loves us all, hating the sin but not the sinner. This assumption conflicts with Scripture. Although God pours out His benevolence on the entire human race, this includes those from whom He is estranged. He pours out this benevolence on people who count Him as their enemy.

If you ask an atheist why he hates God, he will most likely reply, "I don't hate Him; I just don't believe there is a God." Even the agnostic says: "I don't know whether there is a God. But if there is, I don't have anything against Him. I'm not opposed to Him." In other words, people will not admit that their hearts are filled with enmity and hostility toward their Creator. The Bible says that this hostility runs so deep that we do not even want to think about God. In his sermon "Man, Naturally God's Enemy," Jonathan Edwards speaks about those divine attributes that provoke fallen humanity's animosity toward the Creator. Men do not by nature love God's holiness, power, omnipotence, knowledge, omniscience, constancy, or immutability, all of which combine to make God the most formidable opponent of, and obstacle to, our desire to rule our lives without His intrusion.

Some theologians have argued that, as people who are alienated from God, we face the problem of trying to make peace with One who is angry and ill disposed toward us. In their view, the way redemption took place was that Christ, the second person of the Trinity, came into the world and not only sought to get us to overcome our hostility toward God but also sought to change the Father's hostility toward us. In simple terms, God the Father was angry until God the Son came, interjected Himself into this hostile relationship, and persuaded the Father to be more graciously disposed toward us.

That sort of thinking is denied at the very beginning of chapter 8 of the confession, which shows that God was pleased from all eternity to provide us with a Mediator. It was the Father Himself who took the initiative in this work of reconciliation. The One who had been most violated in this relationship was the One who provided the mediation necessary to effect reconciliation. This should be clear from John 3:16, "For God so loved the world, that he gave his only Son."

To choose and ordain the Lord Jesus. When we hear words like choose and ordain with respect to God's work, we normally think of the doctrine of predestination or, more specifically, election. In trying to sort through this biblical doctrine, we often make election an abstract concept, removed from its redemptive context. But through election, God begins to bring about His eternal plan of redemption. The first elected One is Jesus Himself, the firstborn of many brethren. Believers are chosen in Christ Jesus to participate in the benefits that the Father will bestow on the Son.

God chose and ordained the Lord Jesus, his only begotten Son, to be the Mediator. In his first letter to Timothy, Paul writes that Christ is the only Mediator between God and man (1 Tim. 2:5). Yet many Old Testament figures function as mediators. Moses, for example, is called the mediator of the old covenant (Gal. 3:19) because God brought the law to His people through the agency of Moses. Others in the Old Testament were also intermediaries between God and His people.

Mediators in the Old Testament held one of three offices: prophet, priest, or king. Prophets were God's spokesmen, speaking to the people of Israel on behalf of God. God spoke first to His prophet, and then the prophet spoke to the people on God's behalf, usually prefacing his announcement by saying, "Thus says the Lord."

Priests, also ordained by God to work as mediators, offered intercessory prayers for the people. The priest both spoke to the people on God's behalf and spoke to God on the people's behalf.

While new covenant ministers do not hold these offices, elements of the offices appear in the church's worship. The call to worship, for example, is prophetic; the prophets also called for the solemn assembly, requiring the people to gather to hear the word of God. Reading Scripture and preaching the sermon are also prophetic. The invocation, pastoral prayer, and benediction are priestly.

Israel's kings also functioned as mediators. The Bible teaches that governmental authorities no less than priests or prophets are ordained and instituted by God (see Rom. 13:1). At first, this authority was exercised in Israel not by kings but by judges. The judges were charismatically endowed leaders whom God raised up to meet a particular need during that time when Israel was a loose federation of tribes. The people grew weary of the judges and demanded to be ruled by a king. God was not pleased, seeing in this demand a rejection of His lordship over them. Nevertheless, He allowed them to have a king, but with conditions attached: The king was accountable to God for how he ruled. The king was understood to be the Lord's representative, ruling the people in dependence on God. The king was to mediate the rule of God to the people.

Radical corruption overtook these rulers, who were supposed to be mirroring and reflecting the reign of God over the people. They began to do what was right in their own eyes, turning the people away from God. Ahab, for example, built altars to pagan deities. The corruption of the kings became symptomatic of the disobedience of the whole nation, as seen in the books of Kings and Chronicles.

Prophets, priests, and kings functioned as mediators in the Old Testament, yet Paul says that there is only one Mediator between God and man (1 Tim. 2:5). Paul, of course, is not repudiating what was done in former days. Instead, he is speaking of a Mediator in the ultimate sense. Only one Mediator is both truly God and truly man. Only one Mediator has a divine nature and a human nature. Only the God-man participates in both deity and humanity, and in that regard Christ is utterly unique. Only one Mediator has the ability to effect the ultimate goal of mediation, our redemption and reconciliation. That was beyond the ability of Elijah, Jeremiah, Ezekiel, Aaron, Levi, or any other prophet or priest. The work of ultimate redemption could not be mediated by David, Hezekiah, or any of the other kings. It could not even be accomplished by Moses, the mediator of the law. He was not the one who brought about reconciliation by his own person and work.

Paul is speaking in an ultimate sense when he speaks of the only Mediator and His work of mediation. That Mediator is Christ. That may raise the hackles of people who embrace relativism and pluralism, who can tolerate no claim of religious exclusivity. Western culture assumes that there are many paths to God, and that there are many mediators, such as Buddha, Confucius, and Muhammad. People are repulsed by the idea that there is only one way of salvation. But the fact is that only one man qualifies to be the Mediator. No one but Christ has the necessary qualifications to effect reconciliation between God and man. Missing from all other religions is an atonement that satisfies the justice of God. They have only men; Christianity alone has a God-man, One who shares in both the nature of God and the nature of our humanity.

Christ is traditionally called the "only begotten" Son of God, the *monogenēs*, and even the English word *only* does not sufficiently capture the exclusivity of that concept. Nor is the word *unique* adequate. As the New Testament speaks about Christ offering His sacrifice once for all (Rom. 6:10), He and His work are more than unique. The singularity of Christ as the *monogenēs* lies in the fact that He is the one and only begotten of the Father. His atonement occurred once for all, and He alone is God incarnate. No one else will ever do it. There will never be another incarnation.

From all eternity, God aimed to bring about the plan of redemption that was pleasing to Him by sending One who would be his only begotten Son, . . . the Mediator between God and man, the Prophet, Priest, and King. These three offices in the Old Testament were mediatorial. One of John Calvin's important contributions to theology was the doctrine of Christ's threefold office of Prophet, Priest, and King. People see in Jesus the fulfillment of the Old Testament prophecy that a prophet like Moses would arise. Christ's office as a Prophet was also unique in other ways.

The Old Testament prophets were given the word of God to proclaim to the people, making these men mediators. Christ not only proclaimed the word of God, but He is the Word of God (John 1:1), the very incarnation of the divine Word. He not only says the word but reveals it in His own person.

Old Testament prophets spoke about things beyond themselves. The principal content of their prophecies of the future concerned Christ, who is both the subject and the object of biblical prophecy. When He prophesies, He speaks about Himself. Old Testament prophets were prophesying not about themselves but about another who would come, Christ.

Christ is also the subject and object of His priesthood. In the Old Testament, Israel's priests offered sacrifices. The objects of their sacrifices were the bulls and goats they presented before God. Christ, who functions as Priest in the New Testament, both makes the offering and is the offering. He is the Priest who offers Himself as the perfect sacrifice to satisfy the demands of God's justice. In working out His priestly ministry, Jesus is both the subject and the object of His priesthood. He is the perfect Priest, our Great High Priest, whose sacrifice is offered once for all. He fulfills the Old Testament shadows, whose validity and grounds were not in the actual bulls and goats but in their typifying of the perfect sacrifice that would satisfy God's demands, the sacrifice of Christ Himself.

In the Old Testament, a high priest was appointed, and when he died, his office was assumed by a successor. But Christ is our High Priest forever. He has no successor. He is uniquely the High Priest of the people of God. He enters the heavenly sanctuary, the heavenly Holy of Holies, where He continues His ministry of intercession for His people forever.

In the Old Testament, royal succession was a great concern. Kings tried to establish dynastic succession in preparation for their own demise. Few of these dynasties endured. The house of David lasted for a season, and the house of Omri for a short period, but Christ's kingship is forever. He is anointed and crowned in heaven itself to become the King of kings and the Lord of lords. He is the King in the superlative degree, the ultimate King to whom the Father gives all authority in heaven and on earth.

In all these mediatorial offices, Christ is the perfect Mediator: the perfect Prophet, the perfect Priest, and the perfect King. The Father established each office for our redemption. It pleased God to ordain Christ as our **Prophet, Priest, and King.**

The Head and Savior of his church. Today, when people discuss what it means for Christ to be the Head of the church, some contend that it means only that Christ founded the church. The New Testament likens the church to a human body (Eph. 4:15–16), and it is in this metaphorical context that Christ is called the Head of the body, in the sense that the head rules the rest of the body. The head (or the mind or the brain) controls everything that happens in the earthly tabernacle. So Christ is the Head in the sense that to Him is given the authority to rule over His church. We are to live in submission to Him. It bears repeating that the church's mission, identity, and agenda are to be determined not by the church but by the church's Head. We are to be subordinate to Christ as the Head, the Lord of His church.

The confession says that Christ is not only the Head of the church but also its Savior. He is the church's Redeemer and Lord. When Scripture sets forth for us lesser levels of authority—such as parents' authority over their children, teachers over their students, masters over their servants, and husbands over their wives—all these levels of authority fall under the supreme authority of Christ. All authority in this world is delegated from the office of Christ's headship. In the church, there is no equality of authority between the church and its Head.

When Scripture says, "Wives, submit to your own husbands, as to the Lord" (Eph. 5:22), some women chafe at that, and in many cases are in open rebellion against God's authority at that level. Likewise, men are often in outward rebellion against Christ's authority because He commands them to "love [their] wives, as Christ loved the church and gave himself up for her" (v. 25). To women who are upset about being submissive to their husbands, I ask, "Would you have a problem submitting to Christ if He were your husband or if your husband loved you the way Christ loves His church?" Few women still say: "I don't want to submit. I would demand a fifty-fifty relationship." In Christ's relationship with His bride, authority is not divided fifty-fifty. He is the head, and the church is to submit to and obey Him. Jesus does not tyrannize the church. He bought the church, owns the church, paid for His church with His own blood, and gave His life to save the church.

The framers of the confession at this point do not mention Christ as Savior of the world, but refer specifically to Him as the Savior of the church. That He is the church's Savior does not mean He that could not at the same time be the world's Savior. If He were the Savior of everyone in the world, then clearly He would be the Savior of the church. To be the Savior of the church, however, does not require that He be the Savior of the whole world. We will address the question of the specific goal of His saviorhood in another chapter. This Christ, who is Prophet, Priest, and King, and who is the Mediator, is also the Head and the Savior of the church, **the Heir of all things.**

God has also appointed Him as **Judge of the world,** so He whom God has appointed as this Judge is also our Lord and Savior. In the final analysis, everyone will have to stand before Christ's judgment seat. Paul spoke about this to the Athenians at the Areopagus: "The times of ignorance God overlooked, but now he commands all people everywhere to repent, because he has fixed a day on which he will judge the world in righteousness by a man whom he has appointed; and of this he has given assurance to all by raising him from the dead" (Acts 17:30–31). Here the Apostle announces to Athenian philosophers that they will be judged on the day of judgment by the Judge whom God has appointed and whom He has vindicated by the resurrection.

> 2. The Son of God, the second person in the Trinity, being very and eternal God, of one substance and equal with the Father, did, when the fullness of time was come, take upon him man's nature, with all the essential properties, and common infirmities thereof,

yet without sin; being conceived by the power of the Holy Ghost, in the womb of the virgin Mary, of her substance. So that two whole, perfect, and distinct natures, the Godhead and the manhood, were inseparably joined together in one person, without conversion, composition, or confusion. Which person is very God, and very man, yet one Christ, the only Mediator between God and man.

The Reformation built on the truths that had been confessed in the early ecumenical councils, such as Nicaea, Constantinople, Ephesus, and Chalcedon. The Reformers did not jettison that body of historic Christian doctrine.

In chapter 2, we looked at the doctrine of the Trinity and referred to church councils to help develop some of the important Christological foundations. But here we encounter a more specific reference to the person of Christ, so it would be good to reiterate the teaching of those historical confessions.

Section 2 affirms that Christ is the Son of God, the second person in the Trinity, being very and eternal God, of one substance and equal with the Father. Our previous discussion addressed the importance of the term one substance. At the Council of Nicaea (AD 325), participants debated and then adopted the term *homoousios*, a Greek word meaning "the same substance or essence," to describe the fact that the persons of the Trinity are one God. The classic formula for the Trinity is that God is one in essence, being, or substance and three in person.

The teaching of Arius provoked the Council of Nicaea. Arius wanted to prevent any undermining of pure monotheism. He believed that to refer to Christ as God would undercut monotheism and result in two gods—or three, if you include the Holy Spirit. Arius vigorously opposed Trinitarian Christianity. He was opposed by Athanasius, who championed Trinitarianism.

Arius believed that Christ is a creature and therefore had a beginning in time. He pointed out that the New Testament speaks of Christ as the firstborn of all creation (Col. 1:15) and as the only begotten of the Father (John 1:14). He said that generation requires a beginning in time. Thus, Christ, the Logos, is not eternal or divine. Arius declared that the Son is "like" the Father (*homoiousios*) but that the Son's being is not the same as the Father's.

After much debate, Arius and his followers were condemned as heretics. Trinitarian Christianity was upheld and maintained in the Nicene Creed. From that time onward, the orthodox church has insisted that the second person of the Trinity is *homoousios* with the first person of the Trinity. The Father and the Son (and the Holy Spirit) are one in essence, having the same substance. After a revival of Arianism, the Council of Constantinople in 381 expanded the Nicene Creed into the Niceno-Constantinopolitan Creed (though it is usually still called the Nicene Creed), which says that the Son of God is "eternally begotten of the Father" and "consubstantial with the Father." This teaching was reinforced by the Chalcedonian Creed (AD 451), which was produced amid the Christological controversies of the fifth century.

The Nicene Creed affirms that Christ is not only consubstantial (of the same essence) with the Father but also coeternal—that is, that there never was a time when He was not. The Nicene Creed says that He was "begotten, not made," emphasizing that He is not a creature.

The New Testament uses the terms *firstborn* and *only begotten* to refer to the Son's unique relationship with the Father. The Son is the heir of all things in terms of His relationship to the covenant of Israel. In the Old Testament, the inheritance is given to the firstborn son. Since Christ is the heir of all things, He fulfills the role of God's firstborn. That is not the same thing as saying that He was begotten in time. As the only begotten, His begottenness is unique. The New Testament speaks of Christ's being begotten in the context of John's revealing that He was in the beginning with God and was God (John 1:1). From all eternity, the Son is always the Son in relationship to the Father. Begottenness in this context does not refer to biological beginnings in time through normal procreation or any other creative act.

The Son of God . . . did, when the fullness of time was come, take upon him man's nature, with all the essential properties, and common infirmities thereof, yet without sin; being conceived by the power of the Holy Ghost, in the womb of the virgin Mary, of her substance. The fullness of time is a concept taken from the New Testament (Gal. 4:4).

It places redemption in the arena of ordinary history. God is working out salvation in and through history. The Old Testament reveals to us God's progressive unfolding of His divine plan of salvation, beginning with Adam and Eve and continuing with Noah, Abraham, Isaac, Jacob, and Moses. There is a clear progression of redemptive history, and a developing clarity in what God reveals to His people. Christianity is inseparably bound up with history. It is married to time and space, not something that occurs merely in some spiritual sphere. That is why the New Testament makes such statements as this: "In those days a decree went out from Caesar Augustus that all the world should be registered. This was the first registration when Quirinius was governor of Syria" (Luke 2:1–2). There was a historical setting for the entrance of Christ into the world. The incarnation happened in real history. The Roman governor, Pontius Pilate, is mentioned in the Apostles' Creed. Christianity is about real people, places, and events. God promises us that there is a future for the people of God in time and space.

In Galatians 4:4, the "fullness" of time is the *plērōma* of time. The English language falls short in translating that idea. If we took a glass and filled it to the brim with water, we would say that the glass is full. But *plērōma* suggests a glass under the faucet, with water cascading over the sides of the glass, full to the point of overflowing. This is what the Bible means when it refers to the "fullness" of time. History was overflowing with anticipation; all of history, from the creation onward, was converging in that moment in history when Jesus Christ would be born.

So that two whole, perfect, and distinct natures, the Godhead and the manhood, were inseparably joined together in one person, without conversion, composition, or confusion. This sentence has in view the formula that was set forth at the Council of Chalcedon in AD 451. Church historians and theologians have often regarded the Council of Chalcedon as having taken us to the very limit of our ability to comprehend the mystery of the incarnation. Chalcedon established the boundaries beyond which we dare not tread in our speculations, lest we plunge ourselves into serious error. If we move away from Chalcedon in either direction (exaggerating either the divinity or the humanity of Christ at the expense of the other), we will fall into heresy.

The confession affirms that Christ has two whole, perfect, and distinct natures that are joined together in one person. These natures are joined inseparably . . . without conversion, composition, or confusion. This formula is taken from the Chalcedonian Definition, and it is known as the hypostatic union. To understand this definition, we must see what the church faced during the crisis that led up to the Council of Chalcedon in the middle of the fifth century. The church was besieged by heresies from two different sides: the heresies of Eutyches and Nestorius.

The Eutychian heresy is better known as the Monophysite heresy. The Monophysite heresy attributes to Christ one nature (*physis*), not two. Eutyches taught that Christ had a single theanthropic nature, a mixture of deity and humanity. According to him, Christ had a deified human nature, or, if you will, a humanized divine nature. It is neither completely divine nor completely human, but rather a mixture or blend of deity and humanity. Here we see a confusion of Christ's two different natures.

Nestorius separated Christ's divine nature too much from His human nature, almost to the point of saying that Christ has two separate personalities. He was charged with dividing Christ into two persons and was condemned by the Council of Ephesus in 431.

The Eutychian or Monophysite heresy confused or blended the two natures, and the Nestorian heresy divided the two natures. In response, the church declared that Christ is one person with two natures, and at Chalcedon, the union of the two natures was affirmed using the phrase that Christ was *vere homo, vere Deus*—"truly man, truly God." Christ has both a human nature and a divine nature, and those two natures are perfectly united in one person.

At Chalcedon, the church was careful to define the limits of speculation regarding the mystery of this union of two natures, using a method of definition that we call the way of negation. That is, it is difficult to say much about the union of a divine and a human nature in one person, but we can at least tell you what it is not. The four famous negatives of Chalcedon are these: the two natures of Christ are without mixture, confusion, division, or separation.

When the church said that the two natures are without mixture or confusion, it had in mind the Eutychian or Monophysite heresy. Chalcedon goes on to say that the two natures are without division or separation, which was aimed at the Nestorian heresy. By using those four negatives— without mixture, confusion, division, or separation—the church rejected both the Monophysite and Nestorian errors.

One other phrase added by the Council of Chalcedon is often overlooked in the discussion: "The two natures are without mixture, confusion, division, or separation, each nature retaining its own attributes." That last phrase is absolutely crucial. Hymns and sermons are often heard that have God setting aside His deity when He becomes incarnate. That is heretical. The divine nature of Christ during the incarnation was fully divine. Christ did not give up any divinity when He took upon Himself a human nature. All the divine attributes are retained in the person of Christ. And when the divine nature adds a human nature, the human nature does not lack any of its humanity. Christ's human nature is fully human.

The natures of Christ were a burning theological issue in the fourth, fifth, and nineteenth centuries, and again today, the biblical doctrine of Christ is severely under attack, not just from outside the church but from inside it as well. Let's consider this, using the terms *liberal* and *conservative* broadly as convenient labels for theological tendencies. The basic tendency of liberalism is to deny the deity of Christ or to so focus on His humanity that His deity is swallowed up by it. This reduces Jesus to the status of a great and insightful human being. In reaction to that, conservatives, zealous to protect the deity of Christ, have a tendency to deny the reality of His humanity and allow it to be swallowed up by His deity. In contrast to both tendencies, we must maintain a full confession, both of the true and complete deity of Christ and of the true and complete humanity of Christ.

Where does this make a difference in the life of the church? Each Sunday, in cities all over the world, the Lord's Supper is observed and celebrated in a multitude of different denominations. Roman Catholics believe in the miracle of the Mass, that the elements of bread and wine are supernaturally transformed into the actual body and blood of Christ while retaining the outward characteristics of bread and wine. Therefore, the body and blood of Christ are supposedly present in different places all over the world at the same time. But do His body and blood belong to His deity or His humanity? Since God does not have a body, they obviously belong to His humanity. So how is Christ present in the Lord's Supper? In His deity, He can of course be present all around the world at the same time. But since omnipresence is not a human attribute, how can the humanity of Jesus be present in the Lord's Supper everywhere at once? It cannot, if Christ's two natures retain their own properties and attributes. That is why the Reformers strenuously objected to the idea of the omnipresence of the physical body and blood of Jesus. The sacramental debate in the final analysis was a Christological debate. The Reformers charged that Rome, while supposedly endorsing Chalcedon, actually violated it in its view of the Mass, falling into a form of the Monophysite heresy.

The Roman Catholic Church says that the body and blood of Jesus can be at more than one place at the same time by virtue of what is called the *communicatio idiomatum* (communication of attributes). Rome says that the divine nature communicates divine powers and properties to the human nature, specifically the power of omnipresence, enabling it to be present wherever the Mass is celebrated. But that notion involves a confusion or mixture of the two natures. It involves the deification of the human nature of Jesus. If His human nature is no longer restricted by time and space, He is no longer human.

The Reformers did believe in the real presence of Christ at the Lord's Supper, but they insisted that He is there in His divine nature, not His human nature. The response from Rome would be that if His divine nature is there and His human nature is not, we have fallen into the Nestorian error of dividing and separating the two natures. The Reformed response is that two things can be distinguished without being separated. For example, we can distinguish someone's body from his soul without harming him at all. But if we separate his body from his soul, we kill him. The Reformation view is that the physical nature of Jesus ascended into heaven and is there now—not anywhere else. But His divine nature is never absent from us. That is what Jesus said to His disciples, "A little while, and you will see me no longer; and again a little while, and you will see me" (John 16:16). In one sense, Jesus is no longer here; in another sense, He is.

The person of Christ is still a perfect union of a divine nature and a human nature. The human nature is in heaven. The divine nature is not limited to the physical confines of the body of Jesus. When God became incarnate in Christ, God was not confined to the place where Jesus was in Palestine. The divine nature retained its property of omnipresence. The person of Christ can be everywhere, but that ability is through the power of the divine nature, not the human nature.

That is why we can say, when we come to the Lord's Supper, that we enter into communion with the risen Christ. He is with us by virtue of His divine nature. When we commune with the divine in the Lord's Supper, we commune with the whole person, because Christ's divine nature is not separated from His human nature. The person is here, but only by way of His divine omnipresence, not by bringing His body with Him.

3. The Lord Jesus, in his human nature thus united to the divine, was sanctified, and anointed with the Holy Spirit, above measure, having in him all the treasures of wisdom and knowledge; in whom it pleased the Father that all fullness should dwell; to the end that, being holy, harmless, undefiled, and full of grace and truth, he might be thoroughly furnished to execute the office of a mediator, and surety. Which office he took not unto himself, but was thereunto called by his Father, who put all power and judgment into his hand, and gave him commandment to execute the same.

This is a lengthy paragraph, but the accent is in the first line: The Lord Jesus, in his human nature thus united to the divine, was sanctified. Notice that the confession is careful to maintain the perfect union of the two natures of Christ. It does not fall into Nestorianism, which involves a separation of the two natures. The church has always found it necessary to distinguish between the two natures yet to maintain that they are perfectly united, though not blended, mixed, or confused. One reason for distinguishing the two natures is that we distinguish between divine attributes and human attributes. For example, sometimes Jesus was hungry or thirsty. There were times when He was weary, when He wept, and when He slept. All those things manifested His human nature, because the divine nature is never hungry, thirsty, or weary and neither weeps nor sleeps.

In the transfiguration, the deity of Christ broke through. But for the most part, during His earthly life, Jesus concealed the deity that was part of who He was. The redemption that is carried out by Christ for us is linked in the Bible to His ministry as the last Adam. In Christ's taking the place of Adam and being the Mediator between God and man, it was critical that His work was done in His human nature. It was not done in a human nature that was separated from His divine nature, but His human nature was distinguished from His divine nature.

It is not possible for God to die, but human beings do die. On the cross, Jesus Christ died, but God did not die. The divine nature does not die; Jesus, the person, experienced death in His human nature. The divine nature, prior to the death of Christ, was united with a living, breathing human nature. The death of Christ did not destroy the union of the two natures. During the time that Christ was in the tomb, the divine nature was united with a human nature whose spirit was in paradise. On the cross, the Lord said, "Father, into your hands I commit my spirit!" (Luke 23:46). When Jesus' physical body was in the grave, the divine nature was still united with it. The union of the two natures was not severed by the death of Christ, but the divine nature did not die.

An interesting and speculative question arises with respect to the manifestation of the power that Jesus exhibited during His earthly ministry. He walked on water, He raised people from the dead, and He restored sight to the blind and hearing to the deaf. Was that power a manifestation of His divine nature or His human nature?

That is a difficult question because the miracles that Christ performed were, in the main, duplicated in biblical history by other people who were surely only human. For example, Elijah raised a widow's child from the dead. We see the miracles of Moses, of the Apostles, of some of the prophets, and of others. The power for all miracles obviously comes from God. We know that the human nature does not have the power in itself to walk on water, to change water into wine, or to raise people from the dead. When Jesus did these things, was it the divine nature working or was it the human nature working as it was empowered by God?

The Lord Jesus, in his human nature thus united to the divine, was sanctified, and anointed with the Holy Spirit, above measure. There is no essential difference between the divine nature of Christ and the Holy Spirit. They are one being, but they are two persons of the Trinity. In the union of the human nature with the divine nature, the human nature is united with the Father and the Son and the Holy Spirit. In other words, the union is with God, and God has three persons. Now, in the economy of the Trinity, we normally speak of the second person's being incarnate in Christ, but the second person is never separated from the first person or the third person. We are just distinguishing the manner of operation and the manner of working.

Here the confession says that Christ was sanctified and was anointed by the power of the Holy Spirit without measure. Elijah performed His miracles by the power of the Holy Spirit. The Holy Spirit came upon Elijah and empowered him, but the work was still done by Elijah.

In the New Testament, we do not read about Jesus' performing miracles until after the inauguration of His public ministry, after His baptism at the age of about thirty. No miracles are reported in the accounts of His birth and youth.

But the Gnostics in the second century tried to fill in the gap. Their apocryphal gospels contain fantasies about Jesus that are incompatible with the sober tone of the New Testament. They tell of Jesus' making mud pies and turning them into birds with which He could play. In another story, Jesus casts spells over playmates who taunt him. These stories are obviously fictional.

The confession is saying, albeit somewhat speculatively, that at His baptism Jesus was anointed by the Holy Spirit and empowered in his human nature to fulfill the role of the Messiah. The Holy Spirit descended like a dove and empowered Him. The prophet Isaiah, speaking of the coming Messiah, said, "The Spirit of the Lord GOD is upon me, because the LORD has anointed me to bring good news to the poor; he has sent me to bind up the brokenhearted, to proclaim liberty to the captives, and the opening of the prison to those who are bound" (Isa. 61:1). That was the text that Jesus read in the synagogue at the very beginning of His earthly ministry. After reading it publicly, Jesus said, "Today this Scripture has been fulfilled in your hearing" (Luke 4:21). Jesus was saying that Isaiah had written about Him. The word *Messiah* (from the Hebrew), or *Christ* (from the Greek), means "one who is anointed." When we speak of Jesus Christ, *Christ* is not His name but the title that He was given. When we say "Jesus Christ," we are saying "Jesus the Messiah." He was anointed by the Holy Spirit to carry out the functions of this office.

When John the Baptist was locked in prison and had his crisis of faith, he sent a message to Jesus: "Are you the one who is to come, or shall we look for another?" (Matt. 11:3). Jesus sent this message back: "Go and tell John what you hear and see: the blind receive their sight and the lame walk, lepers are cleansed and the deaf hear, and the dead are raised up, and the poor have good news preached to them" (vv. 4–5).

Jesus was saying that John should read Isaiah 61 and understand what the ministry of the Messiah was to be. The earthly ministry of Jesus was the work of the Messiah prophesied in the Old Testament. It was a mission to be carried out by a human person anointed by the Holy Spirit. From the time He was born, Jesus was God incarnate and His human nature was in perfect union with the divine nature. He may have had the ability at any time to call upon the power of His divine nature to do whatever He wanted to do. But part of His mission was to fulfill the law of God in His human nature as the second Adam. In other words, Jesus couldn't just appear here as God and do everything correctly that Adam failed to do. God required a human sacrifice, a human fulfillment of the law. We do not have that if God keeps the law. It is the God-man who must keep the law for us.

The best theologians, past and present, have been divided on the question of whether Jesus could have sinned. It seems best to say that since Jesus was truly human, it was possible for Him to sin. Obviously, the divine nature cannot sin. But if Christ's divine nature prevented Him from sinning, then in what sense did He obey the law of God as the second Adam? At His birth, Jesus' human nature was exactly the same as Adam's before the fall, with respect to His moral capabilities. Jesus had what Augustine called the *posse peccare* and the *posse non peccare*, that is, the ability to sin and the ability not to sin. Adam sinned; Jesus did not. Satan did everything in his power to corrupt Jesus and tempt Him to sin.

That would have been an exercise in futility had he been trying to tempt God to sin. Satan was not trying to get God to sin. He was trying to get Christ to sin according to His human nature, so that He would not be qualified to be the Savior.

At the same time, Christ was uniquely sanctified and ministered to by the Holy Spirit. In order to sin, a person must have a desire for sin. But Jesus' human nature throughout His life was marked by a zeal for righteousness. "My food is to do the will of him who sent me" (John 4:34), He said. As long as Jesus had no desire to sin, He would not sin. It seems wrong to think that Christ's divine nature made it impossible for His human nature to sin. If that were the case, the temptation, the tests, and His assuming of the responsibility of the first Adam would have all been charades. This position protects the integrity of the authenticity of the human nature because it was the human nature that carried out the mission of the second Adam on our behalf. It was the human nature uniquely anointed beyond measure by the Holy Spirit.

The confession tells us that Jesus' anointing with the Holy Spirit above measure was to the end that, being holy, harmless, undefiled, and full of grace and truth, he might be thoroughly furnished to execute the office of a mediator, and surety. Which office he took not unto himself, but was thereunto called by his Father. The office that Christ had to execute was to satisfy the demands of the law. For our redemption, the law had to be satisfied by a perfect man, not by God or an angel. In our justification, we are redeemed not only by Christ's death but by His life. His life of perfect obedience is crucial to our redemption, as one man fulfilling the demands of the law for others. It is also important that His sacrifice on the cross was offered in His human nature. This was a man paying the price for men. He is our substitute man when He offers Himself on the cross. The difference between Him and us, with respect to our humanity, is that He and He alone is the sinless man.

In one respect, Christ's sinlessness is more astonishing than His resurrection. Other people have come back from the dead, but no other person has lived a sinless life. His perfect life is amazing because no one of us has ever loved the Lord with all his mind, heart, and strength. None of us has loved our neighbor as much as we love ourselves. There is just too much sin in us being manifested every hour of every day. Can you imagine some-one living every minute of His entire life loving God with an undiluted, perfect affection, whose whole mind is devoted to the Father, who has no other desire than to obey the Father's will? That is more difficult for me to comprehend than that Jesus came out of the grave.

We struggle with the resurrection today because of its biologically anomalous character. It is a law of biology that when someone is dead, he's dead. How likely is it that someone would be dead for more than twenty-four hours and then come back to life? That people do not come back from the dead has been elevated to the level of a natural law of biol-ogy, which some people say can never be broken. They therefore cannot embrace the teaching of the resurrection because it is deemed impossible as measured against the fixed laws of nature. It is a critical ingredient of natural law that all sinners can expect to die and remain dead, because death is understood biblically to be inseparably related to sin.

Before the sin of Adam and Eve, there was no human death. The biblical law is that if there is no sin, there is no death. How then could Jesus die, since He never sinned and didn't participate in original sin? The only way that Jesus could die and come under the divine judgment of death for sin was for Him to take on Himself the guilt of other people's sin. Taking our guilt on Himself is exactly what He did. In and of Him-self, He was not vulnerable to death. He says: "For this reason the Father loves me, because I lay down my life that I may take it up again. No one takes it from me, but I lay it down of my own accord. I have authority to lay it down, and I have authority to take it up again" (John 10:17–18). He always had at His disposal the authority to call on legions of angels who stood ready to defend Him at any moment. But He willingly died because He desired to obey the will of the Father that He be the Mediator and take upon Himself the guilt of His people.

Once He allowed the transfer of the guilt of His people onto Himself, He was susceptible to death. The New Testament, when it speaks about the biological and ontological possibilities with respect to Jesus, takes a view that is radically different from that of secular biology. The New Tes-tament principle is that it was not possible for death to hold Him (Acts 2:24). After Christ made the sacrifice and was deemed acceptable to God, having finished the work of atonement and having paid for sin, death had no claim on Him. It was impossible for Him not to rise from the dead, because He was sinless, and death has no claim to, or hold on, sinless people. If we can understand and embrace the sinlessness of Jesus, the rest is easy. We are able to embrace the record and testimony of Jesus' resurrection once we are convinced that it is the resurrection of a sinless man.

The Bible also teaches that Christ was raised for our justification. We understand how the cross contributes to our justification because it involves a payment for our sin and a satisfaction of the demands of the righteousness of God against us. But how are we justified by His resurrection? This is an elliptical statement. The Bible is saying that Christ was raised by the Father to proclaim to the world, as Paul says in Acts, that His work of satisfaction was accepted by the Father (Acts 17:30–31). We are justified because Christ has finished the work of paying for our sins, so death no longer has any hold over Him. If He has finished His work of satisfaction, there is nothing left for us to do for our own justification. It has been accomplished fully and perfectly by Him. That was clearly shown when God raised Christ from the dead. When He raised Christ from the dead for our justification, Christ became the firstborn of many brethren (Rom. 8:29).

Therefore, if the penalty for our sins has been paid, what claim does death have on us? We have been delivered from death and from judgment by the perfect work of our Mediator, so death has no claim over us.

"I am the resurrection and the life. Whoever believes in me, though he die, yet shall he live" (John 11:25), Jesus said. That was accomplished in the incarnation under the blessing, and by the empowerment, of the Holy Spirit.

4. This office the Lord Jesus did most willingly undertake; which that he might discharge, he was made under the law, and did perfectly fulfill it; endured most grievous torments immediately in his soul, and most painful sufferings in his body; was crucified, and died, was buried, and remained under the power of death, yet saw no corruption. On the third day he arose from the dead, with the same body in which he suffered, with which also he ascended into heaven, and there sitteth at the right hand of

his Father, making intercession, and shall return, to judge men
and angels, at the end of the world.

In this segment, there is a mini-version of the Apostles' Creed, setting forth the highlights of the life of Jesus and calling attention to what He has accomplished for us. It gives a brief summary of the work of Jesus as He progressed from humiliation to exaltation.

We make a distinction between the person of Christ and the work of Christ. We are concerned about who Jesus is and also about what Jesus has done. Although we distinguish between the person and the work of Christ, we do not want to separate them. How we understand His identity as a person has tremendous impact on our understanding of His work. For example, if we viewed Jesus merely as an insightful human being, endowed with prophetic gifts, we would interpret His activity in a particular way. If we understand Christ to be the God-man, it sheds new light on what He achieved. And an understanding of the work He performed is important for understanding who He is.

Christ's work began in humiliation. His work began in the humiliation of the incarnation, being conceived and born in human flesh. We tend to think that His transition from humiliation to exaltation came at the resurrection. However, it really came in His burial. Isaiah prophesied that the Messiah would make his grave with the rich. He was not relegated to the garbage heap of Gehenna. Then, of course, in the blaze of glorious resurrection, His exaltation was manifested.

Jesus was born to a poor family, and grew up in obscurity in the town of Nazareth. "Can anything good come out of Nazareth?" was the question that Nathanael asked (John 1:46). The quiet, silent years before the start of His public ministry further obscured Christ's presence on earth. He "emptied himself, by taking the form of a servant" (Phil. 2:7). He set aside His divine glory and willingly embraced the humility that was part of His official vocation. The life of Jesus was lived out basically in humiliation, and it worsened as it moved toward the suffering of the cross.

When we distinguish between Jesus' humiliation and His exaltation, we tend to absolutize these two states. That is a mistake. In the gospel accounts, at points along the way, there are little insights or vignettes of glory and exaltation that attend the humiliation. Various episodes manifested the glory of Christ during His earthly pilgrimage, and these episodes grasped the Apostles and other disciples. John, in the prologue to his gospel, speaks of Jesus' becoming flesh and dwelling among us, and he adds, "We have seen his glory, glory as of the only Son from the Father, full of grace and truth" (John 1:14).

The Hebrew word for "glory" is *kavod*. In the midst of a calamity in Israel's history, when the ark was captured by the Philistines, a baby was born and named Ichabod, which means "the glory has departed" (1 Sam. 4:21). The Old Testament is much concerned with the manifestation of God's glory. For God's glory to depart from Israel meant that His redemptive presence was removed.

The root meaning of *kavod* is "heaviness" or "weightiness." This word became an important metaphor to describe the nature of God. God is not literally "heavy," but He is in a figurative sense, just as we say in English that something particularly profound or meaningful is "heavy." If someone treats us in a disrespectful manner, we may say, "They took us lightly," or "They gave no weight to what we said." In an ultimate sense, the God of Israel is known for His heaviness, His weightiness, because of His eternal significance and majesty.

The divine glory was manifested throughout the Old Testament by the shekinah, which was a "glory cloud" that radiated brilliant light. It is described in Scripture as a light brighter than the noonday sun. Its brilliance is so great that it overwhelms all those who are caught in its presence. We see that glory attending Jesus on specific occasions during His otherwise humble life.

At Christmas, as we celebrate His birth, we sing carols such as "Away in a Manger." We talk about there being no room in the inn, and the baby's being wrapped in swaddling clothes. All the images that surround the birth of Jesus dramatize His entrance into this world in a state of humiliation. But even as the record tells us of this descent into poverty by the second person of the Trinity, we have a wonderful announcement by the angels in the field outside of Bethlehem.

At the edge of the town, there is a little stone wall where you can sit and look over a large, empty plain. From there, one can imagine what happened that night when the world was visited with a great sound-and-light show. The glory of God shone round about, the heavens opened, and the voices of angels declared the nativity of Christ.

We are told in classic understatement in the King James Version about the response of the shepherds: "And they were sore afraid" (Luke 2:9). Their knees were knocking and their teeth were chattering. The Father turned on the lights for the shepherds, manifesting the glory of this One who had been born in humble circumstances.

Many years later, John the Baptist protested about baptizing Jesus: "I need to be baptized by you, and do you come to me?" Jesus responded, "Let it be so now, for thus it is fitting for us to fulfill all righteousness" (Matt. 3:14–15). Jesus said that His baptism was necessary to fulfill all righteousness. God had imposed upon Israel a new requirement for ritual cleansing, indicating that they were filthy and needed to be prepared for the breakthrough of the kingdom of God. By the voice of the prophet John, this new requirement was announced to the whole nation. Jesus, as the new Adam, who would save His people, had to submit to every requirement that God placed upon His people. He required them to be circumcised, and so Jesus was circumcised. God required them to be baptized, as announced by John the Baptist, and so Jesus was baptized. He was not baptized for the cleansing of His own sin, for He had none; rather, He was baptized to identify with the sinful nation that God had appointed Him to save. This new rite of cleansing had previously been prescribed only for gentiles, who were "unclean." Baptism was scandalous in the eyes of the Pharisees, and they viewed it as humiliating. And yet, Jesus willingly submitted to it.

During Jesus' baptismal experience at the river Jordan, the heavens opened and the Spirit of God descended visibly upon the head of Jesus in the form of a dove. God's voice was heard saying, "This is my beloved Son, with whom I am well pleased" (Matt. 3:17). God speaks audibly from heaven three times in the New Testament, and on each occasion it is to direct people's attention to the One whom He has sent. So, on this occasion, Christ was glorified in the midst of His humiliation.

Perhaps the most magnificent glorification of Jesus during His period of humiliation came at His transfiguration. Jesus had withdrawn with

His disciples to the northern edge of the nation for reflection and contemplation. At that time Peter confessed, "You are the Christ, the Son of the living God" (Matt. 16:16). Jesus concurred, but He "began to show his disciples that he must go to Jerusalem and suffer many things from the elders and chief priests and scribes, and be killed, and on the third day be raised" (v. 21). Six days later, Jesus took Peter, James, and John with Him up a mountain. There Jesus was transfigured before their eyes. An intense light shone out of the face of Jesus, and His clothes were dazzling white. The disciples were overwhelmed. They fell to the ground in fear at this dazzling display of the glory of Jesus (17:1–8).

There is one other instance in the Bible where someone's face shone because of the glory of God. Moses had gone up on Mount Sinai to meet with God. When Moses came down from the mountain, his face shone with such intensity that the people were afraid, and so he began veiling his face when speaking with them (Ex. 34:29–35). The radiance of his face was the reflected glory of God. It was not the glory of Moses but a reflection of God's glory.

The glory that the disciples witnessed on the Mount of Transfiguration, however, was not a reflection. It was the glory of God—of the second person of the Trinity—breaking through the cover that concealed the deity of Christ. It pierced through Jesus' humanity, and the disciples beheld it. Peter later referred to this moment in his letters (2 Peter 1:17–18), and John referenced it (John 1:14). Upon witnessing this event, His disciples fell on their faces and were terrified. Jesus said, "Rise, and have no fear" (Matt. 17:7).

In the midst of that awful moment of preparation for Jesus' final visit to Jerusalem, there is glory and truth. We see it again at the empty tomb with the angelic presence. We see it in the ascension, when Christ was carried up into heaven on the shekinah cloud. The disciples did not want to see their master leave them. He had told them, "It is to your advantage that I go away" (John 16:7), but they could not imagine how His absence would be better for them than His presence.

The disciples watched the taking up of the Son of Man to heaven (Acts 1:9), going to His coronation as King of kings. Angels then appeared and asked, "Men of Galilee, why do you stand looking into heaven? This Jesus, who was taken up from you into heaven, will come in the same way as you saw him go into heaven" (Acts 1:10–11). The Bible records that "they worshiped him" just before His ascension and then "returned to Jerusalem with great joy" (Luke 24:52).

When He announced that He was going to leave, they were depressed. When He actually left, they rejoiced. His resurrection and ascension mean that right now He is reigning as the King of kings in heaven. That puts us in a better position now than the disciples were in during His earthly ministry. Jesus sits in the seat of cosmic power. He holds the highest office in the universe. He has taken His throne in glory.

> 5. The Lord Jesus, by his perfect obedience, and sacrifice of himself, which he, through the eternal Spirit, once offered up unto God, hath fully satisfied the justice of his Father; and purchased, not only reconciliation, but an everlasting inheritance in the kingdom of heaven, for all those whom the Father hath given unto him.

This paragraph summarizes important points that are distinctive to Reformed theology. The first reference to the mediatorial work of Christ is to his perfect obedience. Christians often have a tendency to think that the redemptive work of Christ was accomplished solely through His sacrificial death on the cross. But the life of Jesus was just as important to our salvation as His death. He was born as the second Adam, and He submitted Himself to the law at every point.

Christ had an obligation as our representative not only to die for us but also to live for us. By achieving a life of perfect obedience, He fulfilled all the terms of the Old Testament covenant. Stipulations were imposed in the covenant by way of the law. The dual sanctions of the covenant included both the blessing and the curse. The blessing of God is promised to all who obey the terms of the covenant, but the curse of God is pronounced upon all who fail to keep the terms of that covenant.

Jesus was the only one who ever fully kept the terms of the covenant. Everyone else earned God's curse. In His death, Christ took upon Himself the curse deserved by the covenant-breakers. Furthermore, by His life of complete obedience, Jesus achieved the blessing that was promised to those who keep the terms of the covenant.

We make a distinction between the *active* obedience of Christ and the *passive* obedience of Christ. The active obedience refers to His life of perfect obedience to God's law, by which He merited the blessing of God for Himself and all whom He represents. When we say that we are justified by faith, we mean that our faith links us to Jesus and His righteousness. The ground of our justification is Christ's righteousness, His merit. When Christ lived a life of perfect obedience, He did it for us. His obedience was full, complete, and perfect, and by the imputation of it to all those who believe, it is counted as our full, complete, and perfect obedience.

That is why, when we looked at the covenant, we made the distinction between the covenant of works and the covenant of grace. At the beginning, God entered into a relationship with Adam and Eve that was based on works, and they failed their probation and lost the blessing. But instead of destroying the human race, God gave us an opportunity to be redeemed. We call that the covenant of grace because we are saved by God's grace, based on what someone else did for us. It is not because we have earned anything. However, the basis for our redemption always remains good works. The only way anyone is saved is by works. But it is Christ's good works, not ours. When we say that we are justified by faith, that does not mean that our faith is so righteous that it satisfies the demands of God's law. When we are justified by means of our faith, we are united to the One who does the good works necessary for God to declare us righteous. That is the gospel in a nutshell. We are justified by the righteous works and the merit of someone else, who acts as our Mediator, who is our champion, who is the substitute for us in the sight of God.

The Lord Jesus, by his perfect obedience, and sacrifice of himself, which he, through the eternal Spirit, once offered up unto God, hath fully satisfied the justice of his Father. This section is complex, and we have not arrived at the end of the first sentence yet. It says that we are saved through the perfect obedience and righteousness of Jesus and by the sacrifice of Himself that He offered to God. To understand that, we must go back to the beginning, to the basic understanding of worship.

God was originally worshiped by His people submitting to His authority in obedience and offering Him glory, honor, reverence, homage, and adoration. After the fall of Adam, worship took on a sacrificial dimension. Sacrifices were offered by Cain and Abel, and that practice continued down through the centuries, until an elaborate ceremonial system was instituted under Moses.

In Genesis 4, we read that Cain's offering, or sacrifice, was not acceptable to God, but that Abel's offering was pleasing to God. That passage doesn't tell us what it was about Cain's offering that made it unsatisfactory to God. It has been suggested that Cain's offering was unacceptable because there was no blood involved in it. However, in the Mosaic sacrificial system there were grain offerings. There is no hint that animal sacrifices were acceptable and vegetable sacrifices were not. Furthermore, the book of Hebrews tells us, "By faith Abel offered to God a more acceptable sacrifice than Cain" (Heb. 11:4). What was unacceptable about Cain's sacrifice was not what was offered but who offered it: someone lacking faith. Offerings that are acceptable to God are expressions of the giver's love, submission, and veneration.

Throughout the Old Testament, any worship given to God without faith is unacceptable to Him. When God said, "I hate, I despise your feasts, and I take no delight in your solemn assemblies" (Amos 5:21), it was because the Israelites' worship was insincere. People went through the motions but were not making an authentic sacrifice of praise to God. Although the sacrificial system of the Old Testament has ended, we are still to bring to God the sacrifice of sincere praise.

The Apostle Paul tells us, "I appeal to you therefore, brothers, by the mercies of God, to present your bodies as a living sacrifice, holy and acceptable to God, which is your spiritual worship" (Rom. 12:1). All this sets the stage for the ultimate sacrifice of Christ, which is a sacrifice given to satisfy the demands of God's justice.

In the Middle Ages, Anselm of Canterbury wrote a famous little book titled *Cur Deus homo*, which is usually translated "Why the God-man?" Anselm set forth the satisfaction view of the atonement. It is also called the substitutionary view of the atonement because the satisfaction is offered not by us but by our Mediator in our place, as our substitute. These ideas are often linked together as the substitutionary satisfaction view of the atonement.

Anselm understood that the Scriptures express the concept of atonement in several ways, using different metaphors. We must not have a simplistic view of the atonement of Christ. For example, the Bible sometimes speaks of the atonement as a purchase. We read in the text of the confession that Christ **purchased** our salvation.

We are also told that He came "to give his life as a ransom for many" (Matt. 20:28), and so there have been various ransom theories of the atonement. One such theory is that Christ paid a ransom to God the Father, to purchase His people. Another view is that Satan holds us hostage, and that Christ paid off Satan to buy us back. The latter view is problematic, in that it is inconceivable that God could owe a debt to Satan, but it has been popular historically.

Another view is called the *Christus Victor* view. This view states that on the cross, Christ was victorious over the powers of Satan and the powers of darkness. This view has its roots in God's promise in the garden of Eden that the seed of the woman would crush the head of the serpent and in the process have his heel bruised (Gen. 3:15).

As the New Testament unfolds, the significance of the work and the death of Christ on the cross and the concepts of satisfaction, substitution, and ransom are there. We learn in Exodus that an indentured servant, when freed, has his wife and children released with him. However, if he marries the daughter of the man to whom he is indentured, his wife and children stay. He would then have to pay a bride price in order to redeem his wife and children. That whole system is taken up in the metaphor of the ransom of Christ, in which He purchased His bride, the church. He paid the bride price to buy His wife out of slavery. That is why Paul says that we are not our own but have been purchased at a price (1 Cor. 6:20; 7:23), the price of Christ's blood. There is that strong element of ransom, but it is not a ransom paid to the devil. It is a ransom paid to the Father, whereby we are purchased by the blood of Christ.

The substitutionary satisfaction view of the atonement is rejected in liberal theological circles. In the view of many today, God loves everyone unconditionally. He is like a cosmic grandfather or a heavenly Santa Claus who freely and unilaterally forgives our sins without worrying about such quaint things as vindicating His righteousness and justice. This view has had a pervasive impact on the church and modern culture.

When Paul explains the gospel in Romans, he states that God, in providing redemption through the cross of Christ, demonstrates both that He is just and that He is the justifier of those who have faith (Rom. 3:26). The cross is the clearest expression of God's grace and mercy that we find anywhere in Scripture. There are those who say they prefer the God of the New Testament because he's a God of love, grace, and mercy, while the Old Testament God is vengeful, angry, and concerned about law and justice. It is important to note in response that the most vivid demonstration of the wrath and justice of God that we find in Scripture is found in the New Testament, at the cross. In the violence of that act, the wrath of God was poured out on One who, in and of Himself, was completely innocent but who took upon Himself our transgressions and our guilt.

The Father executed His full vengeance. On the cross, Christ endured hell, was cursed, and was forsaken precisely because God would not compromise His justice or set aside His own righteous demands. He required that the moral debt be paid, and it was paid. When Christ said from the cross, "It is finished," He indicated that the debt had been paid in full.

In the satisfaction view of the atonement, what is being satisfied is the requirement of God—His justice and righteousness. We have broken His law and incurred His wrath, and He would be completely just to require us to pay the penalty. If someone else offered to pay the penalty, He would not have to accept it, since we are talking about our personal sins against His grace and mercy. Yet He has agreed (and indeed arranged) to accept the death of Christ as satisfaction for our debt.

The basic stance of modern America is not that we owe God but that He owes us. He owes us a good and happy life, where nothing ever goes wrong. We don't really grasp what happened at the cross or what Christianity is all about. We say, "Forgive us our debts," but we do not really understand the extent of that debt. Every time we sin, our debt increases. The Lord Jesus sacrificed Himself and satisfied the justice of His Father on the cross for His own glory, and for the benefit of the elect.

For all those whom the Father hath given unto him. The Father did not give everyone to the Son. On the night He was betrayed, Jesus prayed for those whom the Father had given Him. He was not praying at that time for those whom the Father had not given Him (John 17:9). He thanked the Father that none of those had been lost—except for Judas, who really was not lost because he was a devil from the beginning (17:12). "All that the Father gives me will come to me," Jesus said (John 6:37). He prayed that none of those whom the Father had given Him would be lost.

If Christ's purchase of redemption is only for those whom the Father has given to Him, and the Father has not given all people to Him, then the next question is, Has Christ purchased redemption for all people? Not according to the Westminster Confession.

> 6. Although the work of redemption was not actually wrought by Christ till after his incarnation, yet the virtue, efficacy, and benefits thereof were communicated unto the elect, in all ages successively from the beginning of the world, in and by those promises, types, and sacrifices, wherein he was revealed, and signified to be the seed of the woman which should bruise the serpent's head; and the Lamb slain from the beginning of the world; being yesterday and today the same, and forever.

The confession is affirming here that the basic distinction between the Old Testament economy and the New Testament economy is the difference between promise and fulfillment. The Old Testament saints, born before Christ came, believed in God's covenant promises. The promises increased over time as God revealed more of the content of His plan of redemption. The point made in the confession is that those people were not given to understand all that would unfold in the work of Christ. The only information they had was the basic promise of the crushing of the serpent's head in Genesis 3. Those who trusted in that promise were trusting in the promise of the Christ who was to come, and they were justified by their faith.

Section 6 explains that the benefit of Christ's righteousness extends not only to those who believe in it after it is accomplished but also to those who believed in it before it was accomplished. Abraham believed in the promise of the coming Messiah, and through that faith he received the righteousness that Christ earned through His work, even though that work had not yet been performed. God sees the value of the work of

Christ as having everlasting significance—both into the future and back into the past. The author of Hebrews emphasizes this point when he talks about the inadequacy of the types and shadows of the Old Testament sacrificial system in and of themselves to effect redemption. He argues that the blood of bulls and goats cannot take away sin (Heb. 10:1–4).

On what basis, then, were the Old Testament saints forgiven when their sacrifices were offered? They were forgiven on the grounds of the reality to which the shadow or the type pointed. The blood of the bulls and goats and lambs pointed to the reality of the Lamb who was slain from the foundation of the world (Rev. 13:8), even Christ.

We see this shadow or type in Old Testament circumcision, which became the sign of the covenant and of God's promise. Circumcision was not only a covenant sign but also a fiduciary sign. It was a sign whose content was linked to faith. Abraham was circumcised as an adult, after faith was present, but his son Isaac was circumcised as a child, before faith was present. There is a distinction between the receiving of the sign of the covenant in the Old Testament and the timing of the actualization of faith. Abraham first had the faith, and then the sign. Isaac first had the sign, and later the faith.

This is the point that Calvin made when he drew a parallel between circumcision in the old covenant and baptism in the new covenant. The *sign* of faith is not tied to the *time* of faith. Calvin would argue two things about infant baptism: First, the giving of the sign does not produce the faith; that is, baptism does not create faith in the infant. Second, a person does not have to wait until faith is actualized before he receives the sign.

Although the work of redemption was not actually wrought by Christ till after his incarnation, yet the virtue, efficacy, and benefits thereof were communicated unto the elect, in all ages successively from the beginning of the world. Everything that Christ accomplished for New Testament believers was accomplished for Old Testament believers as well. All the benefits that we derive from the work of Christ were given also to Abraham. This is what Jesus refers to when He says, "Abraham rejoiced that he would see my day" (John 8:56).

The benefits of Christ's work were communicated to the elect in and by the promises, types, and sacrifices in which Christ was revealed. We are not denigrating the value of the types, sacrifices, and shadows that came before, because they were part of the revelation that God gave to His Old Testament people about redemption. The actual benefits of Christ's work were communicated through these means before His incarnation.

Wherein he was revealed, and signified. The Old Testament rites were signs, pointing beyond themselves to a higher reality. The sign is not the reality. The sign signifies something other than itself, and that is what the Old Testament signs did. They pointed forward to the seed of the woman, who would crush the serpent's head, to the Lamb slain from the beginning of the world, who is the same yesterday and today and forever.

> 7. Christ, in the work of mediation, acts according to both natures, by each nature doing that which is proper to itself; yet, by reason of the unity of the person, that which is proper to one nature is sometimes in Scripture attributed to the person denominated by the other nature.

Section 7 touches on a very difficult theological issue. Christ is called in this chapter the Mediator, and in a special sense is the lone Mediator between God and man, insofar as He alone is the God-man. Others have functioned in mediatory activities, such as priests and prophets and especially Moses, who was the mediator of the old covenant, but they did not function in the transcendent sense in which Christ is the Mediator, in that He partook of both the divine nature and the human nature. This section repeats the earlier affirmation of the dual nature of Christ, echoing the ecumenical creeds of the past.

Christ, in the work of mediation, acts according to both natures, by each nature doing that which is proper to itself. This statement harks back to section 2 and its reiteration of the Definition of Chalcedon, where the church affirmed that each nature retained its own attributes, and were united without mixture, confusion, separation, or division. There are certain things that Christ does in His humanity and certain things that He does in His deity.

For example, Christ stated that no one knows the day and the hour of His return, except the Father—not even the Son (Mark 13:32). That has long puzzled Christians, including eminent theologians. Did not Christ have to know the day and the hour, since He was God incarnate, and God is omniscient?

It would be a mistake to think that anything Christ knew according to His divine nature He also knew according to His human nature. Each nature retained its own attributes, and the incarnation was not a mixture or confusion of the two natures. Christ, according to His human nature, did not gain divine omniscience from the incarnation.

Jesus' human knowledge was limited, just like anyone else's knowledge. There were times when He demonstrated supernatural knowledge, but that did not then mean that His human nature had taken on divine omniscience, thereby violating His humanity. God communicated supernatural information to the prophets without deifying their human nature. It is one thing to communicate information and it is another thing to communicate, or share, divine attributes.

Yet, by reason of the unity of the person, that which is proper to one nature is sometimes in Scripture attributed to the person denominated (i.e., designated) by the other nature. In Acts 20:28 we read, "Pay careful attention to yourselves and to all the flock, in which the Holy Spirit has made you overseers, to care for the church of God, which he obtained with his own blood." And 1 John 3:16 says, "By this we know love, that [God] laid down his life for us, and we ought to lay down our lives for the brothers."

In these texts, we see references to God's blood and God's death. But this does not mean that Christ perished on the cross according to His divine nature. Since there is a perfect unity between the human nature and the divine nature, anything that can be attributed to either nature can be attributed to the person, and sometimes, as in the examples above, we even see attributes of one nature attributed to the one person of Christ by way of referring to the other nature.

8. To all those for whom Christ hath purchased redemption, he doth certainly and effectually apply and communicate the same; making intercession for them, and revealing unto them, in and by the Word, the mysteries of salvation; effectually persuading them by his Spirit to believe and obey, and governing their hearts by his Word and Spirit; overcoming all their enemies by his almighty

power and wisdom, in such manner, and ways, as are most consonant to his wonderful and unsearchable dispensation.

To all those for whom Christ hath purchased redemption, he doth certainly and effectually apply and communicate the same. Here we see the doctrine of definite atonement. Both Reformed people and semi-Pelagian groups are particularistic in their theology—that is, they believe that not everyone was saved or is saved by Christ. There are some who are lost. The Reformed faith teaches that there is a vast multitude of people who are saved, but not all people, and that those who are saved are those who are elect. Only the elect receive the saving benefits of the work of Christ. In the semi-Pelagian view, God's commitment to redemption is limited, since all God does in that scenario is make salvation possible. He makes it possible for everyone but certain for no one. Since people are truly dead in sin, without further help from God, no one would be saved, and the atonement would be useless.

Even more importantly, if Christ actually satisfied the demands of God's justice for all the sins of all people in the world, it would then be an injustice for God to punish anyone with damnation. Their sins would already have been atoned for and covered. The confession here affirms that the atonement that Christ offered was both real and effectual. It certainly brought to pass what God intended to accomplish by it.

He doth certainly and effectually apply and communicate the same. Here we see that God's plan of salvation is a definite plan that definitely works and definitely comes to pass. Christ does, in fact, effectively atone for the sins of the elect, and He communicates the benefits of His death to them.

Making intercession for them. Christ objectively purchases redemption for the elect. He certainly and effectually applies and communicates that redemption to them. And He makes intercession for them. This is a summary of Jesus' farewell prayer recorded in John 17, wherein Jesus prays for those whom the Father has given Him, and He distinguishes them from the world. He intercedes for the elect in a way that He does not intercede for the rest of the world.

We tend to undervalue Christ's work of intercession. We focus our attention on His priestly work of making the atonement, but that is only part of His priestly work. The high priest not only offers the sacrifice but also attaches to it the priestly prayer of intercession for the application of that sacrifice to those who are in need.

At the Last Supper, Jesus announced to His disciples that one of them was going to betray Him, and yet in the ensuing events we find out that two of them did so. One is called a betrayal, and the other is called a denial, but that is just another word for betrayal. When Judas asked, "Is it I, Rabbi?" Jesus replied, "You have said so" (Matt. 26:25), and "What you are going to do, do quickly" (John 13:27). He dismissed Judas into the night. We know what happened to Judas, who is described as a son of perdition (i.e., a son of damnation) from the beginning. It is not the case that Judas was saved and then lost his salvation. He was never included among the elect. He was never one whom the Father had given to the Son.

Simon Peter publicly and disgracefully denied Jesus. When Jesus had earlier told him that this would happen, Peter insisted that it would never happen. Jesus said: "Satan demanded to have you, that he might sift you like wheat, but I have prayed for you that your faith may not fail. And when you have turned again, strengthen your brothers" (Luke 22:31–32).

This is a joyous thing for every Christian to know. Christ not only has died for our sins and purchased our redemption on the cross, but He is making intercession for us every day in heaven. That is why there must be no pride in believing that we are numbered among the elect. The whole point of election is that we are dependent from beginning to end on the mercy and grace of God and on the work of Jesus to rescue us. He is the One who rescues us, body and soul. He does not just make it possible and offer us that rescue. He actually intercedes on our behalf so that His rescue effort will be efficacious.

And revealing unto them, in and by the Word, the mysteries of salvation. That which is hidden from the lost of this world is revealed to the elect by the divine and supernatural light that brings them to faith in the first place. This section assigns the work of the Holy Spirit in **revealing . . . the mysteries of salvation** to the work of Christ because it is Christ and the Father who send the Holy Spirit to apply the benefits of Jesus. We say that the Trinitarian work of redemption is designed and planned by the Father, who sends the Son into the world. It is accomplished by the Son and it is applied by the Holy Spirit. When the Holy Spirit applies the work of the Son, the Son works through the Spirit in the application of that ministry.

Effectually persuading them by his Spirit to believe and obey. This hints at the doctrine of effectual calling. When the Holy Spirit convicts us of sin and brings us to faith, His work is effective. He does not merely woo us. He does not just try to persuade us to believe. He effectively brings us to faith and obedience.

And governing their hearts by his Word and Spirit; overcoming all their enemies by his almighty power and wisdom, in such manner, and ways, as are most consonant to his wonderful and unsearchable dispensation. This is an exultation on the power and the real sufficiency of the mediatory work of Christ. It is sufficient because it is efficient. That which He has done for us as our Mediator is effective because He makes it effective. He came into this world to save His sheep, and He accomplished that mission of redemption. He came to seek and to save those who were lost. He found them, and He saved them, and He will keep them by the power of the Holy Spirit forever.

Section 8 articulates the doctrine of limited atonement (also called definite atonement), which is the most controversial point of Reformed theology. It is the *L* in TULIP, the famous acrostic of the so-called five points of Calvinism. This acrostic contains five points:

T: Total Depravity
U: Unconditional Election
L: Limited (or Definite) Atonement
I: Irresistible Grace
P: Perseverance of the Saints

In the evangelical world, some people get upset when they hear about TULIP. It indicates to them that Christ did not die for everyone. What does this do to evangelism? How can an evangelist say to people, "Christ has died for your sins"? Surely, we have the freedom to declare boldly to everyone we meet: "Jesus died for you. All you have to do to be saved is to put your trust and faith in Him." People who are accustomed to declaring the gospel in those terms get upset when they hear this doctrine that says, in effect, that Christ did not die for everyone.

The Bible says, "For God so loved the world, that he gave his only Son, that whoever believes in him should not perish but have eternal life" (John 3:16). Does not the New Testament say that Jesus died not only for our sins but for the sins of the whole world? How could anyone come to the conclusion that He did not die for everyone? The answer is that God gave certain people to the Son, and the Son provided a sacrifice for them—to all those for whom Christ hath purchased redemption.

The doctrine of unconditional election, as formulated biblically, leads inescapably to limited atonement. From all eternity, God has planned to save certain people, the elect. They will all certainly be saved because His decree of election cannot fail. Unconditional election means that salvation is of the Lord, that God has intended from all eternity to save His people, and that He does it. Now, if God has determined from all eternity to save the elect, and part of His plan of redemption is to send a Savior to save them—and only them—then it follows that Christ died for the elect—and only for them. In other words, it follows that Christ's atonement is limited or definite in its design and purpose. Christ died to save only the ones whom God intended to save.

The point of limited atonement is that salvation is entirely of the Lord. It comes from God's design, from His plan, and from His intervention, and it comes through the work of Christ on behalf of His people. Christ's work is applied to the elect by the Holy Spirit. The Father designs it, the Son carries it out, and the Holy Ghost applies it to the elect by quickening us, awakening us from spiritual death, and creating faith in our hearts so that we come to Christ. It is a Trinitarian work, and everyone whom God intends to be saved receives the benefits of Christ, because God the Holy Spirit makes sure that those benefits are realized in us.

The value of Christ's atonement is not limited; the perfection of His work is not limited. His death on the cross provides all the necessary merit and righteousness that would be required to satisfy the wrath and justice of God for all the sins that have ever been committed by all the people in the world. Had God chosen to save every person, Christ would have to have done nothing more than what He did to save the elect. His atonement on Calvary two thousand years ago—had God willed to apply it to every person who has ever lived—could cover everyone's sin. Calvinists and Arminians agree on the point that Christ's death is of enough worth to save everyone.

But Calvinists and traditional Arminians also agree that this worth is not applied to all people who have ever lived. The atonement leads to salvation for only some people in both Calvinist and Arminian theology.

At these two points, broadly considered, there is nothing distinctively Reformed about the view that Christ's work on the cross has enough worth and value to save all sinners. There is also nothing distinctively Reformed about the view that Christ's death will not save every sinner, that not everyone will have the benefits of the atonement applied to them. This is simply an affirmation of particularism over against universalism. Universalism teaches that everyone will be saved. Particularism teaches that only some people will be saved. Both Reformed theology and traditional Arminian theology affirm particularism.

The difference between Reformed theology and Arminian theology, then, is in how each system explains *why* some are not saved. In both systems, the reason why some are not saved is grounded in the system's view of the intent of the atonement. Arminians are saying that in the atonement, God intended to provide for the potential forgiveness for all people through the death of Christ but that He did not intend to provide for the actual forgiveness for anyone. In Arminian thought, saving grace is ultimately resistible. Some people are not saved because they do not cooperate with the grace of God in order to be saved. On the other hand, the Reformed believe that in the atonement God intended to provide for the actual forgiveness of the elect but that He did not intend to provide for the potential forgiveness of all people. In Reformed thought, grace is ultimately irresistible. Some are not saved because God has not given them saving grace, which finally converts all to whom it is given.

If Christ died for all people and actually satisfied the demands of God's justice and made a perfect atonement for all the sins of the entire world, what would be the point of a judgment? It would be unjust for God to punish someone if Christ has already paid the penalty for his sins. We said that Christ sacrificed Himself perfectly for the elect, and we do not deny that Christ's death would be enough to cover every sin had that been God's intent in the atonement. What we affirm is that Christ's death was intended to cover *only* the sins of the elect. He did not intend to die for the nonelect. Though His sacrifice was enough for the nonelect as well, our triune God did not have the nonelect in view when He planned and executed the atonement. So, the nonelect do not have a perfect sacrifice made on their behalf. Christ did not die to offer the nonelect either a potential forgiveness or an actual forgiveness.

Arminian thought—which is quite popular today—essentially says that Christ's atonement, His work of satisfaction, is made effective by our faith. In this view, God requires something else besides the atonement for our salvation, namely, our faith. God's justice is not fully satisfied unless and until we believe. What Christ did on the cross is not effectual for our salvation until we believe, and our belief is not guaranteed by the death of Christ or by the irresistibility of saving grace. Though Arminians would not put it quite this way, in their system there is a deficiency with respect to the work of Christ and how it provides for our salvation. Christ's work needs our faith to accomplish God's intent behind it. This is ghastly thinking.

The Reformed do not say that faith is necessary to accomplish God's intent behind the atonement. Rather, the intent of the atonement was to save the elect, and it actually saves the elect. We must believe in Christ in order to be saved, but our faith is a gift to us out of God's irresistible saving grace, which comes as a consequence of the atonement. We do not add our faith to the work of Christ to secure our forgiveness; Christ's work secures our forgiveness and our faith is a consequence of Calvary.

On the other hand, some say that the atonement is intended to pay for the sins of all people, unless a person rejects it in unbelief. But that would mean that Christ died for all the sins of the world except for the sin of unbelief. We do not want to say that either. Remember, when we say that Christ's death on Calvary two thousand years ago could cover the sins of all if God had intended it to do so, we mean that the value of His death cannot be augmented. We do not mean that it was actually directed to all. If a death of such value were directed to all people, then it would save all people.

Jesus said: "I lay down my life for the sheep. . . . My sheep hear my voice" (John 10:15, 27). He lays down His life for those whom the Father has given to Him. What took place on the cross was not just an abstract act of total atonement for all human sin. Rather, Jesus died specifically for His own, His elect.

How do our prayers for the unsaved fit into this equation? Our prayers cannot make someone elect who is not elect, but our prayers can be the means that God may use to bring that person's election to realization. God has ordained from all eternity to save certain people, and He has ordained from all eternity to save them through the foolishness of preaching, through the prayers of His people, and through the means of grace. We covered this earlier, but it is vital to remember. God has ordained from all eternity not just what would happen but how it would happen.

What, then, is the purpose of the nonelect? As Paul explains in Romans 9, their purpose, as vessels fit for destruction, is to bring glory to God. In God's plan of salvation, His glory is manifested in two directions: through the sweetness and wonder of His grace and mercy, and through His perfect, holy, righteous justice. The elect receive the mercy of God; the nonelect receive the justice of God. No one is treated unfairly or unjustly. When God manifests His justice, He does it for His glory. When He manifests His grace, He does that for His glory as well. And we, when we are in glory, fully sanctified, will rejoice in both manifestations of His glory.

Of Free Will

1. God hath endued the will of man with that natural liberty, that it is neither forced, nor, by any absolute necessity of nature, determined to good, or evil.
2. Man, in his state of innocency, had freedom, and power to will and to do that which was good and well pleasing to God; but yet, mutably, so that he might fall from it.
3. Man, by his fall into a state of sin, hath wholly lost all ability of will to any spiritual good accompanying salvation: so as, a natural man, being altogether averse from that good, and dead in sin, is not able, by his own strength, to convert himself, or to prepare himself thereunto.
4. When God converts a sinner, and translates him into the state of grace, he freeth him from his natural bondage under sin; and, by his grace alone, enables him freely to will and to do that which is spiritually good; yet so, as that by reason of his remaining corruption, he doth not perfectly, nor only, will that which is good, but doth also will that which is evil.
5. The will of man is made perfectly and immutably free to good alone, in the state of glory only.

We come now in our study of the Westminster Confession to a separate treatment of the subject of free will. Every time Reformed theology is presented in open discussion, it seems inevitable that the subject of free will arises. For many, the idea of God's sovereignty is antithetical to one of the most precious and axiomatic principles of human understanding—the idea of free will.

When we examine the question of free will from the viewpoint of biblical theology, we are pressured by the massive impact that secular views of free will have had on our thinking. If there is any place where secular humanism has undermined a biblical view of human nature, it's with respect to the idea of free will. The prevailing view of free will in the secular culture is that human beings are able to make choices without being encumbered by sin. In this view, our wills have no predisposition either toward evil or toward righteousness but remain in a neutral state from birth.

This view of human freedom is on a collision course with the biblical doctrine of the fall, which speaks of the radical corruption of our human condition. The whole person is caught up in the fall, including the mind, the heart, the will, and the body. The ravages of sin have affected us profoundly and deeply. Nonetheless, we are still able to think. Similarly, although the will has been tragically marred by the fall, we have not lost our ability to make moral choices. We still have wills, which are able to make choices without being coerced by God. The fact remains, however, that when the Bible speaks of our condition, it speaks of bondage or slavery to sin, which the confession addresses.

1. God hath endued the will of man with that natural liberty, that it is neither forced, nor, by any absolute necessity of nature, determined to good, or evil.

Here the confession speaks of **natural liberty**, a liberty that is part and parcel of our nature as human beings. We were given a will that is not coerced or forced to make any decision **by any absolute necessity of nature**. The confession distances itself from every form of moral determinism, which would subject human choices to fixed, mechanical, or physical forces, or even to the arbitrary influences of fate. In a word, Reformed theology categorically rejects fatalism and any determinism based upon the forces of nature. We are not coerced or forced by natural causes, or by our environment, either to do good or to do evil.

Section 2, however, goes on to make an important distinction between the state of the human will as it was created and its state after the fall.

2. Man, in his state of innocency, had freedom, and power to will and to do that which was good and well pleasing to God; but yet, mutably, so that he might fall from it.

Here the confession asserts and affirms that in creation the human will had freedom and power to do what is good, to do what is well pleasing to God. Before the fall, human beings had the moral capacity or the moral ability to choose righteousness and obedience before God. But this endowment from God was mutable. Man was capable of change and falling away from his original disposition.

Augustine of Hippo stated that in creation we were both *posse peccare* (able to sin) and *posse non peccare* (able not to sin). After the fall, we continued to be able to sin, *posse peccare*, but we lost the power or ability not to sin, *posse non peccare*. We were left in what Augustine called a state of moral inability.

This truth can be illustrated from a rational perspective and from an analytical perspective. According to Jonathan Edwards, free will is freedom to choose what we want—the ability to choose according to our own inclinations. Not only are we able to choose according to our strongest inclinations, but, in a very real sense, we must choose according to our strongest inclination in order to be free. This is the essence of freedom: to be able to choose what we want, rather than what someone else wants for us. We also recognize that we are creatures who have multitudes of conflicting desires. We are pulled in more than one direction, and the intensity with which we want things changes and vacillates.

If we desired only to obey God, we would never sin. As Christians, we have some desire in our hearts to please Christ. Unfortunately, we still desire to please ourselves, to gratify our own lusts, and to do what we want to do rather than what Christ wants us to do. Now, we are confronted with a choice between obeying Christ and disobeying Christ. If our desire to please Christ is greater than our desire to please ourselves at this point, what will we do? Whenever our desire for obedience is greater than our desire for sin, we will obey Christ. However, whenever our desire for sin exceeds our desire to please God, we will sin. In a real sense, we are slaves to our own freedom. We not only can be free but must be free. We are volitional creatures, and to be volitional means that we choose according to our wills. We make choices according to what seems best or most pleasing to us at the moment of decision.

What does that say for our sanctification? Is there any way that we can fool ourselves? This is important for our realization of how we function as sinners, having conflicting desires in our soul. We want to grow in grace, we want to please God, we want to obey Christ, and yet we still have desires for self-fulfillment that are sinful. We are told in the New Testament to feed the new man and starve the old man, to put the old man to death and seek the renewal of the new man, the strengthening of the inward man.

What can we do to strengthen our sanctification? The level of our desire to obey Christ has to increase, and the level of our desire for the things of this world has to diminish. Because we are always going to follow our strongest inclinations or desires, the only way to grow in grace is to feed and strengthen our positive desires for God and to starve our negative desires.

What are some things that we can do to strengthen the inner man? It certainly helps to spend time in the Word of God. Paul says, "Do not be conformed to this world, but be transformed by the renewal of your mind" (Rom. 12:2). When we read Scripture and hear the Word of God reinforced, we begin to understand that certain behavioral patterns that are acceptable in the culture in which we live are totally unacceptable to God. When we sin, we know that we are sinning, but we trivialize our sin. We say, "I know I am not supposed to do that, but it's not that important." As we come under the scrutiny of the Word of God, we begin to see that things that we do not regard as important are indeed very important to God. We get a deeper understanding of righteousness and of evil.

The Scriptures also encourage us to obey God and discourage us from sinning. So the Word of God is what we call a means of grace. When we spend time in the Bible, something happens to the inward man. Our minds get changed. We start to think differently, and we approach decisions in a different way, all because our minds are saturated with the truth of God.

Many times we resolve to spend time in Scripture, but we do not, because something else comes up that we want to do more than we want to read Scripture. The desire is not compelling enough to cause us to act in a diligent and disciplined manner to feed the new man in Christ on the Word of God.

OF FREE WILL • 235

What can we do about that? We can make a commitment and enter a group. We can become part of a group that is going to root for us and cheer when we succeed. That group is the church of Christ. We come to church partly to lose the excess baggage that we brought into the kingdom of God with our conversion. We come to church for help in killing the old man. We come to church so that our souls can be nurtured and so that we can be instructed in the things of God in a way that is going to change our lives. Going to church changes our lives by strengthening our resolve to do one thing rather than another. If we want to learn the Bible, and we are not doing it on our own, we can get into a Bible study group. We can get into a Sunday school class, not just for one hour a week, but to study and work on assignments for the rest of the week. The whole Christian battle is a battle of the will. It is a battle to overcome a will that by nature is bent in the wrong direction.

3. Man, by his fall into a state of sin, hath wholly lost all ability of will to any spiritual good accompanying salvation: so as, a natural man, being altogether averse from that good, and dead in sin, is not able, by his own strength, to convert himself, or to prepare himself thereunto.

The Reformers believed that the will, although in a fallen state, could still achieve civic virtue or civic righteousness. Fallen man can still obey the traffic lights and so on, but he cannot incline himself to the things of God.

Jesus said, "This is why I told you that no one can come to me unless it is granted him by the Father" (John 6:65). "No one can" means that no one is able. One of the key doctrines of the Reformation was *sola gratia*, meaning that we are saved by God's grace alone and not from our own efforts. Does fallen man have the ability to turn to Christ and to choose Him before he is born of the Holy Spirit? Most professing evangelical Christians today believe that faith comes first and then rebirth. This presupposes that the unconverted person has the ability to incline himself, or to choose to come, to Jesus Christ. Augustine, Luther, Calvin, and Edwards said that no one is able to do that. If we continue to think that in our fallen state we have the moral ability to come to Christ apart from the grace of God, we do so at your own peril. In John 6:65, our Lord clearly says that no one is able to come to Him unless the ability to do so is given to him by the Father.

Fortunately for us, Jesus puts the word "unless" in that statement. That word points to what we call a necessary condition, a *sine qua non*. A necessary condition has to be met before a desired result can occur. The desired result is coming to Christ; the necessary condition is that the ability to come must be given to each person by the Father. Only God gives that ability. No one can come to Christ on his own; we are not able to, unless God gives us the moral ability to do it.

Jacobus Arminius was a sixteenth-century theologian who opposed the Calvinist doctrine of salvation and whose teachings were rejected at the Synod of Dort in 1618–19. And yet, even he agreed that God has to do something to make it possible for a person to come to Christ. In a narrow sense, even Arminius would say that the Spirit must work in a person before he can choose Christ. However, Arminius' understanding of what the Holy Spirit does here differs radically from the Augustinian tradition that was carried forward in the Reformation. Arminius says that God makes people able. However, in his view, even when God gives us the grace to come to Christ, we still have the ability to refuse that grace. Some people accept that grace (the assistance to come to Christ), while other people reject the help. Ultimately, the reason one person perishes and another person is saved is that one person cooperates with grace and is saved while the other person refuses to cooperate with grace and perishes. It all comes down to a person's choice.

The problem with this kind of thinking is that in the end someone who is saved must say that he is saved, while his neighbor isn't, because the one who believes is more righteous. The one who believes has done the right thing to get saved, while his neighbor has not—and now he has something to boast about. But the Bible says that we who believe may not boast before God, because it is God and God alone who enabled us to choose Christ (cf. 1 Cor. 4:7; Eph. 2:8–10). He actually worked faith in our hearts, not only giving us release from prison, but giving us the positive inclination by which we then willingly came to Christ. Since the fall, the human will has been in bondage to sin, until liberated by God. He gives us what we lack, a positive desire for Christ.

The next chapter of the confession is on effectual calling. When the Holy Spirit gives us the grace of regeneration, its purpose is to bring us to Christ. God does not just give us the ability to come to Christ (John 6:65), but He also draws us to Him: "No one can come to me unless the Father who sent me draws him" (v. 44). Many evangelicals look at that text and say: "That means they will never come on their own initiative unless they are enticed or lured or encouraged or wooed. The Holy Spirit comes and woos people, encouraging them and drawing them like the flame draws the moth. But all that enticing and drawing is merely the external influence of the Holy Spirit. He will not invade your soul or shape your will. He will try to encourage you, saying, 'Come on now; it's a beautiful thing. Come to Christ.' Some will be persuaded, and some will not."

The Greek word translated "draw" in John 6:44 is the same verb that is used in the book of Acts when some men in Philippi dragged Paul and Silas before the authorities for casting an evil spirit out of their slave girl (Acts 16:19). Those men did not try to entice them to come before the magistrates; they compelled them to come. It is also used in reference to drawing water out of a well. We do not stand at the top of the well and invite it to come up; the water lies inert in the bottom of the well unless and until someone lowers a bucket into the water and drags it up to the surface.

Jesus' point in John 6:44 is that people cannot come to Him unless they are compelled to come by the Father—unless God drags them. However, it is important to note that for those of us who are in Christ, God did not drag us kicking and screaming against our wills. This is because the Holy Spirit changed our wills before we came. Had He not changed the disposition of our hearts, had He not put into our hearts a desire for Christ, we would still be strangers and aliens to the kingdom of God, because our wills, while free from coercion, would still be in bondage to sin. Our wills, far from being free as some conceive of it, would still be slaves imprisoned to ourselves. Prior to conversion, our wills are enslaved to our dispositions, to our desires, which, the Bible says, are wicked continually.

That sounds like determinism. B.F. Skinner, in his book *Beyond Freedom and Dignity*, argued that human decisions are the result of materialistic determinism. He claimed that people have no control over their destiny and no real freedom, because their decisions are determined by the physical forces around and within. In truth, we do have freedom in the sense that we have the capacity to do what we want to do, but we are also subject to a kind of determinism, which we call self-determination.

Self-determination is virtually synonymous with freedom or liberty. To be self-determined means that we are not forced or coerced to do something against our wills; we are able to do what we want to do; we determine our destiny and make our choices, so it is the self that determines the will. But the problem is that the self is fallen and spiritually dead. It gives us desires and inclinations that are sinful. If we accordingly make sinful decisions, they may be made freely (that is, free from coercion), but they are still made in bondage to sin. Therefore, the capacity to make our own decisions does not give us the liberty we need.

4. When God converts a sinner, and translates him into the state of grace, he freeth him from his natural bondage under sin; and, by his grace alone, enables him freely to will and to do that which is spiritually good; yet so, as that by reason of his remaining corruption, he doth not perfectly, nor only, will that which is good, but doth also will that which is evil.

5. The will of man is made perfectly and immutably free to good alone, in the state of glory only.

Before conversion, we are free to sin; after conversion, we are free to sin or to obey God. In heaven, when we are in glory, we will be free only to obey. That is what we call royal freedom, the most wonderful freedom, where our choices will only be good. We will have no inclination whatsoever to do anything wicked or evil. The humanistic view, that true freedom means that we have an equal ability to go to the left or to the right, to do what is sinful or what is righteous, is a myth. It is not only unbiblical but irrational. We must rid our minds of that notion and realize that at the heart of this matter is original sin. Prior to conversion, we are enslaved to wicked impulses. But when the Spirit sets us free from bondage to sin, then we are truly free.

Of Effectual Calling

1. All those whom God hath predestinated unto life, and those only, he is pleased, in his appointed and accepted time, effectually to call, by his Word and Spirit, out of that state of sin and death, in which they are by nature, to grace and salvation, by Jesus Christ; enlightening their minds spiritually and savingly to understand the things of God, taking away their heart of stone, and giving unto them a heart of flesh; renewing their wills, and, by his almighty power, determining them to that which is good, and effectually drawing them to Jesus Christ: yet so, as they come most freely, being made willing by his grace.

2. This effectual call is of God's free and special grace alone, not from anything at all foreseen in man, who is altogether passive therein, until, being quickened and renewed by the Holy Spirit, he is thereby enabled to answer this call, and to embrace the grace offered and conveyed in it.

3. Elect infants, dying in infancy, are regenerated, and saved by Christ, through the Spirit, who worketh when, and where, and how he pleaseth: so also are all other elect persons who are incapable of being outwardly called by the ministry of the Word.

4. Others, not elected, although they may be called by the ministry of the Word, and may have some common operations of the Spirit, yet they never truly come unto Christ, and therefore cannot be saved: much less can men, not professing the Christian religion, be saved in any other way whatsoever, be they never so diligent to frame their lives according to the light of nature, and the laws of that religion they do profess. And, to assert and maintain that they may, is very pernicious, and to be detested.

Chapter 10 of the confession is titled simply "Of Effectual Calling." Section 1 is somewhat complex and lengthy, with many commas and semicolons.

1. All those whom God hath predestinated unto life, and those only, he is pleased, in his appointed and accepted time, effectually to call, by his Word and Spirit, out of that state of sin and death, in which they are by nature, to grace and salvation, by Jesus Christ; enlightening their minds spiritually and savingly to understand the things of God, taking away their heart of stone, and giving unto them a heart of flesh; renewing their wills, and, by his almighty power, determining them to that which is good, and effectually drawing them to Jesus Christ: yet so, as they come most freely, being made willing by his grace.

This section is a good example of the remarkable clarity and precision of the confession. The gracious operation of the Holy Spirit on our hearts and minds, by which we are brought savingly to Christ, cannot be expressed any more precisely and carefully than it is here. We are told that God effectually calls **all those whom God hath predestinated unto life, and those only.** Whom does God effectually call? The elect—and only the elect.

Effectual calling has also been called irresistible grace because of its inclusion as the *I* in the famous acrostic TULIP, which represents the five points of Calvinism. The five points emerged out of a dispute that occurred in the Netherlands in the early seventeenth century, when the so-called Remonstrants protested against five particular points of classic Reformed theology. They accepted that grace brings us to salvation, but they insisted that God's grace is resistible. The church responded to the Remonstrants and excommunicated them for their errors. The theological points defended by the church came to be known as the five points of Calvinism. Popularly, they were symbolized by the acrostic TULIP.

The term *irresistible grace* is somewhat inadequate because we are able to resist grace to a certain extent. Indeed, we are, as sinners, inclined to resist it. On the other hand, grace is irresistible in the sense that God's saving work overcomes whatever resistance we set up against it. In order to avoid the confusion that sometimes arises from the phrase irresistible grace, it is better to call it *effectual grace*.

In these days of high-tech industry and management, all the management textbooks talk about the importance of efficiency. In fact, the computer has made the business world much more efficient, due to the ease and speed with which information can now be stored and analyzed. However, Peter Drucker, a famous management consultant, makes an important distinction between being *efficient* and being *effective*. Sometimes we obscure that difference by using the two terms as if they were synonyms. Drucker defines *efficiency* as "doing things right." But he defines *effectiveness* as "doing the right things." There is a difference between doing things right and doing the right things. The more efficiently we do the wrong things, the worse off we become. It would be much better to do the right thing inefficiently than to do the wrong thing efficiently. The goal, of course, is to do the right thing right. We want to be efficiently effective.

No one is more efficiently effective than God the Holy Spirit. When the Holy Spirit comes to perform spiritual surgery on our souls, to bring us to faith, He is not only efficient but effective. The point of effectual calling is that when the Holy Spirit comes to change our natures, He has the power to bring the effect to pass. It happens. That is what we mean when we speak of effectual calling.

Effectual calling must be distinguished from the general call that goes out to everyone to believe the gospel. We are given the commission, as the people of God, as the church, to proclaim the gospel to every person, to the whole world. We know that faith comes by hearing, and hearing by the Word of Christ (Rom. 10:17). But not everyone who hears the gospel outwardly responds to it.

Many people hear the gospel and never seem to respond in faith. It appears as if the Word of God has had no effect in such cases. But the Scriptures tell us that God's Word does not return to Him void (Isa. 55:11). The proclamation of the gospel is an outward call and can by itself have no effect. But the call of God, when He works inwardly by the Holy Spirit in the soul and in the heart of an unregenerate person, is effective every time. That call cannot fail; it is the re-creative agency of God's power.

242 • TRUTHS WE CONFESS

When God created the universe, He did it by His sovereign, omnipotent power and authority. He did not simply invite the stars to shine. He did not woo the lights to come on. He said, "Let there be light," and there was light (Gen. 1:3). He called it into being. How effective was that divine imperative? How effectual was that call? When God, through His creative agency, called the world into being, it came into being.

Jesus raised Lazarus from the dead (John 11). With a loud voice, Jesus called him: "Lazarus, come out" (v. 43). He had been dead for four days. He was in the tomb, with no brain waves, no heartbeat, and no circulation; already his body was beginning to decay. But Christ called, "Come out." The instant Jesus said that, brain waves started, and Lazarus' heart began to beat. Blood flowed to every cell in his body. Strength returned to Lazarus' limbs and organs, and he got up and walked out of the tomb. That is the effectual call of the Holy Spirit. It is the same power that is unleashed in re-creation or redemption.

There are particular aspects of the call. He is pleased, in his appointed and accepted time, effectually to call, by his Word and Spirit, out of that state of sin and death, in which they are by nature, to grace and salvation, by Jesus Christ; enlightening their minds spiritually and savingly to understand the things of God. The effectual call of the Holy Spirit in the first instance provides a divine and supernatural light, a light that is not possessed by unregenerate people.

Jonathan Edwards became famous through an early sermon that he preached titled "A Divine and Supernatural Light Which Lighteth the Soul." Edwards probed this element of effectual calling, which is complicated when we come to the Scriptures. In Romans 1, for example, we are told by the Apostle Paul that one of the reasons why the wrath of God is revealed to the whole human race is that God has plainly revealed Himself to everyone. Every human being suppresses that general knowledge that God provides. People twist it and distort it and begin to serve and worship the creature rather than the Creator. The creature refuses to honor God as God; neither is he grateful. Because of this, the wrath of God is revealed. Paul says: "For his invisible attributes, namely, his eternal power and divine nature, have been clearly perceived, ever since the creation of the world, in the things that have been made. So they are without excuse. For although they knew God, they did not honor him as God or give thanks to him, but they became futile in their thinking, and their foolish hearts were darkened" (Rom. 1:20–21).

Here is where some confusion comes in. In the first chapter of Romans, Paul clearly says that the natural man has a knowledge of God; the revelation is clear. And not only is it plain, but it gets through, so that the sinner apprehends the reality of God, which he represses, exchanges, and denies, and for which he is everlastingly guilty. Yet when Paul writes to the Corinthians, he makes it clear that the natural man—the unregenerate person—does not know God (1 Cor. 2:14). Do we have a contradiction in Scripture?

There are different ways in which something can be known. In saying that unbelievers "knew God" (Rom. 1:21), Paul uses the Greek word *ginōskō*, which means "to know." It can be used in more than one sense, in a way that is similar to the Old Testament Hebrew concept of knowing. In Hebrew, a distinction can be made between cognitive awareness or intellectual knowledge of something and a knowledge that goes to a deeper level of personal intimacy. For example, Genesis 4:1 says that Adam "knew" his wife and she conceived. The Bible is not usually given to euphemisms when it comes to sexual relations; it usually speaks plainly and candidly. The author is not playing with euphemisms here but is saying that the pregnancy was a result of the most intimate form of knowledge that two people can have of each other.

When Paul says in Romans 1 that the natural man knows God, he is not saying that the natural man has an intimate, personal, saving, filial relationship with God. All he is saying is that man has a cognitive awareness of God. He knows that God exists, and he knows something about His eternal power and attributes, but he does not know God in a saving, personal, intimate way. In 1 Corinthians 2, Paul states not only that the natural man does not know God in a personal, intimate way, but also that he cannot know God that way unless the Holy Spirit enlightens his understanding.

This is an important point because it could be so easily misunderstood, reducing Christianity to mysticism and turning Christian apologetics into subjectivism. We can hide from our critics forever behind that wall of subjectivism, so we have to be very careful. It is true that someone cannot know the sweetness of Christ, the excellency of Christ, as long as his foolish mind is darkened, until the Holy Spirit illumines or enlightens his mind spiritually. No one knows the mind of God except the Spirit of God, and the Spirit is the One who searches the deep things of God and who communicates them to God's people.

There is a sense in which, if we know Christ, we have a knowledge of something that we can never communicate to someone else unless they, too, participate in the Holy Spirit. But we can present sound, rational, objective evidences about the person of Christ and about the Word of God. Even though evidences will, by themselves, never persuade an unbeliever of the truth, they will prove the things of truth. Calvin made a distinction between proof and persuasion. He said that the objective evidence for the nature of Christ is there, but if we give this objective evidence, however rationally conclusive, to a person who is absolutely, adamantly opposed to this truth, that person will not surrender to the truth. That person will not embrace the truth, not because he cannot understand it intellectually, but because he does understand it intellectually and hates it. He has to have his soul changed; he has to have the disposition of his heart changed. In this whole process of changing the heart, there is also a changing of the mind. What the confession affirms is that the Holy Spirit works on the mind to enlighten a person.

In the previous chapter, Jonathan Edwards' brief definition of free will was mentioned. The will, he says, is the mind choosing. Even though we commonly distinguish between the faculty of choosing, which we call the will, and the faculty of thinking, which we call the mind, we should not separate them to such a degree that we divorce the mind from the will, as if our choices were thoughtless. Edwards focuses on this and says that choosing involves an apprehension that esteems one thing better than another, so that at the very heart of choosing is an evaluation made by the mind.

If we do not want to choose Christ, and we have no desire for God, and if God is going to operate on our souls to make us willing to come to Christ, even though we were previously unwilling to come, would He not first show us the sweetness of Christ and give us that enlightenment that we did not have before? Once we were blinded by the prince of this world; our minds were darkened and dead in sin. We did not see the beauty of Christ until the Holy Spirit enabled us to see.

Remember, we are by nature children of wrath. We must be converted; we must be regenerated; we must be effectually called. The most dire warning in the whole Bible comes near the end of the Sermon on the Mount, where Jesus teaches that on the last day many will say to Him, "Lord, Lord, did we not prophesy in your name, and cast out demons in your name, and do many mighty works in your name?" He will say to them, "I never knew you; depart from me, you workers of lawlessness" (Matt. 7:22–23). It is always important that we examine ourselves. We are supposed to step back every now and then and ask: Is it well with my soul? Do I belong to Christ? We will never love Christ perfectly or love Him as much as we ought to. But if we have love for Him at all, we can be assured of our salvation.

However, we can deceive ourselves. The Christ we think we love may not be the biblical Christ. Can we read the Scriptures and know that the Christ who is set forth on those pages is the object of our affection? If we can say yes, then we must know that we could not have generated an affection for the biblical Jesus out of our fallen nature. The only way we can have any affection for Christ is if the Holy Spirit has changed the disposition of our hearts and given us an affection for the One whom we formerly despised. That is where Reformed theology can be very comforting in giving us assurance.

The Holy Spirit effectively calls the elect, **enlightening their minds spiritually and savingly to understand the things of God, taking away their heart of stone, and giving unto them a heart of flesh; renewing their wills, and, by his almighty power, determining them to that which is good, and effectually drawing them to Jesus Christ.** He illumines and enlightens the mind, exchanges the heart of stone for a heart of flesh, and renews the will. So the mind, the heart, and the will are changed by the sovereign power of almighty God and by His determinate counsel are effectively changed. He does not simply offer to change these aspects of our humanity and ask us to cooperate with Him. Rather, He does what He sets about to do. He changes that heart.

Does that mean that we are brought kicking and screaming against our wills into the kingdom? No, He does this in such a way that we come to Christ willingly, for He changes our wills. Whereas we were unwilling before, now we are willing, because He has illumined our minds. He has softened our hardened, recalcitrant hearts, and He has renewed our wills, so that what we formerly did not want, now we want. He created the desire in our hearts for Him. That is the graciousness of our salvation. All the debate over predestination, election, semi-Pelagianism, Calvinism, and Arminianism comes down to this question: Is conversion the sovereign work of God the Holy Spirit working monergistically—unilaterally—or is it a cooperative venture between God and us, wherein we cast the final vote?

The confession states clearly that the operation of the Holy Spirit in effectual calling or regeneration is the work of God alone. This is the divine initiative by which we are brought to faith. After He makes this change in us, we are the ones who do the believing, who profess faith, and who embrace Christ. We can do none of these things until and unless God first changes us.

> 2. This effectual call is of God's free and special grace alone, not from anything at all foreseen in man, who is altogether passive therein, until, being quickened and renewed by the Holy Spirit, he is thereby enabled to answer this call, and to embrace the grace offered and conveyed in it.

Do you remember the difference between monergism and synergism? The historic difference between Augustinian theology and all forms of semi-Pelagianism can be reduced to the distinction between these two words, and that is why it is important that we understand what they mean, in view of this section on effectual calling.

The little word *erg*—a unit of work—is found in the middle of both words, *monergism* and *synergism*. They have in common the same suffix. If you put *-ism* at the end of some harmless words, you can get into all kinds of problems. It is all right to be human, but it is another thing to embrace humanism. It is one thing to exist, another to embrace existentialism. The suffix *-ism* indicates some kind of philosophy or viewpoint.

Monergism and synergism are two conflicting philosophies about something that has to do with work. The prefix of the first word is *mono-*, meaning "one." When we speak of monergism, we are talking about work that is accomplished by a single worker.

On the other hand is synergism. We talk about synchronizing our watches or the dangers of syncretism. The words *synchronize* and *syncretism* start with the prefix *syn-*, which means "together with." When we synchronize our watches with someone else's, we set it together with (at the same time as) the other one. Syncretism is the blending or mixing of one religion with another one. The prefix *syn-* means "with" or "together with."

Monergism describes a kind of work that is accomplished by one person; synergism refers to a kind of work that is done by two or more people. These two words contain the essence of the difference between classical Augustinian theology and all forms of semi-Pelagianism. The issue is whether the initial work of our salvation is accomplished by God working by Himself or by God working with the sinner, changing his constituent nature, but requiring the cooperation of the sinner for the change to take place. Is our regeneration, our being made alive from spiritual death to spiritual life, something that God does on His own, or does He offer us the grace necessary to be reborn, grace with which we must cooperate?

Monergism sees the grace of regeneration as being operative or working grace. Synergism is cooperative, meaning that there are two or more people working. And so synergism sees the grace of regeneration as being cooperative grace.

A person who is dead in sin and trespasses has no inclination to turn to Christ. His will is held captive by his wicked desires, he is in bondage to his sin, dead to the things of God, and he hears the outward call of the gospel: "Believe in the Lord Jesus, and you will be saved" (Acts 16:31). For him to be saved, he must respond. He has to believe; he has to embrace Christ. But what has to happen before he will in fact embrace Christ? The disposition of his heart has to change. Does God simply try to persuade him to change his thinking, or offer him help to change his thinking? Does God do 99 percent of this, but leave the final 1 percent up to us to accomplish on the strength of our flesh?

Luther says that God does the work 100 percent. That is monergism. We are speaking here with respect to the first step of our salvation, not the whole process by which we are saved. We are talking about the initial position, where the change of heart has to take place. The first step, regenerating the sinner, God does by Himself. We are completely passive; we cannot respond in faith and embrace Christ until God first changes us. Once God has created faith in our heart, our faith becomes active. Regeneration precedes faith.

Why does this issue come up when the subject of divine election is being discussed? If regeneration is a monergistic work of God brought to pass by His sovereign power, why doesn't everyone believe the gospel? The answer is that not everyone who receives the outward call of the gospel receives the grace of the inward call of the gospel. If everyone who heard the gospel received the inward call, they would all believe.

Let's review the formula. Regeneration precedes faith. You don't have to have faith in order to be born again. Rather, you have to be born again before you can ever have faith. No one can even see the kingdom of God, let alone enter it, according to our Lord (John 3:3, 5), until he has been quickened from spiritual death by the Holy Spirit. The necessary condition for faith is regeneration. The Arminian believes just the opposite, that you have to have faith before God will effectively change you. They put the cart before the horse. At issue is whether God's grace is operative or cooperative, monergistic or synergistic.

The reality is that multitudes of people hear the gospel but reject it. Arminians say that God gives grace both to the person who responds and to the person who does not, but that grace is not irresistible. It is not in and of itself effectual; it is cooperative grace, demanding a synergistic response. They explain that those who cooperate with this grace are saved, while those who repudiate it are lost. In their view, election merely involves God's looking down the corridors of time and seeing in advance who will cooperate with this proffered grace. On the basis of this foreknowledge, He elects those people whom He knows will respond positively to His offer of grace.

The Reformers taught that when God elects people, He elects them not on the basis of what He foresees them deciding to do but rather on the basis of His sovereign good pleasure, that the determinate counsel of His grace may be shown forth and that His Son Jesus Christ may have an inheritance. God sovereignly determines to give the grace of effectual calling only to the elect. When that grace is given to the elect, it works. The monergistic grace of God brings to pass what He intends for it to bring to pass. This is integral to the whole concept of election and sovereign grace.

There is a connection between effectual grace, effectual calling, and the sovereignty of God's election. God works unilaterally and effectually to change a person's heart and bring him to faith, but He does not do that for everyone. When God reaches down into fallen humanity, He raises from the grave some of those who are spiritually dead. The problem people have is that He does not raise all the corpses from the tomb. Is there any reason why He should? No, He owes them nothing other than punishment. If He chooses to be gracious to some and gives justice to the rest, there is no unrighteousness in Him.

We enter the house of God as people who understand that once we were dead, and now we are alive. We were blind, and now we see. We had no affection in our heart for the Lord Jesus Christ, and now our heart pants for the Lord as a deer pants for the water. This is not because we pulled ourselves up by our own bootstraps but because God, in the great love and mercy that He has poured out upon us, has rescued us from the grave. This should overwhelm us with joy and gratitude. G.C. Berkouwer, a professor at the Free University of Amsterdam, once said that the essence of theology is grace, and that the essence of Christian ethics is gratitude, because we respond to Christ as people who understand that grace is truly graciousness, that we have not earned our status in His kingdom.

> 3. Elect infants, dying in infancy, are regenerated, and saved by Christ, through the Spirit, who worketh when, and where, and how he pleaseth: so also are all other elect persons who are incapable of being outwardly called by the ministry of the Word.

Remember that this chapter is about effectual calling, and effectual calling has to do with the inward operation of the Holy Spirit. There is the outer call, which is the proclamation of the gospel. And there is the inner call, which is the work of the Holy Spirit on our souls. Usually, we think of the effectual call of God as the inward call that attends the outward call. But this section is about those who have never heard the outward call. What about those people who live in a distant corner of this world where the outward call never goes? What about babies who cannot possibly understand the gospel? Does every single baby who dies in infancy perish? Is every person who has never heard the gospel lost?

The confession introduces this section about elect infants by affirming that God alone has the sovereign right and power to work when, where, and how He pleases, even on those who have never heard the gospel or who are too young to understand it. The first point is that God can save a baby while the baby is still a baby. The Holy Spirit doesn't necessarily withhold the grace of regeneration until a person reaches the age of accountability. The Holy Spirit can save an infant by changing his heart, giving grace, and applying the merit of Christ to him. The Westminster divines certainly believed that babies can be saved. They did not teach that all infants are necessarily saved; rather, they taught that only an undetermined number of elect infants are saved. Obviously, an elect infant is going to be saved, and any saved infant is elect, but the divines did not speculate on which infants those would be.

Reformed tradition has held that the children of believers are numbered among the elect and are saved. Babies who die in infancy don't go to heaven simply because they die in infancy. People assume that the reason they go to heaven is that they are innocent, but every baby is conceived in a state of original sin, is alienated from God, and is by nature a child of wrath. Nonetheless, we can be confident that the children of believers who die in infancy are elect. Our reason for this belief is the confidence that King David exhibited at the death of his baby (2 Sam. 12:23).

We can hope for the salvation of people who have never heard the gospel, but we dare not rest on it. God, by the power of the Holy Spirit, can choose to search out someone in a remote place in the world and change him. No one would argue about that. But does He do it? If He does, He must not do it very often. But whether He does or not, our marching orders do not change. We are to take the gospel to every nation, every tribe, every tongue, and every living creature. Our job is to proclaim the outward call. Paul plants, Apollos waters, but God alone gives the growth (1 Cor. 3:6). That does not release us from planting and watering. Our obligation, as the church, is to be actively engaged in missionary outreach.

4. Others, not elected, although they may be called by the ministry of the Word, and may have some common operations of the Spirit, yet they never truly come unto Christ, and therefore cannot be saved: much less can men, not professing the Christian religion, be saved in any other way whatsoever, be they never so diligent to frame their lives according to the light of nature, and the laws of that religion they do profess. And, to assert and maintain that they may, is very pernicious, and to be detested.

Look closely at this closing statement from the Westminster divines: **And, to assert and maintain that they may, is very pernicious, and to be detested.** That is strong language. It would be repugnant to most Americans, who are told that there are many ways to God, and that any claim to exclusivity is a manifestation of religious bigotry and a fundamental denial of the pluralism of our country.

As a young Christian in college, I had an English teacher who had been a war correspondent during World War II. She was hostile toward Christianity, and she never missed an opportunity to attack the Christian faith in her classroom. On one occasion, she asked, "How many of you think that Jesus is the only way to God?" She did not take a poll, but she berated those who thought that Jesus was the only way. In the middle of her diatribe, knowing that I was a Christian, she addressed me: "Mr. Sproul, do you believe that Jesus is the only way to God?" I knew that I was under the gun here. I also knew that if I said, "Yes, Jesus is the only way to God," I would incur the wrath of the teacher and the hostility of the rest of the class. I had to weigh that against saying, "No, I don't believe that He is the only way," because then I would incur the wrath of God. I remembered the words of Jesus: "Whoever denies me before men, I also will deny before my Father who is in heaven" (Matt. 10:33). I was terrified, and I sort of mumbled, "Hmmm, yes."

Well, the skyrockets that I had expected went off immediately, and in front of the whole class, in great agitation, she snapped, "That's the most bigoted, narrow-minded statement I've ever heard coming from anyone's lips." I did not respond, but after the class was over, I spoke to her: "You said that I am narrow-minded and bigoted and arrogant, and maybe I am. But I think you need to understand one distinction. If I believed that Jesus is the only way to God because He is my way, indeed, that would be arrogant, bigoted, and narrow-minded. But may I ask you a question? Do you think it is remotely possible that Jesus could be one way to God?" Not being a religious lady at all, she thought for a second, and said, "Well, I grant that's a possibility." I continued, "I am persuaded that He is the Son of God, and He is my Lord. He is the One who has declared that He is the only way to God. It was Jesus Himself who said, 'I am the Way, the Truth, and the Life. No one comes to the Father but by Me.' The New Testament declares, 'There is no other name under heaven by which men may be saved.' I did not invent the idea that Christ is the only way; it is integral and foundational to the teaching of the New Testament." My professor then said: "I can understand that you could be persuaded to believe that, if you believe in Jesus. But how can you believe in a God who is so narrow that He provides only one way and one religion? There are billions of people in the world who are religious and who worship God in their own way. They were indoctrinated into Shintoism, Hinduism, Buddhism, Islam, Judaism, Taoism, and a host of other -isms that are part and parcel of the religious experience of the human race." My reply was, "One of the things we learn from Scripture is that God requires that we worship God in His way, and that the fundamental sin of fallen humanity is the sin of idolatry."

In the first chapter of Romans, the Apostle Paul says that the wrath of God is revealed from heaven against all unrighteousness and ungodliness of men (Rom. 1:18). We struggle with the fact that God might have wrath. Yet, it is utterly reasonable for a God who is perfectly holy and perfectly righteous to be angry with unrighteousness and ungodliness. Those two terms—*ungodliness* and *unrighteousness*—are general terms. There are specific actions in the Bible that are defined or described as unrighteous. Any sin is an act of unrighteousness. There are also sins that are specifically called ungodly. They include irreverence and blasphemy.

In the context of Romans 1, when Paul speaks about God's wrath being poured out or revealed against all ungodliness and unrighteousness of men, the terms *ungodliness* and *unrighteousness* describe the same thing. God is not angry about two different sins—one irreligious and the other unethical—but about one sin that is both ungodly and unrighteous. Paul specifically describes it as the sin of repressing, suppressing, or holding down the knowledge that God has given of Himself in and through the created realm. Paul goes on to say that, from the creation of the world, the things of God have been clearly perceived through the things that are made (v. 20). God has manifested Himself clearly, but men have suppressed this knowledge and have exchanged the truth of God for a lie and have refused to honor God as God.

Paul is talking about idolatry, which is the substitution of a counterfeit deity for the genuine one, a refusal to honor God as God. Instead of giving God the honor that belongs to Him, we attribute the glory of the eternal God to the sun, or to animals, or to other created things. The first commandment in the Decalogue is, "You shall have no other gods before me" (Deut. 5:7). It should not be thought strange that the Christian faith, which is rooted in the Old Testament, makes a claim to exclusivity, when the very first commandment that God gave is "no other gods."

The history recorded in the Old Testament is the history of syncretism—religious blending. God gave the descendants of Abraham the promised land. When the conquest took place, God told the people not to intermarry with the pagans or to get involved in pagan religion. But they decided to combine a little bit of Yahweh, some of Baal, and a touch of Dagon. They had their synagogues, but they also had their high places, where they worshiped Ashtoreth and other gods. Throughout the Old Testament, the Jewish people repudiated the exclusive claim that God had upon them and dabbled in other religions.

The United States was formed in large part by people fleeing religious persecution in Europe. They came to the shores of America looking for a place where they could practice their faith without fear of government persecution. Therefore, they established the principle of toleration. Our founding fathers refused to establish one official national religion or church—unlike England, with its established Church of England. The fundamental right of the free exercise of religion was enshrined in the First Amendment to the U.S. Constitution for all who come to these shores.

We have grown up with the idea of religious toleration. However, equal toleration under the law does not mean equal validity in the eyes of God. A Buddhist in America has as much freedom to worship and to be free from persecution as a Christian does. But that does not make his religion just as true or valid. In fact, from the Christian perspective, his Buddhism is a profanation and an abomination to God because, instead of worshiping God as He commands to be worshiped, the Buddhist follows the teachings of Siddhartha Gautama (the Buddha), who is not the only begotten Son of God, Jesus Christ.

Muhammad, Buddha, Confucius, and Moses are all dead. Jesus is risen. There is a difference. Muhammad never died for the sins of his followers. Not Muhammad, nor Buddha, nor Confucius, nor Moses met the qualification of sinlessness; therefore, they could not die for their people. What is missing from other religions but that is present in Christianity is an atonement.

God has spoken clearly to us in creation and in His Word. He has provided, out of His mere good pleasure, a means of salvation. He has promised to greatly bless all those who place their faith in Christ. No one can say that He is too narrow-minded or that He should have done more. No one can say that He hasn't done enough or that He is unjust to require faith in Christ while rejecting allegiance to Muhammad.

When Jesus was put to death, God shook the world, and He removed the rock that stood in front of His tomb. He raised Jesus from the dead in order to prove to the world who He was.

The men who wrote this confession wrote it at a time when they were risking their lives for the faith that they were proclaiming. But they boldly wrote: Others, not elected, . . . cannot be saved: much less can men, not professing the Christian religion, be saved in any other way whatsoever, be they never so diligent to frame their lives according to the light of nature, and the laws of that religion they do profess.

What this affirms is that no matter how devout and obedient people are to their religion, they cannot be saved apart from the Christian religion. Let's go a step further: the more devout someone is in the pursuance of idolatry, the more exposed he becomes to the wrath of God. And, to assert and maintain that they may be saved through these other religions is very pernicious, and to be detested. How do we get to a degree of wickedness beyond pernicious? Not only are they pernicious, they are very pernicious. This view is not only pernicious but to be detested.

If we love Christ, we must detest everything that degrades or demeans Him. This does not mean that we detest the people who demean and degrade Him, but we must hate the demeaning of Christ and recoil in horror at the abasing of Him.

We need to clarify to people that God is not being narrow-minded at all. The question is not, Why has God given us only one way to be saved? The real question is, Why has God given us any way to be saved?

Of Justification

1. Those whom God effectually calleth, he also freely justifieth: not by infusing righteousness into them, but by pardoning their sins, and by accounting and accepting their persons as righteous; not for anything wrought in them, or done by them, but for Christ's sake alone; nor by imputing faith itself, the act of believing, or any other evangelical obedience to them, as their righteousness; but by imputing the obedience and satisfaction of Christ unto them, they receiving and resting on him and his righteousness, by faith; which faith they have not of themselves, it is the gift of God.

2. Faith, thus receiving and resting on Christ and his righteousness, is the alone instrument of justification: yet is it not alone in the person justified, but is ever accompanied with all other saving graces, and is no dead faith, but worketh by love.

3. Christ, by his obedience and death, did fully discharge the debt of all those that are thus justified, and did make a proper, real, and full satisfaction to his Father's justice in their behalf. Yet, inasmuch as he was given by the Father for them; and his obedience and satisfaction accepted in their stead; and both, freely, not for anything in them; their justification is only of free grace; that both the exact justice and rich grace of God might be glorified in the justification of sinners.

4. God did, from all eternity, decree to justify all the elect, and Christ did, in the fullness of time, die for their sins, and rise again for their justification: nevertheless, they are not justified, until the Holy Spirit doth, in due time, actually apply Christ unto them.

5. God doth continue to forgive the sins of those that are justified; and, although they can never fall from the state of justification, yet they may,

by their sins, fall under God's fatherly displeasure, and not have the light of his countenance restored unto them, until they humble themselves, confess their sins, beg pardon, and renew their faith and repentance.

6. The justification of believers under the old testament was, in all these respects, one and the same with the justification of believers under the new testament.

The doctrine of justification is the most controversial issue in the history of Christendom. It was the material cause of the Protestant Reformation, the issue that led to the most serious fragmentation of the Christian church in its history. The debates it raised in the sixteenth century were not over minor details of theology. Both the Roman Catholic Church and the Protestant Reformers understood that what was at stake in the controversy was nothing less than the gospel itself. When, at the Council of Trent in the middle of the sixteenth century, the leaders of the Roman Catholic Church condemned the Reformed doctrine of justification by faith alone and placed their anathema upon it, it was not their intention to place an anathema on the gospel. But if the Reformers were right, then that is exactly what they did, and they thereby anathematized themselves.

Luther declared in the sixteenth century that the doctrine of justification by faith alone is the article upon which the church stands or falls. Calvin used a different metaphor; he said it is the hinge upon which everything turns. At one point, when Luther was engaged in debate with Desiderius Erasmus of Rotterdam, Erasmus turned on Luther and attacked his position. Luther thanked Erasmus for not attacking him on trivial matters and expressed his appreciation that the debate in which they were engaged touched the very heart of the church itself. If Luther's assessment is true, and justification is the article upon which the church stands or falls, then it follows that justification is the article upon which we stand or fall as individuals.

Justification has to do with the justice and righteousness of God. God is just. Biblically, justice is always defined in connection with righteousness. To say that one is just is at the same time to say that one is righteous.

God is the absolute standard of all righteousness. As our Creator, He is also the supreme, sovereign judge of heaven and earth. The Bible clearly indicates that the One who is the judge of all is Himself perfectly just and righteous.

In one sense, that is very good news for us. To live in a world governed by an unjust being would be a dreadful thing to contemplate. We would have no hope for the ultimate triumph of justice in such a world. So it is good news for us that the ruler and judge of all things is Himself good and righteous.

In another sense, that is very bad news for us, because we are not just. The Scriptures make it clear that this just and righteous God has appointed a day in which He will judge the world, including all of us who are not just and righteous.

People today hardly get exercised about the doctrine of justification, which was a matter for which our forefathers were willing to die, and many did die. In Oxford, England, in the sixteenth century, Nicholas Ridley and Hugh Latimer were burned at the stake for their confessed faith in the Reformation doctrines, including the doctrine of justification by faith alone. On a particular street in Oxford, a tiny sign marks the spot where they were executed. I watched people cross the street paying no attention to the mark or to the commemorative plaque. Although people today do not get exercised about a doctrine like justification, it was the issue that changed the whole Western world in the sixteenth century.

Part of the reason for this modern disinterest may be our concept of the last judgment. The idea of a final judgment to which all people will be subjected has all but disappeared from our thinking, and even from the preaching in most of today's pulpits—despite Jesus' repeated warning that we all will stand before God, and that every idle word that we speak will be judged.

Here is the dilemma. If God judges people according to His perfect standard of righteousness, then those who are unjust will be in serious trouble. The psalmist asks, "If you, O LORD, should mark iniquities, O Lord, who could stand?" (Ps. 130:3). The obvious answer is that no one could stand. We are all guilty of violating the commandments of our Creator, and at some point, we will be called on to stand before His judgment seat.

Even people who believe that there will be a judgment often believe that God is so kind and merciful that He will overlook our sins and grant unilateral pardon and forgiveness, so there is nothing to fear. That idea is foreign to the New Testament. The sober warning of Christ and of the Apostles is that God, in His perfect judgment of us, will judge all men according to their works and will reward the righteous and punish the unrighteous. We can look forward to receiving a reward that corresponds to our merit or punishment for our demerit. That may seem fine until we realize that we have no merit of our own, and that all we will have to offer God on the day of judgment will be our demerits.

The psalmist declares, "Where shall I go from your Spirit? Or where shall I flee from your presence? If I ascend to heaven, you are there! If I make my bed in Sheol, you are there!" (Ps. 139:7–8). "You know when I sit down and when I rise up; you discern my thoughts from afar. . . . Even before a word is on my tongue, behold, O LORD, you know it altogether" (vv. 2, 4). The Scriptures reveal a God who is omniscient, so He does not need someone to give Him a list of what we have done. He knows everything about our lives.

We must not flee to the popular understanding that when God *forgives* our sins, He also *forgets* our sins. When the Scriptures tell us that He remembers our sins no more when He forgives them, the point is not that He has a sudden lapse in His divine memory. Rather, the point is that He does not hold what we have done against us ever again.

God's forgiveness is not automatic and universal, but it is part of justification. When a person is guilty before a righteous God, there is nothing more important than to understand how that guilt can be removed and how God's forgiveness can be attained. How can an unforgiven person become forgiven? How can an unjust person be justified or be considered just in the sight of God? There are not many issues in theology more serious than that. The controversy of the sixteenth century boiled down to this: How can we be saved? How can we, as unjust people, possibly be reconciled to a holy and righteous God? This is the greatest issue we face in our entire lives—the question of our personal redemption. Therefore, it behooves us to get a clear understanding of this doctrine of justification if we hope to survive the last judgment.

1. Those whom God effectually calleth, he also freely justifieth: not by infusing righteousness into them, but by pardoning their sins, and by accounting and accepting their persons as righteous; not for anything wrought in them, or done by them, but for Christ's sake alone; nor by imputing faith itself, the act of believing, or any other evangelical obedience to them, as their righteousness; but by imputing the obedience and satisfaction of Christ unto them, they receiving and resting on him and his righteousness, by faith; which faith they have not of themselves, it is the gift of God.

There is enough in this one paragraph to warrant the writing of an entire book. Let us consider what the central thrust of this paragraph is. The Westminster Confession sets forth the Protestant doctrine of justification against the background of the Roman Catholic doctrine of justification. After all the serious efforts to reach a compromise agreement ended in the sixteenth century, the chief question upon which the two sides could never agree was this: What is the ground of a sinner's justification before God? That is, on what basis will God pardon or declare righteous a sinful person in His sight?

The dispute came down to two different words: *infusion* and *imputation*. The difference between infusion and imputation is basically the difference between the Roman Catholic view of justification and the Protestant view of justification. One of the best ways to learn the distinctives of Reformed theology is first to learn classic Roman Catholic theology. You cannot really understand Protestant thought until you understand what the Reformers were protesting against.

For Rome, the meaning of *justification* was to be found, first of all, in the Latin root of that word. The English word *justification* is the translation of the Greek word *dikaiosunē*. But the English word came into our language from the Latin verb *iustificare*. That Latin word combines two root words to make one word. *Iustus* means "justice" or "righteousness." And *facere* means "to make" or "to do." So *iustificare* means, literally, "to make just" or "to make righteous." This concept had a profound meaning under Roman Catholic law, having to do with the rehabilitation of unrighteous or unjust people. A person is justified when he is changed from being unjust to being just.

Roman Catholicism worked on the assumption that what happens in justification is that an unjust person is changed and made righteous. The fundamental thesis of Rome was this: God will never declare a person to be righteous until that person actually is righteous. That is the worst of all possible news, for it means that before we can be justified, we must first be sanctified, and a person who still sins cannot enter heaven. That would leave us without any hope of heaven at all.

However, Rome said that God understands that man does not have the capacity in and of himself to make himself righteous. As a parenthetical statement, we should note that the first three canons of anathema at the Council of Trent were directed against the ancient Pelagian heresy, which taught that original sin is not part of our human condition, that we are not born in a state of corruption, and that we have the power in and of ourselves to live a life of perfect obedience. According to Pelagius, some people have in fact achieved sinless lives. For Pelagius, grace is not necessary to enter heaven. He was not opposed to grace, for he argued that grace facilitates redemption in the sense that it makes it easier, but he did not deem it a necessary condition. Grace is not absolutely required, because we have the innate moral ability to get into heaven by our good works. Although Pelagius was condemned early in the fourth century, he was condemned again at the Council of Trent, along with the Protestants. Thus, Rome was not saying that people can work their way into heaven on their own, by their own power.

There are well-meaning Protestants who mistakenly say that Roman Catholics believe in justification by works, while Protestants believe in justification by faith. The Roman church does not believe that a person is justified by works without faith or by merit without grace. They grant that we are fallen, that we are unjust, and that we do not have the power within ourselves to become good enough to pass the bar of God's final judgment. In order for that to happen, according to Rome, we must receive grace through their sacramental system, beginning with baptism.

The Roman church explains it this way: In baptism, the grace of justification, sometimes called the grace of the righteousness of Christ, is poured into the soul. This is called infusion. Without the assistance of the grace of justification, a person cannot be saved. Roman Catholicism teaches that we need to have the righteousness of Christ infused into our souls in order to be saved.

To be saved, several things have to happen. First, we must cooperate with, and assent to, this grace to such a degree that righteousness truly inheres within us. This grace is necessary, but its presence alone is not enough for salvation. We must cooperate with it, agree to it, and work with it to such a degree that righteousness is truly in us. When that happens, we are placed in a state of justification before God. We remain in that state as long as we do not commit a mortal sin. Mortal sins are so serious that they kill the infused grace in the soul and leave a person in an unjustified state. If a person dies in a state of mortal sin, he is damned.

One might think that if the grace that is infused in baptism is completely lost, the remedy would be to get rebaptized and be reinfused with grace. But Rome does not practice rebaptism. They say that there is an indelible mark placed on the soul in baptism, and so one need not be rebaptized. Instead, the way to be rejustified, if we commit mortal sin, is through the sacrament of penance. In penance, we receive a renewed infusion of grace, and if we cooperate with it, we can be restored to a state of grace.

If we die without mortal sin on our souls, but we have lesser, or venial, sins, we will not go to hell, but neither will we go to heaven. Instead, we will go to purgatory, where we may remain for five minutes or five million years, depending upon how many imperfections remain in our lives. Purgatory is called the place of purging, where the dross is burned away from the gold until we become righteous enough to enter heaven. Heaven is available only when we have enough inherent righteousness.

The controversy in the sixteenth century initially focused not on baptism but on penance, and it started innocuously enough. The church needed a large sum of money to build St. Peter's Basilica in Rome. So the pope authorized indulgences for those who contributed to the building program. What is an indulgence? In the Roman Catholic view, the church, specifically the pope, has the power to dispense forgiveness or pardon from required punishment. The pope can do this by issuing an indulgence, which reduces a person's sentence in purgatory.

The pope does not do this gratuitously. A moral price must be paid for the reduction of time in purgatory. In other words, if we have a certain level of demerits on our accounts, we cannot get out of purgatory until we have made up for those demerits. The church can grant a transfer of merit from somewhere else to the sinner's account, sort of like a bank transfer. The treasury of merit is the depository of the Roman Catholic Church that contains not only the merit of Christ but also the merit of Mary and of the great saints of the ages. That account of merit contains what is called supererogatory merit for work that is done above and beyond what is necessary. Certain saints, such as Francis of Assisi, who at the time of their death had accrued more merit than they needed to get into heaven, had surplus merit to deposit into the treasury of merit. The church can make use of that merit for less fortunate people who have a deficit in their merit account.

Some people today think that the sixteenth-century system that caused all the controversy is now gone. However, in the catechism of the Roman Catholic faith, there is a reaffirmation of the treasury of merit and of indulgences. To this day, there are pilgrims in Rome who come to ascend the *Scala Sancta*, a marble staircase reputed to be the stairs from Pontius Pilate's palace that Christ climbed. Luther famously scaled the stairs and had a spiritual crisis during a pilgrimage. Pilgrims kiss each stair as they go up the stairs on their knees, saying their prayers as they go. There is a sign beside the stairs that explains how many indulgences a trip up the stairs is worth. The indulgence system continues.

In sixteenth-century Germany, an unscrupulous representative of the church named Johann Tetzel sold indulgences to the poor peasants in a crass way, which made people think that they could buy indulgences and get their relatives out of purgatory and into heaven. His slogan was, "Every time a coin in the coffer rings, a soul from purgatory springs." Luther was a theologian who understood the teaching of the church, and he knew that Tetzel's view on the sale of indulgences was opposed to the church's teaching on penance.

Restoration to salvation through penance requires confession of sins, repentance, and absolution from the priest (as a representative of Christ, who promises forgiveness to all who earnestly repent). The controversy in the sixteenth century pertained to the next step. In order for the sacrament to be complete and effective, works of satisfaction have to be performed. A priest assigns the work. It might be something as simple as saying five "Our Fathers" and three "Hail Marys," and a person, by that work of satisfaction, can earn what Rome calls *congruent merit*. That means it is fitting or congruous for God to reward this work of satisfaction in order for the person to be justified. There is also a higher merit, *condign merit* or absolute merit.

In the medieval framework, there were many kinds of works of satisfaction that people could perform in order to meet the requirements of penance. All of them had to be done with a proper motive of humility and an honest desire to manifest one's repentance, not as a commercial transaction to purchase salvation. When Rome authorized contributions to St. Peter's to be used as indulgences, it authorized it as part of the sacrament of penance, as part of the giving of alms, with the proviso that the transaction had to be motivated by a proper spirit.

Tetzel failed to make the church's position clear to the peasants. He received a commission, and he wanted to get as many ducats as he could into that pot. Initially, Luther tried to correct the abuse, but when he analyzed it, he began to raise questions about the whole system of purgatory and of a treasury of merit. He pondered such questions as, If the pope has at his disposal a treasury of merit, why doesn't he just use it to let everyone out of purgatory?

This led to a discussion of justification and the idea of being justified by infused grace. Luther understood Rome to be saying that justification was by the sacraments rather than by faith, as the New Testament taught. Luther and the Reformers asserted that a person can be justified only if he possesses perfect righteousness in the sight of God. The only perfect righteousness was achieved by Christ in His life of perfect obedience. Therefore, the only objective merit in God's sight is the merit that Christ earned in and through His own obedience.

It is not the righteousness of Christ working in us that justifies us. It is the righteousness of Christ that He worked in His own life, which God now counts toward us. God transfers righteousness from the account of Christ to the account of everyone who believes. In justification, there is a double transfer. Our sin was transferred to Christ on the cross; His righteousness is transferred to us. He was not punished by God for any wickedness or sin in His own life. He was the Lamb without blemish. He had no sin. And yet, the full wrath of God was poured out upon Christ because our sins were imputed to Him. That is, our sins were legally transferred from our account to His account.

To *impute* means "to account," "to reckon," "to deem," "to transfer legally." In Genesis 15, God promises to Abraham that he will be the father of a great nation. We read, "Abraham believed God, and it was counted to him as righteousness" (Rom. 4:3). This is the first clear example in Scripture of the doctrine of justification by faith alone. Abraham was reckoned or counted to be righteous the moment that he believed. That is what Paul labors to demonstrate in Romans 3 and 4. Half of our salvation is accomplished when God imputes, accounts, or reckons our guilt to Jesus. Then He transfers the righteousness of Christ to our account when we put our trust in Him. Our sin is transferred to Christ; His righteousness is transferred to us.

Luther said that the righteousness by which we are justified is a foreign righteousness, rather than an inherent righteousness. It is not the righteousness of Christ *in* us; it is the righteousness of Christ *for* us. The righteousness by which we are justified is not our own; rather, it is outside of us. That does not mean that the Holy Spirit does not indwell us. When we come to faith, the Holy Spirit does indwell us, and Christ is in us and we are in Christ. But what is in dispute here is the basis for our justification. Does God look at some righteousness that we have cooperated with, in us, or does God look strictly at the righteousness of Christ that was produced in His own life for us? That is all the difference in the world. Rome talks about the increase of justification, and we talk about the increase of sanctification. Our justification cannot be increased or diminished. Because the righteousness by which we are justified is Christ's righteousness, it is perfect. There is nothing that we can do to add to the righteousness of Christ or to subtract from the righteousness of Christ. We have to receive that righteousness by faith, not through the sacraments.

2. Faith, thus receiving and resting on Christ and his righteousness, is the alone instrument of justification: yet is it not alone in the

> person justified, but is ever accompanied with all other saving
> graces, and is no dead faith, but worketh by love.

In the previous section, we examined the difference between the *imputation* of the righteousness of Christ, which is the Reformed view, and
the *infusion* of the righteousness of Christ, which is the Roman Catholic
view. We read this statement in section 2: Faith, thus receiving and resting
on Christ and his righteousness, is the alone instrument of justification.
Let's stop at this point and spend some time on this affirmation.

The Reformation doctrine of justification is frequently summed up
in the slogan *sola fide*, which means "by faith alone." The phrase *sola fide*
stands for the teaching that justification is by faith alone.

The Roman Catholic Church, historically, has also taught that justification is by faith. They say that faith is the initial stage of justification.
It is the foundation and root of our justification.

Rome insists on the necessity of faith for justification. So the *fide*
in *sola fide* is clearly affirmed by Rome. What is not affirmed by Rome
is the *sola*, because even though faith is the initiation, the foundation,
and the root of justification, its mere presence is not enough to effect
justification. There must be something besides faith in order for us to be
justified—a necessary condition. A necessary condition is something that
must be present in order for an effect or consequence to follow, but its
presence does not guarantee the result.

For example, under normal circumstances, a necessary condition for
fire is the presence of oxygen. But, fortunately for us, the mere presence
of oxygen is not enough to cause a fire. If it were, we would catch on fire
every time we took a breath of air. So we distinguish between a *necessary*
condition and a *sufficient* condition. A sufficient condition absolutely
guarantees that the result will follow.

Given that distinction, we can see the difference between the Roman
Catholic view and the Reformation view of the relationship between
faith and justification. In the Roman view, faith is a necessary condition
for justification, not a sufficient condition for it. In the Protestant view,
faith is not only a necessary condition but also a sufficient condition for
justification. That is, when we put our faith and trust in Christ, God
will most surely declare us justified in His sight. The Reformation view,

which is the biblical view, is that if faith is present, justification is inevitably present as well.

What is unthinkable in the Reformation view is that we could have faith without justification. We cannot have justification without faith, and we cannot have faith without justification. Rome says that we cannot have justification without faith, but we can have faith without justification. We can keep our faith but commit a mortal sin that will destroy the grace of justification, so that we will be damned (without proper penance). But for the Reformers, the mere possession of genuine faith is all that is required in order for us to receive the grace and maintain the state of justification.

The confession says this: Faith, thus receiving and resting on Christ and his righteousness, is the alone instrument of justification. An instrument is a tool that is used for a particular purpose. When the framers of the Westminster Confession wrote that faith is the alone instrument of justification, they were aware of the sixteenth-century dispute regarding the instrumental cause of justification. It is necessary to have a clear understanding of this doctrine—the instrumental cause of justification—because it is about how we are saved.

The term *instrumental cause* goes back in history to the fourth century before Christ, to the philosophy of Aristotle. He was concerned to explain motion and change. In that process, he tried to isolate various causes that contribute to something's change of state or status. How does that relate to our question here? We, by nature, are not justified. We are unjust, and our status before God is that we deserve his unmitigated wrath. We need a change of our status, from a state of damnation to a state of justification.

We previously considered Aristotle's attempts to determine what causes change. He distinguished four kinds of causes: the formal cause, the efficient cause, the final cause, and the material cause. He did not include the instrumental cause. His four causes, however, formed the basis for the idea of instrumental cause.

He used the illustration of a statue that starts out as a block of stone from the quarry. Aristotle defined the block of stone as the material cause, the stuff out of which something is made. The formal cause is the idea in the sculptor's mind, or his blueprint or sketch, of the way that he wants the finished product to look. There has to be an idea before there can be a result. The efficient cause is that which brings about the change from stone to statue, and in this case it is the sculptor. He is the one who makes it happen. The final cause is the purpose for which the thing is made, which in this case may be to beautify a garden.

To these four causes we may add the idea of the instrumental cause, which is the means by which the change takes place. If the sculptor wants to change the block of stone into a statue, he has to chip away at the stone to shape, form, and smooth it. His chisel and his hammer are the instruments, the means by which the change is wrought. In English, we often indicate means with the words *by* and *through*.

When the Reformers said that justification is by faith or through faith, they affirmed that the means or the instrument by which we are justified is faith and faith alone. The only instrument that we need, the only tool required to move us from a state of damnation to a state of justification is faith, but faith is not the only thing that we need in order to be justified. We also need Christ in order to be justified. That is, in order to be justified, we need His perfect righteousness and His atonement on the cross. Everything that is required by God to meet His standard of righteousness and justice has been fulfilled objectively in and through the work of Christ. He has done it all. The whole Roman Catholic–Protestant debate on justification is not over the objective work of Christ so much as it is over how we receive the benefits of His work. How is the objective work of Christ subjectively appropriated? The answer that the Reformers gave, based on the teaching of the Apostle Paul, was "in and through, or by and through, faith alone." But it is not faith alone that saves us. When we say that justification is by faith alone, we are saying that justification is by and through our faith in Christ alone.

The instrumental cause of justification, according to Rome, is baptism and penance. Rome defines these sacraments as the instruments by and through which a person is justified. The difference is between salvation that is accomplished sacerdotally (that is, through the church's administration of the sacraments) and salvation that is experienced through faith in Christ alone. This is all the difference in the world. The confession says that faith is the only instrument of justification because it is through faith alone that we rest on and receive the righteousness of Christ. The righteousness of Christ, the benefits of His atonement, the objective merit or grounds of our justification, are freely offered to anyone who believes. "The righteous shall live by faith" (Rom. 1:17). We are justified not by faith plus works but by faith alone. All that is needed to enter the kingdom of God is faith or trust in the work of Christ alone.

Faith is not the grounds of our justification. The grounds of our justification is the righteousness of Christ, His merit. The Reformers said that the meritorious cause of our justification is the righteousness of Christ alone. The instrumental cause of our justification is faith, but when we say that we are justified by faith alone, we do not mean that faith is a meritorious work that adds anything to the ground of our justification.

What difference does that make practically? There are people who say they believe in justification by faith alone but who rely on their faith as if it were meritorious or a good work that will satisfy the demands of God's justice. The fact that a person possesses faith adds no merit to his account. It adds infinite merit to his account by imputation, but it is the merit of Christ that is imputed to him. We can receive Christ's merit only by faith, and there is no merit to that. The only One who can save us is Christ, and the only way we can get access to Him is through faith. We do not rest on anything else in our lives except Christ and His righteousness for our salvation.

The end of section 1 of chapter 11 of the confession reads, ... but by imputing the obedience and satisfaction of Christ unto them, they receiving and resting on him and his righteousness, by faith; which faith they have not of themselves, it is the gift of God. A gift, by definition, is not something earned or bought but something received gratuitously through the benevolence of someone else. If faith is a gift of God, we have nothing about which to boast.

Anyone who is a self-conscious evangelical, or who has any understanding of what evangelicalism is, will affirm the doctrine of justification by faith alone. But only a small percentage of these people will acknowledge that they are justified only because God, from the foundation of the earth, sovereignly chose to redeem them. Most evangelicals will say that

God, from the beginning, looked down the corridors of time from all eternity and saw which people, when they heard the offer of the gospel, would say yes and which people would say no. God then elected those whom He knew ahead of time would say yes but did not elect those whom He knew ahead of time would say no. In this view, it is up to each person to decide whether to believe and be justified.

Now let's ask this question: Can we believe that last statement and at the same time believe that faith is a gift? No, because we would have to say that God knows from all eternity—and He does—to whom He will give that gift and on that basis elects them. That is a reversal of the order. People are elected to receive the gift because He is the giver. If God's gift were dependent upon anything that we did, it would not be gratuitous and we would have something about which to boast. But the Apostle Paul insists that we have nothing about which to boast. He taught *sola fide* and *sola gratia*. We are saved by grace through faith. "For by grace you have been saved through faith. And this is not your own doing; it is the gift of God" (Eph. 2:8). When Paul is finished, he banishes works altogether. Reformed theology is the only theology that consistently holds to that.

Let us review what the confession says: **Faith, thus receiving and resting on Christ and his righteousness, is the alone instrument of justification: yet is it not alone in the person justified, but is ever accompanied with all other saving graces, and is no dead faith, but worketh by love.** What is anticipated here is the Reformation formula, "Justification is by faith alone, but not by a faith that is alone."

The Roman Catholic Church believes that justification is by faith plus works. Rome says that we cannot be justified without faith and that we cannot be justified without works either, because faith alone is not enough.

In the Reformation view, justification is by faith alone. But the faith that justifies is not alone. That means that true faith, if present in the soul, will immediately and inevitably yield the fruit of good works. True faith is the instrument by which we are justified, and works flow out of it. Those works contribute nothing to justification, because the only ground of our justification is the merit of Christ. It is His work by which we are justified. We lay hold of the benefits of His work by faith. When we do that, we are justified. But true faith will manifest its presence in the fruit of a changed life.

The antinomian view, advocated by some within dispensationalism, is that it is possible to have faith and justification and never have any fruit. A person can be what is called a "carnal Christian," one who professes faith in Christ but may be involved in sin, sometimes scandalous sin. A Reformed person would call a totally carnal Christian a non-Christian, an unregenerate person. A person cannot be born of the Holy Spirit, have the gift of faith, and continue to live exactly as he lived when he was a pagan.

That does not mean that the instant we have true faith and are regenerated, we are perfect. However, we do come alive to righteousness and our lives do begin to change immediately. The change takes the rest of our lives to complete, and we will struggle all along the way. But the notion that we can stay completely carnal is one of the most insidious heresies that affects the Christian world.

Luther made it clear that the Protestant formula is justification by faith alone, but not by a faith that is alone. Luther said that the only faith that saves is a living, vital faith that yields the fruit of righteousness. A dead faith has no fruit and justifies no one. We are justified not by a profession of faith but by a possession of faith.

Chapter 11, section 2, concludes with this affirmation: Faith . . . is ever accompanied with all other saving graces, and is no dead faith, but worketh by love. This affirms the Reformation formula that justification is by faith alone, but not by a faith that is alone. That phrase, "not by a faith that is alone," had some undergirding. One was Luther's understanding of the teaching of James. Early on in the justification controversy, the Roman church used the second chapter of James so frequently to refute the idea of justification by faith alone that Luther began to wonder if James really belonged in the New Testament canon. At one point, he concluded that James should not be in the canon. When we discussed the doctrine of Scripture, I said there is a difference between one's view of the nature of Scripture and one's view of which books constitute Scripture. A person can believe that all the books of the Bible are inspired by God but then argue that a particular book does not belong in the Bible. That was the situation with Luther.

Luther later changed his mind and accepted the Apostolic authority of James. Yet, James 2:21 asks, "Was not Abraham our father justified by works when he offered up his son Isaac on the altar?" It would seem that James is clearly saying that justification is not by faith alone, but also by works. You can feel the weight of the criticism that was leveled against Luther at the Council of Trent in the middle of the sixteenth century. When the Roman Catholic Church responded to the Reformation doctrine, it made several references to the second chapter of James in an effort to combat the doctrine of justification by faith alone.

Luther had two problems. One was the exegetical problem presented by James. The second problem was that people misrepresented him as teaching a doctrine that gave people a license to sin. If all a person has to do to be saved is to believe, he does not have to amend his life or be righteous in any way other than through imputation. You can see how people would hear in this a license to sin. The Reformers had to respond to these issues.

Luther explained that the faith that justifies is *fides viva*. The word *fides* means "faith," and *viva* means "living." Luther said that the kind of faith that justifies is a vital faith, a faith that is alive. James, in chapter 2 of his epistle, criticizes dead or barren faith—one that yields no fruit.

Nonetheless, there does seem to be a real tension between Paul's teaching on justification in Romans 3 and James' teaching in James 2. Paul, in Romans 3, says that we are justified by faith, apart from the works of the law. But James says that we are justified by works and not by faith alone.

The problem is compounded when Paul, in Romans 3 and 4, uses Abraham as his chief example of justification by faith alone. He quotes Genesis 15:6, "And he believed the LORD, and he counted it to him as righteousness." Paul emphasizes that God declared Abraham justified the moment he believed, before he was circumcised, before he offered Isaac on the altar, and before he did anything else to obey the law of God.

When James makes his case for justification by works, his chief example is also none other than Abraham. James appeals to Genesis 22, where Abraham offers Isaac on an altar. "Was not Abraham our father justified by works when he offered up his son Isaac on the altar?" (James 2:21). Paul says that justification is by faith *apart* from the works of the law;

James is saying that justification is by faith *with* the works of the law. Paul says that Abraham is justified in Genesis 15; James has Abraham being justified in Genesis 22. What are we to make of that? Some scholars think the two are irreconcilable. They say that if James was written earlier than Romans, then Paul was writing to refute the error of James. But if Romans was written earlier than James, then James was writing to refute the error of Paul. Or perhaps the two men wrote without any knowledge of what the other had said, and this proves that we have multiple theologies in the New Testament.

So, is there any way to reconcile the two positions? Attempting to do so requires that we pay careful attention to the context of each passage and that we determine what questions each author is trying to answer. In Romans 3, the issue clearly is, How can a sinner be declared righteous by God, who is holy? But the question that James is addressing is different: If a man says he has faith but has no good works, will that faith save him?

The Bible teaches that justification is by the *possession* of faith and not by the mere *profession* of faith. Many people may tell us that if we have ever raised our hand at an evangelistic meeting or come down the aisle, that is enough to get us saved. It is not. It is virtually impossible to have genuine faith and never profess it. However, it is possible to profess faith and not possess it. James was acutely conscious of that. He had heard Jesus talk about those who pay only lip service to Him. So if a person says he has faith, but he has no works, that empty kind of faith will not save him. Genuine faith makes itself evident by works. James goes on to say in 2:26 that "faith apart from works is dead." Faith without works is not true faith, so it won't save anyone.

Rome teaches that faith and works together justify. Luther taught that faith alone justifies, but that if it is true faith, works necessarily and inevitably follow. Luther did not believe in justification by faith without works. There is an important difference between justification by faith alone and justification by faith without works. "By faith alone" means that all we need to do to be justified is to have faith; the moment we have faith, we will be justified. If it is true faith, then works will follow, but neither our faith nor our works contributes to our justification. The only grounds or basis for our justification is the righteousness of Christ, which is imputed to us. The only way we receive the benefit of His righteousness is by believing in Him. We are justified by faith alone, apart from any consideration of our works, but not by faith that is without works.

James says that faith is shown to be true faith by works. He is saying, "Show me your faith by displaying your works." Abraham shows his faith in Genesis 22. James was aware of what Genesis 15 says—that Abraham believed God, and it was counted to him for righteousness. Before Genesis 22, God of course knew that Abraham had genuine faith. But we can look only at outward behavior, and that is provided in Genesis 22.

Outward appearances are important. Jesus calls us to be discerning, and He says, "Thus you will recognize them by their fruits" (Matt. 7:20). But even that is not an absolute. Sometimes we can be fooled by the fruit, but God looks at the heart.

The verb *dikaioō* does not always have precisely the same meaning in the New Testament. It can mean "to justify," "to demonstrate," "to vindicate," or "to manifest." Both Paul and James use that word, but we cannot assume that they are necessarily using it in exactly the same way. Jesus once commented, "Wisdom is justified by her deeds" (Matt. 11:19). He is saying that wisdom is demonstrated to be wise when it produces good results.

Likewise, when James says that a man is justified by his works and not by faith alone, he is saying that the man's claim to faith is justified—that is, shown to be legitimate, demonstrated, or made manifest—when he shows good works. This is how we reconcile Paul and James. James says that only living faith justifies. Living faith is always vindicated or justified by the presence and outflowing of the fruits of obedience.

Saving faith, according to the Reformers, has three essential elements, without which there is no salvation. They are *notitia, assensus,* and *fiducia. Notitia* refers to the information or content of saving faith. What this means—and Rome agrees with this—is that faith must have an object. In order to be saved, we have to believe something.

We have all heard the idea expressed in our culture that it doesn't matter what we believe, as long as we are sincere. We might call this "justification by sincerity alone," and it is antithetical to the teaching of the New Testament. When the New Testament speaks about the necessity of faith for justification, it refers to believing some actual content. We have to believe in the Lord Jesus Christ. There are essential elements or truths that form the minimally required content to be saved, but it is hard to say how much a person has to understand about God, about Christ, about his own sinfulness, or about the cross before he can have saving faith.

In the Old Testament, Adam and Eve had very little information. Abraham had more understanding than they did, but he did not have all the information proclaimed in the New Testament. Abraham believed in the information he had, as sparse as it was, and God justified him. That leads me to think that the requirements for justification are quite minimal. On the other hand, if we reject something that is essential to the Christian faith, that can be enough to damn us. We may not understand all the nuances of the deity of Christ, but if we hear a statement of the deity of Christ and reject it, we are in trouble.

The first part of saving faith, according to both Rome and the Reformers, requires us to have faith in something. There has to be some information. When the gospel was carried to the gentiles, the Apostles did not have a textbook filled with information or even the Scriptures with them. There was an outline of the gospel that the Apostles proclaimed in the book of Acts. It is called the *kerygma*, and it was the essential core message of the proclamation of the gospel. It told of Christ, who came in the fullness of time, who fulfilled the law, who died on the cross as an atoning death, and who was raised from the dead. That minimal outline was proclaimed to the gentile world. It was *notitia*—information.

The second part of saving faith is *assensus*, "assent." It is possible to know what information the gospel consists of and yet not affirm its truthfulness or provide intellectual assent to it. So we must have not only *notitia*, the information, but also *assensus*, assent or affirmation that the information is true. To be Christians, we have to accept the truth claims of the gospel. We have to believe that Jesus died on the cross for our sins and rose from the tomb. We have to be convinced that these things are true. If we do not believe these things, then we are not justified.

But faith is still more than *notitia* and *assensus*. If we have a synopsis of the person and work of Christ and we say that they understand and believe it is true, that will not save us. James says: "You believe that God is one; you do well. Even the demons believe—and shudder!" (James 2:19). Sarcasm seems to bleed from the pen of James. The demons were quick to recognize Christ during His earthly ministry. Satan, in the wilderness, understood that he was dealing with God incarnate. He knew it was true, but he hated the truth. He opposed Christ.

In order to be justified, we not only must have the content and believe it is true but also must have *fiducia*—personal trust or reliance. James Kennedy tells the story of talking to a person about a chair. He explains all the characteristics of it. It has four steel legs, and they are well braced and so on. He asks the person, "Do you understand that this is a chair? Are you convinced that this chair is able to bear your weight and hold you up if you were to sit in it?" Kennedy says it is one thing to believe the chair will support you, but we do not really trust that chair until we sit down in it. It is similar to believing that Jesus is the Christ and that He is truly our Christ, able and qualified to save us. But until we put our personal trust and reliance in Him, He is not saving us. *Fiducia* has to do with the personal trust and reliance, as well as the state of the heart or the soul, which we call religious affection.

What happens when God gives us saving faith is not only that we trust Christ and rely on Him for salvation but also that the disposition of our hearts is changed. Previously, we were estranged from God, but now God is pleasing to us. Christ is now the object of our delight and our affections. That change of heart is wrought by the Holy Spirit, and for this reason anyone who has *fiducia* has had his heart changed by God. It is not possible to have a love for Christ and never show any fruit of that love. Luther and the Reformers were not saying that *fiducia* is the grounds of our justification, even though we cannot be justified without it. The merit for our salvation belongs to Christ. It is appropriated by faith alone—by all who trust in Christ. All who trust in Christ will also have the works that flow from it. Justification is by faith alone, but not by a faith that is alone. True faith, like Abraham's faith, will show itself to be true faith through its works.

3. Christ, by his obedience and death, did fully discharge the debt of all those that are thus justified, and did make a proper, real, and full satisfaction to his Father's justice in their behalf. Yet,

inasmuch as he was given by the Father for them; and his obedience and satisfaction accepted in their stead; and both, freely,
not for anything in them; their justification is only of free grace;
that both the exact justice and rich grace of God might be glorified in the justification of sinners.

Because of our sin, we are debtors to God and cannot pay our debt. We
are spiritually and morally bankrupt in the sight of God, and we do not
have the resources to pay our debt. When we studied the atonement,
we distinguished between a moral indebtedness and a pecuniary indebtedness. When we talk about our debt being paid by Christ, we are not
talking about a financial or a pecuniary debt. We are talking about a moral
indebtedness that Christ paid on our behalf. The Father is not bound by
justice to accept that payment. But, in His grace, He willingly accepts the
payment that has been made on our behalf, the vicarious satisfaction of
His justice by Christ. The confession teaches that moral indebtedness has
been fully discharged, so that at the heart of the doctrine of justification
is the concept of remission.

We have many words linked to the Latin words *mitto*, "send," and
missio, "sending." We know what missiles are. Sometimes we get letters
that are called missives. When we send people to a foreign field to represent Christ, we call them missionaries. Remission, then, means "sending
again" or "sending away."

This happens in justification. Because of the application of the work
of Christ to the believer, the believer's sins are remitted. They go into
remission and are sent away.

To better understand the relationship between Christ's death on
the cross and the remission of our sins, it helps to consider the Day of
Atonement in Leviticus 16. On that day, a goat called the scapegoat was
involved. The high priest laid his hand on the head of the scapegoat to
transfer, or impute, the guilt of the people to the goat. We use the term
scapegoat today for someone who gets blamed for something that someone else has done. In the Old Testament, the goat received the blame, or
guilt, of the whole people. The goat was then sent outside the camp, into
the wilderness, away from the blessed presence of God.

There is a vertical dimension to the Day of Atonement, where the blood of a bull and of a goat is sprinkled on the mercy seat, on the throne of God. There is also a horizontal dimension, where another goat (the scapegoat) is sent away, loaded with the sins of the people. Similarly, Jesus not only satisfied the demands of God's justice and wrath by taking God's punishment for us, but He also became the scapegoat who bore our sins and took them away.

Christ was killed under Roman law, not under Jewish law. He was killed as a curse, outside Jerusalem. In every detail of His death, He fulfilled the Old Testament principle and prophecy of the coming Messiah who would bear the sins of His people, be cut off from the presence of God, become a curse for us, and be sent outside the camp. He takes our sin away, and by His doing so, our sins are remitted.

Do we have to understand the doctrine of justification by faith in all its complexities in order to be saved? No, we do not; however, if we understand it and reject it, we will not be saved. We do need at least a simple, basic understanding of the doctrine in order to be saved. We must understand that we are sinners and that we cannot save ourselves, that we are in need of a Savior, that God is holy, and that we need to put our trust in something other than our own works—in Jesus and His righteousness—in order to satisfy Him.

The whole point of justification by faith alone is that justification is by Christ alone—not Christ assisting us, nor working in us, but Christ working *for us* in terms of His perfect, active obedience. He actively satisfied every demand of the law of God, and He passively received the punishment for our sin on the cross.

Imagine three circles on a chalkboard. The first circle represents God. If I were to indicate His sin by shading in an area of the circle, I would of course not shade any of it. The next circle represents Christ; again, I would not shade any of it, since He was and is sinless. The third circle represents mankind. If we were humanists, we would put very little shading in the circle—perhaps a few specks out around the edge. The humanist view is that sin is on the peripheral edge, but not at the core, of mankind. If we took the semi-Pelagian view, we would shade it all over, except for a small area of righteousness in the middle, unaffected by the fall; by exercising that righteousness, we can save ourselves.

In the Reformed view, all the circle will be shaded in. This doesn't mean that we are as bad as we could possibly be, but it does mean that sin penetrates to the very core of our being and touches every part of our lives. In Christ's circle, there is no sin, but there is merit, because He has obeyed the law of God perfectly and has earned the blessing of God. We have no merit, only demerit, so we should never ask God for justice. The worst thing that could ever happen to us would be for God to treat us justly. If a just judge treats someone justly who has no merit, and only demerit, that person will receive nothing but punishment.

On the cross, our demerit was transferred or imputed to Christ. He bore all our demerit or sin by Himself. Christ became the most obscene, filthy object ever set before God's eyes. Christ took on Himself all our guilt and pollution and became a curse for us. We cannot grasp what was going on in that transaction. It is no wonder that Christ said on the cross, "My God, my God, why have you forsaken me?" (Matt. 27:46). On that cross, in the sight of the Father, Christ was absolutely repugnant.

Once our demerits have been transferred to Christ, all the shading in our circle is removed in the sight of God. He looks at us and regards us as sinless, because instead of us, He sees Christ. Is this enough to justify us? We have said that if all Jesus did was to pay the penalty for our sins and do away with our demerit, it would only move us back to square one, back to Eden, where Adam and Eve were created. Though sinless, they were in a probationary period, and they had to achieve positive obedience in order to be given the reward of the tree of life. But they did not pass the test.

If all Jesus did was to take away our sin, then we, like Adam and Eve, might fall as they did. It is not simply that Jesus took our demerit; there was a double transfer. Our sins were transferred to Christ, and His righteousness or merit was transferred to us. The ground of our justification is not our faith but the merit or righteousness of Christ imputed to us. All that faith does is trust, lay hold of, receive, and appropriate that righteousness. Faith is our subjective response to the objective grounds of our salvation, and it rests upon a double transfer of our guilt to Him and His perfect righteousness to us. That occurs the second we believe—not a moment before, not a moment later. The moment we put our trust in

Christ, all that Christ is and all that He has becomes ours, and all that we are becomes His.

This happens that both the exact justice and rich grace of God might be glorified in the justification of sinners. This way of salvation demonstrates that God is both just and the justifier (Rom. 3:26). In this whole process, God's justice is displayed, because sin must be punished. He does not negotiate His justice, nor does He stop being just. He demands that the price be paid. He does not simply waive the debt. But He also demonstrates His graciousness by accepting Christ's payment of that debt for us.

> 4. God did, from all eternity, decree to justify all the elect, and Christ did, in the fullness of time, die for their sins, and rise again for their justification: nevertheless, they are not justified, until the Holy Spirit doth, in due time, actually apply Christ unto them.

Section 4 affirms that the Holy Spirit doth, in due time, actually apply Christ unto the elect. And when does He do that? As soon as we believe. In fact, it is the Holy Spirit who creates that faith in us.

> 5. God doth continue to forgive the sins of those that are justified; and, although they can never fall from the state of justification, yet they may, by their sins, fall under God's fatherly displeasure, and not have the light of his countenance restored unto them, until they humble themselves, confess their sins, beg pardon, and renew their faith and repentance.

The Roman Catholic view is that we are justified by faith and works, and the antinomian view is that we are justified by faith without works. In the Reformed view, we are justified by faith alone, which inevitably produces good works. But the antinomian view says we are justified even if we never produce good works. Paul addressed that when he said: "Are we to continue in sin that grace may abound? By no means!" (Rom. 6:1–2). When we experience God's free, gracious forgiveness of our sins, how can we possibly say, "I might as well keep sinning because I'm free from the law now"? Such an attitude is not the fruit of genuine repentance or of authentic faith.

This section of the confession says that God continues to forgive the sins of those who are justified. God does not wipe the slate clean and say, "We are going to start over again." He wipes the slate clean and keeps it clean. From that day forward, the only way we can possibly be justified is by the righteousness of Christ. We will continue to sin, and the remedy for that sin will continue to be the gospel. Because of our ongoing sins, we incur the displeasure of God and grieve the Holy Spirit. Our sins are all forgiven the moment we are justified, but that moment is just the beginning of a lifelong process of being molded and shaped into the image of Christ, the process that we call sanctification. God not only declares us holy in His sight, but He also begins to make us holy—a process that is not completed until we reach heaven. That is why we have an ongoing struggle.

> 6. The justification of believers under the old testament was, in all these respects, one and the same with the justification of believers under the new testament.

The last section in chapter 11 informs us that Old Testament believers were justified in the same way that New Testament believers are justified. Abraham was justified through faith in the promise, and the ground of his justification was the finished work of Christ. Abraham believed God's promise to perform this work in the future. We are living on the other side of the atonement, and we trust in the fulfillment of that promise. That is the only difference. The objective ground for Abraham's salvation, as well as for our salvation, is Christ and His work.

There are those who believe that the way of salvation in the Old Testament is different from the way of salvation in the New Testament. But that goes against the clear teaching of the New Testament, which teaches that Abraham was justified by faith alone, just as we are.

Of Adoption

1. All those that are justified, God vouchsafeth, in and for his only Son
   Jesus Christ, to make partakers of the grace of adoption, by which they
   are taken into the number, and enjoy the liberties and privileges of the
   children of God, have his name put upon them, receive the Spirit of
   adoption, have access to the throne of grace with boldness, are enabled
   to cry, Abba, Father, are pitied, protected, provided for, and chastened
   by him, as by a father: yet never cast off, but sealed to the day of redemption; and inherit the promises, as heirs of everlasting salvation.

When Paul gives his exposition of the doctrine of justification in
Romans, he says, "Therefore, since we have been justified by
faith, we have peace with God through our Lord Jesus Christ. Through
him we have also obtained access by faith into this grace in which we
stand" (Rom. 5:1–2). The alienation and estrangement that we enter into
at birth is removed when God declares us just in Christ. The first result of
our justification is a peace treaty. "Therefore, since we have been justified
by faith, we have peace with God." We have a tendency to underestimate
the significance of that. Peace in this world is always fragile. It is nothing
more than a guarded truce, and when the enemy rattles his sword, it can
explode into another conflict of enormous magnitude.

But peace with God is not like that. When a person is justified, he
receives a peace that passes understanding. Full-scale conflict can never
erupt again. With the peace treaty that God makes with those who were
formerly estranged from Him comes adoption. God is not an abusive or
brutal father. He is totally committed to the well-being and the preserving

of His children. We may displease Him, but once we are welcomed into His family, we are truly His sons and daughters, and there is no more war. We dare not underestimate the importance of that condition of peace that has been won for us by Christ.

Peace is the chief legacy of Jesus to believers. When Jesus died, He had only His robe, and it was taken from Him by the soldiers. He did not leave a large estate for His disciples or an inheritance of silver and gold, but He did give His last will and testament in the upper room on the night when He was betrayed. He said: "Peace I leave with you; my peace I give to you. Not as the world gives do I give to you. Let not your hearts be troubled, neither let them be afraid" (John 14:27). All who are adopted into the family of God have been granted this legacy of peace.

Christ is God's single heir by nature. He is the Father's Son. We who are adopted become heirs of God, joint heirs with Christ, and ours is the most valuable and rich inheritance that anybody can have. The inheritance is given by God the Father to His Son, and everything Christ possesses is given to us, as His adopted brothers and sisters, including the gift of eternal life. He is called the firstfruits of those who are raised from the dead. As God the Father has raised our elder brother from the grave, so He promises to do the same for us. It is an incalculable inheritance that God has preserved for His people, and at the last day God will say to His children, "Come, you who are blessed by my Father, inherit the kingdom prepared for you from the foundation of the world" (Matt. 25:34).

In the nineteenth century, liberal theology swept through the continent of Europe, then crossed the sea to the United States and undermined many churches and seminaries. A new science arose called the science of comparative religion. This new science sought to analyze all the great religions of the world and find the essential beliefs that were common to them. These scholars were looking for that lowest common denominator, that essential kernel of truth, that is found in all the world's religions.

Adolf von Harnack, for example, wrote a book translated into English as *What Is Christianity?* Harnack argued that the essence of Christianity is found in two principles: the universal fatherhood of God and the universal brotherhood of man. Ironically, those two principles are actually foreign to Christianity. God is not the father of everyone, except as their Creator.

When the Scriptures speak of God's fatherhood, they describe a filial relationship that exists only between God and His redeemed children. Only those who are in Christ have the privilege of addressing God as Father.

Another German scholar, Joachim Jeremias, studied the concept of fatherhood in Judaism. He described how the children of the Jews were taught to memorize several appropriate titles that they might use when addressing God in prayer. Noticeably absent from that list was "Father." Jeremias could not find a Jewish person in any extant literature who addressed God directly as "Father" until the tenth century AD. It was unthinkable in Judaism that anyone would have the audacity to address God in such a familiar fashion. Yet, in the New Testament, every prayer that comes from the lips of Jesus, except one, begins with Jesus' addressing God as "Father." That practice provoked the hostility of Jesus' contemporaries.

Jesus taught His disciples to pray, "Our Father in heaven, hallowed be your name . . ." (Matt. 6:9). Jesus alone had the right to address God with this kind of filial language, and yet He instructed His followers to do the same. We now take it for granted that God is our Father. That is why it is so insidious when people talk about the universal fatherhood of God. It is an extraordinary privilege that we can address the Creator of heaven and earth in terms of filial and personal intimacy.

When Christians pray out loud, they usually address God as their Father. It has become so commonplace that we tend to forget what it cost for us to be able to have such a relationship with God. The Bible speaks of a universal neighborhood, not a universal brotherhood. That is, every person is our neighbor, but only fellow Christians are the adopted children of God. Only if someone is in Christ is he our brother, in the biblical sense.

Chapter 12 of the confession begins: All those that are justified, God vouchsafeth . . . to make partakers of the grace of adoption. To vouchsafe to do something is to graciously condescend to do it. Almighty God graciously condescends, in and for his only Son Jesus Christ, to make all those who are justified partakers of the grace of adoption. It is always in Christ Jesus that God adopts us. Only those who are in Christ Jesus are adopted into the family of God.

If we read this too quickly, we may miss the fact that our adoption is not only *in* Christ but also *for* Christ. We tend to think that the only purpose of our adoption is to confer a benefit to us, but the confession says that our adoption is really for Christ's benefit. Because the Father loves the Son, He wants Christ to see the travail of His soul and be satisfied, becoming the firstborn of many brethren.

In His Bread of Life Discourse, Jesus declared, "All that the Father gives me will come to me" (John 6:37). God will not allow any of those whom He has given to the Son to be lost. He promises the benefits of adoption to all those who are justified, because they are the Father's gift to the Son. Christ's body, the church, is made up of His people, whom the Father has given to Him.

Our salvation is a gift. Our adoption is a gift of God's grace. It is not something that we earn or are entitled to. It is through the grace of God that we are brought into the family of God through adoption. And we, in turn, are the Father's gift to the Son. From all eternity, the Father and the Son were in agreement in this enterprise, and so the Father was pleased to give us to the Son, and the Son was pleased to receive us from the Father. The Son was so pleased about this gift that He laid down His life for us while we were still His enemies, so that we might be His brothers and sisters.

People who say that Christ died potentially for everyone, but not certainly and particularly for anyone, do not understand the whole drama of redemption. God guaranteed from eternity that Christ would have progeny. Those who believe in Christ are children of God because Christ died specifically for them.

Those who are justified God condescends to make partakers of the grace of adoption, by which they are taken into the number, and enjoy the liberties and privileges of the children of God, have his name put upon them. Everyone who is adopted into the family of God receives a new name. That is why we are called Christians. We bear the very name of our brother.

All those receive the Spirit of adoption, have access to the throne of grace with boldness, are enabled to cry, Abba, Father. This is a reference to Romans 8:14–17:

For all who are led by the Spirit of God are sons of God. For you did not receive the spirit of slavery to fall back into fear, but you have received the Spirit of adoption as sons, by whom we cry, "Abba! Father!" The Spirit himself bears witness with our spirit that we are children of God, and if children, then heirs—heirs of God and fellow heirs with Christ, provided we suffer with him in order that we may also be glorified with him.

In his epistles, the Apostle Paul frequently tells us that if we are not willing to participate in the humiliation of Christ or to be despised by the world for righteousness' sake, we will never participate in His exaltation. Jesus told us that if we are ashamed of Him in this world, He will be ashamed of us before the Father. We should add that if we are truly born of God the Holy Spirit and are adopted into that family, we will participate in His humiliation. We will confess Him before men and not be ashamed of your Redeemer. You will participate in His exaltation and in His glorification. Baptism, the sign of our inclusion in the new covenant with Christ, signifies, among other things, our participation in His death and resurrection, and his humiliation and exaltation.

The confession goes on to say that they **are enabled to cry, Abba, Father, are pitied, protected, provided for, and chastened.** All the adopted children of God are pitied by Him. The word *pity* usually has somewhat negative connotations in modern usage, but here it describes something positive: divine compassion. When God adopts us into His family, He cares about us. We often look for sympathy because we want people to care what happens to us. We can call upon the living God, and He will care for us. "As a father shows compassion to his children, so the LORD shows compassion to those who fear him" (Ps. 103:13). That is a precious aspect of our adoption. And we are not only pitied but also protected and provided for.

When Jesus spoke about how God cares for the plants and for the birds, He added, in effect, "How much more does your heavenly Father care to protect you and to provide for you?" (see Matt. 6:26–30; 10:29–31). David once remarked, "I have been young, and now am old, yet I have not seen the righteous forsaken or his children begging for bread" (Ps. 37:25). The Father provides. That is what the doctrine of providence is about—God's provision for His people, His protection of His people.

Those who are adopted are **chastened by him, as by a father**. This comes from an Old Testament proverb, the exact meaning of which is debated: "Train up a child in the way he should [or will] go; even when he is old he will not depart from it" (Prov. 22:6). This proverb is commonly interpreted to mean that if a child receives proper instruction, he will live a godly and productive life when he becomes an adult. This is a companion text to "Whoever spares the rod hates his son, but he who loves him is diligent to discipline him" (Prov. 13:24). The great lie of Satan is that if we really love our children, we won't discipline them. In fact, normal discipline is often considered "child abuse." But the greatest abuse parents can give their children is to let them do whatever they want without any correction, chastening, or discipline. A truly loving and caring father will rebuke, admonish, and chasten his children. Similarly, God says that He chastens or disciplines His children because He loves them (cf. Heb. 12:5–6).

God loves His children enough to chasten them, but notice the character of that chastening: **chastened by him, as by a father: yet never cast off**. The Father never writes us off. His hand can be heavy upon us at times, but it is the pressure of holy, fatherly, gracious love. It is not the punitive wrath that is received by the ungodly. This is one of the most important distinctions in theology, the distinction between the corrective wrath of God and the punitive wrath of God. Those who are in Christ never have to fear the punitive wrath of God. That has been taken for us by Christ on the cross. However, we still face the corrective wrath of God when He chastens us.

Not only are we never cast off, but we are also **sealed to the day of redemption**. One of the fruits of justification and adoption is being sealed by the Holy Spirit. In the ancient world, kings (and others) had signet rings with they put their indelible impression in wax on documents and decrees to guarantee their authenticity. Similarly, all those who are born of the Spirit and justified are sealed by the Holy Spirit for the day of redemption. God places His indelible mark on our souls. He puts His name on us and seals us forever.

Another aspect of this in the New Testament is that the Holy Spirit is given to all who are adopted. The Holy Spirit is like a down payment or guarantee, or like earnest money in the real estate market. Earnest money is paid when people want to buy a house and want to show that they are serious about their intent. If they do not go through with the deal, they forfeit that money.

This is the language, taken from the commercial world, that the Apostle Paul uses when he says, "You also . . . were sealed with the promised Holy Spirit, who is the guarantee of our inheritance until we acquire possession of it" (Eph. 1:13–14). We are given the seal and guarantee of the Holy Spirit when God gives us the initial indwelling of the Holy Ghost. That is a guarantee that He is going to take us safely home, all the way, until we are totally glorified in heaven. He will not take His Holy Spirit from us once He has bestowed Him upon us. The Spirit is a down payment; the best is yet to come and will be ours forever, an inheritance that God has promised to deliver to those whom He has adopted.

The final words, **sealed to the day of redemption; and inherit the promises, as heirs of everlasting salvation,** tell us that all these things come with adoption. They come when God takes home a child who was not His natural-born child but who is now His supernaturally born child, whom He welcomes into His family. That is who we are, if indeed we are in Christ.

Of Sanctification

1. They, who are once effectually called, and regenerated, having a new heart, and a new spirit created in them, are further sanctified, really and personally, through the virtue of Christ's death and resurrection, by his Word and Spirit dwelling in them: the dominion of the whole body of sin is destroyed, and the several lusts thereof are more and more weakened and mortified; and they more and more quickened and strengthened in all saving graces, to the practice of true holiness, without which no man shall see the Lord.

2. This sanctification is throughout, in the whole man; yet imperfect in this life, there abiding still some remnants of corruption in every part; whence ariseth a continual and irreconcilable war, the flesh lusting against the Spirit, and the Spirit against the flesh.

3. In which war, although the remaining corruption, for a time, may much prevail; yet, through the continual supply of strength from the sanctifying Spirit of Christ, the regenerate part doth overcome; and so, the saints grow in grace, perfecting holiness in the fear of God.

God the Father is holy, Jesus the Son also is holy, and yet when we distinguish among the persons of the Godhead, it is the Spirit who is called "Holy." In the economy of redemption and the functions that are performed by the persons of the Godhead, the Father initiates the plan of redemption, the Son accomplishes that redemption, and the Spirit applies the work of redemption to our lives personally. It is by the Holy Spirit that we are regenerated in the first place, through His indwelling work. He is the One who is working in us to effect our sanctification, to make us actually holy. It is not by accident that the Spirit, whose chief work is to bring us to a state of holiness or sanctification, is called "the Holy Spirit."

The word *sanctification* comes from the verb *to sanctify*, which means "to set apart," "to consecrate," or "to make holy." In the Old Testament, the high priest was allowed to go only on the Day of Atonement into what is called the *Sanctum Sanctorum*, the Holy of Holies. We see that there is a link between sanctification and holiness. What does the word *holy* mean in the Bible? What do we mean when we say that God is holy or that we are holy?

The easiest way to state this briefly is in the words of the childhood prayer that many of us learned, and that was a table grace: "God is great, God is good, and we thank Him for this food." Two things were ascribed to God in that prayer: greatness and goodness. There is one word in the Scripture that incorporates both greatness and goodness, and that is *holy*. God's holiness expresses the fact that He is greater than all His creatures. He transcends us and everything else in the universe in terms of His own majesty. When we speak of God's holiness, it is primarily His greatness— His self-existent, transcendent majesty—that is in view.

The secondary meaning of the term *holy* in the Bible has to do with purity. When we say that God is absolutely holy, we mean that there are no blemishes in His character. There is no shadow of turning in Him. The One who is transcendently majestic is also perfectly pure in all that He does. When He sets apart a people to bear His name, He says to them, "You shall be holy, for I am holy" (1 Peter 1:16). He is not saying to them, "You shall be self-existent, transcendently majestic, as I am"; rather, He is making specific reference to our responsibility to mirror and reflect His character. We cannot be God, but we can be like Him by imitating His behavior. This is our call to holiness.

Our problem, as fallen creatures, is that we are not holy in either sense of the word—transcendent or pure. We have been addressing this fallen condition throughout our study. During the sixteenth-century controversy regarding justification, Luther described the justified person as *simul justus et peccator*, "at the same time just and a sinner." He said that because we are justified before we are sanctified, we are declared to be just because God legally imputes or transfers the righteousness of Christ to our account while we are still sinners, so that a justified person is at the same time a sinner and just. We are just, legally and vicariously, because Christ's righteousness has been imputed to us, yet, at the same time, we are still sinners in terms of our behavior. We don't have to wait until we stop being sinners before we can be justified.

In the Roman Catholic view, however, God would never declare a person just until that person is inherently just. In that view, a person has to be sanctified before he can be justified. The doctrine of justification by faith alone affirms that we can be just before we are righteous. We are justified because of someone else's righteousness, namely, the righteousness of Christ. Are we still sinners? Yes. Are we changed people? Yes.

The changing of a person's heart is called regeneration. It changes the inclination of the soul. It involves a quickening from spiritual death to spiritual life. Until that happens, we are dead in our sins and trespasses. At regeneration, the Holy Spirit comes into us and does something to us, the fruit of which is faith itself. Before conversion and justification, we don't have faith or regeneration, nor are we indwelt by the Holy Spirit. At the moment of salvation, we are regenerated by the Holy Spirit, God creates faith in our heart, and we are indwelt by the Holy Spirit. These are significant changes. No one can have these supernatural things take place in his life without being changed.

The idea that a person can be justified and fail to show any fruits of sanctification is completely contrary to the teaching of Scripture. It is a misunderstanding of the doctrine of justification by faith alone. But the idea that someone can be justified by faith and yet remain in the flesh completely, without any change in his life, is also contrary to the teaching of Scripture. Anyone who has faith is necessarily a changed person, and thanks to the indwelling of the Holy Spirit, obedience is part of the justified person's life.

In the evangelical world, techniques have been developed to win people to Christ, such as the altar call, the raising of the hand, the saying of the sinner's prayer, the signing of a card, and other outward expressions of affirming the gospel. However, we have to remember that justification is by faith, not by the profession of faith. A mere profession of faith justifies no one. There are people who make a profession of faith and evidence absolutely no difference in their lives. Justification must be distinguished from sanctification, and sanctification is never the grounds of justification, but if there is no sanctification going on in one's life, that is the clearest evidence that there is no justification. Sanctification follows justification *necessarily, inevitably*, and *immediately*.

The power of the Holy Spirit makes it necessary for sanctification to follow justification. When Christ raised Lazarus from the dead, Lazarus was necessarily changed from death to life. A similar change is wrought in all who receive the benefit of the Spirit's work of regeneration. When Christ raised Lazarus from the dead, He brought the same Lazarus back to life. That was a radical change from death to life, but there was no new creation in the sense that the old Lazarus was gone and a new Lazarus was created from nothing. There was continuity.

The Bible says that before we are regenerated, we are biologically alive but spiritually dead in sin and trespasses (cf. Eph. 2:1–3). When the Holy Spirit regenerates us, we are the same people as before. We are delivered from captivity to sin, but our old nature, with its inclination to sin, is not eradicated. Regeneration does not take imperfect people and make them perfect.

Before regeneration, our direction is not toward the things of God, but when we are justified, our direction takes a dramatic turn. We still have a long way to go to finish the work of renovation, to reach glorification. Perfection is the goal of sanctification, but our conversion does not get us there. We are still sinners. When we are justified, sanctification begins necessarily, inevitably, and immediately. There is an actual change in us. The moment we are regenerated, a changed life begins. The change is real, and it happens instantly.

Luther said that the justified person is a sinner who is truly justified. He now possesses the righteousness of Christ, though he remains a sinner. Luther gave the illustration of a man who has been raised from the dead but is still weak, still mortal, and he remains so until the resurrection. Similarly, God will not make the justified sinner completely holy until the resurrection. Until then, he must undergo the lifelong process of sanctification, by which he is being conformed to the image of Christ.

This is important to note because the church has been assaulted in every generation by the heresy of perfectionism. It has appeared in different guises. Some believe that there is a second work of grace (beyond the work of regeneration) by which the Holy Spirit perfects and completely sanctifies a person immediately. Recipients of that second grace then become sinless believers in Christ. Others dilute the definition of sin to such a degree—saying, for instance, that it is only conscious or intentional acts that qualify—that they can claim to have been perfected.

This is not simply a problem of theology. The error of perfectionism is devastating to real Christian living. For a person to be convinced that he is without sin in this life, he must make a radical adjustment downward of the requirements of God. He has to discount what obedience requires and lower it to a level that fits where he is. At the same time, the person must have an exaggerated view of his own performance in meeting the standard of God's law. Usually what happens is a combination of these things. God's standards are brought down, and the person's self-evaluation is raised up. Both of these involve serious delusion. God does not lower His standards so that we can meet them. In His work of redemption, God raises us up to His level through Christ. But to think that one has attained perfection in this life is to deceive oneself. There is a failure to make an honest and sober evaluation of one's own performance, which manifests a lack of humility and a proclivity to become arrogant.

Conversely, there is a pattern in the lives of those whom the church recognizes as the greatest Christians of all time. The older they became, the more sanctified they became, and the more they were aware of their own imperfections. And that is the irony here. The more holy someone becomes, the more unholy he realizes he is. That is why Paul could call himself the "foremost" of sinners (1 Tim. 1:15). He was not indulging in hyperbole, but he began to understand, as Isaiah did in Isaiah 6, what true holiness is.

Paul says of those who commend themselves, "But when they measure themselves by one another and compare themselves with one another, they are without understanding" (2 Cor. 10:12). If we see everything that a hardened criminal does wrong and compare ourselves to him, we can think that we are very righteous by contrast. However, the true standard of righteousness is God's own character. If we judge ourselves by the standard of real holiness, we begin to realize how far short of the mark we fall. Scripture says, "The heart is deceitful above all things, and desperately sick" (Jer. 17:9). We can deceive ourselves into thinking we are more righteous than we are.

When the publican and the Pharisee went to the temple to pray, the Pharisee prayed, "God, I thank you that I am not like other men, extortioners, unjust, adulterers, or even like this tax collector" (Luke 18:11). He was judging himself by himself, and was puffed up with his self-importance and his self-righteousness. The publican, knowing his sinfulness, couldn't even raise his head up to heaven, and he prayed, "God, be merciful to me, a sinner!" (v. 13). The Pharisee's perfectionism was his undoing. Jesus said, "I tell you, this man went down to his house justified, rather than the other. For everyone who exalts himself will be humbled, but the one who humbles himself will be exalted" (v. 14).

The old doctrine of holiness, in its crassest form, that promised instant perfection has largely disappeared from the evangelical landscape. But the basic concept still has a stranglehold on the American church. It comes in different forms, with different descriptions and different terminology. One such is the Keswick movement, originating in England, which talks about the higher Christian life or the victorious Christian life. Most common in our culture today is the notion of the Spirit-filled life, which teaches that some Christians are filled with the Spirit, while others are not. The former group is living the victorious Christian life. One of the leaders of that movement said on television, "I try to confess my sins to God, if I have any."

In the Scriptures, the people who are called holy—saints such as Abraham, David, Peter, and Paul—struggled their whole lives to overcome the ongoing temptations to sin. Paul talks about a war that goes on in the Christian life between the spirit and the flesh (Rom. 7). Jesus says, "The spirit indeed is willing, but the flesh is weak" (Matt. 26:41). The word "flesh" in these contexts refers to our fallen nature. We do not escape from our flesh in this life.

When Jesus told Nicodemus that he had to be born again, He said, "That which is born of the flesh is flesh, and that which is born of the

Spirit is spirit" (John 3:6). Jesus also said, "The flesh is no help at all" (John 6:63). When we are regenerated, born of the Spirit, the Holy Spirit comes to this mass of flesh, this fallen humanity, and liberates it from the dominion of sin, changing the heart and making it come alive spiritually, but the flesh is not destroyed. Before, we were just flesh; now we are flesh and Spirit. When we get to heaven and all the remnants of that flesh are removed from us, we will have one heart and one will and one mind-set to please God and God alone. Only then will we become fully conformed to the image of Christ.

We want the future promise now. The doctrine of perfectionism is a premature grasping for the eschatological gift. That does not mean that we should not want to be as sanctified as we can be. But we should be leery of people who promise an easy path to sanctification and holiness. It doesn't work like that; sanctification is a lifelong battle. It takes determination to lay hold of the riches of God's grace. It takes diligent discipline, devotion to prayer, and a serious reading of Scripture. No one gets sanctified with five minutes of Bible reading a day. The Word has to be our meat and drink if we want to grow in grace. We don't get sanctified by going to church once every six weeks and neglecting corporate worship or fellowship or service. Through all these means of grace, the Holy Spirit works with us to bring us to spiritual maturity. All these disciplines are necessary and involve work. "Work out your own salvation with fear and trembling, for it is God who works in you, both to will and to work for his good pleasure" (Phil. 2:12–13). Growth in the Christian life is labor-intensive. We have to work at it, to study, to pray, to worship, and even after we do all of those things on a regular basis, we are still sinners.

We are called to be transformed people. Paul says, "Do not be conformed to this world, but be transformed by the renewal of your mind" (Rom. 12:2). He points to the renewing of the mind because if transformation is not in our minds, it can never be in our hearts. And if it is not in our hearts, it will never be in our lives. Paul is giving us a hint here that if we want to be transformed, what we need is a new mind. We won't live like Christ until we start thinking like Christ. To know what Christ thinks, we have to know the Word of God. We cannot dabble in it and expect to see changes in our life. It is interesting that the word for "repentance" in the Bible is *metanoia*, which means "a changing of the mind." We think differently as our minds are renewed.

1. They, who are once effectually called, and regenerated, having a new heart, and a new spirit created in them, are further sanctified, really and personally, through the virtue of Christ's death and resurrection, by his Word and Spirit dwelling in them: the dominion of the whole body of sin is destroyed, and the several lusts thereof are more and more weakened and mortified; and they more and more quickened and strengthened in all saving graces, to the practice of true holiness, without which no man shall see the Lord.

We have looked in an introductory way at the doctrine of sanctification in its broader categories. Now we will look at the confession itself. Section 1 of chapter 13 begins with these words: They, who are once effectually called, and regenerated, having a new heart, and a new spirit created in them, are further sanctified, really and personally, through the virtue of Christ's death and resurrection, by his Word and Spirit dwelling in them.

Notice that the confession begins its discussion of sanctification by referring first to effectual calling and regeneration. One of the things that the Westminster divines were concerned about is known as the *ordo salutis*, Latin for "the order of salvation." That is, in what order do certain things take place that pertain to our salvation? In Romans 8, Paul gives an abbreviated order of salvation: "For those whom he foreknew he also predestined. . . . And those whom he predestined he also called, and those whom he called he also justified, and those whom he justified he also glorified" (Rom. 8:29–30). There is a progression or an order of steps in our salvation.

The word *save* is used in Scripture in every verb tense in Greek, which has more tenses than English does. When the Bible speaks of salvation, it speaks of it in the sense that we were saved from the foundation of the world, and also in the sense that we were being saved, and then in the sense that we were saved at a distinct moment in the past when we came to faith. There are also past, present, and future dimensions to our salvation—we were saved, are being saved, and will be saved. Our salvation will not be fully completed or realized until we enter heaven and are glorified.

The order of our salvation has to do with the sequence of God's work of redemption on our behalf. When we talk about the order of salvation, the order is one of *logical priority*, not necessarily *temporal priority*. For example, we say that justification is by faith. How long must a person have faith before God declares him just? How much time must elapse between the presence of faith and the presence of justification? None, not even a nanosecond. There is no passage of time between the presence of one and the presence of the other. There is, however, a logical priority. When we are justified by faith, faith precedes justification, not in time but in logic, because the necessary condition for justification is faith. We are justified by faith; we are not "enfaithed" by justification. Justification is the consequence of faith; faith is not the consequence of justification.

In the confession, reference is made at once to effectual calling and regeneration. We see that faith precedes justification and that regeneration and effectual calling precede faith. Regeneration and effectual calling lead to faith, faith yields justification, and then comes sanctification, followed by glorification. Thus, the order, from a Reformed perspective, is: effectual calling, regeneration, faith, justification, sanctification, and glorification.

Most evangelical Christians believe that faith precedes regeneration. A person has to believe in order to be born again, and then comes justification. But Reformed theology says no one will ever believe unless the Holy Spirit first does a creative work in the soul of that person, to bring forth the faith. The terms *effectual calling* and *regeneration* are often used interchangeably, but at a technical level they are not exact synonyms. Regeneration is what God brings to pass in the soul of a person. It refers specifically to the quickening of the soul from spiritual death to spiritual life.

Regeneration occurs through the direct and sovereign work of the Holy Spirit when He calls a person inwardly in the creative way in which He called the world into existence outwardly. Analogously, Jesus called to Lazarus with a loud voice, "Lazarus, come out." That is the effectual call of the Lord, the power through which Lazarus was raised from the dead.

Lazarus was physically reborn as a result of that. Effectual calling is the Holy Spirit's work of bringing about a change in someone. The change that is brought about in and through the effectual call is regeneration.

Effectual calling yields regeneration, which yields faith, which yields justification, which yields sanctification. When we understand the order of salvation, we apprehend our radical dependence upon the grace of God, who saves us out of darkness and death and brings us safely home. The order of salvation traces God's plan of redemption, and what comes out boldly through this order is both the sovereignty and the graciousness of God. Once we figure out where we are in the scheme of this order, we can have great comfort and consolation. Most importantly, our assurance of salvation rests not on our achievements but on the God whose plan of salvation it is.

Because Reformed theology puts such great stress on monergism at the point of regeneration in the order of salvation—that is to say, God works alone in bringing sinners to new spiritual life—many people have the misunderstanding that Reformed theology teaches that salvation is monergistic from start to finish, which is not the case. Semi-Pelagian theology from start to finish is synergistic, which simply means that there is a working together of God and man to bring about salvation. Some people assume that Reformed theology teaches that a human being is passive or a robot throughout his whole spiritual pilgrimage, and that it is God alone who starts the process and drags us through it to the end of our lives. No, Reformed theology teaches that salvation is monergistic at first and then synergistic after effectual calling and regeneration.

The dominion of the whole body of sin is destroyed, and the several lusts thereof are more and more weakened and mortified; and they more and more quickened and strengthened in all saving graces, to the practice of true holiness, without which no man shall see the Lord. The result of regeneration is the liberation of the will from slavery and bondage. The dominion of sin over the person is destroyed. This does not mean that sin is completely conquered, but its stranglehold on the will has been released. In addition to that, real changes take place within the person who is regenerated. As the confession states, several lusts . . . are more and more weakened and mortified. That is to say, the old man is now being put to death, or robbed of its strength, so that it is no longer able to keep us in captivity. At the same time, the new man is made alive and strengthened in all the saving graces.

The dominion of the whole body of sin is destroyed and our lusts are weakened and mortified **to the practice of true holiness, without which no man shall see the Lord.** The goal of this process of sanctification is holiness, a holiness that is manifest in practice. Without this holiness, no one will ever see the Lord. Again, this does not mean that holiness becomes the ground of our justification, but it is the purpose of our justification, as sanctification leads us to this end.

The New Testament makes it abundantly clear that the process of sanctification is a joint venture, a cooperative enterprise. We remember Paul's admonition to the Philippians: "Work out your own salvation with fear and trembling" (Phil. 2:12). The first word in that command is "work." God commands the justified person to work out his salvation. That does not mean that we are to work out our justification. We do not work to become justified, but once we are justified, our work starts. Before we were justified, there was only one rider on our horse, and he was the devil. Now there are two riders fighting for the same horse, as Augustine put it. Life becomes complicated because we are engaged in a constant conflict between the flesh and the Spirit, between virtue and vice. Although we are justified, we are still sinners, and the flesh wars against the Spirit throughout our lives. If we are to grow in our Christian faith and become conformed to the image of Christ, it is necessary for us to work toward that end.

"Work out your own salvation with fear and trembling." Notice the conjunction of those two words, "fear" and "trembling." They communicate that the work called for in sanctification is not to be undertaken in a casual or a cavalier manner. To do something with fear and trembling is to approach it with the utmost seriousness and earnestness. It is a matter of life and death, and is to be our top priority. Our Lord Himself said to His disciples, "Seek first the kingdom of God and his righteousness" (Matt. 6:33). The seeking of the kingdom of God should be the main business of every Christian. This gets obscured in the evangelical world when interested non-Christians are called "seekers," and "seeking" is said to be what one does before committing oneself to Christ.

We are told, "None is righteous, no, not one; no one understands; no one seeks for God" (Rom. 3:10–11). Unregenerate people in this world do not seek after God. They seek only the benefits that He can give them. They seek happiness, they seek meaning, they seek relief from guilt, but they want to receive these things while turning their backs on the only One who can give them. We want the gift, but not the Giver, because we are uncomfortable, by nature, in the presence of God Himself.

We hear evangelists say: "Jesus stands at the door and knocks. Sinner, if you hear His voice and open the door, He will come in and sup with you." This plea is usually on the lips of Arminians, who believe that regeneration is a cooperative venture. Jesus is knocking at the door of our hearts, and He will certainly come in and save us, but first we have to let Him in. It is as if Jesus stood outside of the tomb of Lazarus and called out: "Lazarus, I am standing here with the power of resurrection. I will bring you back from the dead, I will make your heart beat afresh, I will give you new brain waves, but first you must open up the door so that I can get in there and do this for you." What could be more ridiculous than that?

When we read in the Bible that Jesus stands at the door and knocks, we see from the context that He is addressing Christians (Rev. 3:20). He is knocking on the door of the church, not on the door of the world. He is calling for redeemed people to cooperate with Him, for only they have the spiritual power to do so. Once we are regenerated by the Holy Spirit, we can work (or not work) with God in our quest for sanctification. We can so easily become lax, thinking that our quest is over the moment we are saved. No, that is when our quest begins. That is when Jesus says to His people, "Seek first the kingdom of God and his righteousness" (Matt. 6:33). Seek the kingdom first—not just in chronological sequence, but in the order of importance. The most important task that any Christian has in his life is the quest for the kingdom of God. Every Christian should be involved in a passionate pursuit of righteousness, but not to establish the grounds for our justification. The quest for righteousness is the quest of a person who has already been justified. We are justified on the basis of Jesus' righteousness, but now that God has pronounced us just, He wants us, with fear and trembling, to seek to conform our lives to the standards of the righteousness of God.

Christians often say, "I want to be a spiritual person." There is nothing wrong with that desire, but being spiritual is not the goal of the Christian life. The goal of the Christian life is to be righteous. Being in touch with spiritual things is only an aid to reaching the real goal. If spirituality becomes the end, we miss the point of it.

Jesus strongly denounced the Pharisees, who defined themselves as people who were committed to the pursuit of righteousness. However, they pursued self-righteousness, for which they were condemned. Jesus never condemned the pursuit of righteousness.

> 2. This sanctification is throughout, in the whole man; yet imperfect in this life, there abiding still some remnants of corruption in every part; whence ariseth a continual and irreconcilable war, the flesh lusting against the Spirit, and the Spirit against the flesh.

The confession affirms that sanctification is not simply on the periphery of our human nature, but extends throughout the whole person. Although it remains imperfect in this life, the process is moving toward our glorification, which will be the complete sanctification of the whole person. We struggle as Christians because the residual elements of the old nature still remain in us. There remain **some remnants of corruption**, which touch **every part** of us. As a result, evil inclinations persist to our dying day, making the Christian life a constant battle. It has been called the war between the Spirit and the flesh. In this life, the old man never completely surrenders to the conquering Spirit. The flesh continues to fight against the Spirit, and the Spirit against the flesh. The pursuit of righteousness requires work that is intense, that involves working out our salvation with fear and trembling. In this process of sanctification, we have to fight a war on two fronts, for there are two heresies that seek to undermine the pursuit of righteousness in the life of the Christian. Those enemies are legalism and antinomianism. We will look at them at some length as we proceed in this chapter.

Our Lord says, "Seek first the kingdom of God and his righteousness" (Matt. 6:33). He also says, "Unless your righteousness exceeds that of the scribes and Pharisees, you will never enter the kingdom of heaven" (5:20).

Jesus tells us to make the number one priority in our lives the pursuit of righteousness. Can we say with conviction that the top priority of our Christian experience from the beginning has been personal righteousness? Because we are still sinners when we come into the faith, it is unnatural for us to say that what we want more than anything else in our lives is to be godly people. We have a desire for godliness, but we have too many other desires that fight against making righteousness our top priority. The whole call of the Bible is for us to get our priorities in order.

When Paul tells us, "Work out your own salvation with fear and trembling" (Phil. 2:12), he is telling us that we have a job to do. But there is good news. "For it is God who works in you, both to will and to work for his good pleasure" (v. 13). This is a classic biblical text for synergism. We work because God is working. We know that our labors will not be in vain because God is working. It is not that regeneration is God's work, and then the rest of the Christian life is our work. No, the whole process of sanctification is a joint effort.

Why is that important? Because when we're working at something that is hard, it helps to have someone working with us. As Christians, we are called to do hard work, but never by ourselves. God promises to help every Christian who is engaged in the pursuit of godliness. He is not going to do it for us, but He promises to do it with us. That is why we do not surrender to despair when we fail—and frequently we do fail—in our pursuit of sanctification. God will give us the grace, and He promises His help.

The relationship between our working and God's working in sanctification is often misunderstood, and it has been distorted in two serious errors. The first error is called *activism*. Activism sees our entire progress in sanctification and growth in righteousness as due solely to our own efforts. Activism leads to the sin of self-righteousness. We are called to "work out [our] own salvation with fear and trembling, for it is God who works in [us], both to will and to work" (Phil. 2:12–13). The activist pays attention only to the first half of that admonition, to work out our salvation with fear and trembling, forgetting that God is at work in us. The opposite error is *quietism*, the credo for which is "Let go and let God." The idea is that all that is necessary to be sanctified is to remain passive and wait for God to do the work, while not being engaged in any strenuous spiritual effort. Both of these views distort the biblical call to earnest pursuit of righteousness in reliance upon the help of God.

Two heresies undermine the doctrine of sanctification. The first is *legalism*, and the second is *antinomianism*. At issue is how the law of God applies in the Christian's spiritual development or process of sanctification.

Let us consider legalism first. Legalism is often misunderstood, in part because there are different kinds of legalism. The first biblical group of people who come to mind as legalists are the Pharisees, who sought their salvation through keeping of law. One form of legalism is the view that people can get to heaven by doing good works, by obeying the law scrupulously. Those who believe that they are justified by their works or by their achievements represent one form of legalism.

The Pharisees were zealous for the law. In fact, the very word *Pharisee* came from a word denoting the people who were separated from the rank and file. During the intertestamental period, as the nation of Israel became more secular and the Old Testament covenant was more and more forgotten, a group of pious and devout Jews remained faithful to the old covenant. They were the spiritual conservatives of the era, who wanted to reform their society and rekindle some fervor for the ancient covenant that God had made with His people. The members of that group dedicated themselves to being separate from the paganism and the secularism of their day, and they devoted themselves to obeying all the terms of the Old Testament covenant. These puritans of Israel, if you will, called themselves the Pharisees. The first generation of Pharisees was one of the most godly groups of people that ever arose in Israel. They were genuinely sincere, but by the second generation, as happens in most reform movements, the pursuit of obedience to the old covenant became formalized and externalized. The Pharisees began to take pride in their own righteousness and became corrupt. They began to pretend a kind of godliness that they didn't really possess. That is why the chief criticism that Jesus leveled against the Pharisees was that they were hypocrites: "Woe to you, scribes and Pharisees, hypocrites!" (Matt. 23:13). They feigned righteousness that they had not attained.

We are not being legalists when we obey God. If God's law tells us to do something or tells us not to do it, then it is our responsibility to obey. That is not legalism. The Pharisees, though, substituted the traditions of men for the law of God. They legislated their own laws, and they made their laws, rather than the law of God, the test of true godliness. They put people in chains where God had left them free. One of the most important doctrines in Reformed theology is the doctrine of Christian liberty. That does not mean that Christians are free to behave in any way they want to behave. The doctrine of Christian liberty applies to matters that are *adiaphorous* (those things that the Bible does not prohibit or enjoin).

In the Bible, drinking alcohol is adiaphorous. It is not a sin, but it is a sin to get drunk. Because drunkenness and alcoholism are such problems, some Christian groups prohibit drinking entirely, giving the idea that to drink at all is a sin. But if that's the case, we are without a Savior, because Jesus drank. If Jesus drank, and if drinking is a sin, then He wasn't holy enough to save Himself, let alone us. Efforts have been made to prove that Jesus didn't really drink, that the water He turned to wine was not really wine, and that the wine of the New Testament was not fermented. From an exegetical and scholarly perspective, that is sheer folly. Those who take this position have twisted the Bible in order to substantiate their own ethic. As a matter of prudence, a person may choose never to let wine touch his lips. But as soon as that decision is elevated to a rule of Christian conduct, it becomes legalism, pure and simple. It is legislating where God has left people free.

God does not leave us free to get drunk, but when we go beyond what God requires and impose obligations that God does not impose and do it in His name, we are doing what the Pharisees did. There are conservative churches that are so zealous for the righteousness of God that they fall into this trap. They tell people that they can't wear makeup or that they can't dance, and they make other nonbiblical rules, and then those rules become the test of whether a person is a Christian. It is important that we don't make rules that God doesn't make. We expect responsible behavior, but as soon as we begin to define things in terms not specified by God, we have legislated where God has left people free and have miscommunicated the nature of the gospel.

When we look at the true requirements of the law of God and understand what godliness actually means, we tremble at the moral obligations that are imposed on us by almighty God. But we should not tremble at the requirements of men that have only the appearance of righteousness.

The Judaizing heresy in the New Testament involved the demand that Christians had to keep the portions of the law of Moses that were no longer in effect. For example, the Judaizers insisted that gentiles had to be circumcised in order to be saved. Paul resisted them openly and accused them of undermining the very gospel itself (Gal. 5:1–6). When the question was raised about eating meat offered to idols, Paul taught that if people wanted to eat meat offered to idols, they could (1 Cor. 8). If they had a scruple about it, they shouldn't do it. They were free. It is adiaphorous.

Another dimension of legalism is majoring in minors. Jesus rebuked the Pharisees: "You tithe mint and dill and cumin, and have neglected the weightier matters of the law: justice and mercy and faithfulness" (Matt. 23:23). The Pharisees were so scrupulous about tithing that not only did they give 10 percent of their income from all their produce, but if they walked down the street and found a dime on the sidewalk, to put it in American terms, they would make sure that they added a penny to the collection plate on Sunday morning. If they had some mint growing outside their door, they would give 10 percent of those little mint plants.

Jesus did not say that they didn't have to tithe their mint. He didn't rebuke them for being overly scrupulous in obeying the law of God, but He did say that it is much more important to live for justice and mercy, which the Pharisees tended to ignore. The Pharisees majored in the letter of the law and ignored the spirit of the law. Godliness requires obeying both. A person who is seeking to be sanctified must have a passionate desire to obey both the letter and the spirit of the law of God.

That requires, first of all, knowing what the law of God is. Sometimes we erect substitutes for God's law because we realize that the real law of God is hard to obey. It is a lot easier to go without wearing lipstick than it is to go without being a gossip. It is easier to refrain from dancing than it is to refrain from pride. In light of the law of God, we are not very successful in achieving authentic spiritual growth and authentic righteousness.

Jesus said, "Unless your righteousness exceeds that of the scribes and Pharisees, you will never enter the kingdom of heaven" (Matt. 5:20). Jesus may have meant one of two different things. He could have meant that no matter how much righteousness we think we have, it's not enough unless we have His righteousness, because His righteousness is the only righteousness that will get us into the kingdom. In other words, this could have been a thinly veiled announcement of justification by faith alone. Or He could have been saying that the test of the faith that truly justifies is the fruit of true righteousness, which exceeds that of the Pharisees. If that is the case, then Jesus is saying that the true fruit of a Christian should go beyond the achievements of the Pharisees.

Let's consider that. We've already talked about tithing. The Pharisees were scrupulous in paying their tithe. A mere 12 percent of people who claim to be evangelical Christians in America tithe; 88 percent do not. By withholding their tithe, they rob God financially (Mal. 3:8–10). They do not even reach the standard of the Pharisees.

Jesus said to the Pharisees, "You search the Scriptures because you think that in them you have eternal life" (John 5:39). There is perhaps no greater problem among professing evangelical Christians than abysmal biblical illiteracy and ignorance. The Pharisees searched; they didn't just have a fifteen-minute daily devotional. They searched the Scriptures; they were diligent in their study of the Bible.

Jesus said, "Woe to you, scribes and Pharisees, hypocrites! For you travel across sea and land to make a single proselyte, and when he becomes a proselyte, you make him twice as much a child of hell as yourselves" (Matt. 23:15). They were willing to go to great lengths just to convert one person. They were zealous for evangelism and world missions.

These Pharisees had a passion for righteousness, and they tithed their income scrupulously. They went over land and sea to be faithful witnesses to God, they were diligent in their study of Scripture, and they prayed all the time. The problem was that they prayed to be seen by men, instead of praying in secret. They prayed regularly, they tithed regularly, they studied the Bible regularly, they were involved in missions and evangelism, and yet Jesus said, "Unless your righteousness exceeds that of the scribes and Pharisees, you will never enter the kingdom of heaven" (Matt. 5:20). That is frightening, isn't it?

The Pharisees got lost in legalism, in the details of the ceremonial law, the externals. The moral law of God went right past them, right over their heads. The true mark of sanctification is found in the Old Testament saints and in the attitude found in Psalm 119:97: "Oh how I love your law!"

Psalm 1 tells us, "Blessed is the man who walks not in the counsel of the wicked, nor stands in the way of sinners, nor sits in the seat of scoffers" (v. 1). That means we don't live the lifestyle of a pagan, we don't participate in the ungodly pleasures of the world, and we are not to be cynical and skeptical and mock the things of God. The psalm goes on:

> But his delight is in the law of the LORD,
>   and on his law he meditates day and night.
> He is like a tree
>   planted by streams of water
> that yields its fruit in its season,
>   and its leaf does not wither.
> In all that he does, he prospers.
> The wicked are not so,
>   but are like chaff that the wind drives away. (vv. 2–4)

Here we see the stark contrast between the godly person and the ungodly person. The godly person has deep roots that are substantively planted, bringing forth fruit because those roots are being nurtured and nourished every moment by drinking deeply of the law of God. The godly person does not have a casual understanding of the law of God. He meditates on it; he thinks about it, studies it, and exposes himself to it. The ungodly person ignores the law of God and has a superficial religion, a religion of externals, not a religion that takes hold of the soul and of the heart and says: "I'm going to live my life for God, and I want to please Him. O Lord, reveal what pleases you." And God says, "Here is what pleases Me; here is My law." Jesus said, "If you love me, you will keep my commandments" (John 14:15).

It requires working with fear and trembling to go beyond the surface to the depth and to develop integrity in the inner person. It means, as James says, that our yes means yes (James 5:12). The test is not if we dance or smoke, but it does matter if people can trust us when you say yes. The New Testament makes that a priority, and we substitute other things. If we want to know what righteousness looks like, we look at the law, because in it God reveals His righteousness.

We turn our attention now to antinomianism. *Anti* means "against," and *nomos* means "law" in Greek, and so antinomianism is a repudiation of the authority of the law of God over one's life.

Perhaps the most significant work that appeared in the last half of the twentieth century encouraging an antinomian viewpoint was *Situation Ethics*, written by Joseph Fletcher. This book has had a significant impact on churches and professing Christians. Fletcher discusses antinomianism and actually seeks to distance himself from it. He is careful to point out that he is not opposed to all law. Rather, he reduces the law of God to one law, the law of love. It is expressed in these terms: We are always called to do what love requires in a given situation.

In one respect, that sentiment is in perfect agreement with orthodox Christianity, because the Scriptures tell us that he who loves obeys the law, and even Augustine said, "Love God and do as you please." That could have been better stated by the great saint, because he meant that if you love God, you will be pleased to do only what pleases Him. We can do as we please if we no longer take pleasure in violating the will of God. But someone could easily take Augustine's statement to mean, "If you have an affection for God, you can go out and live however you want."

Antinomianism is the spirit of the person who seeks to take advantage of God's grace and love. He thinks that "where sin increased, grace abounded all the more" (Rom. 5:20) means that he should intensify the pursuit of sin so that he can get more grace. However, the Apostle Paul goes on to ask his readers the rhetorical question, "Are we to continue in sin that grace may abound?" (6:1). He answers his own question: "By no means!" (v. 2). Other translations read, "May it never be" or "God forbid." Paul says that to continue in sin so that grace may abound is a gross distortion of the grace of God. Even though we have been saved by grace through faith, we are still called to flee from sin and to pursue a life of righteousness with all our strength and might.

Let's get back to Fletcher, who says that there is only one law that we have to keep in front of us, the law of love, and that we must always do what love requires in a given situation. His idea is that we have to determine in each situation what the right thing to do is. Fletcher gives the example of a husband and a wife who were captured by the Nazis during World War II and interned in the same camp, one in the male quarters and one in the female quarters. A guard came to the wife and said, "Unless you agree to sleep with me, I'm going to kill your husband." So she slept with the guard. After the war ended and the camp was liberated, the husband found out from his wife that she had slept with the guard under those conditions, and he sued her for divorce on the grounds of adultery. Some would say he was right to do so because the woman committed adultery.

Consider another situation. A woman is on her way home one night, and a man jumps out of the shadows, knocks her to the ground, holds a knife to her throat, and rapes her. Does the husband have grounds for divorce on the basis of adultery? Many of those same people would say that is not adultery; it is rape. She was coerced and forced by the threat to her own life. But is it coercion if the threat is not to the woman's life but to someone else's life? What if the man came with a gun to her child's head and said, "Sleep with me or I will kill your child"? In the case of the woman in the concentration camp, wasn't she likewise coerced? We could argue whether she should have resisted to death, but did her husband have grounds for divorce when the wife's submission was coerced by the guard's threat to kill her husband? It seems better to say that the husband did not have grounds for divorce, and Fletcher says that in this situation love demands that the woman submit to the guard out of her love for her husband.

All of God's laws, given to us as principles by which we are to live, have to be applied to real situations. So, Christian ethics always have to be applied to particular situations. But that is not the same thing as saying that the situation determines your action. The problem is that Fletcher's one principle, the law of love, is so vague that sinful people can apply it in ways that justify their sin. That's why we need the Bible's explanation of what love really entails. Paul, for example, talks about how important it is for us to "walk in love, as Christ loved us" (Eph. 5:2). And then he goes on to say, "But sexual immorality and all impurity or covetousness must not even be named among you, as is proper among saints" (v. 3).

Paul gives the principle, "Walk in love," and then explains that if we do so, we will never be engaged in sexual immorality. Adultery is completely incompatible with love. If we love God, we will never steal from another person, because stealing is a violation of our love for God. Paul is saying that we are called to live by our love for God, but the whole purpose of the law of God is to show us what it is that love requires.

God doesn't give just one law—love Me and do what you want. He gives a multitude of laws to regulate human behavior, all of which reveal to us what love requires. It is our duty as Christians to master that body of law, not simply so that we will have the moral power to obey the law of God—which is the biggest problem we have—but so that we can know what it is that God requires. To do the right thing, we first have to know what the right thing is. Having then learned what the right thing is, we must have the moral courage to do it.

The law is given to instruct us as to what is right. What does it mean to be righteous? A righteous person, in the simplest definition, is the person who does what is right. Righteousness, according to the Bible, is defined by the law of God, and sin is also defined by the law of God. The Westminster Shorter Catechism, which summarizes all these things in the Westminster Confession of Faith, asks, "What is sin?" And the answer is, "Sin is any want of conformity unto, or transgression of, the law of God" (Q&A 14). Where there is no law, there is no sin, because sin is defined as a violation of the law. The law is absolutely vital to our understanding of what is right. The pursuit of the law of God only really begins at conversion. It is a pernicious distortion of Christianity to say that as soon as we become Christians, we are done with the law. If we are done with the law, we don't care anymore about being righteous or about sin.

Situation ethics is very subtle. The one who practices it says, "I'm not an antinomian. I believe in the law, but there is only one law of God, and that is the law of love." He then negotiates every other law that Scripture reveals. That is antinomian. If God would reveal to us a thousand laws and we would deny only one of them, we would still be antinomian— just to a lesser degree than the person who denies all of them.

Historically, the battle of antinomianism had its roots in the six- teenth-century Reformation. The principal focus of the debate at that time was the question of the Old Testament law. Does the law of God, revealed in the Old Testament, have any claim on the Christian, who now is not under law but under grace? Can we safely distance ourselves from the law of the Old Testament? That is not an easy question to answer, because it is clear that some of the laws of the Old Testament have been specifically abrogated, such as circumcision.

That issue actually first came up in the early church, and Paul announced that the question of circumcision was adiaphorous. It is morally neutral, without any ethical or righteous reference (Gal. 6:15). The Old Testament covenant was fulfilled in Jesus Christ. He fulfilled all that was meant by circumcision, so there is now no need to be circumcised. Paul said that circumcision will neither help you nor hurt you.

Then things changed radically. The Judaizers began to follow the Apostle Paul around, insisting that any gentile who was converted to the Christian faith had to abide by all the regulations of the Old Testament, including circumcision. They tried to institute a doctrine of salvation by works of the law, and were actually undermining the very essence of the gospel. When Paul wrote to the Galatians, he said of the Judaizers, "I wish those who unsettle you would emasculate themselves!" (Gal. 5:12). He used some of his strongest language in his writing against the Judaizers. Peter had to go through this business with the question of unclean foods (Acts 10). Do Christians have to eat kosher? No, we can eat pork if we want. We understand that some of the laws in the Old Testament are not binding on Christians.

It is a big move from saying that some of the Old Testament laws are not binding on the Christian to saying that none of them are binding. This is no easy issue, yet it is important if we are to pursue our sanctification in a way that will please God.

Dispensational theology is a nineteenth-century aberration away from historic, orthodox, biblical Christianity. There was no dispensationalism before the nineteenth century, and even though it has swept through America and has become the dominant view among evangelicals, many dispensationalists don't know much about church history or theology. They grow up being taught nothing but dispensationalism. They don't hear that dispensationalism is often antinomian. This because dispensationalism encourages believers to ignore the Old Testament almost completely because it had to do with the Jews, not Christians.

The Old Testament reveals to us what pleases God and what He hates. Once God principally reveals something that reflects His character, He doesn't have to keep repeating it in every new era in order to maintain its moral obligation upon His people. I hear this about tithing. The Old Testament sets forth the principle of tithing and makes it no small matter. In Malachi, God accuses the people of robbing Him by not paying their tithes (3:8–10). We do not have a command to tithe in the New Testament, but we have a command to give as the Lord prospers us. The New Testament teaches us that the new covenant is better than the old covenant. It is richer and provides greater benefits and blessings to us from God. Are we no longer responsible to manifest gratitude for the blessings of God by returning to Him the sacrifice of praise in worship by tithing? The obligation in the New Testament is greater.

Before Christians were called Christians, which was a derogatory term, they were called "people of the way," in response to Jesus' teaching, "I am the way" (John 14:6). The Old Testament teaching reiterated by Paul in Romans, that all have sinned, continues: "All have turned aside; together they have become worthless; no one does good, not even one" (Rom. 3:12). The Bible speaks of two ways or two paths. One is the way or the path of godliness, and the other is the way or the path of ungodliness. "Blessed is the man who walks not in the counsel of the wicked, nor stands in the way of sinners" (Ps. 1:1). That is, the person who avoids the path or the way that is divorced from the way of Christ is blessed. It is not so with the man who "sits in the seat of scoffers," mocking the Word of God and reducing it to scorn.

Every spokesman for God—the patriarchs, the prophets, Jesus, and His Apostles—was subjected daily to the scorn of his contemporaries. One of the reasons why the Christian church nationally and internationally is so weak is that we are intimidated by scorn. We do not want to be scorned. We do not want to be mocked. We do not want anybody to laugh at us.

> Blessed is the man
>   who walks not in the counsel of the wicked,
> nor stands in the way of sinners,

> nor sits in the seat of scoffers;
> but his delight is in the law of the LORD,
>   and on his law he meditates day and night. (Ps. 1:1–2)

But that law was in the Old Testament. Does that mean that the godly person no longer has to take any delight in the law of the Lord?

> He is like a tree
>   planted by streams of water
> that yields its fruit in its season,
>   and its leaf does not wither.
> In all that he does, he prospers.
> The wicked are not so,
>   but are like chaff that the wind drives away. (vv. 3–4)

The righteous man is likened to a tree that is planted by rivers of water and brings forth its fruit in its season. Jesus still cares about our bringing forth fruit. Paul says that grace removes the curse of the law from us. Although we are no longer under the damning power of the law, Paul says that we establish the law, that we still delight in the law, and that we still learn from the law of God, because we want to please God, who, by His grace, has redeemed us.

Our study of justification showed how the demands of God's law upon our lives are met for us by someone else's perfect righteousness and how the justice of Christ is imputed to us. After we are saved on the basis of His works and by grace, we are called to be conformed daily to Christ, to grow in that grace to the achieving of righteousness. We do it not by despising the law of God or by substituting our laws for God's laws as the legalist does but by delighting in the law of God that does apply to our lives. If the Old Testament moral law reveals to us what is pleasing to God, and the new covenant commands us to live in a way that pleases God, that tells us that we must give serious attention to the Old Testament law.

3. In which war, although the remaining corruption, for a time, may much prevail; yet, through the continual supply of strength from the sanctifying Spirit of Christ, the regenerate part doth

> overcome; and so, the saints grow in grace, perfecting holiness in the fear of God.

Despite the obstacles that stand in the way of our growth in grace and our pursuit of righteousness, we are comforted by the certainty that victory will be ours. Section 3 of this chapter suggests that although there are low moments when it seems the old man has the upper hand and is prevailing, the constant supply of the weapons that we need for triumph are given to us by the Holy Spirit. Because of this supply and because of the Holy Spirit's actions within us, it is most certain that the regenerate nature will ultimately overcome. We speak then of the process of growing in grace. This growth toward spiritual maturity is driven by **the sanctifying Spirit of Christ, so that the saints grow in grace, perfecting holiness in the fear of God.**

Of Saving Faith

1. The grace of faith, whereby the elect are enabled to believe to the saving of their souls, is the work of the Spirit of Christ in their hearts, and is ordinarily wrought by the ministry of the Word, by which also, and by the administration of the sacraments, and prayer, it is increased and strengthened.

2. By this faith, a Christian believeth to be true whatsoever is revealed in the Word, for the authority of God himself speaking therein; and acteth differently upon that which each particular passage thereof containeth; yielding obedience to the commands, trembling at the threatenings, and embracing the promises of God for this life, and that which is to come. But the principal acts of saving faith are accepting, receiving, and resting upon Christ alone for justification, sanctification, and eternal life, by virtue of the covenant of grace.

3. This faith is different in degrees, weak or strong; may be often and many ways assailed, and weakened, but gets the victory: growing up in many to the attainment of a full assurance, through Christ, who is both the author and finisher of our faith.

The Westminster Confession is precise in its language. Each word is chosen with great care. Chapter 14 begins with a crisp statement of the Reformed understanding of how faith is actually wrought in the human soul.

> 1. The grace of faith, whereby the elect are enabled to believe to the saving of their souls, is the work of the Spirit of Christ in their hearts, and is ordinarily wrought by the ministry of the Word, by

which also, and by the administration of the sacraments, and prayer, it is increased and strengthened.

First, **faith** is described in terms of **grace**. The connection between faith and grace is a repeated theme in the New Testament, particularly in the writings of the Apostle Paul. He writes, "For by grace you have been saved through faith. And this is not your own doing; it is the gift of God" (Eph. 2:8).

Grace is the instrumental power or the means by which we are saved through faith. Paul continues, "And this is not your own doing." The word "this" must have an antecedent, which would normally be the closest preceding noun. In this case, "this" would refer back to "faith." Paul is not saying that grace is not our own doing. That would be redundant, because if it were our own doing, it would not be gracious at all. Rather, he says that faith is not our own doing. That does not mean that faith is not found in us; it is found in us. It does not mean that it is someone else's faith by which we are justified. It is, properly speaking, our faith, for we are the ones who have it, the ones who are exercising it. But it is not our own doing, meaning that we are not the origin of it. It is not something that we have generated by our own power, nor does it originate in our flesh.

That simple statement is the death blow to all forms of semi-Pelagianism. It contains the primary point that distinguishes Reformed theology. The Reformers affirmed that the faith by which we are justified, by which we are united to Christ and which is the instrumental cause of our justification, did not originate in some activity or decision of our will. It did not come from our unregenerate flesh. Rather, our faith is a gift to us from God. He made a promise that He would save every person who responds to the gospel with faith. The most famous verse in the entire Bible, known by every Christian, is, "For God so loved the world, that he gave his only Son, that whoever believes in him should not perish but have eternal life" (John 3:16). Whoever believes will be saved. Faith is a necessary condition for salvation. Faith is a necessary requirement for justification. Those who do not have faith will not be justified. Faith determines whether we are redeemed.

The semi-Pelagians say that salvation is of grace, that grace assists us, and that no one can really come to faith unless God offers His help. However, they further say that there is an unaffected part of the soul where this offer of saving grace can be accepted or rejected. Whoever accepts that grace and then exercises faith is saved, but whoever rejects the grace of God will not be saved. In this view, everything depends on a person's response to the offer of God's grace. But that was not the belief of the Westminster divines, nor was it the belief of Luther, Augustine, Calvin, or Edwards; nor is it the teaching of the New Testament. The New Testament tells us that we are fallen and dead in sin, so that unless the Holy Spirit raises us from that spiritual death, God's offer of all the grace in the world to us would be like an offer of water to a dead man. That man is not going to drink the water unless he is first resurrected.

In Ephesians 2, Paul writes: "And you were dead in the trespasses and sins in which you once walked, following the course of this world, following the prince of the power of the air, the spirit that is now at work in the sons of disobedience. But God . . . even when we were dead in our trespasses, made us alive together with Christ. . . . For by grace you have been saved through faith. And this is not your own doing; it is the gift of God" (Eph. 2:1–2, 4, 6, 8). The Apostle is teaching, and the divines are responding, that God in His grace supplies the necessary condition that He requires for salvation. That condition is faith. He requires us to exercise faith in order to be saved, but we are unable to do so unless He first gives faith to us.

This is difficult for some people to accept. They want to know how God can require something of people that they cannot perform. This was what started the debate between Augustine and Pelagius. Pelagius was upset with the lethargy of Christians and the scandalous behavior of many members of the church, and he wanted to see the Christian community become more righteous. He knew Augustine had prayed, "Oh Lord, grant what You command, and command whatever You will." Pelagius agreed that one could pray, "God, grant whatever You will," because that humbly acknowledges God's authority and right to command His creatures to do His will. However, Pelagius could not agree with Augustine's words, "Grant what You command."

Pelagius asked why we should ask God to give us grace to do something that He commands us to do, for surely, He wouldn't command us to do something that we couldn't do, apart from His intervention. Pelagius waged a long campaign against Augustine and ended up being declared a heretic because he concluded that grace is not really necessary for salvation. You can be saved without it, he said, because you can be righteous without it. If God requires us to be holy—and God does say, "You shall be holy, for I the LORD your God am holy" (Lev. 19:2), and Jesus adds, "You therefore must be perfect, as your heavenly Father is perfect" (Matt. 5:48)—then He would be unjust, Pelagius argued, to require us to do something that we cannot possibly do. Augustine's response was that man, as originally created, was able to be holy and could have achieved perfection. When Adam fell, the punishment that came upon him and all whom he represented was that God removed their righteousness from them. He punished sin with sin, so that we are born in sin. We are all born in a fallen condition that is called original sin. Augustine said that since the fall, we cannot do what God commands, but our fallen condition does not absolve us of the responsibility to do what we were supposed to do in creation.

Suppose God said to a man, "I want you to mow the grass this afternoon for Me. Here is the tractor and all the equipment you need. The gas is in the machine. Everything works perfectly. All you have to do is start the engine, sit in the chair, steer the mower, and mow this field. Just be careful of that one area over there, because there is a deep pit in it. If you fall into that pit, you won't be able to get out." Imagine that as soon as God left, the man jumped down into the pit, and, as hard as he tried, could not climb out of it.

Later, when God returned and asked the man what he was doing down in that pit, the man replied that he had jumped into it. God inquired why the grass was not cut, and the answer was, "How do you expect me to cut the grass? I'm down in this pit. I can't possibly do the job that You assigned me, because I am in this pit." That is basically what Augustine was saying to Pelagius. The fact that we are fallen in Adam does not mean that God's law has changed. We are still responsible to mirror and reflect His righteousness and holiness. We are still to be holy, as He is holy. Perfect obedience is still required, even though we no longer have the moral power to give it. Augustine argued that people can be justly held accountable by a holy and righteous God to do things that they are no longer able to do because of Adam's fall.

God requires faith in Jesus Christ as a necessary condition for salvation, but that does not necessarily imply that we have the innate ability, on our own, to exercise faith. We cannot "make a decision" to believe what we do not believe. Charles Finney, who perfected the techniques of mass evangelism, taught that by making a "decision," a person could become a Christian and live a perfectly righteous life. That is how "decision evangelism" came into the fabric of American religion.

What we can make a decision about is action. We can decide to investigate the truth claims of Christianity, to attend church every Sunday for the next fifty-two weeks and listen to the gospel about Jesus Christ. We can also decide to follow the Jesus we believe in, but we can't decide to believe any more than we can decide to love someone affectionately whom we don't love. We can treat someone in a loving manner and be kind to him, but we cannot decide to have an affectionate, emotional feeling toward him by an act of the will. When we talk about faith in its saving sense, we are talking about all those different dimensions. We assent to the truth of certain concepts, not only intellectually but also with genuine affection. The person who receives Jesus Christ not only embraces Him as the true Savior but also embraces Him with positive affection, which the flesh can never produce. If we have affection in our soul for Christ, it is because the Holy Spirit has changed our hearts and has given us an affection for Christ that we never could have conjured up by ourselves. That is the heart and soul of what the Reformed faith is all about and what the Westminster Confession affirms—that God Himself gives the gift of faith.

He doesn't give it to everyone. He gives it only to the elect. The doctrine of election is a distinctive of Reformed theology, but it is not an esoteric doctrine that doesn't touch the rest of our faith or theology. Martin Luther said that the doctrine of election is at the very heart of the church. The church is called the *ekklēsia* (the assembly, those called out) because all the elect come to faith, and all who come to faith are numbered among the elect. The gift of faith is given to all of God's elect and to no one else, because from all eternity God has had a plan of salvation that includes a certain number of people whose names He knows. He has moved heaven and earth to secure the salvation of the elect. One of the things that God does for the elect is give them faith. He regenerates them by the Spirit. He calls them inwardly; He changes their hearts. He gives them the gift of faith; He keeps them in the faith. "For those whom he foreknew he also predestined to be conformed to the image of his Son, in order that he might be the firstborn among many brothers. And those whom he predestined he also called, and those whom he called he also justified, and those whom he justified he also glorified" (Rom. 8:29–30). This plan of salvation rests upon the grace of God from beginning to end. It is at the heart of our whole relationship with God.

The grace of faith, whereby the elect are enabled to believe to the saving of their souls, is the work of the Spirit of Christ. God enables us to believe because, by ourselves, we are morally unable to do so. The elect believe to the saving of their souls, and that the work of the Spirit of Christ in their hearts. Many people ask at this point, if it is God who brings people to faith, not our powers of persuasion, why should we be engaged in evangelism at all? The answer is that faith is ordinarily wrought by the ministry of the Word. The Holy Spirit changes the disposition of the heart, to be sure, but the ordinary way by which the Spirit does that is the ministry of the Word. He gives the gift of faith through the power of the Word. "So faith comes from hearing, and hearing through the word of Christ" (Rom. 10:17). The Spirit ordinarily works through the Word, and the wonderful thing is that God calls His people to proclaim that Word.

The power of the Word is never in the proclaimer. The only thing we can do to help the cause is to be as accurate and faithful as we can possibly be when we communicate God's Word. The Word of God is like a two-edged sword. It pierces and penetrates the soul, and it cuts between the muscle and the sinew as it reaches the deepest chambers of a person's heart and does its work, because the Spirit accompanies the Word (Heb. 4:12). The Spirit normally does not work apart from the Word, but rather in and through and with the Word. Preachers often pray for the Spirit to proclaim the Word, knowing that the Word of God will never return to Him void (Isa. 55:11). Of course, we can give the outward call to all listeners to believe in Jesus Christ. But we are powerless to give the internal call (the effectual call). Only the Holy Spirit can do that.

That is what the divines are teaching here. Faith is ordinarily wrought by the ministry of the Word, by which also, and by the administration of the sacraments, and prayer, it is increased and strengthened. When we discussed justification, we saw that one of the differences between the Reformers and the Roman Catholic Church was that the Roman church believes that justification can be increased or diminished. The Reformers insisted that there is no increase or decrease in justification, because the only ground of justification is Christ's life of perfect obedience, his righteousness, which is imputed to us. His righteousness is the only possible ground for our salvation.

Our justification can't be augmented or diminished by anything we do, because the only basis for it is Christ's righteousness. However, our faith can increase or decrease. It fluctuates, and we say, "I believe; help my unbelief!" (Mark 9:24). We are not consistent in our faithfulness. Faith that is wrought in our heart by the Spirit can be, and needs to be, strengthened. In fact, this is what sanctification is all about. There is a reason why this chapter follows the chapter on sanctification. Our growth in sanctification is directly related to our growth in faith, because our growth in faith is closely related to our faithfulness. The more faithful we are, the more sanctified we become. We must work hard to strengthen our faith.

There are various ways that we can strengthen our faith. One of the most important is faithful attendance at corporate worship. Some people think that you can get along without the body of Christ, without the means of grace, without hearing the preaching of the Word. But like a piece of wood that is removed from the fire, sooner or later such people lose their warmth. When God saves a person, although He saves him as an individual, He never leaves that person alone. He always places him in His body, the church.

Another way our faith is strengthened is through the administration of the sacraments. When we see a person—adult or infant—baptized, we see dramatized the covenant promise of God to His people and to their seed. When we worry about whether God is going to keep His promises, we can be reminded in this sacred rite that God keeps His word. God makes promises to His people and to their seed. Likewise, when we partake of the Lord's Supper, we are reminded of Christ's sacrifice on our behalf, so that we can have our sins forgiven and have communion of Him. We are reminded of His promise to come again to take us to be where He is.

> 2. By this faith, a Christian believeth to be true whatsoever is revealed in the Word, for the authority of God himself speaking therein; and acteth differently upon that which each particular passage thereof containeth; yielding obedience to the commands, trembling at the threatenings, and embracing the promises of God for this life, and that which is to come. But the principal acts of saving faith are accepting, receiving, and resting upon Christ alone for justification, sanctification, and eternal life, by virtue of the covenant of grace.

When they talked about justification by faith alone, the Reformers had to answer the charge of easy-believism. Some thought the Reformers were teaching, "All you have to do is believe, and you can live any kind of riotous, licentious life and still be saved." It was important, in responding to those charges and to the teaching of James that faith without works is dead, to determine the necessary ingredients of saving faith. James had written, "What good is it, my brothers, if someone says he has faith but does not have works? Can that faith save him?" (James 2:14). He also wrote, "You believe that God is one; you do well. Even the demons believe—and shudder!" (v. 19). This seems to say that if all you have is faith, you are no better off than a demon!

Having the correct information about Jesus and believing it to be true—*notitia* and *assensus*—are necessary elements of saving faith, but they are not sufficient. We cannot have saving faith without them, but we can have them and still not be redeemed. For example, we believe that George Washington was the first president of the United States, but that doesn't mean that we trust him for salvation or that we pray to or worship him. We have the information about George Washington and we believe it to be true, but we have no commitment to him. Personal trust and commitment, *fiducia*, is the third element of saving faith.

By this faith, a Christian believeth to be true whatsoever is revealed in the Word. Christians assent not only to the information contained in the gospel but also to everything that is revealed in the Word of God, the Bible. This brings us to another idea that first appeared in the Roman Catholic Church and was used in a particular way during the Middle Ages, and then was used in a different way by the Reformers. This is the concept of implicit faith (*fides implicita*).

An implicit faith is the automatic acceptance of whatever a particular source says, simply because that source is considered trustworthy. Because God is omniscient and incapable of lying or being deceived, we know that whatever He says is true. Since He is completely trustworthy, we can believe whatever He says *implicitly*. When the Bible talks about a childlike faith, it does not mean a childish faith; rather, as a child trusts his parents implicitly, so we are to come before God in a spirit of humility, saying, "Lord, Your word is true, and we will live by every word that proceeds from Your mouth." This is not a naive faith; rather, it is a reasonable faith, given the nature of God. The Roman church demanded that Christians have implicit faith also in the Roman church's teachings as well as in the Bible, but the Reformers said that we should have an implicit faith only in God and His Word.

By this faith, a Christian believeth to be true whatsoever is revealed in the Word. As Christians, we have been regenerated by the Holy Spirit and by the grace of God, and saving faith has been imparted to our souls. By this faith, we grasp Christ and receive our justification, and by that same faith we should confidently trust in every word that proceeds from the mouth of God. We can believe everything that is revealed in Scripture because the authority of God stands behind it. The fundamental issue that led to the fall of the human race was the trustworthiness of God. When Satan tempted Jesus in the wilderness, he questioned the trustworthiness of God's word, but Jesus replied that He lived by every word that proceeds from the mouth of God.

The confession says that a Christian, when believing what is revealed in the Word, **acteth differently upon that which each particular passage thereof containeth.** A person who does not have the gift of saving faith can hear Scripture, read it, understand it, and be completely unmoved by it. But the Christian believes what it says and yields obedience to its commands. Remember that saving faith is not destitute of works; true faith yields the fruit of obedience. When the believer hears the warnings and admonitions of Scripture, he trembles before God. As the hymn says, we do have a friend in Jesus, but our friend is also the Holy One of Israel and the King before whom we bow.

Here the confession speaks wonderfully about the difference that faith makes in the Christian life. The believer is to be found embracing the promises of God for this life, and that which is to come. How is this done? The confession explains that the principal acts of saving faith are accepting, receiving, and resting upon Christ alone. This is *fiducia*. The Christian trusts in Christ for justification, sanctification, and eternal life, by virtue of the covenant of grace. The principal fruit of saving faith is justification. But faith is also vital to our sanctification. It is by faith that we tremble at the commands of God, that we yield obedience to the mandates of Christ, and that we put our trust in the promises of God for now and for the future. Faith is critical from the beginning of the Christian life until we are brought home, full and free into the presence of Christ. And this is not our own doing. Not unto us, O Lord, not unto us, but unto Your name be all glory.

> 3. This faith is different in degrees, weak or strong; may be often and many ways assailed, and weakened, but gets the victory: growing up in many to the attainment of a full assurance, through Christ, who is both the author and finisher of our faith.

When we studied the doctrine of justification by faith alone, we saw that there is only one ground for our justification. The sole ground upon which God declares us righteous is the righteousness of Jesus, whose righteousness is perfect. That which is perfect cannot be improved. Since the righteousness by which we are justified is Christ's righteousness, it does not admit to augmentation or diminution.

However, the faith by which we lay hold of Christ is a varying faith. Our trust in Him does admit to augmentation and diminution. Our faith can increase, and it can grow weaker. This brings us out of the theoretical realm of Christian theology right to where we live every day, because it is by faith that we live out the Christian life, and that faith vacillates. We pray, "I believe; help my unbelief!" (Mark 9:24). Our faith is always mixed with some measure of doubt, and our fidelity is always mixed with some measure of infidelity. None of us possesses a perfect faith. If our faith were perfect in this world, our obedience would also be perfect.

The confession addresses here the vacillating aspect of faith itself. This faith is different in degrees, weak or strong, and it may be assailed and weakened. Luther wrote about experiencing the unbridled and at times relentless assault from Satan. Luther was a prime target for the fiery darts of the evil one, whose attacks left him struggling in his faith. The Apostle Paul tells us to put on the whole armor of God (Eph. 6:10–17), that we may withstand the things that assail our faith and cause us to stumble, to struggle, to doubt, to be paralyzed.

As we have seen, there are three elements to faith: *notitia*, *assensus*, and *fiducia*. The first two are established in the mind, and the third can be given to us only by the work of the Holy Spirit. We cannot argue anyone into the kingdom of God. Nevertheless, we are called to clearly set forth the content of the gospel and to show the basis for belief in its truth claims. Having done all those things, we realize that unless the Holy Spirit does His work, no one will come to saving faith.

The task of apologetics—defending the faith—does not end at conversion. The principal purpose of defending the faith is to strengthen the faith of believers. High school students, new to the faith, go to college and there find the Christian faith constantly assailed. One of the tasks of apologetics is to edify and equip those whose biblical faith is attacked. Satan may not be able to snatch our souls away from Christ, but he can certainly paralyze us with doubt and insecurity, decreasing our boldness as Christians and as witnesses for Christ. One of the tasks of the ministry, as we nurture and edify the people of God, is to produce an army of brave warriors who are not intimidated by the power structures of this world, who can withstand the assaults of Satan, and who can be bold and courageous—not arrogant but confident in their faith.

Christian faith is often fragile. Every Christian knows what it is like to go through what has classically been called the dark night of the soul. Martin Luther, when the Diet of Worms met, stood alone before the authorities of this world, the emperor of the Holy Roman Empire and the princes of the church, and he was commanded to recant. He mumbled an answer that no one could hear. When told to speak up, he asked finally,

"May I have twenty-four hours to think about it?" He had gone through several years of preparation to get to this moment, and yet when the time came, he begged for twenty-four more hours, which he was granted. He spent the whole time in bold prayer and cried out to God in agony, "The cause is Yours, and I am Yours. I cannot do this unless I know You are with me." We can peer into the window of his soul and see the struggle that every Christian faces at one point or another, because faith vacillates.

Faith is assailed, the confession says, and it is weakened, but it is always victorious. The doctrine of the perseverance of the saints does not mean that the Christian life is one of steady, upward growth with no failures. No, a Christian is capable of falling into serious sin. There is likely no sin, except blasphemy against the Holy Spirit, that a truly regenerate Christian is incapable of committing. Regenerate people have committed murder, have committed adultery, and have publicly denied Christ, but not persistently. A Christian can fall radically and seriously but not fully and finally. We cannot read the state of other people's souls. We know them by their fruits, but we do not know them to the degree that God knows them, because only He can read the heart.

A person who has fallen into sin may be subjected to church discipline, where the church steps in, counsels him, and calls him to repentance. He may persist in disobedience and eventually be excommunicated, after being censured and then suspended for a season from the Lord's Table. Those who don't repent were never believers in the first place. Judas betrayed Jesus and went out and hanged himself; Peter denied Jesus but was restored because he came to repentance and his faith was strengthened.

The confession acknowledges that our faith is weak; it is fragile and is subjected to all these assaults. Anyone "who thinks that he stands" is warned to "take heed lest he fall" (1 Cor. 10:12). We do fall, but never fully or finally, because those who possess true faith will be victorious, although we may be bloodied in the process.

Christians know that their faith is fragile and that there are moments of failure and lack of confidence. There are those who think that Christians are supposed to pretend that this doesn't happen, that there is not a struggle. That is sad, because we are supposed to encourage one another. There are several different ingredients that go into courage, but the one absolutely necessary ingredient is fear. Courage is not required to do something if we are not afraid to do it. The reason we are called to encourage one another is that we are people given to fear. But the first prohibition that Jesus gave to His disciples was "Fear not."

We have failed to recognize that as a negative command. Our Lord understands that we are easily frightened or intimidated, and that cowardliness is contagious. In battle, when one person runs, everyone wants to run; but if one person steps forward into the line of fire, other people are encouraged to join him. One of the greatest problems we have in the church today is a lack of courage. We have plenty of fear, but the victory comes by faith that is strengthened not only by the Holy Spirit but also by the people of God as we encourage one another.

We are encouraged by the examples in Scripture of people who were faithful. Hebrews 11 contains the classic roll call of the heroes of the church. In every generation, Christians need to have heroes. Some people object to that, thinking that it isn't spiritual to look for heroes, but the Word of God understands our need, and that is why the eleventh chapter of Hebrews is set before us.

"Now faith is the assurance of things hoped for, the conviction of things not seen" (Heb. 11:1). This is a wonderful definition of faith: "the assurance of things hoped for." The Bible speaks of the three virtues, faith, hope, and love, the greatest of which is love (1 Cor. 13:13). We hear about love in the church, and we also hear about faith, but when is the last time you heard a sermon on hope? In today's church, the concept of hope is commonly misunderstood.

In our culture, hope is a desire that a future event or action will take place. When the Bible speaks about hope, it describes the anchor of the soul. Biblical hope refers to those things in the future that God has promised to bring to pass. They have not yet taken place, but they certainly will. We talk about the return of Christ as the blessed hope of the church. We do not merely desire that Jesus win; we know He is going to win. We trust the God who, in ages past, has always fulfilled His word and has never broken a promise. Our trust in the future is based on something of substance. It is not ephemeral and wishful but has substantive reality, based on the certainty of God's promises.

In our culture, with the massive impact of existential philosophy, we have seen an unprecedented divorce between what is called faith and what is called reason or rationality. The general assumption of the modern era is that faith demands belief against the evidence. It intimates that a person must take a leap of faith into the darkness, for no reason whatsoever. But the Bible never tells us to jump into the darkness and hope that Jesus will catch us. Rather, we are told to run out of the darkness into the light, to the solid foundation of the manifold evidence provided by God that Christ is His beloved Son.

The Bible doesn't suggest that there is not enough evidence to prove that Christ is the Son of God but that we have to believe it anyway. That is not faith. The Bible declares, "For we did not follow cleverly devised myths when we made known to you the power and coming of our Lord Jesus Christ, but we were eyewitnesses of his majesty" (2 Peter 1:16). Luke lets us know that he is giving us eyewitness testimony of what took place in real history that can be evaluated rationally (Luke 1:1–4). He says that it was predicted centuries ago on the pages of sacred Scripture, and it has been fulfilled in our midst. We are to submit to the evidence, not believe against it.

Some things in the Bible, admittedly, seem to go against the evidence. For example, God told Abraham, "I have made you the father of a multitude of nations" (Gen. 17:5). At that point, there seemed to be no possibility of children for Abraham and Sarah. But there was one piece of evidence that still had to be evaluated, namely, who it was that said Abraham would have children. God said it. Sarah's age and barrenness could not prevent God from fulfilling His promise. It would be utterly irrational not to trust a declaration if we knew that it came from God. It is never unreasonable to believe God; it is totally unreasonable not to believe God.

But how does one know that a declaration has come from God? That was Moses' question when God sent him to Pharaoh (Ex. 3–4). He said, "You want me to do what? You want me to go see whom? Pharaoh? Tell him what? Let this free labor force go? You want me to tell people, who are powerless and enslaved by the strongest military power in the world, to stop working and leave the country?" Moses knew he was talking to

God, but he persisted: "How are they going to believe that You sent me?" That is one of the most significant questions in biblical history. And God gave him this answer: "Put your hand in your shirt; now take it out." His hand was leprous. Moses then followed God's instruction to put his hand back in his shirt and then remove it, and it had been made clean. Many people mistakenly think that miracles prove the existence of God. But miracles are never used in the Bible to prove the existence of God; rather, they demonstrate that a human being is an agent sent from God and authorized by Him. From Moses through the New Testament, God accredits writers and speakers through the working of miracles, including the fulfilling of Old Testament prophecies concerning the person and work of Christ.

Faith is the assurance of things not seen, but those things have been promised by One whose word has been demonstrated to be reliable over and over again. As Christians, we serve and seek to obey a God we cannot see, and yet whose presence we trust. Where is He? At this moment, there is an ontological barrier between where we live and where the being of God is. He is here, but there is a dimensional barrier between us, and even the best microscope is not going to make Him visible to us. But we have visible evidence of the presence of the invisible God. God makes His invisible power and deity known through the things that are made. The visible is used by God to reveal His invisible reality (Rom. 1:20).

We trust that, and faith provides the evidence of things unseen, not only of realities that are invisible but also of events that have not yet taken place. There is the future, which is not seen by anyone except God, and there is the present dimension of reality that we do not penetrate. We walk through this world as if we were blindfolded, because the presence, the manifestations, and the signs of the glory and majesty of God are all around us. The Bible tells us that the whole world is filled with His glory, but we tend to think that, if we are lucky, maybe two or three times in our life we will have some kind of spiritual encounter that will strengthen our faith that God is really out there. All around us, the glory of God fills the world. We are surrounded by it, yet we do not see it.

By faith "the people of old received their commendation. By faith we understand that the universe was created by the word of God, so that what is seen was not made out of things that are visible" (Heb. 11:2–3). The worlds were framed by the Word of God. The worlds came from Him, and we know that if something exists now, then something must have the power to create, or nothing could possibly exist. The Scriptures declare to us that God is the One who called the world into existence. We believe that, we trust that, and it is not irrational.

And "by faith Abel offered to God a more acceptable sacrifice than Cain, through which he was commended as righteous, God commending him by accepting his gifts. And through his faith, though he died, he still speaks" (v. 4). "By faith Abraham obeyed when he was called to go out to a place that he was to receive as an inheritance. And he went out, not knowing where he was going" (v. 8). Abraham did not know, nor could he see, where he was going. He had no map, but he knew the tour director, and the tour director said, "Trust me"—and Abraham did. "By faith he went to live in the land of promise, as in a foreign land, living in tents with Isaac and Jacob, heirs with him of the same promise. For he was looking forward to the city that has foundations, whose designer and builder is God" (vv. 9–10). We also read of the faith of Enoch, Noah, and Sarah. Then we come to verse 13: "These all died in faith, not having received the things promised, but having seen them and greeted them from afar, and having acknowledged that they were strangers and exiles on the earth."

That is what it means to be a Christian—to die in faith, not in one's sins. They died in faith, not having received what was promised. Every Christian who is now in heaven passed from this world without living to see the consummation of the kingdom of God. We might also die before all those promises are fulfilled. But "having seen them and greeted them from afar," they "acknowledged that they were strangers and exiles on the earth." Faith enables us to understand that we are strangers and pilgrims on this earth.

This faith is different in degrees, weak or strong; may be often and many ways assailed, and weakened, but gets the victory: growing up in many to the attainment of a full assurance, through Christ, who is both the author and finisher of our faith. That last clause is of vital importance. Faith is not something that comes from our flesh, nor is it something that is evoked by our decision. Faith is a gift of God. It is worked in the soul by the Holy Spirit. It is the gift of Jesus, who is its author. We are not the authors of our own faith. Christ is, and He who has begun a good work in us will perform it to the end. That is the promise: that the same One who authored faith in our soul will finish what He began. Because He finishes what He starts, the framers of the confession can say that we will be victorious. We have this assurance because of the One who gives us faith in the beginning. Reformed theology relies on the grace of God from beginning to end. Thanks be to God that He is the author and the finisher of our salvation.

Of Repentance unto Life

1. Repentance unto life is an evangelical grace, the doctrine whereof is to be preached by every minister of the gospel, as well as that of faith in Christ.

2. By it, a sinner, out of the sight and sense not only of the danger, but also of the filthiness and odiousness of his sins, as contrary to the holy nature, and righteous law of God; and upon the apprehension of his mercy in Christ to such as are penitent, so grieves for, and hates his sins, as to turn from them all unto God, purposing and endeavoring to walk with him in all the ways of his commandments.

3. Although repentance be not to be rested in, as any satisfaction for sin, or any cause of the pardon thereof, which is the act of God's free grace in Christ; yet it is of such necessity to all sinners, that none may expect pardon without it.

4. As there is no sin so small, but it deserves damnation; so there is no sin so great, that it can bring damnation upon those who truly repent.

5. Men ought not to content themselves with a general repentance, but it is every man's duty to endeavor to repent of his particular sins, particularly.

6. As every man is bound to make private confession of his sins to God, praying for the pardon thereof; upon which, and the forsaking of them, he shall find mercy; so, he that scandalizeth his brother, or the church of Christ, ought to be willing, by a private or public confession, and sorrow for his sin, to declare his repentance to those that are offended, who are thereupon to be reconciled to him, and in love to receive him.

1. Repentance unto life is an evangelical grace, the doctrine whereof is to be preached by every minister of the gospel, as well as that of faith in Christ.

We see a crisis in the modern church, in which cheap grace has achieved the upper hand. People are told that God loves them unconditionally and that we are acceptable to God no matter what we have done. No mention is made of the necessity of repentance. And if people are called to faith in Jesus Christ, faith is too often defined as a fleeing to Christ for salvation, but not as a fleeing from our sin in true repentance. If repentance is not preached, the message is a false gospel.

2. By it, a sinner, out of the sight and sense not only of the danger, but also of the filthiness and odiousness of his sins, as contrary to the holy nature, and righteous law of God; and upon the apprehension of his mercy in Christ to such as are penitent, so grieves for, and hates his sins, as to turn from them all unto God, purposing and endeavoring to walk with him in all the ways of his commandments.

The essence of what is found in section 2 may be illustrated by going back in American history to the First Battle of Bull Run (known in the South as the First Battle of Manassas), which took place on July 21, 1861, outside Washington, D.C. This was the first significant conflict of the Civil War. In the nation's capital, it was assumed that the Southern rebellion would be quashed in a matter of days or weeks. The sense of assurance was so great that the First Battle of Bull Run was attended by a host of spectators. The wealthy women of Washington went out in their carriages to observe the quick and decisive victory that the North would inflict on the South.

What most people overlooked in this conflict—which ultimately led to the death of six hundred thousand Americans—was that two different wars were being fought. The North was fighting a war of conquest, while the South was fighting a war of attrition. The objective of the

Confederacy, both politically and militarily, was simply to be free of any formal relationship with the North. They had no desire to conquer the North or to incorporate the Northern states into the Confederacy. The objective of the Northern states, both politically and militarily, was to force the Southern states back into the union.

For the North to achieve its objective, it had to conquer the Southern states and force them to surrender, to turn in their arms, and to submit to the federal government. All the Southern states had to do was to hang on, fight a defensive war, and hope that as the casualties mounted, the North would lose its resolve to force its will on the South.

In a war of attrition, people get worn out because the cost of the war, in casualties and finances, is too heavy. In fact, the Civil War went on for four years, but it was within a forty-eight-hour period that everything turned around at the Battle of Gettysburg on July 3, 1863, and the fall of Vicksburg on July 4. If those two battles had gone to the Confederates, historians agree, the South would have won the war. People in the Northern states had had enough war. They didn't believe it was worth pursuing any further.

Historians say that if Abraham Lincoln had not been assassinated and had run for reelection, he would not have been reelected, because by that time the war was so unpopular in the North. The national attitude during the Vietnam War was similar. Lyndon Johnson didn't even seek a second elected term because the people were tired of losing American lives in a war that they didn't care about. The Vietnamese were not trying to conquer America; they were fighting a war of attrition. How did our Colonial fathers achieve victory over the major world power of the day, Britain, in the Revolutionary War? They won because the British did not want to expend the necessary money and manpower to force the American colonists to submit.

What do wars of attrition have to do with repentance? There are two different kinds of repentance, one of which is authentic and acceptable to God, and the other of which is not acceptable. The kind of repentance that is not acceptable to God is the repentance of attrition. That is a repentance, or a decision to change one's behavior, that is motivated purely by counting the cost or the consequences and deciding that continuing the old behavior is not worth it. It is the kind of repentance that every parent has observed in a child who is caught in an act of disobedience, when the parent appears with a wooden spoon. The child says, "Oh, I'm sorry; I won't do it again; don't spank me." Sorrow is produced by a fear of punishment and shame for having been caught, but there is no real remorse for having broken the rule of the household. The motive for the repentance is to escape punishment.

Repentance that is not acceptable to God is repentance that is motivated by seeking a ticket out of hell, an escape from divine retribution. In the Roman Catholic prayer of contrition, the words are to this effect: "O God, I am heartily sorry for having offended You. Help me, in thought, word, and deed, not only for fear of the consequences of Your wrath and of the punishment of hell, but because I have offended You." People who have been caught in gross and egregious sin pour out their sorrow and remorse to escape punishment. We do not have to look beyond the mirror to find that kind of attitude expressed by the human heart.

Genuine repentance, or contrition, comes from a heart that is broken because we have become acutely aware of how awful our sin really is. We then detest our sin and are genuinely contrite. We have a broken spirit because we have injured and violated the holiness of God.

Bennett Cerf, when he was with Random House Publishing Company, brought together a large group of people in the arts to write critical essays on the great classics of Western literature. Included in the list of books was *The Confessions* of Augustine. The review of Augustine's *Confessions* was written by Rod Serling, creator of *The Twilight Zone*. In his review, Serling panned the book, saying that it did not deserve to be considered a classic of Western literature because of its naivete.

What provoked Serling's wrath was that Augustine, in reflecting upon his life, went into great detail about his deep remorse for a sin that he committed as a youth, when he stole pears from someone's pear tree. Serling thought it ridiculous that a grown man would parade his remorse for a childhood peccadillo. Serling completely missed Augustine's point. His point was that he could understand sexual sin because of the passions of the body, or stealing bread when one is hungry, or stealing money when one is impoverished. But he couldn't understand why he stole pears, when he didn't even like pears. He stole pears on a full stomach. When he reflected on this boyhood act, he realized that the only motivation that he had for stealing those pears was the sheer joy and pleasure of doing something that he knew was wrong.

It is extremely difficult to look in a mirror and see a person there whose heart is a heart of darkness. None of us has a clue as to the depths of the capacity for evil that resides in our hearts even now, as converted people. The capacity that we have for sin is incalculable, and we have a deeply distorted view of our own righteousness, particularly in these days, because we live in an era of narcissism that is unprecedented in American history and certainly in church history. The church seems to have decided that the most significant way to minister to people is to help them increase their self-esteem. We are not to make them feel unworthy.

We have no desire to destroy the dignity of human beings. God would have us treat people in such a way that we do not demean them. However, we need to make a sober evaluation of who we are in the presence of God. The more the Holy Spirit works in our lives and the more sanctified we become, the more we realize how much we have taken God's grace for granted. True contrition makes us realize, "For I know that nothing good dwells in me, that is, in my flesh" (Rom. 7:18)—that we have absolutely nothing in our hand to present to God.

The hymn "Rock of Ages" confesses our utter, total dependence on grace, which is the fruit of true repentance. As long as we think that God owes us something, our repentance is not genuine. Here are the words of a song written in 1861 by Horatius Bonar:

Not what my hands have done can save my guilty soul;
not what my toiling flesh has borne can make my spirit whole.
Not what I feel or do can give me peace with God;
not all my prayers and sighs and tears can bear my awful load.

Your voice alone, O Lord, can speak to me of grace;
Your power alone, O Son of God, can all my sin erase.
No other work but Yours, no other blood will do;
no strength but that which is divine can bear me safely through.

I praise the Christ of God; I rest on love divine;
and with unfaltering lip and heart, I call this Savior mine.
My Lord has saved my life, and freely pardon gives;
I love because He first loved me, I live because He lives.

Horatius Bonar was a Scottish Calvinistic minister. If ever a hymn captures the essence of what our theology should be, this is it.

The supreme prayer of contrition penned by David in Psalm 51 has the notation, "To the choirmaster. A Psalm of David, when Nathan the prophet went to him, after he had gone in to Bathsheba." Remember the story of David and Bathsheba, and David and Nathan (2 Sam. 11–12). Not only did David commit adultery with Bathsheba, but he also wanted to possess this woman, who was already married to Uriah, one of his faithful soldiers. David had Uriah put on the front line of battle, hoping that he would be killed there. David, who is called a man after God's own heart, not only was involved in adultery, but he also committed murder by proxy, for Uriah was indeed killed in battle. David then moved Bathsheba into his palace to be his wife.

The Lord sent Nathan the prophet to David with a parable about two men, one rich and one poor. The poor man had one small ewe lamb, a pet of his children, and the rich man had extensive flocks and herds. One day a visitor was invited to dinner with the rich man, but rather than slaying a lamb from his own abundant flock, the rich man took that pet lamb from the poor man, killed it, prepared it, and served it to his visitor. When David heard that story, he was angry, and he ordered that the rich man die and from his estate the poor man be given fourfold. Nathan looked David in the eye and said, "You are the man!" (12:7)—and David disintegrated. This is the way we are. It is much easier to see other people's sins and to be angry about them, while we shield our souls from our own transgressions. We refuse to see it until the Word of God comes and says to us, "You are the man." After this happened to David, he prayed the greatest prayer of confession ever:

Have mercy on me, O God,
    according to your steadfast love;
according to your abundant mercy
    blot out my transgressions. (Ps. 51:1)

David was not asking that God treat him according to justice. Instead, he pleaded with God to deal with him according to His mercy, His loving-kindness. A deeply important concept in the Old Testament is the loyal love of God. David asked, "God, I appeal to that; treat me according to Your mercy." "Blot out my transgressions. Wash me thoroughly from my iniquity, and cleanse me from my sin!" (vv. 1–2). Shakespeare's Lady Macbeth, after she stained her hands with the murder of King Duncan, tried everything to clean them and she cried, "Out, damned spot!" Nothing could erase those bloodstains from her hands. That was how David felt when he cried out, "Blot out my transgressions." He did not want God to look at his sins, nor did he want to have to see them. "My sin is ever before me" (v. 3). David was aware of his sinfulness and was broken and haunted by it.

> Wash me thoroughly from my iniquity,
>   and cleanse me from my sin! (v. 2)

He felt dirty, filthy, and a bath would not help. He needed to be washed thoroughly, and he needed God to do it because he needed to be cleansed from his sins. The real crux of true repentance and contrition comes in verses 3 and 4:

> For I know my transgressions,
>   and my sin is ever before me.
> Against you, you only, have I sinned
>   and done what is evil in your sight,
> so that you may be justified in your words
>   and blameless in your judgment.

There is a little bit of hyperbole when David says, "Against you, you only, have I sinned." In one sense, that is true; but in another sense, it is not true, because David also sinned against his wives, against Bathsheba, against Uriah, and against Uriah's family. He sinned against every one of the troops who fought for Israel. By violating one soldier under his command, David was betraying them all, and as the king of Israel, he violated the trust of every person in the nation. He sinned against everyone.

David said his sin was only against God. What part of that is true?

Ultimately, sin is sin because we are breaking a law. Where there is no law, there is no sin. The law that was broken was the law delivered by the lawgiver, who is the covenant God and David's Creator. David violated and injured other human beings, but, ultimately, his offense was against the holiness of God. David understood that, and he directed his repentance toward God.

When David said, "that you may be justified in your words and blameless in your judgment" (v. 4), he was saying: "God, I am guilty, I have no excuse, and You have every right to do with me whatever You want. I am begging You to treat me according to Your mercy, and not according to Your justice. If You give me justice, I am finished, because I know I deserve to be punished. I will not complain if You remove me from the kingship. I will not complain if You take my life." This is the real crux of genuine repentance.

God let David live, and He let Bathsheba live. He granted clemency and did not require the death penalty from them for their adultery, but He took the child of their union. David fasted and prayed for seven days, begging for the baby to be spared. When the baby died, everyone was afraid to tell David, for fear he would kill himself. Instead, he got up, changed his clothes, anointed his head, and went to the house of the Lord to worship, because he was still repentant. He never said, "It is not fair." David's repentance was not attrition, but real contrition.

> Purge me with hyssop, and I shall be clean;
>> wash me, and I shall be whiter than snow.
> Let me hear joy and gladness;
>> let the bones that you have broken rejoice.
> Hide your face from my sins,
>> and blot out all my iniquities.
> Create in me a clean heart, O God,
>> and renew a right spirit within me.
> Cast me not away from your presence,
>> and take not your Holy Spirit from me. (Ps. 51:7–11)

David begged God not to break fellowship with him. And that was after he had said, "You have every right to abandon me. You have every right to forsake me, but please, God, don't do it." He begged and pleaded:

Restore to me the joy of your salvation,
and uphold me with a willing spirit.
Then I will teach transgressors your ways,
and sinners will return to you. (vv. 12–13)

Perhaps you have heard the cliché that a Christian evangelist is one beggar telling another beggar how to find bread, one forgiven person trying to tell another person how to find forgiveness. This is seen in verses 15–17:

O Lord, open my lips,
and my mouth will declare your praise.
For you will not delight in sacrifice, or I would give it;
you will not be pleased with a burnt offering.
The sacrifices of God are a broken spirit;
a broken and contrite heart, O God, you will not despise.

That is what repentance is. When we repent of our sin, we come before God, not whole, but broken. An excellent illustration of this is Isaiah in the temple, where he sees the holiness of God and cries out: "Woe is me! for I am undone" (Isa. 6:5, KJV). He was saying, "I've come apart; I am no longer whole. I am broken." And one of the seraphim put a hot coal on his lips and cleansed his mouth, an act of grace for a man who was truly contrite before the holiness of God.

> 3. Although repentance be not to be rested in, as any satisfaction for sin, or any cause of the pardon thereof, which is the act of God's free grace in Christ; yet it is of such necessity to all sinners, that none may expect pardon without it.

The Westminster Confession was written by a team of godly scholars whose goal was to articulate the essence of the faith that was confessed by British Protestants. This seventeenth-century confession had as part of its background the major controversies of the sixteenth-century Reformation. Many of its doctrines, such as the doctrine of justification, were defined vis-à-vis their Roman Catholic counterparts, so that there could be a clear understanding of the difference between the English Reformation and the teaching of the Roman Catholic Church. What is in view in this chapter is the difference between the Reformation understanding of repentance and the Roman Catholic Church's sacrament of penance.

In the Roman Catholic Church, there are seven sacraments, not two as in Protestantism. The first sacrament is the sacrament of baptism, in which an infant is cleansed of original sin and receives an infusion of the grace of justification, which is the righteousness of Christ poured into the soul of the infant (or of the adult, if it is an adult baptism). That infused grace enables the person to become righteous if he cooperates with this assisting grace and the assisting righteousness of Christ that is poured into him. If he cooperates with it and assents to it, then he can become truly righteous and be in a state of justification, unless he commits mortal sin. Mortal sin, such as murder, adultery, drunkenness, and missing Mass on Sunday, is sin that is so serious that it kills the grace of justification that was infused into the soul at baptism. (Lesser sin is called venial sin.)

A person at this stage can have faith but can still be without justification. So for him to be saved, he has to be restored to the state of justification. There is a second sacrament that is designed to restore people who have fallen into mortal sin. It is the sacrament of penance, which the Roman Catholic Church defined in the sixteenth century as "the second plank" of justification for those who have "made shipwreck" of their souls.

If mortal sin is committed, the remedy is the second plank of justification, which is popularly called confession. It is here that a person receives the sacrament of penance. There are several aspects to the sacrament of penance, but one is confession. Protestants sometimes object to the practice of confessing one's sins to a priest and receiving absolution, saying that they can confess their sins directly to God. But we should be reminded that at the time of the Reformation, even though the sacrament of penance was at the heart of the controversy, what made it controversial was not the idea of going to a priest to confess sins. There was no real objection to that. In fact, Luther wanted to retain the confessional in his church because he understood how important it was for people to go in confidentiality to someone who would minister to them in the name of Christ and allow them to empty their souls and rid themselves of burdens. Protestant ministers spend a great deal of time hearing the confessions of the people. Although it is true that we can go to God directly, the New Testament admonishes us to confess our sins to one another.

A nationwide poll of college students once measured not just the sensitivity of their consciences but also their unresolved guilt, their guilt complexes. Students at a Baptist college, where the gospel was freely communicated, college ranked in the ninety-ninth percentile of unresolved guilt problems in American colleges. Obviously, the gospel was not coming across. Either people don't know the doctrine of justification by faith alone, or they don't understand it and are still trying to work their way into heaven, or they have the antinomian view that "I can sin all I want." The downside, of course, is the antinomian solution: "All I've got to do is go to confession, and I am fixed."

To go to confession was not an issue in the sixteenth century, and neither was it an issue for the priest to pronounce absolution. Jesus communicated to His Apostles what we call the power of the keys: "I will give you the keys of the kingdom of heaven, and whatever you bind on earth shall be bound in heaven, and whatever you loose on earth shall be loosed in heaven" (Matt. 16:19). The Roman Catholic Church does not believe that the priest has an inherent power to forgive sins. When a priest says, "I absolve you," it is meant to be understood that he is speaking in the name of Christ. This is the same in the Protestant service of worship, when, after a prayer of confession and an assurance of pardon, the minister stands up and says to the congregation, "The Word of God declares, 'If we confess our sins, he is faithful and just to forgive us our sins and to cleanse us from all unrighteousness'" (1 John 1:9). A minister does that not on his own authority but on the authority of God, whose Word makes that declaration.

It was the next part of the sacrament of penance that caused trouble in the sixteenth century, and that was the part called satisfaction. Before people can be restored to a state of justification, they must do works of satisfaction. This is closely linked to the biblical concept of restitution, wherein, say, someone who stole fifty dollars from another could not simply ask forgiveness without repaying the money. If he was truly repentant, he would do everything he could to make restitution. He would return the money. (And actually, the biblical principle is that one should repay more than was stolen.)

The works of satisfaction were designed partly for restitution, to impress on people the importance of being careful the next time, and partly as a deterrent to further sin, to show people that sin has consequences. There is a cost to it, and the person must satisfy the demands of God's justice. We make a fine distinction even in Protestantism between eternal guilt and temporal guilt. We often hear of people on death row in our prisons who profess faith in Christ, and I think many of those professions are genuine. One of the places where the ministry of the gospel is really focused in our time is in prison. There are ministries that focus on people who are incarcerated. So yes, there are people who come to Christ even on death row. There are those who believe that if an inmate becomes a Christian, he should not have to finish out his sentence or be executed. However, while Christ and the cross cover our eternal guilt, we still have to pay the consequences for our sins in this world. Faith and repentance can get one approved by God for the hereafter, but we still have to pay our debt here.

The distinction between eternal guilt and temporal guilt in Roman Catholicism is not only about making restitution but also about being restored to a state of justifying grace. To be restored, we have to do the works of satisfaction. We have to do penance.

By doing the works of satisfaction, a person can gain *congruous merit*. The quality of congruous merit is not so high that it obligates God to reward us, but it is still merit. It is called congruous because it is fitting for God to reward it. Luther objected to this, saying, "Do you mean that if we do these works of satisfaction, and God doesn't restore us to a state of justification, then God has done something that is not fitting? No, with one flash of lightning and one thunderbolt, the gospel destroys all merit, condign and congruous." We are justified only by the free grace of God, based solely on the righteousness of Christ, not on anything we do. We have nothing to contribute to our salvation.

In Roman Catholicism, if you die in mortal sin, you go to hell. That is why the sacrament of penance is so important. It is necessary to restore fallen sinners to grace and to keep them out of hell. Those who die without mortal sin, but with venial sin or any impurity, go to purgatory, where they stay as long as it takes to be purified, so they can get into heaven. The

Protestant understanding is that the minute we put our trust in Christ, we are translated from the kingdom of this world to the kingdom of God. We receive the righteousness of Jesus, and that righteousness can never be augmented or diminished.

One of the works of satisfaction, according to the Roman church, is almsgiving. And the giving of alms, if done out of a genuinely contrite heart, can count as a work of satisfaction to get someone restored to justification. But it can also be used to gain indulgences. Keep in mind that for the Roman Catholic Church in the sixteenth century and even now, as detailed in the latest Catechism of the Catholic Church, there is a treasury of merit. The treasury of merit is like a storehouse in heaven that holds merit obtained by Christ, Mary, Joseph, Peter, Paul, James, John, Francis of Assisi, Thomas Aquinas, and other saints who, when they died, not only had enough merit to get into heaven but had more merit than they needed. They had excess merit because, in addition to doing the normally demanded works, they did what are called *supererogatory works*, which are works that are above and beyond what is necessary. That excess merit was then deposited into the treasury of merit.

The benefit of this to people like us is that if we are deficient in our own merit, the church can transfer to our account some merit from the treasury of merit. The Roman Catholic Church repudiates the imputation of the merit of Jesus to us in justification, but the concept of imputation is used when Rome talks about the transfer of merit from the treasury of merit.

That is the background for section 3: Repentance be not to be rested in, as any satisfaction for sin. This statement is a repudiation of Roman Catholic practice. Repentance is not to be rested in, as any satisfaction for sin, or any cause of the pardon thereof, which is the act of God's free grace in Christ; yet it is of such necessity to all sinners, that none may expect pardon without it. Our repentance adds nothing to the grounds of our justification. We can't trust at all in our contrition to satisfy God. It is not an act of satisfaction; it gives us no merit whatsoever. We can't be saved without repentance, but repentance itself adds nothing to the grounds of our salvation. It is the same with faith. We can't be justified without faith, but we are not justified on the grounds of our faith. Faith is not a meritorious work that does for us what we failed to do with our lives. If we sin and are not sorrowful about it, that adds to our guilt and to our demerit; on the other hand, if we sin and are sorrowful for your sin, there is no merit in that—you have simply escaped further demerit.

> 4. As there is no sin so small, but it deserves damnation; so there is no sin so great, that it can bring damnation upon those who truly repent.

There are places in the confession when John Calvin's teaching is quoted word for word. This teaching, directed against the idea that only the worst sins are mortal, is one of them. Calvin said that every sin is mortal in the sense that it deserves damnation. Every sin that we commit is an act of treason against God, and the Bible says the soul that sins shall die. Because the civil code of Israel limits the number of sins that are capital offenses, people come to the conclusion that God wouldn't kill anyone for the minor peccadilloes we commit. However, no sin is so insignificant or so small that it does not deserve damnation, because the smallest sin is an act of blasphemy against God and an act of treason. Calvin said that all sin is mortal in the sense that it deserves death. But no sin is mortal in the sense that it actually destroys the saving grace that Christ has given to His people. What about blasphemy against the Holy Spirit? As we will see later in this chapter, the unforgivable sin of which Jesus warns is a sin that no Christian will ever commit.

Even though the Reformers rejected the Roman Catholic distinction between venial sin and mortal sin, that does not mean that they taught that all sin is equally heinous. All sin is equally worthy of damnation, but some sins are still worse than others. This gradation of the degrees of sin is established by at least twenty-five texts in the New Testament. Jesus told Pilate that the one who had delivered Him up was more guilty than he was (John 19:11). He compared the sins of Chorazin and Bethsaida to those of Tyre and Sidon, and those of Capernaum to those of Sodom (Matt. 11:20–24). He spoke of certain sins' being particularly wicked and heinous. And there is a difference between that sin that is covered ("Love covers a multitude of sins"; 1 Peter 4:8) and those sins that are so grievous that they require church discipline.

Section 4 insists that no sin in the Christian life is so serious that it brings damnation on the penitent. However, many earnest Christians struggle with the questions raised by Jesus' severe warnings regarding the unforgivable sin. But there is no sin so grave that repentance is of no avail.

King David was guilty of the sin of adultery, and he was also guilty of conspiracy to commit murder. In spite of the depths of his sin, David repented, gave to the church a model prayer of contrition, and was forgiven by God for his heinous sin. By no means does this minimize the seriousness of the sins of murder and adultery, but to say that they are unforgivable or unpardonable is to miss the clear message of Scripture. If it is not adultery or murder, what is the unforgivable sin? Jesus describes the unpardonable sin as the sin of blasphemy against the Holy Spirit. But what is blasphemy against the Holy Spirit?

In Luke 12:8–10, we read: "And I tell you, everyone who acknowledges me before men, the Son of Man also will acknowledge before the angels of God, but the one who denies me before men will be denied before the angels of God. And everyone who speaks a word against the Son of Man will be forgiven, but the one who blasphemes against the Holy Spirit will not be forgiven." In Matthew 12:31–32, Jesus adds that any sin against the Son of Man can be forgiven in this world or in the world to come, but he who blasphemes against the Holy Spirit will not be forgiven either in this world or in the world to come.

Jesus makes a distinction between speaking a word against the Son of Man and speaking blasphemy against the Holy Spirit. Why would it be more serious to blaspheme the third person of the Trinity than it would be to blaspheme the first or second person of the Trinity? First, we have to look at the context in which Jesus gives this dire warning. Jesus gave the warning about blasphemy against the Holy Spirit after the Pharisees charged Jesus with casting out Satan by the power of Satan. In other words, they accused Jesus of being in league with the devil.

Casting out demons was unprecedented in Israel. Almost all the miracles that Jesus performed during His earthly ministry were of a type that had been performed at one time or another in Old Testament times. In the Old Testament, there were resurrections, healings, and other miraculous things. But Jesus' exorcism of demons was unique. He said in

Matthew 12:28, "If it is by the Spirit of God that I cast out demons, then the kingdom of God has come upon you." In other words, the clear sign of the presence of the kingdom of God was His exorcising of the power of Satan, who is the prince of this world.

The scribes and Pharisees didn't deny that Jesus was casting out demons. What they denied was that He did so by the power of the Holy Spirit. They claimed He was casting out demons through the power of Satan. Our Lord was patient with the Pharisees, but here He stopped them in their tracks. He warned them that they were coming perilously close to committing a sin that would never be forgiven, namely, the sin of blasphemy against the Holy Spirit.

We need to understand the nature of that sin, and what it was that provoked this warning. They accused Jesus of being in league with the devil. Whatever else the unforgivable sin is, it involves blasphemy. It has to do with words; it is a verbal sin. Jesus did not say that all forms of blasphemy are unforgivable and that anyone who has ever blasphemed God has no hope. If we use the sacred name of God in an inappropriate, insulting manner, or as a casual curse word, we have blasphemed against God. We have failed to give proper reverence and adoration to the sacred name of God. On television, certain kinds of language are censored, but it is perfectly OK to blaspheme God. We often hear "Oh my God!" when it is clearly not a prayer. Our culture has not taken seriously the commandment to honor the name of God.

If every kind of blasphemy is unpardonable, then few of us have any hope of heaven. We must not minimize the evil of blasphemy, but clearly blasphemy, in and of itself, is forgivable, or else we would have no hope.

Jesus distinguishes between blaspheming the Son of Man and blaspheming the Holy Spirit. How are we to understand that? Let's make it even more complicated by looking at some related texts. In Hebrews 6:4–6, we find one of the most controversial texts in the whole New Testament: "For it is impossible, in the case of those who have once been enlightened, who have tasted the heavenly gift, and have shared in the Holy Spirit, and have tasted the goodness of the word of God and the powers of the age to come, and then have fallen away, to restore them again to repentance, since they are crucifying once again the Son of God to their own harm and holding him up to contempt."

When the author of Hebrews warns against the impossibility of restoring someone, it is related to crucifying Christ afresh. This sin, from which there is no restoration, is directed against the second person of the Trinity, not against the Holy Spirit. Do you see how the plot is thickening? We have Jesus' warning in Luke, "You can sin against Me, you can say a word against Me, but watch out what you say about the Holy Spirit," but the author of Hebrews says, "If you crucify the Son of God afresh, there is no hope of renewal."

Hebrews 10:26–31 reads:

> For if we go on sinning deliberately after receiving the knowledge of the truth, there no longer remains a sacrifice for sins, but a fearful expectation of judgment, and a fury of fire that will consume the adversaries. Anyone who has set aside the law of Moses dies without mercy on the evidence of two or three witnesses. How much worse punishment, do you think, will be deserved by the one who has trampled underfoot the Son of God, and has profaned the blood of the covenant by which he was sanctified, and has outraged the Spirit of grace? For we know him who said, "Vengeance is mine; I will repay." And again, "The Lord will judge his people." It is a fearful thing to fall into the hands of the living God.

In Hebrews 6, there is a warning against crucifying the Son of God afresh. Here the language is of trampling the Son of God underfoot and insulting the Spirit of grace. In Luke, the rejection of Christ is distinguished from a sin against the Holy Spirit, but in Hebrews 10 it involves a sin against the Holy Spirit. The distinction that Jesus makes in the gospel falls away in the epistle. In Matthew 12, Jesus says that if a person says a word against Him, he can be forgiven, but not if one blasphemes the Holy Spirit. But in Hebrews we read that if someone crucifies the Son of God afresh and tramples Christ underfoot, he is doing violence to the Holy Spirit.

The context in Hebrews 6 and 10 is *after* we have already been made aware of the true identity of Christ, *after* the Holy Spirit has revealed to us that Christ is indeed the Son of God. Now with the full knowledge of Christ's true identity granted to us by the Holy Spirit, if you crucify Him afresh, if we accuse Him of being in league with the devil, then we have sinned against the Son and the Spirit.

The gospel accounts of the crucifixion help us see this. One of the things that Jesus did on the cross was pray for the forgiveness of those who were killing Him. His grounds for asking for their pardon were that "they know not what they do" (Luke 23:34). The Apostles in Acts 3:17 told the people that they had crucified Jesus in ignorance. We can argue whether they should have known who Christ was and what they were doing. If they had studied the Scriptures carefully, they would have known (cf. Luke 24:25). But even though they were culpably ignorant, Jesus prayed for their forgiveness.

If the Pharisees, by working to condemn Jesus, had committed the unforgivable sin, Jesus would not have prayed for their forgiveness. After Christ rose from the dead, and after the Holy Spirit bore witness to the character of Jesus, if those Pharisees then knew that He was the Son of God and they were still ready to crucify Him again, there would be no forgiveness for that. So we conclude, as do many biblical scholars, that the unforgivable sin is blasphemy against Christ when we *know* better—when we already know who He is.

There are many scholars in our Western culture who are hostile to the Christian faith. They have leveled absurd, cynical, and ridiculous charges against the credibility of the Scriptures. But even people like these are usually careful not to say nasty things about Jesus. They criticize the church, the Bible, the clergy, and orthodox believers, but they exalt Jesus as a paragon of virtue or as a great moral leader and teacher. George Bernard Shaw, who was hostile toward Christ, in his worst criticism against Jesus, could only say that there were occasions when Jesus did not behave as a Christian. Even Shaw, in trying to demean Christ, could find no higher standard than Christ by which to judge Him. We rarely hear the critics of Jesus say that He was a madman or that He was in league with the devil. Why, given the enmity of natural man toward Christ, do so few unbelievers actually express their hostility toward Jesus with incautious language? Perhaps it is the restraining power of God that people are kept from that.

The unforgivable sin is when someone calls Christ the devil after the Holy Spirit has revealed Christ's true identity to him. If that is the case, is it possible for a Christian to commit the unpardonable sin? The answer to that question is yes in one sense and no in another sense.

The sense in which a Christian is capable of committing blasphemy against the Holy Spirit is this. We have all the necessary equipment to commit the unpardonable sin: a mouth, the ability to speak sinful things, and the capacity to sin. We are still capable in our flesh of virtually every sin imaginable. So in that sense we have to conclude that we could commit the unforgivable sin.

In another sense, however, we cannot commit the unforgivable sin. It is not because we cannot; it is because we will not. The reason we will not is that Christ, the captain of our salvation, who has begun a good work in us, has promised to continue that work until it is completed, and part of that work is to protect us, as it were, from ourselves. The Holy Spirit who regenerated us now restrains us from committing some sins that we are capable of committing.

Of course, this presupposes that a Christian will never lose his faith completely, will never fall completely. Christians can fall radically and seriously, but not fully and finally. Peter blasphemed Christ at the campfire, cursing and swearing that he never knew the man, and he denied Christ publicly. That was not blaspheming against the Son, saying a word against the Son. Peter denied knowing Him, but he did not accuse Him of being Satan. Thus, Christians do not need to worry about committing blasphemy against the Holy Spirit because the Holy Spirit Himself restrains us from doing so if we are ever tempted to do so. It is by God's grace that we do not do it.

Hebrews 6:4–6 warns us against crucifying Christ afresh: "For it is impossible, in the case of those who have once been enlightened, who have tasted the heavenly gift, and have shared in the Holy Spirit, and have tasted the goodness of the word of God and the powers of the age to come, and then have fallen away, to restore them again to repentance, since they are crucifying once again the Son of God to their own harm and holding him up to contempt." The author is describing the Judaizers' heresy that was threatening the Christian community, particularly the Hebrew Christian community. In verse 9 he says, "Though we speak in this way, yet in your case, beloved, we feel sure of better things—things that belong to salvation."

Verse 9 is a huge caveat, warning us not to jump to conclusions from the admonition of verses 4–6. The conclusion that most people jump to is that if the author warns us about falling away, then it must be possible that we could fall away. If that were all that is said, that would be a reasonable inference. But then comes the caveat: "Although I am speaking to you in this manner, I am convinced of better things of you—that is, things that accompany salvation." In other words, saved people do not crucify Christ again. The warning not to do so is one that we can give to the community in general, just as the author of Hebrews frequently does, comparing the New Testament community with the Old Testament community, which was a mixed body of believers and unbelievers. He is saying, "I am convinced of better things from you, things that accompany salvation," meaning, "I do not expect you to do this." But he stresses, "If you do crucify Christ again, and if you do reject the cross, you will have no way back." Once someone has rejected the cross, he has rejected the only grounds for salvation.

Blasphemy of the Holy Spirit can be committed only by someone to whom the Spirit has revealed who Christ is, and yet then accuses Christ of being the devil. Notice that we have not connected Jesus' warnings of blasphemy against the Holy Spirit and the Apostle John's teaching about the "sin that leads to death." In 1 John 5:16, John says that if we see our brother sinning a sin that does not lead to death, we are to pray for him. Then he says that if we see our brother committing the sin that leads to death, "I do not say that one should pray for that." John does not say that in that situation you should *not* pray for him. Rather, he says, "I will not command you to pray for him."

It is one thing to say we are *not commanded* to do something; it is another thing to say we are *commanded not* to do it. John does not say that we are not allowed to pray. He simply says that we are not commanded to pray in that situation. The problem is, the recipients of John's letter knew what the sin that leads to death was, but we do not. John does not tell us what the sin is that lifts our responsibility to pray for a person. What is the sin that leads to death? Usually, the assumption is that there is a connection between Jesus' warning about blasphemy against the Holy Spirit and John's warning about committing a sin that leads to death. It's hard to make that connection, because we do not know what the sin that leads to death is.

There is another text that may be related. In 1 Corinthians 11:29, Paul warns against eating and drinking the Lord's Supper unworthily, adding, "That is why many of you are weak and ill, and some have died" (1 Cor. 11:30). Paul is saying that if we participate unworthily in the Lord's Supper, it may cause our death. That is not the same thing as saying that God will send us to hell. It just means we will die. We may die and go to heaven, but we will still die. Perhaps this is the sin that John refers to as the sin that leads to death. John could be talking about blasphemy or the unworthy participation in the Lord's Supper—or another sin that we don't know about.

Things are not always as simple as they may appear to be at first glance. There are often, as here, several texts in Scripture that must be dealt with and studied in conjunction with each other. Do not get the idea that where the Bible is less clear, we do not have to worry about it because we are ignorant. The Bible is basically a clear book. The Holy Spirit is not the author of confusion. There are portions of Scripture that are much clearer than others, and the obscure has to be interpreted in light of the clear. The greatest obscurity in the Scriptures comes from our muddle-headedness. When we come to the Scriptures, and we are not diligent, or we haven't searched the Scriptures completely, or we don't understand something, that is the time to worry about the seriousness of our devotion to Scripture, not about the trustworthiness of it. One of the great advantages of studying Scripture is that we learn more with each reading. That which once was difficult becomes open as we study the Bible more deeply.

There are subjects like this one, however, where Scripture is silent. There is no way to know the impact that John's statement had on the first hearers of it, since it has not been spelled out.

If we have done everything we can to learn what Scripture says about a particular subject, and if it is silent on the subject, then we, like Calvin, must say, "Where God closes His holy mouth, I will desist from inquiry, and I will also desist from worry."

5. Men ought not to content themselves with a general repentance, but it is every man's duty to endeavor to repent of his particular sins, particularly.

In one sense, the psalmist asks God to forgive his sins in general when he requests that the Lord purge him from his secret sins (Ps. 19:12). Nevertheless, the model for true repentance contains a confession of specific and particular sins against God and against our neighbor. It is a weak form of repentance merely to pray, "Dear God, please forgive all my sins." Repentance in general does not get to the root of the matter. It does not exhibit godly sorrow for the specific manner in which we have transgressed the law of God and violated His holiness. Therefore, the confession maintains that we should not be at ease in Zion, reaching an easy level of spiritual contentment that is found by resting on a general repentance. Rather, it is our duty to be specific when we confess our sins to God.

> 6. As every man is bound to make private confession of his sins to God, praying for the pardon thereof; upon which, and the forsaking of them, he shall find mercy; so, he that scandalizeth his brother, or the church of Christ, ought to be willing, by a private or public confession, and sorrow for his sin, to declare his repentance to those that are offended, who are thereupon to be reconciled to him, and in love to receive him.

Section 6 goes on to say not only that particular confession of sin is a duty before God but also that we are to look at the people whom we have offended in this world. If we have scandalized our brothers and sisters, we have violated and besmirched the purity of the church to such a degree that in our repentance we need to direct our apology to those whom we have offended. When David said in Psalm 51:4, "Against you, you only, have I sinned," he was speaking in ultimate categories. Ultimately, sin is an offense against God. However, proximately, we also violate each other, and part of the remedy for our guilt is to repent of our sins specifically to those whom we have offended. We ought to be willing in true penitence to make either a private or a public confession manifesting our genuine sorrow for sin and to speak to our offended brothers and sisters. The goal of such confession is to seek the forgiveness on which true reconciliation can be established.

Of Good Works

1. Good works are only such as God hath commanded in his holy Word, and not such as, without the warrant thereof, are devised by men, out of blind zeal, or upon any pretense of good intention.

2. These good works, done in obedience to God's commandments, are the fruits and evidences of a true and lively faith: and by them believers manifest their thankfulness, strengthen their assurance, edify their brethren, adorn the profession of the gospel, stop the mouths of the adversaries, and glorify God, whose workmanship they are, created in Christ Jesus thereunto, that, having their fruit unto holiness, they may have the end, eternal life.

3. Their ability to do good works is not at all of themselves, but wholly from the Spirit of Christ. And that they may be enabled thereunto, beside the graces they have already received, there is required an actual influence of the same Holy Spirit, to work in them to will, and to do, of his good pleasure: yet are they not hereupon to grow negligent, as if they were not bound to perform any duty unless upon a special motion of the Spirit; but they ought to be diligent in stirring up the grace of God that is in them.

4. They who, in their obedience, attain to the greatest height which is possible in this life, are so far from being able to supererogate, and to do more than God requires, as that they fall short of much which in duty they are bound to do.

5. We cannot by our best works merit pardon of sin, or eternal life at the hand of God, by reason of the great disproportion that is between them and the glory to come; and the infinite distance that is between us and God, whom, by them, we can neither profit, nor satisfy for the debt of

our former sins, but when we have done all we can, we have done but our duty, and are unprofitable servants: and because, as they are good, they proceed from his Spirit; and as they are wrought by us, they are defiled, and mixed with so much weakness and imperfection, that they cannot endure the severity of God's judgment.

6. Notwithstanding, the persons of believers being accepted through Christ, their good works also are accepted in him; not as though they were in this life wholly unblamable and unreprovable in God's sight; but that he, looking upon them in his Son, is pleased to accept and reward that which is sincere, although accompanied with many weaknesses and imperfections.

7. Works done by unregenerate men, although for the matter of them they may be things which God commands; and of good use both to themselves and others: yet, because they proceed not from an heart purified by faith; nor are done in a right manner, according to the Word; nor to a right end, the glory of God, they are therefore sinful, and cannot please God, or make a man meet to receive grace from God: and yet, their neglect of them is more sinful and displeasing unto God.

Chapter 16, "Of Good Works," is a rather lengthy section of the confession, which is not surprising, considering that the subject has been controversial throughout church history. It begins:

1. Good works are only such as God hath commanded in his holy Word, and not such as, without the warrant thereof, are devised by men, out of blind zeal, or upon any pretense of good intention.

The Westminster divines begin by defining good works, and they affirm that a work is good because God says it is good, not because we say it is good. Let's look at this by way of contrast. Obviously, a sinful act is a bad work. Sin is defined biblically as *any* violation of the law of God (every sin is worthy of death). In Romans 5:14, the Apostle Paul says that death reigned from Adam to Moses. There could not have been death unless there was sin, and there could not have been sin unless there was law, because sin is defined by the law. Paul's point is that the law did not start with Moses. From Adam onward, there was a knowledge of righteousness, which God had implanted in the hearts of all His creatures.

We can describe good works as the opposite of bad works or sin. Just like bad works, good works are defined by the law. Bad works involve sin, which is a lack of conformity to, or a transgression of, the law of God. Conversely, good works involve conformity to, and the obeying of, the law of God.

If our work conforms only outwardly to the law, it is not a good deed, because God's law requires not only that our behavioral patterns meet certain standards that are defined in the law but also that our works are motivated by a right heart.

Consider the story of the rich young ruler and his encounter with Jesus (Matt. 19:16–22; Mark 10:17–22; Luke 18:18–23). He eagerly came to Jesus and said, "Good Teacher, what must I do to inherit eternal life?" (Luke 18:18). He was asking Jesus the ultimate question of redemption: What do I have to do to get into heaven? Jesus replied: "Why do you call me good? No one is good except God alone" (v. 19). Jesus did not say, "I am not God, so why are you calling Me good?" He knew that the rich young ruler was not aware that he was speaking to God incarnate. Jesus picked up on the loose way in which this man was using the term good. "Why are you calling Me good? Don't you know that only God is good?"

In any study of good works, this should be the major premise: Only God is good. That teaching of Jesus cuts right across everything we learn about behavioral standards from the world. We have been immersed in the spirit of humanism and taught that people are basically good. Ligonier Ministries' State of Theology survey has found that about two-thirds of people, including more than half of evangelicals, believe that human beings are basically good. But the Apostle Paul says, "None is righteous, no, not one" (Rom. 3:10, quoting Ps. 14:3). That is a radical idea in today's culture—the idea that no one under normal circumstances does good. Paul says that no one does good, and Jesus says that only God is good. So Paul and Jesus agree.

Jesus then went to the next stage and said, "You know the commandments: 'Do not commit adultery, Do not murder, Do not steal, Do not bear false witness, Honor your father and mother'" (Luke 18:20). The response of the rich young ruler was, "All these I have kept from my youth" (v. 21). He had not read Paul's letter to the Romans, of course, because Paul hadn't written it yet, but the young man should have known from the Psalms that what he had just said was nonsense. Jesus did not reply by commending the young man and telling him that he had nothing to worry about.

Jesus was masterful in the way He revealed things to people. He said to the ruler, "One thing you still lack. Sell all that you have and distribute to the poor, and you will have treasure in heaven; and come, follow me" (v. 22). The young man walked away sorrowfully because he had many possessions.

Why did Jesus ask him to sell all that he had? Nowhere does Jesus lay down such a universal precept, nor does God in His law require people to divest themselves of all worldly goods. There is no vow of poverty commanded by the law of God. Yet Jesus commanded it from this man. When the man said he had kept all the law from his youth, Jesus put him to a test. He started with the first law, Exodus 20:3: "You shall have no other gods before me." Jesus knew that this man's god was his possessions, for "where your treasure is, there your heart will be also" (Matt. 6:21). So Jesus told him to get rid of his possessions, to give them away.

The rich man walked away sorrowfully, but perhaps he realized that he had not kept the law to the degree that he had thought he had. We have said before that some people thought Martin Luther was insane because he was so concerned about his own sin that he spent two, three, or even four hours in the confessional every day agonizing over his sins. We forget that he had had intense training in law before he went into the priesthood, and that he examined himself against the law of God. According to the rigorous standards of the monastery of which he was a member, he fared quite well. In fact, he was considered to be a monk among monks. But he examined himself not by the laws of the monastery but by the laws of God. "Love God?" he said. "Sometimes I hate Him." He looked at God's law, saw how far short he fell, and was stripped of his righteousness.

If we examined ourselves by the law of God with Luther's rigor and intensity, we would have to say, "I have committed great transgressions."

Theologians have given many different explanations of the unforgivable sin, but no one has tried to make a case that the unforgivable sin is a failure to love God with all of one's heart or mind. If that were the unforgivable sin, no one would be saved. Not one of us keeps the Great Commandment and loves God with all our heart every second of the day.

If we loved the Lord our God with all our heart, with no mixture of self, and if we had a pure and perfect love for God every second of our existence, loving Him totally with our mind, so that we searched the Scriptures and knew exactly what His law required and forbade, we wouldn't commit any sins.

Even if we devote our minds to a certain degree to the Lord, it is no good if the heart isn't there, too. We dwell in the midst of people of unclean lips, and none of us has given to God the honor that He deserves. There are still portions of our hearts that are far from God. Luther concluded that if the Great Commandment is to love God with all our heart, mind, and strength, then the great transgression would be the failure to obey the Great Commandment.

But we know that no one keeps the Great Commandment, so we think it is impossible, and if it's impossible, why worry? Our Creator, however, commands us to do it, and He won't judge us on the basis of how we measure up against others.

The first point of chapter 16 of the Westminster Confession is that good works are defined by God, by correspondence to His law. We should understand that outward conformity to the law of God is not enough. The Pharisees conformed outwardly, but their hearts were far from God. Their outwardly good works were despicable in the sight of God. Let's look at an illustration of this.

There was a man who liked to drive his car in a fifty-five-mile-per-hour zone. It was his favorite traveling speed. He drove down the highway at the speed limit, fifty-five miles an hour. Everyone else passed him at sixty-five, seventy, or more. A policeman saw him driving in a fifty-five-mile-per-hour zone, pulled him over, and gave him a commendation as the safe driver of the month. The driver took the award with him, and then drove down the street into the school zone marked fifteen miles per hour. He drove through the school zone at his regular fifty-five miles per hour. His reason for driving fifty-five miles per hour on the highway had nothing to do with desiring to obey the civil magistrate. His only reason for driving at that speed was that he liked to drive at fifty-five. Now and then, he drove within the speed limit, but that was accidental, not intentional. Unlike the policeman, God sees beyond the outward, and He sees the heart. He sees that there is no love for God, that there is no desire to honor God with obedience to His law. Outwardly good works without proper motivation are evil in God's sight.

One of the most misunderstood passages in Romans is in the second chapter, where Paul brings the whole world before the tribunal of God and shows that all human beings are under the judgment of God for their sins. Paul begins with the Jewish people. They had been privileged to have the oracles of God; they had the law of God in a clear way that was not available to the Greeks or to the Romans. Paul says in effect, "These people are proud of themselves because they possess the law." However, he speaks of when "Gentiles, who do not have the law, by nature do what the law requires" (Rom. 2:14). That is a difficult text, and some people think that Paul is teaching that the Jews who have the law do not keep it, whereas the gentiles who do not have the law do keep it. But if that were what Paul is saying, then his whole argument, that both Jew and gentile are guilty under the law, would fall apart. What he is really saying is that even though these gentiles don't have the Ten Commandments in written form, they still have their moral codes and are concerned about many of the same things with which the Jewish law is concerned. He then goes on to show that the people who have a reduced view of law don't even keep the laws that they do have. In our culture, the ethical standards are far beneath God's standard, but we cannot even keep to a standard invented by human beings, which in many cases are a substitute for the law of God.

We have been born again to do good works, redeemed for good works. Our good works do not contribute anything to our justification, but if we are truly people of faith, the goal of our lives should be to please God and to seek first His kingdom and His righteousness. In our pursuit of sanctification, we try to be good. The first problem, then, is to discover what it means to be good. Christians argue about what is proper and appropriate behavior and what are the right things to do.

Is it right for Christians to have abortions? Polls show that on major social issues like abortion, divorce, and adultery, there is little difference in the behavioral patterns of professing evangelical Christians and of pagans in America. The reason for this is that we get many of our standards from the culture around us. In the 1950s, abortion was despised by the culture, and the only place a person could get an abortion was in the back alley. But today the culture thinks that abortion is OK. We also take our cue from the law—from what the state accepts, from what the government allows. We think that if something is legal, it must be right. But we need to ask what the relationship is between the law of our state and the law of God.

Even a cursory reading of the Bible and theology reveals that God hates abortion. He considers it a gross and heinous sin, a sin so wicked that He threatens to judge an entire nation that tolerates it. It is not a stretch to say that abortion and its tolerance are as evil as the systematic genocide carried out by Hitler. At least the people who were killed in the death camps during World War II had some years of life on this planet, and they were not murdered in their mothers' wombs.

The point of the confession is that goodness and evil are defined by the law of God, not by our self-serving legislation. There is no act so heinous in this world that someone isn't out there politicking for its legitimacy or defending the rightness of it. Part of the fallenness of humanity is that we call good evil and evil good. The real "good" consists of knowing what is good and having the moral strength to do it. These two things— knowing the good and doing the good—can and must be distinguished, but they can never be separated. Here is why: the stronger the conviction of what is right becomes, the easier it is to perform it.

We must search the Scriptures to know what is good. Psalm 1 clearly shows us the contrast between the godly and the ungodly. The godly person does not walk according to the counsel of paganism. He shuts his ears to the maxims and ethics of the ungodly. He does not sit in the seat of the scornful or make fun of the law of God. He takes his cue from God's law, and he meditates upon it day and night. As our understanding increases of how wicked wickedness is and how much God hates particular forms of behavior, the easier it is for us to avoid it. Even as Christians, who are regenerate, we have the flesh to contend with, and that is why we need to reinforce our understanding of the Word of God.

> 2. These good works, done in obedience to God's commandments, are the fruits and evidences of a true and lively faith: and by them believers manifest their thankfulness, strengthen their assurance, edify their brethren, adorn the profession of the gospel, stop the mouths of the adversaries, and glorify God, whose workmanship they are, created in Christ Jesus thereunto, that, having their fruit unto holiness, they may have the end, eternal life.

The Westminster divines were given to a kind of theological precision that was unparalleled in church history. Here we see them heaping up phrases about the significance of the Christian's good works. Each phrase crystallizes an important purpose for good works that has been set forth in sacred Scripture.

These good works are defined as **the fruits and evidences of a true and lively faith.** There is a method in the arrangement of the articles of doctrine as they are set forth in the confession. We have gone from the fall and sin to justification, sanctification, the nature of faith, the nature of repentance, and now to the function of good works. It is not by accident that this treatment of good works comes after the exposition of justification. In Reformed theology, justification does not flow from good works; rather, good works flow out of our justification. We should remember the Reformation motto, "Justification is by faith alone, but not by a faith that is alone." Good works will accompany genuine faith.

When we say that justification is by faith alone, we really mean that it is by Christ alone. The only works that count toward our justification are those that Christ performed in His lifetime. Luther defined saving faith as *fides viva. Viva* is the Latin word for "living," so *fides viva* refers to a faith that is vital or alive, a lively faith. Luther said that the faith that justifies is never a dead faith. As James 2:17 points out, a dead faith is a faith that does not bear fruit.

The Reformation doctrine of justification affirms that faith produces justification. If it is true faith, good works will absolutely, immediately, inevitably, and necessarily ensue from that faith. Where one puts works in the formula makes all the difference. It is not that we have faith plus works in order to get justification. It is faith alone that yields justification, and if it is true faith, works will follow. If works do not follow, there was not true faith. If there was not true faith, there was no justification. That is what the confession means by saying that good works are the fruits and evidences of a true and lively faith.

In addressing the relationship between faith and works, James was answering a question: "What good is it, my brothers, if someone says he has faith but does not have works? Can that faith save him?" (2:14). The clear answer is no, because faith without works is dead (v. 17). Works provide evidence or an outward manifestation of an internal reality. If there is true faith, that faith will be manifested by works, so that "you will recognize them by their fruits" (Matt. 7:20). Good works are the fruit of faith and provide evidence of a true and living faith.

And by them believers manifest their thankfulness. Good works are an outward manifestation of thankfulness. When we have received the full pardon of God, based strictly on the free mercy that He has given to us, undeserved and unearned, the godly response to such favor is obedience. Obedience is motivated not by a desire to get to heaven but by the sheer delight and joy of thankfulness.

In Romans 1, Paul says that all people, in the flesh, repress, bury, and reject the general revelation that God gives of Himself. The primordial, fundamental sin of fallen humanity is expressed in two aspects. First, man, while he knows God, refuses to honor Him as God. Second, man is not thankful. We live and move and have our being in God; everything good comes from His hand—and yet, we live our lives as ungrateful people. Our whole lives should be nothing but a song of praise and gratitude to a God who mercifully bestows every good and perfect gift that we receive.

In Luke 17:11–19, Luke gives an account of Jesus' healing of ten lepers. In those days, a leper was doomed to an existence of total misery. He was exiled from his family, his friends, and his community. He had to live outside his village, and if anyone came near, he had to cry out, "Unclean, unclean." The only people he could associate with were other lepers. And then, one day, Jesus came by and ten lepers asked Him to heal them. He instructed them to go and show themselves to the priests. As they did,

He caused their leprosy to disappear. But only one of the ten returned to thank Jesus. All ten men were grateful to be healed, but only one made an effort to find Jesus and express his gratitude to Him. The other nine were so excited about being clean that they headed straight home to see their loved ones. It is easy to feel grateful and not express it. How many times have people done wonderful things for us, but we never took the time to write them a note, or give them a call, or go out of our way to thank them? What the confession points out is that our good works are, in a sense, an offering to God of our thanksgiving. We outwardly say "Thank you" by showing obedience to the One who has redeemed us. We are showing our love for Christ, who told His disciples, "If you love me, you will keep my commandments" (John 14:15). We show our love for Christ by obeying His commandments.

By their good works, believers **strengthen their assurance.** How is our assurance of salvation related to our good works? One of the things that weakens our assurance of salvation is the presence of sin in our lives. If we're honest in analyzing ourselves, we have to say, "How can I be a Christian? I say that I'm a Christian, I say that I believe, that I love God, but I know that what I'm thinking and what I'm doing are often contrary to the law of God. Maybe I'm not a Christian after all." If we let ourselves fall captive to that horrible thought, if we look at our sin and listen to the accusations of Satan, our assurance will be destroyed.

When we think of Satan's activity, we generally think of him as the tempter, the one who entices us to sin. He certainly does that, but the number one function of Satan in the life of the Christian is to accuse. He accused Joshua the high priest of wearing dirty clothes while ministering in the name of God. But God silenced him: "Is not this a brand plucked from the fire?" (Zech. 3:2). Of course Joshua still had dirt on him, but God had snatched him out of the fire. Then God ordered that new clothes be given to Joshua. Like him, we too are brands snatched from the fire. We sin, and when we sin, we have to deal with two voices that come into our head. One is Satan, who says, "You're guilty, you're guilty." And then there is the Holy Spirit, who says, "You're guilty, you're guilty." Isn't it interesting that they are both saying the same thing? They are both right, but there is a difference. The Holy Spirit is the Spirit of truth, and Satan is a liar from the beginning, who distorts and twists the truth to his own use.

When Satan reminds us of our sin, he tells us the truth, but it is only to cause us to despair of our salvation, to paralyze us with our guilt, and to keep us from being productive Christians. Guilt is one of the most powerful forces of paralysis. At that point, we must quote Scripture to Satan: "Who shall bring any charge against God's elect?" (Rom. 8:33). It is God who justifies us; it is Christ who was raised again for our justification. Our justification rests on Christ, and Satan knows it. We should tell him to depart, because "he who is in you is greater than he who is in the world" (1 John 4:4). Not only our justification but also our sanctification is rooted and grounded in faith. We must trust in the gospel in every circumstance.

When the Holy Spirit tells us that we are guilty and convicts us of sin, He never destroys us with that conviction. His purpose is to heal us, to restore us, to cause us to repent and rely on Christ. Repentance is not a pleasant experience, and yet, is it not sweet when we finally unburden ourselves before the Lord and confess our sin? As humiliating as it may be, to come back to the forgiveness of Christ is salutary. It is sweet and wonderful. It does not leave us groveling in the dirt, but it leaves us restored, healed in the middle of our brokenness. When Satan accuses, he does it relentlessly with no relief, in order to leave us in the dirt. There is a huge difference between the accusation of Satan and the conviction of the Holy Spirit, and we must learn the difference in our Christian lives or we will be sifted like wheat by the enemy.

When we look at our lives and see our sin, it can be discouraging. That's why it's important to understand that good works flow from our being born again and being given the gift of faith. If we have any true faith at all, it will manifest itself in works of obedience and in a spirit of repentance. So we can look at our lives and ask, Do we have any fruit of justification in our lives? Is there any sense in which our lives are different now from what they were before? Are we obeying God?"

We previously discussed these three questions. First, do we love Christ perfectly? The answer to that question is no, we don't love Him perfectly. We will someday, but not now. Second, do we love Him as much as we ought to love Him? No. If we don't love Him perfectly, we don't love Him as much as we ought to love Him, because we ought to love Him perfectly. Now, let's get down to the big question. Third, do we love Christ at all? Yes, we do love Him, but not as much as we should. We are not talking about some cultural idea of Christ; we are talking about the biblical Christ. Could we love the biblical Christ at all if we were not born again? No. Could we be born again if we were not elect? No. If we love Christ at all—and loving Him is a fruit of regeneration, which is based upon election—then we can have assurance of our salvation. We have assurance because we understand that all whom God elects, He preserves to the end.

That is why theology is important for our assurance. If we are not sure about the doctrine of election, we are not sure that regeneration precedes faith. We can say we have a love for Jesus now, but we could lose it tomorrow. Then everything depends upon what we do. There is no assurance that way. The Westminster divines say that obedience in our lives helps our assurance because they understand the role of works in the whole order of salvation. They have already taught that a person cannot do any good works apart from regenerating grace, and that one cannot be regenerated unless elected, so if there are any good works, that is evidence to our souls that we are elect. If we have assurance of our election, that strengthens our assurance of salvation.

By their good works, believers **edify their brethren.** We rarely think of it as a reason for obeying God, but good works do edify our brothers and sisters in Christ. Our bad works, on the other hand, discourage other Christians, and can be harmful to them.

By their good works, believers **adorn the profession of the gospel and stop the mouths of the adversaries.** What does it mean to adorn something? The purpose of adorning anything is to enhance or to increase its beauty. The confession says that the good works of the saints add beauty to the profession of faith of the Christian community. If we profess faith and then live corrupt lives, we make our professions ugly to other Christians and to the world. But our good works cause others, especially the watching world, to show more respect for the gospel.

In referring to **adversaries,** the confession acknowledges that we will face opposition in this world. In fact, if we profess faith in Christ and yet have never been falsely accused or slandered, then there may be something wrong with our Christianity. Christians are accused of being hypocrites and any number of other things. Our works can be used against us falsely. However, even the unrighteous person will see our good works and come to recognize that they are beautiful, that they do adorn our profession of faith, and they stop the mouths of the obstreperous.

If we do the works that Christ has called us to do, if we love our neighbors, are honest, patient, gentle, and kind, even pagans stop their criticism of us. If we display contemptuousness toward them as unbelievers, they will complain about how self-righteous and hypocritical we are.

By their good works, believers stop the mouths of the adversaries, and glorify God, whose workmanship they are, created in Christ Jesus thereunto, that, having their fruit unto holiness, they may have the end, which is eternal life. This harks back to Ephesians 2, where we are told that we are the workmanship of God. We have been crafted by Christ unto good works. The great craftsman who is changing us, who has rescued us from the fire, who has given us spiritual life where there was only spiritual death, does this so that we will glorify God. The beauty of a statue honors and glorifies the sculptor. We extol Michelangelo because of the beauty of the work of his hands. We are the craftsmanship of Christ, who is forming and shaping us, so that God may be glorified. The Westminster Shorter Catechism begins by asking, "What is the chief end of man?" The answer is, "Man's chief end is to glorify God, and to enjoy Him forever."

> 3. Their ability to do good works is not at all of themselves, but wholly from the Spirit of Christ. And that they may be enabled thereunto, beside the graces they have already received, there is required an actual influence of the same Holy Spirit, to work in them to will, and to do, of his good pleasure: yet are they not hereupon to grow negligent, as if they were not bound to perform any duty unless upon a special motion of the Spirit; but they ought to be diligent in stirring up the grace of God that is in them.

The elements in this third section are loaded with theological assumptions that flow out of the Reformation and Reformed theology. The first assertion is that even the Christian's ability to do good works is not at all of ourselves but completely and wholly from the Spirit of God. What is behind this somewhat radical statement is the Reformed doctrine of the *moral inability* of fallen man.

We have seen that the essence of the Reformed understanding of original sin is expressed in the concept of moral inability. It is perhaps this concept more than any other that distinguishes Reformed theology from other theologies. This has to do with our anthropology, our understanding of man and the fall of man. We distinguished three positions: Pelagianism, semi-Pelagianism, and Augustinianism. The Pelagian position teaches that the fall of Adam affected only Adam. There was no transmission of any corruption to the progeny of Adam. Every person is born in a state of innocence and has the moral power to live not only a good life but a perfect life. Although the grace of God facilitates perfection, in this view, such grace is not required to attain perfection, because we are not fallen.

The semi-Pelagian position says that the fall of Adam does affect his progeny, that we do have an inherited condition of original sin. We are so weakened by the fall and weakened by the sin that dwells within us that we cannot possibly be good or do any good apart from the assistance of divine grace. However, we are not so weakened that all moral ability is extinguished. We still have within us the moral ability to cooperate with the grace of God or to refuse to cooperate with the grace of God.

The Augustinian position is that the corruption of fallen man is so deep and so severe that we are left in a state of spiritual death. We cannot incline ourselves to righteousness or cooperate with the offer of grace from God unless He first quickens us from spiritual death by the work of the Holy Spirit. This work of the Spirit is called regeneration. We are in a state of total moral inability until the Spirit performs a supernatural work in our souls, changing the disposition of our hearts.

When the confession says at the beginning of this section that **their ability to do good works is not at all of themselves, but wholly from the Spirit of Christ,** it has in view the doctrine of the fall and of original sin that teaches total moral inability. It also has in view our absolute need of divine election in order to be saved. All three of the doctrines that are in dispute basically come down to this point.

Some object at this point that unbelievers, who show no evidence of being born again, often do all kinds of virtuous deeds, performing caring works and altruistic service, and making sacrificial gifts. When we define moral inability, we use Paul's quotation of Psalm 14:1–3 in Romans 3:10–12: "None is righteous, no, not one; no one understands; no one seeks for God. All have turned aside; together they have become worthless; no one does good, not even one." There is a difference between superficial goodness, which is simply external conformity to the law of God, and internal conformity to God's law that is motivated by a love for Him. God looks not only at the actual outward action but also at the motivation behind it. For a work to be truly good, it has to have not only the external conformity but also the internal motivation of wanting to please God.

Moral inability, or what we will call spiritual inability, is contrasted here in the third section with the *ability* to do good works with respect to God, which comes wholly from the Spirit of Christ. The confession explains that in order that they may be enabled thereunto, beside the graces they have already received, there is required an actual influence of the same Holy Spirit, to work in them to will, and to do, of his good pleasure: yet are they not hereupon to grow negligent, as if they were not bound to perform any duty unless upon a special motion of the Spirit. In contemporary terms, people have no right to say, "I didn't do that because the Spirit didn't lead me to do it." Our responsibilities cannot be passed off to God. We cannot blame Him for our inaction.

As we have seen, the beginning of the Christian life (in regeneration) is monergistic, but afterward, our sanctification is synergistic. It is a cooperative effort, a joint venture between us and God. When Paul says, "Work out your own salvation . . . , for it is God who works in you" (Phil. 2:12–13), he indicates that God is working and also that we are working. How hard are we supposed to work? As hard as we possibly can. When God tells us to work out our salvation "with fear and trembling," that means that we should be sweating blood in our efforts to gain progress in holiness and in sanctification. It is not that we can work out our salvation without any further assistance from the Holy Spirit; that is the creed of activism and a distortion of what the Apostle teaches. Neither is that we are to expect the Holy Spirit to work unilaterally and to effect a second work of grace, an instant sanctification, or an instant leap forward in sanctification. That is the creed of quietism, which says, "Let go and let God." Rather, we are to cling to God, to depend on His help and His grace, and not just on our own efforts. We are to look to God and to the Holy Spirit for help in our spiritual growth as we strive to advance in our sanctification.

Yet are they not hereupon to grow negligent, as if they were not bound to perform any duty unless upon a special motion of the Spirit; but they ought to be diligent in stirring up the grace of God that is in them. In many churches, new members take vows, and one of the vows they take is the vow to make diligent use of the means of grace. This is where we need to be active and where the active and quiet aspects come together. To make diligent use of the means of grace is to be earnestly disciplined and to be engaged in regular Bible study. It means being engaged in regular prayer. It means being regular in church attendance, experiencing Christian fellowship, participating in the sacraments, and engaging in outreach. These activities are means of grace. They are instruments by which we make use of and expose ourselves to the assistance of God's grace in our personal growth.

Self-discipline usually is a result of having first been disciplined by another. Our parents disciplined us as children. As we grew, they helped us establish certain habits, some of which we have maintained. Some of the areas in which we were not disciplined, we have not to this day gotten under control. Patterns of behavior are usually formed under the authority or under the disciplining pattern of other people. Few people are self-disciplined in every respect.

How then are we to make diligent use of the means of grace? The best way to learn the truths of God is to go where a knowledgeable person is teaching them. If we want to learn how to pray, we join a prayer group. If we are not studying the Bible diligently on our own, we can get into a Bible study program, which increases our diligence or persistence and helps us overcome a lack of motivation or a lack of discipline. We can make it a policy never to miss church on Sunday morning, because we know that we need that constant, consistent reinforcement for our spiritual growth. God has chosen the foolishness of preaching to save the world, and we may not remember all the points from the sermon, but for the twenty minutes or longer we hear it, it is getting into our heads. God will use sermons from His Word to strengthen and develop our souls. Even if we can't pass an examination on what we heard, just hearing the Word of God will have a cumulative effect on our souls. It is not the technique, it is not the methodology, and it is certainly not the eloquence of the preacher. The power is in the Word; the Holy Spirit works through the Word.

The responsibility of a preacher and teacher is to set forth the Word. He is to be diligent and to learn communication techniques that make it easier for us to understand. But in the end, the impact on our life will be the impact of the Word of God through the power of the Holy Spirit. We each have a responsibility to make diligent use of the means of grace; we are told by the Westminster divines that we **ought to be diligent in stirring up the grace of God** that is in us.

People ask, "Should our reward in heaven motivate us to do good works?" Jesus certainly promised rewards in heaven. There are at least twenty-five texts in the New Testament that make it clear that we will be rewarded in heaven according to our works. The formula for the Reformed faith on this point is, "Justification is by faith alone, but our reward in heaven will be according to our works"—though not because those works merit or deserve any reward whatsoever. Augustine said that our best works, even as Christians, are splendid vices. Our best works are still tainted by whatever sin abides in our heart until we die. We will always have some measure of abiding sin until we are glorified in heaven. No work that we do proceeds from a heart that is absolutely pure; no work that we ever do in this world is completely untainted. Since our works are tainted, they have no claim upon God to reward them. That God does reward them is, as Augustine said, God crowning His own gifts.

4. They who, in their obedience, attain to the greatest height which is possible in this life, are so far from being able to supererogate, and to do more than God requires, as that they fall short of much which in duty they are bound to do.

They who, in their obedience, attain to the greatest height which is possible in this life, are so far from being able to supererogate. . . . What is supererogation? Works of supererogation are those works that are above and beyond what is necessary. According to Roman Catholic teaching, there have been a few saints who lived lives of such extraordinary righteousness that they accumulated more merit than they needed in order to gain direct entrance into heaven. Their excess merit was then deposited in the treasury of merit, where it is available to others.

We remember that the Reformation grew out of Luther's objections to the manner in which Johann Tetzel was selling indulgences in Saxony. As a representative of the church, Tetzel was promising the peasants that the more money they gave, the sooner their dead relatives would exit purgatory and enter heaven. Luther then questioned the whole system of indulgences and the concept of a treasury of merit. He asked whether any Christian's life could ever be more righteous than what God requires.

The confession says that those Christians who, in their obedience, reach the greatest height possible in this life still **fall short of much which in duty they are bound to do.** No matter how good we are, we are never so good as to gain more merit than we need. So there is no supererogation. This is further explained in section 5.

> 5. We cannot by our best works merit pardon of sin, or eternal life at the hand of God, by reason of the great disproportion that is between them and the glory to come; and the infinite distance that is between us and God, whom, by them, we can neither profit, nor satisfy for the debt of our former sins, but when we have done all we can, we have done but our duty, and are unprofitable servants: and because, as they are good, they proceed from his Spirit; and as they are wrought by us, they are defiled, and mixed with so much weakness and imperfection, that they cannot endure the severity of God's judgment.

There is much in section 5 that amplifies section 4. We recall that the sacrament of penance was called "the second plank" of justification for those who have "made shipwreck" of their souls. In Roman Catholic theology, those who cooperate with the grace they receive at baptism remain in a state of justification until they commit a mortal sin. If someone loses his justification by committing a mortal sin, he can be justified again through penance. Penance involves confession, priestly absolution, and the assignment of the works of satisfaction. By doing the works of satisfaction, the repentant sinner gains congruous merit.

The Roman Catholic Church makes a distinction between *condign* merit and *congruous* merit. Condign merit is so good that it earns the reward of a just God. Congruous merit is not that good. It is merely good enough that it would be fitting or congruous for God to reward it. The reward is restoration to a state of justification.

Rome is reluctant to speak of merit today as much as it did in the past, even though it still does in its catechism. It is quick to point out that any meritorious work flows from God's grace. In other words, we couldn't have merit if we didn't first have grace. But the Reformers objected to this view. Even with grace, they said, our best works are but splendid vices and are never good enough to earn any merit. The only merit that we should talk about is the merit of Christ.

In section 5, we find a Reformed response to the Roman Catholic concept of merit: We cannot by our best works merit pardon of sin, or eternal life at the hand of God. Also, we can neither profit nor satisfy for the debt of our former sins. In the Roman view of penance, these are works of satisfaction. But the Reformers said that when we have done all we can, we have done but our duty, and are unprofitable servants. If we skipped over this lightly, we could miss one of the most important concepts in the entire confession. We don't really understand the gospel until we understand that whatever we do as Christians in this world is at best nothing more than our duty. There is nothing meritorious about doing what one is obligated to do.

When the Bible calls us unprofitable servants, that does not mean that we are unproductive servants. Jesus calls His disciples to be fruitful, to be productive, to bring forth the fruits of our labor, of our ministry, of our righteousness. The parable of the talents (Matt. 25:14–30) speaks to that. There is a difference between being unproductive and being unprofitable. The church does not exist to make a profit. A profit means that we have some net gain to show for our labor. But in moral terms, if we yield all the righteousness that we can, and then measure that against what God requires, there is no net. We are always debtors who cannot possibly pay our debt. The biblical view is that God is perfectly holy and righteous, and He requires perfect holiness and righteousness from His creatures. When we sin against God, our sin is against an infinitely good and infinitely great God. As a result, our sin is infinitely heinous, and there is no possible way that we could ever pay the debt that we owe. In fact, even in eternal punishment in hell, one still cannot pay the debt, because it is not simply an eternal debt but an infinite debt. No matter how long a person is in hell, he is still a finite creature who cannot undo the dishonor that he has given to his Creator.

One sin makes us less than perfect, and we can work for the rest of our lives and still not make up for that one sin. We are still imperfect. The only perfect person who has ever lived is Christ. That is why we must depend upon His merit and His righteousness for our salvation.

There is a common recognition in our society that no one is perfect, but the idea continues, "I try to live a good life, I'm doing the best that I can, and so God should certainly be pleased with that." Most people are resting on their performance, on what they perceive to be a net balance of goodness in their life, to get them past the judgment seat of a holy and righteous God. But they are sadly mistaken.

Even if we could obey the law of God perfectly, of what could we boast? We would simply have done our duty. The confession affirms not only that we come to the gospel for our initial redemption and our justification but also that we continue in that gospel to carry us through our entire lives. We have to look to the gospel for our sanctification, as well as for our justification. Even though we are trying to be fruitful, the minute we begin to look at the fruit of our sanctification and become smug about it and think that we have done something worthy of a reward, we have missed the point.

God gives us rewards, and He gives us blessings, but they are completely gracious. The best works that we do in this world have no merit before God. That is why salvation has to be of grace at the beginning, in the middle, and at the end. We cannot rely on our own righteousness at all, lest we miss the kingdom of God.

And because, as they are good, they proceed from his Spirit—"they" being our best works—and as they are wrought by us, they are defiled. That is, whatever good is in our works comes from the Holy Spirit working in us. Yet, because we are the ones who do them, they are defiled and tainted to some degree by the flesh.

They are defiled, and mixed with so much weakness and imperfection, that they cannot endure the severity of God's judgment. The reference here is to Isaiah 64:6: "We have all become like one who is unclean, and all our righteous deeds are like a polluted garment." Even our best works cannot withstand God's holy judgment.

> 6. Notwithstanding, the persons of believers being accepted through Christ, their good works also are accepted in him; not as though they were in this life wholly unblamable and unreprovable in God's sight; but that he, looking upon them in his Son, is pleased to accept and reward that which is sincere, although accompanied with many weaknesses and imperfections.

When the confession says that notwithstanding, the persons of believers being accepted through Christ, their good works also are accepted in him, it doesn't say "accepted *by* Him." What a difference a preposition makes. Our good works are accepted by God, but how and why are they accepted? They are accepted *in* Christ. It is only in Christ that we are accepted in any way before the Father. He sees us in Christ, and He accepts our works because they are in Christ. If they were not in Christ, they would be odious to God. But their imperfections are covered by the righteous robes of Christ. The imagery of the cover appears throughout the Scriptures from the early days of the Old Testament all the way through the New Testament.

Isaiah says that our righteousness is "like a polluted garment." We remember the story in Zechariah 3 about Joshua, the high priest with dirty clothes. Christ takes His own clothes, which are spotless, and covers Joshua with His cloak of righteousness. That is a metaphor, the chief image, of the atonement. In the Old Testament, the lid of the ark of the covenant was the mercy seat, where the throne of God was represented as

His seat of judgment. On the Day of Atonement, the high priest went to the mercy seat and put the blood of the sacrifice on it. That symbolized the covering that we receive through the righteousness of Christ. The only way our righteousness is acceptable to God is if it is done in and through Christ.

Our good works in this life are not blameless in God's sight. But He, looking upon them in his Son, is pleased to accept and reward that which is sincere, although accompanied with many weaknesses and imperfections. This is pure Augustinian theology. Augustine taught that when God gives rewards to His people in Christ Jesus, He is crowning His own gifts. The blessing is at the beginning and all the way through.

> 7. Works done by unregenerate men, although for the matter of them they may be things which God commands; and of good use both to themselves and others: yet, because they proceed not from an heart purified by faith; nor are done in a right manner, according to the Word; nor to a right end, the glory of God, they are therefore sinful, and cannot please God, or make a man meet to receive grace from God: and yet, their neglect of them is more sinful and displeasing unto God.

In our discussion of section 3, we observed that civic virtue and outward conformity to the law of God can be manifested even by non-Christians. Here, in section 7, it is stated that even if unregenerate people outwardly do those things that God commands, they are judged by their intent, by their motive, by the internal disposition that brings them forth. Their deeds proceed from a heart that is not purified by faith. They are not done in the right manner, according to the Word, nor are they done to the right end, for the glory of God. Therefore, they are not righteous but sinful, and they cannot please God.

In the Old Testament, the Israelites observed the feast days and performed the ceremonies that God had set forth in the law of Moses, and they did so meticulously. However, they did not have a broken and contrite heart (Ps. 51:17). So God said in Amos 5:21–22: "I hate, I despise your feasts, and I take no delight in your solemn assemblies. Even though you offer me your burnt offerings and grain offerings, I will not accept them; and the peace offerings of your fattened animals, I will not look upon them." He sent Jeremiah to the temple (Jer. 7:1–15), and Jeremiah said to the people: "Thus says the LORD of hosts, the God of Israel: Amend your ways and your deeds, and I will let you dwell in this place. Do not trust in these deceptive words: 'This is the temple of the LORD, the temple of the LORD, the temple of the LORD'" (vv. 3–4). Jeremiah said, "You trust in deceptive words to no avail" (v. 8). And then he said to them, "Go now to my place that was in Shiloh, where I made my name dwell at first, and see what I did to it because of the evil of my people Israel" (v. 12). Shiloh, formerly a central sanctuary for the Jews, was then in ruins. God said that is what the temple would look like, and that is what Jerusalem would look like. Why? Because the people were honoring God with their lips while their hearts were far from Him. The confession reminds us that the unregenerate person can go through all the motions, do all the outward things that the law of God requires, but still will not survive the judgment of God.

We need to examine ourselves against God's standards of what is good and what is not, and not by the cultural standards or by the customs or even by the laws of the nation in which we live. Not only does the world have a warped sense of righteousness, but also we Christians often have a warped sense of what is good. That is why we constantly have to measure ourselves against the perfect law of God. Every time we do this, it sends us rushing to the cross and to the gospel, to the One whose good works alone suffice for us.

The only way any person can satisfy the demands of God is through the works of Christ. The only works that ever avail to justify us are the works of Christ. The only way one can receive and appropriate those works is by faith. The ground of our justification is works—not our works but His. When we stand before God on the judgment day, we will rest either on our works or on Christ's works. It is terrifying to think of anyone relying on his own works, because there is a vast gulf between what God commands and what we have done.

Of the Perseverance of the Saints

1. They, whom God hath accepted in his Beloved, effectually called, and sanctified by his Spirit, can neither totally nor finally fall away from the state of grace, but shall certainly persevere therein to the end, and be eternally saved.

2. This perseverance of the saints depends not upon their own free will, but upon the immutability of the decree of election, flowing from the free and unchangeable love of God the Father; upon the efficacy of the merit and intercession of Jesus Christ, the abiding of the Spirit, and of the seed of God within them, and the nature of the covenant of grace: from all which ariseth also the certainty and infallibility thereof.

3. Nevertheless, they may, through the temptations of Satan and of the world, the prevalency of corruption remaining in them, and the neglect of the means of their preservation, fall into grievous sins; and, for a time, continue therein: whereby they incur God's displeasure, and grieve his Holy Spirit, come to be deprived of some measure of their graces and comforts, have their hearts hardened, and their consciences wounded; hurt and scandalize others, and bring temporal judgments upon themselves.

Chapter 17 of the Westminster Confession encapsulates the Reformed concept of what some tend to call eternal security, that is, "once in grace, always in grace." Another way to put it is this: If you have it, you never lose it, and if you lose it, you never had it. This is a controversial doctrine, because everyone knows someone who has made a profession of faith in Christ and was enthusiastic about his faith, but who, at some time thereafter, left and repudiated the faith. We have seen people fall away or commit what is called apostasy.

Apostasy means literally "standing away from." It is the condition of people who, having made a profession of faith and joined the church, later repudiate that profession and depart from the church. We have records of apostasy in the Old Testament and also in the New Testament. There were those who departed from the apostolic community, and John observed that "They went out from us, but they were not of us" (1 John 2:19). We need to know how to evaluate apostasy.

Can a person, in fact, lose his salvation? Or are those who commit apostasy simply those who have made a false profession of faith in the first place? This situation is similar to what is described in the parable of the sower (Luke 8:4–15). In that parable, whether the plant that comes up from the ground is genuine or spurious depends on the kind of soil in which the seed is sown. The spurious plant springs up quickly but is choked by the thorns, or it is without roots and dies under the heat of the sun. Those plants represent people who initially respond positively to the gospel but are not truly converted. Jesus warned His contemporaries, "This people honors me with their lips, but their heart is far from me" (Matt. 15:8). People often make a profession of faith without possessing authentic faith. For good reason, we speak of the perseverance of the saints, not the perseverance of all who profess faith.

When we use the term *saint*, we are not speaking about Roman Catholic "saints" such as Augustine. Rather, we are using the term *saint* the way it is used in the New Testament. All believers are called "saints" in the New Testament—not because they have achieved a super level of spirituality or righteousness but because they are those whom the Holy Spirit has regenerated, consecrated, and worked within for their sanctification. The saints are the elect, the true believers, those who have been redeemed by Christ and have been regenerated by the Holy Spirit. Those who persevere are those who are truly saints, that is, those who are truly believers, who are numbered among the elect. All who are elect come to faith and are preserved in that state of faith until the end of their lives. The goal and purpose of election is completely realized in them.

Having said that by way of introduction, let's see how this doctrine is set forth by the confession.

1. They, whom God hath accepted in his Beloved, effectually called, and sanctified by his Spirit, can neither totally nor finally fall away from the state of grace, but shall certainly persevere therein to the end, and be eternally saved.

Section 1 begins by saying that those who have been accepted and called and sanctified **can neither totally nor finally fall away**. This does not mean, however, that a true believer is incapable of a partial fall or a temporary state of apostasy. The key words here are **totally** and **finally**.

The doctrine of perseverance does not teach that once a person becomes a genuine Christian, he never backslides or strays from the path of righteousness. The classic exhibits, of course, are of David in the Old Testament and Peter in the New Testament. David was a man after God's own heart, a believer who was redeemed. He was a regenerate man, and yet, in his state of grace, he fell into the sordid sin of adultery, as well as murder by proxy, and so his fall was a radical one, with serious consequences for the whole nation. When Nathan confronted David and the Spirit convicted him of his sin, David became a model of repentance and restoration, so that his fall was neither total nor final.

Think of the difference between Peter and Judas in the New Testament. Both Peter and Judas were disciples who had followed Christ. Each made a profession of faith, and each seemed to be converted. But when our Lord gathered His disciples together for the Last Supper in the upper room, He predicted that one of them would betray Him and that another one would deny Him. And even as Christ predicted, Judas went out and betrayed Jesus into the hands of His enemies for thirty pieces of silver. Afterward, in his remorse, Judas committed suicide. In His High Priestly Prayer, Jesus said that He had preserved all whom the Father had given Him, and that none of them would be lost, except Judas, who was the son of perdition (John 17:11–12) and had been known as such to Jesus all along (John 6:70). Judas was never anything but a son of perdition. He was not a true believer who repudiated the faith.

Peter's denial of Jesus was, in many respects, as wicked as Judas' betrayal of Him. Jesus warned Peter of his upcoming denials, but Simon Peter declared that he would never deny Jesus. Less than twenty-four hours later, however, on three occasions, Peter denied that he had ever known Jesus. In his final denial, he even employed curses. He tried to put as much distance between himself and Christ as he could. This was not in the presence of authorities who were threatening him with imprisonment or execution but in the presence of a servant girl. Peter was so terrified that he would suffer the consequences of being close to Jesus that he repudiated Him. But after Peter made the third denial, Jesus, being led from the judgment hall in chains, looked up and His eyes met the eyes of Peter (Luke 22:61). Jesus did not need to say a word.

In the upper room, when Jesus predicted that Simon Peter would deny Him, Jesus also said, "Simon, Simon, behold, Satan demanded to have you, that he might sift you like wheat" (v. 31). That is, "You are an easy target for Satan; you tell Me that you won't deny Me, but I know who you are. I know what Satan will do with you, and you will crumble like dust." But Jesus continued: "But I have prayed for you that your faith may not fail. And when you have turned again, strengthen your brothers" (v. 32).

We wonder why Jesus didn't say the same thing to Judas. Rather, Jesus told Judas, "What you are going to do, do quickly" (John 13:27), and He dismissed him. It is not that Jesus didn't care about Judas, but He knew that Judas was not one that the Father had given Him. He knew that Peter was one of the gifts that the Father had given to Him, one for whom He was going to die, and who was going to be redeemed by His death. He knew that the plans and purposes of the Father would be accomplished. He knew that Peter was going to fall in a serious and radical way, but He also knew that it would not be total or final. So He said to Peter, "When you have turned again"—not *if* you turn again— "strengthen your brothers."

One of the most significant aspects of perseverance is the intercession of Christ. In the High Priestly Prayer, Jesus prayed that the Father would keep His elect from falling (John 17:11). We persevere only because God, in His grace and power, preserves us. In and of ourselves, each of us is capable of serious and radical falling, such as we saw in the life of David and in the life of Peter. Even as regenerate creatures, we are capable of full and final falling, if left to ourselves. But God does not leave His people to their own devices. The Lord intercedes for us constantly, so that we will not fall away. Just as Christ prayed for Peter, so He intercedes for us. He prayed for His disciples in the upper room, and He prays for us as well. He said, "I do not ask for these only, but also for those who will believe in me through their word" (v. 20). Even as early as the High Priestly Prayer that is recorded in John 17, Christ began His intercessory ministry on our behalf, praying that we would be preserved. Therefore, believers **can neither totally nor finally fall away from the state of grace, but shall certainly persevere therein to the end, and be eternally saved.**

> 2. This perseverance of the saints depends not upon their own free will, but upon the immutability of the decree of election, flowing from the free and unchangeable love of God the Father; upon the efficacy of the merit and intercession of Jesus Christ, the abiding of the Spirit, and of the seed of God within them, and the nature of the covenant of grace: from all which ariseth also the certainty and infallibility thereof.

Our confidence in our perseverance does not rest on us or on the exercise of our wills. Even though we have a changed and liberated will in Christ, there is enough remnant of sin that we still are vulnerable to temptation. Left to our weak wills, we would not persevere.

Wherein does our confidence lie? Our perseverance depends, first of all, on **the immutability of the decree of election.** We could look at this abstractly and say that our perseverance is a matter of logical deduction in Calvinist theology. However, that is only one aspect of the situation, and it is misleading to think that our confidence rests simply on a logical deduction. What it is really based on is the character of God. The doctrine of God's immutability is not just an abstract concept from which logical deductions can be made; it is part of the revelation of the Word of God, which tells us who God is and what He is like. When we rest upon the immutability of God, that means that God is consistent, that He is constant and trustworthy, and that He does not have a plan B. We humans have plan B because we never know for sure if our plan A is going to work, but God does not need a plan B because He has never had and will never have a plan that fails. He has an eternal purpose that He is executing in His plan of salvation for His people, for the elect. From the foundation of the world, He has known His people and He has chosen them to be saved in Jesus Christ. Having made that decree from all eternity, He is not going to change His mind.

Peter wrote that we are to confirm our calling and election (2 Peter 1:10). That is one of the most important support systems for our Christian pilgrimage and sanctification. We need to know whether we are in a state of grace. If we do know that we are in a state of grace now, then we can rest assured that we are going to remain in that state of grace tomorrow, the day after, and forever, because God's calling does not change. He does not change His mind. Once He has set our salvation in motion, the final outcome is assured. That was what Paul wrote to the Philippians: "He who began a good work in you will bring it to completion at the day of Jesus Christ" (Phil. 1:6). He promises to finish what He starts. The first thing on which our perseverance depends, according to the confession, is the immutability of God's decree of election.

Second, our perseverance flows **from the free and unchangeable love of God the Father.** The love with which God loves us in His eternal choice of us is entirely free and not based upon any foreseen merit or righteousness in us. Just as His decrees are immutable, so this love with which He loves us is immutable. He will not change His mind, His heart, or His disposition because He is a loyal, covenant God.

The Hebrew word *hesed* is frequently translated "loving-kindness" or "mercy." It is what the story of Hosea is all about. The ESV translates it as "steadfast love." Paul had this in view when he gave us the golden chain in Romans 8:29–30: "For those whom he foreknew he also predestined. . . . And those whom he predestined he also called, and those whom he called he also justified, and those whom he justified he also glorified." Our salvation starts with foreknowledge and ends with glorification. "Foreknew" could also be rendered "foreloved": those whom God foreloved, He also predestined. God's loyal love is the most astonishing thing about the Christian faith. It provoked the Apostolic amazement of John, who exclaimed, "See what kind of love the Father has given to us, that we should be called children of God; and so we are" (1 John 3:1).

This is a love that will not let us go, because it is a love that is eternally and immutably loyal.

The Bible nowhere uses the expression "unconditional love." There are preachers who announce indiscriminately to people, "God loves you unconditionally." It is true that God loves the elect unconditionally, but He works in them to meet certain conditions for salvation. He creates faith in people and brings them to repentance. The last thing an impenitent sinner should hear is that he does not need to meet any conditions to be right with God.

In this world, we realize that loyalty is sometimes blind. But there is nothing blind about the steadfast love of God, and there is no fault in His steadfast love. In His love, we have transcendent loyalty. When God saves us, He saves us no matter what. No matter how much we let Him down or how much we fail to persevere on our own, He has given us a love that will not let us go. For our preservation, God has taken hold of us. If it were up to us, we would let go, but He will not let go. We do not fall because He keeps us from falling. The second thing upon which our perseverance depends, according to the confession, is the unchangeable love of God.

Third, our perseverance depends on **the efficacy of the merit and intercession of Jesus Christ.** That which is efficacious is the cause; the effect is the result. The confession teaches that our perseverance depends on the efficacy of the merit of Christ, His righteousness. The only merit by which anyone can ever be saved or justified in the sight of God is the merit of Christ. The only kind of merit that we have to offer God is demerit. But Christ comes to the Father with perfect merit, which purchases the redemption of His people.

The ground and basis of our justification is perfectly adequate to cover us. Christ's merit works. It is not only perfect in itself but also perfectly effective to do what it was designed to do. The reason Christ earned this merit was to save His people on the basis of it, and His merit does not at some future point lose its efficacy.

Join His merit with His intercession, and we are utterly secure. The only way we could ever lose our salvation would be if our Savior got lost somewhere, or if He mislaid His righteousness, or if He stopped loving us, or if He decided to sleep in tomorrow morning rather than praying for us. But those things will never happen. They are totally foreign to the character of Christ.

Frequently, the question is whether the doctrine of election can be reconciled with the biblical statement that "The Lord is . . . not wishing that any should perish" (2 Peter 3:9). There are two ambiguities in this text. First, there is ambiguity with respect to the word "wishing." It is sometimes translated "willing." There are two distinct Greek words that are translated by the English word "will": *thelēma* and *boulē*. Each of these words has several different nuances. Let's say there are eight of them. One of the three most familiar and common ones is that the will of God refers to His sovereign, efficacious will, by which He brings to pass whatsoever He decrees. When He created the universe, He said, "Let there be," and there was; He willed it, and it happened. The will of God can also refer to His commands, which we call His preceptive will: He says we are not allowed to do this, we must do that, and so on. That is the will of God that, of course, we can violate. We cannot violate His sovereign, efficacious will. The third and most frequent use of the word *will* has to do with God's basic disposition or attitude toward the world. God has "no pleasure in the death of the wicked" (Eze. 33:11). That describes His will of disposition. He may decree or require the death of the wicked, but He does not have pleasure in it.

Which view of God's will is in this text? If the text teaches that God is not willing in the sovereign, efficacious sense that any should perish, then no one would perish. So those who want to use this text against election have to be universalists, and most of them are not. However, we could say that God is not willing in the sense that His law does not allow any to perish. But that does not make a lot of sense. It would fit with the rest of Scripture to say that God's disposition is such that He does not want any to perish. Nonetheless, it seems best to say that the text does refer to the sovereign, efficacious will of God. Peter is saying that God sovereignly decrees that He will not allow any to perish.

The other ambiguity is in the word "any." To whom does "any" refer? The antecedent of "any" is the word "you": "The Lord . . . is patient toward you, not wishing that any should perish" (2 Peter 3:9). Those who are included in the word "you" are addressed in this epistle as "brothers" who are called and elect (1:10). Peter is explaining why it is that Jesus has not come back yet: because He is not willing that any of us—the elect—should perish before we come to faith. This is actually one of the strongest texts in the Bible for election. God will not permit any of His elect people to perish.

We have looked at half of these principles on which our perseverance depends and examined the efficacy of the merit of Christ and of His intercession on our behalf. Now let us look at the final principles: **the abiding of the Spirit, and of the seed of God within them, and the nature of the covenant of grace.**

First, our perseverance does not rest on our ability to persevere, but rather on the preserving activity of God. The Holy Spirit abides with us to this end. We are familiar with the Spirit's work in regenerating us, in quickening us from spiritual death to spiritual life. The Holy Spirit also ministers in us and on us in the process of our spiritual growth and sanctification. The Spirit convicts us of sin and of righteousness. There are other aspects of the Holy Spirit's work that are of crucial importance for our perseverance in the faith.

We do not believe, in the Reformed tradition, that an indelible mark is placed on the soul by baptism. We do believe, however, that for all who are truly saved, who are regenerate, there is an indelible mark—the seal of the Holy Spirit, by which we are sealed for everlasting life.

The second aspect of the Spirit's contribution to perseverance is the guarantee or down payment of the Spirit. When the Holy Spirit is our guarantee and God's Word promises final and complete redemption, no one would think that it would be remotely possible that the Holy Spirit would fail to keep His promise. God would not fail to keep His promise to finish what He has started. This is what Paul said: "He who began a good work in you will bring it to completion at the day of Jesus Christ" (Phil. 1:6). That is what the confession has in mind when it says that our perseverance does not depend on our ability to pay. If it were left to us, even in our redeemed state, we might default at some point along the way. To overcome our weaknesses, God not only gives His word about our future but backs up that word by giving us the guarantee of the Spirit.

The Holy Spirit is present in us and is given to us by the Father as His promise to finish this work of redemption.

The confession says the perseverance of the saints depends not on us or on our free will but on the immutability of the decree of election, flowing from the free and unchangeable love of God the Father. Our perseverance depends in the first place on the work of the Father, His election and immutable love. Second, it depends on the efficacy of the merit and intercession of Jesus Christ, which is the ground of our salvation. The effect that is wrought by Christ's perfect righteousness is of eternal and everlasting efficacy. It will not and cannot fail us and is supported by the continuing intercessory work of Christ. We look to the work of the Son, the second person of the Trinity, to confirm our confidence in perseverance. Third, the saints look to the abiding of the Spirit, and of the seed of God within them. The Holy Spirit dwells in us and seals us, being the guarantee of our inheritance. The work of perseverance, or the preservation of the saints, is a Trinitarian operation; our future is guaranteed by the Father, the Son, and the Holy Spirit. The confession concludes by observing that our perseverance depends on the nature of the covenant of grace: from all which ariseth also the certainty and infallibility thereof.

In Genesis 15:6, we read that Abraham believed God and that it was counted to him for righteousness. Abraham asked God: "How can I know? How can I know for sure? Right now, I cannot see my final redemption." Then God had Abraham cut up animals and birds and lay them end to end. When the sun went down, a deep sleep fell upon Abraham. Then a smoking pot and a flaming torch moved between the pieces. On the same day, the Lord made a covenant with Abraham (Gen. 15:8–21).

That smoking pot, that flaming torch, was a theophany, a visible manifestation of God. God passed through the animal and bird pieces, saying to Abraham in a graphic way, "Abraham, if I fail to keep My promise to you, may I be like these animals that you've cut in half." The author of Hebrews picks up on this later and says that because God could swear by nothing greater, He swore by Himself (Heb. 6:13). He said, "I swear to you by Myself, by My eternal immutable being. May I be cut in half just like you have cut these animals in half, if I do not keep My word."

Our faith and our salvation rest on trust in the promise of God. Without the promise of God, we have nothing. It is one thing to believe that God exists or to believe *in* God. It is quite another to *believe* God. The Christian faith is about believing God. It is about trusting God, and that means relying on Him and taking Him at His word. That is not gratuitous or blind faith. It is not irrational or absurd faith, because the more we learn about the character of God, the more trustworthy we realize He is and the more absurd it becomes that we would not trust Him. If there is anyone's word we ought to trust, it is the word of the perfectly righteous God, who is able and always willing to stand by His word. That is what God said to Abraham: "I will not just sign a document; I promise you by My own character, by My own nature, that I will see you through to the end."

The Westminster Confession states that the perseverance of the saints depends, finally, on **the nature of the covenant of grace**. We can hope to make it to the end because God Himself promises us the final redemption. That is not promised in the covenant of works. If our perseverance rested on the covenant of works, we could have no confidence. Our perseverance rests on the covenant of grace. God, in His grace, initiates our salvation and accomplishes it. God, in His grace, applies our salvation and preserves it. Our election is by His grace. The merit of Christ is transferred to us with perfect efficacy by His grace, as is the intercessory ministry of Christ as our High Priest. The indwelling of the Holy Spirit, the sealing of the Spirit, and the giving of the earnest is by His grace. These are all aspects of the covenant that God makes, not because we deserve it, but because He is gracious to us. So, in all these things taken together, we have reason to be confident that we will persevere.

3. Nevertheless, they may, through the temptations of Satan and of the world, the prevalency of corruption remaining in them, and the neglect of the means of their preservation, fall into grievous sins; and, for a time, continue therein: whereby they incur God's displeasure, and grieve his Holy Spirit, come to be deprived of some measure of their graces and comforts, have their hearts hardened, and their consciences wounded; hurt and scandalize others, and bring temporal judgments upon themselves.

388 • TRUTHS WE CONFESS

In section 3, we get the downside: Nevertheless, they may, through the temptations of Satan and of the world, . . . fall into grievous sins. In section 2, the Westminster divines told us why it is that we will persevere and on what our perseverance depends. With this section comes a warning that even though our final destiny is secure because of God's preservation, there can be serious and radical falls along the way—not because of some weakness in God but because of some weakness in us. One of the factors that contribute to our less-than-perfect performance during our earthly pilgrimage is Satan and his temptation of us.

When Jesus predicted Judas' betrayal, He said, "What you are going to do, do quickly," and He dismissed him. When He predicted Simon Peter's denial, He said to him, "Simon, Simon." That repetition of the personal form of address was emphatic, but it also communicated deep personal intimacy. It was an affectionate form of address by which Jesus said to him, "Simon, as strong as you think you are, as bold and courageous as you may feel, as sanctified as you presume to be, you will be an easy target for the tempter when he comes to you." That is why we have these warnings in Scripture: "Let anyone who thinks that he stands take heed lest he fall" (1 Cor. 10:12). "Your adversary the devil prowls around like a roaring lion, seeking someone to devour" (1 Peter 5:8). And yet: "He who is in you is greater than he who is in the world" (1 John 4:4). "Resist the devil, and he will flee from you" (James 4:7).

Satan does not limit his temptations to pagans. He works overtime with his minions against us, so that we have to deal with his temptations as well as those of the world. Luther saw the three enemies of the Christian faith as the world, the flesh, and the devil. That is a formidable triad of opponents, because we still have the remnants of our fallen corruption that work against the Spirit. Paul said they are at war with each other. We have to deal with the flesh and with the carnal desires that are still part of our life.

The means of grace—the sacraments, the reading of Scripture, preaching, prayer, worship, fellowship, and service—enable us to strengthen our walk with Christ. If we neglect them, we become weaker and more exposed to the impact of the world, the flesh, and the devil. We must use the means of grace diligently.

For Jesus, long times of prayer were not rare, and neither were they rare for David. Luther would characteristically spend a couple of hours in prayer every day. He was asked, "What would you do if you were really busy?" He answered, "If I had a really full day ahead of me, then I would make it three hours." The greater the burden, the more time he went to the Lord for his strength. He made diligent use of the means of grace. We often make casual use of the means of grace, and we wonder why we backslide or fall into the traps of Satan.

The reason for our fall is the work of Satan, the weakness of the flesh, the impact of the world, and the neglect of the means of grace. Spending time in the Word reinforces the things of God in our thinking. Paul says, "Whatever is true, whatever is honorable, whatever is just, whatever is pure, whatever is lovely, whatever is commendable, if there is any excellence, if there is anything worthy of praise, think about these things" (Phil. 4:8). It is hard to think about these when the TV is on and we are watching some of the worst programming. Our mind is distracted and not focused on the truth that comes from God. When that happens, our spiritual growth suffers.

They may . . . fall into grievous sins; and, for a time, continue therein. A Christian is capable of a serious and radical fall, but not a full or final fall. We can fall into grievous sin and persist in that sin, but not forever. David fell into sin and persisted in it, but God brought him back. The little phrase for a time is significant. We can fall like this for a time, but not for all time, not forever.

Whereby they incur God's displeasure. Just as a parent will scold a child to correct that child, so God may have a heavy hand upon us, and He corrects us. That is not at all inconsistent with His love. God uses His wrath to correct His wayward children as a manifestation of His holy love.

The way it is stated here in the confession is that we incur God's displeasure. We know when we have done something that is not pleasing to God, and we know that He is displeased with us. That is why we keep coming back to the cross. We keep coming back to Christ because the Father is never displeased with the Son, and our only hope is that we will be hidden in the folds of the righteousness of Jesus. When we fall into sin, we incur the displeasure of God and He is angry with us. We grieve his Holy Spirit.

They . . . come to be deprived of some measure of their graces and comforts, have their hearts hardened, and their consciences wounded.

That is perhaps one of the most dangerous things. The longer we continue in sin, the more our hearts become hardened, the more our souls become calloused. Jeremiah spoke God's word of judgment upon the Israelites when he said, "You have the forehead of a whore" (Jer. 3:3). In other words: "You have lost your capacity to blush. You can say things and do things without even having a red face anymore. You are not even embarrassed." That is where we are today in our culture. People will speak openly, without embarrassment, about behavior that no one would have dared to speak about just a few decades ago. People did such things then, but they would not talk about them. Some claim that there is just less hypocrisy today, but in reality our hearts have become hardened. Our consciences have been seared. Jeremiah was saying in effect that their consciences have been wounded. They have been wounded in the sense that they have become covered with scar tissue and they are not as sensitive as they once were.

What is the final result? They hurt and scandalize others, and bring temporal judgments upon themselves. When we sin, we incur the displeasure of God and grieve the Holy Spirit. We also wound, hurt, and scandalize others in the faith. And we suffer consequences for our sins. The Westminster divines were fully cognizant of the depth to which Christians can fall and do fall—and how much that can hurt others. The good news is that God refuses to leave us in that state. He who rescued us the first time will continue the rescue operation until He brings us home to Himself, safe and sound.

The whole concept of perseverance presupposes one very important thing, and that is that perseverance is promised only to the saints. God promises to preserve only those who are His. He promises to preserve only true believers who have been justified in Christ. How then can we know that we have received the promise of God's preservation? That question brings us to the question of assurance of salvation. The perseverance of the saints and the assurance of salvation, although two different matters, are so closely related that we can barely speak of the one without the other. Thus it is not by accident that the next chapter in the confession deals with the assurance of salvation.

Of the Assurance of Grace and Salvation

1. Although hypocrites and other unregenerate men may vainly deceive themselves with false hopes and carnal presumptions of being in the favor of God, and estate of salvation (which hope of theirs shall perish): yet such as truly believe in the Lord Jesus, and love him in sincerity, endeavoring to walk in all good conscience before him, may, in this life, be certainly assured that they are in the state of grace, and may rejoice in the hope of the glory of God, which hope shall never make them ashamed.

2. This certainty is not a bare conjectural and probable persuasion grounded upon a fallible hope; but an infallible assurance of faith founded upon the divine truth of the promises of salvation, the inward evidence of those graces unto which these promises are made, the testimony of the Spirit of adoption witnessing with our spirits that we are the children of God, which Spirit is the earnest of our inheritance, whereby we are sealed to the day of redemption.

3. This infallible assurance doth not so belong to the essence of faith, but that a true believer may wait long, and conflict with many difficulties before he be partaker of it: yet, being enabled by the Spirit to know the things which are freely given him of God, he may, without extraordinary revelation, in the right use of ordinary means, attain thereunto. And therefore it is the duty of everyone to give all diligence to make his calling and election sure, that thereby his heart may be enlarged in peace and joy in the Holy Ghost, in love and thankfulness to God, and in strength and cheerfulness in the duties of obedience, the proper fruits of this assurance; so far is it from inclining men to looseness.

4. True believers may have the assurance of their salvation divers ways shaken, diminished, and intermitted; as, by negligence in preserving of it, by falling into some special sin which woundeth the conscience and grieveth the Spirit; by some sudden or vehement temptation, by God's withdrawing the light of his countenance, and suffering even such as fear him to walk in darkness and to have no light: yet are they never utterly destitute of that seed of God, and life of faith, that love of Christ and the brethren, that sincerity of heart, and conscience of duty, out of which, by the operation of the Spirit, this assurance may, in due time, be revived; and by the which, in the meantime, they are supported from utter despair.

Chapter 18 begins with these words:

1. Although hypocrites and other unregenerate men may vainly deceive themselves with false hopes and carnal presumptions of being in the favor of God, and estate of salvation (which hope of theirs shall perish): yet such as truly believe in the Lord Jesus, and love him in sincerity, endeavoring to walk in all good conscience before him, may, in this life, be certainly assured that they are in the state of grace, and may rejoice in the hope of the glory of God, which hope shall never make them ashamed.

This section teaches that unregenerate people may possess a false sense of assurance but that genuine believers may attain a true sense of assurance. Assurance must be considered for the four kinds of people in the world.

The first group of people are not saved and are aware that they are not. They are unregenerate and they know it. They have no interest in becoming Christians.

The people in the second group are in a state of grace, but they are not sure that they are saved. The confession, as we will see, says that assurance of salvation is possible and indeed should be sought. Nevertheless, not everyone who is in the state of grace has yet arrived at the conclusion that he is in that state. Such people may think or hope they are saved but may not have full assurance that they are. Their degree of assurance vacillates from firm to shaky. During our study of the perseverance of the saints, we indicated that they can fall seriously and radically, but not fully and finally. When people are in the midst of a serious fall, they can have grave questions about the state of their soul.

The third group of people is easy to explain. They are in a state of grace and are assured of their salvation.

What complicates the whole question of assurance is the fourth group: those who are not saved but think that they are. There are two groups who possess assurance of salvation, but only one of those groups actually has salvation. So if someone has assurance of salvation, how can he be sure that his assurance is genuine, and not the false assurance of the hypocrite and the unbeliever? And how can people who are not saved nonetheless have full assurance that they are?

The main way that people acquire a false sense of assurance of their salvation is by having a false understanding of the way of salvation. Many people hold to justification by death, which is the creed of the universalist. The reasoning goes like this: "All people are saved by a loving and merciful God. Since I am a person, it follows that I am saved and cannot lose my salvation." Our purpose here is not to debate the claims of universalism, which cannot be substantiated from the Bible, but to show how people can come to a false sense of assurance by being universalists.

Probably the most prevalent doctrine of justification in modern culture is the doctrine of justification by works. Most Americans, including those who call themselves evangelicals, believe that people will get into heaven if they live a good life. They think: "I am pretty good. I do the best that I can, and haven't done anything terribly wrong. God will be satisfied." Christians may think: "I look forward to the day when I will be welcomed into heaven. After all, I've gone to church for forty years, I have been a Sunday school teacher, I've given money to the church and other good causes, and I've never murdered anyone or committed adultery." The confidence of such people is based upon their own goodness, which is not the biblical understanding of salvation.

This false concept of salvation is pervasive in our culture, and it is as pernicious as it is pervasive, because it completely obscures and denies the true gospel. What is so damaging about it is that it gives people a false sense of security. Jesus warns us about that in the Sermon on the Mount (Matt. 5–7). Near the end of the sermon, He says of the day of judgment, "On that day many will say to me, 'Lord, Lord, did we not prophesy in your name, and cast out demons in your name, and do many mighty works in your name?'" (Matt. 7:22). They do not say "Lord" twice for emphasis but for intimacy. About fifteen times in the Bible, the personal form of address is used twice to express a deep level of personal intimacy. That is why this warning of Jesus is so terrifying. Jesus is saying that people are going to come to Him on the last day not only confessing Him as Lord but also claiming an intimate, personal relationship with Him. He is talking about people who will approach the judgment with a strong sense of assurance of their state of grace and of their personal relationship with Jesus Christ. They will claim to have cast out demons in His name, to have preached, to have worked, to have been engaged in the missionary activity of the church, and to have been involved in evangelism. But Jesus says, "And then will I declare to them, 'I never knew you; depart from me, you workers of lawlessness'" (v. 23).

Our destiny is not determined by whether we know Jesus but by whether He knows us. Obviously, He knows everyone's name, but when He says, "I never knew you," He means, "I never knew you in a personal, intimate, saving way; you are pretending." It is frightening, but possible, that we may have false assurance. That is why we must examine ourselves carefully to make sure that our profession of faith is in fact genuine.

The first and basic reason why people arrive at a false sense of assurance is that they have a false understanding of salvation. They think that they are saved by their good works. Other people believe that they are saved automatically through the sacraments of the church. In this view, the classic Roman Catholic view, the gifts of God are communicated *ex opere operato*, "by the working of the works," through the sacramental ministry of the church. There are literally millions of people whose confidence rests on the ministrations of the church. This mentality is not restricted to Roman Catholics but is shared by many Protestants who think that if they are church members, that is all it takes to be saved.

When there is a false sense of assurance, the doctrine of salvation is probably wrong. There are people who say: "Doctrine doesn't matter. All you need to know is Jesus." The question then is, "Who is Jesus?" If we answer that question, we are engaged in doctrine. Our theology has to do with the content of the Christian faith, with the teaching of the Bible, with the most important issues of human existence, namely, how we can relate to the living God. That is a doctrinal question. If our doctrine is wrong, it can lead to a wrong sense of assurance. On the other hand, even if our doctrine is right, that is not enough to give us real assurance of salvation. We are not justified by holding to the doctrine of justification. The devil can earn a perfect score on a systematic theology exam. The devil knows the truth, but he hates it, and his heart remains estranged from it. Just having the doctrine of justification correct in one's mind is not a guarantee of salvation. One can have an incorrect understanding of the doctrine of justification and still be justified. It is possible to have the wrong doctrine, but the right content in the mind and heart, and not be able to articulate it.

Suppose the right doctrine is the doctrine of justification by faith alone, which means justification by Christ alone, and someone says he understands that the only way he can be saved is by putting his faith in Jesus and resting on His righteousness alone. He says further that he is indeed resting on Christ, that he has faith, and that therefore he is sure that he is in a state of salvation. Can a person delude himself about the state of his faith? Yes. Can we think we have saving faith and not have it? Can we have it and not be sure we have it? Yes, we can really have it and not be sure that we have it. We can really not have it and be sure we do have it. That is why we have to study the Scriptures diligently and prayerfully, so that we can learn to distinguish between true assurance and false assurance.

This chapter of the confession is designed to help us make that distinction and learn the difference between false assurance and true assurance. Section 1 again: hypocrites and other unregenerate men may vainly deceive themselves with false hopes and carnal presumptions of being in the favor of God. Each word in this confession of faith is carefully thought out and is so expressive. We read of hypocrites, unregenerate men, vain deceit, false hopes and carnal presumptions of being in the favor of God, and estate of salvation (which hope of theirs shall perish): yet such as truly believe in the Lord Jesus. . . . Now we are beginning to be shown the real marks of assurance, and the real mark of true Christians is genuine faith, for they truly believe in Christ and love him in sincerity, endeavoring to walk in all good conscience before him. They may not actually walk in all good conscience, but they try to do so. When they do so, these people may, in this life, be certainly assured that they are in the state of grace, and may rejoice in the hope of the glory of God, which hope shall never make them ashamed.

We may, in this life, be certainly assured. The divines are saying that the Word of God as the basis for our confidence in our salvation is so overwhelmingly powerful that it leaves us without doubt. It leaves us without anxiety, and it leaves us confident of the state of our souls. The greatest assurance in our own lives comes not from syllogisms but from the Word of God. When we read the Word of God, we receive assurance. We are not talking here about formal certainty, such as is derived from mathematical equations, but about certainty in and through God's Word.

> 2. This certainty is not a bare conjectural and probable persuasion grounded upon a fallible hope; but an infallible assurance of faith founded upon the divine truth of the promises of salvation, the inward evidence of those graces unto which these promises are made, the testimony of the Spirit of adoption witnessing with our spirits that we are the children of God, which Spirit is the earnest of our inheritance, whereby we are sealed to the day of redemption.

We mentioned above the difference between philosophical certainty of a formal nature and assurance that comes with respect to our inner confidence. One of the oldest questions encountered in philosophical investigation is, How do we know what we know? That is the study of epistemology. The debate that has raged for millennia tends to focus either on the knowledge that we gain through the mind or the knowledge that we gain through the senses. Our Creator has made us with minds by which we think, reason, and reach conclusions. He has also made us as creatures who have bodies. The only contact we have with the world outside of our mind is through the five bodily senses—hearing, sight, smell, touch, and taste.

How do we learn what we learn? Some people say that the mind has priority, because only the mind operates at the logical, formal, and deductive level. The standard syllogism is, "All men are mortal; Socrates is a man; therefore, Socrates is mortal." That syllogism represents deduction and indicates a logical progression of thinking, in which one moves from the initial premise to the conclusion. If indeed all men are mortal, and if Socrates is a man, then we know with absolute, formal certainty that Socrates is mortal, because of the laws of inference. This is a logical and formal conclusion, like the conclusions we get from mathematics. That is what we mean by formal certainty. But notice that we said "if" all men are mortal. The only way we could know that with absolute certainty would be posthumously. Even if there were only one person left alive, that person might be the first example in history of someone who did not die.

We do not know with certainty that Socrates was a man, either. He may have been a fictitious character, a creation of Plato's imagination. Then again, he could have been an alien from outer space disguised as a human. We do not know; none of us has ever seen Socrates. We hear a lot of skeptics say: "I don't believe in God. I've never seen, tasted, touched, smelled, or heard Him. I believe only what I can see with my eyes or hear with my ears." The Bible says that we see the creation of God with our eyes; nevertheless, we do not see God. This is one of the most difficult problems for the Christian: to worship and serve a Being whom we have never seen or heard.

However, on the other side of the coin, I believe that the mind absolutely requires—it doesn't just suggest a probability—that we affirm the existence of God with formal certainty. That is another discussion, but the present discussion is about the relationship between the mind and the senses. Anything that we know through the senses of hearing, seeing, smelling, tasting, and touching gives us less than absolute certainty.

Timothy Leary was a professor of psychology at Harvard during the 1960s. He experimented with a synthetic drug that was nicknamed LSD and with other hallucinogenic drugs. He claimed that LSD was not hallucinogenic but rather psychedelic, or mind-expanding. A hallucinogenic drug gives a distorted perception of reality. But a psychedelic drug, according to Leary, enhances one's ability to perceive what is actually there. In court, Leary brought in artists to give testimony that under the influence of LSD, they could discern nuances of color tones that they could not perceive in their normal conscious states. Likewise, musicians testified that when they used LSD they could hear tonal patterns at a much more discrete level than they could with their natural auditory ability.

There are limits to our senses. We cannot hear dog's whistles. We have microscopes and telescopes. There is a realm of reality out there that we cannot perceive with our unaided senses.

Our senses not only are limited, but they also can deceive us. Augustine talked about the bent oar. When a rowboat is taken out on the water, as the oar dips into the water, it looks like the oar goes into the water and bends. That is because of light refraction, and though the oar is not bent, it looks that way.

We learn to make adjustments in those areas of our normal experience that we know to be distortions. However, how do we know that the outside world is at all the way we perceive it? That is the oldest philosophical question there is—the so-called subject-object question. That is why some people argue that any knowledge based upon sense perception is less than certain. Philosophically, that is true, but when we talk about assurance in the theological sense, we are not in the realm of technical epistemology. We are talking about the confidence we have in our souls that is associated with a proposition or with an idea. Part of our confidence comes from our belief that the supreme source of truth in all the universe is divine revelation.

Christianity affirms that we have a revealed religion. We learn things from God that we could never learn through pure human speculation, rational deduction, or sense perception. What we call revelation does not eliminate the mind or the senses. How do we know that we have divine revelation? How do we get in touch with its content? Mystics might say that although they can't conceive of it mentally or rationally or encounter it empirically with the senses, they have an "inner light" that tells them what is true. How do we distinguish between this inner light of revelation and indigestion? We are thinking beings encapsulated in bodies. The only path from our interior thoughts in the mind to that which is outside of us is through the senses.

Some Christian philosophers say that there is so much weakness inherent in the senses that the only truly Christian philosophy is one that is completely skeptical with regard to the senses and that Christian philosophy must start with the Bible and not with the senses. But how can we know about anything in the Bible unless we read it with our eyes, listen while someone else reads it out loud, or, if we are blind, feel it in Braille? The only access we have to this Book is through our senses.

The Book itself does not despise the physical. Throughout Scripture is recorded the testimony of the prophets and the Apostles who declare to us, "For we did not follow cleverly devised myths when we made known to you the power and coming of our Lord Jesus Christ, but we were eyewitnesses of his majesty" (2 Peter 1:16). When the Apostle Paul sets forth his case for the resurrection of Christ, he says in 1 Corinthians 15:5–8 that Christ appeared to Peter and to the Twelve, to five hundred people at one time, and to Paul himself. Luke informs Theophilus that the gospel narratives relate what "those who from the beginning were eyewitnesses" handed down (Luke 1:1–4). Thus, the testimony of the writers of Scripture is not that they have revealed to us some inner light, but rather that they have revealed what they have seen with their eyes and heard with their ears. Christ came in the flesh partly for that reason.

God gives revelation through His spokesmen that is not available from any other source. Once we know with our minds and with our senses that God is there, and once we become convinced that this is His Word, then we come in touch with a source of truth that transcends anything else that we can have in this world. God endorsed His spokesmen by His miracles. When Nicodemus came to Jesus, he said, "Rabbi, we know that you are a teacher come from God, for no one can do these signs that you do unless God is with him" (John 3:2). The primary function of miracles in the Bible is to authenticate agents of revelation, to prove that the speaker has the endorsement of God. God does not give the ability to do miracles to impostors, nor does He give that power to the devil.

Many evangelicals believe that Satan can perform miracles because the Bible says to watch out in the last days for the lying signs and wonders that the Antichrist does. What is a lying sign or wonder? Is it a real miracle done on behalf of falsehood? It is a clever trick, because if Satan can actually perform miracles, then Nicodemus would have to have acknowledged that Jesus could have come from the devil. If the devil can part the Red Sea, if he can make an ax head float, and if he can bring about the resurrection of Christ from the grave, then the whole appeal of the early church to the hand of God in the miracles, proving Christ to be who He claimed to be, is a false appeal.

God empowered Moses to perform miracles, not to prove the existence of God but to prove that God was behind Moses' message. We can know with certainty that God exists apart from miracles, but in the sphere of history the presence of miracles helps us understand something about the presence of divine revelation. That is why we spend so much time studying the nature of sacred Scripture. If we believe that the Bible is the Word of God, then we have an arbiter to settle any dispute that we have about what is truth, as long as we can agree as to what the Bible says. If we disagree on whether predestination is true, we can see what the Bible says. If the Bible convinces us that predestination is true, then the dispute is over, as long as we believe that the Bible is God's revealed Word. If we do not believe that it is the Word of God, then we have to argue our case on other grounds.

For the Christian, the highest court of appeal is the Word of God. That was settled at the beginning of our study of the Westminster Confession. The doctrine of Holy Scripture is discussed in chapter 1 of the confession because Reformed theology is derived from Scripture. God's truth doesn't need any human approval. It is important to understand that if God says something, it is settled. Scripture says, "If we confess our sins, he is faithful and just to forgive us our sins and to cleanse us from all unrighteousness" (1 John 1:9). What higher court of appeal is there? Where can we possibly get more assurance of our forgiveness than from God's own Word? If God came to us and said, "I forgive you all your sins," how would we feel? Would we feel liberated? Would we feel free from the paralysis of our guilt? We certainly would. No wonder Isaiah was willing to give his life—because he really believed the Word of God. The Christian life is about believing God, not just believing that there is a God. When God says it, it's settled. That's the advantage of having information and knowledge that comes from God.

You may wonder why we are spending all this time on revelation and epistemology when our subject is the assurance of salvation. The answer is that the second section of this chapter of the confession teaches that the assurance we have of our salvation is infallible. The confession is not suggesting that we are infallible. We have no doctrine of the infallibility of individuals in the Reformed church; we have no doctrine of the infallibility of the church and no doctrine of the infallibility of the confession. Only the Scriptures are infallible. Our assurance does not rest on our own reasoning or desires. It is not a bare conjectural and probable persuasion grounded upon a fallible hope; but an infallible assurance of faith founded upon the divine truth of the promises of salvation.

Our confidence is founded on the promises of the God who is infallible. He knows with absolute certainty who is saved, who is not, and who is in a state of grace. If God confirms our state of grace, then He is the ground of our assurance. The assurance of faith is infallible because it is founded upon the promises of salvation made by our infallible God.

The confession goes on to say that our assurance is also based on the inward evidence of those graces unto which these promises are made, the testimony of the Spirit of adoption witnessing with our spirits that we are the children of God, which Spirit is the earnest of our inheritance, whereby we are sealed to the day of redemption. We have already discussed the guarantee of the Spirit and the sealing of the Spirit, and we won't repeat that discussion here, except to say that the confession speaks here about the inward evidences of those graces unto which the promises are made. The scriptural allusion is to 2 Peter 1:2–4, 10–11:

> May grace and peace be multiplied to you in the knowledge of God and of Jesus our Lord. His divine power has granted to us all things that pertain to life and godliness, through the knowledge of him who called us to his own glory and excellence, by which he has granted to us his precious and very great promises, so that through them you may become partakers of the divine nature, having escaped from the corruption that is in the world because of sinful desire. . . . Therefore, brothers, be all the more diligent to confirm your calling and election, for if you practice these qualities you will never fall. For in this way there will be richly provided for you an entrance into the eternal kingdom of our Lord and Savior Jesus Christ.

We skipped from verse 4 to verse 10; now we will quote verses 5–9:

> For this very reason, make every effort to supplement your faith with
> virtue, and virtue with knowledge, and knowledge with self-control,
> and self-control with steadfastness, and steadfastness with godliness,
> and godliness with brotherly affection, and brotherly affection with
> love. For if these qualities are yours and are increasing, they keep you
> from being ineffective or unfruitful in the knowledge of our Lord Jesus
> Christ. For whoever lacks these qualities is so nearsighted that he is
> blind, having forgotten that he was cleansed from his former sins.

Those words are from the Apostle Peter, not from the Apostle Paul. Peter's
list of Christian qualities resembles Paul's famous list of fruit of the Spirit
in Galatians 5:22–23. But in this context, Peter says, "Therefore, brothers, be all the more diligent to confirm your calling and election, for if
you practice these qualities you will never fall" (1:10). Peter wants us to
be fruitful in the Christian life, confident in the knowledge that the Holy
Spirit dwells in us. If we are sure that we have the indwelling of the Holy
Spirit, that goes a long way toward helping us become productive in manifesting the fruit of the Spirit.

Some churches believe that at conversion a person begins a process by
which he is eventually deified, because Peter speaks here of our becoming "partakers of the divine nature" (v. 4). However, the way in which
we partake of the divine nature is that the Holy Spirit changes us in our
regeneration and dwells in us for our sanctification. Insofar as the Holy
Spirit is dwelling in us, He is not making us God, but the Holy Spirit
is God inside of us. In that sense, we are partaking of, and participating
in, the divine nature. Peter says we are to "be all the more diligent to
confirm [our] calling and election" (v. 10), that is, to seek assurance of
salvation. The practical reason for looking for assurance of our salvation
is to enhance our sanctification. The Christian who is not sure is more
vulnerable to every wind of doctrine. People who are able to stand in
times of adversity are those who have things settled. They know who they
are; they know to whom they belong and in whom they have believed.
Their assurance gives them spiritual strength to deal with the world, the
flesh, and the devil, particularly the latter.

We generally think of Satan's great work as that of being the tempter, the seducer, but perhaps his strongest efforts are made as the accuser. He constantly reminds us of our sinfulness, which is what the Holy Spirit does to convict us of sin. The one time that Satan does not totally lie is when he holds our sin up before us and tells us that we really are sinners. But then he twists that truth and tells us that we are not in Christ, that we do not have any security. He takes away our confidence as believers.

If Satan can cause us to lose confidence in our standing before God, he can paralyze our fruit-bearing and performance. It is hard to be a Christian, with all our weaknesses and failings, and to maintain a high level of confidence. But we are called, even while we are still in the process of being sanctified, to go out with boldness to serve Christ.

If we are going to serve Christ, we had better know how we are saved, what the grounds of our salvation are, who our Savior is, and where our confidence rests, or else Satan will threaten to run rampant over us. Satan constantly attacked Martin Luther until Luther said, "Get away from me; I'm baptized." Luther did not believe that his baptism secured his salvation. What he meant was this: "I have the promise of God in my body, and I am resting on the Word of God. I am resting on the righteousness of Christ for my salvation. If the righteousness of Christ isn't good enough for you, Satan, don't expect me to exceed it. But I have all the merit that He has, so go after Jesus if you think you can get Him." Luther knew in whom he had placed his trust and his faith.

In section 2 of this chapter, there is a reference to Romans 8:15, where Paul says that we are adopted by God and enabled by the Spirit to cry, "Abba! Father!" He is our Father, and the Holy Spirit bears witness with our spirits that we are the sons of God (v. 16). That text could easily be ripped out of its context and made the proof text for a mystical inner light, but the internal testimony of the Spirit is a confirmation that comes in and through the Word. How does the Spirit bear witness to our spirits? He does it through the Bible. There is no time when we receive greater assurance of our salvation than when we are in the Word of God. That is how the Spirit bears witness, because He does not leave us alone to read this book. As we are searching for the truth of God, the Holy Spirit is working through the Word of God. The Word is infallible, and the Spirit's testimony is infallible. That combination of Word and Spirit is what pulls us out of the morass of doubt and lack of confidence in our standing before God.

> 3. This infallible assurance doth not so belong to the essence of faith, but that a true believer may wait long, and conflict with many difficulties before he be partaker of it: yet, being enabled by the Spirit to know the things which are freely given him of God, he may, without extraordinary revelation, in the right use of ordinary means, attain thereunto. And therefore it is the duty of everyone to give all diligence to make his calling and election sure, that thereby his heart may be enlarged in peace and joy in the Holy Ghost, in love and thankfulness to God, and in strength and cheerfulness in the duties of obedience, the proper fruits of this assurance; so far is it from inclining men to looseness.

Section 3 begins with an important caution: This infallible assurance doth not so belong to the essence of faith, but that a true believer may wait long, and conflict with many difficulties before he be partaker of it. In other words, possessing the assurance of one's salvation is not essential to one's faith; it is not essential to salvation, as is faith in Christ as one's Savior.

The Christian faith has literally hundreds of doctrines about which Christians disagree at many points. Yet all Christians agree on the essentials of the faith. For example, the deity of Christ is essential to the Christian faith. If someone denies the deity of Christ, he is not an orthodox Christian. That is why orthodox Christians have not recognized such groups as Jehovah's Witnesses and Mormons as Christian churches. Both groups deny the deity of Christ, and that is an essential of Christianity.

Much more controversial is the Reformation dispute over the doctrine of justification by faith alone. The Reformers insisted that this doctrine is an essential of Christian faith, so that its denial would preclude an institution from being considered Christian. Therefore, in the sixteenth century, when the Roman Catholic Church condemned justification by faith alone at the Council of Trent, the Protestant community believed that Rome had become apostate. This dispute goes on to this day. When it comes to other essential doctrines, such as the deity of Christ and the Trinity, the Roman Catholic Church has defended them heroically through the ages. But if there are ten essentials and we deny one of them, we are still denying something that is essential to historic Christianity.

The Westminster divines are saying in section 3 that the doctrine of the assurance of salvation is not essential to our salvation. It is not one of those doctrines that a person has to believe in order to be a Christian. Moreover, we don't have to possess assurance of our salvation in order to be in a state of grace. We may be plagued with doubts, yet be saved.

Since assurance of salvation is not an essential part of Christian experience, we may fail to have it without losing or failing to possess an essential of the Christian faith. However, in the absence of assurance, we will lack a measure of Christian well-being. There are certain things that may not be necessary for our salvation, but they are important to our sanctification and to our spiritual growth.

One of those things is the doctrine of the inerrancy of Scripture. Is Scripture verbally inspired by God, or is it simply a set of ancient human writings that contains errors? Many Christians would say that the doctrine of the inerrancy of Scripture is essential to the Christian faith. However, it is better to say that the doctrine of inerrancy is necessary to the well-being of the church, but it is not essential for salvation. Without the doctrine of inerrancy, there will be great confusion, suffering, and intrusion of error into the life of God's people, but one does not have to affirm the inerrancy of Scripture in order to be saved. It is understandable how a genuine believer who is exposed to the avalanche of academic criticism of the Bible could have real questions about the extent of the Bible's veracity and the extent of its infallibility without losing his faith.

Let's be clear. A person does not have to believe in the inerrancy of Scripture to be saved, but he must believe the basic teachings of Scripture to be saved. A person can't be saved if he does not believe that Jesus is who the Bible says He is. A person can't be saved if he does not believe in the resurrection of Christ. There are a lot of reasons why people do not believe the Bible. One is that they do not believe the message of the Bible, and in that case they cannot be saved. But it is possible for a person to believe the essential message of the Bible and still have questions about the nature of Scripture. However, if we give up inerrancy, the next thing will be to doubt the character of God. It is a very short step from denying inerrancy to denying the truths that are essential for salvation, since they come to us in the Word of God. It is possible for a Christian to be so battered by the modern criticisms of the Bible that he abandons inerrancy. However, if we start to doubt that it is God's Word, we are coming perilously close to denying the God whose Word it is.

Let's look at another example of the distinction between something's being essential to the *being* of the church and its being vital to the *well-being* of the church. Devout evangelicals differ over the question of whether infants should be baptized. Both sides are convinced that their position is scriptural. Both sides are trying to do what God wants them to do. But they disagree on what the Bible teaches. This is an important matter, but it is not essential for salvation. Others, however, say that it is an essential of Christian faith and Christian fellowship. Infant baptism is an important matter, but the correct position on the matter is not essential to salvation. Similarly, the confession speaks about the assurance of salvation as being important, but not as being essential to salvation.

This infallible assurance doth not so belong to the essence of faith, but that a true believer may wait long, and conflict with many difficulties before he be partaker of it: yet, being enabled by the Spirit to know the things which are freely given him of God, he may, without extraordinary revelation, in the right use of ordinary means, attain thereunto. Reformation theology was defined in comparison to Roman Catholic doctrine, because it was important for people to understand the difference between what they were embracing and what Rome had been teaching. That is true not only with regard to justification and sanctification but throughout systematic theology. Here, the confession clearly has the Roman Catholic position in view when it says that when a true believer is enabled by the Spirit to know the things which are freely given him of God, he may—now here is the phrase—without extraordinary revelation, in the right use of ordinary means, attain thereunto.

The key words are without extraordinary revelation. The Roman Catholic Church, going back to the Council of Trent, taught that, as a general rule, Christians could not have assurance of salvation unless God gave them some extraordinary, special revelation. People like Mary or Francis of Assisi or Thomas Aquinas could receive this extraordinary revelation and have full assurance of salvation, but the ordinary means of pursuing a personal assurance of salvation would not be successful, according to classic Roman Catholic theology.

The confession affirms, on the contrary, that assurance is attainable by ordinary means. To be sure, true believers can go for a long time through struggles and difficulties without achieving the assurance of salvation; nevertheless, that goal of the sweet assurance of salvation is readily available to us without any extraordinary revelation. The ordinary means of grace are sufficient to achieve assurance.

Therefore it is the duty of everyone to give all diligence to make his calling and election sure. This statement is based on 2 Peter 1:10, where the Word of God exhorts and mandates us to confirm our calling and election. Since the Bible calls us to do that, it is our duty to obey. So if we do not have the assurance of salvation, it is our duty to pursue it. One should do this that thereby his heart may be enlarged in peace and joy in the Holy Ghost, in love and thankfulness to God, and in strength and cheerfulness in the duties of obedience, the proper fruits of this assurance; so far is it from inclining men to looseness. That is a magnificent statement. We should diligently seek the assurance of salvation so that our hearts may be enlarged in peace and joy in the Holy Ghost.

In 2 Peter, we are called to find assurance of salvation so that we might be productive and fruitful Christians. To settle the assurance question is a key to bearing the fruit of the Spirit. The particular virtues that Peter elaborates parallel the Apostle Paul's teaching in Galatians on the fruit of the Spirit. The confession here mentions two of the fruits of the Spirit, namely, peace and joy.

If God never bestowed another blessing upon us for the rest of our days, we would still have every reason to be joyful for the blessings He has already poured out on us. We have an insatiable appetite for more and more blessings before we can be joyful. If we are poverty-stricken or unemployed, if we are doubled over in pain from a chronic or an acute illness, we still are blessed people because our names are written in the Lamb's Book of Life. That is the most wonderful thing for which anyone could rejoice. The Apostle Paul could go through all the misery he recounts for us in 2 Corinthians 11 and still be the Apostle of joy. He understood that he had received the pearl of great price, and he never tired of rejoicing in what he had. Even in the midst of the travails and pains that come with age, many Christians find that the older they get, the more joy they have. It comes from an increasing understanding of who God is and what a wonderful assurance it is to belong to Him. That gives joy.

The other fruit mentioned here is peace. Peace is set forth as the first fruit of our justification: "Therefore, since we have been justified by faith, we have peace with God" (Rom. 5:1). Peace with God does not end our conflict with the world, the flesh, and the devil. However, we can possess peace in the midst of conflict, turmoil, persecution, and pain. With the assurance of our salvation comes peace with God, which is permanent and lasting. It is not a guarded truce, where the first time we step out of line, God rattles the sword. The chief legacy of Christ to the believer is peace. He says in John 14:1–2, 27: "Let not your hearts be troubled. Believe in God; believe also in me. In my Father's house are many rooms. If it were not so, would I have told you that I go to prepare a place for you? . . . Peace I leave with you; my peace I give to you. Not as the world gives do I give to you. Let not your hearts be troubled, neither let them be afraid." We have the peace of Christ given in His last will and testament. We have the peace that passes understanding and the peace that transcends every earthly peace. This peace is rooted and grounded in the assurance that the Spirit gives to our soul that we are children of God.

How much would we spend to get peace and joy? **That thereby his heart may be enlarged in peace and joy in the Holy Ghost, in love and thankfulness to God.** The more certain we are of our salvation, the greater is our love and thanksgiving to God. **And in strength and cheerfulness in the duties of obedience.** Assurance of salvation gives us not only peace but also joy. It increases our love and our gratitude to God, and it strengthens our resolve to be obedient. Here is where the assurance of salvation facilitates sanctification. If Satan can keep us unsure of our salvation, he can accuse us and keep us from being productive. The more certain we are of our salvation, the more resolved we are to obey God. Assurance gives us cheerfulness in the duties of obedience, the proper fruits of this assurance; so far is it from inclining men to looseness.

The confession is responding again to Rome, which attacked this concept of assurance, fearing that it would breed antinomianism and licentiousness. Rome was afraid that assurance would create a smug attitude among Christians, making them anything but diligent in the pursuit of righteousness and sanctification.

The Reformers reply that just the opposite is the case. When we have assurance and the Holy Spirit comforts our heart, that fuels our love, joy, and peace with the Lord. It strengthens our resolve to obey the One who has assured us that we are His. Love is the most powerful motivational force. It barely edges out hate, which is a powerful force as well. Real love is what induces people to give their lives for their children, spouses, neighbors, or country. It is the love that we have for God that fuels our pursuit of obedience to Him. God wants us to obey Him because we love Him. He bestows assurance on us freely when we know we do not deserve to be His children and we know we do not deserve to be justified. When we understand the gratuitous nature of our salvation and are sure that Christ's work has availed for us, that fuels the fires of love for Him in our souls and makes us say, "Lord, You have given me such a wonderful gift; what can I do to show my love for You?" Jesus answers that question: "If you love me, you will keep my commandments" (John 14:15). Our obedience is not motivated by a desire to earn salvation, nor by a grim duty that is imposed upon us by the divine will; rather, it is rendered to God as a sacrifice of love.

Paul connects Romans 12 to the previous eleven chapters with the word "therefore." After eleven chapters of heavy theology, he turns to practical application. He writes: "I appeal to you therefore, brothers, by the mercies of God, to present your bodies as a living sacrifice, holy and acceptable to God, which is your spiritual worship. Do not be conformed to this world, but be transformed by the renewal of your mind" (vv. 1–2). Paul calls on us to respond with sacrifice, but not the Old Testament sacrifices of bulls, goats, lambs, or turtledoves. We are to sacrifice ourselves to God, which is our logical response to everything that God has done for us. The confession is following in the footsteps of the Apostle, calling us to the duties of obedience.

4. True believers may have the assurance of their salvation divers ways shaken, diminished, and intermitted; as, by negligence in preserving of it, by falling into some special sin which woundeth the conscience and grieveth the Spirit; by some sudden or vehement temptation, by God's withdrawing the light of his countenance, and suffering even such as fear him to walk in darkness and to have no light: yet are they never utterly destitute of that seed of God, and life of faith, that love of Christ and the brethren, that sincerity of heart, and conscience of duty, out of which, by the operation of the Spirit, this assurance may, in due time, be revived; and by the which, in the meantime, they are supported from utter despair.

The divines warn that a host of things can diminish our assurance. We can be negligent in attending worship, in reading the Scriptures, and in prayer. We can remove ourselves from those means of grace by which our assurance is strengthened daily. If we get careless, there will be consequences. The level of our assurance will begin to diminish. We can fall into some grave sin or be exposed to what is called **vehement temptation**. This can happen to any Christian. If we crumble in such situations, it can so wound our consciences and so grieve the Holy Spirit that we can fall into what the saints of old called "the dark night of the soul."

We are down, but we are never out. We never, ever abandon hope, no matter how rough things may be. Even if, for all the reasons mentioned in the confession, the strength of our assurance is attacked and we fall away for a season, we never fall so far as to be in **utter despair**. If we come to the place in life where we think, "God, this is all I can take," we shouldn't say it, because it seems that every time a Christian says that, God gives us something else. He seems to say: "Don't tell Me how much you can take. I'll be the judge of that, because with everything that I put on you, I give you the grace to bear it." That is why we never surrender. To give up would be a complete repudiation of the assurance of God and His grace that He has bestowed upon us.

Of the Law of God

1. God gave to Adam a law, as a covenant of works, by which he bound him and all his posterity to personal, entire, exact, and perpetual obedience, promised life upon the fulfilling, and threatened death upon the breach of it, and endued him with power and ability to keep it.

2. This law, after his fall, continued to be a perfect rule of righteousness; and, as such, was delivered by God upon Mount Sinai, in ten commandments, and written in two tables: the first four commandments containing our duty towards God; and the other six, our duty to man.

3. Beside this law, commonly called moral, God was pleased to give to the people of Israel, as a church under age, ceremonial laws, containing several typical ordinances, partly of worship, prefiguring Christ, his graces, actions, sufferings, and benefits; and partly, holding forth divers instructions of moral duties. All which ceremonial laws are now abrogated, under the new testament.

4. To them also, as a body politic, he gave sundry judicial laws, which expired together with the State of that people; not obliging any other now, further than the general equity thereof may require.

5. The moral law doth forever bind all, as well justified persons as others, to the obedience thereof; and that, not only in regard of the matter contained in it, but also in respect of the authority of God the Creator, who gave it. Neither doth Christ, in the gospel, any way dissolve, but much strengthen this obligation.

6. Although true believers be not under the law, as a covenant of works, to be thereby justified, or condemned; yet is it of great use to them, as well as to others; in that, as a rule of life informing them of the will of God, and their duty, it directs and binds them to walk accordingly; discovering also

the sinful pollutions of their nature, hearts, and lives; so as, examining themselves thereby, they may come to further conviction of, humiliation for, and hatred against sin, together with a clearer sight of the need they have of Christ, and the perfection of his obedience. It is likewise of use to the regenerate, to restrain their corruptions, in that it forbids sin: and the threatenings of it serve to show what even their sins deserve; and what afflictions, in this life, they may expect for them, although freed from the curse thereof threatened in the law. The promises of it, in like manner, show them God's approbation of obedience, and what blessings they may expect upon the performance thereof: although not as due to them by the law as a covenant of works. So as, a man's doing good, and refraining from evil, because the law encourageth to the one, and deterreth from the other, is no evidence of his being under the law; and, not under grace.

7. Neither are the forementioned uses of the law contrary to the grace of the gospel, but do sweetly comply with it; the Spirit of Christ subduing and enabling the will of man to do that freely, and cheerfully, which the will of God, revealed in the law, requireth to be done.

Chapter 19 of the Westminster Confession is full of important content that is often overlooked or misunderstood. What relevance does the Old Testament law of God have for Christians today? This chapter of the confession provides some significant guidelines in answer to that question.

When we study the law of God, we usually think first of Mount Sinai and the giving of the law through Moses. But the confession begins with God's law at creation:

1. God gave to Adam a law, as a covenant of works, by which he bound him and all his posterity to personal, entire, exact, and perpetual obedience, promised life upon the fulfilling, and threatened death upon the breach of it, and endued him with power and ability to keep it.

The initial section of the confession's treatment of the law looks back to creation, to what theologians call the "creation ordinances." In an earlier chapter of the confession, we saw the distinction between the covenant of works and the covenant of grace. The covenant of grace does not annihilate the covenant of works; rather, God agrees to save us on the basis of someone else's fulfillment of the covenant of works, rather than our own. Paul, in Romans 5:19, contrasts the work of Adam and the work of Christ, whom he elsewhere calls the last Adam (1 Cor. 15:45) and the second man (v. 47). Through Adam's disobedience, the world is plunged into ruin; through Christ's obedience, we are redeemed. Where Adam failed, Christ succeeded. Adam failed to keep the covenant of works, whereas Christ kept the covenant of works on our behalf.

To understand the significance of the creation ordinances, we have to understand the covenant in which they were given. We can distinguish the various covenants in the Bible as the covenant with Adam, the covenant with Noah, the covenant with Abraham (and Isaac and Jacob), the covenant with Moses, and the new covenant instituted by Christ in the New Testament. They are all distinguished from one another by their specific content.

In the covenant of creation, announced to Adam, God set up an arrangement with the entire human race. This is vitally important in our day, because controversies rage in the political arena about the relationship between church and state. We understand the difference between the two institutions. They do not have the same role to perform. There have been times when the government has tried to usurp the role of the church, and other times when the church has tried to usurp the role of the state.

There is probably no more emotionally charged issue in our culture today than the issue of abortion. It simply will not go away. Those who are pro-abortion get upset when churches protest the government's making it lawful to have an abortion on demand. They say that the church is interfering in the business of the state. Now, if the government tried to promote one church over another, or decided to regulate the administration of the sacraments, then it would clearly be in violation of the terms that were established at the founding of the American republic. The United States was founded on the idea that no religious group would be favored over another, and all groups were guaranteed the free exercise of religion. But when religious groups say to the state that there ought to be a law against abortion, we are not asking the state to be the church; we are asking the state to be the state. We are reminding the civil government of its God-given responsibility to protect and defend human life. God gives the sword to the civil magistrate, not to fight wars of aggression, but to defend human life. When the government abdicates its responsibility to protect human life, then the church may exercise its prophetic role by calling upon the government to be the government. The sanctity of life is not a Christian issue; it is a human issue. It is rooted and grounded not in the law of the New Testament or in the law of Mount Sinai but in creation, in the creation ordinances.

Here's another illustration. In our day, we have seen the collapse of one of the oldest institutions in human history, namely, the institution of marriage. We can trace the institution of marriage beyond the advent of Christianity, beyond the advent of Old Testament Judaism. We find this institution in virtually every culture, going all the way back to creation. Marriage was instituted not by Moses or Jesus but by God in creation for our first human parents and the first human family. God ordained marriage in the covenant that He made with mankind. Today, many people despise this institution and elect instead for cohabitation without marriage. Or they redefine marriage so that it can encompass unions between two people of the same sex. These distortions are a rebellion against creation and against the law of God established in the creation.

A non-Christian may respond that this argument still flows from the Bible. Yes, we are looking to the Bible, because we are convinced that we get the truth of God from it. But we are not trying to impose a Christian value on the world. Rather, we are saying that all people in this world are inescapably in a covenant relationship with God simply by virtue of their humanity. When God entered into a covenant relationship with Adam, it was not just with him as an individual. Adam represented the whole human race. When God entered into a covenant with Adam, He entered into a covenant with humanity.

A person may object that he doesn't believe in God, in Adam, or in the Bible. But, if the Bible is true, the fact that someone does not believe that it is true does not change its truth. A person's refusal to believe in the existence of God does not excuse him from keeping the terms of the creation covenant. All people are in a relationship with God whether they want to be or not. If God exists, would He not be related to human beings? Whether they acknowledge it or not, everyone is inescapably in a covenant relationship with God by virtue of His creation ordinances.

When we talk about being in a covenant relationship with God, some may assume that we are talking about a wonderful, loving relationship. However, covenant relationships can be either positive or negative. In biblical language, people can be either covenant keepers or covenant breakers.

In this covenant relationship made with all mankind, there are various ordinances. One of them is marriage. God instituted marriage for the well-being of the whole world; it is not just for Christians. Obviously, there are certain restrictions about whom and under what conditions a Christian may marry. But a person does not have to be a Christian to get married. Marriage is a creation ordinance given by God to all people.

There is an ongoing debate about whether the Sabbath law was a creation ordinance instituted for all mankind or only part of the Mosaic law given to Israel. Was there a weekly Sabbath before Moses? Many states used to have "blue laws," which governed certain behaviors on Sunday. The laws did not require people to go to church, but they did prohibit commerce on the Sabbath day, except for necessities, such as the prescription counter of the drugstore for people who had to have emergency medicine.

States observed these laws on the assumption that a day of rest was good for all people, no matter what their religious persuasion was. So that workers would not be unduly exploited, it was mandated by the state that there be a day of rest, one day out of seven.

If the Sabbath is a creation ordinance, and if the state is called by God to maintain the law of God outside the church, then it would be the state's duty to legislate with respect to the Sabbath. That sounds radical today, even to Christians, because we live in a culture that has completely repudiated that way of thinking. Civil government in the United States has now declared its independence from God and from His law, and has become godless, pagan, and barbarian. There is still enough liberty and influence from previous generations of Christian commitment alive in our culture to lead us to think we are still living in a Christian nation. But in terms of the actual structures of society, it has been a long time since Christian influence has prevailed.

Many people in the secular culture are hostile toward the church and to Christians because they see us as a potential threat to their freedom. They fear that Christians will impose restrictions and demands on them.

Every law that is enacted by the federal government of the United States is backed up by the entire arsenal of our government. Government is legal force. Any government that has the right to enact laws also has the right to enforce those laws. Every law that is passed limits someone's freedom. The secular culture is afraid that we as Christians will use the power of the ballot, the political power of this world, to force Christianity on people. That is not the mandate we have from God, nor is it the mandate we have from Christ. We cannot use the sword to turn America back into a Christian nation. So we as Christians need to be very careful about how we use our electoral power. We must not try to use the ballot to enforce the distinctives of the Christian community.

The first level of understanding of the law begins with creation, and that is where this section of the confession starts: **God gave to Adam a law, as a covenant of works.** God's laws are given to us in the context of a covenant. Jesus stated it for the Christian this way: "If you love me, you will keep my commandments" (John 14:15). The laws are the stipulations or the terms of the agreement. In creation, God set before the human race a blessing and a curse, and the terms are spelled out in Genesis: "You may surely eat of every tree of the garden, but of the tree of the knowledge of good and evil you shall not eat, for in the day that you eat of it you shall surely die" (Gen. 2:16–17). If Adam had obeyed, he would have received blessing. The promise of blessing, the promise of damnation—those are the terms. The stipulations are the laws.

The death penalty for murder was not established at Mount Sinai. It was established in the covenant that God made with Noah in Genesis 9:6: "Whoever sheds the blood of man, by man shall his blood be shed, for God made man in his own image." The rationale for the original establishment of capital punishment was that if a person murders someone with malice aforethought (first-degree murder), that person has willfully taken the life of someone who is made in the image of God. The heinousness of the sin of murder is rooted in the sanctity of human life, which is tied to the image of God borne by humans. Ultimately, an attack on the image bearer of God is an attack on God Himself, and the penalty for that is death. God does not mention capital punishment for murder as an option; rather, it is a mandate. Therefore, if a government does not carry out that mandate, it is acting in rebellion against God.

The creation ordinances are found not only in the narrative pertaining to Adam and Eve but also in the narratives all the way through Noah. Capital punishment is a creation ordinance that Christians should support and should tell their state governments to uphold. That is not asking the state to be Christian but asking the state to be the state. That is what God has mandated just rulers to do. Paul reiterates in Romans 13 that it is God who gives the power of the sword to the civil magistrate. He does not give the power of the sword to a killer or an aggressor. To protect the sanctity of life and to enforce justice are tasks of the civil magistrate.

The law was given to Adam **as a covenant of works, by which he bound him and all his posterity.** God bound Adam and every other human being coming after him **to personal, entire, exact, and perpetual obedience to** His law, **promised life upon the fulfilling, and threatened death upon the breach of it, and endued him with power and ability to keep it.** We know that the power and ability to keep God's law was lost by Adam, but the obligation to keep the law was never set aside.

All law finds its origin in God. Law finds its validity in terms of its conformity to the character of God. Law is not simply a matter of arbitrary societal convention. If there is no God, all things are permissible. If there is no transcendent norm or standard or lawgiver, then laws are merely an expression of the will of whatever individual or group is in power.

We accept lobbyists as part of the American way. We hear of "special-interest groups," and no one bats an eye. Public officials follow public-opinion polls because they are more interested in what is pragmatic than in what is right or just. We are reverting to the law of the jungle, where might makes right. It may be economic might or political influence. But Christians cannot live like that, for we are bound not by our vested interests but by the law of God.

> 2. This law, after his fall, continued to be a perfect rule of righteousness; and, as such, was delivered by God upon Mount Sinai, in ten commandments, and written in two tables: the first four commandments containing our duty towards God; and the other six, our duty to man.

In Psalm 119, the psalmist expresses in a multitude of ways his love for God's law. Such sentiments are often foreign to Christians today. People today will speak in an affectionate manner of the Word of God but not of the law of God. In Old Testament times, there was no distinction between the Word and the law, because the people of Israel understood that the Word of God is law, and that whatever God says becomes a duty, a command.

The law that God gave at Mount Sinai was not the first expression of His law, because it was first given to Adam and Eve in creation. The Apostle Paul, in Romans 5:14, makes that point by saying that death ruled from Adam to Moses. Death implies the presence of law because without the law there is no sin, and without sin there is no death. Since death reigned from Adam to Moses, we can infer, as the Apostle did, that God's law must have been in force from Adam to Moses.

In the Old Testament, there are different kinds of law. There is *apodictic* law and *casuistic* law, both of which may be distinguished from proverbs. A proverb is not a commandment but rather an expression of practical wisdom that can be applied to situations in life. A proverb is not binding on the conscience. If we read proverbs as if they were commandments, we end up in deep confusion. For example, one proverb says, "Answer not a fool according to his folly," and another one says, "Answer a fool according to his folly" (Prov. 26:4–5). If both of these proverbs were universal commandments, we would have a difficult time obeying them.

Proverbs are practical snippets of wisdom and prudence, such as we have in our own culture. We hear sayings like "Look before you leap" and "He who hesitates is lost." Wisdom requires that we do not act rashly or impulsively. We must be careful not to jump into things before first examining all the costs and the consequences. As Jesus Himself says, the wise man counts the costs before he begins a construction project, and a military leader considers the strength of his enemy before he goes into battle (Luke 14:28–31). But there are other times when swift and decisive action is required. In that case, he who hesitates is lost. There are real-life situations where wisdom requires care and thought in advance, but there are other situations where we must act without that benefit. Both adages are nuggets of wisdom for different situations, yet on their face they appear to be contradictory.

That is the case with the proverbs instructing us both to answer a fool according to his folly and not to answer a fool according to his folly. It is foolish to continue investing time and energy in a discussion if the other person is obstinate and has no interest in learning. Jesus says in Matthew 10:14 to shake off the dust of our feet and leave those people. On the other hand, there are occasions in which, by answering someone's foolish assertions carefully, he may come to understand that he is not as wise as he thought.

One of the most clever types of arguments used by the Apostle Paul was made famous by the philosopher Zeno. It is called the *reductio ad absurdum* argument. The premise of the opponent is granted for the sake of argument, and then the logical inferences from that premise are demonstrated to lead to an absurd conclusion. In that case, a fool is being answered according to his folly in order to help him see the foolishness of his premise. Perhaps we have all been instructed in that way.

Casuistic law is what we call case law. The Word of God is designed to give us guidance for glorifying God in our behavior. God's law is a light for our path. But if God set forth specific laws to apply to every conceivable human exigency, the Bible would be larger than a multivolume encyclopedia.

Therefore, God gives case law: "If your ox tramples your neighbor's roses, then the penalty is. . . ." The law could go on to say, "But if your ox tramples your neighbor's daffodils, then the penalty is. . . ." And what if a mule is involved, not an ox? The point is that a few concrete examples from real-life situations are set forth, and judges who hear specific cases of negligence or damage can use them as guidelines by which to apply principles of justice.

Casuistic law is expressed in the Old Testament in conditional language, called the "if-then" formula. *If* someone's ox tramples his neighbor's flowers, *then* he is required to pay. These laws apply general principles to specific situations.

The apodictic law consists chiefly, though not exclusively, of the Ten Commandments. The commandments express universal principles and absolute norms that are to govern the life of the people. They are communicated in the literary form that begins with either "You shall" or "You shall not." They express the divine norms upon which biblical ethics are based.

In our culture, the terms *ethics* and *morality* are used interchangeably. Another term, *values*, can be added. For example, people today are saying that we have a "crisis in values." But value is an ethical matter only indirectly. It involves assigning worth to things. No two of us place the same value on things, and that makes for interesting marriages. A marriage is the union of a man and a woman with different values and a finite amount of disposable capital. Suppose a couple has a thousand dollars of disposable, discretionary income. The husband wants to buy a new set of golf clubs, but the wife wants a new refrigerator, and they are off and running for marriage counseling. The man values golf clubs more than a new refrigerator, and the woman values the refrigerator more than golf clubs.

Value is primarily a question not of ethics but of taste or preference, of what's important to us. Indirectly, it becomes a matter of ethics, because as Christians we are trying to discover a value system for ourselves that matches God's. Sanctification involves loving what God loves, hating what God hates, and embracing God's priorities. We are to have the mind of Christ. God's priorities and His values conflict with most of our priorities and values. In that sense, a value system is enormously weighted with ethical concerns. In our culture, when politicians talk about values in the school system, values in the culture, and values in the government, they are not talking about divine values. This is a not-so-subtle assumption of relativism, because subjective tastes are relative. When we say that virtue is a matter of preference, we have relativized ethics. We have taken the position of those who say, "Whatever you like, that's what's right; that's what's good."

When lexicographers write dictionaries, they pay attention to three things: the etymological derivation of words (their origin in Latin,

Greek, or whatever), their historical meanings (how their meanings have changed or grown over time), and, most importantly, how they are being used today. If a word is misused long enough and frequently enough, the misuse becomes the new standard use. Even though, historically and ety-mologically, the words *ethics* and *morality* differ significantly, dictionaries will likely eventually treat them as synonyms.

Originally, there was a distinction between these two terms. *Ethics* comes from the word *ethos*, which refers to the philosophical assump-tions of a given society and to the conceptual base or foundations on which a civilization is established. *Morality* comes from the word *mores*, which describes the behavioral patterns, customs, and habits of a particu-lar social group. The word *ethos* has to do with an underlying philosophy; the word *mores* has to do with actual practice.

Historically, the science of ethics seeks to discover laws or norms that govern the behavior either of material things in the realm of physics, biology, or chemistry, or of people in social science. Ethics has to do with normative principles of law and of behavior. Morality, on the other hand, is a descriptive science.

To understand the difference between a normative science and a descriptive science, we say that ethics is concerned with "oughtness," while morality defines "isness." The study of ethics is the study of what we ought to do; the study of morality is the study of what we actually do—which may or may not conform to what we ought to do.

How does this work out practically? Some time ago, a group of schol-ars evaluated and rated the literature of the twentieth century. The worst scientific book on their list was Margaret Mead's study of the behavioral patterns of Samoans, which proved to be completely wrong. Number two on the list was the Kinsey Reports, a pair of studies of the sexual behavior of Americans. They purported to reveal that Americans were funda-mentally hypocritical. Although the customs and taboos from earlier generations were still in place, they were not being followed by the new generation. The reality of actual practice was completely out of step with the so-called outmoded traditions and outmoded ethics of Christianity.

The Apostle Paul, writing to the first-century church, said, "But sex-ual immorality . . . must not even be named among you, as is proper among saints" (Eph. 5:3). In the middle of the second century, the apologist Justin Martyr wrote to Antoninus Pius, the emperor of Rome, to defend the truth of Christianity. In setting forth his philosophical arguments, Justin Martyr informed the emperor that if he wanted to see how the Christians back up their creed, he should examine the chastity of the Christian people. I don't think any apologist in the twenty-first century would dare issue a challenge like that.

The Kinsey Reports sought to show that the cultural taboos and customs should be changed because the behavior and the morality of Americans was not measuring up to their ethic. If 51 percent of first-time brides in America were not virgins when they got married, then the conclusion was that the lack of virginity was normal. If it is normal, then it is good, because it is a good thing to be normal. Standards must change to match behavior. That's the old "Everyone's doing it" ethic.

There are some obvious flaws in this approach. Let's say 90 percent of students at one time or another have cheated in school. Therefore, it is statistically normal for students to cheat on their examinations. If it is statistically normal, then it is good and we should encourage students not to be abnormal, but to be normal and to cheat. We should even encourage students to become more proficient at their cheating. Thus is revealed the folly of this sort of thinking.

All the morality studies in the world only indicate how fallen people are behaving. What is statistically normal among fallen creatures can never be the norm or the standard of godliness. God's law is based not on the practices of fallen human beings but on His own character, which is not fallen. From a Christian viewpoint, there should always be a significant difference between ethics and morality. Christians are to look to the imperative, to what we ought to be doing, not to the indicative, what we are doing. We are called not to be conformed to this world but to be transformed, to live according to a higher norm than the standards that are acceptable in the culture. Sadly, most people, as Nietzsche said, follow the herd. They pick up their cues from what is legal, what society allows, and, more importantly, what those around them allow or approve.

In 1970, it was against the law in many places for a woman to have an abortion. In 1973, it was within the law. In 1970, most Americans said that abortion on demand was wrong. Today, the statistics are reversed. Now most Americans say that women should have the right to choose. Is there something inherently wrong about abortion on demand, or is it merely a matter of cultural preference? We can hardly say that it was wrong in the sight of God in 1970, but that God approves of it now. What has changed is the civil law and morality, not the character of God. We will not be judged in the last judgment by what our culture approves or disapproves, or by what our government allows or does not allow. We will be judged by the law of God. That is why it is important to understand the law of God.

It doesn't matter what everyone else is doing. What matters is what each of us is doing with respect to the law of God. Section 2 reads: This law, after his fall, continued to be a perfect rule of righteousness. In other words, man fell, but God's standards did not change. God's law became a perfect rule of righteousness; and, as such, was delivered by God upon Mount Sinai, in ten commandments, and written in two tables: the first four commandments containing our duty towards God; and the other six, our duty to man.

> 3. Beside this law, commonly called moral, God was pleased to give to the people of Israel, as a church under age, ceremonial laws, containing several typical ordinances, partly of worship, prefiguring Christ, his graces, actions, sufferings, and benefits; and partly, holding forth divers instructions of moral duties. All which ceremonial laws are now abrogated, under the new testament.

This section of the confession is somewhat controversial today, as there is disagreement in the Reformed community regarding the extent to which the Mosaic law has been abrogated.

It has been traditional in Reformed theology to distinguish between the *moral* law and the *ceremonial* law. The moral law is the portion of the Old Testament law that is still in effect, but the ceremonial law is the part that is no longer in effect.

To the Jew in Old Testament days, however, the keeping of the ceremonial law was an intensely moral matter. It was the Jew's moral obligation and solemn duty to obey every portion of the law, including the dietary regulations and the ceremonies governing the cultic life of Israel. These were divine obligations.

There is another distinction that pertains to God's law: the natural law of God is distinguished from His legislative law. God's natural laws and precepts are based upon His eternal character, and come from the very nature of God Himself. If God were to do away with natural laws, it would require His very nature to change and would do violence to His own character.

During the Senate confirmation hearings of Justice Clarence Thomas, he said he was an advocate of natural law. Senator Joe Biden was dismayed and replied abruptly, "Nobody believes in natural law anymore. They don't teach natural law in the law schools of our country in this day and age." The natural law to which Justice Thomas and Senator Biden referred is not the same as God's law. Natural law is the theory that there are certain moral precepts that one can learn simply by studying the laws of nature. This is called the *jus gentium*, the law of the nations. The laws and customs of civilizations all over the world, in different times and different places, are examined to find a common thread of basic moral precepts. The theory is that one can learn these from nature. There is a statement in the U.S. Declaration of Independence that God has made all men equal and that our Creator has endowed us with certain inalienable rights, such as life, liberty, and the pursuit of happiness. There was an effort, particularly among eighteenth-century jurists, to look beyond the Bible to nature itself to find the basic principles of the sanctity of life, private property, and other rights.

When we refer to the natural law of God here, we are speaking not of the natural (created) order but of the nature or essence of the being of God. The natural law of God consists of those laws that are based on His own immutable being. For example, in the Ten Commandments, God said, "You shall have no other gods before me" (Ex. 20:3). If God were to set that law aside and permit the practice of idolatry, He would be violating His own holiness and character.

When we look at the moral and ceremonial laws of the Old Testament, we must ask: Were these laws based on the eternal character and nature of God? Or were these laws legislated by God for a particular, redemptive, historical reason? Were these laws imposed for a particular period of time, for a salvific reason? The confession teaches that God gave to the people of Israel, as a church under age, ceremonial laws, containing several typical ordinances. When we use the word *typical* in our ordinary conversation today, we mean "commonplace" or "ordinary." "Typical" behavior is behavior that we expect. But when the confession speaks of typical ordinances, a different meaning is in view.

The confession uses the word *typical* to refer to typology, in which an archetype, or primary type, symbolizes a more fully developed reality that comes later. For example, in the Old Testament system, there was an elaborate sacrificial system, climaxing on the Day of Atonement. But the author of the book of Hebrews makes the point that the blood of bulls and goats cannot take away sins (10:4). So were all the sacrifices of the Old Testament an exercise in futility? They had no intrinsic or inherent value. They could not themselves atone for anything, but they were shadows and symbols pointing forward to the sacrifice of Christ.

Those animal sacrifices had value in pointing beyond the shadows to a future sacrifice that would be made once and for all. Suppose that the year after Christ died on Calvary, the Christian community gathered on the Day of Atonement and sacrificed bulls and goats. That would have indicated that Christ's atonement did not work, and that Christians had to go back to the old system, back to the shadows. That is what confronted the early New Testament church with the Judaizing heresies, which encouraged the people to continue observing the ceremonies of the Old Testament. Paul, in his letter to the Galatians, had to rebuke the people for going backward. That message also comes across clearly in the book of Hebrews. Once the shadow has been fulfilled by the reality, the typological ordinances pass away. The Mosaic ceremonies were not based upon the eternal, immutable character of God (although their symbolism certainly reflected something of the character of God). The reality to which they pointed was the work of Christ for our redemption. After that work was perfectly completed, it would have been an insult to Christ and to God to observe the former ceremonies. So Christians no longer observed them.

That explains the confession's use of the term *typical*—meaning "typological." However, we must be careful when using typology in our biblical interpretation. There are certain occasions when the New Testament interprets the Old Testament typologically in a manner that one would not normally interpret history. For example, after Jesus was born, Joseph was warned by an angel to take Jesus and Mary to Egypt, because Herod was about to slaughter all the baby boys in and around Bethlehem in an attempt to kill Jesus. So Joseph took his family and fled to Egypt. After the threat was over, Joseph brought Mary and Jesus back into the Holy Land, fulfilling the Old Testament prophecy, "Out of Egypt I called my son" (Matt. 2:15). However, the Old Testament passage quoted (Hos. 11:1) refers to the children of Israel at the time of the exodus. Under the inspiration of the Spirit, Matthew was calling attention to an event in the Old Testament that was a type of something in the life of Jesus. Jesus was the sin bearer of Israel, and there was a corporate solidarity between Him and His people Israel. There was a sense in which His life recapitulated the Old Testament history of Israel. One event in which that was seen was in the exodus. Jesus had an exodus from Egypt, just as His people Israel did.

We are edified when the New Testament interprets the Old Testament typologically. We get a sense of awe at the intricacy and symmetry of the two testaments and the amazing way that the Scriptures fulfill themselves. Also, typological interpretation reveals all that God did in history to prepare the world for the coming of Christ. There were no cavalier redemptive actions initiated by God. The whole history of Israel was under His sovereign plan and direction to lead up to that moment in the fullness of time when His Son would appear. The Apostolic preaching of the first-century church showed God's hand over eons of time, bringing history forward to the redemption that took place in the person and work of Christ.

The Westminster divines teach that we are to distinguish the moral laws from the ceremonial laws, which were not maintained in the Apostolic period. We see a similar situation with respect to the dietary laws of the Old Testament. At the Council of Jerusalem (Acts 15), the question the church faced was how the gentiles fit into the new covenant. In biblical times, there were four distinct groups of people. First, there were the Jews. Second, there were gentile converts to Judaism who stopped short of full ceremonial conversion. They were accorded certain privileges in and around the temple that were less than the full privileges of the Jewish people. They were called God-fearers. The third group was the Samaritans, who were despised by the Jews. Fourth, there were the gentiles, who were strangers to the covenant that God had made with Abraham and his seed. For them to be converted, they not only had to be circumcised, but they also had to undergo a ceremonial rite of purification called proselyte baptism, because they were considered unclean.

Before He ascended into heaven, Jesus told His disciples that they were to be His witnesses "in Jerusalem and in all Judea and Samaria, and to the end of the earth" (Acts 1:8). When Luke wrote the book of Acts, he began his account in Jerusalem, dealing with the Jewish community. The church spread into Judea, which was still part of the Jewish community. Then the gospel was taken to Samaritans, and some of them were converted to Christ. From chapter 13 onward, Luke follows Paul's missionary outreach as the Apostle to the gentiles. There was a tremendous influx of people into the Christian community who were not Jews. Each group—Jews, God-fearers, Samaritans, and gentiles—experienced in turn the power of Pentecost. The inference drawn by the Apostles was that God had made them all one body. All believers would receive full membership in the body of Christ since they had all received the same Holy Spirit. In the new covenant community, part of the Old Testament law would be maintained, but not the dietary restrictions and not the ceremonial law.

Throughout the Old Testament, there was the problem of syncretism when the Jewish people, who were called to be separate, different, and holy, began to intermingle and intermarry with the pagans in their midst. They adopted pagan religions. Conflict arose because they failed to maintain their purity. However, God had set the nation of Israel apart, because it was through the Jews that He would save the world.

> 4. To them also, as a body politic, he gave sundry judicial laws, which expired together with the State of that people; not obliging any other now, further than the general equity thereof may require.

Section 4 is controversial today among those in the theonomic movement. The Greek word *nomos* means "law," and *theos* is the Greek word for "god." *Theonomy* means, literally, "the law of God." Moral or ethical obligations are distinguished by the words *autonomy* and *heteronomy*. *Auto* means "self," and *nomos* means "law." Autonomy is the view that people are a law unto themselves. Someone who is autonomous is not obligated to anyone or anything beyond himself. Adam and Eve reached for autonomy in the garden of Eden. The serpent told Adam and Eve that they wouldn't die if they disobeyed God; rather, they would become as gods and be a law unto themselves. He promised that they would be free from any restrictions imposed by God or anyone else.

Heteronomy means that one is subject to the law of someone other than oneself. The supreme form of heteronomy is theonomy, because God is the supreme other. All Christians are theonomists in the sense that they are subject to the law of God. However, the movement that bears the name *theonomy* is particularly concerned with applying the civil laws in the Mosaic law to today. For example, some thirty-five offenses were listed as capital crimes in the penal code of Israel. They included the disobedience of children to their parents, public blasphemy, consorting with fortune-tellers, wizards, necromancers, or spiritual mediums, and homosexual behavior. Theonomists believe that these and the other civil laws in the Old Testament should be enacted in the legislation of nations today.

The Westminster Confession, however, says this: He gave sundry judicial laws, which expired together with the State of that people; not obliging any other now, further than the general equity thereof may require. This becomes rather complicated, but the key point is that these laws that were given to Israel expired when the Jewish state expired in the first century. There is a big difference between living as a Christian in first-century Rome, living as a Christian in the United States today, and living as a Jew in Old Testament Israel. The Jewish people had their own government, called a theocracy. The kings of Israel and Judah were subject to God and the law that He had given to Moses. There was a marriage of church and state in the theocratic establishment of Israel. The New Testament church, on the other hand, was founded in the Roman Empire, and it had to live in a pagan environment where the civil magistrates were often hostile to Christians. That is where we find ourselves today, living in a pagan nation that has embraced secularism. As Christians, we are trying to function as believers in a pagan environment.

Should we try to make the United States a theocracy? The confession says that we should not. The judicial laws were set forth in Israel for the purpose of their redemption and are no longer applicable since that theocratic state has expired. However, it is conceivable that there could be another theocracy today, molded according to the legislation of the Old Testament. It could be made a capital offense to profane the name of God publicly. Such a penalty would not be inherently unjust, for that would mean that God was unjust to impose such a sanction in the Old Testament community.

Since the Old Testament came from God, who is holy and righteous, we should not be offended by any laws that we read there. If we are offended by them, it is because our thinking has been distorted by a secular perspective on law, righteousness, and ethics. God's standards, revealed to His people in the Old Testament, are as foreign to us today as they were to the ancient worshipers of Baal. We must go to the pages of Scripture and ask ourselves if it is really the law of God. If it is, it teaches us what is pleasing to God and what is odious to Him.

5. The moral law doth forever bind all, as well justified persons as others, to the obedience thereof; and that, not only in regard of the matter contained in it, but also in respect of the authority of God the Creator, who gave it. Neither doth Christ, in the gospel, any way dissolve, but much strengthen this obligation.

Jesus said, "Do not think that I have come to abolish the Law or the Prophets; I have not come to abolish them but to fulfill them. For truly, I say to you, until heaven and earth pass away, not an iota, not a dot, will pass from the Law until all is accomplished" (Matt. 5:17–18). When Jesus used the word that is translated "abolish," He used a form of the verb that means "to loose" or "to destroy." He does not destroy the law or release us from all its obligations. His duty as the second Adam was to obey the law for us in every respect, and in that sense He fulfilled the law. He also fulfilled the ceremonies that were typified in the Old Testament law, and since they were fulfilled, we are no longer obligated to keep them. But here the confession is speaking not of the ceremonial or dietary laws but of the moral law of the Old Testament, which was not destroyed by the ministry of Christ but is still binding, even for justified people.

This is further expounded in section 6.

6. Although true believers be not under the law, as a covenant of works, to be thereby justified, or condemned; yet is it of great use to them, as well as to others; in that, as a rule of life informing them of the will of God, and their duty, it directs and binds them to walk accordingly; discovering also the sinful pollutions of their nature, hearts, and lives; so as, examining themselves thereby, they may come to further conviction of, humiliation for, and hatred against sin, together with a clearer sight of the need they have of Christ, and the perfection of his obedience. It is likewise of use to the regenerate, to restrain their corruptions, in that it forbids sin: and the threatenings of it serve to show what even their sins deserve; and what afflictions, in this life, they may expect for them, although freed from the curse thereof threatened in the law. The promises of it, in like manner, show them God's approbation of obedience, and what blessings they may expect upon the performance thereof: although not as due to them by the law as a covenant of works. So as, a man's doing good, and refraining from evil, because the law encourageth to the one, and deterreth from the other, is no evidence of his being under the law; and, not under grace.

The first statement of section 6, **Although true believers be not under the law, as a covenant of works, to be thereby justified,** acknowledges that we are not in a position in which our only way to be justified is to fulfill the works of the law. In that sense, then, we are not under the law. **Yet is it—the law—of great use to [Christians], as well as to others; in that, as a rule of life informing them of the will of God, and their duty, it directs and binds them to walk accordingly.**

Calvin spoke of the revelatory use of the law; that is, the law reveals to us what is pleasing to God and what He would have us do. We are now going to skate along the edge of heresy and peer down into the abyss of antinomianism, where there is a fine distinction to be made. The confession says we are no longer under the covenant of works, and that is true. Entering into a covenant relationship with God involves taking an oath. The oath places us under the burden of the terms and stipulations of the covenant. In the Old Testament law, the Ten Commandments were delivered to Israel as part of the terms of the covenant that God made through Moses. We call that the Mosaic covenant, the Sinaitic covenant, or the old covenant, as distinguished from the new covenant.

As Christians, we are not bound by the Ten Commandments since they are part of the old covenant, and we are not subject to the stipulations of the covenant that God made with Moses. We Christians are in a new and different covenant, the new covenant. Although the new covenant flows out of the old covenant, in a very real sense it supersedes the old covenant. However, some Jewish converts in the early church insisted that gentile converts had to be brought under all the terms of the old covenant, including circumcision. This was the Judaizing movement that was fiercely combated in New Testament letters to the Colossians, to the Hebrews, and especially to the Galatians. If we entered that old covenant and were circumcised as a religious rite, we would, in effect, be taking a sacred oath to keep all the terms of the old covenant and to be exposed to its blessings and curses.

Paul told the Galatians and the Judaizers that Jesus bore the curse of the old covenant in His death: "For it is written, 'Cursed is everyone who is hanged on a tree'" (Gal. 3:13). Then Paul said he hoped that the Judaizers be cut off or accursed, the punishment that circumcision signifies. Paul wondered what was wrong with the Judaizers. "Christ has fulfilled all the Mosaic covenant stipulations. You have embraced Christ as your Redeemer and have trusted in His perfect work for His fulfillment of the curse. You are now going back to the old situation, as if Christ did not really fulfill the covenant." Paul warned them that the last thing they wanted to do as Christians was to put themselves back under the stipulations and terms of the old covenant. There is a very real sense in which the Christian is no longer under that covenant. If we insist that we are under that covenant, we are falling into the Judaizing heresy. It is a kind of legalism, and we have, in effect, denied the perfection of the work of Christ.

We said we would skate along the edge of antinomianism and look right down into that hideous pit but not jump into it. So far, what we have said could be construed as unvarnished antinomianism. What we mean is that we are not under the damnation, the bondage, the power of the law. Nor are we under covenantal obligation to the Old Testament law. However, as New Testament Christians in the new covenant, we are called to please God and to imitate Christ. The Old Testament moral law reveals to us what is pleasing to God, so we still have a spiritual and moral obligation as part of the new covenant to meditate on that law day and night. We are under the law in the sense that its instructions and guidelines are a revelation of what is pleasing to God. We are no longer in a legal relationship with the covenantal structures of blessing and curse, through circumcision or through ceremony.

Someone may be thinking that, for all practical purposes, we are saying that we are still just as much bound by the Ten Commandments as we would have been had we lived in Old Testament times. That is true. That is why we will not cross the line and fall into antinomianism. We are still morally obligated to keep the moral law of God. We no longer have a covenantal relationship through Moses, but we do have a covenantal relationship through our Mediator, Jesus Christ. It is important to understand this so that we will not fall into the other trap of legalism or into the Judaizing heresy by placing ourselves under the Old Testament covenant. We are walking a fine line between our continuity with the people of God under the Old Testament and the discontinuity with them that comes from being in the new covenant.

The law is of great use to believers in discovering also the sinful pollutions of their nature, hearts, and lives; so as, examining themselves thereby, they may come to further conviction of, humiliation for, and hatred against sin, together with a clearer sight of the need they have of Christ, and the perfection of his obedience. According to Calvin, the law functions in this manner as a mirror. The confession agrees with Calvin that through the law we get a clear revelation not only of what is pleasing to God but also of our own imperfections and sinfulness. By examining ourselves, we will come to further conviction of, humiliation for, and hatred against sin.

As we have seen, the human will is free in the sense that we still have the capacity to make choices. We still have the faculty of the will and still are moral agents, even though we are fallen. What we lack is what Augustine called *liberty*—what Edwards called *moral ability*. We lack the moral persuasion or desire or inclination, by nature and in the flesh, to choose the things of God. We are completely in the flesh in our fallen condition, and the desires of our heart are wicked continuously. God has to raise us up from spiritual death. We have to be quickened by the Holy Spirit before we can be inclined to righteousness or to the things of God.

Given the fact that Christians have been quickened by the Holy Spirit, why is it that we still sin? We have been set free from prison, where, the Bible tells us, we were by nature slaves to sin. We were in bondage but were liberated by the Spirit. The disposition of our hearts was changed. Before our liberation, we had no desire for the things of God. Now we do have a desire for such things. However, there is still continual spiritual warfare between the flesh and the Spirit. In the midst of that struggle, our sanctification proceeds, as we are nurtured more and more by the Word and come more and more to hate our sin.

Jesus said: "If you love Me, keep My commandments, and if you want to know what My commandments are, get in the Book, read the Word. This is what I want My people to do." This is what the confession affirms here in section 6, that the law is of great use to believers as a rule of life informing them of the will of God. A big question that people ask is, "What is the will of God for my life?" The answer is, "Your sanctification" (1 Thess. 4:3). If we want to know what that looks like, we are going to have to meditate on His law day and night. To know what the will of God is for our lives, you must study the law of God all our lives. His will is for us to obey Him.

As a rule of life informing them of the will of God, and their duty, [the law] directs and binds them to walk accordingly; discovering also the sinful pollutions of their nature, hearts, and lives; so as, examining themselves thereby, they may come to further conviction of, humiliation for, and hatred against sin. The moment we are reborn of the Spirit, the

Holy Spirit convicts us of sin, but the conviction doesn't purify us from sin. The process of sanctification requires further conviction of sin, and that comes by seeing ourselves in the mirror of the law.

There also may come humiliation for, and hatred against sin, together with a clearer sight of the need they have of Christ, and the perfection of his obedience. It is likewise of use to the regenerate, to restrain their corruptions, in that it forbids sin. The second use of the law is that it restrains sin. The threatenings of it serve to show what even their sins deserve; and what afflictions, in this life, they may expect for them, although freed from the curse thereof threatened in the law. The promises of it, in like manner, show them God's approbation of obedience, and what blessings they may expect upon the performance thereof: although not as due to them by the law as a covenant of works. So as, a man's doing good, and refraining from evil, because the law encourageth to the one, and deterreth from the other, is no evidence of his being under the law; and, not under grace.

> 7. Neither are the forementioned uses of the law contrary to the grace of the gospel, but do sweetly comply with it; the Spirit of Christ subduing and enabling the will of man to do that freely, and cheerfully, which the will of God, revealed in the law, requireth to be done.

Neither are the forementioned uses of the law contrary to the grace of the gospel, but do sweetly comply with it. It is good that the divines included the adverb "sweetly." This is not just dry, abstract, theological language. The law of God is not opposed to grace. Not only does it comply with grace, but the law's compliance is sweet. That is how we started our study of the law when we went to Psalm 119. The psalmist says he loves the law of God, that the law of God is more precious than emeralds and rubies and fine stones, and it is also sweeter than honey. We don't usually like laws. We think of the law as a bad thing, but the Christian loves God, loves His Word and His law, and sees that grace and law are not incompatible. Grace complies with the law, and the law complies with grace, and it does so in a manner that is sweet. Therefore, the more we grow in grace, the more we love God's law. We have tasted of the Lord and found that He is good, and we love the sweetness of His law.

Of Christian Liberty, and Liberty of Conscience

1. The liberty which Christ hath purchased for believers under the gospel consists in their freedom from the guilt of sin, the condemning wrath of God, the curse of the moral law; and, in their being delivered from this present evil world, bondage to Satan, and dominion of sin; from the evil of afflictions, the sting of death, the victory of the grave, and everlasting damnation; as also, in their free access to God, and their yielding obedience unto him, not out of slavish fear, but a childlike love and willing mind. All which were common also to believers under the law. But, under the new testament, the liberty of Christians is further enlarged, in their freedom from the yoke of the ceremonial law, to which the Jewish church was subjected; and in greater boldness of access to the throne of grace, and in fuller communications of the free Spirit of God, than believers under the law did ordinarily partake of.

2. God alone is Lord of the conscience, and hath left it free from the doctrines and commandments of men, which are, in anything, contrary to his Word; or beside it, if matters of faith, or worship. So that, to believe such doctrines, or to obey such commands, out of conscience, is to betray true liberty of conscience: and the requiring of an implicit faith, and an absolute and blind obedience, is to destroy liberty of conscience, and reason also.

3. They who, upon pretense of Christian liberty, do practice any sin, or cherish any lust, do thereby destroy the end of Christian liberty, which is, that being delivered out of the hands of our enemies, we might serve the Lord without fear, in holiness and righteousness before him, all the days of our life.

4. And because the powers which God hath ordained, and the liberty which Christ hath purchased, are not intended by God to destroy, but mutually to uphold and preserve one another, they who, upon pretense of Christian liberty, shall oppose any lawful power, or the lawful exercise of it, whether it be civil or ecclesiastical, resist the ordinance of God. And, for their publishing of such opinions, or maintaining of such practices, as are contrary to the light of nature, or to the known principles of Christianity (whether concerning faith, worship, or conversation), or to the power of godliness; or, such erroneous opinions or practices, as either in their own nature, or in the manner of publishing or maintaining them, are destructive to the external peace and order which Christ hath established in the church, they may lawfully be called to account, and proceeded against, by the censures of the church.

It is significant that the Westminster divines included this chapter, because Christian liberty is one of the most important fruits of our redemption that was won for us by Christ. It is also an extremely important element of Christian ethics if we are to avoid antinomianism on the one side and legalism on the other.

1. The liberty which Christ hath purchased for believers under the gospel consists in their freedom from the guilt of sin, the condemning wrath of God, the curse of the moral law; and, in their being delivered from this present evil world, bondage to Satan, and dominion of sin; from the evil of afflictions, the sting of death, the victory of the grave, and everlasting damnation; as also, in their free access to God, and their yielding obedience unto him, not out of slavish fear, but a childlike love and willing mind. All which were common also to believers under the law. But, under the new testament, the liberty of Christians is further enlarged, in their freedom from the yoke of the ceremonial law, to which the Jewish church was subjected; and in greater boldness of access to the throne of grace, and in fuller communications of the free Spirit of God, than believers under the law did ordinarily partake of.

Christian liberty consists of **freedom from . . . the condemning wrath of God and bondage to Satan.** Augustine contrasted the state of man at the time of his creation with his condition after the fall. In creation, he said, God gave to man two things: free will and liberty (*libertas*). It is significant that he distinguished between free will and liberty, because we tend to think of them as synonymous. Augustine said that even though we were plunged into the ruination of the fall, we didn't lose our humanity. We still have our human faculties: our minds, wills, and affections. We have free will in the sense that we still have the power and the ability to make choices. What we lost, Augustine said, was our liberty. When the Bible speaks of our condition after the fall, it describes us as prisoners, in bondage to sin. This bondage does not destroy our humanity or annihilate the faculty of the will, but we are willing prisoners of sin. In our fallen natures, we have lost the power to incline ourselves toward heavenly things. We are slaves to the passions of this world, to our own corruption and fallenness. We still make choices, but we choose according to our base passions and not according to the things of God. Therefore, we are left in the wretched state of being bondservants to sin.

The confession teaches that the redemptive work of Christ brings us liberation. He is the supreme liberator. On Palm Sunday, the people hailed His entrance into Jerusalem, waving palm branches and shouting the acclamation of "Hosanna." They hoped that He would liberate them from bondage to Rome. The irony is that He came to free them not from Roman bondage but from a far worse bondage. He came to free people from the bondage of Satan, death, the power of the grave, and guilt that would destroy them.

The confession's first phrase speaks of **the liberty which Christ hath purchased for believers under the gospel.** Exodus 21 contains laws regarding bondservants. The law said that if a man could not pay his debt to another man, he could become an indentured servant. He could bind himself to the other man until such time as he worked off that indebtedness. Then he had to be set free, and he was allowed to leave with everything that he had brought in. If he became an indentured servant after he was married and had children, he would bring his wife and children with him during that period of bondage. When he had fulfilled his obligations and was set free, his wife and children would also go with him.

If the man became a bondservant while unmarried, but during his servitude took a wife from the family of other servants or from his master, then, upon his release, his wife and any children could not go with him. From our perspective, that seems cruel and harsh. However, he had obtained his wife without paying the bride price to the woman's father. He could return, pay the bride price, and get his wife and children back.

Paul uses the language of redemption when he says, "Do you not know that your body is a temple of the Holy Spirit within you, whom you have from God? You are not your own, for you were bought with a price" (1 Cor. 6:19–20), referring to the bride price. Paul calls himself a slave who is owned by his Lord. He says that he has been purchased. On the cross, Christ paid the bride price. He purchased the freedom of His bride, which is the church. That is why, at the beginning of the statement about Christian liberty, the Westminster divines use the word "purchased." We are set free by virtue of a ransom that was paid for us by our Redeemer.

The liberty which Christ hath purchased for believers under the gospel consists in their freedom from the guilt of sin. *The Pilgrim's Progress* is one of the greatest pieces of literature ever written in the English language. It is an allegory, in which each character has symbolic significance. The hero of *The Pilgrim's Progress*, named Christian, goes on a pilgrimage where he encounters Mr. Worldly Wiseman, and in the Slough of Despond he is beset with many problems. His biggest problem is the burden that he carries with him, which weighs him down and almost crushes him.

Christian is weighed down with the burden of the guilt that he has amassed as the result of his sin. With every sin we commit, there is a corresponding measure of guilt. Guilt is objective, not subjective. Guilt feelings are subjective, but guilt itself is objective. Guilt arises when we break the law. We may not feel guilty, but we are guilty. With every transgression against the law of God, we incur guilt, and the sum total of our guilt increases daily. Paul speaks of the reprobates who are "storing up wrath for [themselves] on the day of wrath" (Rom. 2:5). With every transgression, their burden becomes heavier. That is what Christian in *The Pilgrim's Progress* was feeling until he reached the foot of the cross and his burden was removed as his guilt was taken away. The first freedom that is mentioned in the confession is **freedom from the guilt of sin**. We are in bondage to sin and under the curse of the law. We are under the judgment of God, held captive, and imprisoned by our guilt. First, we are freed from the guilt of sin, and second, we are freed from the condemning wrath of God.

The question is sometimes asked, "If we've been forgiven, why do we keep asking for forgiveness?" When we seriously ask for forgiveness, we acknowledge our sin and repent of it. Our need to do that will end only when we enter glory. The guilt of our sin has been taken by Christ. He has given us the remission of sin, whereby our guilt has been removed. Nevertheless, every time we come into His presence, we ask for a fresh awareness of our forgiveness. The objective ground of our forgiveness is the work of Christ on the cross once and for all, but we still acknowledge our dependence upon that. "If we confess our sins, he is faithful and just to forgive us our sins and to cleanse us from all unrighteousness" (1 John 1:9). There is a distinction between *eternal* guilt and *temporal* guilt. The eternal guilt was taken for us by Christ on the cross, but we are still left with temporal guilt. The main reason we keep asking for God's forgiveness is that our Lord taught us to do that in the Lord's Prayer. He told us to pray, "Forgive us" (Matt. 6:12). We ask for forgiveness, even though He has already forgiven us. We ask for a fresh appropriation, if you will, of the grace that is given to us already in the cross.

We can't imagine how horrible it was for Jesus to have the wrath of God poured out upon Him on the cross. Who could stand in the presence of God and face His wrath? Our salvation saves us from the wrath of almighty God. We are set free from the curse of the moral law. We are liberated from the condemning wrath of God.

Thanks to the influence of nineteenth-century liberalism, the idea of God's condemning wrath has become unpopular in many quarters of the church. But people who do not know the law and how it condemns them to the wrath of God cannot get excited about a gospel that frees them from that wrath. The guilt and weight of sin, to many people, is no more than the weight of a feather, unlike Christian's burden in *The Pilgrim's Progress*. The world is not afraid of the judgment of God. There are preachers who say, "God loves you with unconditional love, and there is no wrath in God." If there is no wrath in God, then there is no justice in God. If there is no justice in God, then there is no goodness in God. And if there is no goodness in God, then there is no God. A God without wrath is not God. The biblical God promises to pour out His wrath with a vengeance against an impenitent, rebellious world. That day has been fixed, and we will all be there. Either we will face the wrath of God on our own or we will be dressed in the robes of Christ, who has received that wrath for us. What greater liberation is there than to escape from the wrath of God?

God demonstrated His wrath in the exodus. He sent His angel of death against the Egyptians, and in every home in that nation the first-born child was killed. Only those homes that were marked above the door with the blood of a lamb escaped His wrath. God told the people that He wanted them to celebrate that day every year so that they would never forget that He excused them from the visitation of His wrath and of His judgment. It is hard to see how anyone can read the Bible and not see that God is indeed a God who will punish wickedness.

We have been set free from that sentence. We have been liberated from the wrath of God. We have been freed from the curse of the moral law. When God set His law before the people, He gave them two options, blessing and curse. The blessing was articulated in the famous Hebrew benediction:

> The LORD bless you and keep you;
> the LORD make his face to shine upon you and be gracious to you;
> the LORD lift up his countenance upon you and give you peace.
> (Num. 6:24–26)

To be "blessed" to the Jew was to be brought close to the face of God, into His presence, where the light of His countenance shines. He gave peace. The exact opposite of that is the curse. Instead of seeing the light of God's countenance, one is sent into the outer darkness, where God turns His back on the person. To be cursed is to be cut off from the presence of

God. The Old Testament law said, "Cursed is everyone who is hanged on a tree," so when Paul wrote to the Galatians about the nature of their liberty, he explained to them that Christ became the curse for His people on the cross (Gal. 3:13). The lights went out in the middle of the afternoon; the sunlight was blocked. Jesus died outside of the camp, outside of Jerusalem, at the hands of the gentiles. He became cursed for us and bore God's awful wrath. He fulfilled His work as the liberator. He released us from guilt, from the wrath of God, and from the curse that goes with it.

Liberty for Christians also consists in their being delivered from this present evil world, bondage to Satan, and dominion of sin. In Ephesians 2:1–6, we are told that God made us alive when we were dead in sin and trespasses. We used to walk according to the prince of the power of the air, following the lusts of our flesh, but He delivered us from sin's dominion. We have been rescued from slavery to the flesh, the world, and the devil. The whole world is fallen, and by nature we follow the course of this world set by the prince of darkness. Doing what comes naturally is doing what comes sinfully. Salvation involves liberation from that bondage to Satan.

We are freed from the evil of afflictions, the sting of death, the victory of the grave, and everlasting damnation. Christ liberates us, not only from the dominion of sin and bondage to Satan and this present evil world, but also from afflictions and from the sting of death. We are not freed from death, because we still have to die, nor from the grave, because we still have to go there. But we are freed from the sting of death and the victory of the grave because those who are in Christ participate in His triumph over this last enemy. The point that Paul labors in 1 Corinthians 15 is that Christ's resurrection was not a unique event merely for the purpose of vindicating His perfection and demonstrating God's acceptance of His payment for His bride. He was also raised for our justification (Rom. 4:25). But at the heart of the good news is that Christ is the firstborn of many brethren. Just as He has been raised from the grave, so also shall those who are in Him participate in His resurrection. Even though we die, we shall live. The message of the New Testament is that there is no more sting to death. There may be pain in dying, and none of us looks forward to a difficult death; but we need not be afraid of death itself. We are souls and bodies, and right now we cannot conceive of our souls' living apart from our bodies. When our bodies die, we die. The New Testament tells us that though this body dies, the soul stays alive, free of all the encumbrances of the body.

When we die, we will open our eyes in the kingdom of God. Our bodies will be put in the grave, but that is insignificant. The grave has no victory over us, because it cannot hold us, just as it couldn't hold Jesus. The grave had no right to hold Christ because He was sinless, and death had no claim on Him. Death did have a claim on us until we were covered with the righteousness of Christ. Once our guilt was removed and we were liberated from our sin, then all the consequences of sin were removed from us as well, including the power of the grave. The grave has no power over people who are justified, who are wearing the righteousness of Christ.

That is liberation far beyond what people dreamed of when they waved palm branches at Jesus as He made His way into Jerusalem. We also are liberated from everlasting damnation. The consequence of the condemning wrath of God for those who are still in their sins is everlasting damnation or hell. But death, the grave, and hell have no claim on those who have been set free by Christ.

The liberty of Christians also consists in their free access to God, and their yielding obedience unto him, not out of slavish fear, but a child-like love and willing mind. Paul begins Romans 5 with this statement: "Therefore, since we have been justified by faith, we have peace with God through our Lord Jesus Christ. Through him we have also obtained access by faith into this grace in which we stand, and we rejoice in hope of the glory of God" (vv. 1–2). Before the work of Christ was accomplished, we had no right to come into the presence of God. The first thing that God did after He expelled Adam and Eve from the garden of Eden was to set an angel with a flaming sword at the entrance to the garden. He did that to make certain that those fallen creatures could not get back into the garden where they had been in the immediate presence of God. But in Christ, we have obtained again free access to the Father.

One of the reasons we worship the Son of God and why we are so grateful to Him is that He is the Mediator who redeems us, reconciles us, and restores free access to the Father. Ultimately, salvation is not just from God but by God and to God. Before, we could not approach Him. He turned His back on us. But now He gives us free access to His presence and invites us to come boldly before His throne. Once again, we can draw near and know that when we die, we will see Him face-to-face.

The first positive benefit of our liberation is free access to God. The second positive benefit is our **yielding obedience unto him, not out of slavish fear, but a childlike love and willing mind.** We are called to fear God, and Luther described that fear not as a servile fear, like that of a tortured prisoner for his tormentor, but as a filial fear, similar to that which we have for a parent whom we love and do not want to disappoint. It is not that we fear the loss of certain privileges or other punishment but that we do not want to displease that parent. That change in our disposition is what the Holy Spirit works in our regeneration. We were by nature the children of wrath, walking according to the prince of the power of the air, and the desires of our heart were only wicked continually (Eph. 2:3; cf. Gen. 6:5). The Spirit changed our hearts, so that we obey God now willingly. We obey Him because we want to please Him.

All which [benefits] were common also to believers under the law. People were saved the same way in the Old Testament as they are saved in the New Testament. They were justified by faith. There were Israelites then who believed and acted upon the promises that were set forth in types and ceremonies. The ground of Abraham's salvation was Christ. Abraham believed in the One who was promised to come, and he was justified by faith in Him and on the basis of what He would do. The only difference between Abraham and us is that Abraham looked ahead to Christ, and we look back. But we both trust in the same Savior.

2. God alone is Lord of the conscience, and hath left it free from the doctrines and commandments of men, which are, in anything, contrary to his Word; or beside it, if matters of faith, or worship. So that, to believe such doctrines, or to obey such commands, out of conscience, is to betray true liberty of conscience: and the requiring of an implicit faith, and an absolute and blind obedience, is to destroy liberty of conscience, and reason also.

Throughout this study of the confession, we have noticed the amazing precision with which every statement has been crafted. However, there is an awkwardness in this section that we may find confusing. We will examine it carefully to determine what it means. The message is one that touches each of us and raises issues of supreme importance.

The section begins with a thematic statement: **God alone is Lord of the conscience.** That is almost self-evident. The sovereign God certainly has an inherent right to rule over His entire creation. When He commanded light to shine out of the darkness on the first day of creation, there was no opportunity for the darkness to do anything but flee. There was no possibility that the light would do anything but shine. If God sovereignly commands something, it occurs. When the prophets in the Old Testament rebuked the people of Israel for their willful disobedience to God, they contrasted the people with the dumb animals, who know their master and obey. The people were also contrasted with the stars in the sky, which follow the courses established for them by God. It is man who manifests a rebellious attitude that rejects God's sovereign rule over him.

The first assertion we have is that God is Lord of our consciences. That means that God has the inherent right to impose obligations upon us and to compel us to obey His commands. We live constantly under various authorities—the authority of the police officer on the corner, of the boss at work, and of our parents in the home. Sometimes we don't agree with those who are in authority over us, and we balk at their commands. We may ask, "Says who?" When we do that, we are inquiring, "Who is the source of this command, and does that source have the authority to require me to do it?"

God Himself is the one who ordains other authorities in this world. He calls on us to submit to the civil magistrate. He calls on wives to submit to their husbands. He calls on children to submit to their parents, employees to their employers, students to their teachers. God has established this structure of authority by which He governs all things. For example, the civil magistrate commands us to obey the law. If we disobey that civil law (assuming that it does not require us to disobey God), we are consequently disobeying God. It is God who instructs us to obey the civil magistrate; it is not the civil magistrate who has lordship over our conscience. It is God who instructs children to obey their parents and not parents who have lordship over the conscience of their children. The only one who has authority to bind anyone's conscience is God. That is the thematic statement. **God alone is Lord of the conscience.**

To understand this statement, we must define the word *conscience*. The conscience has to do with our moral sense, our mental awareness of right and wrong. Thomas Aquinas defined the conscience as that inner voice that the Creator has planted in us that either accuses or excuses, that either disapproves or approves our behavior. We have heard the advice, "Let your conscience be your guide." There is some wisdom in it, for to act against one's conscience is to do something that is believed to be sinful, which is therefore wrong to do.

However, the Bible teaches us that our consciences can become corrupt and inured to the impulses of the Word of God. When Jeremiah complained that Israel had developed "the forehead of a whore" (Jer. 3:3), he meant that through their repeated sinning, they had lost their capacity to blush. If we knowingly commit a sin for the first time, our conscience will give us a sense of guilt. But if we keep repeating that sin, or find out that others do it and that the culture accepts it, our conscience will become ambivalent. Eventually, it will permit us to continue in that sinful practice with a sense of impunity. We begin to approve of the very thing that God condemns, and we call evil good. This is how sin runs its course in the life of fallen creatures.

That being the case, we must be careful about following our conscience. Our conscience can lie to us. Our conscience can excuse what it ought to accuse, and approve of what it ought to disapprove of. That is one reason why the work of the Holy Spirit is so important in the Christian's life. The Spirit overrules the corruption of the human conscience and convinces us that our sin is sin. The classic example is David, after he committed adultery and had Uriah sent to the front lines to be killed in battle. At that point, his heart was so hardened that he was oblivious to his own guilt. But through the prophet Nathan, God convicted David of his sin. David was broken as his conscience was brought to life once again. God alone is the Lord of the conscience.

Throughout a person's lifetime, there will be many pretenders to that throne. Satan will claim to be the lord of our conscience. Our friends, the boss, and the government would like to control our conscience. Even the church may seek to control the conscience. History is replete with instances of the church trying to be God, taking authority and saying, "Since we are God's earthly representative, we can bind your conscience by telling you what you must believe and how you must behave."

Indeed, the church is to be God's divinely appointed institution to communicate His Word to His people. The church has the solemn obligation to communicate the law of God faithfully and accurately, but that is not always what the church does. The chief point of conflict that Jesus had with the Pharisees, the church authorities of the day, was that they substituted their own human traditions for the law of God. When Jesus violated their human traditions, they wanted to kill Him. In order to be faithful to His vocation as the Messiah, Jesus was responsible to obey every law of God. He kept running into conflict between His Father's will and the will of the Pharisees. They represented an attempt of the church of the time to usurp the law, the will, and the authority of God. Even the Christian church can rob people of their Christian liberty. This is especially bad because we are called to model the highest ethical standards before a watching world. The prophets were the conscience of Israel, but they had the right to function as such only when they were faithful to the Word of God. Had they substituted their own traditions for the Word of God, they would have been no different from the Pharisees.

In every denomination, there are distinctive traditions that may or may not be grounded in an accurate and faithful understanding of Scripture. The fact that there are many denominations indicates that someone somewhere has misunderstood and distorted the Word of God. Although the Reformation churches sought to achieve unity, one of the things that hindered unity was their conviction that the church must be *semper reformanda*, always reforming. They recognized that the church is capable of error. That is why we are called to be patient and long-suffering with Christians of other persuasions. Many different denominations want to be and try to be faithful to the Word of God, but wherever they differ, someone must be in error. Where we are in error and we teach that error, if we try to bind people to that error, then we are usurping the role of God.

The statement that **God alone is Lord of the conscience** has its roots in Luther's defense at the Diet of Worms. There, before the emperor, nobles, and leading churchmen of the Holy Roman Empire, he was called on to recant his teaching of justification by faith alone. Luther replied, "Unless I am convinced by sacred Scripture or by evident or plain, manifest reason, I cannot recant, because my conscience is held captive by the Word of God."

Luther was not claiming infallibility. He told them that if they could show him that the pope is infallible, that church councils are infallible, or that the doctors of the church are infallible in their interpretation of church teachings, then he would submit to them. He said that they all agreed that the Bible is the Word of God, but they did not agree on what it teaches. Luther declared that if they would show him from the Scriptures where he was wrong, he would recant. But unless he was convinced by sacred Scripture, he couldn't recant because, as a matter of conscience, he was convinced that the Word of God teaches justification by faith alone. His mind was held captive by that. His conscience was held captive not by church councils or by papal decrees, but rather by the Word. He believed that to act against conscience is neither right nor safe. He said, "Here I stand. I can do no other. God help me." That was how the Reformation started. That was when the principle of *sola Scriptura* was born. That principle says that Scripture, being the Word of God, is our final authority in matters of faith.

The issue is whether we find the Word of God in the Bible alone or also in church tradition. We are studying the Westminster Confession. It is not the Bible, and we are not required to submit absolutely to it. It has no right to rule over our conscience. It states what we believe to be the truth, but it is truth from the Bible that we believe. If anyone can show that something in this confession is not consistent with what is taught in Scripture, then the confession must be corrected. That does not mean that we despise the history of biblical interpretation. Luther did not say that every generation has the right to interpret the Bible any way it wants and to ignore the teachers whom God has given the church over the years. Luther had respect for what had been taught in the church down through the centuries. But that teaching did not rise to the level of the Word of God.

The requiring of an implicit faith, and an absolute and blind obedience, is to destroy liberty of conscience, and reason also. We should respect our ministers and other leaders, but that respect does not mean slavish devotion to everything they say. We are often at the mercy of the so-called expert. If a doctor tells us something, we tend to accept it because doctors know so much more than we do about health problems. If a repairman comes to fix the air conditioner, we tend to accept that what he says is needed is needed. That is implicit faith. We must be careful lest we have an absolutely implicit faith in any human authority. Only God deserves that.

To believe doctrines or obey commands that come from men, not from God, out of a sense of duty, is **to betray true liberty of conscience and to destroy liberty of conscience.** One can betray liberty, injure liberty through the betrayal, and still not destroy it altogether. But implicit faith destroys it altogether. There is no liberty left.

We are free to use and enjoy things as long as they do not rule our lives. Many good things can be abused, and it is the abuse that is the sin, not the use. Our tendency is to think that the only proper corrective to an abuse is complete disuse. We start posting rules and regulations governing all kinds of things that God allows His people to use in the liberty of conscience, and we try to take away their liberty in order to protect them from falling into abuses.

Paul told Timothy to take a little wine for his stomach's sake (1 Tim. 5:23). The Scriptures also tell us that drunkenness is a great sin. Are we to turn to Timothy and say, "Disregard Paul's advice; take no wine, lest you become a drunkard"? To guard against the abuse of something that God allows, we prohibit it altogether. That destroys Christian liberty, and that principle was important to the Apostle Paul. Where God has left us free, we must be careful not to usurp His authority and take away from people the freedom that He has given.

It is important to master the law of God. One of the great benefits of mastering the law is to know not only what we are not allowed to do but also where God has left us free, so that we can discern the difference between the law of God and the rules of men.

3. They who, upon pretense of Christian liberty, do practice any sin, or cherish any lust, do thereby destroy the end of Christian liberty, which is, that being delivered out of the hands of our enemies, we might serve the Lord without fear, in holiness and righteousness before him, all the days of our life.

Christian liberty is abused when it becomes an excuse for libertinism or licentiousness. Paul's teaching on Christian liberty in Romans begins: "As for the one who is weak in faith, welcome him, but not to quarrel over opinions. One person believes he may eat anything, while the weak person eats only vegetables. Let not the one who eats despise the one who abstains, and let not the one who abstains pass judgment on the one who eats, for God has welcomed him" (Rom. 14:1–3).

Paul develops here the same principle that he spelled out to the Corinthian Christians who had disputes about eating meat offered to idols. Meat offerings were made to the pagan deities at Corinth. After the religious ceremonies, that meat was put on sale in the marketplace. Some Christians took advantage of the discount prices of that meat and ate it. Other members of the church were horrified by this and wondered how they could eat meat after it had been used in pagan religious ceremonies. These people had a strong scruple against eating such meat.

Paul dealt with the meat issue according to the principle set forth in Romans 14. He addressed matters that are called *adiaphora*, which means "things that are indifferent" and refers to things whose use God has neither commanded nor prohibited. He has left the use of these things up to the judgment of the individual. Paul included meat offered to idols among the *adiaphora*.

A related ethical question has to do with separation from sin. There is a distinction in Christian ethics between primary and secondary separation. Primary separation from sin means that we do not commit particular sins. Secondary separation means that we separate ourselves from any person or institution that is involved in sinful practices. To apply secondary separation from wickedness means to remove oneself from any involvement whatsoever with a person or institution. If we applied that principle across the board, we would have to leave the planet, because there is sin in every company and institution.

The same thing goes with taxation. We pay taxes to the government because God commands us to pay taxes to the government. But then we do not like what is done with the money that is turned over to them. Some Christians have suggested that the only way to fight abortion is to stop paying taxes. The problem is that God does not give us that option. If the government takes our taxes and then uses them to support abortion clinics, that does not make us guilty; it makes them guilty.

There are differences within the Christian community with respect to certain scruples. In the Corinthian case, there was a difference pertaining to meat offered to idols. In Romans, Paul says, "As for the one who is weak in faith, welcome him" (14:1). The weaker brother is one who has not reached spiritual maturity, has a simplistic understanding of the things of God, and is an infant in the faith. He becomes upset if he sees something with which he disagrees and may become contentious. Paul says that we do not refuse these people; we are to welcome them. They are not to dispute over doubtful things. They are not allowed to apply pressure and cause conflicts over indifferent things.

"One person believes he may eat anything, while the weak person eats only vegetables" (v. 2). It would be wrong for a church to tolerate a movement that would require vegetarianism of all its members. Should someone decide that it is wrong for anyone to eat meat at all—offered to idols or not offered to idols—and try to make a rule that members may eat only vegetables, it would be the duty of the church to resist. Should such a policy prevail, it would be the tyranny of the weaker brother.

It is certainly all right to choose to be a vegetarian. God does not command us to eat meat, nor does He command us to be vegetarians. Whether we are vegetarians is a matter of *adiaphora*. We should not allow such matters to be major issues in the church.

"One person believes he may eat anything, while the weak person eats only vegetables. Let not the one who eats despise the one who abstains, and let not the one who abstains pass judgment on the one who eats, for God has welcomed him. Who are you to pass judgment on the servant of another? It is before his own master that he stands or falls. And he will be upheld, for the Lord is able to make him stand" (vv. 2–4). This is a principle of Christian liberty that is most important in matters of adiaphora.

When Christians disagree, both parties must understand the principle that we both belong to Christ, and that each of us is trying to serve the same Master, to whom we are accountable. Christ will judge us, but in the meantime we are not to judge each other. This applies only to matters of indifference, where God has not legislated. If someone decides not to be a total abstainer, and his Christian brother sees him inebriated, that is a different matter. God has spoken about drunkenness.

Paul continues:

One person esteems one day as better than another, while another esteems all days alike. Each one should be fully convinced in his own mind. The one who observes the day, observes it in honor of the Lord. The one who eats, eats in honor of the Lord, since he gives thanks to God, while the one who abstains, abstains in honor of the Lord and gives thanks to God. For none of us lives to himself, and none of us dies to himself. For if we live, we live to the Lord, and if we die, we die to the Lord. So then, whether we live or whether we die, we are the Lord's. For to this end Christ died and lived again, that he might be Lord both of the dead and of the living.

Why do you pass judgment on your brother? Or you, why do you despise your brother? For we will all stand before the judgment seat of God; for it is written,

"As I live, says the Lord, every knee shall bow to me, and every tongue shall confess to God."

So then each of us will give an account of himself to God.

Therefore let us not pass judgment on one another any longer, but rather decide never to put a stumbling block or hindrance in the way of a brother. (vv. 5–13)

The stumbling block is put in the way most frequently when the weaker brother tries to legislate his position for others. Paul goes on to say here and in 1 Corinthians, "If my eating meat causes you to stumble, I'll stop eating meat, because the basic principle is for me to show love and consideration for my brother."

There is often a fine line, and we must be considerate. Paul continues in Romans 14:14, "I know and am persuaded in the Lord Jesus that nothing is unclean in itself." However, "It is unclean for anyone who thinks it unclean." If a person does something that he mistakenly believes is wrong, then he sins. Paul continues:

> For if your brother is grieved by what you eat, you are no longer walking in love. By what you eat, do not destroy the one for whom Christ died. So do not let what you regard as good be spoken of as evil. For the kingdom of God is not a matter of eating and drinking but of righteousness and peace and joy in the Holy Spirit. Whoever thus serves Christ is acceptable to God and approved by men. So then let us pursue what makes for peace and for mutual upbuilding. Do not, for the sake of food, destroy the work of God. Everything is indeed clean, but it is wrong for anyone to make another stumble by what he eats. It is good not to eat meat or drink wine or do anything that causes your brother to stumble. The faith that you have, keep between yourself and God. Blessed is the one who has no reason to pass judgment on himself for what he approves. (vv. 15–22)

Paul is not saying that for the sake of the weaker brethren we are required to give up our liberty. If that were the case, our ethic would be determined by the weaker brother and not by the Word of God. Paul says that if we can eat and drink in faith, we should do it before the Lord. But do not flaunt it in front of our neighbors. If a person drinks wine, and he is going out with others who he knows will be troubled by that, then he should not have wine that night. Have it at home before the Lord, who will not stumble.

That could make one vulnerable to the charge of hypocrisy, when liberty is exercised in private or only with those who are of like mind. However, the only way that is hypocritical is if you claim that you never indulge in a particular matter or practice when you actually do.

> The faith that you have, keep between yourself and God. Blessed is the one who has no reason to pass judgment on himself for what he approves. But whoever has doubts is condemned if he eats, because the eating is not from faith. For whatever does not proceed from faith is sin. We who

are strong have an obligation to bear with the failings of the weak, and not to please ourselves. Let each of us please his neighbor for his good, to build him up. For Christ did not please himself, but as it is written, "The reproaches of those who reproached you fell on me." (Rom. 14:22–15:3)

We are to remember that these people belong to Christ, and we are to receive them as Christ has received them and as Christ has received us. This is one of the most important principles in the entire matter of Christian liberty. This is not about liberty; it is about Christian liberty, a liberty that is given to us in Christ, who receives us. We are to practice a love that covers a multitude of sins. We are to be patient and long-suffering with our brothers and sisters when we notice their sins, unless they are scandalous and destructive. We are to be patient with one another and know the difference between serious matters and indifferent matters.

The Pharisees majored in minors. They created righteous indignation over peccadilloes. The fruit of the Spirit involves patience, kindness, long-suffering, goodness, joy, and peace. This is how we are to live, rather than arguing over every jot and tittle of the faith.

They who, upon pretense of Christian liberty, do practice any sin, or cherish any lust, do thereby destroy the end of Christian liberty, which is, that being delivered out of the hands of our enemies, we might serve the Lord without fear, in holiness and righteousness before him, all the days of our life. Much of our study of Christian liberty has put the accent on the areas where we are free from the requirements of God's law, and how often those liberties are destroyed in the context of legalism. Those who take away our Christian liberty fall into the legalistic camp, and those who use their alleged liberty as a license to commit sin become antinomian in their approach to the law of God.

Two terms, often used to describe liberty as a license for sin, are *libertinism* and *licentiousness*. The term *licentiousness* is based on the idea that the spiritual liberty that is ours in Christ gives us a license to go out and commit sin. This is a serious affront to the Holy Spirit. Licentiousness most frequently arises when people put their private views and desires above the clear teaching of the Word of God.

Sometimes people engage in activities that are clearly in opposition to the revealed Scriptures. They might defend their actions by saying that they prayed about it and God gave them peace. Not only do these people violate the law of God and sin against Him, but they make it worse by claiming that God endorses their sin.

The Holy Spirit inspired the Apostolic word. Through the ministry of the Holy Spirit, God superintended the text of Scripture, so that the Word of God is the fruit of the Spirit of God. Scripture tells us that the Holy Spirit is not the author of confusion. If we think that we are being led by the Spirit to do something that is contrary to Scripture, then our leading is not from the Holy Spirit at all. It could be a spirit leading, but it is from an unholy spirit.

When we think of licentiousness, libertinism, and antinomianism, we think of the decadent lives of people who have no involvement in the things of God or of the church. The danger, spoken of in the confession, comes into the church and the Christian community when we distort our license and our liberty and turn it into libertinism or licentiousness.

They who, upon pretense of Christian liberty, do practice any sin, or cherish any lust, do thereby destroy the end of Christian liberty. Pretense is pretending; it is phony and hypocritical. Anyone who sins in such circumstances destroys **the end of Christian liberty.** The "end" of Christian liberty is its purpose or goal. The purpose of Christian liberty is never to incite us to sin or to lust, but to send us to Christ and to cause us to grow in grace. That end is defined here: **that being delivered out of the hands of our enemies, we might serve the Lord without fear, in holiness and righteousness before him, all the days of our life.** Not only is the end of the law our sanctification and our holiness, but the purpose of liberty is to the same end. Where God has commanded, the goal is our sanctification; where God has left us free, the goal is still our sanctification. It is a monstrous evil to take that liberty and use it to destroy the purpose for which God intended it in the first place.

4. And because the powers which God hath ordained, and the liberty which Christ hath purchased, are not intended by God to destroy, but mutually to uphold and preserve one another, they who, upon pretense of Christian liberty, shall oppose any lawful power, or the

lawful exercise of it, whether it be civil or ecclesiastical, resist the ordinance of God. And, for their publishing of such opinions, or maintaining of such practices, as are contrary to the light of nature, or to the known principles of Christianity (whether concerning faith, worship, or conversation), or to the power of godliness; or, such erroneous opinions or practices, as either in their own nature, or in the manner of publishing or maintaining them, are destructive to the external peace and order which Christ hath established in the church, they may lawfully be called to account, and proceeded against, by the censures of the church.

The Westminster divines, writing in the seventeenth century, had no idea of what was coming politically in the New World. There would be an experiment in democracy, where a spirit of rugged individualism would prevail, the likes of which the world had never before seen. We live in a society whose cultural attitude of individualism is unique. Since the 1960s in the United States, there has been a massive revolt against corporate authority, which always stands as an obstacle to individual liberty. The libertine says, "No one can tell me what to do. I am the captain of my soul, the master of my fate."

There are **powers which God hath ordained**. We have liberty, but our liberty ends where the lawful authority that God has ordained begins. The civil magistrate is established by God and given power and authority by Him. The civil government does not always act in accordance with the will of God. Government can be demonized, even as the Roman Empire was at the time of the Apostle Paul's letter to the Romans. He tells us that we are not to resist the authorities whom God has placed over us, because they are ministers for the public good and for righteousness. Unless the magistrate commands us to do something that God explicitly forbids or forbids us to do what God explicitly commands, we are to obey. If Caesar says we may not pray, may not preach, or may not give our money to the church, we not only may disobey Caesar but must do so.

This is true whether the powers are **civil or ecclesiastical**. Notice that the confession speaks of the powers (plural) that God ordains. On the one hand, there is civil government; on the other hand, there is ecclesiastical government. The Reformers tried to determine how we can recognize a true church. When is a church not a church? When does a church become apostate and lose its authority? Different churches had arisen, and people wondered how they could all be genuine. The Reformers named three necessary marks of a true church. The first one is that the gospel is truthfully preached. Any church that officially denies the gospel is not a true church. That is why the Reformers rejected Rome. They said that Rome had become apostate because it condemned the gospel itself at the Council of Trent in the sixteenth century. The next mark is the right administration of the sacraments, and the third mark is that the church exercises discipline. A church that does not exercise discipline over its members and does not function as spiritual overseer of the body of Christ is not a true church.

The session of a church in Presbyterianism is a court (other churches have similar bodies, such as a board of elders). It is not a civil court but an ecclesiastical court, before which disputes may be brought and decisions and verdicts may be rendered. If a dispute emerges between two or more members of the congregation, they can come to the session for mediation. The court itself can summon the parties and give mediation or dispense ecclesiastical discipline. The court, the session of the church, has authority invested in it to take through the steps of discipline anyone who is involved in public, scandalous sin. They may be summoned and confronted by the session of the church and called upon to repent. If they refuse to do so, they may go through the steps of discipline, ending with censure. They may be suspended from the sacraments while being disciplined. Many ministers warn the congregation before the Lord's Supper is administered that anyone who is suspended from the Lord's Table by another church should not partake of the sacrament; they want to honor the authority of other church courts. Such ministers recognize that other churches have not only the right but also the duty to exercise discipline.

The strongest censure is excommunication. There may be members who have left a fellowship without ever withdrawing their membership. They have gone to another church. Our first duty is to contact the other church and ask if our members have been received into membership. If they have, we transfer their membership and remove them from our rolls.

Suppose they have just stopped going to church altogether. We contact them to determine why they have not been engaged in worship or involved in the sacraments. We seek to restore them to worship and service in the church. There may come a point where it is the duty of the session to say, "If you neglect the responsibilities that you swore before God that you would maintain when you joined this church or another church, it is our duty to exercise spiritual oversight and call you to repentance. If you steadfastly refuse to become involved in the life of the church, then it is our duty to excommunicate you." When a person joins a church, he submits to the spiritual oversight of that church. Any church that is a true church has the responsibility to exercise discipline over its members. That comes as a shock to many people in the United States.

Excommunication means that a member is removed from the fellowship of the body of Christ and is to be regarded as an unbeliever. He is turned over to Satan to be buffeted by him. The hope is that if he is truly a Christian, his isolation from the means of grace and the body of Christ and his exposure to the onslaught of the enemy will bring him to his senses and that he will then repent and be restored to the body of Christ. No one should join a church if he does not want to be in submission to its spiritual authority.

This idea of ecclesiastical authority has almost disappeared from the thinking of evangelical Christians today, and the normal response is, "I don't need some session to tell me how to live my life." The church members' spiritual well-being is the primary concern of the session. The session is called to give spiritual oversight—not to act as a police department, but to be ministers for our spiritual well-being. God does not give the sword to the ecclesiastical authorities; He gives the sword to the civil authorities. We have a tendency to think that without the sword, there is no such thing as spiritual or ministerial authority. That is what the confession addresses at this point, helping us see that Christian liberty does not give a person the right to destroy either civil or ecclesiastical authority.

There are those who, **upon pretense of Christian liberty, shall oppose any lawful power, or the lawful exercise of it.** If the session is acting in a way that is unbiblical or is being tyrannical over its people, then it can be opposed. But if it is lawfully exercising its authority, then to resist the session is to resist the ordinance of God. If there are those whose words or deeds, as either in their own nature, or in the manner of publishing or maintaining them, are destructive to the external peace and order which Christ hath established in the church, they may lawfully be called to account, and proceeded against, by the censures of the church. No Christian is above the authority of the church in regard to promulgating heresy. Before we defy a lawfully established ecclesiastical authority, as Luther did, we had better be sure that we are fighting for the angels and not being obstreperous. That is why Luther said that he saw himself in a conflict between loyalty to Christ and loyalty to the church, and at Worms he declared, "Unless I am convinced by sacred Scripture, I cannot recant." The church is derelict when it fails to discipline those who promote erroneous opinions or engage in erroneous practices in the name of Christian liberty.

The confession cautions against an invalid appeal to Christian liberty—"I am free in Christ; I am free to do with my own body what I want to do, including abort a baby that is growing within it; I am free to do this, no matter what anyone says." This destroys the whole concept of Christian liberty.

Of Religious Worship, and the Sabbath Day

1. The light of nature showeth that there is a God, who hath lordship and sovereignty over all, is good, and doth good unto all, and is therefore to be feared, loved, praised, called upon, trusted in, and served, with all the heart, and with all the soul, and with all the might. But the acceptable way of worshiping the true God is instituted by himself, and so limited by his own revealed will, that he may not be worshiped according to the imaginations and devices of men, or the suggestions of Satan, under any visible representation, or any other way not prescribed in the Holy Scripture.

2. Religious worship is to be given to God, the Father, Son, and Holy Ghost; and to him alone; not to angels, saints, or any other creature: and, since the fall, not without a Mediator; nor in the mediation of any other but of Christ alone.

3. Prayer, with thanksgiving, being one special part of religious worship, is by God required of all men: and, that it may be accepted, it is to be made in the name of the Son, by the help of his Spirit, according to his will, with understanding, reverence, humility, fervency, faith, love, and perseverance; and, if vocal, in a known tongue.

4. Prayer is to be made for things lawful; and for all sorts of men living, or that shall live hereafter: but not for the dead, nor for those of whom it may be known that they have sinned the sin unto death.

5. The reading of the Scriptures with godly fear, the sound preaching and conscionable hearing of the Word, in obedience unto God, with understanding, faith, and reverence, singing of psalms with grace in the heart;

as also, the due administration and worthy receiving of the sacraments instituted by Christ, are all parts of the ordinary religious worship of God: beside religious oaths, vows, solemn fastings, and thanksgivings upon special occasions, which are, in their several times and seasons, to be used in an holy and religious manner.

6. Neither prayer, nor any other part of religious worship, is now, under the gospel, either tied unto, or made more acceptable by any place in which it is performed, or towards which it is directed: but God is to be worshiped everywhere, in spirit and truth; as, in private families daily, and in secret, each one by himself; so, more solemnly in the public assemblies, which are not carelessly or willfully to be neglected, or forsaken, when God, by his Word or providence, calleth thereunto.

7. As it is the law of nature, that, in general, a due proportion of time be set apart for the worship of God; so, in his Word, by a positive, moral, and perpetual commandment binding all men in all ages, he hath particularly appointed one day in seven, for a Sabbath, to be kept holy unto him: which, from the beginning of the world to the resurrection of Christ, was the last day of the week; and, from the resurrection of Christ, was changed into the first day of the week, which, in Scripture, is called the Lord's day, and is to be continued to the end of the world, as the Christian Sabbath.

8. This Sabbath is then kept holy unto the Lord, when men, after a due preparing of their hearts, and ordering of their common affairs beforehand, do not only observe an holy rest, all the day, from their own works, words, and thoughts about their worldly employments and recreations, but also are taken up, the whole time, in the public and private exercises of his worship, and in the duties of necessity and mercy.

Chapter 21 of the Westminster Confession, "Of Religious Worship, and the Sabbath Day," is a lengthy chapter that covers issues relating to proper worship and observance of the Sabbath day. It begins as follows:

1. The light of nature showeth that there is a God, who hath lordship and sovereignty over all, is good, and doth good unto all, and is therefore to be feared, loved, praised, called upon, trusted

in, and served, with all the heart, and with all the soul, and with all the might. But the acceptable way of worshiping the true God is instituted by himself, and so limited by his own revealed will, that he may not be worshiped according to the imaginations and devices of men, or the suggestions of Satan, under any visible representation, or any other way not prescribed in the Holy Scripture.

The light of nature showeth that there is a God. The affirmation in the first half of this section is that the knowledge of the essential nature and reality of God, which reveals His character, is not restricted to the pages of sacred Scripture but is part of what we call natural revelation or general revelation. The heavens themselves declare the glory of God. As Paul explains in Romans 1, nature so manifestly reveals the character of God to everyone that all people know that it is their duty to glorify Him. The heavens not only declare the glory of God but also reveal to us that we ought to glorify that God of glory.

God . . . hath lordship and sovereignty over all, is good, and doth good unto all, and is therefore to be feared, loved, praised, called upon, trusted in, and served, with all the heart, and with all the soul, and with all the might. The light of nature makes it abundantly clear not only that God exists but also what kind of God He is. This revelation makes clear to mankind God's eternal power and very deity—His holiness, moral character, goodness, eternity, and omnipotence. All these things God reveals through the light of nature, so that we have a natural obligation to render to our Creator worship that is appropriate to who He is.

In Romans 1–2, Paul tells us that the whole world is brought before the divine tribunal and judged to be guilty, both Jew and Greek. The primordial sin of mankind, rejecting the revelation of God through nature, was to fail to honor God as God or to be grateful to Him (1:20–21). Most people have refused to render to God the worship that is owed Him. They "exchanged the truth about God for a lie and worshiped and served the creature rather than the Creator" (1:25). By nature, not only do we fail to honor God as God, but we take the honor that should be given to Him and give it to another. It is not that we stop being religious, for in fact, all idolatry is religious. One of the great myths of humanism is that all religions are equally valid. That could be true only if they also are equally invalid, equally false.

Our basic disposition as fallen creatures is to create worship alternatives or substitutes. What is most important, we think, is to be sincere and zealous. That would have made even the priests and the prophets of Baal pleasing to God, because they were zealous in their religion. The message of sacred Scripture, however, is quite different. There is only one true God, and only one Mediator, and only one true religion.

John Calvin saw the chief need for the reformation of the church to be in the area of worship. He believed that the church's worship had degenerated to superstition and idolatry because the church's doctrine had been neglected. He believed that unless sound doctrine informs our worship, our worship will go astray. God wants people who will worship Him in spirit and in truth and who will give glory to Him in a way that reflects His true nature and His true character.

In Old Testament times, the ram's horn (the shofar) sounded forth into the community, calling the people to solemn assembly. The people of God joined together before God, invoking His presence in their midst. But if God is omnipresent, why invoke His presence? We are not asking God to concentrate His being here and not out there. We are asking Him to be present in a special way, to give to us a visitation. We are told, "Blessed be the Lord God of Israel, for he has visited and redeemed his people" (Luke 1:68), which He does by concentrating His grace in their midst.

What we have seen in our culture is an avant-garde revolution of worship motivated by a desire to reach out to a secularized America turned off to "churchiness" and ecclesiastical traditions. There has been an attempt to disguise or mask the gospel, so that people will not think they are in church. There is no chancel, but a stage. There is no choir, but a worship team. This has been enormously successful as an innovation, and it will probably define evangelical worship in the United States for some time. However, when we begin to pander to the "audience" rather than to God, we are in serious trouble. The Old Testament worship service where the people were the most enthusiastic and energetic consisted of the singing of praise songs by an overflow congregation while dancing around a golden calf (Ex. 32:17–19).

Worship is not an arena for open experimentation. If we "worship" by doing what we enjoy, rather than by doing what is pleasing to God, our worship will gravitate toward idolatry. It is our duty, as much as possible, to learn what true worship is supposed to be like.

True worship should delight the soul of every Christian, but that will not always happen, because our souls are still tainted with sin. We may be offering worship to God, yet nodding off to sleep. Our wandering thoughts may be "I am bored" or "I did not get anything out of that." What did we put into it? To worship is to actively offer a sacrifice of praise and glory and honor to him, to attend to the proclamation of His Word, and to celebrate the sacraments.

The acceptable way of worshiping the true God is instituted by himself, and so limited by his own revealed will, that he may not be worshiped according to the imaginations and devices of men, or the suggestions of Satan, under any visible representation, or any other way not prescribed in the Holy Scripture. That "visible representation" refers to visible representations of God the Father. When God prescribed worship to His people in the old covenant, the very first commandment established pure monotheism: "You shall have no other gods before me" (Ex. 20:3). That first commandment was not just an establishing of one God but, by implication, a total prohibition of idol worship. The words "before me" are not a demand for preference but mean, literally, "You shall have no other gods in My presence." God's presence is everywhere. God is saying, "I don't want to see a golden calf anywhere." Old Testament history is replete with stories of Israel's worshiping at pagan altars. God ordered the kings, through the prophets, to tear down those places. He was jealous about the integrity of His people's worship and commanded that there be no idols.

The second commandment is explicit: "You shall not make for yourself a carved image, or any likeness of anything that is in heaven above, or that is in the earth beneath, or that is in the water under the earth" (Ex. 20:4). This is not a universal prohibition against art, because the tabernacle and later on the temple, designed on God's instructions, were veritable art museums. The first people anointed by the Holy Spirit in the Old Testament were the artisans whom God called to fashion the furniture and the rest of the sacred vessels for the tabernacle. The Holy of Holies contained a beautiful carving of the cherubim over the ark of the covenant. Art was not prohibited, but images of God Himself were prohibited. What we have here is called the regulative principle of worship, which states that God not only institutes worship but regulates it through His Word.

By analogy, God not only institutes sacred worship but also regulates it. He regulates it by His Word. We see this especially in the Old Testament story of Nadab and Abihu, the sons of Aaron, who were trained in all the proper procedures of worship in the religious community of Israel (Lev. 10). On one occasion, they offered "unauthorized fire" on the altar, and fire came out of the altar and consumed them on the spot (v. 2). They were executed for their experimental worship, for doing what God did not authorize, institute, or sanction. At that time, Moses said to Aaron, "This is what the LORD has said: 'Among those who are near me I will be sanctified, and before all the people I will be glorified'" (v. 3). The most important ingredient of worship is that the holiness of God is made manifest. We are to honor our holy God and to acknowledge and give glory to His majesty and His transcendent greatness. There should be an atmosphere of fear and trembling in our worship.

According to polls, the number one reason why people go to church on Sunday morning is for fellowship. Most people go to church in America to be with other people. There is nothing wrong with fellowship, and there is certainly a place for it. Some churches have a ritual of friendship in the worship service when they give a moment for people to greet each other. At that point, the emphasis is not on God but on those who have been brought together as His people. But our primary purpose for being together in worship is to come into His presence with thanksgiving and praise, giving honor and glory to Him.

2. Religious worship is to be given to God, the Father, Son, and Holy Ghost; and to him alone; not to angels, saints, or any other creature: and, since the fall, not without a Mediator; nor in the mediation of any other but of Christ alone.

We have looked at how God is known through the light of nature. Universally, however, the knowledge that God gives of Himself, in and through creation, is suppressed by fallen man. Even though man knows God in terms of His eternal power and deity, he refuses to honor God or to express the proper gratitude toward his Creator. He then moves to exchange the truth of God for a lie, and to serve the creature rather than the Creator. Paul teaches, in the first chapter of Romans, that there is a universal propensity among fallen humanity to make idols and to substitute false gods for the true God. This is our most primordial sin and a very subtle one that is not instantly cured by conversion. We read in the Bible a clear revelation of the character of God, and there may be some disturbing aspects to it. At times, He pours out His wrath on people. He sends people into judgment and to hell according to His justice, and He is sovereign in the distribution of His saving grace. We react by saying, "That's not fair," or, "That's not very nice." We want God always to be merciful, gracious, and loving according to our standards of love. Certain aspects of the character of God are then discounted. We treat God's revelation as if it were a smorgasbord, to which we may go and select only the attributes that please us. We leave those we do not like on the table. If our deity is incapable of wrath, not sovereign, not immutable, not like the Scripture reveals God to be, then we have created an idol.

Religious worship is to be given to God . . . alone. Scripture tells us that when Paul approached the city of Athens, the cultural center of the ancient world, he was distressed and heartbroken. His spirit was provoked within him because he saw that the whole city was given to idolatry. What the rest of the world applauded as high culture, Paul viewed as idolatry. When he confronted the philosophers at the Areopagus on Mars Hill, Paul said to them, "I perceive that in every way you are very religious" (Acts 17:22), and then he exposed their religion to be a false religion.

Our culture teaches that it doesn't matter what we believe or how we worship, just as long as we are sincere, because all God cares about is that we are sincerely religious. The point of Romans 1, Acts 17, and this section of the confession is that a person can be exceedingly religious and at the same time completely alienated from God. If the religion we embrace and practice is based on a distorted, false view of God, then it is idolatry. God is exceedingly displeased with idolatry. He is displeased when we substitute something other than who He is for the true God.

In Romans 1, Paul speaks about an exchange that takes place. Paul states that after we receive the natural revelation of God, we exchange the truth for a lie and worship and serve the creature rather than the Creator. We exchange the glory of the incorruptible God for the glory of corruptible things—animals, trees, and totem poles. We do not trade the true God for no god (atheism) but for a false god—some created thing (1:20–25). That propensity is deeply imbedded within the human heart.

The most famous verse in the New Testament is John 3:16, "For God so loved the world, that he gave his only Son, that whoever believes in him should not perish but have eternal life." Verses 17–18 continue: "For God did not send his Son into the world to condemn the world, but in order that the world might be saved through him. Whoever believes in him is not condemned, but whoever does not believe is condemned already, because he has not believed in the name of the only Son of God." Christ was sent to a world that was already under the condemnation of God. Verse 19 explains: "And this is the judgment: the light has come into the world, and people loved the darkness rather than the light because their works were evil." We are told that, by nature, we are children of darkness; we love the darkness rather than the light, because when the light comes in, it exposes our evil deeds. We prefer to read John 3:16–17 and stop. We do not want to hear verses 18–20, which show the truth of what those verses teach. It is our nature to resist and to quench the light that has come into the world. We are not to engage in mere "religion" when we worship God. That is a subtle form of idolatry. We are to worship the living God, the God of Scripture, to whom we are to give glory.

Religious worship is to be given to God, the Father, Son, and Holy Ghost; and to him alone; not to angels, saints, or any other creature: and, since the fall, not without a Mediator; nor in the mediation of any other but of Christ alone. God is one Being in three persons, and all three persons of the Godhead are worthy of our worship. Thomas, in the upper room, after Christ appeared to him, confessed, "My Lord and my God!" (John 20:28). He was worshiping the second person of the Trinity at that point. We are to adore and glorify the Spirit, the Son, and the Father because all three are God. This section also teaches that we are to worship no one else—not saints, angels, images, or icons. Only God is ever to be worshiped, and we bring our worship to Him only through mediation. There is only one Mediator between God and us, and that Mediator is Jesus Christ, God's only begotten Son.

The idea that there is only one Mediator between God and us is contrary to our culture. The mountain analogy—where God is at the top of a mountain and there are many routes up the mountain to Him—is standard today. Some routes up the mountain are circuitous and some are direct, but there are many different paths to God. It doesn't matter which path is chosen, whether the path of Buddhism, Islam, Judaism, Christianity, or any other. All these paths will ultimately lead to God, according to the world.

To the contrary, the confession and the Apostle Paul teach that there is only one way to God. Jesus Himself said: "I am the way, and the truth, and the life. No one comes to the Father except through me" (John 14:6). That is a radical claim to exclusivity made by our Lord Himself. He also said: "I am the door. If anyone enters by me, he will be saved" (10:9) and "I am the good shepherd. I know my own and my own know me" (10:14). Other religions, far from leading to God, consistently lead away from Him, because they are idolatrous substitutes. To say, in today's culture, "There is only one way to God," may be unpopular, but that is exactly what the Apostles taught and proclaimed in the first century: the exclusive mediatory work of Christ.

Christ is the only Mediator because He is the only begotten and divine Son of God, the only God incarnate, and He is alive. No one else can do the work of mediation that He does for us. All those other religious leaders are dead. They were sinners, and none of them had the credentials necessary to reconcile us to God.

A famous West Coast preacher was once interviewed on television, and he was excited about a conversation with a so-called evangelical leader who had opened his eyes to what he called the wideness in God's mercy. This wideness was interpreted to mean that God does not require that we come to Him only through Christ; we may come through a number of other ways as well. Even one of the popes, some years ago, stated that people who are Muslims can be redeemed. However, when the pope says that, he means that the church has the authority to apply the benefits of Christ to people of other religions. These are examples of the kinds of pluralism that we encounter today.

It is certainly narrow-minded to say that there is only one way, and it is socially unacceptable. It is the nadir of political incorrectness to make that statement, but that is exactly what the Bible teaches. Christ Himself claims to be the *only* Mediator.

> 3. Prayer, with thanksgiving, being one special part of religious worship, is by God required of all men: and, that it may be accepted, it is to be made in the name of the Son, by the help of his Spirit, according to his will, with understanding, reverence, humility, fervency, faith, love, and perseverance; and, if vocal, in a known tongue.

Although section 3 is short, it contains enough information to keep us busy for a long time. It lists the requirements and characteristics of prayer that is acceptable in the sight of God.

The Scriptures make it clear that unless we pray through the one Mediator, Christ, then God abhors our prayers of unbelief. In a sense, the prayers are insulting to God. That is why He used such strong language when He said through the prophet Amos: "I hate, I despise your feasts, and I take no delight in your solemn assemblies" (Amos 5:21). God is not happy with worship that is not sincere and not according to His requirements. When empty ritual is offered, God will not accept it. That is the teaching of the prophets.

The confession uses the phrase **prayer, with thanksgiving**. The New Testament teaches that when we pray, we ought always to pray with thanksgiving. Paul says, "Do not be anxious about anything, but in everything by prayer and supplication with thanksgiving let your requests be made known to God" (Phil. 4:6). Prayer with thanksgiving is one special part of religious worship that God requires of all men.

God requires everyone to pray to Him, but that does not mean that He is pleased with the prayers of everyone. **And, that it may be accepted, it is to be made in the name of the Son.** God requires all people everywhere to pray in the name of Christ because He is the Mediator. Not only was He the Mediator during His earthly ministry, bearing our sins on the cross and earning righteousness for us, so that we might be adopted into the family of God, but He is still our Mediator. As our Great High Priest, He is interceding for us. The greatest advantage of prayer is gained when Christ prays for us. When we pray, we direct our prayer to Christ, so that He may bear our prayers to the Father. That is His priestly role, and it is different from His prophetic role. In the Old Testament, the priest spoke to God on behalf of the people. Christ is our Priest, speaking to the Father on our behalf.

We do not always know how to pray as we ought, and so we have another mediator. He is not a mediator of salvation, the way that Christ is, but He is another advocate who helps us to pray as we ought. The Holy Spirit helps us to articulate to the Son what we want Him to take to the Father. Our prayers are Trinitarian. By the help of the Spirit, we give our requests to the Son, so that the Son may take them to the Father. God, in three persons, is involved in our prayer.

The prayers that are required of all people, in order to be acceptable, are to be made **in the name of the Son, by the help of his Spirit, according to his will, with understanding, reverence, humility, fervency, faith, love, and perseverance; and, if vocal, in a known tongue.** Prayers are to be made not only in the name of the Son, by the help of the Spirit, but also in accordance with His will. It is a blasphemous thing to pray for anything that God, in His Word, prohibits. People not only break the law of God but ask God to sanction their sin by praying for His blessing on sinful undertakings. His will is made known to us through sacred Scripture, and we are never to pray against the revealed will of God.

There are some people who seem to have a track record of answered prayer. One of the reasons for this is that they know how to pray according to the will of God. They don't come to prayer and "name it and claim it," nor do they ask God to do what He has never promised, nor do they demand that He allow them to do what He prohibits. Matthew 18:19 says, "If two of you agree on earth about anything they ask, it will be done for them by my Father in heaven." Let us assume that the only thing the Bible teaches about prayer is that if any two of us agree on anything, God will do it. Would we like to have a cure for cancer, or have all wars in the world cease, or be rid of all famine and hunger? We would have no trouble getting two people to agree on these things. Should we therefore assume that Matthew 18:19 is not true? Of course not, for that statement presupposes everything else that the Bible teaches us about prayer. It is an elliptical statement. There are things left out that are tacitly understood, namely, that if we pray about what God has promised to do, and we agree that this is one of those situations, it will be done. It is not a blanket order attached to our door that guarantees room service as soon as we have agreement with our prayer partner. God is not a celestial bellhop who is obligated to give us everything for which we ask.

"If we confess our sins, he is faithful and just to forgive us our sins and to cleanse us from all unrighteousness" (1 John 1:9). When we confess our sins, we can confidently pray for God's forgiveness and claim the promise. In that event, we can name it and claim it. But God does not promise a job that pays seven figures or freedom from all trouble, tribulation, or disease in this world. If we claim those things in prayer, we don't understand the Word of God, nor are we praying according to the will of God. "For this is the will of God, your sanctification" (1 Thess. 4:3). The will of God for your life is our holiness. We ought to pray for that. That is the kind of prayer that pleases Him.

We are supposed to pray **according to his will, with understanding, reverence, humility, fervency, faith, love, and perseverance; and, if vocal, in a known tongue.**

Reverence. This may be the most difficult. We are among the most casual and disrespectful people who have inhabited the earth. That disrespect carries over even into our worship and prayer life. We tend to approach God as if we are His peer. We talk to Him as if we were talking to our next-door neighbor, with no sense of awe, adoration, or reverence before Him. Simple instruction on the mode of praying requires that we practice two things. The first is to remember who it is to whom we are speaking, and the second is to remember who we are who are speaking. It is incredible that we are allowed to open our mouths in the presence of God.

Humility. That the next virtue or requirement is humility should go without saying, since reverence and humility are two sides of the same coin. We come into the presence of God with our prayers, on our faces before Him in awe and adoration, saying, "God, I know I have no right whatever to mumble in Your presence, except that You have invited me to be here, clothed with the righteousness of Christ." It is only because we have been justified by faith that we now have access to the Father. We must always remember who He is.

Fervency. James tells us that the effective, fervent prayer of a righteous man avails much (James 5:16). Noise and emotion do not prove that we are fervent. The posture of the body can be indifferent or earnest. The confession, following James' teaching, says that God is pleased with people who pray to Him in earnest and who are serious about their prayers, who mean what they say before the living God. One does not have a casual conversation with God. It is a serious matter to come into His presence through prayer.

With . . . fervency, faith, love, and perseverance. We hear about the "prayer of faith" that saves or about "faith healing." A prayer of faith is simply a prayer in which the heart is poured out to God with trust. To pray in faith is to plead one's case before God and then leave it in His hands and trust Him. It is to have the attitude of Job, who said, "Though he slay me, I will hope in him" (Job 13:15). That is the prayer of faith and the prayer of love. Finally, we are to persevere in prayer, as did the persistent widow before the unjust judge (Luke 18:1–8).

If our prayers are spoken out loud, they are to be uttered in a known tongue. That statement was not directed, back in the seventeenth century, against modern-day charismatics, who claim to be speaking in tongues. It was directed against the Roman Catholic practice of praying in Latin, an ancient tongue that people no longer understood. We are always to pray in a language that is known and understood by those assembled.

We ask if, in regard to praying for an unsaved child or friend, prayer changes God's mind. This is a dangerous question, and the answer is no. What could we possibly tell God to cause Him to change His mind? It suggests that His plan was bad until we corrected it or gave Him information that He lacked before He made His own plan. It assumes that we can give Him counsel to correct His bad decision. God, from all eternity, determined whom He would save, and we cannot change that eternal decree by our prayers. However, in His eternal plan of salvation, God chose to save people through means, including the prayers of His people. There is every reason to be encouraged that our intercessory prayer for our unsaved children or for unsaved friends may be used by God to help bring about their salvation. But there is no guarantee. We could pray for someone for fifty years without apparent effect, because our prayers do not save anyone. However, when we have a burden to pray for someone, that may be a good indication that God is working. If God has laid that burden upon us, our prayers can be a part of the means by which He will bring that person to salvation. We certainly are encouraged by God to pray fervently for the lost, just as we are encouraged to proclaim the gospel to all people.

> 4. Prayer is to be made for things lawful; and for all sorts of men living, or that shall live hereafter: but not for the dead, nor for those of whom it may be known that they have sinned the sin unto death.

We have repeatedly noted the great care, the sound articulation of the biblical faith in the Westminster Confession. The wisdom manifested by those who framed this document is awe-inspiring—until we get to this section.

It starts out well: **Prayer is to be made for things lawful; and for all sorts of men living, or that shall live hereafter: but not for the dead.** But then it says that we are not to pray **for those of whom it may be known that they have sinned the sin unto death.** The biblical basis for that instruction is found in 1 John 5:16, which reads as follows: "If anyone sees his brother committing a sin not leading to death, he shall ask, and God will give him life—to those who commit sins that do not lead to death. There is sin that leads to death; I do not say that one should pray for that."

Scripture says that if we see our brother engaged in sin, we should pray for him in the hope that he will repent and be fully restored. We have a command from God to pray for our friends who are involved in sin. Then John goes on to say of the sin that leads to death, "I do not say that one should pray for that." Now, there is a difference between saying, "You must not pray for someone who does a particular thing," and, "If you see someone doing this particular thing, I do not tell you that you have to pray for him." This is the difference between saying that we *must not* and saying that we *do not have to*. The first is a prohibition and the second is open-ended, posing no obligation in either direction.

The chief cause for misunderstanding the Scriptures is drawing unwarranted inferences from the text. The Westminster divines seem to be drawing an inference from the text that is unwarranted. Where the Scripture text says that we *do not have to* do something, the divines are saying that we *must not* do it. If those great and godly minds could collectively make a slip like that, it should alert us to our own tendencies to do the same. One can see how easy it is to draw a conclusion from Scripture that is unwarranted by the text. The confession says that we are not allowed to pray for people whom we know to have committed the sin that leads to death. The Bible actually says that we do not have to pray for them, and that is quite different. For a treatment of the sin unto death, see our discussion above of chapter 15, sections 4–6.

Having said that, let's go back to the beginning of section 4. **Prayer is to be made for things lawful.** On a television talk show a few years ago, there was a man who owned and operated the most financially successful brothel in the West. This wealthy entrepreneur was asked, "What is the secret of your success?" He replied: "I prayed this business to its level of success. When I started this business, I gave it to God and said, 'God, if you will prosper my business, I will give you 10 percent of the proceeds.' I have done that from the beginning, and God has poured out the blessings of heaven upon me." He was serious. He had prayed for God to bless his enterprise, one that is explicitly prohibited by the Word of God. His prayer was an insult to God, a blasphemous assault on the character of God. God was not pleased with that prayer, because it was not for anything lawful. When we come before God in prayer, we are to ask for what His Word teaches to be in accordance with His law.

Prayer is to be made . . . all sorts of men living, or that shall live hereafter: but not for the dead. The confession says that we should pray for all sorts of people who are alive now and even for those who are not yet born. Unborn children need prayer. We now know that the most dangerous place in America is in the womb. We do not pray just for the unborn coming to term, but also for our own children and grandchildren. We pray in advance. The Word of God does not prohibit praying for the unborn. Indeed, in Scripture God speaks of His intimate knowledge of His people before they are born. He says that He knew Jeremiah while he was still in the womb (Jer. 1:5). Throughout the Scriptures, we see God sanctifying people before they are born. To pray for the unborn is a legitimate enterprise.

For what possible reason would we pray for people who have died? If a saint passes into glory, how can we improve his lot by praying for him at that point? The Bible says "It is appointed for man to die once, and after that comes judgment" (Heb. 9:27). At the end of life, a person moves immediately into the presence of God. The framers of the confession put into this statement on prayer the essence of Reformation theology. If we affirm justification by faith alone, we should not deny it by assuming that prayers for the dead will have any efficacy.

5. The reading of the Scriptures with godly fear, the sound preaching and conscionable hearing of the Word, in obedience unto God, with understanding, faith, and reverence, singing of psalms with grace in the heart; as also, the due administration and worthy receiving of the sacraments instituted by Christ, are all parts of the ordinary religious worship of God: beside religious oaths, vows, solemn fastings, and thanksgivings upon special occasions, which are, in their several times and seasons, to be used in an holy and religious manner.

The next aspect of worship that is pleasing to God is **the reading of the Scriptures with godly fear.** Not only are the Scriptures to be read in worship, but they are to be read in an atmosphere and spirit of fear. Is anyone afraid to listen to the Bible being read? That fear is qualified as godly fear, which refers to the attitude of reverence, sacredness, and honor that the occasion demands. In the wisdom literature of the Old Testament, we are told that "the fear of the Lord is the beginning of wisdom" (Ps. 111:10). This fear of the Lord is not a servile fear like that of a prisoner who is terrified of his tormentors. It is the fear that a child has for a father whom he adores, a father he never wants to let down or disappoint. Luther called it filial fear. Filial fear is born out of a spirit of enormous respect, love, and admiration.

True worship involves the reading of Scripture in an attitude of reverence, where we cling to every word and delight in hearing it. Today's worship is different from the Puritan worship of our nation's early history, which often involved the reading of a chapter from the Old Testament and a chapter from the New Testament. We are told that today the average attention span for listening to the reading of the Word is about ten verses. So a Scripture text is selected on the assumption that more than ten verses will lose the audience.

Next the confession mentions **the sound preaching and conscionable hearing of the Word.** This addresses the shepherd and the sheep. Not only does God want the Scriptures to be read, but He wants the Scriptures to be interpreted by preaching. Nothing is said about dynamic, exciting, interesting, eloquent, fascinating preaching. Only one word is used to describe the preaching: *sound.* God's concern is that preaching be sound and biblical. Today, people jump from church to church because they are seeking sound preaching, not psychology lessons, entertainment, or essays on self-esteem. The churches are not empty where ministers preach the Word of God faithfully and soundly. There is no reason why we should abandon our commitment to the sound preaching of the Word of God.

Preaching is only part of the equation. Not only is the preacher held accountable to God for sound preaching, but also the congregation is held accountable to God for the **conscionable hearing of the Word.** As the preacher is to preach soundly, so the congregation is to listen soundly.

Calvin wrote that even the greatest saints, while they are praying, have minds that wander. This is how we deal with God. We go to sleep during the preaching of His Word. Our minds wander while we are on our knees praying to Him, when we should be most fervent in our intercession. Even the disciples couldn't stay awake with Jesus. It is not in our nature always to be eager to hang on every word of the proclamation of Scripture. But it is our duty as believers to do whatever is necessary to keep ourselves awake and attentive. We are responsible for the **conscionable hearing of the Word.**

Singing of psalms with grace in the heart; as also, the due administration and worthy receiving of the sacraments instituted by Christ, are all parts of the ordinary religious worship of God. This reference to singing mentions only the singing of psalms. Because of this, some churches have practiced exclusive psalmody. They believe that in corporate worship God approves of the singing of the Psalms, which constituted the choral music of Israel, and nothing else. Other Reformed groups that follow the Westminster Confession have also included in their worship the singing of hymns and spiritual songs. Paul, in Ephesians 5:19, speaks of psalms, hymns, and spiritual songs. The church has a rich history of hymnody that has informed her worship.

In every generation, there are enormous controversies over which hymns are appropriate for singing in worship. Probably few periods in church history have had more controversy about church music than we currently have, particularly in the United States. We have seen a vast movement of contemporary and experimental worship motivated by a desire to reach out to a culture that has become more and more secularized. New songs and new hymns have been written and introduced into the life of the church.

In this controversy over contemporary forms of worship, some people assume that if a church uses only contemporary music, it has embraced the full paradigm of contemporary worship. That is not necessarily the case. We have to distinguish between contemporary music and contemporary forms of worship. Virtually all churches that are experimenting with contemporary forms of worship use contemporary music, but not all churches that use contemporary music are committed to a totally contemporary form of worship.

Every hymn sung in the church today, at some point in church history, was new. There is nothing particularly sacrosanct about a song's being old. What generally happens is that the better songs and hymns survive the test of time and endure in the life of the church.

There is a difference between good music, mediocre music, and poor music. The confession stresses that the kind of music we use in worship, in terms of both the tune and the words, is important. The Psalms were vital in the life of God's people, and singing was a significant element of biblical worship as it was designed by God. Therefore, it certainly is clear from Scripture that we ought to be raising our voices in song in the context of worship. The music that we use, obviously, ought to bring honor and glory to God. The singing of songs has a unique ability to penetrate the mind and the heart, and if we are singing songs that express bad theology, we are undermining the truths of God's Word.

The confession says that we are to sing psalms **with grace in the heart**. Those who argue in favor of contemporary music often make the point that the old style of music is foreign to people in today's culture. It is not moving to their souls, and when they sing the older hymns, they are only going through the motions. There has been an effort to put the content of the music into the forms, structures, and sounds with which young people are familiar. The confession teaches that when we sing, it is to be with grace in our hearts. We are to sing in a spiritual mood and not in empty recitation, mouthing the words. We are to think about what we are singing.

One of the difficulties in the life of the church is to achieve a balance of nurture. The New Testament calls upon us to move beyond the milk of the Word to the meat, to the weightier matters, as we grow to spiritual maturity (Heb. 5:12–14). The same principle can be applied to the music that we use. There is a nurturing process, where part of our growth is to learn how to express ourselves with great music.

The Scriptures tell of occasions when songs were sung to celebrate God's victory on behalf of His people. At the time of the exodus, there was the Song of Moses (Ex. 15:1–18)—"The horse and his rider he has thrown into the sea" (v. 1)—celebrating the victory over the Egyptians. In Judges 5, we have the Song of Deborah, celebrating the victory that God gave to the Israelites. In the New Testament, there are several hymns celebrating the birth of Jesus. There is the *Benedictus* of Zacharias (Luke 1:68–79), the *Nunc Dimittis* of Simeon (Luke 2:29–32), and the *Magnificat* of Mary (Luke 1:46–55). In Revelation 5:9–10, we are told that in the new heaven and the new earth, the Lord will give us a new song. The purpose of that song will be to celebrate the final consummation of the kingdom of our Lord. These great songs celebrate the victory of God on behalf of His people, and so we are to sing them from the heart and with grace.

As also, the due administration and worthy receiving of the sacraments instituted by Christ, are all parts of the ordinary religious worship of God. Here the importance of the proper administration and the worthy receiving of the sacraments in a solemn and sacred manner is emphasized. The word *sacrament* indicates that these are special forms of worship that Jesus Himself instituted during His ministry. These sacraments are to be handled in a spirit of profound reverence.

The church has historically established rules for the observation of the sacraments. When the church establishes rules and regulations, there must be some biblical basis for them. The administration of the sacraments is typically restricted to the clergy and to the elders in the church, a regulation that is rooted is the injunction that the Lord's Supper is not to be observed in an unworthy manner. We know that in the Corinthian church, great abuses arose with respect to the celebration of the Lord's Supper. This caused the Apostle Paul to write to those at Corinth and spell out in some detail the importance of celebrating the Lord's Supper in a godly and proper manner (1 Cor. 11:20–34). The responsibility for the oversight of the congregation is given to the pastors and elders, and part of their duty is to make sure that the sacraments are administered properly. The elders are to protect the people from eating and drinking the sacraments in an unworthy manner. Even though most churches restrict the administration of the sacraments, unordained people are often allowed to administer the sacraments in cases of extreme necessity. For example, Christians in a prison camp during a war with no ordained minister available can appoint someone in their midst to lead them in worship and in the administration of the Lord's Supper. But under ordinary circumstances, the sacraments may be administered only by those who have been ordained and set apart.

These, we are told, are all parts of the ordinary religious worship of God: beside religious oaths, vows, solemn fastings, and thanksgivings upon special occasions, which are, in their several times and seasons, to be used in an holy and religious manner. This indicates that there are special services that the church holds in addition to its normal weekly corporate worship. There may be a feast, for example, at Thanksgiving or at Christmas, or special holy days during the week before

Easter, as on Maundy Thursday, when there are special opportunities for worship.

> 6. Neither prayer, nor any other part of religious worship, is now, under the gospel, either tied unto, or made more acceptable by any place in which it is performed, or towards which it is directed: but God is to be worshiped everywhere, in spirit and truth; as, in private families daily, and in secret, each one by himself; so, more solemnly in the public assemblies, which are not carelessly or willfully to be neglected, or forsaken, when God, by his Word or providence, calleth thereunto.

Neither prayer, nor any other part of religious worship, is now, under the gospel, either tied unto, or made more acceptable by any place in which it is performed, or towards which it is directed. In the prescriptions for praying to God, our prayers, made to Him in the privacy of our home, are as acceptable to God as the prayers that we make in church on Sunday. We are not constrained, like people in other religions, to face toward the east, or toward Mecca, or toward Jerusalem while we pray. As Jesus taught the woman of Sychar (John 4:23), "True worshipers will worship the Father in spirit and truth, for the Father is seeking such people to worship him."

God is to be worshiped everywhere, in spirit and truth; as, in private families daily, and in secret, each one by himself; so, more solemnly in the public assemblies, which are not carelessly or willfully to be neglected, or forsaken, when God, by his Word or providence, calleth thereunto. It is our sacred duty to be engaged in worship that is acceptable to God daily, not simply to be engaged in worship on a weekly basis.

In addition to the corporate worship on the Lord's Day in our solemn assemblies, we are also to have a daily devotion unto God with our families, as well as by ourselves. We are to enter His presence in prayer, study His Word, and worship Him in private and in our families. We are especially warned in Scripture not to neglect the assembling together of the saints (Heb. 10:25). Christians have a special obligation to gather on the Lord's Day for corporate worship, to participate in what is called the communion of the saints, the body of Christ. One's relationship to a wife, to a husband, to children, or to parents will never save one in the sight of God. The only faith that is acceptable to God is the faith that we ourselves have. In that sense, Christianity employs a kind of rugged individualism. On the other hand, every time the Lord redeems an individual, He places that individual in a group, in a body, because no Christian is to live in isolation from other Christians. We are to be part of the body of Christ.

The group itself is gifted. Paul teaches in 1 Corinthians 12 that God empowers the body with different offices and with different gifts. Using that metaphor of the body, the ear cannot say to the eye, or the eye to the nose, "I don't need you." Just as our physical body is a marvelous unity of different parts, so each member of the church serves the whole spiritual body in a significant way. Not everyone is called to be a preacher, a teacher, an administrator, or an evangelist. Different gifts are given by God to individual people. However, the whole church is to be involved in preaching, teaching, and evangelism. There are many things that we can do, without being an actual evangelist, to make sure that evangelism takes place. We may not teach in the church, but we must make sure that there is proper teaching going on in the church.

Every Christian has been gifted by the Holy Spirit for ministry. That is the big difference between the Old and the New Testaments. In the Old Testament, an isolated group of people were especially endowed by God. They were empowered by the Holy Spirit to lead the people. But on the Day of Pentecost, the Spirit of God was poured out on all of God's people, and Paul tells us that every person in the body has been gifted by the Spirit with different gifts. A person may not yet know what his gift is, but there is a gift and a God-given ability to serve Him and His church. Every Christian is supposed not only to be present in the worship of the church, but also to be involved in some measure in the ministry of the church. The whole church is to do the ministry, not hire someone to do it for them. The minister's job is to watch over the flock and to enable the church to perform its outreach.

The Lord says that we are not to neglect the gathering together of ourselves in corporate worship (Heb. 10:24–25). It is as if the church operates in concentric circles. It has been observed that 20 percent of the people do 80 percent of the work and give 80 percent of the financial support. The people in the center of the circle are the core of the church. They are the people who are in church every Sunday that they can possibly be. They are the ones who attend Sunday school, who are present for every special event, who are involved in the building program, and who come out for the work days. They are actively serving.

The second circle is that group that comes to church on a regular basis, but only on Sunday morning, never Sunday evening, and never for special events during the week. They never participate in any of the outreach and service programs or projects of the church. Third, there are those people who are peripherally involved in the church. They come once a month or once every two months. They attend sporadically. They are involved at the edges of the life of the church.

The confession here incorporates the New Testament command not to neglect the assembling together of the saints. It is our spiritual duty to be present every single week in corporate worship, unless we are providentially hindered. We should enjoy it and want to be there. There are, of course, times when we don't feel like participating and are not enthusiastic about corporate worship. At those times, we must come anyway because it is our duty. Our duty does not stop with church attendance on Sunday morning. The duty of every Christian is to exercise whatever gifts God has given him in the life and ministry of the church.

One of the principles of the Reformation expounded by Martin Luther was the principle of the priesthood of all believers. Luther and the confession made the point that the work of the church is not limited to the clergy. Every person in the church is to participate in the priesthood of Christ and to be Christ to our neighbor. As a member of a visible church of the body of Christ, we become an arm, a leg, an eye, or an ear, and though we partake and are nurtured, we are also there to serve Christ in the work of the ministry of the church. We are all called to that task.

7. As it is the law of nature, that, in general, a due proportion of time be set apart for the worship of God; so, in his Word, by a positive, moral, and perpetual commandment binding all men in all ages, he hath particularly appointed one day in seven, for

a Sabbath, to be kept holy unto him: which, from the beginning of the world to the resurrection of Christ, was the last day of the week; and, from the resurrection of Christ, was changed into the first day of the week, which, in Scripture, is called the Lord's day, and is to be continued to the end of the world, as the Christian Sabbath.

It is the law of nature, that, in general, a due proportion of time be set apart for the worship of God. The confession appeals initially to the law of nature. This can be understood in more than one way. On the one hand, in Romans 1, the Apostle Paul speaks about the general revelation that God gives of Himself in and through the created order, or what we would call natural revelation. Natural revelation reveals the eternal power and deity of God. This revelation leaves men without excuse because the fundamental sin of the human race is the refusal to honor God as God or to be grateful. We see the proclivity among fallen people to exchange the glory of God for a lie, and to serve and worship the creature rather than the Creator, thus entering into idolatry. Paul says in Romans 1 that, in and through nature, God so manifests Himself and reveals enough of His character that the creature is obligated to worship Him. Nature itself teaches us that we ought to give due attention to the worship of the Creator.

That is one way in which to understand the opening line of section 7, and it seems to be the proper one. However, there could be an underlying assumption here that is not spelled out in detail. That has to do with the institution of the Sabbath day. The debate goes on among biblical scholars as to whether the Sabbath was instituted as a creation ordinance, which was the view of the Puritans and many Continental believers. Others argue that it was not instituted until the time of Moses.

The question of the Sabbath's time of institution is closely related to the question of its scope. If the Sabbath day was instituted in creation, it was given to all mankind, like the institution of marriage. In that case, the Sabbath day should be honored and regulated by the civil government, just as marriage is. On the other hand, if the Sabbath was given as part of the law of Moses, it was arguably given only to Jews and perhaps also to Christians to observe.

If the Sabbath was instituted in creation, that would explain why many states instituted blue laws, which regulated behavior on the Sabbath day. These laws did not command people to go to church, but they limited commerce on that day to what was "necessary," so that people could have a regular opportunity to rest from their labors. Those laws were based upon the principle that the Sabbath was a law of nature, established by God for the welfare of all people, not simply the tenet of a particular religion.

The idea that the Sabbath was instituted in creation is challenged by some scholars who argue that there is no record of people (such as the patriarchs) observing it until the time of the Mosaic covenant. This, of course, is an argument from silence. Is the practice of people before the time of Moses—or the Bible's silence about it—really normative for us? Would the practice of polygamy at that time be normative for us?

What really matters is whether the Bible explicitly teaches that the Sabbath was instituted in creation. The Old Testament record of creation shows that God's work of creation extended through six days, and that He rested on the seventh day and hallowed it. Because of that account in Genesis, the majority report throughout church history has been that God did sanctify the Sabbath day in creation. By "hallowing" the Sabbath, God consecrated it, setting it apart as special and holy.

One could argue that the Sabbath day was hallowed in creation, but that the obligation to keep it holy was not given until Moses. However, it would seem that if God hallowed something in creation and made it holy, He was not doing that for Himself, but for us, and therefore that we are obligated to keep it holy.

So, in his Word, as distinct from the law of nature, by a positive, moral, and perpetual commandment, God has established the Sabbath. God did not institute the Sabbath and just leave it at that, but gave specific, particular rules and regulations regarding the Sabbath under the Mosaic economy. This positive legislation implements the commandment to keep the Sabbath day holy (Ex. 20:8–11), found in the moral law, the Ten Commandments, which state the universal and perpetual norms upon which specific legislation is based.

According to the Reformers, the ceremonial law and the dietary laws were fulfilled in Christ and are therefore abrogated. But the moral law of the old covenant remains in force in the Christian economy. The Westminster divines speak of the Sabbath in terms of moral and positive law, and, in their judgment (unlike that of Augustine), the Sabbath day is part of the moral law of the Old Testament.

The next statement makes it all the more clear which position the confession is taking. In his Word, by a positive, moral, and perpetual commandment binding all men in all ages, he hath particularly appointed one day in seven, for a Sabbath, to be kept holy unto him: which, from the beginning of the world to the resurrection of Christ, was the last day of the week. The confession clearly takes the position that the Sabbath is a perpetual obligation, not just for Jews, but for all men in all ages. From the beginning of the world to the resurrection of Christ, the Sabbath day was the seventh day of the week. The Sabbath was the seventh day of the week from creation onward—not just from Moses but from the beginning of the world.

But from the resurrection of Christ, the Sabbath was changed into the first day of the week, which, in Scripture, is called the Lord's day, and is to be continued to the end of the world, as the Christian Sabbath. The Sabbath day itself is simply one day in seven, not a particular day. The Puritans, especially Jonathan Edwards, argued that the Sabbath day is to be observed simply on a one-day-in-seven rotation. Calvin declared that it could be every Wednesday if the church agreed on it. There is ample evidence that the earliest Christians came together on the first day of the week to worship God and celebrate the Lord's Supper because Christ rose from the dead on that day. The first day of the week became known as the Lord's Day (Rev. 1:10). Christ's resurrection sanctified the first day of the week. He is the Lord of the Sabbath (Mark 2:28), and He brings His people together for worship on His day.

The resurrection provides a strong testimony to one of the elements of the classic Sabbath. The Sabbath day in the Old Testament looked to the past, to the work of creation. God created the world in six days and rested on the seventh day, and that was recalled by observing the Sabbath day. In addition to looking to the past, there is also a looking ahead to the future. The Sabbath day in Israel was a sign, something that signifies something greater. For example, the sign of the Noahic covenant was the rainbow. God took an ordinary thing like a rainbow and gave it significance, so that when it is seen in the sky, it corroborates God's promise to every living creature. In that sense, the Sabbath day is an outward sign of God's promise to give everlasting rest to His people. Every time the Sabbath day is observed, it not only looks back to the past and recalls God's work of creation, but it also points to the future, underscoring God's work of redemption for us.

On Sunday mornings, when the saints gather to worship God corporately, it should be a foretaste of heaven. We have an opportunity to stop our normal labor, to come together for spiritual refreshment, and to serve and worship God by offering our praise to Him. We should delight in the promises that He gives to His people regarding the future as we look forward to joining the heavenly assembly.

Tombstones used to carry the standard abbreviation RIP, "Rest in Peace." Our forefathers understood that death was the transition to our heavenly rest, which is not a rest that indicates inactivity. When God rested on the Sabbath day, He did not sleep for twenty-four hours. He rested from His work of creation and delighted in His own glory. When we enter into our rest, we rest from travail, from struggle, and from the sweat of our brows. We rest from pain, from internal conflict, and from anguish. We enter the joy and peace that the Holy Spirit will give us in heaven. That promise of heaven is communicated every Sabbath day. That is why there is perpetual, ongoing, sacramental significance to the Sabbath day, at least until the final consummation of heaven and earth and the restoration of creation.

8. This Sabbath is then kept holy unto the Lord, when men, after a due preparing of their hearts, and ordering of their common affairs beforehand, do not only observe an holy rest, all the day, from their own works, words, and thoughts about their worldly employments and recreations, but also are taken up, the whole time, in the public and private exercises of his worship, and in the duties of necessity and mercy.

We find a division among Reformed theologians on how the Sabbath day is to be observed. Both the Continental believers and the Puritans believed that the seventh day was to be observed, but they differed as to how it was to be observed. They agreed that Christians are required to worship on the Sabbath day, which is set apart in the New Testament as the day when the people of God come together. We are not to neglect the assembling together of the saints on the Lord's Day (Heb. 10:24–25).

The communion of saints includes us and the saints who have gone before us, who are now in glory. When we gather to worship, we are in a mystical situation where we enter the heavenly sanctuary, not only the earthly sanctuary. We enter the presence of the Lord, the angels, the arch-angels, and the spirits of just men made perfect (Heb. 12:22–24), and we are part of the corporate worship of the body of Christ everywhere. We are in a huge congregation, spiritually speaking, as we engage in worship. There is a common time throughout the world when the people of God come together.

This Sabbath is then kept holy unto the Lord, when men, after a due preparing of their hearts, . . . observe an holy rest. The confession calls on people not only to keep the Sabbath day holy but to prepare for the Sab-bath day—an idea that has been all but completely eclipsed in our culture today. That preparation includes a spiritual preparation and preparation in other ways. Think, for example, of the gathering of the manna by the people of Israel in the wilderness. A double portion fell on the sixth day of the week, and the people collected twice the usual amount, so there would be no need to gather more on the seventh day. There was cessation from normal domestic chores, since the preparations for the Sabbath day were made in advance. The entire day could then be given over to rest from normal labor and for worship. That tradition extended long into Christian history, particularly among the Puritans. They would prepare double meals on the sixth day, so that there would be no need for that kind of labor on the seventh day.

Jesus taught that it was lawful to do good on the Sabbath day, such as pulling an animal out of a pit. His disciples picked corn on the Sabbath day because they were hungry, and the Pharisees rebuked Him for per-mitting such work on the Sabbath. Jesus responded that they needed to eat, and that the Sabbath is made for man, not man for the Sabbath. He, as the Lord of the Sabbath, gave His verdict on some of these matters.

The church, through the ages, has followed Jesus' teaching by permitting *works of mercy* and *works of necessity* on the Sabbath. We need to keep this in mind as we study this section.

In addition to preparing for physical needs, there is also the idea of spiritual preparation. For example, the Puritans looked in joyous anticipation to the coming of the Sabbath day. They gave extra diligence to their prayers to ready their souls for the taste of heaven involved with the Lord's Day. In practical terms, that meant that on the night before the Sabbath, they had a good sleep in order to be rested. They didn't attend church tired and inattentive because of late hours on Saturday night. The preparation was both a physical and a spiritual preparation for the enjoyment of the Sabbath day.

The notion exists that Jonathan Edwards' idea of God was that of a wrathful tyrant, always exercising His judgment and sending people to hell. But a search of all his writings revealed that the two words that occur most frequently are "sweetness" and "excellency." Edwards constantly extolled the sweetness and the excellency of God. He was a man who took delight in the things of God.

The Puritans prepared their souls and looked forward to the Sabbath day as the highlight of the week, not because they could cease from work, but because it was the opportunity for their soul to bask in the things of God and take full delight in them. Their worship services lasted two or more hours.

Christians should be prepared to **observe an holy rest, all the day, from their own works, words, and thoughts about their worldly employments and recreations.** Here is the chief and principal point of difference between the Continental view of the Sabbath and the Puritan view of the Sabbath. It was the Puritan view that won out in the Westminster Confession. The Puritans believed that the Sabbath day was to be taken up in worship, in the study of the things of God, and in doing errands of mercy. It was not to include things like going on picnics, playing badminton, swimming, or any of the recreational activities that are commonplace on the Sabbath day in our culture. The Continentals believed that though the Sabbath day should indeed be given principally to worship, there still was an opportunity for restful recreation. The whole idea of recreation was that the body was re-created by having rest and fellowship on the Sabbath day.

To see how these views collided, imagine the consternation of John Knox, who was expelled from England during the reign of Bloody Mary and first sought refuge in Germany and finally went to Calvin's Geneva. Knox was shocked when he arrived in Geneva and found Calvin, with his family, lawn bowling on the Sabbath day. Calvin took the Continental view, while Knox took the Puritan view. This difference among Reformed thinkers has gone on for a long time.

The difference is based on Isaiah 58:13:

> If you turn back your foot from the Sabbath,
> from doing your pleasure on my holy day,
> and call the Sabbath a delight
> and the holy day of the LORD honorable;
> if you honor it, not going your own ways,
> or seeking your own pleasure, or talking idly. . . .

If God's people do these things, then He promises to bless them. The Puritans inferred from the word "pleasure" in this passage that any kind of recreation was prohibited, because recreation is an indulgence in pleasure.

This would indicate that the prophet Isaiah, as an agent of revelation, added a new restriction to the Sabbath day that was not earlier set forth in the law of the Old Testament for regulating the Sabbath day. If God wanted to add a new stipulation to the law given through Moses, it would have been His prerogative to do so, and He could have done so through the mouth of the prophet Isaiah. However, the Old Testament prophets functioned more broadly as the reformers of Israel, not as lawgivers. From a covenant perspective, their chief function was that of prosecuting attorneys. God had entered into a covenant, a legal pact with stipulations or terms, with the people of Israel. Part of the law, or the stipulation of that covenant agreement between God and Israel, had to do with the observance of the Sabbath day. God told His people what they were allowed to do and what they were not allowed to do on the Sabbath day.

When the people broke the contract, they broke the law, and God sent His prosecuting attorneys, the prophets, to call them to task. The prophets weren't revolutionaries; they were reformers. They didn't come to change the law of Israel. For example, in Jerusalem, Jeremiah saw the people involved in temple worship and chastised them because they kept repeating, "This is the temple of the LORD, the temple of the LORD, the temple of the LORD." He said, "You trust in deceptive words to no avail" (Jer. 7:4, 8). Jeremiah warned that God would destroy Jerusalem and the temple because the people made a mockery out of true religion by mindlessly going through the motions of worship. The religion of Israel had degenerated into formalism, externalism, and ritualism. Their hearts were not in their worship.

God, speaking through the prophets, said:

> I hate, I despise your feasts,
> and I take no delight in your solemn assemblies.
> Even though you offer me your burnt offerings and grain offerings,
> I will not accept them;
> and the peace offerings of your fattened animals,
> I will not look upon them. (Amos 5:21–22)

It may seem that the prophets were saying, "Get rid of the sacrifices; get rid of the temple; get rid of the rites and the forms and the externals of Jewish worship," but their concern was to stop the pagan rites, to get rid of what had been brought into the religious life of Israel from the Canaanites. The prophets called the people back to the original terms of their covenant with God. The function of the prophets wasn't to add new burdens but to call the people back to the original terms. That is why it is unlikely that Isaiah was adding new regulations regarding the celebration of the Sabbath day.

The Puritans misunderstood the word "pleasure." The Israelites knew God's law, but they were violating it commercially. They didn't want to lose their profits by closing their business on the seventh day or giving their fields a rest every seven years or giving their domestic animals and servants one day off in seven. Their "pleasure" was what pleased them: to continue doing business on the Sabbath day. God said, "If you turn from your pleasure and do what I commanded you and honor Me, then I will open up heaven and bless you." The rebuke of the prophet was, "You people are doing what you please and what you want to do on the Sabbath day, instead of what God wants you to do." It really had nothing to do with recreation; it had to do chiefly with commerce.

Both the Continental and the Puritan views on the Sabbath are tolerated within the Reformed community. Each takes a strong view of the central importance of worship and delighting in the things of God. The Westminster Shorter Catechism, which is built on the substance of the confession, asks as its very first question, "What is the chief end of man?" The answer is, "Man's chief end is to glorify God, and to enjoy Him forever."

The allure of sin is its pleasure for a season, but no sin has ever given joy. Practically speaking, we know the difference between pleasure and joy. When we are in God's presence and we are pleased to do what He wants of us, there is real joy. It is not the fleeting pleasure that the culture describes, but the joy the Scriptures speak of in terms of blessedness. Something profound and substantive, which penetrates into our very souls and gives us a sense of well-being, is that which we call joy. When in prison, Paul said, "Now I rejoice in my sufferings for your sake" (Col. 1:24), even though he was experiencing pain, not pleasure. He experienced joy because he knew for whom he was suffering, and he was willing to participate in the pain for Christ's sake. That is why he could command us to rejoice and to learn the joy of the Lord, which is one of the fruits of the Spirit.

We should be the world's most joyful people because we are the most blessed. It is difficult to understand why Christians violate the tenth commandment—"You shall not covet" (Ex. 20:17). How could we envy anyone when we have inherited the riches of eternity and have been given the pearl of great price? Anything else, any other benefit that we get in this world, is just the sprinkles on top of the ice cream cone. We are to enjoy God and to do what pleases Him.

Men . . . are taken up, the whole time, in the public and private exercises of his worship, and in the duties of necessity and mercy. This is also problematic, and it's a question again of logic. This sentence contains the idea that the only things we are allowed to do on the Sabbath day is worship and do works of mercy, like visiting shut-ins, going to the hospital, and doing mercy ministry. The argument that the Puritans gave for this was that the New Testament shows Jesus doing these things on the Sabbath day. He got into controversies with the Pharisees because He healed on the Sabbath day, and He did works of mercy on that day.

The example of Jesus doing works of mercy on the Sabbath day shows us that if Jesus, who was sinless, did works of mercy on the Sabbath day, then it is permissible for us to do works of mercy on the Sabbath. However, the fact that Jesus did works of mercy on the Sabbath day does not imply that we *must* do works of mercy on the Sabbath day. To infer that would go beyond what the text of Scripture actually says.

It is a good idea to follow Jesus' example of doing works of mercy, but there is also plenty of time on the Sabbath day to be engaged in worship and the study of the Scriptures, to visit people in the hospital, and to take an hour's nap on Sunday afternoon. We may rest on the Sabbath day. The primary focus of the Sabbath day originally was to provide rest for people. So it is not best to say that our whole time has to be taken up with worship and doing works of necessity and mercy. There is also time to enjoy fellowship and to rest.

Of Lawful Oaths and Vows

1. A lawful oath is a part of religious worship, wherein, upon just occasion, the person swearing solemnly calleth God to witness what he asserteth, or promiseth, and to judge him according to the truth or falsehood of what he sweareth.

2. The name of God only is that by which men ought to swear, and therein it is to be used with all holy fear and reverence. Therefore, to swear vainly, or rashly, by that glorious and dreadful Name; or, to swear at all by any other thing, is sinful, and to be abhorred. Yet, as in matters of weight and moment, an oath is warranted by the Word of God, under the new testament as well as under the old; so a lawful oath, being imposed by lawful authority, in such matters, ought to be taken.

3. Whosoever taketh an oath ought duly to consider the weightiness of so solemn an act, and therein to avouch nothing but what he is fully persuaded is the truth: neither may any man bind himself by oath to anything but what is good and just, and what he believeth so to be, and what he is able and resolved to perform.

4. An oath is to be taken in the plain and common sense of the words, without equivocation, or mental reservation. It cannot oblige to sin; but in anything not sinful, being taken, it binds to performance, although to a man's own hurt. Nor is it to be violated, although made to heretics, or infidels.

5. A vow is of the like nature with a promissory oath, and ought to be made with the like religious care, and to be performed with the like faithfulness.

6. It is not to be made to any creature, but to God alone: and, that it may be accepted, it is to be made voluntarily, out of faith, and conscience of duty, in way of thankfulness for mercy received, or for the obtaining of what we want, whereby we more strictly bind ourselves to necessary duties; or, to other things, so far and so long as they may fitly conduce thereunto.

7. No man may vow to do anything forbidden in the Word of God, or what would hinder any duty therein commanded, or which is not in his own power, and for the performance whereof he hath no promise of ability from God. In which respects, popish monastical vows of perpetual single life, professed poverty, and regular obedience, are so far from being degrees of higher perfection, that they are superstitious and sinful snares, in which no Christian may entangle himself.

N ormally, when creedal statements are made, the focal point is on doctrine, on theological principles. We may wonder why the Westminster divines would consider lawful oaths and vows important enough to devote an entire chapter to the subject. The answer may be found in the book of James, which articulates many important spiritual and ethical principles that are to inform our lives. Near the end of the book, he writes: "But above all . . ." (James 5:12), evidently introducing something of special importance.

The early church indicated that the author of this book was Jesus' brother James, who was converted after Christ's resurrection. If that is true, James would have been familiar with his brother's teachings. From a historical perspective, then, James would have had insights into the teachings of Jesus that others in the early church did not have. That adds credibility and significance to the admonitions he gives.

James writes, "But above all, my brothers, do not swear, either by heaven or by earth or by any other oath, but let your 'yes' be yes and your 'no' be no, so that you may not fall under condemnation" (James 5:12). There are some people who understand this text to mean that the ultimate test of a Christian is whether he uses bad words in his vocabulary. But that is not at all what James meant. When he used the word "swear," he was talking about the solemn taking of oaths and vows.

It might seem as if he is saying that it is unlawful ever to take an oath or a vow. He then states positively, "Let your 'yes' be yes and your 'no' be no." That statement means that, among other things, a Christian should be a person whose word can be trusted. When we say yes, that should be what we mean. When we say no, we should not be dissembling. We should always say what we mean.

To understand what James is concerned about, we need to see what Scripture teaches us elsewhere about oaths and vows. Indeed, Scripture has much to say, and that is why there are seven sections in chapter 22 of the confession on this subject. In the Sermon on the Mount, Jesus gave a similar admonition to the one in James. He warned His disciples not to swear by the heavens, the altar, the temple, or that sort of thing (Matt. 5:33–37). He restricted and qualified that by which one may swear. There is a narrow range of legitimate vows and oaths, and a wide range of illegitimate ones.

The Apostle Paul frequently confirmed the truthfulness of what he was proclaiming by taking a vow or swearing an oath. For example, in Romans 9:1–4, he wrote: "I am speaking the truth in Christ—I am not lying; my conscience bears me witness in the Holy Spirit—that I have great sorrow and unceasing anguish in my heart. For I could wish that I myself were accursed and cut off from Christ for the sake of my brothers, my kinsmen according to the flesh. They are Israelites, and to them belong the adoption, the glory, the covenants, the giving of the law, the worship, and the promises." That was an extravagant statement, so he confirmed it with an oath.

The reason we have oaths and vows is that all people are liars. Romans 3:4 says so. As fallen men and women, we have an aversion to truth—not just to receiving the truth of God, but also to speaking the truth. The first liar encountered in Scripture was the serpent in Eden. That is why Jesus says in John 8:44 that Satan is "a liar and the father of lies." The difference between God and us is that God's word is always trustworthy. He never lies, whereas our words cannot be trusted implicitly.

The first assault against God recorded in Scripture is an attack on His truthfulness: "Did God actually say?" the serpent asked (Gen. 3:1). When Eve defended the truth of what God had said, the serpent suggested the very opposite. He lied to her, and he is therefore called the father of lies (John 8:44). On the other hand, God keeps His word. Our hope for redemption rests in our confidence that He will keep His promises. The covenants in the Bible are promises made by God. In Genesis 15, God confirmed His promise to Abraham by taking an oath.

It is one thing to believe that God exists. James 2:19 says that even the devils know that God exists. But Christianity is about believing God, not just believing that He exists. We must believe His Word and live on the basis of our trust that what He declares is the truth.

We have wedding services, where promises are made in the presence of every authority in the culture: friends, family, church, secular government, and God. It is one thing to promise fidelity to another person when no one is listening; it is something else to make that same promise in front of many people and many authorities. When we promise something out loud and there are witnesses, those people can call us on it and say, "You aren't keeping your promise." And even if the government, the church, friends, and family don't care, God does care. He gives the warning, "It is better that you should not vow than that you should vow and not pay" (Eccl. 5:5).

God established marriage and gives to us the sacred vow and oath that calls attention to the special, holy, and sacred dimension of the promise. Because we are weak and fallen, and because our words are not inherently trustworthy, God has given us the holy vow and oath, because it makes a difference.

Why do witnesses in a courtroom have to put their hand on the Bible, raise their right hand, and swear "to tell the truth, the whole truth, and nothing but the truth, so help me God"? Why doesn't the judge just say to the witness, "Please make sure you tell us the truth today"? While people try to throw God out of everything else in the culture, the government most likely isn't going to throw God out of the courtroom, because people understand the seriousness of taking an oath and they know the difference between telling a falsehood and committing perjury.

In the Decalogue, the third commandment is, "You shall not take the name of the LORD your God in vain" (Ex. 20:7). When we hear that, our first thought is that it prohibits blasphemy or cursing. Certainly it does prohibit those things, by extension, but mainly it has to do with using the name of God in an oath or a vow. The third commandment protects the sanctity of truth, which is vitally important to human relationships, and doing the truth—keeping our promises.

When we buy something on credit, we sign a promissory note that someone else is counting on for their livelihood. When we fail to pay the bill on time, we are breaking our word and stealing from someone else. That person who trusted our "yes" is harmed. When we say yes, we are going to do something—yes, we are going to be somewhere; or yes, we are going to pay our bill—and then we do not honor our commitment, we have broken trust. Think about how many problems have arisen in life because people break their word.

Just as the first commandment protects the purity of our worship, and the second commandment sets up barriers against idolatry, so the third commandment also deals with idolatry. We can swear on my mother's grave, on the pulpit, or on the Bible, but none of those things have any power to enforce our promise. There is only One who hears every promise we make and sees everything we do subsequent to making a promise. The only One who has the power to enforce that promise or to punish us if we break it, ultimately, is God. If we swear an oath by anything less than God, we are attributing divine dimensions to it, which is idolatry. Not to take the name of the Lord in vain means not to take an oath or a vow without full submission to the true character of God.

Having addressed some of the issues involved in the swearing of oaths and the taking of vows, let us turn our attention to the text of the confession.

1. A lawful oath is a part of religious worship, wherein, upon just occasion, the person swearing solemnly calleth God to witness what he asserteth, or promiseth, and to judge him according to the truth or falsehood of what he sweareth.

The confession has in view that a lawful oath is a part of religious worship. We don't usually think in those terms, but one of the ways in which we worship God is by calling on Him to be the witness and the enforcer of the oaths and the vows that we take.

Notice what is involved in a lawful oath: wherein, upon just occasion, the person swearing solemnly calleth God to witness what he asserteth, or promiseth. When we enter a courtroom or an ecclesiastical court to bear testimony, we are sworn in, and under oath we promise to tell the truth, the whole truth, and nothing but the truth, "so help me God." We are calling on God to be a witness to our testimony, so that if we bear false testimony against a person, we have not only violated the commandment that prohibits that, but we have also violated our relationship to God. We violate two commandments when we bear false witness. One is the ninth commandment: "You shall not bear false witness against your neighbor" (Ex. 20:16). The other is the third commandment: "You shall not take the name of the LORD your God in vain" (v. 7).

When we call on God to bear witness to us when we are lying, that is the ultimate insult to God. While we are falsely accusing our brother, we are calling on God to verify the truth of our accusation. A human being can sink no lower than that. Not only does our false testimony do violence to a fellow human being, but it also desecrates the character of God.

The traditional marriage ceremony begins, "Dearly beloved, we are gathered here in the presence of God and of these witnesses to unite this man and this woman in the holy bonds of marriage." The first appeal is a call on God to be a witness to the oaths or the promises that are about to be made.

The person taking an oath calls on God to judge him according to the truth or falsehood of what he sweareth. In the oath, we are calling on God not simply to witness it but also to judge what is said. We do that in the courtroom and also when we take a sacred oath in a marriage service, in an ordination service, or when joining a church. When we become a member of the church of Jesus Christ, we are required to make a public profession of faith and take vows of fidelity.

There are those who say, "I don't believe in doctrine." Every word of God is doctrine; every truth that is revealed to us about the person and work of Christ is doctrine. How can a person say, "I embrace Jesus Christ, but I don't believe in any doctrine"? That is a contradiction in terms. With the opposition to doctrine, denial of objective truth, and casual relativism of our day, truth is slain in the streets.

Underlining this entire section of the Westminster Confession is the sanctity of truth. It matters whether we keep our vows, because to keep a vow is to honor the truth. To make true statements in our testimony is not only to honor our fellow neighbor, but also to honor God, who is the fountain and source of all truth. "Let God be true though every one were a liar" (Rom. 3:4). We should be acutely conscious that, in our flesh, there is an enormous propensity for falsehood, deceit, promise-breaking, and covenant breaking. Conversion does not remove our corruption instantly. We have to struggle with lying for our entire life. Our own personal pilgrimage is more difficult when we live in a truth-denying world.

> 2. The name of God only is that by which men ought to swear, and therein it is to be used with all holy fear and reverence. Therefore, to swear vainly, or rashly, by that glorious and dreadful Name; or, to swear at all by any other thing, is sinful, and to be abhorred. Yet, as in matters of weight and moment, an oath is warranted by the Word of God, under the new testament as well as under the old; so a lawful oath, being imposed by lawful authority, in such matters, ought to be taken.

It's hard to imagine anyone writing a theological statement in our day that includes the word *abhorred*. We live in a culture that abhors abhorrence. The one thing we are not allowed to do is to hate anyone or anything. But here, the confession says, there are certain things that are so despicable, so noxious to God, that a Christian ought to abhor them. When we abhor something, we hate it with all our might. The bearing of false witness and the irreverent and flippant use of the name of God should make our blood curdle. We should hate lies so much that we would rather die than tell one. But many people will shrug and say, "We shouldn't lie under oath, and we shouldn't give false testimony, but everyone does it."

To swear vainly, or rashly, by that glorious and dreadful Name . . . is sinful, and to be abhorred. Who would call the name of God dreadful? The Westminster divines did, and they were learned and godly men, who wrote the confession with great care. They did not waste words or use them casually, and they wrote that the name of God is full of dread. Dread is a profound fear of something frightening. The first petition of the Lord's

Prayer is "Hallowed be your name" (Matt. 6:9). Every time we pray the Lord's Prayer, we pray that the name of God would be treated with supreme reverence and respect. It should involve a holy fear and trembling, so dreadful is that name. When people have a holy fear of misusing God's name, they will be careful not to swear by it falsely or use it in a vain and irreverent way. But when someone insincerely makes a promise before God or insincerely gives testimony asking God to be his witness and judge, he shows nothing but contempt for God and will indeed be judged by Him for that.

We are people whose ears have been deafened by the din of the culture around us, which routinely misuses God's name. We are surrounded by people who have no fear of God before their eyes and suffer from no dread. There is no trembling when they hear His name. We must not become calloused by living in that kind of environment. When we hear the name of God, a hush should come over our souls and we should be prepared to tremble.

The time of corporate worship is a sacred hour when we come into the presence of the living God to listen to His Word, to lift our prayers to Him, to offer the sacrifice of our praises. It is the most sacred hour of the week. The place where that takes place should be regarded as a dreadful, as well as a holy, place. We are coming into the presence of a holy God. We need to be reminded of the holy and of the sacred, because we live most of our lives in a profane environment.

The word *profane* originally meant "outside the temple," and it referred to anything that took place outside of the church. It did not necessarily mean something bad. Martin Luther said that every Christian is called to be a profane Christian, not in the sense that we are supposed to be wicked or corrupt, but in the sense that we are to take the truth of God out of the temple and into the world. The world is the mission field into which we go after we have been in the presence of the sacred in worship and have been energized and enabled to go out into the world. In current use, *profane* means something else, because the world is secular and pagan.

We live in a pagan country with pagan values and philosophies, and it is becoming more and more barbarian. We live in a nation that slaughters more than one million unborn babies every year. In God's sight, this is unspeakably evil and utterly abhorrent. Yet, the law of our land permits this. The sooner we understand where we live, the quicker we will understand that we are called to live a different kind of life, to embrace a different kind of ethic, and to minister to a profane world.

> 3. Whosoever taketh an oath ought duly to consider the weightiness of so solemn an act, and therein to avouch nothing but what he is fully persuaded is the truth: neither may any man bind himself by oath to anything but what is good and just, and what he believeth so to be, and what he is able and resolved to perform.

Whosoever taketh an oath ought duly to consider the weightiness of it. The Bible speaks about the glory of God, and in the previous section the confession spoke of His glorious name. The Bible tells us that the ark of the covenant was captured by the Philistines on the day that the sons of Eli were killed in battle. At the same time, Eli's daughter-in-law bore a son, and as she was dying she named him Ichabod, meaning "the glory has departed" (1 Sam. 4:21). The Hebrew word for "glory," *kabod*, literally means "heaviness or weightiness." We speak of weighty concepts or of a matter being taken lightly. We use this metaphor drawn from weight and apply it to the level or the realm of importance. To the Hebrews, the ultimate weightiness or significance was the *kabod* of God, the glory of God. The confession teaches that when we call on God in sacred oaths and vows, this is a weighty matter, because the glory of God is involved.

This section reminds us of the sober weightiness of any vow that is taken, any oath that is sworn. Ecclesiastes 5:5 says that it is better not to vow than to vow and not pay. So, before we take vows and make solemn promises under oath, we need to understand the seriousness of it. We tend to be somewhat cavalier in entering into marriage vows, church membership vows, ordination vows, and congregational vows.

The subject of this chapter is not simply oaths and vows but *lawful* oaths and vows. The Westminster divines understood that people sometimes take unlawful, unrighteous, and unjust oaths and vows. We are told that we ought not to vow to do anything that we are not fully persuaded is proper. A person may not bind himself by an oath to anything except what is **good and just, and what he is able and resolved to perform.** For

OF LAWFUL OATHS AND VOWS • 501

example, if someone promises to do something and then realizes that if he does what he promised, he will be sinning, then not only may he break that vow, but he must break it. He should never have entered into it in the first place. We find this problem when reading of Jephthah's vow in Judges 11:30–40.

> 4. An oath is to be taken in the plain and common sense of the words, without equivocation, or mental reservation. It cannot oblige to sin; but in anything not sinful, being taken, it binds to performance, although to a man's own hurt. Nor is it to be violated, although made to heretics, or infidels.

In the sports world, athletes often want to renegotiate their contracts. They have one good year and they want to tear up their contract and demand a raise. When they have a bad year, they are never heard to say, "Can we renegotiate my contract downward?" A contract is a contract, and the reason they get a three-year contract or a five-year contract is that the person who is paying the money takes the risk that they will be able to perform for three or five years. The athlete is taking the risk that he won't explode into such greatness that he could make ten times what he has already agreed upon. People make promises and then want to renege on their promises.

An oath is to be taken in the plain and common sense of the words, without equivocation, or mental reservation. That means we don't take a vow while never intending to keep it or while assigning an unusual or unexpected meaning to the terms of the vow. There is a saying in theological circles: "No one can write a creed so precise or tight that some dishonest person can't sign it." People sign creeds with studied ambiguity, with reservations, or by playing with words. That this happens in the church is, of course, a ghastly thing. A studied ambiguity is a word or a phrase that is ambiguous by design, so that people are free to interpret it in different ways. Words are used to equivocate.

It is to our shame when we tamper with the laws of perjury and of vows and oaths. The Westminster divines instruct: An oath is to be taken in the plain and common sense of the words. When we make a promise, we must not use language that gives us an escape hatch, so that we can later claim, "Well, that's not what I meant." We are to use language that is plain and clear and to use the words according to their commonsense meaning, because that is how they will be interpreted by those who hear them.

5. A vow is of the like nature with a promissory oath, and ought to be made with the like religious care, and to be performed with the like faithfulness.

6. It is not to be made to any creature, but to God alone: and, that it may be accepted, it is to be made voluntarily, out of faith, and conscience of duty, in way of thankfulness for mercy received, or for the obtaining of what we want, whereby we more strictly bind ourselves to necessary duties; or, to other things, so far and so long as they may fitly conduce thereunto.

These sections are here because of the third commandment: "You shall not take the name of the LORD your God in vain" (Ex. 20:7). It is also here because of the second commandment: "You shall not make for yourself a carved image" (v. 4), and because of the first commandment: "You shall have no other gods before me" (v. 3). That is, it is here to protect against our propensity toward idolatry. The oath is to be sworn to the true God, not to some part of the creation. To swear by the creature is to endow the creature with divine attributes, which is to engage in idolatry, whereby we serve and worship the creature rather than the Creator.

7. No man may vow to do anything forbidden in the Word of God, or what would hinder any duty therein commanded, or which is not in his own power, and for the performance whereof he hath no promise of ability from God. In which respects, popish monastical vows of perpetual single life, professed poverty, and regular obedience, are so far from being degrees of higher perfection, that they are superstitious and sinful snares, in which no Christian may entangle himself.

The Westminster Confession often articulates Reformation theology with contrary Roman Catholic thinking in view. The Reformers and the

Puritans disavowed the idea of perpetual vows of celibacy, of remaining unmarried, or of taking vows for lifelong poverty, as there is no necessary virtue in such vows. We do not take vows that ought not to be taken in the first place, and we certainly do not take vows that we know we cannot keep.

In summary, vows and oaths must be guarded jealously. They are not to be taken in a cavalier manner. Nor are they ever to be sworn before any creature as to assign or ascribe to the creature attributes that belong to God alone.

Righteous people are called to live by faith. To live in this manner means more than trusting God. It involves being trustworthy and faithful with respect to promises, oaths, and vows. As people of the Word, our word should be our bond.

Of the Civil Magistrate

1. God, the supreme Lord and King of all the world, hath ordained civil magistrates, to be, under him, over the people, for his own glory, and the public good: and, to this end, hath armed them with the power of the sword, for the defense and encouragement of them that are good, and for the punishment of evildoers.

2. It is lawful for Christians to accept and execute the office of a magistrate, when called thereunto: in the managing whereof, as they ought especially to maintain piety, justice, and peace, according to the wholesome laws of each commonwealth; so, for that end, they may lawfully, now under the new testament, wage war, upon just and necessary occasion.

3. Civil magistrates may not assume to themselves the administration of the Word and sacraments; or the power of the keys of the kingdom of heaven; or, in the least, interfere in matters of faith. Yet, as nursing fathers, it is the duty of civil magistrates to protect the church of our common Lord, without giving the preference to any denomination of Christians above the rest, in such a manner that all ecclesiastical persons whatever shall enjoy the full, free, and unquestioned liberty of discharging every part of their sacred functions, without violence or danger. And, as Jesus Christ hath appointed a regular government and discipline in his church, no law of any commonwealth should interfere with, let, or hinder, the due exercise thereof, among the voluntary members of any denomination of Christians, according to their own profession and belief. It is the duty of civil magistrates to protect the person and good name of all their people, in such an effectual manner as that no person be suffered, either

upon pretense of religion or of infidelity, to offer any indignity, violence, abuse, or injury to any other person whatsoever: and to take order, that all religious and ecclesiastical assemblies be held without molestation or disturbance.

4. It is the duty of people to pray for magistrates, to honor their persons, to pay them tribute or other dues, to obey their lawful commands, and to be subject to their authority, for conscience' sake. Infidelity, or difference in religion, doth not make void the magistrates' just and legal authority, nor free the people from their due obedience to them: from which ecclesiastical persons are not exempted, much less hath the pope any power and jurisdiction over them in their dominions, or over any of their people; and, least of all, to deprive them of their dominions, or lives, if he shall judge them to be heretics, or upon any other pretense whatsoever.

Why we have government, what its purpose and role are, and how governmental authority relates to the sovereign authority of God Himself are important considerations in this chapter on the civil magistrate.

1. God, the supreme Lord and King of all the world, hath ordained civil magistrates, to be, under him, over the people, for his own glory, and the public good: and, to this end, hath armed them with the power of the sword, for the defense and encouragement of them that are good, and for the punishment of evildoers.

Chapter 23 of the confession begins with the words **God, the supreme Lord and King of all the world, hath ordained civil magistrates, to be, under him, over the people, for his own glory, and the public good.** Virtually every aspect of this opening statement is in opposition to the assumptions that hold sway in our culture with respect to civil government. There was a crisis in the role of government in the first half of the twentieth century, which produced the greatest level of international conflict, violence, and warfare in recorded history. The level of armed conflict each century was calculated several years ago by a professor at Harvard University. The greatest era of peace was the first century. The second most peaceful century was the nineteenth century. The most violent century was the twentieth century. There is, therefore, a tendency on our part to assume that international conflict is normal.

Adolf Hitler and his Third Reich and Joseph Stalin and his Soviet Union illustrate what happens when government rebels and declares its independence from God. Increasingly, we hear rhetoric from people in the government and in the press about the separation of church and state. What they mean is the separation of the state from God. Their idea is that the civil government is not under God but independent of Him, that it has its own autonomous authority. Hitler, Stalin, and Mao Zedong in communist China all held that same assumption. It is a fearful thing to see governments declaring independence from God Himself.

In many European and Asian nations, a particular faith is supported financially by government taxation and politically by the power of the sword. Such a faith is called *established*. Those who oppose the establishment of a church are called *disestablishmentarians*. Pilgrims from many nations came to the shores of the New World to flee persecution because they were not in concert with the established church. Among the most significant of those groups were the English Puritans, who were Nonconformists—they refused to conform to the form of worship and government prescribed by the established Church of England. They found themselves under severe persecution in England, not only from the Roman Catholic Church during the reign of Mary I, but also from her successor, Queen Elizabeth, whose rigorous persecution of the Puritans caused them to flee. Various colonies in America had their own established churches, and they could not agree on an established church for the new nation. Instead, the principle of freedom of religion was enshrined in the First Amendment to the U.S. Constitution. This meant that the federal government could not establish a particular church.

The First Amendment does not express the idea that our nation is independent of God or that it was founded on atheism. It was actually self-consciously theistic in its origin, but refused to grant any particular theistic group favored status under the law.

First of all, the Westminster divines describe God as **the supreme**

Lord and King of all the world. It is significant that in the discussion of the role of the civil magistrate, they begin with an affirmation of the supremacy of God in His lordship and kingship over the world.

In the Old Testament, two of the most important titles given to Yahweh are *adonai* and *melek*. *Adonai* means "the one who is absolutely sovereign." It is translated in our English Bibles as "Lord" (as opposed to "LORD," which translates His personal name, Yahweh). *Melek* is translated as "king." To the Jew in Israel, God was viewed as both the sovereign Lord and the King of the nation of Israel, the supreme King over all the world. "The earth is the LORD's and the fullness thereof, the world and those who dwell therein" (Ps. 24:1). He is the Creator of all things; therefore, His realm and reign extend beyond the borders of Israel. He is the Most High God, and the theater of His operation is universal.

When the people of Israel clamored for a king, God spoke to them through the prophet Samuel and told them that because they rejected Him as their king, He would let them have a king. But their king would be like everyone else's kings. He would conscript their young people into the army, tax their property and income, and do other objectionable things. God let them have a king, but the king was never autonomous. He was always held accountable to the King's law.

When David sinned in his affair with Bathsheba, Nathan rebuked and confronted him. It was then that David penned his penitential psalm, Psalm 51. One of the statements that he made in that psalm was "Take not your Holy Spirit from me" (v. 11). David was not worried that God would take away the regenerating power of the Holy Spirit, because God never does that. What concerned him was that God might rescind His anointing of him as king. There, at least, David recognized God's authority over him. This became a major crisis in the history of Israel, when the wicked kings, such as Ahab, ruled as if the Lord could be ignored. They sought to be independent from the reign of God.

One of the central motifs in the Old and New Testaments is that of the kingdom of God. The New Testament work of Christ is couched in the language of the breaking through of the messianic kingdom. Almost every parable that Jesus told was a parable of the kingdom: "The kingdom of God is like. . . ." The gospel that Jesus preached, which was previously declared by John the Baptist, was a gospel of the kingdom: "The kingdom of God is at hand; repent and believe in the gospel" (Mark 1:15). The culmination of the ministry of Christ was not the resurrection but the ascension, when He was elevated and escorted on the clouds of glory into heaven. There, He received the throne of His Father, where He is and will be our King and Priest forever.

The Old Testament passage most frequently quoted in the New Testament is Psalm 110:1: "The LORD says to my Lord: 'Sit at my right hand, until I make your enemies your footstool.'" At the center of God's work of redemption is a political consideration. It is the city of God, the reign of God. The person who holds the highest political office in the universe is the Lord Jesus Christ. To Him we are to give our supreme allegiance and devotion. We are not Americans first and Christians second. Our highest loyalty, our first allegiance, is to the King of kings and the Lord of lords. That concept is seldom mentioned even in devout Christian circles.

John Guest came to the United States from Liverpool, England, as an evangelist in the 1960s. He spent most of his first week in Philadelphia, visiting all the historic sights. He went to antique stores that specialized in Revolutionary War memorabilia. He saw placards that said, "Don't tread on me" and "No taxation without representation," as well as an earlier one that declared, "We serve no sovereign here." John said to me, "That's in your blood as an American. How can I preach the kingdom of God to a people who have a built-in cultural allergy to monarchy?" That is a problem we have as we seek to understand the Bible. The kingdom of God does not exist by referendum. It is not a democracy. It is rooted and grounded in a principle of absolute monarchy, absolute sovereignty, where the Lord God Almighty reigns. Americans resist that.

Before we talk about government, we must understand that God is the supreme Lord and King of all the world. It is He who has ordained civil magistrates. In Romans 13, Paul says: "Let every person be subject to the governing authorities. For there is no authority except from God, and those that exist have been instituted by God" (v. 1). Another way to translate that last clause is, "The powers that be are appointed by God." We may struggle to think that God cast the deciding ballot in our national elections or that He appointed Adolf Hitler to be the chancellor of Germany and Joseph Stalin to rule over Russia. What Paul is saying, of course, is that all government is under God's authority. The Scriptures say, "The Most High rules the kingdom of men and gives it to whom he will" (Dan. 4:25). If, in His sovereign government of the earth, He installs a despicable person, that does not mean that God therefore sanctions everything the corrupt official does. He used Nebuchadnezzar, Belshazzar, and others to chasten His own people. He uses evil powers to achieve His own righteous goals. When Paul said that the governing powers are appointed by God, he was writing to the Roman Christians, who were on the threshold of living under the oppressive tyranny of Nero. Under Nero's decree, the Apostle Paul was executed.

What is government? The simplest, most basic definition is this: government is legal force. Governments are agencies that have the power and the legal right to coerce people to obey their dictates. Their laws are not simply suggestions but requirements. Laws are backed up by the law enforcement agencies that are established to ensure that the law is maintained. Every law that is passed restricts someone's freedom and exposes people to the violence of law enforcement if they fail to submit to that law. Governments must have legal force. If they don't, they are no more than advisory committees.

Earthly government started in the garden of Eden after the fall, when God sent Adam and Eve out of the garden and prohibited them from returning. He put a "No Trespassing" sign up in front of the gates to Paradise. He put an angel there with a flaming sword, which was an instrument of force. Had Adam and Eve tried to return, they would have been stopped by force.

Government is necessary because of evil. Augustine said that civil government is a necessary evil made necessary because of evil. We are sinners, and we have a propensity to violate other human beings, to commit injustices or cause bodily harm. We may take property or threaten life. People need to be protected by the civil magistrate, who is instituted and ordained by God to bear the sword. The magistrate has legitimate power and authority to protect us from one another.

The hierarchical structure of the universe, as God has ordained it, finds God Himself at the top. Immediately under God is Christ, to whom He has given all authority in heaven and on earth. Under Christ are the civil magistrates, such as kings, senators, presidents, governors, parents, employers, and teachers. There is an order of authority and of law. The definition for sin given by the Westminster Shorter Catechism is "any want of conformity unto, or transgression of, the law of God" (WSC 14). Where there is no law, there is no sin. God has delegated the right and authority to enact laws to lesser magistrates. He has not delegated to them the right to enact unjust laws. He never gives anyone the right to do wrong or to do evil. Authorities are there biblically, but the basic structure of government is to be under God and over the people.

Is vengeance bad? No, if vengeance were a bad thing, then God would have no part of it, because God cannot sin. But private vengeance—personal, vigilante vengeance—is bad, for God tells us, "Vengeance is mine, I will repay" (Rom. 12:19, quoting Deut. 32:35). He prohibits us from being the avengers of the wrongs that are done to us, because He knows that we are never interested in getting even; we want to get one up. If vengeance is left to us, we will commit an injustice by seeking our vindication. However, God does delegate vengeance to the civil magistrate. In the Old Testament, those who were wronged could go to the court for justice and for satisfaction. The same principle operates in the New Testament. The session of the church is a court, and if one person in the congregation violates another person in the congregation, the victim has the right to appeal to the session for justice. The victim does not have the right to take matters into his own hands and inflict punishment on the other person. Government is under God and over the people. However, our culture increasingly understands government to be over the people and independent of God.

Francis Schaeffer once said that his biggest concern for the church and for the people in the United States was statism, the increasing encroachment and dominion of the federal government in the lives of people: in the school, in the community, in the church, in all areas. One cannot turn around without bumping into the federal government. That was his major concern, and since he said that, the intrusion of the federal government in the lives of people has greatly increased.

God has ordained government **for his own glory, and the public good.** God did not create us for our glory. He created us for His glory, and God is glorified in His grace. When He saves a fallen sinner who does not deserve to be saved and so manifests His grace, that glorifies God. When He withholds His grace from a willful sinner and punishes with judgment, He manifests His justice, which glorifies God. There are two places where God is given all glory: heaven and hell. The sinner gets no glory in hell, but God does. Perfect righteousness is vindicated by divine punishment.

God ordains government, first of all, **for his own glory.** Nothing is more insulting to God's glory than our sin. God refuses to let insults to His glory go unpunished. Therefore, He established government to uphold righteousness and to punish wickedness and evil. That is why a sword guarded the gate of Eden. Why must we obey the civil magistrate? The Apostle Peter tells us to obey the civil magistrate for Christ's sake (1 Peter 2:13). How can my civil obedience glorify Christ? When I am a law-abiding citizen, I am submitting to a magistrate who is under the authority of Christ. If Christ delegates authority to that lesser authority, my submission to the lesser authority redounds to the honor of the One who delegated it. That is the principle that Paul sets forth in Romans 13. The main reason that we are called to be obedient to civil magistrates is to glorify God and honor Christ.

God has also ordained government for **the public good.** He has established government to protect people. There may be times when we think the best of all possible worlds would be a world without human government, but anarchy is absolute lawlessness. That is why, historically, political theorists have said that the most corrupt government is preferable to anarchy. That is why our forefathers tried to establish a system of government with checks and balances, so that there would be a division of power at the top to put restraints and restrictions on those in government to guard against moving toward oppressive dictatorship. Government exists both for God's glory and for our good, so that we can be protected from ourselves. It is to this end that God has armed government **with the power of the sword.**

> 2. It is lawful for Christians to accept and execute the office of a
> magistrate, when called thereunto: in the managing whereof,

> as they ought especially to maintain piety, justice, and peace, according to the wholesome laws of each commonwealth; so, for that end, they may lawfully, now under the new testament, wage war, upon just and necessary occasion.

Section 2 of chapter 23 begins, It is lawful for Christians to accept and execute the office of a magistrate, when called thereunto: in the managing whereof, as they ought especially to maintain piety, justice, and peace, according to the wholesome laws of each commonwealth. It may seem strange that the Westminster divines took the time to include in the confession an affirmation that it is legitimate for Christians to serve in offices of the state and to serve in the government. Throughout our country's history, we have assumed the lawful right of Christians so to serve, and we are accustomed to Christian believers running for elected office and being elected.

The confession was written, however, in the seventeenth century. The Reformation in the sixteenth century had opened up broad and spirited debate about the relationship between church and state. The particular nuances of this debate became exceedingly complex. We can, for simplicity's sake, reduce the views that arose at that time to three. One is what we call the *unity of church and state*. In this view, the church is subsumed under the state, or vice versa. The civil magistrate is also the ecclesiastical magistrate, or the ecclesiastical magistrate is also the civil magistrate. For much of church history, the papacy controlled political territories as well as exercising ecclesiastical jurisdiction. In this approach, there is a merging or confusing of church and state, with the tendency for the two to be grouped as one. There are those who believe that the goal of the Christian church, the earthly kingdom, is to manifest the heavenly kingdom, with the kingdoms of this world under the authority of the church. That would be a kind of theocracy, such as existed in the Old Testament.

In the theocratic state of Israel, there was a clear division of responsibility between the king and the priesthood. It was not the king's responsibility to offer sacrifices on behalf of the people; that was done by the priests. One of the five greatest kings in the Old Testament, who reigned for over fifty years, was named Uzziah. He ranked alongside David, Solomon, Hezekiah, and Josiah. For most of his reign, Uzziah was a godly and able ruler. His economic policies and military strength were assets to the nation. However, he provoked a crisis late in his life when he went into the temple and assumed the right to offer sacrifices. The priests were horrified that the king would do such a thing. God punished Uzziah with leprosy, making him incapable of finishing his reign. Before he died, his son ascended to the throne. Even in Israel's theocracy, with a union between church and state, there was a division of labor.

The second view is the *separation of church and state*. In certain Anabaptist groups of the Reformation, there was such a radical separation of church and state, that Christians were not permitted to be involved in the ministry of the state at all. Some of the Anabaptists believed that a Christian could not serve in secular government because that would involve compromise with his commitment to Christ. They declared that church and state are not only different spheres but spheres that are not to have any kind of joint activity. Some Anabaptists refused to take oaths in the civil courts. They would not serve in the army or in the government. They would have nothing to do with the evil in the secular state.

The third view is that of the *two kingdoms*, or the two spheres, which was set forth in antiquity by Augustine in his work on the city of God. Luther also talked about the two kingdoms, the kingdom of the government and the kingdom of the church. Calvin embraced this idea of the distinction between the two kingdoms. There were nuanced differences between Luther and Calvin. The idea was that both the state and the church are ordained by God, and when the state is carrying out its God-given mandate, a Christian certainly may be involved in the fulfilling of that mandate.

Part of this has to do with the Reformation concept of vocation, which has been largely obscured in our culture today. The idea of vocation is that God calls people to their life's work in many different spheres. God gifts people in different ways, and it is not only church-related jobs that are to be considered a calling or a vocation. Just as God calls people to the gospel ministry, so He also calls the ministers of the state to perform their tasks. He calls farmers to farming, businessmen to business, and artists to art. The first people said to be filled with the Holy Spirit were the artisans whom God called to fashion the holy vessels and the furniture for the tabernacle in the Old Testament (Ex. 31:1–11). The Spirit did not come upon them to preach the gospel or to minister as priests or prophets. The Spirit gifted them to produce works of art, to be musicians, and to be sculptors.

As Christians, we should think of our careers as vocations. We should be a banker because God calls us to be a banker. If banking is a legitimate enterprise and contributes to the general welfare of human beings, then it is a legitimate sphere of labor in which a Christian may be engaged. God will and does call people to that and to other vocations.

The Reformation concept of vocation is that God's calling is not limited to the isolated realm of the church. His calling can involve tasks outside the church and can include government service. We have two kingdoms with different job descriptions and responsibilities, but God can call people to be engaged in either one. He calls people to the gospel ministry; He also calls people to be civil magistrates. Sometimes lost in current debates on the nature of these two kingdoms is that Jesus reigns over them both. We do not want to conflate the two kingdoms. Neither, however, do we want to deny that Christ is Lord over the whole of creation. Some would argue that the church has nothing to say to the broader culture and should be silent before it. This view, often called radical two kingdom or R2K, largely leaves the realm of creation to its own devices. The Reformed view affirms that Jesus calls us to work with Him to bring all things into subjection.

The concept of vocation does not mean that every job is something that a Christian can, in good conscience, do. God does not call people to be prostitutes, because that business is forbidden by the Word of God. We have to be careful not to assume that any job we want is sanctioned by God.

So, for that end, they may lawfully, now under the new testament, wage war, upon just and necessary occasion. This was written to rebut the Anabaptists, who developed the theory of pacifism, arguing that Christians are not permitted to participate in warfare. They cannot serve in the military. They must be pacifists, and they should exercise, wherever possible, the right of conscientious objection. Even if the state does not give them the right of conscientious objection, they must still refuse to be involved in the military or in law enforcement. Contrary to that position, the Westminster Confession affirms the classic Christian "just war" theory, which accepts the just involvement of Christians in warfare.

This can be a complicated matter. The just war theory goes back again to Augustine and was given fuller exposition by Thomas Aquinas in the Middle Ages. This theory states that all wars are evil. People are not to take up arms to harm and to kill each other. But not everyone's involvement in war is evil. For example, God has given the civil magistrate the power of the sword, and that gives the magistrate not only the right to use the sword but also the obligation to use it under certain circumstances. The magistrates in Israel were rebuked by God for failing to execute criminals convicted of capital crimes. The law in Israel for premeditated murder required capital punishment. If the civil magistrate failed to follow through, God would call him to task for his failure to carry out the punishment.

If the civil magistrate has the sword, and his domain or jurisdiction is invaded by a hostile force, it is not only the right of that nation to defend its borders but the obligation of the civil magistrate to protect his citizens from harm or death by the invader. A war of aggression, where one nation invades another nation's territorial boundaries, is basically murder on a grand scale.

In a war, is there always one side that can claim justice? There have been wars in history where neither side had a justifiable basis for engaging in armed conflict. There have also been wars where one side was clearly the aggressor. When Hitler marched into Poland and into the Low Countries, it was a classic example of unprovoked aggression, though he claimed to be justified in his action. What the confession teaches is that a Christian in Germany should not have participated in Hitler's aggressive war. One may participate in war, but only when the cause is just. We cannot hide behind the slogan "My country, right or wrong," because that assumes that our country is always entitled to blind loyalty or obedience. History is replete with examples of nations engaging in military activities that are morally unjustifiable. When our government is so involved, we cannot and must not participate.

In this age of sophistication, it is often difficult to know who is right and who is wrong. In the Civil War, Christians stood staunchly on both sides of the conflict. Christians in the South believed that their states' rights were being violated by an aggressor, and the states in the South did not want to wage war. They wanted peace and the freedom to withdraw from an alliance with the North into which they had freely entered. Many Christians in the South believed that since they had been invaded by a hostile foe, they had the right and the obligation to defend themselves.

In the meantime, there were people in the North who believed that the Confederate rebellion was an ungodly, unjustified disruption of the union. They believed that the action of the federal government was proper and just and that their involvement in this war was legitimate. At least one side in that war was wrong, even though Christians on both sides fought in good conscience.

Christians who believed that it is never right to rebel against an established government refused to participate in the American Revolution. Other people who were devout Christians believed that lesser magistrates had the right to overthrow the superior magistrate if the superior magistrate becomes corrupt. They willingly engaged in armed conflict against the king of England. The biblical principle and the confession say that we have the right to wage war if the war is just. If it is not just, we are morally obligated to stay out.

In World War II, the atrocities by the German high command included the organized genocide of six million Jews, along with millions of others. Think how many people had to be involved in that activity. There were those who engineered the trains and those who herded people into boxcars and carried them off to death camps. There were soldiers who shot these people in the back and put them into mass graves. There were people who herded them into the "showers" to be gassed. Many people were involved. The excuse during the war crimes trial was that they had to follow orders. The United States took the position at the Nuremberg trials that they did not have to follow those orders. If they saw their government performing a criminal activity, it was their moral duty to refuse to serve. The government of the United States, at that point, was following the principle of just war and necessary-at-times conscientious objection.

Up until the middle of the Vietnam War, the position of the United States government was that people who had conscientious objections to war had the opportunity to be excused from armed conflict. They might be assigned to some peaceable enterprise, but they could receive conscientious objector status. No war in American history provoked the use of this claim as did the Vietnam War. Never in our history, except for the Civil War, was the populace of America so divided over our government's involvement in a war.

3. Civil magistrates may not assume to themselves the administration of the Word and sacraments; or the power of the keys of the kingdom of heaven; or, in the least, interfere in matters of faith. Yet, as nursing fathers, it is the duty of civil magistrates to protect the church of our common Lord, without giving the preference to any denomination of Christians above the rest, in such a manner that all ecclesiastical persons whatever shall enjoy the full, free, and unquestioned liberty of discharging every part of their sacred functions, without violence or danger. And, as Jesus Christ hath appointed a regular government and discipline in his church, no law of any commonwealth should interfere with, let, or hinder, the due exercise thereof, among the voluntary members of any denomination of Christians, according to their own profession and belief. It is the duty of civil magistrates to protect the person and good name of all their people, in such an effectual manner as that no person be suffered, either upon pretense of religion or of infidelity, to offer any indignity, violence, abuse, or injury to any other person whatsoever: and to take order, that all religious and ecclesiastical assemblies be held without molestation or disturbance.

Civil magistrates may not assume to themselves the administration of the Word and sacraments; or the power of the keys of the kingdom of heaven; or, in the least, interfere in matters of faith. We are not examining the Constitution of the United States of America, but a theological confession concerning the proper relationship between the state and the church. Nevertheless, section 3 of chapter 23 is an American revision of the original confessional text. The words quoted here follow the original version in substance from "Civil magistrates may not assume" to "the keys of the kingdom of heaven." After that, the American text goes on to set forth a theory of church-state relations substantially different from that of the seventeenth-century British Reformers. In the view of the writers of the confession, it was the responsibility of the state to suppress heresy, to prevent or reform corrupt worship, and so forth. The idea of an institutional church-state separation developed later in the American context.

We previously mentioned King Uzziah, and how he arrogated to himself the role of the priesthood, for which God punished him with leprosy. Uzziah stepped across the line, usurped the role of the priesthood, and violated the distinction between the two orders of church and state. Civil magistrates are not to assume the authority to administer the Word and sacraments or the power of the keys of the kingdom of heaven.

Even though, in our culture, there may be no danger of the state's taking to itself the right to administer the sacraments, what about the power of the keys of the kingdom? Historically, in the United States, the so-called wall of separation between church and state became part of the fabric of American tradition. The concept says that the exercise of church discipline is not the state's business but is a matter for the church in conducting its affairs. According to the Reformation, the third necessary mark of a true church, in addition to the preaching of the gospel and the administration of the sacraments, is the exercise of discipline. It is the church's function to determine who may or may not be members of its body. The state cannot tell the church who must be accepted into membership. We do have the right to discriminate *according to creed* because we are a confessional body, and there is a minimal content of affirmation that a person must embrace in order to become a member of the body of Christ. For example, one who does not believe in the deity of Jesus Christ would not qualify for membership, nor would he be permitted to receive the sacrament of the Lord's Supper. That is discriminating according to creed. It is not done in the secular world, but in the church we not only may but must do so in order to maintain the integrity of the church.

We have seen some incidents in recent years where the civil authorities have encroached on the church's right to discipline by excommunication.

The civil government has heard some lawsuits, ruled in favor of the excommunicated person, and ordered churches either to pay damages or to receive the person back into their fellowship. That is not only a gross breach of our traditional wall of separation but also a violation of this principle in the confession. It is a radical violation of the First Amendment, which guarantees the right of the free exercise of religion. Part of the exercise of the Christian religion involves the exercise of church discipline. Church discipline is the "power of the keys." The church has the power to impose moral sanctions for the ungodly behavior of church members, starting with rebuke, followed by censure and then temporary suspension from the sacraments, and concluding with excommunication.

According to the confession, civil magistrates never have the right, in the least, interfere in matters of faith. Yet, as nursing fathers, it is the duty of civil magistrates to protect the church of our common Lord, without giving the preference to any denomination of Christians above the rest— there is the principle of disestablishmentarianism—in such a manner that all ecclesiastical persons whatever shall enjoy the full, free, and unquestioned liberty of discharging every part of their sacred functions, without violence or danger. What Americans call the separation of church and state would, from a Reformed viewpoint, be described as a "separation of powers and duties." We distinguish between the role of the state and the role of the church, because they are two separate institutions. That does not mean that they cannot support each other. Just as the church has a responsibility to honor the civil magistrates, to pray for them, and to render obedience to them, so, by the same token, the civil magistrate has the responsibility to honor the functions of the church. They are to support, rather than oppose, each other.

And, as Jesus Christ hath appointed a regular government and discipline in his church, no law of any commonwealth should interfere with, let, or hinder, the due exercise thereof, among the voluntary members of any denomination of Christians, according to their own profession and belief. There was once a man who was involved in a divorce process, and he was the innocent party. However, the session of the church met with his wife and heard her complaints, without interviewing him, which is a violation of ecclesiastical law. Why didn't they interview him? The wife's attorney had gotten a court order that prohibited him from coming within so many yards of her or the church, and the church was afraid of civil sanctions if it carried through with the normal due process of ecclesiastical discipline. That was an outrageous act of cowardice on the part of the church leaders to obey the civil magistrate at that point. They should have said to the civil magistrate, "You are out of order." They should have exercised their duty to give due process to that man in the ecclesiastical court.

Problems arise when authorities collide with one another. For example, in marriage and divorce cases, we understand that the civil magistrate has the right to perform marriages and also the right to dissolve them. Historically, the church also has had the right to perform marriages and dissolve them. So the church and the civil magistrate have overlapping jurisdiction and could come into conflict. In such a situation, the state should only have the right to dissolve a marriage performed by the civil court, and only an ecclesiastical court should render the decision in ecclesiastical cases. Historically, however, the church in America has failed to exercise its duty in hearing cases of divorce. Most churches have to deal at some point with a divorce among its membership. Often the attitude is, "That's none of the church's business," but that is exactly the church's business. It is a matter for the church's spiritual oversight.

When we join a church, we submit ourselves and our conduct to the spiritual oversight of that Christian body. That is what church discipline is all about. Secular thinking has now so infiltrated the church that even people who are faithful and obedient in their church involvement have the idea that the church should play no role in their spiritual discipline.

Jesus Christ hath appointed a regular government and discipline in his church. Church government and church discipline were not invented by mean-spirited people but by Christ Himself for His church. The Reformers declared there is no church without church discipline because the church that Jesus Christ established included government and discipline. A cursory reading of the Pastoral Epistles and of 1 Corinthians makes that clear. Paul rebuked the Corinthians for failing to exercise discipline in their community (1 Cor. 6:1–11).

Because Christ has set up church government and discipline, no law of any commonwealth should interfere with, let, or hinder, the due exercise thereof, among the voluntary members of any denomination of Christians, according to their own profession and belief. Private organizations and public officials have come under increasing pressure from groups opposed to biblical standards for sexual relationships and the definition of marriage.

It is the duty of civil magistrates to protect the person and good name of all their people, in such an effectual manner as that no person be suffered, either upon pretense of religion or of infidelity, to offer any indignity, violence, abuse, or injury to any other person whatsoever. This puts restraints on Christians. Christians do not have the right to carry the sword, nor do they have the right to slander anyone. Slander and libel are prohibited under civil law.

It is the duty of civil magistrates . . . to take order, that all religious and ecclesiastical assemblies be held without molestation or disturbance. As the church is called to honor the magistrate, the magistrate also has the duty to protect the church from being hindered in carrying out its duties. This touches the U.S. Bill of Rights, specifically the First Amendment, which guarantees the "free exercise" of religion.

4. It is the duty of people to pray for magistrates, to honor their persons, to pay them tribute or other dues, to obey their lawful commands, and to be subject to their authority, for conscience' sake. Infidelity, or difference in religion, doth not make void the magistrates' just and legal authority, nor free the people from their due obedience to them: from which ecclesiastical persons are not exempted, much less hath the pope any power and jurisdiction over them in their dominions, or over any of their people; and, least of all, to deprive them of their dominions, or lives, if he shall judge them to be heretics, or upon any other pretense whatsoever.

It is the duty of people to pray for magistrates. The emphasis is switching to our Christian responsibility toward the civil magistrates. The first duty is to pray. This mandate is given repeatedly in the Scripture, and our prayers are not to be limited to pleas for judgment. We are to pray that God will bless our rulers and give them wisdom and integrity. We are also to honor their persons, to pay them tribute or other dues, to obey their lawful commands, and to be subject to their authority, for conscience' sake.

If the magistrate is not a Christian or is a different kind of Christian, that does not excuse us from our responsibility to pray for him and to submit to his authority in the civil sphere.

Infidelity, or difference in religion, doth not make void the magistrates' just and legal authority, nor free the people from their due obedience to them: from which ecclesiastical persons are not exempted, much less hath the pope any power and jurisdiction over them in their dominions, or over any of their people; and, least of all, to deprive them of their dominions, or lives, if he shall judge them to be heretics, or upon any other pretense whatsoever. Being a Christian—including an ecclesiastical person (that is, a church leader)—does not exempt us from obeying the civil magistrate and the laws of the state. Church leaders are not to interfere in civil matters, just as civil magistrates are not to interfere in the free exercise of religion.

Is there ever a time when a Christian has the right to disobey the law or to disobey the civil magistrates? This question arises because of what the confession reaffirms here and what we read in Romans 13, where Paul emphasizes the need for civil obedience. Peter similarly writes that we are to obey the civil magistrate for the Lord's sake, because Christ is the one who redeems us from lawlessness. When laws are passed and we disobey them, we take our stand on the side of lawlessness rather than on the side of divinely sanctioned obedience. But that does not mean that every law is just or binding upon the conscience of the Christian.

The fact that a law is unjust does not give us the right to disobey it. Every legal system in our world includes laws that are unjust or unrighteous. There are laws that inflict inconvenience, suffering, and pain upon its citizens, but that is not an excuse to disobey the civil magistrate. When is it right to disobey? The answer is easy to articulate but difficult to apply to real-life situations. The principle is this: whenever any authority (civil magistrate, employer, father in the home, husband in the marriage) commands us to do what God clearly forbids or forbids us to do what God clearly commands, we not only *may* disobey but *must* disobey.

We see examples in the book of Acts where the Sanhedrin, the legal body that ruled over the Jews, stopped Peter and the Apostles from preaching and forbade them to preach Christ. Peter replied, "Whether it is right in the sight of God to listen to you rather than to God, you must judge" (see Acts 4:19). Christ had commanded the disciples to preach the gospel to every creature. They were fulfilling that mandate in Jerusalem. The civil authorities came and ordered them to stop preaching, and the disciples said that they could not obey the civil authorities. That is one of the reasons why Paul spent so much time in jail. He had to disobey human authorities in order to obey God.

When the human authorities inconvenience or inflict suffering upon us, what are we to do? It wasn't convenient for Joseph and his wife to undergo an arduous journey to Bethlehem because the emperor wanted to take a census so he could increase his taxes on the Jews. Yet Joseph risked the life of his wife and of their promised child to obey the civil magistrate, through which the Scriptures were fulfilled. "But you, O Bethlehem Ephrathah, who are too little to be among the clans of Judah, from you shall come forth for me one who is to be ruler in Israel, whose coming forth is from of old, from ancient days" (Mic. 5:2). Here we have a heroic example of obedience to the civil magistrate. Our emotions say they would have been justified to stay in Nazareth, but God had not commanded Joseph and Mary to stay there. God doesn't command us to be happy or to be wealthy. If we don't like the income tax structure and think the government is unjust, that is no excuse for us to disobey, even though it may inconvenience us and cause us discomfort.

We see examples in the Old Testament where, with the sanction of God, people were disobedient to the magistrates. Hebrew midwives, under the capricious decree of Pharaoh, were to kill all the male children born to the Israelites. The midwives delivered those male babies and hid them, rather than killing them. They even lied to cover up what they had done in order to save the lives of those babies, and they received the blessing of God for their acts of civil disobedience (Ex. 1:15–21). Shadrach, Meshach, and Abednego were in the fiery furnace because they wouldn't serve Nebuchadnezzar's gods or worship the golden image as they were ordered to (Dan. 3:12–18). What about Mordecai in the book of Esther and Daniel in the lion's den? They were being obedient to God, rather than to the magistrates. There are occasions when we not only *may* disobey, but we *must*.

The debate continues to this day regarding the Revolutionary War, through which the United States became a free nation. One of the ideas advanced during the Reformation was that lesser magistrates may revolt against higher magistrates if the higher magistrates are operating in an unjust and illegal manner. Not all Christians adopted that principle, and not all Christians supported the Revolutionary War. There is no doubt that the magistrates who were in favor of revolution were duly appointed magistrates. It wasn't just a grassroots rebellion, for the lesser magistrates were protesting against Parliament and the king for violating British law and the terms under which the Colonies were to be governed.

In the civil rights movement in the United States in the 1950s and 1960s, Martin Luther King Jr. followed Gandhi's principles of peaceful resistance and intentionally engaged in acts of civil disobedience. The question then was, May Christians participate in civil rights protests with Dr. King?

The justification was that no state has the right to enact a statute that denies a guaranteed right of the Constitution. Every individual in the United States of America has certain constitutional rights that no magistrate and no majority has the right to take away. This country was established as a republic and not as a democracy. In a democracy, the majority rules, and the rights of a minority can be trampled underfoot. Majority rule can become mob rule, where the individual or minority falls victim to the desires of the majority. Because of the Bill of Rights, the citizen has the right to peaceably force a test case in the courts to determine the legitimacy of a statute. That was behind King's strategy. He wanted to test the laws and show that individual states, through their majority, had enacted legislation that discriminated against individuals unconstitutionally. The Reformers would likely have considered that a legitimate form of civil disobedience.

Of Marriage and Divorce

1. Marriage is to be between one man and one woman: neither is it lawful for any man to have more than one wife, nor for any woman to have more than one husband, at the same time.

2. Marriage was ordained for the mutual help of husband and wife, for the increase of mankind with legitimate issue, and of the church with an holy seed; and for preventing of uncleanness.

3. It is lawful for all sorts of people to marry, who are able with judgment to give their consent. Yet it is the duty of Christians to marry only in the Lord. And therefore such as profess the true reformed religion should not marry with infidels, papists, or other idolaters: neither should such as are godly be unequally yoked, by marrying with such as are notoriously wicked in their life, or maintain damnable heresies.

4. Marriage ought not to be within the degrees of consanguinity or affinity forbidden by the Word. Nor can such incestuous marriages ever be made lawful by any law of man or consent of parties, so as those persons may live together as man and wife.

5. Adultery or fornication committed after a contract, being detected before marriage, giveth just occasion to the innocent party to dissolve that contract. In the case of adultery after marriage, it is lawful for the innocent party to sue out a divorce: and, after the divorce, to marry another, as if the offending party were dead.

6. Although the corruption of man be such as is apt to study arguments unduly to put asunder those whom God hath joined together in marriage: yet, nothing but adultery, or such willful desertion as can no way

be remedied by the church, or civil magistrate, is cause sufficient of dissolving the bond of marriage: wherein, a public and orderly course of
proceeding is to be observed; and the persons concerned in it not left
to their own wills, and discretion, in their own case.

---

1. Marriage is to be between one man and one woman: neither is
   it lawful for any man to have more than one wife, nor for any
   woman to have more than one husband, at the same time.

The Westminster divines affirmed that saving faith is a direct result
of the operation of the Holy Spirit in our hearts, and that the Holy
Spirit ordinarily creates faith in our hearts through the ministry of the
Word. This study of the Westminster Confession seeks to strengthen our
faith through a deeper understanding of the Word of God. Insofar as our
faith is strengthened, our Christian lives will be more productive and
effective.

The subject of marriage and divorce is important for us to understand from a biblical perspective. In a wedding ceremony, the opening
words usually are, "Dearly beloved, we are assembled here today in the
presence of God and of these witnesses to unite this man and this woman
in the bonds of holy matrimony." We go on to consider other aspects of
marriage and acknowledge that it was instituted by God and further consecrated by Christ. Then we add this statement: "Marriage is regulated by
God's commandments." Marriage is a gift of God to the human race. It is
an institution that He has commanded, ordained, and instituted. He did
not simply create the estate of marriage, give it to the human race, and
allow us to do with it whatever we want. Rather, God circumscribed the
institution of matrimony by His law, and He set forth certain principles
to govern it. He determined who may enter into marriage, when one may
enter into it, and what constitutes a valid marriage and a valid dissolution
of it.

We live in a time when biblical law and God's regulations for marriage are rejected or ignored in a wholesale manner, even by many church

members. It is important that we examine once again the biblical principles that regulate marriage.

Marriage is to be between one man and one woman: neither is it lawful for any man to have more than one wife, nor for any woman to have more than one husband, at the same time. Set forth here is the principle of monogamy, that a man has but one wife, and a wife has but one husband, at the same time. Prohibited are bigamy and polygamy, which are shades of the same thing. Polygamy refers to marriage to several wives (or, rarely, several husbands) simultaneously. Bigamy refers to having two wives at the same time, as Jacob did with Leah and Rachel.

To understand this call to monogamy, we start with the creation of the human race. When God created man in His own image, male and female, He provided for the sacred union that we call marriage. He gave a mandate to Adam and Eve to be fruitful and to multiply. One of the reasons for marriage is the propagation of the human race. Originally, marriage was defined as a relationship between one man and one woman: "Therefore a man shall leave his father and his mother and hold fast to his wife, and they shall become one flesh" (Gen. 2:24). The principle of leaving and cleaving was set forth at creation, and it follows throughout Scripture.

The Old Testament record gives many examples of otherwise godly men who had multiple wives—and, in the case of Solomon, many wives and many concubines. David had several wives, and he was called a man after God's own heart. What are we to make of this? It doesn't mean that God sanctioned polygamy in the Old Testament. Polygamy never received God's positive sanction. Rather, we see God's forbearance and long-suffering with his people, despite their flagrant disobedience. Jacob's taking of two wives did not nullify the creation mandate that one man and one woman are to enter into the sacred and holy union of marriage.

The New Testament clearly sets forth the practice of monogamy as the biblical principle. In the qualifications for elders, 1 Timothy 3:2 says that an elder must be the husband of one wife. Some have said that this makes it impossible for a man who was once divorced and then remarried ever to be an elder in the church. If that is what the text means, it also prohibits a widower from remarrying and becoming an elder, because he would also have had more than one wife. Most scholars agree that Paul's teaching is a prohibition of polygamy or bigamy of any kind. Monogamy is clearly established in the creation account of the Old Testament and by Apostolic teaching in the New Testament.

Polygamy and bigamy are not serious issues in our culture today. However, they are serious matters for missionaries who go into cultures where polygamy is practiced. When a man who has multiple wives becomes a Christian, what is he supposed to do about them and their offspring? Should he divorce all but one of his wives, abandon the others, and cease to fulfill the obligations of his marriage contracts? No. The usual way this situation is handled is for the missionaries to communicate God's laws regarding marriage and to instruct the people that from that day forward, they should not take multiple wives. In the meantime, men with more than one wife must carry out their commitment to care for their wives and their offspring. It is a difficult situation, but the church has handled it this way throughout church history.

Although we don't have a glaring problem with polygamy in our culture, we have tension with the principle that marriage is to be contracted between one man and one woman. There is no biblical provision for same-sex unions. This has become a major ecclesiastical issue where various denominations either have or are contemplating marriage services for same-sex unions. The civil magistrate, since the Supreme Court's decision *Obergefell v. Hodges*, has affirmed that civil marriages may include couples of the same sex, a deviation from God's law unheard of in human history.

Churches approving same-sex unions have an inadequate view of scriptural authority. They may argue that the Bible is historically conditioned and is therefore not binding on us today. However, the clarity of the biblical text with respect to this matter is evident. Any sexual relationship between two men or between two women is clearly prohibited by the Word of God. These relationships are not only prohibited but grossly sinful and an abomination in God's sight.

2. Marriage was ordained for the mutual help of husband and wife, for the increase of mankind with legitimate issue, and of the church with an holy seed; and for preventing of uncleanness.

The reasons given for marriage start with its being ordained for the mutual help of husband and wife. There is a clear recognition of the mutuality of the marital relationship. Clearly, the Reformation church of the seventeenth century held that wives are to be subordinate to their husbands. Nevertheless, the church recognized that there is to be mutual concern, care, and responsibility between husband and wife. The wife is not accorded the role of chattel or slave but fully shares the image of God.

Eve was created initially to be Adam's helpmate, and God prescribed a deep bond between those first two human beings. With each aspect of His creation, God "saw that it was good" (Gen. 1:25). But it was "not good that the man should be alone; I will make him a helper fit for him." So God said, "I will make him a helper fit for him" (2:18).

When Adam saw Eve, he was filled with delight, because God had made the perfect helpmate. God then made both Adam and Eve vicegerents over the entire creation. Eve had joint rule over their household and over all nature. She was placed in an exalted position, but she was still subordinate to her husband. That doesn't mean that she was inferior. She was equal in dignity, value, and honor to her husband, but she was still expected to be submissive to him (Eph. 5:22).

Marriage was established for the mutual help of husband and wife. Even though Eve was created to be Adam's helpmate, he also had responsibilities to help her. The heaviest burden to provide support and help is given to the man, because he is commanded by God to love his wife as Christ loved the church and to give himself to his wife as Christ gave Himself to the church. Christian women who struggle with the biblical mandate to be submissive to their husbands will seldom, if ever, say that they would have a hard time submitting to Christ if they were married to Him. A woman in that situation could trust Him, knowing that her husband loves her and is prepared to die for her at any moment. He would provide for her all that He has and give her all that He is. That is the burden that God puts on men in marriage. Marriage is the deepest kind of personal commitment into which any two people can enter, and so the first purpose of marriage is to provide mutual help for husband and wife.

Marriage was also established for the increase of mankind with legitimate issue. The context for the bearing of children is marriage.

Producing children outside the sacred bond of marriage is the producing of "illegitimate" children. In our culture, we see the proliferation of childbearing outside of marriage, just as we have seen a wholesale attack on the very institution of marriage. There is a public embracing of fornication, or sexual activity outside of marriage, which is totally opposed to the law of God in the Decalogue, to the teaching of Christ, and to the Apostolic admonition that we read in the New Testament. "But sexual immorality and all impurity or covetousness must not even be named among you, as is proper among saints" (Eph. 5:3). Paul wrote that to people who were living in an immoral, pagan environment. He told them: "You Christians have to live differently from the world around you. You are called to a different standard."

It is amazing how many professing Christians have followed the world in repudiating marriage and embracing sexual relationships outside of it. It was not the Puritans or Queen Victoria who declared a sexual relationship outside of matrimony to be sinful; it was God. This is one of the laws that God writes on the human heart. A Christian must understand that neither we nor society makes the rules. God makes the rules. Christians today too readily take their cues from the culture. If our culture accepts certain kinds of behavior, then we tell ourselves that it is acceptable, even when we know it isn't.

Children are to be born inside the marriage covenant, into an environment that under normal circumstances includes a mother and a father. That is the most fundamental unit of society as established by God. That is verified not only by the Word of God but by the history of civilization. The most basic, foundational unit of society is the family, and it is that very unit that is under such fierce attack in our culture today.

One of the issues behind the scenes during the Reformation was the Roman Catholic Church's view of the superiority of celibacy. Rome argued that the only justification for sex in marriage is the need to propagate the species. Therefore, all forms of birth control are considered evil, since they prevent that purpose from being realized. The Reformers insisted that the mutual joy and pleasure of the marriage bed is undefiled, and that the husband and the wife have every legitimate reason to enjoy each other's bodies, even if it doesn't result in bearing children.

Marriage was also established for the **increase . . . of the church with an holy seed.** Many people today look at children as a burden and at large families as irresponsible. But in the Bible, a large family is viewed as a tremendous blessing of God for the parents. Some argue that this is true only in an agrarian society, where having many children ensures cheap labor to work on the farm. But now that we are city dwellers, they say, having more than two children is an economic burden.

Children may indeed be an economic hardship. But it is a great blessing of God to have children. When parents invest time in nurturing their children in the Word of God, they are strengthening the church through the bearing of children. "Be fruitful and multiply" has not been rescinded in our day.

Finally, marriage was established **for preventing of uncleanness.** When Paul said, "It is better to marry than to burn with passion" (1 Cor. 7:9), he was implying that some of the people to whom he was writing were living in sexual sin. He is talking about burning with lust. God plants a sexual drive in people because He created them for reproduction. God also says that marriage is the only context in which that drive may properly be exercised. A person may try to be chaste yet have impulses and desires that control him. In that situation, it is better to look for a husband or a wife to alleviate that problem.

> 3. It is lawful for all sorts of people to marry, who are able with judgment to give their consent. Yet it is the duty of Christians to marry only in the Lord. And therefore such as profess the true reformed religion should not marry with infidels, papists, or other idolaters: neither should such as are godly be unequally yoked, by marrying with such as are notoriously wicked in their life, or maintain damnable heresies.

Section 3 affirms the specific and unique requirements that are imposed on God's people. The restriction placed on believers from Old Testament times through the New Testament is to **marry only in the Lord,** so as to be equally yoked (2 Cor. 6:14). Paul's correspondence with the Corinthians indicates that some of them were involved with mixed marriages. There was no provision in the early church for a Christian to marry a non-Christian. Presumably, those mixed marriages arose when one of the spouses was converted. That puts a strain upon the marriage.

If a believer in Christ is yoked in the closest possible way with someone who does not share that deep commitment, there will be trouble. There is a mandate from the Apostolic word that Christians are not allowed to marry unbelievers.

Furthermore, the confession prohibits marriage between people who embrace the Reformed faith and **papists**, or people who embrace the Roman Catholic faith. The church takes this very seriously. This is a matter of prudence and wisdom, yet we live in a culture where people often get married on the basis of emotion rather than on the basis of principle.

When marriages were arranged by families, it was rare that young people determined their own marital destiny. The church, after the Reformation, came to the conclusion that parents ought not to impose arranged marriages upon their children without their consent. Part of this confessional statement says that those who marry should be **able with judgment to give their consent.** When marriages were arranged, they tended to be long lasting. The present system, where young people are allowed to make personal commitments without parental supervision, is not working as well.

It is not that we should go back to the matchmaker and arranged marriages. But when parents are opposed to the marriage of a young couple, that couple ought to take seriously the wisdom of their parents when they contemplate marriage.

> 4. Marriage ought not to be within the degrees of consanguinity or affinity forbidden by the Word. Nor can such incestuous marriages ever be made lawful by any law of man or consent of parties, so as those persons may live together as man and wife.

Marriage ought not to be within the degrees of consanguinity or affinity forbidden by the Word. There is a distinction between a relationship of consanguinity and a relationship of affinity. Consanguinity refers to a blood relationship. The confession is saying that we are not allowed to intermarry in incestuous relationships. We are not to marry blood relatives.

A relationship of affinity is created by marriage. For example, if you marry a woman, you gain a relationship of affinity with her family members.

Some people have asked, Whom did the children of Adam and Eve marry? The Bible tells us that they had sons and daughters (Gen. 5:4) but mentions no one else of their generation. The presumption is that their sons married their sisters. In the beginning, then, marriages were necessarily incestuous.

How do we respond to that ethically and theologically? The answer is that the prohibition against intermarriage was not established in creation but only later in history. We also know that biological problems from intermarriage do not ordinarily arise in the first generation. Only after repeated generations do we begin to see birth defects and other problems resulting from the intermarriage of blood relatives. Initially, the populating of the earth required blood relationships, but God refused to allow that to continue once there were spouses available who were not immediately related by blood.

Nor can such incestuous marriages ever be made lawful by any law of man or consent of parties, so as those persons may live together as man and wife. This means that a son cannot marry his mother, a daughter cannot marry her father, nor can brother and sister enter into marriage.

> 5. Adultery or fornication committed after a contract, being detected before marriage, giveth just occasion to the innocent party to dissolve that contract. In the case of adultery after marriage, it is lawful for the innocent party to sue out a divorce: and, after the divorce, to marry another, as if the offending party were dead.

Adultery or fornication committed after a contract, being detected before marriage, giveth just occasion to the innocent party to dissolve that contract. This refers to an engagement contract prior to marriage. If sexual infidelity with another person occurs during the period of engagement, then that infidelity is grounds for breaking the engagement. In some places, historically, engagements involved more than a simple personal promise. There was a certain legal basis as well. We see that in the case of Joseph and Mary. They were not married when she conceived, but they were betrothed, so Joseph had legal recourse to sue Mary for adultery during their betrothal. He decided to be gracious enough to her to put her away privately. Then God revealed to him that Mary had conceived supernaturally by the Holy Spirit, and he married her.

In the case of adultery after marriage, it is lawful for the innocent party to sue out a divorce: and, after the divorce, to marry another, as if the offending party were dead. Some churches believe that there are no valid grounds for divorce. This issue depends on how one interprets Jesus' discussion with the Pharisees, recorded in Matthew 19. The Pharisees came to Jesus with a dilemma, saying that Moses, in Deuteronomy 24:1, makes provision for the divorce of a wife on the basis of "some indecency in her." At the time, there was an ongoing debate about the interpretation of this "indecency" among the rabbinical schools. There was a conservative (narrow) interpretation given by the school of Shammai, and a liberal (wide) interpretation by the school of Hillel. The followers of Hillel said that the indecency refers to anything that displeases the husband. For example, if the wife accidentally breaks his favorite dish, the husband could write a bill of divorcement and dissolve the marriage. But the followers of Shammai said that divorce is justified only on the grounds of sexual indecency, that is, adultery. The Hillelites replied that the indecency in view couldn't be adultery because the punishment for adultery in the Mosaic law was execution, not divorce.

The debate continued for years among the scholars of Israel, and they brought the question to Jesus. Jesus said that the provision for divorce in the Old Testament was a permission on God's part because of the hardness of people's hearts, and that from the beginning it was not so. Jesus reminded the people that marriage was originally intended to be a lifelong contract without dissolution. He then concluded, "Whoever divorces his wife, except for sexual immorality, and marries another, commits adultery" (Matt. 19:9). Jesus prohibited divorce with an exception. The exceptive clause of that text is "except for sexual immorality."

Added to that is the teaching of Paul in 1 Corinthians, where he allows a believer to be freed from an unbeliever in the case of the desertion by the unbeliever (1 Cor. 7:15). Those churches that seek to be confessional and biblical in the matter of divorce generally reduce the legitimate grounds for divorce to two: adultery and desertion. Some people include physical abuse within the scope of desertion, arguing that the abuser has in effect deserted the spouse. That becomes a matter for church courts to interpret.

The options in the traditional marriage vows, "for better or for worse, for richer, for poorer, in sickness and in health," are illustrative, not exhaustive. We rarely anticipate that things are going to be worse, rather than better, but the vow we take is to live together ever after. First Corinthians 13 reveals the standard of love that God has given to us. It provides one of the most thorough indictments of human behavior that we will ever see. In 1 Corinthians 13, we meet a standard of love so high, holy, and righteous that it convicts us of sin and sends us running to the Savior. Love is so much more than a warm puppy or a handful of roses and a romantic ballad. It is living out the vows that we take before God.

On many occasions, the church must establish the innocent party and the guilty party in a divorce case. If there is a married couple in the church, and one spouse files for divorce without biblical grounds, the church has a responsibility to step in and say, "You can't do that." If the person persists in divorcing a spouse without just grounds, it is the duty of the church to discipline that person. The guilty spouse is to be disciplined to the point of excommunication in order to protect the innocent party and to allow the innocent party to remarry according to biblical law. However, since secular law does not require excommunication before remarriage, most churches abandon their responsibility at that point.

6. Although the corruption of man be such as is apt to study arguments unduly to put asunder those whom God hath joined together in marriage: yet, nothing but adultery, or such willful desertion as can no way be remedied by the church, or civil magistrate, is cause sufficient of dissolving the bond of marriage: wherein, a public and orderly course of proceeding is to be observed; and the persons concerned in it not left to their own wills, and discretion, in their own case.

When people's interests aren't compatible, there ensues a conflict of values and a clash of wills, and they heap up a variety of reasons to justify their

536 • TRUTHS WE CONFESS

sinful behavior. The confession teaches that divorce has to be according to the law of God, not according to the will of the participants.

Even if there are just grounds for divorce, be it adultery or desertion, it doesn't mean that a person *must* dissolve the marriage. It simply means that he or she may seek a divorce. When God gives the right to a Christian to dissolve a marriage, the person who exercises that right ought not to be criticized by the rest of the community. It is an unjust and unbiblical burden to suggest that the victim of adultery, if he or she were spiritual enough, would remain in his or her marriage.

If a man commits adultery and then pleads for forgiveness from his wife, it is her Christian duty to forgive him. She has no other option. But that doesn't mean that she must stay married to him. She must forgive him and receive him as a brother in Christ, but she does not have to receive him as a husband in Christ. His behavior radically undermined the trust that is foundational to an intimate marital relationship. If she cannot continue in such a damaged relationship, God gives her the freedom to dissolve it. The innocent party has that right, and it is wrong to condemn that Christian for exercising his or her right.

Of the Church

1.   The catholic or universal church, which is invisible, consists of the whole number of the elect, that have been, are, or shall be gathered into one, under Christ the Head thereof; and is the spouse, the body, the fullness of him that filleth all in all.

2.   The visible church, which is also catholic or universal under the gospel (not confined to one nation, as before under the law), consists of all those throughout the world that profess the true religion; and of their children: and is the kingdom of the Lord Jesus Christ, the house and family of God, out of which there is no ordinary possibility of salvation.

3.   Unto this catholic visible church Christ hath given the ministry, oracles, and ordinances of God, for the gathering and perfecting of the saints, in this life, to the end of the world: and doth, by his own presence and Spirit, according to his promise, make them effectual thereunto.

4.   This catholic church hath been sometimes more, sometimes less visible. And particular churches, which are members thereof, are more or less pure, according as the doctrine of the gospel is taught and embraced, ordinances administered, and public worship performed more or less purely in them.

5.   The purest churches under heaven are subject both to mixture and error; and some have so degenerated, as to become no churches of Christ, but synagogues of Satan. Nevertheless, there shall be always a church on earth, to worship God according to his will.

6.   There is no other head of the church but the Lord Jesus Christ. Nor can the pope of Rome, in any sense, be head thereof.

1. The catholic or universal church, which is invisible, consists of the whole number of the elect, that have been, are, or shall be gathered into one, under Christ the Head thereof; and is the spouse, the body, the fullness of him that filleth all in all.

The invisible church is made up of those who truly are in Christ, and it is called invisible because we cannot read the hearts of people. However, those who are God's are known to Him perfectly. He can read the heart; we cannot. The invisible church exists substantially within the visible church but cannot be identified with it. It refers to the elect, to those who make genuine professions of faith. The church, as Augustine taught, is always a "mixed body" in this world. It is made up of wheat and tares. Though the tares are in the visible church, they have no place in the invisible church. It is possible for a true believer to be in the invisible church, while not in the visible church, if providentially hindered or if temporarily blinded by false doctrine. There are four marks of the church as set forth at the Council of Nicaea in the fourth century. The church is one, holy, catholic, and Apostolic. Metaphors used in the Bible to describe the church include the body of Christ, the bride of Christ, and the fullness of Christ.

The word *church* derives ultimately from the Greek word *kyrios*, which means "Lord," the title given to Jesus. The church, then, etymologically, consists of "those who belong to the Lord." The people of God are those who have been purchased by Christ and are owned by Him. The Greek word *ekklēsia*, from which we get the word "ecclesiastical," is commonly translated "church," and means, literally, "those who are called out (from the world)," referring specifically to the elect.

2. The visible church, which is also catholic or universal under the gospel (not confined to one nation, as before under the law), consists of all those throughout the world that profess the true religion; and of their children: and is the kingdom of the Lord Jesus Christ, the house and family of God, out of which there is no ordinary possibility of salvation.

The visible church . . . is also catholic or universal under the gospel. The visible church today is not restricted to one nation, whereas the church in the Old Testament was restricted to the nation of Israel. The Apostle Paul says in Colossians 1:27 that the great mystery that was hidden in the old covenant, but is now revealed, is "Christ in you" (that is, in the gentiles), "the hope of glory." In the book of Acts, we see the gospel taken beyond the borders of Israel to the nations, to the gentiles. Churches were established in Europe, Africa, Asia, and eventually beyond. The visible church is found in its various manifestations all around the globe today. These churches consist of all those that profess the true religion; and of their children: and is the kingdom of the Lord Jesus Christ.

This section of the confession calls the church three things. First, it is called the kingdom of the Lord Jesus Christ. Second, it is called the house . . . of God. And third, it is called the family of God. Section 1 makes reference to the church as the spouse (bride) of Christ and the body of Christ. The New Testament uses these and other metaphors to describe the church. The one we'll consider first is that the visible church is called a *kingdom*.

Many people have been reared in evangelical churches that embrace a theology called dispensationalism, which was created in the nineteenth century. This theology was popularized by the *Scofield Reference Bible*. It carved up the history of the church, going back to creation, into various (often seven) distinct time periods, called dispensations. God supposedly judged the world differently in each of those periods. Most people think of dispensationalism as a set of teachings about the second coming of Christ. In fact, it is a complete systematic theology that has gone through many revisions, particularly at Dallas Theological Seminary, Moody Bible Institute, and elsewhere.

We won't consider the whole scope of dispensational theology, but only one particular aspect of it. The kingdom age, the kingdom of God, according to classic dispensational theology, is something that is completely future. The kingdom has not come yet in any way, shape, or form. Classic Reformed theology, on the other hand, says that the kingdom of God began with the arrival of Christ and with His coronation in heaven as the King of kings and the Lord of lords. That kingdom is not yet consummated, and it won't be consummated until the final return of Jesus, but it has been inaugurated.

John the Baptist prepared the way for Jesus and declared to Israel, "Repent, for the kingdom of heaven is at hand" (Matt. 3:2). The Old Testament prophets said that the kingdom of God was coming someday, but with John there was a sense of urgency about its nearness. "Even now the axe is laid to the root of the trees" (v. 10). "His winnowing fork is in his hand" (v. 12). The time of separation, the time of crisis, has come. John called the people to repentance. When Jesus came on the scene, He also announced the kingdom of God, saying it was "in the midst of you" (Luke 17:21).

That is consistent with what Jesus taught in Luke 11:20: "But if it is by the finger of God that I cast out demons, then the kingdom of God has come upon you." At the center of Jesus' teaching was the message of the gospel of the kingdom. Much of His teaching began, "The kingdom of God is like . . ." (see Matt. 13). Toward the end of Jesus' sojourn on this earth, the disciples asked, "Lord, will you at this time restore the kingdom to Israel?" (Acts 1:6). They were asking: "Are You going to do it, now that You are departing? We have looked for this manifestation of the kingdom ever since You were baptized by John." Jesus replied, "You will receive power when the Holy Spirit has come upon you, and you will be my witnesses in Jerusalem and in all Judea and Samaria, and to the end of the earth" (v. 8).

The word *witness* in the New Testament is the Greek *martyria*. Our English word *martyr* is related to it. The martyrs were called such because they bore witness to Christ with their deaths. In Christian jargon today, the word *witness* is practically synonymous with evangelism. There are actually many ways in which the church bears witness to Christ besides proclaiming the gospel. When we give a cup of cold water to a thirsty person, we bear witness to Christ. When we behave in a just manner in our place of work, we bear witness to Christ. To bear witness is to give testimony, evidence, or a manifestation of something that is not seen. Calvin said that the primary task of the invisible church is to make the invisible kingdom visible. Christ ascended to heaven, to be seated at the right hand of His Father and reign as Lord of lords and King of kings, but how are people on earth to know that? Christ says that "all authority in heaven and on earth has been given to me" (Matt. 28:18). As the psalmist tells us:

> The kings of the earth set themselves,
> and the rulers take counsel together,
> against the LORD and against his Anointed, saying,
> "Let us burst their bonds apart
> and cast away their cords from us."
>
> He who sits in the heavens laughs;
> the Lord holds them in derision. (Ps. 2:2–4)

His reign, now, is invisible, but His church is visible. The visible church is to bear witness to the invisible Christ and to the reality that already exists, that He is now the King of kings and the Lord of lords.

There have been many problems in the church throughout the years because Christians have wrapped their faith in their national flag. We must be careful that our ultimate allegiance as Christians is to the kingdom of Christ. That does not mean that we can't be patriotic or serve and love our nation, but the ultimate authority is Christ. The most powerful political statement that one can ever make is, "My citizenship is in heaven; my number one allegiance is to Christ." Christ calls us to be submissive to earthly magistrates, to honor the rulers of the land in which we live, and we must do that, rendering unto Caesar the things that are Caesar's—but never giving to Caesar the things that are God's.

Luther said that every Christian is called to be Christ to his neighbor. He didn't suggest that we can bear our neighbor's sins or that we can save our neighbor. He meant that we must demonstrate to our neighbor what Christ is like. We are called to mirror and reflect our King because we are His loyal subjects in a land that doesn't want to be subject to His rule. It is significant that the Westminster Confession includes this metaphor of the visible church as the kingdom of the Lord Jesus Christ. We who are true believers, together with our children, are the subjects of the Lord Jesus Christ.

In the legend of Robin Hood, King Richard, who was the rightful king of England, left the nation to go on a crusade. While he was gone, wicked Prince John usurped the throne and began to exercise tyranny over the people of the land. Those who were loyal to King Richard were forced into hiding, and they lived in Sherwood Forest. Robin Hood, previously Sir Robin of Loxley, was disenfranchised because of his loyalty to King Richard and became the leader of those people around him in the woods, who called themselves the Merry Men. The point of my analogy is that they lived as pilgrims in a strange land that should have been theirs because they were loyal to the rightful king. Their king's authority had been usurped by an evil enemy.

When King Richard returned from the Holy Land, he crossed into England in the disguise of a mendicant friar. As he traveled in disguise to reclaim the throne, he went through Sherwood Forest and was stopped at the point of Robin Hood's sword. Richard removed his friar's hood, opened his robe, and the emblem of a lion's heart became visible on his shirt. Robin Hood recognized him and fell to his knees, saying, "My liege," and submitted to his king who had returned. We are in a similar situation. Our King has gone to a foreign land. While He is absent from us, we seek to be His loyal subjects, awaiting His return, when He will vindicate His people who cry unto Him day and night.

The visible church is the house and family of God. Many people think of the church as a building rather than people. We can be a church without a building. We are called chosen stones. We are God's "house." Each Christian is a stone used to build that city whose builder and maker is God. The foundation of that city consists of the Apostles and prophets, and Jesus is the cornerstone. The rest of the edifice is built stone by stone, person by person, so that Jesus can not only say to Simon, "You are Peter, the rock," but to all of us, "You are stones," fit together to form the church.

The church is also called the family of God, a metaphor that is based on a principle that is precious to our faith—adoption. The church is made up of those who are the adopted children of God, brought into his family to be united with Christ, his true child, the only begotten of the Father. God is not the father of everyone. He is the Creator of all people, and, in a poetic sense, all are His offspring. But to have a filial relationship to God, in which He is our Father, is a privilege given only to those who have been reborn by the Holy Spirit and adopted into the family of God. Even though we may have been taught it from childhood, we are not all God's children. We are, by nature, the children of Satan and the enemies of God. It is only through the regeneration of the Holy Spirit and adoption by God that we are welcomed into His family.

Because of the privileged position of adoption, which is at the heart of our salvation, we are not in a universal brotherhood. All men are not our brothers; all men are our neighbors. The brotherhood and sisterhood, however, is restricted to those who are adopted into the family of God. Christ is the only begotten child of the Father. That is why John expressed Apostolic astonishment when he said, "See what kind of love the Father has given to us, that we should be called children of God" (1 John 3:1). For the New Testament church, it was a radical thought that people like us could be considered members of the family of God, actual brothers and sisters of the Lord Jesus Christ. Today we take it for granted, and we miss the significance of what God has wrought in His mercy and grace by including us in this intimate filial relationship. The church is called to be the visible manifestation of the family of God.

Outside of the church, there is no ordinary possibility of salvation. In this confession, the Westminster divines are often responding to issues that have been argued quite thoroughly in church history. There is a long history behind this final phrase of section 2. The early church father Cyprian coined the maxim *Extra ecclesiam nulla salus*, which means "Outside of the church, there is no salvation." In Cyprian's formulation of this principle, it was as necessary to be in the visible church in order to be saved as it was for the people in Noah's day to be physically inside the ark to be saved from the flood.

That concept was embraced by the Roman Catholic Church, and, with certain modifications, it has come down through the centuries. One of the biggest problems that the Roman Catholic Church has had to deal with in the last few hundred years is what to make of the Protestants who left the fold. There was a time when it was taught that those outside the visible Roman Catholic Church could not be saved. But in the nineteenth century, that view began to be modified.

By the twentieth century, it was modified to the point that if someone is sincere in worship and has an implicit desire to be in the Roman church, even though he is an ardent Protestant (or even a fervent Muslim), then he is considered part of the Roman Catholic Church.

That may sound like a very humble position, but it is in fact the height of arrogance. It is based on the belief that the Roman church has the keys to the kingdom and thus can say who is saved and who is not. If someone is a Muslim, a Buddhist, or a Hindu, he may be saved if the Roman church is gracious enough to include him in their body by exercising the power of the keys.

The confession, aware of the traditions relating to Cyprian's formula, says that outside of the visible church there is no ordinary possibility of salvation. At this point, the framers of the Westminster Confession differ from Cyprian and go back to Augustine's position that salvation is found *substantially* but not *exclusively* in the church. People can come to salvation outside the church, but that is unusual. The ordinary way in which people are saved is through the ministry of the church of Jesus Christ.

Since the days in which this was written in the seventeenth century, we have seen an explosion of parachurch ministries, such as the Billy Graham Association, Youth for Christ, Young Life, Campus Crusade, and teaching ministries like Ligonier Ministries. There are many ministries that are basically evangelistic, through which people become Christians outside the pale of the visible church. We hope they are quickly brought into the visible church. Even with all the parachurch ministries in our day, the focal point and the concentration of the means of grace for salvation are still found ordinarily and chiefly in the visible church, because that is where the means of grace are concentrated.

3. Unto this catholic visible church Christ hath given the ministry, oracles, and ordinances of God, for the gathering and perfecting of the saints, in this life, to the end of the world: and doth, by his own presence and Spirit, according to his promise, make them effectual thereunto.

This section is pregnant with theological significance. First of all, it mentions that Christ has given to the visible church the ministry, oracles, and ordinances of God.

The ministry of prayer is one that is given to the entire church. When Jesus cleansed the temple, He rebuked the temple officials for turning it into a place of merchandise when it should be "a house of prayer" (Matt. 21:13). Christ established that one of the most important ministries is that of prayer, because God works through the prayers of His people in order to bring His purposes to pass. Jesus invites, encourages, and even commands us to bring our requests before Him, even though God already knows about our concerns. He invites us into that intimate relationship where we articulate to our Father those things that concern us deeply. God, knowing the content of our concerns and our prayers, works through those prayers as a means by which He brings His plan to fulfillment. Likewise, He does not need us for evangelism. God could call His saints audibly from heaven. He doesn't need the preacher or the missionary. Yet He has been pleased to choose the foolishness of preaching as the means through which He saves the world. God not only ordains the ends but also the means to those ends. The means through which He works include prayer, the Word, and the sacraments.

When we gather to worship, read Scripture, and hear a sermon, we are engaged in an exercise ordained by God to take place in His church. There is to be a ministry of God's Word, and the power to affect people's lives comes in and through that Word. The power is not in the preacher but in the Word of God. We pray that the Word that God promises to attend with the power of His Holy Spirit cuts into people's souls and hearts to bring healing, encouragement, faith, and godliness. Only God can bring forth the fruit of that Word. We plead with God that He will use the proclaimed Word to change people's lives.

The Apostle Paul, in Romans 2, labors the point that both Jew and Greek are exposed and vulnerable to the judgments of God. In chapter 3, he asks what advantage there is to being a Jew. He answers, "Much in every way," because the Jews have "the oracles of God," the Scriptures (Rom. 3:2). What an advantage it is for any person to be able to hear the Word of God. Church is above all a place where we can hear the Word of God and be comforted by it.

It is to the visible church that Christ has given the ministry, the oracles, and the ordinances of God for the gathering and perfecting of the saints, in this life. The function of the church is to gather together the people of God. We have already seen that the Greek word for "church," *ekklēsia*, means "those called out." We are the people called out of the world to solemn assembly.

There is a movement among Christians in the United States that in recent years has picked up a great deal of momentum. People are redoing and rethinking church, according to a new model that is called seeker-sensitive worship. The idea is that to reach the lost, we must do away with the traditional apparatus of church. Some churches that subscribe to this idea have done away with the chancel and replaced it with a stage. There is no pulpit as such, but simply a portable stand. The idea is to create an ambiance that is comfortable for the unbeliever who is "seeking" the things of God.

Sunday morning is devoted to seekers. The believers' special worship service—if there is one—is in the middle of the week in the evening. The whole focus of Sunday morning is to attract those outside the church, a kind of evangelism. It is certainly delightful that people have this kind of zeal for reaching the lost, but it is not so delightful that they think there are such people as unbelieving seekers. According to the Bible, the only people who seek after God are believers. We do not and cannot begin to seek after God until He has found us and brought us to Himself. Our conversion begins a lifelong pursuit, a lifelong quest of seeking after God. As Paul tells us in Romans 3:11, "No one seeks for God" in his natural state; rather, people flee from God. Unbelievers seek the benefits that only God can give them but they aren't seeking God.

The saints do not gather for selfish purposes, and we certainly don't bar the doors to unbelievers. But this gathering on a weekly basis is the gathering of the people of God. Our worship is for Christians and should be designed to enhance the growth and the development of the believer. Christ has given to His saints the ministry, the oracles, and the ordinances for their gathering and for their sanctification and for their perfecting in this life, to the end of the world.

Section 3 goes on to say that Christ doth, by his own presence and

Spirit, according to his promise, make them effectual thereunto. Ligonier Ministries has held seminars around the country on the doctrines of grace, the doctrine of election, and related doctrines. There is probably no doctrine that people struggle with more deeply or fight against more fiercely than the doctrine of election. Ligonier tries to communicate not simply the truth of this biblical teaching but the sweetness of it, the delight of it. Historically, when the people of God come to understand the full measure of the doctrines of grace, it sets their feet to dancing, so to speak. When they see what God has wrought in His mercy and grace, it brings comfort and confidence to believers in this hostile world around us.

The Puritans wrote of their gratitude for the doctrine of election because it focuses not simply on the eternal purposes of the Father but also upon the efficacy of the ministry of the Son. God's eternal purposes will and must come to pass, but in that eternal purpose of God is His determinate counsel to redeem His people. Our election is always *in* Christ, and it is effective and effected *through* Christ. The average evangelical Christian looks at the ministry of Jesus in this way: Jesus obeyed the Father's summons and willingly went to the cross to atone for people's sins—potentially. That is, He made redemption possible for all those who will put their trust in His work. But it was theoretically possible that no one would trust in Him and that He would therefore die in vain. Isaiah said of the Suffering Servant of the Lord, "Out of the anguish of his soul he shall see and be satisfied" (Isa. 53:11). In this view, He atoned for every sin except one: the sin of unbelief. If people persist in unbelief, they will perish.

However, if He atoned for the sins of all people, then all people would certainly be saved. God would be unjust to punish a person for whose sin an atonement had already been perfectly made. We underestimate the value, the purpose, and the power of the atonement when we think like that. The Puritans believed that God sent His Son into the world not only to make redemption *possible* for people but to make it *certain*. Christ's atonement was a perfect atonement that completely satisfied the demands of God's justice for God's people.

That is what the confession affirms: that the Lord gives **the ministry, oracles, and ordinances** to the church. And He gives to the church not only these things but also Himself, **his own presence.** When we come to the Lord's Table, it is not for our own internal fellowship but to feast on the presence of Christ in the sacramental redemption that He offers to us. He promises His presence at the Lord's Table. We won't be able to see Jesus, but He promises to be present, and He will be present. He will never miss that engagement, and the power of His presence will depend not on our faith but on His integrity. He did not come merely to help us through the gates of paradise but to take us into the heavenly kingdom. Like the Puritans, we must gain a deeper understanding of the excellency of Christ.

The Puritans were excited about the doctrine of election not because they enjoyed abstract theology or because it ties everything together so beautifully. They came to see that God had appointed us from the foundation of the world. He was the One who brought us to faith in Christ in the first place, and He would not throw us away after a while. He who has begun a good work in us has determined to bring it to its completion, and He is able to do it (Phil. 1:6). He does it *in* and *through* His Son and through the ministry of the Holy Spirit. Salvation is of the Lord, and the powerful and effective Lord brings His people out of Egypt into the promised land. That is our great comfort. Our only comfort in life and death is Christ and the power of His name and the power of His redemption.

> 4. This catholic church hath been sometimes more, sometimes less visible. And particular churches, which are members thereof, are more or less pure, according as the doctrine of the gospel is taught and embraced, ordinances administered, and public worship performed more or less purely in them.

At the Council of Nicaea, four marks of the church were set forth: that the church is one, holy, catholic, and Apostolic. The church is holy in the sense that it has a holy vocation and has been set apart for a special mission. It has a consecrated task and identity, and it is indwelt by the Holy Spirit. However, that does not mean that the church is perfectly pure. We are always a work in progress. Paul chided the people at Corinth to stop behaving like children. Nevertheless, he addressed them as holy ones (saints) because they had been set apart from the world (1 Cor. 1:2). The confession talks about the church in its visible manifestation, and particular churches as more or less pure, more or less holy.

The church, according to Augustine, is a *corpus permixtum*, "a mixed body," where there are tares growing along with the wheat (see Matt. 13:24–30). That is why any particular visible church can be more or less pure. We want to be committed to the purity of the church. The church can become impure if it crosses the line into apostasy. Then the believer not only may leave but must leave. We are not to be visibly identified with an apostate body.

There is a difference between an apostate and a pagan. Both, of course, are under the judgment of God. A pagan is one who has never made an outward profession of faith. An apostate, on the other hand, has made a profession of faith and then repudiated it. If a person or a particular church or even a denomination makes a profession of faith in Christ and then denies the deity of Christ, that person or institution has become apostate because it has denied an essential truth of the Christian faith.

This is what the Protestant-Roman Catholic controversy in the sixteenth century was about, and what a recent papal encyclical revisited. The Protestant churches of the sixteenth century were condemned by Rome for schism and teaching many false doctrines. In turn, the Protestant churches said that Rome was no longer a church. When Rome condemned the doctrine of justification by faith alone, the Reformers said, she became apostate. Once she denied the gospel, she was no longer a legitimate church, no matter how many other truths she maintained. That was the position of Luther, Calvin, Knox, and the rest of the Reformers. Since the sixteenth century, Roman Catholics and Protestants have not recognized each other as valid churches.

The sixteenth century witnessed not only the Roman Catholic–Protestant split but also splits within the Protestant movement, such as that between the Lutherans and the Reformed. Given the multiplication of churches, people sought to authenticate particular churches and determine whether they were legitimate. The Reformers said there were three criteria that must be met for a group to be a true church.

The first criterion is the gospel. Every true church proclaims the gospel. The essential elements of the gospel are simply the basic creedal formulations of historic Christianity. The essential truths about Jesus are His sinlessness, deity, humanity, atonement, resurrection, and ascension. Essential to the gospel is not only the work of Christ but also how His benefits are appropriated. As Paul indicates, there is only one gospel, and it is the gospel of justification by faith alone. If one believes all the essential truths about Jesus but denies how the benefits of the objective work of Christ are subjectively appropriated, one does not have the gospel.

Some theologians today refuse to say that justification by faith alone is essential to the gospel. Luther said it was the article upon which the church stands or falls. Calvin said it was the hinge upon which everything turns. But these Christian leaders refuse to use the term *essential*. Historically, Protestant theology has always said that *sola fide* is not only part of the gospel but essential to it. Without it, there is no gospel. Without the gospel, there is no church. There can be a religious institution, but without the gospel, it is no church.

Second, the administration of the sacraments is essential to a true church. So, what do we make of the controversy between Protestant bodies who practice infant baptism and those who restrict baptism to so-called believer's baptism? For the most part, Protestants have agreed that the issue of baptism, as serious as it may be, does not determine whether a church is a genuine church. It falls into the category of true churches as more or less pure.

The confession does not say that there must be agreement on every aspect of the doctrine of the sacraments before we can recognize the validity of another church. Protestants disagree not only about baptism but also about the nature of the presence of Christ in the Lord's Supper. Nevertheless, all these groups use baptism as a sign and seal of the promises of God in the new covenant. They all intend to communicate the Lord's death in the Lord's Supper. Some Protestant churches are more pure and others are less pure with respect to the sacraments, but they are sufficiently pure to be true churches of Christ.

The third criterion for a church to be authentic is that it has an organized government by which church discipline can be and is exercised.

Without discipline, gross and heinous sin or heresy can fester openly, leading to the apostasy of a church.

> 5. The purest churches under heaven are subject both to mixture and error; and some have so degenerated, as to become no churches of Christ, but synagogues of Satan. Nevertheless, there shall be always a church on earth, to worship God according to his will.

Section 4 ends with these words: according as the doctrine of the gospel is taught and embraced, ordinances administered, and public worship performed more or less purely in them. Section 5 continues: The purest churches under heaven—not just the least pure churches, but also the most pure churches—are subject both to mixture and error. There is no such thing as a perfect church, nor is there any such thing as an infallible church. Some have so degenerated, as to become no churches of Christ, but synagogues of Satan. Nevertheless, there shall be always a church on earth, to worship God according to his will. A particular church or denomination may pass out of existence or may become apostate, but God will never leave this planet destitute of a visible church that worships Him properly.

> 6. There is no other head of the church but the Lord Jesus Christ. Nor can the pope of Rome, in any sense, be head thereof.

Finally, section 6 adds two brief sentences to say that there is no vicar of Christ on earth. There is no basis for the papacy in the New Testament. Christ and only Christ is the head of His church. That is an axiom, of course, of Protestant Christianity.

Of the Communion of Saints

1. All saints, that are united to Jesus Christ their Head, by his Spirit, and by faith, have fellowship with him in his graces, sufferings, death, resurrection, and glory: and, being united to one another in love, they have communion in each other's gifts and graces, and are obliged to the performance of such duties, public and private, as do conduce to their mutual good, both in the inward and outward man.

2. Saints by profession are bound to maintain an holy fellowship and communion in the worship of God, and in performing such other spiritual services as tend to their mutual edification; as also in relieving each other in outward things, according to their several abilities and necessities. Which communion, as God offereth opportunity, is to be extended unto all those who, in every place, call upon the name of the Lord Jesus.

3. This communion which the saints have with Christ, doth not make them in any wise partakers of the substance of his Godhead; or to be equal with Christ in any respect: either of which to affirm is impious and blasphemous. Nor doth their communion one with another, as saints, take away, or infringe the title or propriety which each man hath in his goods and possessions.

One of the definitions of the church is the communion of saints. The communion of saints is such an important element in the life of the Christian and of the church that the Westminster divines thought it prudent to deal with it separately as a distinct article of faith. In that regard, they followed the ancient fathers of the church, who included the communion of saints as one of the elements in the church's oldest confession, the Apostles' Creed: "I believe in the Holy Ghost, . . . the communion of saints, the forgiveness of sins, the resurrection of the body, and the life everlasting." In Latin, it is the *communio sanctorum*, and it touches one of the richest elements of our Christian experience for two reasons. The communion of saints describes our relationship with Christ and our relationship with each other. There are not many relationships that are as important in our lives as those two.

From the Latin *communio*, we see more clearly the etymology of the word *communion*. The prefix *com* means "with." The root of the word is *unio*, so communion means "union with." Why add the prefix *com* to *unio* when *unio* expresses union by itself? Historically, there's an important distinction between *union* and *communion*.

In classic forms of non-Christian mysticism, such as Gnosticism or Neoplatonism, there was the belief that one has to bypass the mind to apprehend the divine. In some of the Greek mystery religions, the disciples of Dionysus, the god of the vine, engaged in orgies of drunkenness and feasting (known as *bacchanalia*, after Dionysius' other name, Bacchus). There was immoral behavior with the temple prostitutes. The rationale for these orgies was the notion that to apprehend deity, one must silence the rational barrier of reason. To gain entrance into the transcendent realm and mystically apprehend the divine, they believed, one has to bypass the mind and the five senses. The Dionysian frenzy with intoxication and dancing was designed to produce an ecstasy in which contact could perhaps be made with the divine. One could lose consciousness of oneself and become one with God.

That is a concept in Eastern religions also. In these religions, the ultimate goal of religious experience is the loss of personal identity and the experience of losing one's individuality and being swallowed up in "the all" or "the one." It is described as becoming like a drop of water, diffused throughout the entire ocean, losing any sense of particularity or individuation, once merged with the oversoul.

There are mystical elements in New Testament Christianity. Paul talks about being caught up in the third heaven, an incredible experience of transcendence where he had a heightened sense and awareness of Christ (2 Cor. 12). Throughout church history, an element of mysticism has been associated with Christian faith. The difference between pagan mysticism and Christian mysticism is that Christianity never sees the goal of religious faith as the annihilation of personal identity or the loss of the self. Rather, the goal is a heightened understanding of the self as it relates to God. It is the redemption of the personal identity, not the destruction of it, that we see as our goal. One of the reasons why non-Christian religious movements seek to escape from the self and to become one with a greater entity is to escape from personal responsibility. One can then live however one wants without being held accountable, because redemption will be the loss of personal identity. But the Christian faith offers not the destruction but the redemption of the person. Even death does not destroy personal identity. We believe, as Christians, in the continuity of conscious, personal identity at death. We believe that the body dies but that the soul goes on with what we call the *continuity of personal existence* at death. The ultimate goal of pagan mysticism is to lose personal identity and to become one with God—*unio*.

The church has been careful to say that the goal of our redemption is not *unio* but *communio*. That means that there is a mystical union between Christ and His people. Our identity is not swallowed up in the identity of Christ, so that we become gods; rather, we enter into the blessed condition of intense personal fellowship with God. That is what communion means—being with Him, not being absorbed in Him. The person who is in communion with Christ does not lose his personal identity. That is the difference between union and communion.

Two words in the New Testament that need to be distinguished in this connection are *en* and *eis*. The word *eis* is usually translated "into," and the word *en*, "in." If someone is outside a room, he can walk "into" (*eis*) it, whereupon he would be "in" (*en*) it. When Paul says in Acts, "Believe in the Lord Jesus, and you will be saved" (16:31), the Greek word translated "in" is actually *eis*, indicating that we put our faith *into* Him. Then, when Paul talks about how Christians are in Christ and Christ is in them, he uses the word *en*. When we become Christians, we enter by faith into Christ and He enters into us, resulting in a mystical union in which we are in Him and He is in us. We have been initiated and invited into this intimate spiritual fellowship by Christ Himself. We remain distinct persons, and we each have a relationship with Christ, who is the basis of our unity as the church. Our relationships with other Christians need to be based on our mutual inclusion in Christ.

We can't hate someone for whom Christ died. We can be irritated or offended by them, or we can offend them and have altercations, but there is a limit to that hostility beyond which we can't go without at the same time denying Christ. We are to be patient with one another, understanding that our sanctification is still a work in progress. We forbear and love one another because our fellowship is rooted in Christ, who has sacrificed His love and His life for all of us. We must see each other in Christ. As soon as we consider a Christian in that dimension, a remarkable change in our attitude occurs. Our love for Christ and His love for us overcome our tensions and conflicts with one another.

Our mystical union with Christ is effected by the third person of the Trinity, the Holy Spirit. Remember, it is mainly the work of the Spirit to apply the saving work of Christ to us. The Father initiates salvation, the Son accomplishes it, and the Holy Spirit applies it to us. It is the Spirit who causes us to be reborn, who creates faith in our heart, who indwells us and empowers us for our sanctification, and who effects this mystical union of our spirit with Christ. In Romans 8:16, Paul teaches that "the Spirit himself bears witness with our spirit that we are children of God." The Holy Spirit not only brings us into this relationship but also bears witness to our human spirit that we are in this relationship.

1. All saints, that are united to Jesus Christ their Head, by his Spirit, and by faith, have fellowship with him in his graces, sufferings, death, resurrection, and glory: and, being united to one another in love, they have communion in each other's gifts and graces, and are obliged to the performance of such duties, public and private, as do conduce to their mutual good, both in the inward and outward man.

All saints, that are united to Jesus Christ their Head, by his Spirit, and by faith, have fellowship with him in his graces, sufferings, death, resurrection,

and glory. One of the deeply concerning things about modern forms of evangelism is that we are so zealous to win people to Christ and to communicate the benefits of the gospel that we will say, "If you come to Jesus, you can have fellowship with Him in His grace, in His resurrection, and in His glory"—omitting the fellowship in His sufferings. So important is that concept, in terms of our union with Christ, that the Apostle Paul says that unless we are willing to participate in His suffering and death, we will not enter into His exaltation (2 Tim. 2:11–12). If we do enter into the afflictions of Jesus and embrace His humiliation, we will participate in His exaltation and in His glory.

The sacrament of baptism signifies, among other things, that the person being baptized is identified with the sufferings of Christ. Baptism is the sign of our unity with Christ in His death and resurrection. In Colossians 1:24, Paul testifies that he rejoices in his own persecution: "Now I rejoice in my sufferings for your sake, and in my flesh I am filling up what is lacking in Christ's afflictions for the sake of his body, that is, the church." It may sound as if Paul is saying that Jesus did 90 percent of the work of salvation, and we have to do the remaining 10 percent. On the contrary, "what is lacking" refers to the consequences of participation in Christ Jesus. The church is the body of Christ, and thus, in one sense, the continuation of His incarnation. Don't misunderstand; it is not that the church is God incarnate. Rather, the embodiment of Christ in this world today is His church, and He identifies with His church.

Before the Apostle Paul became a Christian, he was on the way to Damascus with authority to drag people out of their homes and throw them into prison. When Jesus stopped him and addressed him from heaven, He said, "Saul, Saul, why are you persecuting me?" (Acts 9:4). He was afflicting Jesus by imposing suffering on those who were in Him and in whom He dwells. By hurting Jesus' body, the church, he was hurting Jesus. In that sense, Paul was filling up what was lacking in the body of Christ by *imposing* the sufferings. After his conversion, he was filling it up by personally *receiving* the sufferings with beatings, stonings, shipwrecks, persecutions, and imprisonment. Jesus said to His people, "In the world you will have tribulation" (John 16:33). He also said: "If the world hates you, know that it has hated me before it hated you. If you were of the world, the world would love you as its own; but because you are not of the world, but I chose you out of the world, therefore the world hates you" (John 15:18–19). We will enter into His sorrows, His pain, His afflictions, and then into His glory. We are "fellow heirs with Christ, provided we suffer with him in order that we may also be glorified with him" (Rom. 8:17).

Paul was referring to that concept and not to any deficiency in the work of Jesus. Through His redemptive suffering at the hands of the Father and the propitiation that He gave us on the cross, His work is finished; that pain is done. Nevertheless, the world is still heaping afflictions on Christ by persecuting His body, the church. When we suffer for the gospel's sake, we fill up the full measure of the sufferings of Christ by virtue of our communion with Him. The confession echoes Paul when it says that we have fellowship with Christ in His grace, in His sufferings, in His death, in His resurrection, and in His glory.

We are united to one another in love. We are in union with Christ as the communion of saints. Anyone who is united with Christ is at the same time united with all others who are united with Christ. Being united to one another in love, they—that is, the saints—have communion in each other's gifts and graces, and are obliged to the performance of such duties, public and private, as do conduce to their mutual good, both in the inward and outward man. Paul describes the diversity of gifts in the body of Christ by using the metaphor of the body, in which a multitude of diverse parts, like eyes, ears, nose, lungs, heart, arms, and legs, work together. Similarly, the church consists of many members working together as one body.

Some may have the gift of giving, administration, evangelism, teaching, or preaching. When a member exercises his gift, we participate in that gift, because it is used for the edification of the whole church. All who give financially receive a return that does not benefit only themselves but the whole body. The spiritual gifts work the same way. The ingredient that makes the communion of the saints cohesive is *agapē*, love.

The discourse on love found in 1 Corinthians 13 is sandwiched between chapter 12 and chapter 14, in which the Apostle Paul admonishes the Corinthian congregation about their abuse of the gifts of the

Spirit. It is in the middle of this that he tells us how the body of Christ is supposed to look. "If I speak in the tongues of men and of angels, but have not love, I am a noisy gong or a clanging cymbal" (1 Cor. 13:1). Paul is not describing love in the abstract; he is telling us how love looks in the midst of a community that has been gifted by God. The purpose of our gifts and of our graces is to benefit everyone in the body of Christ. Not one gifted person can say, "Look at me." First Corinthians 13 is an exposition of the communion of the saints.

Being united to one another in love, they have communion in each other's gifts and graces, and are obliged to the performance of such duties, public and private, as do conduce to their mutual good, both in the inward and outward man. That is communion. Paul wrote to the Corinthians, "And I, when I came to you, brothers, did not come proclaiming to you the testimony of God with lofty speech or wisdom. . . . And I was with you in weakness and in fear and much trembling" (1 Cor. 2:1, 3). Paul was with them in their suffering, and he entered into their suffering. He was part of their community, part of their communion. We weep with those who weep, and we rejoice with those who rejoice (Rom. 12:15). That is communion, and that is the essence of biblical community.

> 2. Saints by profession are bound to maintain an holy fellowship and communion in the worship of God, and in performing such other spiritual services as tend to their mutual edification; as also in relieving each other in outward things, according to their several abilities and necessities. Which communion, as God offereth opportunity, is to be extended unto all those who, in every place, call upon the name of the Lord Jesus.

In sections 2 and 3, we find affirmation and denial; that is, section 2 tells us what the communion of saints does mean, and section 3 tells us what it does not mean. First, the affirmation.

Saints by profession are bound to maintain an holy fellowship and communion in the worship of God. Our purpose for assembling together is to worship God, to offer the sacrifices of praise. If people are leaving church because they are bored, that is revealing. The answer is not to put on dramatic presentations on Sunday morning or to include Christian rock music or any other form of entertainment. If people are bored, they don't have a sense of coming into the presence of God. No one has ever been confronted with the living God and walked away bored. They may burst into tears, faint, or leap with joy, but they are never bored. There is nothing boring about God.

If people leave church saying, "That was absolutely irrelevant," then there are two possible explanations. Either the preacher hasn't preached the Word of God, or the people haven't listened. There is nothing irrelevant about being in the presence of God and hearing his Word.

Fellowship is important, and that is why the church body has times other than worship to be together. It is important to have occasions when we can bond as members of a local congregation. It is amazing how we can edify one another in this way. Luther's principle of "the priesthood of all believers" means that every member of the body of Christ is gifted by the Holy Spirit and is expected to use that gift in the service of Christ and of his kingdom. In that sense, we are all priests and we all participate in the ministry of Christ. The church is an army of gifted people, to be trained, disciplined, and sent into the world for mission. The confession affirms that in the communion of saints we are **bound to maintain an holy fellowship and communion in the worship of God, and in performing such other spiritual services as tend to their mutual edification.**

When we make a profession of faith in Christ and become part of His body, we are indwelt by Christ. He is in us, and we are in Him. From that day forth, we ought never to neglect the assembling together of the saints (Heb. 10:25). The rule of thumb in most of today's churches is that on any given Sunday, a minimum of 25 percent of the church members will be absent. That includes people who are out of town, people who are sick, and people who are otherwise providentially hindered. Still, that is a high percentage of members who are not present with the rest of the body in worship on Sunday morning.

We must rid ourselves of the cavalier, casual attitude that we who bear the name of Christ can fail to participate in worship or in the fellowship of the body of Christ. It is our job to support and edify one another by gathering together for worship. We remember the warnings in Hebrews that it is a dreadful thing to "neglect such a great salvation" (Heb. 2:3). It is our duty to be in church and in fellowship with other Christians, engaged in the worship of God for the mutual edification of the saints.

The saints maintain their communion also in relieving each other in outward things, according to their several abilities and necessities. Which communion, as God offereth opportunity, is to be extended unto all those who, in every place, call upon the name of the Lord Jesus. This last section almost sounds like communism. In fact, the proof texts include the passage in Acts 2 where the disciples in the early church had all things in common. Some people have deduced from that text that there is a mandate in the New Testament to divest oneself of all private property and to live together in communes where all property is held in common. That represents a superficial understanding of that passage and ignores the rest of Scripture. The Decalogue in the Old Testament and the teaching of the New Testament support the right of private property.

The confession is developing the principle that when we see a person weeping, we weep with him. When someone in our fellowship is going through extreme need or want, it is the duty of the congregation to help that person. Most churches have a special fund from which to support people who are lacking food or other necessities. Many of the so-called welfare programs of the government undertake responsibilities that God gave to the church, not to the state. Our responsibility is to make sure that, within the shadow of our church, the outward needs of people are being met.

To find a congregation, Jesus went out to seek and to save those who were lost. He gave His time and His attention to sinners, to those who were sick, to those who were in need of a Savior. He looked for them. That is what it means for the church to be the church. A congregation ought to be so mobilized that it is looking for troubled people to minister to. Some are ill and in need of care. Some are hospitalized and have no one to visit them. Some have family members in prison. There will always be an opportunity to minister for Christ where the pain is.

3. This communion which the saints have with Christ, doth not make them in any wise partakers of the substance of his Godhead; or to be equal with Christ in any respect: either of which to affirm

is impious and blasphemous. Nor doth their communion one with another, as saints, take away, or infringe the title or propriety which each man hath in his goods and possessions.

Section 2 explains what the communion of saints entails; section 3 explains what it does not entail.

This communion which the saints have with Christ, doth not make them in any wise partakers of the substance of his Godhead; or to be equal with Christ in any respect: either of which to affirm is impious and blasphemous. Someone once said, "Every person has a spark of the divine within him." That's not true. All we have is humanity. We may have *reborn* humanity, but it is humanity in the process of sanctification. We may be indwelt by the Holy Spirit, but we never participate in the substance of deity, even though we are created in the image of God. To be made in the image of God does not mean that we participate in His essence, His deity. It means that there are aspects that God imparts that are similar to His own being. Augustine explained the image of God in man as man's memory, his understanding, and his will. God is a rational being. He has a mind and He thinks, and He is also a volitional being. He has a will. He makes choices, and in order to make choices, there is a mind. A mindless response or reaction is not a willful, voluntary action; it is involuntary. In that sense, we are like God, who has given to man a measure of intelligence and volition that is not found anywhere else in creation to the degree that it is given to man. Nevertheless, it is still a finite mind and a finite will. We do not have omniscience in our understanding, which is an incommunicable divine attribute. The substance of deity is not transferred to humanity. In fact, not only did God not create us as little gods, but He could not, because the essence of deity is found only in self-existent eternal being. God could not create another self-existent eternal being. By definition, any created being would not be self-existent and eternal, because it would be created.

The view of the confession is that any person who thinks that he partakes of the substance of Christ's Godhead or is equal with Him in any respect is impious and blasphemous. The highest rung on the spiritual ladder is communion with Christ, but that does not make us divine.

Nor doth their communion one with another, as saints, take away, or infringe the title or propriety which each man hath in his goods and possessions. The confession reaffirms the principle of private ownership. This may seem insignificant, but it isn't simply a statement on economics or political theory. The authors of the confession were concerned about Christian ethics and the Christian faith. They wanted to maintain the right of private ownership as an ethical principle.

The New Testament says, "Let the thief no longer steal" (Eph. 4:28). The Bible prohibits theft, and in doing so it protects the private possession of those who own things. The Bible condemns the sins of greed, envy, and covetousness. If someone has a better job, more money, or a nicer house, the Christian's response is to rejoice in another's prosperity. We are not to be filled with resentment or hostility toward someone who is blessed in outward circumstances more than we are. When we are covetous, we not only do violence and injury to our neighbor, but we insult God, who is the author of every good and perfect gift. We are to be satisfied and content in whatever state we are and to learn with the Apostle Paul how to abound and how to be abased (Phil. 4:11–13).

Some people who are prosperous struggle with enjoying that blessing. One of the beautiful things that God does, related to the handling of private property, is to set down a requirement of giving that is the same for everyone. That was the beauty of the Old Testament principle of the tithe. The widow who was in abject poverty gave the same percentage of her goods as Abraham, who was one of the wealthiest men in the world—10 percent.

There is no graduated income tax or politics of envy with God. Not everyone gives the same, but they all give the same percentage. No one can complain. After they have given what is required, they can enjoy what is left with no guilty feeling.

The first year the Pilgrims were in New England, they held everything in common, and they had nothing to show for their toil. Finally, William Bradford told them that in the second year, they could keep whatever they produced. In the second year and afterward, the community prospered. The difference was that in the first year everyone did as little as possible, knowing that everything they produced was going to be taken away from them. Biblical faith does not follow that concept. It requires stewardship capitalism. We are to be productive and responsible stewards of what we have. That means giving, and that means supporting the ministry of the kingdom, and that means helping the poor. There is a difference between community and communalism. We are to show love and concern to our neighbors, but that does not require us to divest ourselves of private property.

Of the Sacraments

1. Sacraments are holy signs and seals of the covenant of grace, immediately instituted by God, to represent Christ, and his benefits; and to
   confirm our interest in him: as also, to put a visible difference between
   those that belong unto the church, and the rest of the world; and solemnly to engage them to the service of God in Christ, according to his
   Word.
2. There is, in every sacrament, a spiritual relation, or sacramental union,
   between the sign and the thing signified: whence it comes to pass, that
   the names and effects of the one are attributed to the other.
3. The grace which is exhibited in or by the sacraments rightly used, is not
   conferred by any power in them; neither doth the efficacy of a sacrament
   depend upon the piety or intention of him that doth administer it: but
   upon the work of the Spirit, and the word of institution, which contains,
   together with a precept authorizing the use thereof, a promise of benefit
   to worthy receivers.
4. There be only two sacraments ordained by Christ our Lord in the Gospel;
   that is to say, baptism, and the Supper of the Lord: neither of which may
   be dispensed by any, but by a minister of the Word lawfully ordained.
5. The sacraments of the old testament, in regard of the spiritual things
   thereby signified and exhibited, were, for substance, the same with
   those of the new.

The worship experience in the life of the church is usually defined
in terms of Word and sacrament, and chapters 27–29 of the Westminster Confession discuss the two sacraments of baptism and the Lord's

Supper. Chapter 27 discusses sacraments in general, followed by chapter 28 on baptism and chapter 29 on the Lord's Supper. Historically, churches have understood the sacraments in vastly different ways. Because the sacraments are so important to the life of the church, it is understandable that there has been a lot of controversy. It is good that the debates occur, because it indicates that the people of God are taking these aspects of their worship seriously.

There are controversies about the number of the sacraments, their meaning, origin, mode, and efficacy, as well as who may dispense and who may receive them. The word sacrament comes from the Latin *sacramentum*, which translates the Greek *mystērion*, and that's why in some churches the sacraments are referred to as "holy mysteries." The term *mystērion* in the Bible does not mean "mystery" as that word is used in our culture. We think of mysteries as secretive, sinister, or eerie. The biblical *mystērion*, however, refers to a mystery that once was hidden but now is revealed. This differs even from our theological use of the term to denote those things that we do not yet understand. The biblical mysteries are things that were once hidden, particularly in Old Testament days, but are now revealed in the coming of Christ and with the Apostolic revelation.

A mystery, in the sense of a sacrament, is not intended to conceal something, but just the opposite. A mystery reveals something, and thus the sacraments are nonverbal forms of communication. In the Old Testament, God verbally communicated His truth to His people by way of His spoken or written word. His verbal communications were often supplemented or corroborated by nonverbal forms of communication. The prophets frequently gave object lessons, in which they would act out certain of their revelations for the people. They would talk in terms of analogies. "I see a plumb line," Amos said, and that indicated God's intent to measure His people to see whether they were obedient to the norms that He had established (see Amos 7:7–9). Throughout the Old Testament, we see these nonverbal forms of communication.

One of the earliest of these was the sign of the rainbow, by which God signified to Noah that He would never again destroy the world with a flood (Gen. 9:8–17). That sign reminded the people of God's promise.

Also in the Old Testament were circumcision, which became the sign of the old covenant, and the celebratory meal at Passover. There was rich symbolism in the celebration of the Day of Atonement, in which two transactions took place. The priest laid his hands on the scapegoat, dramatically transferring the sins of the people to it. The scapegoat was then sent outside the camp into the wilderness, into the outer darkness. Then an animal was sacrificed on the altar. After an elaborate ritual of purification, the high priest was allowed to go into the Holy of Holies. There he sprinkled the blood of the offering on the mercy seat, which was the lid of the ark of the covenant. In this drama, the promise of God to forgive the sins of His people and to provide an atonement for the people was acted out. Throughout Old Testament history, such ritual is part and parcel of God's communication of His Word to His people. His Word is fortified and confirmed by visible, external, nonverbal forms of communication.

We do not think of those Old Testament visible manifestations as sacraments in the narrow sense of the word, but they are sacramental in the broad sense of the term. In the New Testament, there are sacraments instituted by Christ, and we see God continuing to confirm His Word with actions or nonverbal forms of communication. Ritual is important to the life of God's people. As human beings, we communicate not only with words but also by facial expressions and gestures. These are nonverbal aspects of communication. This is one of the problems we have when we read the Scripture. We must imagine the tone and inflection of the speaker's voice and the look on his face. What was Pilate's tone when he said to Jesus, "What is truth?" Did he say it with cynicism dripping from his lips? Was Pilate taken aback by Jesus' statement that His mission was to bear witness to the truth and that all who are of the truth hear His voice? We don't know, and although sometimes the context gives us hints and clues, we can't know for sure. Words that we speak or write can be strengthened or intensified by the nonverbal apparatus with which they are associated.

In the New Testament, dramatic and important rites were instituted by Christ, called baptism and the Lord's Supper. Baptism had been introduced before the ministry of Jesus, by John the Baptist. The rite that John introduced to Israel was not exactly the same thing as New Testament baptism. John's baptism was intended to prepare Israel for the coming of the Messiah, whereas Jesus assigned a whole new set of meanings and content to His baptism. In both cases, baptism symbolized cleansing, among other things. People underwent a ritual of cleansing that communicated in a graphic way that they were dirty. Their dirtiness was not from the dirt of the ground but from the dirt of their sin. Their baptism symbolized their cleansing from their sinful condition.

Jesus established the Lord's Supper when He gathered His disciples to celebrate the Passover one last time before He died. He went to great lengths to find a place that was suitable for Him to meet with His inner circle. In the middle of the celebration, Jesus changed the significance of the meal. Previously, the Passover had memorialized Israel's deliverance from Egypt, beginning with the blood of a lamb being spread on the doorposts of Israelite homes so that the angel of destruction would pass over them when he went through Egypt killing the firstborn sons. Holding up a cup of wine, Jesus said to His disciples, "This is My blood, the blood of a new covenant, the blood that is shed for the remission of your sins." He attached new meaning to that ancient ritual. Virtually from that night forward, it has been celebrated weekly by the Christian community. The bread of the meal represents His body, and the wine represents His shed blood. The Lord's Supper communicates the significance of the Lord's death nonverbally. "For as often as you eat this bread and drink the cup, you proclaim the Lord's death until he comes" (1 Cor. 11:26). It is a visible manifestation of the verbal content of the atonement, acted out dramatically.

1. Sacraments are holy signs and seals of the covenant of grace, immediately instituted by God, to represent Christ, and his benefits; and to confirm our interest in him: as also, to put a visible difference between those that belong unto the church, and the rest of the world; and solemnly to engage them to the service of God in Christ, according to his Word.

This is a wonderful definition of sacraments. First of all, they are **holy signs and seals of the covenant of grace**. Sacraments are given in the context of covenant. The sign of the old covenant was circumcision, and the sign of the new covenant is baptism. When the people of God entered into the Mosaic covenant, God made promises to the people, and along with the promises came the stipulations, or commandments, of the covenant. The Old Testament covenant included a preamble, a historical prologue, promises, stipulations, and a rite by which people swore their allegiance to their covenant Lord. The sign of the covenant of Abraham, repeated through Moses, was circumcision, which was a cutting rite administered to males. It symbolized two different elements, or dual sanctions. On the one hand, the subordinate party in the covenant, the person being circumcised, was saying, "May I be cut off from the world, set apart from godlessness, and enter into the holy community of the covenant people of God." The cutting of the foreskin was in a sense the cutting out of the person from ungodly humanity, putting him into the privileged position of being numbered among the people of God. It was a mark of consecration, of his being set apart for a holy purpose. That was the positive symbolism behind circumcision.

Conversely, it had a negative symbolism. The circumcised person said with this action, "If I am not faithful to the terms of the covenant and do not obey the law of God, may I be cut off from all His blessings, cut off from His presence, cut off from fellowship with Him, just as I have had the foreskin of my flesh cut off." This was a dramatic image of the terms of the covenant that marked a Jew.

In Genesis 15, God said to Abraham, "Fear not, Abram, I am your shield; your reward shall be very great" (v. 1). Abraham staggered at that announcement and said, "O Lord GOD, what will you give me, for I continue childless, and the heir of my house is Eliezer of Damascus?" (v. 2). God replied, "This man shall not be your heir; your very own son shall be your heir. . . . Look toward heaven, and number the stars, if you are able to number them. . . . So shall your offspring be" (vv. 4–5). Then we read in verse 6, "And he believed the LORD, and he counted it to him as righteousness." This is the first expression of the doctrine of justification by faith alone in the Old Testament.

Moments later, Abraham, who was struggling with his faith, asked, "O Lord GOD, how am I to know that I shall possess it?" (v. 8). God ordered Abraham to kill certain animals, cut them in half, and arrange their body parts to form a path. Half of the body parts would be on one side of the aisle, and the other half would be on the other side. God put Abraham into a deep sleep, in which he saw a smoking fire pot and a flaming torch moving between the pieces (vv. 17–21). By doing this, God was symbolically saying, "Because I cannot swear by anything greater, I swear by Myself. I am dramatizing, by walking through these pieces of animals that have been torn asunder, that I will keep My promises. If I don't, may I be torn apart, just as these animals have been torn apart." God put His eternal deity on the line. When we struggle with faith and wonder whether we can trust God, it is good to go back and read Genesis 15, where He swore an oath by Himself and put His character and being on the line in dramatic fashion.

This was a sacramental act with a small *s*. It was an outward sign that confirmed a promise. In the Old Testament, the sign of participation in the covenant of grace was circumcision. Abraham, who was called after he was an adult and after he had professed faith, was circumcised. Whatever else circumcision represented, it represented his faith. In the case of adult converts to Israel, those from the outside could be circumcised only after they had made a profession of faith. Israel practiced believer's circumcision for those who came into Israel from paganism, but the Israelite children received the sign of their faith in infancy, before they had professed faith. Abraham made his profession of faith as an adult, and then he was circumcised, but God commanded that Isaac be circumcised as an infant. This becomes important when we cross over into the New Testament and see the points of continuity between the Old Testament sign and the New Testament sign. They are not identical, but there are important parallels.

The word *sign* is important. It appears throughout the New Testament (particularly in the book of John), where it translates the Greek word *semeion*. People debate whether there are miracles today or whether they ceased at the end of the Apostolic age. Some say the birth of a baby is a miracle; other people say it is an ordinary event, not an extraordinary one. It all depends on what we mean by "miracle." Some English translations of the Bible use the word *miracle*, but there is no one word in Greek that means "miracle." We extrapolate a concept of miracle from several different words in the New Testament. Sometimes they are called *powers*, sometimes they are called *wonders*, but the word of choice in John's gospel is *sign*. For example: "This, the first of his signs, Jesus did at Cana in Galilee" (John 2:11). The feeding of the five thousand was "the sign that [Jesus] had done" (John 6:14).

This concept runs through the New Testament. A sign points beyond itself to some higher meaning or significance. Baptism is not redemption in Christ; the Lord's Supper is not the crucifixion of Christ. These things point to the realities, but they are not the realities. They are nonverbal confirmations of the promises of God.

People ask: "Does baptism automatically, supernaturally regenerate a person? Does baptism save us?" The Reformation answer is no. If baptism does not convey saving grace, then what good is it? How can it be important if it doesn't do what it is signifying? Some people who are baptized are not saved and never come to salvation. In Romans 2, Paul writes about circumcision of the heart: "But a Jew is one inwardly" (Rom. 2:29). Paul spoke against the idea that developed among the Jews that because they were circumcised, they were saved. They thought they had proof of their salvation in their circumcision; they had the sign of the covenant, so they believed they were saved. Paul's argument was that a person can have the external sign and not have the internal reality to which that sign points.

The efficacy of the sacraments was a major point of controversy between the Reformers and the Roman Catholic Church. Does baptism automatically convey the grace of justification? The Roman Catholic Church said yes; the Reformers said no. Rome charged that the Protestants had reduced the sacraments to a *nuda signa*, a naked sign, devoid of any effect. If baptism doesn't convey the grace of salvation, then it is an empty sign. The Reformers' answer was that when God makes a promise and confirms that promise with a sign, there is nothing empty about the sign. That is why we can say, as Luther did, when Satan comes after us to accuse us, "Get away from me; I'm baptized." We can say to Satan: "I don't trust you because you're a liar, and I put my trust in the promise of God, which was signified to me in my baptism. I bear the ineradicable mark and sign of God's promise."

The promises of baptism are fulfilled only in and through faith, but the integrity of God's promise to us does not rest on our faith. Some people think they need to be rebaptized. Perhaps the person who baptized them turned out a scoundrel, which they fear makes their baptism invalid. But this is not true. The integrity of that sign does not rest with the person who gives it, or the person who receives it, or the parents who were there. The integrity of the sign rests with the One whose promise it is.

Other people were baptized as infants but came to faith later in life. Because they don't remember their baptism and didn't know what was happening, they think it didn't mean anything, and therefore they should get baptized again. Again, this is not true. Saying an infant baptism is meaningless because one came to faith later is like saying the promise of God conveyed in the baptism has failed. But exactly the opposite is the case. His promise has been gloriously fulfilled in the one who later comes to faith. Such people should rejoice that the promise God signified to them in their baptism many years ago is now fulfilled in all its glory.

The fact that people make these requests indicates that even though we practice baptism in a variety of ways in all denominations, there is very little understanding of the meaning of baptism. First of all, baptism is a *sign*. Second, it is a *seal*. It is more than a sign; it is the seal of God's promise.

The word *seal* (Greek *sphragis*) is a rich one in the New Testament. The concept of sealing gets its meaning from kings of the ancient world, who, when negotiating agreements, would sign and seal them with wax and a signet ring. The indentations in that ring were unique to that particular monarch and authenticated his agreement.

When the Holy Spirit seals us inwardly, God puts His stamp of ownership on us with an indelible mark that indicates that we are His and that nothing can change that ownership. That is the inward sealing, which is then signified outwardly by the seal of baptism. Both baptism and the Lord's Supper are outward signs and outward seals of the truth of God's promises. When we celebrate the Lord's Supper, hear the words of institution, and go through the sacrament, we experience in a nonverbal, external way the sign and the seal of all of God's promises of grace. He says, "Let me show you that this is My Word." He gives us the seal of baptism and the seal of the Lord's Supper, which are magnificent things.

This is one of the reasons why the Lord's Supper ought never to be celebrated without preaching, because the signs are never to be given without the Word. The Word and the sacrament may be distinguished but not separated. This is to guard against a pagan kind of ritualism or externalism, where people go through the motions with no understanding of what they are doing. The nonverbal is to enhance the verbal; the nonverbal cannot stand alone. It must always be accompanied by the verbal. Sacrament and Word go together.

> 2. There is, in every sacrament, a spiritual relation, or sacramental union, between the sign and the thing signified: whence it comes to pass, that the names and effects of the one are attributed to the other.

This section reinforces the character of the sacraments as signs and seals of the promises of God. The term **sign** is used because a sign is "significant."

There is, in every sacrament, a spiritual relation, or sacramental union, between the sign and the thing signified. People who use sign language for the benefit of those who cannot hear use two different languages at the same time. One is the spoken language of the signer, which he hears and then conveys to the people who cannot hear the spoken word but can comprehend the signer's second language, which is his sign language. The sign helps to communicate the content of the verbal message. Sacraments in their sign character reinforce the content of the written Word.

If the Lord's Prayer is being signed, hand gestures signify the content of the prayer. There is a relationship between the sign, or the word, and the content of the prayer itself. It is interesting that Christ, as the incarnate second person of the Trinity, is introduced in John's gospel as the *Logos*, or the "Word," who was with God and is God, and who became flesh and dwelt among us (John 1:1, 14). The word *incarnate* indicates the outward expression or the embodied sign of God himself. The *Logos* does not simply *communicate* God but *is* the God whom He communicates. There is a special relationship between Christ as the living Word and God Himself. That, of course, transcends the normal function of language, where words point beyond themselves to realities. The confession affirms that sacraments are not empty signs. There is a spiritual relationship between the sign and that which it signifies. That relationship is established by God, who Himself attaches the significance to the sacrament.

As human beings, we all want to be treated with dignity. We all cherish our dignity. But we have no inherent significance. We are significant only because God says that we are. It is God who takes a pile of dirt and breathes His own breath of life into it and stamps us with His image. We are, in this sense, a living sacrament; we are the outward sign of the very character of God because we bear His image. There is a spiritual relationship between our humanity and the God who declared us significant. Our value as a person ultimately rests in the eternal value of God Himself. Take that away, and our aspiration for significance, our hope and our dignity, is a myth.

Humanists deny God but still claim that people have inherent dignity. They are in an untenable position. They live on borrowed capital, as Francis Schaeffer said, "with both feet planted squarely in midair." Humanists protest around the world for human rights and human dignity, but with no basis for it. They steal it from Christianity, but discard the very foundation, and keep only what they like.

There is a spiritual relationship between the outward sign of the sacraments and what the sign signifies. That does not mean that the sacrament causes what it signifies. Just because we participate in the sacrament of baptism does not mean that we are born again, that we are completely removed from original sin, or that we are indwelt by Christ and participate in His death and resurrection. All those things are communicated by that sign, and it is spiritually tied to the reality because God says it is so. It is as if God is saying: "This is My promise, based on faith. If you believe, I will cleanse you from all your sins. I will raise you from spiritual death to spiritual life. I will bring you into union with Christ. I will baptize you and indwell you with the Holy Spirit. All these things communicated by the sign of baptism are made real by My Word." The sacrament is not just an empty ritual. It has spiritual significance and reality because God assigns that to it. Just as the Word of God does not return to Him void

(Isa. 55:11), neither does the exercise and administration of His sacrament return to Him void.

> 3. The grace which is exhibited in or by the sacraments rightly used, is not conferred by any power in them; neither doth the efficacy of a sacrament depend upon the piety or intention of him that doth administer it: but upon the work of the Spirit, and the word of institution, which contains, together with a precept authorizing the use thereof, a promise of benefit to worthy receivers.

The grace that is exhibited by the sacraments is not conferred by any power in them. *Ex opere operato* is a formula that has been embraced and is still taught by the Roman Catholic Church to explain the efficacy of the sacraments. Literally, the Latin expression means "from the working of the work," which strongly suggests that the sacraments work automatically. It follows that the Roman Catholic Church believes that there is a power inherent in the sacraments, so that those who receive them also receive the reality that is signified by them. If baptism signifies regeneration, then we are regenerated when we are baptized, according to Rome.

It is not quite fair to say that the Roman Catholic Church teaches that the sacraments work automatically, but what is meant by *ex opere operato* is that they work if no hindrance is put forward by the recipient. The person has to receive the sacrament freely—not necessarily in faith, but freely. As long as a person doesn't object to being baptized, he will receive all the benefits of the sacrament. However, if there were someone in the crowd who said, "Don't touch me with that water," and some fell on him, it would have no effect.

The Protestant doctrine of justification by faith alone implies that the sacraments themselves do not have the power to save. But the Roman Catholic Church says that we receive justification first by baptism, and then through the sacrament of penance, if we need it a second time. According to Rome, we are justified sacramentally. The Reformers disagreed, insisting that we are justified by faith and faith alone; the sacraments are important, but they do not confer salvation.

The confession teaches that grace is not conferred by any power in them [the sacraments]; neither doth the efficacy of a sacrament depend upon the piety or intention of him that doth administer it: but upon the work of the Spirit. No power resides in the sacraments, nor does the efficacy of a sacrament depend on the person who administers it. This became a major controversy early in church history—the Donatist controversy, which Augustine addressed. There were those who denied Christ under the threat of persecution and were not willing to die as martyrs but who returned to the faith when the persecution ended. Could lapsed priests, having returned to the church, still administer the sacraments? What about people who had been baptized by them? Were their baptisms valid?

Augustine answered that the validity of the sacrament rests on the One whose promise it is—not on the one who administers it, nor on the one who receives it, but on God. This is God's word in sacramental form, and the ministers carry a treasure in earthen vessels. The sin of the minister does not destroy the validity of God's promise to the one to whom the sacrament is administered. The sacrament does not have power in itself, and the power of the sacrament does not rest in the minister or in a priest or in anyone else. The power of the sacrament rests in God.

Some have been led to Christ by men who later repudiated the faith. That tells me that God can communicate His grace and His truth through pagans, heretics, and apostates. He can even speak through Balaam's donkey (Num. 22:22–35). The power of preaching is not in the preacher. The power of the Word of God is in the Holy Spirit applying the Word to people's hearts. It comes not through the eloquence or the knowledge of the preacher or from the ignorance of the preacher. That is true not only for the Word but also for the sacraments. As the confession goes on to say, the efficacy of the sacraments depends not upon the one who administers them but upon the Holy Spirit.

The only power in the ministry is the power of the Holy Spirit. Without the Holy Spirit, we have no power whatsoever; we have empty rituals and vain words. God has decreed to send His Spirit to accompany the ministry of the Word and the ministry of the sacrament. The power is there, as long as we know whose power it is and where it is vested.

The efficacy of a sacrament depends upon the work of the Spirit, and the word of institution, which contains, together with a precept authorizing the use thereof, a promise of benefit to worthy receivers. The efficacy of a sacrament depends not on the piety or intention of the minister but on the actual working of the Spirit and on the One who instituted the sacraments. The sacraments are Trinitarian. The Father gives authority to His Son, the Son institutes them, and the Holy Spirit applies or empowers them. In redemption, the Father sends the Son, the Son accomplishes our redemption, and the Spirit applies the work of the Son.

Every time we celebrate the Lord's Supper, we repeat the words of institution (1 Cor. 11:23–26). That reminds people that this is not something that we have invented in order to be relevant to our culture today. We are carrying out what the Lord Himself instituted, made sacred, authorized, and commanded to be done in this manner. When Christ gives authority to the sacraments, He is not merely giving permission for the sacraments to be celebrated but is giving a mandate that His people must celebrate them.

Calvin wanted to celebrate the Lord's Supper every Sunday in Geneva because he believed in its importance to the worship of God's people. But to the day he died, the town council of Geneva never permitted it. They allowed the supper only once a month because they were concerned that if it were observed too frequently, it would become a matter of empty externals. We dare not let it become an empty ritual. We understand that Christ does not command us to do it every Sunday, but He does command us to celebrate the Lord's Supper. It is given to us for our edification and for our comfort. In a special way, it enhances the word of promise that comes through the Scriptures.

The words of institution contain a promise of benefit to worthy receivers. The word worthy puts a condition on the reception of benefits. The benefits of the sacraments are not received apart from faith. That is one of the reasons why our Baptist friends oppose infant baptism. They say infants are not capable of having faith, and therefore they do not qualify for baptism. It is true that the promises given to a child at baptism are never actualized or realized unless that child comes to faith. But who is worthy to receive any benefit from God? We certainly are not, regardless of whether we have faith. We have no meritorious worth that requires God to give us a benefit, either through baptism or through the Lord's Supper.

The word **worthy** is not meant in the meritorious sense that we receive a benefit from the sacraments only if we earn it. **Worthy** has in view the use of that word in 1 Corinthians, where Paul warns the church about eating and drinking unworthily, resulting in judgment against them (1 Cor. 11:29). In Corinth, people turned the Lord's Supper into a gluttonous feast, and they showed no concern for the other people who were present. They did not discern the significance of the Lord's Supper or the reality of the ministry of Christ. In that situation, to be worthy meant to come in a proper spirit of reverence and of repentance to the Lord's Table. To be unworthy meant coming impenitently or in a state of cavalier unbelief and merely going through the motions. Going to the Lord's Table without faith and without repentance desecrates the sacrament. Similarly, if we make a mockery of the holy sacraments, we participate in them unworthily and will receive no benefit from them.

> 4. There be only two sacraments ordained by Christ our Lord in the Gospel; that is to say, baptism, and the Supper of the Lord: neither of which may be dispensed by any, but by a minister of the Word lawfully ordained.

There are **only two sacraments ordained by Christ our Lord in the Gospel; that is to say, baptism, and the Supper of the Lord.** The vast majority of Protestant bodies have held that there are two sacraments. The Roman Catholic Church, however, has seven sacraments. They are baptism, confirmation, the Eucharist (Lord's Supper), penance, holy orders, matrimony, and anointing of the sick. Both the Reformed churches and Rome agree that baptism and the Lord's Supper are sacraments. However, there is a significant difference in the understanding of those two sacraments.

We saw in our study of justification that the Roman Catholic Church regards baptism as the instrumental cause of justification. That is, baptism confers the grace of justification by infusing the righteousness of Christ into the recipient. The person is cleansed from original sin, regenerated by the Holy Spirit, and made able, by virtue of regeneration, to cooperate with and to assent to the grace that has been infused into him. People maintain their justification by cooperating with the grace that has been infused into them.

For Rome, this sacrament, as well as the others, functions *ex opere operato*. The grace signified by the sacrament is actually conferred on the recipient, unless he resists it. Thus, everyone who receives baptism also receives regeneration and the infusion of the grace of justification at the same time. That is why baptism is considered the instrumental cause (the means) by which one is brought into a state of saving grace, or justification.

We will consider this philosophically and grammatically. In the ancient world, Aristotle, like most philosophers of that time, tried to explain motion. His inquiry was basically a study of causality—what caused something to move from this place to that place. Aristotle identified various types of causes, using the illustration of the sculptor and the sculpture.

We need to go over Aristotle's illustration again because the various kinds of causes became an integral part of the language of Christian theology in the Middle Ages and through Protestant theology. It is standard to distinguish between material causes and other kinds of causes. The material cause for a statue, according to Aristotle, is that out of which the statue is made, such as marble or stone.

Aristotle also talked about the formal cause: the blueprint, sketch, plan, or idea that the artist has in order to create his statue. The final cause is the purpose for which the statue is made. Perhaps it is to fulfill a commission for a wealthy patron.

The instrumental cause is what the artist uses to bring about the finished work. In the case of a painter, it is his brush and paint; in the case of a literary artist, it is his pen, typewriter, or computer. In the case of the sculptor, the instrumental cause is the chisel and the hammer. But the instruments cannot do it alone. They have to be operated or used by someone (or something) who is the efficient cause, the artist. The Holy Spirit is the efficient cause of a person's being cleansed of original sin or reborn, according to the Roman church. But the means that the Holy Spirit uses to bring that to pass is baptism. The means by which God justifies people, according to Rome, is the instrument of baptism. The Protestant view, however, is that the instrumental cause of justification is faith. Faith is the instrument by which we lay hold of Christ, by whose righteousness we are redeemed. That is the philosophical significance of the term *instrumental cause*.

Grammatically, when we talk about justification, we say that justification is "by faith" or "through faith." The ground of our justification is the righteousness of Christ or the merit of Christ. That is the foundation or the grounds by which God declares us righteous when He transfers the righteousness of Christ to us. God doesn't justify us on the grounds of our inherent righteousness; He justifies us on the grounds of the righteousness of Christ, which is applied to us.

When we say that justification is by faith, we do not mean that faith itself is a merit or is the grounds on which God declares us just. Rather, the word *by* or *through* expresses means. When we say that justification is *by* faith, we are saying that the instrumental cause of justification is faith. Rome, however, says that justification is *by* baptism. That is a significant difference. Even though we both agree that baptism is a sacrament, we disagree dramatically on how it works, what it does, and what it signifies.

The second sacrament, according to the Roman Catholic Church, is the sacrament of confirmation. When a child is confirmed, he or she takes "first communion." In this sacrament, more grace is given to the person who is confirming the vows that were taken by his parents at baptism. Rome understands that when infants are baptized, they aren't cognizant of what is going on. As children grow older, reach the age of accountability, and take instruction, they can confirm publicly, for themselves, what was done for them in the past and, in a sense, fulfill and consolidate their own baptism. This is largely a rite of passage into adulthood.

In many churches, the confirmation rite includes the laying on of hands to symbolize being filled with the Spirit, but that act does not impart the Holy Spirit. In classical Protestantism, baptism is a sign of all that accompanies salvation. Although water baptism signifies the baptism of the Holy Spirit, it does not in itself confer the outpouring of the Spirit. That which baptism signifies does not occur unless or until faith is present.

The traditional Protestant view is that when a person has saving faith, he is indwelt by the Holy Spirit and receives the baptism of the Holy Spirit. The person already has the regeneration of the Holy Spirit, or he wouldn't have the faith necessary to be saved. So, in classical Protestantism, as well as in classical Roman Catholicism, anyone who is truly regenerate or born of the Holy Spirit is, at the same time, baptized with the Holy Spirit. All Christians have the baptism of the Holy Spirit. The baptism of the Holy Spirit means the empowering of the Christian for ministry. There are not two kinds of Christians, those who possess the power of the Holy Spirit for their Christian life and those who do not. Holiness churches, Pentecostals, and charismatics have challenged that view. They argue for two kinds of Christians, those who have been baptized in the Holy Spirit and those who have not. This is a departure from the classical understanding of Catholic and Protestant baptisms.

The fundamental difference between confirmation in the Roman Catholic Church and in Protestant churches is that the Roman Catholic Church regards confirmation as a sacrament, while most Protestant churches do not. The Protestant churches see it as a church rite, or an ecclesiastical ordinance, which falls short of the level of a sacrament. There is debate over what qualifies something to be a sacrament. Protestantism historically teaches that a sacrament has to be directly and immediately instituted by Jesus in the New Testament. There is no doubt that He instituted baptism and the Lord's Supper for all Christians. The rite of confirmation, however, is nowhere set forth by Christ in the New Testament. It was instituted by the church. One of the issues that grew out of the Reformation is whether we find our doctrine in Scripture alone or also in the tradition of the church.

We have a church tradition in Protestantism to which we give great attention. The fact that we pay close attention to tradition is proved by this study of a historic confession of faith. We see the Westminster Confession as an important summary of what is in Scripture, and it has two levels of authority. It has the authority to bind our conscience only insofar as it accurately replicates the Word of God. It also has ecclesiastical authority for ministers and elders, who have to confess its content in order to be in good standing in the church. It is not an infallible source, and it cannot absolutely bind one's conscience. In the Roman Catholic Church, in addition to Scripture, there is ecclesiastical tradition, which has the authority to bind one's conscience. That was, in a measure, what the Reformation was about. One of the things that came out of the debate over authority in the sixteenth century was that, though the Roman church regards confirmation as a sacrament, it doesn't have the mandate of Scripture to support it. Therefore, even though Protestant churches for the most part practice confirmation, they do not see it as a sacrament.

The third sacrament on the Roman Catholic list is the Eucharist, which Protestants call the Lord's Supper. There is no question that the Lord's Supper was instituted by Jesus to be observed regularly in the life of the church. There are significant differences, not only between Protestants and Rome, but also among Protestants themselves, over the meaning, the significance, and the observance of this sacrament.

The fourth Roman Catholic sacrament is penance, also called reconciliation or confession. We discussed penance previously because it was at the heart of the controversy that sparked the Reformation. Penance in the Roman church includes confession, an act of contrition, priestly absolution, and works of satisfaction. Penance is defined as the second plank of justification for those who make shipwreck of their souls. According to the Reformed faith, when we are in a state of grace, justified by the righteousness of Christ through faith, we never lose our salvation. Once we are justified, we are always justified. We may lapse into sin, but we will not ultimately lose all our faith, and therefore we will not lose our justification.

The Roman Catholic Church teaches that if a person who is in a state of grace through baptism commits mortal sin (i.e., a sin that kills the grace in the soul), that person falls from the state of grace. He has killed the saving grace of baptism and must be rejustified. But he doesn't get rebaptized. Instead, there is a restorative sacrament to bring him back to a state of repentance. The practice erupted in the sixteenth century over the selling of indulgences, which were linked to the third step in the sacrament of penance, namely, the works of satisfaction.

After the break with Rome, Luther kept the confessional because he believed that Christians should regularly confess their sins and be assured of their forgiveness and salvation. We try to retain that in Protestant churches by having a prayer of confession in our worship services followed by the assurance of pardon. There is nothing wrong with confessing our sins. The Bible doesn't say that we have to confess our sins to a priest or to a minister, but it does command us to confess our sins to one another. Too many people go through life tormented by their guilt because they haven't had an opportunity to get those painful things out of themselves.

It is true that all we need to do is confess them in secret to God. He will hear us and can confirm us. One of the things that the church and ministers do, through the ministry of the Word, is communicate the assurance of pardon to those who confess their sins. In the Roman Catholic Church, when the priest hears the act of contrition and the confession, he gives priestly absolution and says, "*Ego te absolvo*" (I absolve you).

This upsets some Protestants. They ask, "What right does that priest have to grant the forgiveness of sins?" It is understood historically in the Roman Catholic Church that when the priest grants absolution, he is doing what the Protestant minister does when, from the pulpit, he declares the assurance of pardon to all who genuinely confess their sins. The priest is not forgiving sins by any inherent power that he possesses but is acting basically as a spokesman for Christ.

The Reformers were concerned with the third part of penance, where one had to do works of satisfaction sufficiently meritorious to make it congruous for God to restore him to a state of salvation. Congruous merit is not as high as condign merit, but it is still real merit. One cannot have it without grace, and though it doesn't impose an absolute obligation on God to reward it, it nevertheless makes it congruous and fitting for God to restore that one to justification. Luther said that there can be no mixture of our merit with grace. We are to make restitution wherever possible for our sins, but we are not to think that works we perform after a confession of our sin contribute in any way to the merit of Christ alone, which is the sole ground of our justification. It is through the merit of Christ alone that we are justified.

In support of the sacrament of penance, the Roman church appeals to the New Testament, where the command is, "The time is fulfilled, and the kingdom of God is at hand; repent and believe in the gospel" (Mark 1:15). Jesus certainly commanded people to repent, but He still did not establish it as a sacrament. There is no evidence in the New Testament that Christ instituted a rite of repentance to restore one to the state of justification.

The sacrament of holy orders is reserved for those who are going into church vocations, like monks, priests, and nuns. Rome claims that their life as religious persons gives them a special element of grace.

In the seven sacraments, a Roman Catholic is covered from the cradle to the grave. For all the major transitions in life, he has the assistance of a new sacrament to strengthen him for that occasion. At birth, he receives baptism, and then at the transition to adulthood, he is confirmed. There is the continued infusion of grace through the Eucharist, and penance is there to help when he falls into mortal sin. If one goes into the priesthood or into a religious vocation, he is ordained or set apart and receives grace for that ministry.

In Protestant churches, we also have ordination, and even though Luther taught "the priesthood of all believers," he continued to teach that there is a distinction between laity and clergy. He understood that the New Testament makes such a distinction, and it provides for setting apart people to certain tasks, such as preaching and teaching and ministering. Every Christian is called to participate in the mission of the church. There is a world of lost people, and our mission is to go into the whole world, proclaim the gospel to every living creature, and to make disciples of them.

The sixth sacrament is matrimony. Both Protestant and Catholic churches recognize civil ceremonies. The rite of matrimony was given by God to Adam and Eve and, by extension, to the whole world. Matrimony is not a uniquely Christian estate. Protestants don't see marriage as a sacrament that is to be restricted only to Christians. We see it as a creation ordinance, not a sacrament. In the Roman Catholic Church, matrimony is a sacrament by which supernatural grace is infused into the lives of the recipients to equip them for their new estate. Those who get married receive a measure of grace from God that they would not have outside of marriage.

Finally, there is the sacrament of the anointing of the sick, which is given when one faces death. It is also sometimes called last rites and was previously called extreme unction. The anointing of the sick began as an application of James 5:14–15: "Is anyone among you sick? Let him call for the elders of the church, and let them pray over him, anointing him with oil in the name of the Lord. And the prayer of faith will save the one who is sick." It began in the Christian church as a healing rite, not as a final rite. It was there to encourage people to recover from illnesses. A person could have this anointing not just once but as many times as needed to be restored. Over time, it became the final application of the sacrament of penance, so that people would not die with unforgiven mortal sin and thus go to hell. That is why, when people are in their last moments of life, there are priests available at the hospital to see that they receive their last rites. The last rites are pronounced over people who have already expired, because, in Roman Catholic theology, there is a window of time in which to keep the soul out of hell by giving this sacrament.

Those are the seven sacraments of the Roman Catholic Church. Clearly, much more could be said about them. What is affirmed in the Westminster Confession, however, is that we have only two sacraments.

The final clause of section 4 is frequently disputed among Christians: **neither of which may be dispensed by any, but by a minister of the Word lawfully ordained.**

In the so-called Jesus movement of the 1960s and 1970s, young people reacted against traditional authority structures and created an underground church that dispensed with regularly ordained clergy. People gathered around swimming pools and were baptized by Pat Boone or other celebrities. Church officials were unnerved by these practices and claimed that the sacraments are only to be administered by duly authorized individuals, such as ordained clergy. Over against that was an informal view of the matter that saw little need for ordained clergy.

Added to that was the impact of the charismatic movement, in which people supposedly receive special gifts from the Holy Spirit that empower them for ministry. Most of the New Testament information that we have about the gifts of the Spirit (Greek *charismata*) comes from Paul's letters to the Corinthian church. In Corinth, people who received gifts from the Spirit challenged the authority of those who had been, under normal circumstances, set apart and consecrated for ministry. Paul's two epistles to the Corinthian community deal with that internal disruption.

At the end of the first century, Clement, bishop of Rome, wrote an epistle to the Corinthian community because the crisis had actually worsened after the death of the Apostle Paul. The Corinthian church was in a state of spiritual and ecclesiastical chaos. Clement told the Christians at Corinth to go back and heed the teaching of the Apostle Paul. At the end of the first century, the debate had to do with regular ministers of the church as distinguished from charismatic leaders.

In the Old Testament, the gift of the Holy Spirit was given to people for special tasks at particular times. We read that the Spirit of the Lord came on Jeremiah or on Ezekiel. They were set apart by God for the special charismatic office of the prophet. The kings of Israel were anointed by the priest, as a sign of their anointing by the Spirit, to exercise their office in a godly manner. Before that, God raised up judges like Samson and Gideon as anointed, charismatically gifted leaders to provide some leadership to the loose federation of the tribes of Israel and especially to lead them against an enemy like the Philistines. Moses was also a charismatic leader who was endowed by the Holy Spirit with special gifts. God then anointed Aaron as the high priest and instituted his male descendants as the priesthood. The entire tribe of Levi was set apart for priestly duties and became part of the regular order of the Old Testament ministry.

In the New Testament, the charismatically endowed leaders of the Christian community were the Apostles. They were on the same level as the Old Testament prophets. The power of the Holy Spirit came on them, and they became agents of revelation. When the Apostle Paul established a church, he customarily instructed his assistants to set apart elders who were called to the office of ministry. We find this in his epistles to Timothy and Titus, where he delineates the standards for office. The elders and deacons became the regular officers of the church, and the ordinary ministers were given the responsibility to care for the spiritual needs of the flock.

Their ministry was no longer dependent on a special charismatic gift. In the Old Testament, the Holy Spirit endowed with power only part of the covenant community. At Pentecost, He fell upon everyone assembled, and later He came on the gentile converts. The inference drawn by the Apostles was that all believers, Jew and gentile alike, had the same full membership and status in the New Testament body of Christ. The Holy Spirit has now empowered the entire church to participate in the ministry of Christ. That was why Luther held his view of the priesthood of all believers. Luther said that the ministry of the gospel was entrusted to the whole church, not just to a few people. But Luther also understood that the New Testament established regular church offices for the ministry of the Word and sacrament and for the spiritual care of the people.

Neither sacrament **may be dispensed by any, but by a minister of the Word lawfully ordained.** When the resurrected Jesus gave the Great Commission, He told the Apostles, the first Christian ministers, "Go therefore and make disciples of all nations, baptizing them in the name of the Father and of the Son and of the Holy Spirit" (Matt. 28:19). In 1 Corinthians 11:20–23, Paul states that he received from the Lord the words of institution for the Lord's Supper. He says in 1 Corinthians 4:1, "This is how one should regard us, as servants of Christ and stewards of the mysteries of God." The phrase "stewards of the mysteries of God" is critical. Hebrews 5:4 tells us, "No one takes this honor for himself, but only when called by God, just as Aaron was." We see here a ministry in the church that is instituted by the call of God, and that no one has the right to take it for himself. Included in this ministry is the responsibility of being stewards of the mysteries of God. Just as Old Testament priests were "stewards" of God's mysteries, so that task is also carried out by New Testament ministers.

The word *stewardship* translates the Greek word *oikonomia*. Our English word economy derives from that word. It combines the word *oikos*, meaning "house," and the word *nomos*, meaning "law." So *oikonomia* means "house rule" or "house law." Thus, a steward in the biblical sense is a servant who is responsible for managing the affairs of the household. When we speak of Christian stewardship, we are referring to our responsibility to manage the resources that God has entrusted to us.

The Scriptures teach that God gives to ministers the management or stewardship of the sacred mysteries. When Paul refers to "stewards of the mysteries of God," the church understands that to include being "stewards of the sacraments." Though we must not make an identity between the New Testament use of the word *mystery* and our word *sacrament*, there remains a historic link between the words as the Latin *sacramentum* was used by the church to translate the Greek *mystērion*. One of the pastor's responsibilities in the life of the church is to oversee the sacraments.

Though the biblical evidence is not overwhelming, it seems best to conclude that only ordained people have the authority to administer the sacraments. In addition to biblical references and the biblical concept of what it means to be a bishop, and the responsibilities of eldership as set forth in the New Testament, the church, in her own development, rightly came to the conclusion that the sacraments are so holy that they must be guarded from frivolous or cavalier usage. That becomes particularly clear when we consider the warning not to partake of the Lord's Supper unworthily.

Paul warns about eating and drinking unworthily in 1 Corinthians 11:30: "That is why many of you are weak and ill, and some have died." The New Testament scholar Oscar Cullmann observed that this is one of the most neglected verses in the entire New Testament. He suggested that Paul was saying to the Corinthians, "Some of you people have fallen ill, even unto death, directly as a result of your failure to discern the Lord's body in this most holy event." This need for discernment, along with other concerns, lay behind the church's decision to protect the people from the negative effects of mishandling the sacraments. Therefore, the sacraments must be administered by those who have been set apart for the task of ministry in the church. Not just anyone can administer the sacraments. The responsibility to guard the sacraments is put into the hands of the clergy. That is no guarantee that there will not be abuses, but the situation could otherwise be much worse.

Luther was paralyzed by fear when he sought to administer the Lord's Supper for the first time. Baptism is too important to do at a party in someone's swimming pool. It belongs under the rule and supervision of the church. The confession, following the church practice through the ages, says that the sacraments are to be administered by those who are in positions of ordained authority, the lawfully ordained ministers of the Word.

> 5. The sacraments of the old testament, in regard of the spiritual things thereby signified and exhibited, were, for substance, the same with those of the new.

The principle that is set forth in section 5 is vital to the Reformation understanding and rationale for infant baptism, among other things. The sacraments of the Old and New Testaments, it says, are the same in certain respects. But the Westminster divines are not saying that baptism is the same thing as circumcision (or the baptism in the Red Sea), or that the Lord's Supper is the same thing as the Passover. If there were no difference between them, then it would be meaningless to speak of a "new" covenant.

There is an element of discontinuity from the old to the new, but that discontinuity is not radical. That is, there is no discontinuity at root. The discontinuity is in the leaves of the tree, and not at the trunk or the roots of the tree. The confession is careful to say that the sacraments are the same, not in every respect, but for substance, with respect to the spiritual things thereby signified and exhibited.

For substance means "in essence." We say of the Trinity that God is one in substance and three in person. The distinction of the persons in the Godhead is real, significant, and necessary, but it does not go to the essence of their being. If it were a distinction in essence or in substance, there would be three gods. The Father, the Son, and the Holy Spirit are all the same essence. There is a real difference between them, but not at the point of essence. Likewise, there is an essential continuity between the Passover and the Lord's Supper, and between circumcision and baptism. They are not identical, but in substance they refer to the same ultimate thing.

To understand that, we must know something about the meaning of Old Testament ceremonies. An insight into this is provided by 1 Corinthians 10:1–4: "For I do not want you to be unaware, brothers, that our fathers were all under the cloud, and all passed through the sea, and all were baptized into Moses in the cloud and in the sea, and all ate the same spiritual food, and all drank the same spiritual drink. For they drank from the spiritual Rock that followed them, and the Rock was Christ." Here Paul teaches that in the crossing of the Red Sea, a baptism took place.

All the ceremonies in the Old Testament, down to the very building of the tabernacle, were types, symbols, and shadows of what was to come in fullness and in glory in the person of Christ. The Israelites annually celebrated their redemption from the angel of death, who passed over the Israelite homes in Egypt because of the blood of the lamb on their doorposts and lintels. After that redemption and rescue from judgment by the grace of God, God told the people of Israel never to forget it. He wanted them on a regular basis to sit down at a table, enjoy the Passover meal, and celebrate their redemption from the judgment of God through the blood of the lamb.

The blood that preserved the children of Israel was not really the blood of that lamb that was killed, because the New Testament tells us that the blood of bulls and goats and sheep cannot take away sin (Heb. 10:4). Rather, that blood pointed to the ultimate Lamb who would cause the judgment of God to pass over the people of God forever. That was why Jesus, going into the upper room one last time to celebrate the Passover and seeking to maintain continuity with the Old Testament, said, in effect, "Tonight starts the new covenant in My blood, shed for the remission of your sins." He is our Passover Lamb (1 Cor. 5:7). The substance and essence of what was foreshadowed in the Passover carries over into the New Testament celebration of the Lord's Supper. In the Old Testament, the people survived in the wilderness by eating God-given manna. When Jesus came, He said, "I am the bread of life. Your fathers ate the manna in the wilderness, and they died. This is the bread that comes down from heaven, so that one may eat of it and not die" (John 6:48–50). The manna pointed to the heavenly manna that was Christ.

Even as circumcision was the sign of God's redemptive promises received by faith, which every Jewish man had in his body, so the same promises of salvation are marked by baptism in the New Testament. There is obviously a physical difference between the rite of circumcision and the rite of baptism, but there is also continuity. Both of them signify God's promise to separate people for eternal salvation, and the promise is given to the elect who are justified by faith. Abraham believed God and was justified and counted as righteous. As a sign of the faith that he confessed, God had him circumcised and commanded him to circumcise his sons, giving them the same sign of the same promise. That promise was also received by faith, even before the children had faith. Often, there is a protest against giving the sign of faith before faith is present. But if that argument were valid, it would invalidate circumcision in the Old Testament. Circumcision, among other things, was a sign of faith. God not only permitted the children of believers to be given the sign but also commanded that it to be given to them.

Of Baptism

1. Baptism is a sacrament of the new testament, ordained by Jesus Christ, not only for the solemn admission of the party baptized into the visible church; but also, to be unto him a sign and seal of the covenant of grace, of his ingrafting into Christ, of regeneration, of remission of sins, and of his giving up unto God, through Jesus Christ, to walk in newness of life. Which sacrament is, by Christ's own appointment, to be continued in his church until the end of the world.

2. The outward element to be used in this sacrament is water, wherewith the party is to be baptized, in the name of the Father, and of the Son, and of the Holy Ghost, by a minister of the gospel, lawfully called thereunto.

3. Dipping of the person into the water is not necessary; but baptism is rightly administered by pouring, or sprinkling water upon the person.

4. Not only those that do actually profess faith in and obedience unto Christ, but also the infants of one, or both, believing parents, are to be baptized.

5. Although it be a great sin to contemn or neglect this ordinance, yet grace and salvation are not so inseparably annexed unto it, as that no person can be regenerated, or saved, without it; or, that all that are baptized are undoubtedly regenerated.

6. The efficacy of baptism is not tied to that moment of time wherein it is administered; yet, notwithstanding, by the right use of this ordinance, the grace promised is not only offered, but really exhibited, and conferred, by the Holy Ghost, to such (whether of age or infants) as that grace belongeth unto, according to the counsel of God's own will, in his appointed time.

7. The sacrament of baptism is but once to be administered unto any person.

1. Baptism is a sacrament of the new testament, ordained by Jesus Christ, not only for the solemn admission of the party baptized into the visible church; but also, to be unto him a sign and seal of the covenant of grace, of his ingrafting into Christ, of regeneration, of remission of sins, and of his giving up unto God, through Jesus Christ, to walk in newness of life. Which sacrament is, by Christ's own appointment, to be continued in his church until the end of the world.

This first section gives us a hint of the spiritual riches that are expressed by this sacrament, beginning with the first line: **Baptism is a sacrament of the new testament, ordained by Jesus Christ.**

Baptism is the outward sign of the new covenant, just as circumcision was the external sign of the old covenant. Throughout the history of God's dealings with His people, the making of covenants was serious business, a solemn affair. When the covenants were made between God and Noah, God and Abraham, God and Moses, and God and David, they were consigned by oaths and vows. They always contained stipulations. There was also a ritual, usually a blood ritual, that solemnized the covenant promise.

In the covenant that God made with Noah, the external sign was the rainbow. Even to this day, when we see God's rainbow in the sky, it reminds us of His promise to Noah that He will never again destroy the earth by a flood. In the covenant that God made with Abraham, the sign was circumcision. The new covenant is not divorced from what came before it; there is continuity. In a very real sense, the new covenant is the fulfillment of the promises that God made to Abraham. In the *Magnificat*, Mary praised God for what He had done, "as he spoke to our fathers, to Abraham and to his offspring forever" (Luke 1:55). Mary understood that the announcement from the angel Gabriel showed that God remembered the promise that He had made to Abraham. Jesus spoke to the Pharisees in similar terms about Abraham: "Your father Abraham rejoiced that he would see my day" (John 8:56). The New Testament people of God understood the connection between God's promises in the Old Testament and their fulfillment in the New Testament. Because of the newness of the New Testament, a new sign was given to the people of God. That new sign was baptism. We are told in the confession that baptism was a sign that Christ commanded to be carried to all nations: "Go therefore and make disciples of all nations, baptizing them in the name of the Father and of the Son and of the Holy Spirit" (Matt. 28:19).

New Testament baptism was instituted by Jesus, not by John the Baptist. However, we first encounter the rite of baptism in the Scriptures as it was practiced by John. He announced to the people, "Repent, for the kingdom of heaven is at hand" (Matt. 3:2). He called the people of Israel to be baptized, and he baptized them, as well as Jesus, in the Jordan River.

John did not institute New Testament baptism. He did not administer the sign of the new covenant. The ritual he performed actually belonged to the Old Testament economy, to which John himself belonged. We may read about him in the New Testament, but in redemptive history his place is at the end of the old covenant. The new covenant did not begin until Jesus instituted it at the Lord's Supper, where He gave the Passover rite a new dimension: "For this is my blood of the covenant, which is poured out for many for the forgiveness of sins" (Matt. 26:28). He established the new covenant in the upper room. He ratified it the next day with the blood rite at His death.

Everything that happened from the time of Abraham until the Last Supper belongs to the old covenant. As Jesus said, "The Law and the Prophets were until John" (Luke 16:16). The Greek word for "until" means "up to and including." Jesus said that the period of the law and the prophets incorporated John the Baptist, and then He added: "I tell you, among those born of women none is greater than John. Yet the one who is least in the kingdom of God is greater than he" (Luke 7:28). Here greatness refers to blessedness. Those who are least in the kingdom enjoy greater redemptive blessedness than even John the Baptist enjoyed. The prophets of the Old Testament looked to the far-off day when the Messiah would come and God would inaugurate the kingdom. Isaiah said that one day the King would come (Isa. 40:3–5). The Messiah would appear in world history, but no time frame was given. Shortly before Jesus began His public ministry, God sent a forerunner to call the people to get ready, to prepare themselves for the coming of that promised kingdom.

The prophet selected to make that announcement was John the Baptist. He enjoyed a privilege that no other prophet had ever enjoyed. He didn't simply announce the coming of the King; he ushered in the King. The King had not yet established His kingdom. Even though John was the herald of the King, he was still on the outside of this historical reality, called the kingdom of God, looking in. He had the closest vantage point of anyone in the old covenant, but he was still on that side. He told the people to repent because the kingdom of God was at hand. He said, "Even now the axe is laid to the root of the trees" (Matt. 3:10). The kingdom was about to break through. John's analogy was that the woodsman was cutting down the trees. He was not just chipping away at the outer edge of the bark but cutting to the very heart of the tree. With one more swing of the axe, the tree would come down. It was the time of crisis and of separation. John warned the people that they were not ready for the coming of the Messiah. He called them to a ritual of baptism to cleanse themselves in preparation for His coming.

The ritual of proselyte baptism emerged in the intertestamental period. If a gentile desired membership in the household of Israel, he needed to do three things. He had to embrace the truth of Judaism—to make a profession of faith, as it were. Second, he had to undergo the rite of circumcision. Third, being an "unclean" gentile, he had to go through a ritual of purification, a baptismal cleansing rite. This baptism was only for gentiles, not for Jews. Many gentiles (such as Cornelius in the book of Acts) became God-fearers, not full converts. God-fearers were gentiles who embraced the Jewish faith and underwent the ritual of purification, but did not submit to circumcision. John the Baptist's ritual was radical in that he called Jews to take the ritual bath. He said to them, in effect: "You are as dirty and as unclean in the sight of God as gentiles, who are strangers to the covenant and to the commonwealth of Israel. If you are going to be ready to meet your King, you need to take a bath."

John saw Jesus and said, "Behold, the Lamb of God, who takes away the sin of the world!" (John 1:29). Jesus presented Himself to John to be baptized. John protested, "I need to be baptized by you, and do you come to me?" (Matt. 3:14). Jesus responded, "Let it be so now, for thus it is fitting for us to fulfill all righteousness" (v. 15). That is, "I know you don't understand why this is necessary, John, but I, the Messiah, must represent Israel and fulfill all the law that God imposes upon His nation." He not only went to the cross to die for the sins of the people but also submitted to the law from the time of His birth, because He had to fulfill all the commandments of God on behalf of the people. God added a new requirement that the people had to submit to this cleansing rite. Jesus was to be their representative and fulfill God's command, so He had to submit to the ritual baptism. Jesus was baptized not because He was a sinner but because the people were sinners and He was their Redeemer. So John baptized Jesus.

This baptism had many things in common with the baptism that Jesus later commissioned His disciples to perform as a sign of the kingdom and of the new covenant. Though it certainly was influenced by the preparatory work of John, it was not the same. Jesus' rite of baptism marked people's entrance into fellowship and community with Him. John's was a cleansing rite in anticipation of the coming of the kingdom. John's baptism was a preparatory baptism for the new covenant; Jesus came and said, "Repent, for the kingdom of heaven is at hand" (Matt. 4:17). Later, He said, "But if it is by the finger of God that I cast out demons, then the kingdom of God has come upon you" (Luke 11:20). In Luke 10, He commissioned His disciples to baptize people and to celebrate the breakthrough of the kingdom. New Testament theology does not see the kingdom as something utterly in the future. There remain future elements, but the kingdom of God began with the ministry of Christ and reached a tremendous level of reality at His ascension to the right hand of God, where He now reigns. Baptism, among other things, celebrates the beginning of the kingdom of God as it marks people's entrance into this new covenant community, identifying them as part of the body of Christ.

Baptism is a sacrament of the new testament, ordained by Jesus Christ, not only for the solemn admission of the party baptized into the visible church. When we studied the doctrine of the church, we noted the difference between the visible and the invisible church. It is possible to be a member of the invisible church and not be a member of the visible church. And not everyone in the visible church is in the invisible church. People sometimes make insincere professions of faith. Jesus spoke about His church being made up of tares along with the wheat (Matt. 13:24–30). The visible church will always be a mixed body of believers and nonbelievers. Jesus said that at the last day many people would come to Him and say, "Lord, Lord, did we not prophesy in your name, and cast out demons in your name, and do many mighty works in your name?" (Matt. 7:22). But He will reply, "I never knew you; depart from me, you workers of lawlessness" (v. 23). Jesus understood that people can honor Him with their lips while their hearts are far from Him. Membership in the visible church does not guarantee membership in the invisible church, the true body of Christ.

Baptism is a sign and seal of the covenant of grace and of the promise of redemption. The covenant of grace is God's solemn promise to all who believe that they will be redeemed and will receive all the benefits won for them by and through the ministry of Christ. In the ministry of the Word, the promises of God and the gospel are preached, guaranteeing salvation to all who believe.

In addition to the verbal proclamation of that promise, God gives to His people a visible sign and seal, a nonverbal corroboration of the Word, and that is the sacrament of baptism. God's promise in the covenant of grace is realized only through faith. That was also true in the case of circumcision, as a sign of the covenant of grace in the Old Testament, and not everyone who received that external sign also received what it represented. Paul said, "But a Jew is one inwardly" (Rom. 2:29), meaning that circumcision alone did not save anyone and that the heart had to be circumcised. As in the New Testament, a person in the Old Testament was justified only by faith.

The sign of faith does not communicate faith. The sign of God's promise does not guarantee the fulfillment of the promise. What is guaranteed is God's promise to all who believe. That is why we give the sign to adults and also to the children of believers, just as they did in the Old Testament. In this respect, the covenant community in Israel was no different from the covenant community today. All the people of God and their children are to receive the sign and seal of the promise of redemption. Baptism is not a sign of the child's faith; it is a sign of what the child will receive by faith. It is a sign of God's promise, which is received by faith.

Baptism is a sign and seal to the party baptized of his ingrafting into Christ. Believers can read God's Word and say: "I have in my own body the sign and seal of the King who promised me the remission of my sins. He promised me that I would be ingrafted into Jesus Christ, that I would participate in His death and in His resurrection by faith, and that, if I believe, I can trust the promise of God because I am baptized." How can we ever despise the significance, the value, and the importance of God's promise to redeem us? Jesus instructed His disciples to proclaim the gospel to every living creature and baptize those who respond in the name of the Father and of the Son and of the Holy Ghost. The Word is to be confirmed by the sign of the church and the kingdom, which is the sign of baptism.

Baptism is also the sign and seal of regeneration. Regeneration is conferred sovereignly and solely by the direct and immediate ministry of the Holy Spirit. No one can cause another to be born again. No one can preach someone into regeneration, because it is solely the work of God. Baptism is the external sign of the internal work of regeneration. It is the sign of our cleansing, of our renewal, of our resurrection from spiritual death to spiritual life, from bondage to sin to freedom from sin—a supernatural work performed by God alone. Regeneration is a monergistic work, not a synergistic one. God changes the disposition of the soul. It is not a joint venture; it is not a cooperative activity between us and God. God alone can raise us from spiritual death. Regeneration is an act of re-creation. It is not caused by baptism, but it is signified by baptism.

Baptism is also a sign of remission of sins. In our justification, our sins are remitted, which means that they are removed from us. In our justification, we are declared just, and God redeems us by forgiving our sins. The sign of that justification, or the sign of the gospel itself, is baptism. Part of what is being promised in this sign is that all who believe will have their sins removed from them forever. Baptism is a sign of the remission of sins and of justification through Jesus Christ.

Baptism, finally, is the sign of a commitment to walk in newness of life. It is a sign not only of our justification but also of the whole work of redemption. It signifies our election, our regeneration, our justification, our faith, our sanctification, and our glorification. The scope of our redemption is signed and sealed in the promises of God through this remarkable sacrament. That is why it is a special occasion whenever we see someone receive this blessed promise of God and make his solemn entrance into the visible body of Christ. The means of grace are not exclusively found in His church, but they are heavily concentrated there.

> 2. The outward element to be used in this sacrament is water, wherewith the party is to be baptized, in the name of the Father, and of the Son, and of the Holy Ghost, by a minister of the gospel, lawfully called thereunto.

Christians have historically agreed that water is to be used in baptism, because it was water that Jesus consecrated in His institution of the sacrament. In the Great Commission, He commanded people to be baptized with a Trinitarian formula. A true baptism, therefore, involves the use of water in the name of the Father, the Son, and the Holy Spirit. The one point that tends to be controversial in section 2 is the last one, namely, that it is not lawful for one who is not ordained to administer the sacrament.

We gave considerable attention to this matter when we studied the chapter on the sacraments. In order to protect these sacred rites from misuse or abuse, they have been entrusted to the ministers of the church for supervision and oversight. The church is given not only the ministry of the Word and the task of discipline, but also the administration of the sacraments. It is under the church's authority that they are to be administered.

> 3. Dipping of the person into the water is not necessary; but baptism is rightly administered by pouring, or sprinkling water upon the person.

In the seventeenth century, there was an issue with the Anabaptists. At that time in Protestant history, there were not many adult baptisms. Today in America, probably the majority of evangelical Christians practice only believer's baptism. It is good to remember that throughout church history the vast majority of Christian bodies have understood baptism to apply to the children of believers as well as to adult believers.

Also, throughout the centuries of church history, it has been the practice of Christendom to use various modes of applying water besides immersion. It has only been in recent times that people have raised objections to sprinkling, dipping, and pouring. They have argued that immersion is required to have a genuine baptism. The usual argument is that the word translated "baptize" in the New Testament (*baptizō*) means "to immerse" and never indicates anything other than immersion.

This is simply bad scholarship and bad linguistics. There are numerous places in Greek literature where *baptizō* means something other than "to immerse." For example, in the Septuagint, the Greek translation of the Old Testament, one of the cultic rites calls for the sacrifice of two birds of the same size, where one bird is killed and its blood is drained into a basin. The second bird, which remains alive, is then "baptized" in the blood of the first bird. Manifestly, one cannot get enough blood out of one bird to immerse a second bird in it. There could be dipping or pouring, but not an immersion.

In the New Testament, the Ethiopian eunuch makes a profession of faith to Philip and then asks: "See, here is water! What prevents me from being baptized?" (Acts 8:36). Philip sees "water" and baptizes him on the spot (vv. 36–38). It is doubtful that in that the "desert place" between Jerusalem and Gaza (v. 26) there was enough water for an immersion. Apparently, a minimal amount of water was not a hindrance to baptism. Dipping, sprinkling, and pouring were widely practiced in church history, particularly in arid lands where water was at a premium. The sacrament was administered by sprinkling or by pouring water on the head.

It is commonly assumed that when Jesus was baptized in the Jordan, He was immersed. However, the earliest known depiction of this event in Christian art (dated in the second century) shows Jesus standing next to John the Baptist in waist-high water. In the picture, John is using a ladle of sorts to pour water over Jesus' head. That is not a written record of how John actually baptized. It is simply the earliest graphic representation, but it raises the question whether John practiced immersion at all.

Be that as it may, Calvin, a strong advocate of infant baptism, preferred immersion because baptism signifies our participation in the humiliation and exaltation of Christ, our joining with Him in His death and resurrection. In a remarkable way, putting a person under water pictures his burial with Christ, and bringing him up out of the water pictures his participation in Christ's resurrection. In the Reformed tradition, those who do not restrict baptism to immersion nevertheless are not opposed to immersion, and some see very real value in its use.

4. Not only those that do actually profess faith in and obedience unto Christ, but also the infants of one, or both, believing parents, are to be baptized.

The biggest issue among Christians with respect to baptism has to do with the baptism of infants. It is a vexing question for many people. Christians who practice infant baptism do so because they believe it is what God wants. People who do not practice infant baptism believe that it is displeasing to God. Both sides are trying to please God, but they cannot both be right.

It is important to understand that nowhere in the New Testament do we find an explicit command to baptize infants, nor do we find an explicit prohibition of baptizing infants. The cases for and against infant baptism are both built on inferences drawn from the Scriptures. Such a situation should always give us pause when we disagree with brothers and sisters in Christ. This is an important question, but we should approach it with a spirit of toleration in light of the absence of an explicit biblical mandate.

The single most important objection to infant baptism is that baptism is a sign of faith, which infants are obviously not capable of professing. Furthermore, the command to baptize in the New Testament is linked to commands to repent and believe. The sequence of admonitions that we find in the New Testament tends to be: repent, believe, and be baptized. So Baptists say that the prerequisites for baptism are repentance and faith.

Infant baptism is nowhere found in the New Testament, and every single record of baptism that we have—there are twelve of them—involves the baptism of adults. Each narrative of a baptism involves one or more adults, and there is no specific reference to infants being included with them. It is not until the middle of the second century that we have any surviving record of an infant's being baptized. The silence of early church history with respect to infant baptism is a telling point.

Baptists do recognize a historical continuity between baptism and the Old Testament practice of circumcision, which did include infants. Nevertheless, circumcision marked, among other things, ethnic separation, which passed away in the new covenant community. The idea of marking a sacred race with the sign of circumcision passed away in the New Testament. There would thus be no point in maintaining continuity with the Old Testament practice of marking infants as part of the Jewish race.

Another big concern that Baptists have at this point is a practical one. Some churches teach baptismal regeneration, which can only give people a false sense of security. Because they have been baptized, they may assume they are saved and therefore miss the call to faith, upon which the New Testament places such a premium. Baptists think that for such practical reasons it is important to delay baptism until a person is of the age of accountability, when he can understand the teachings of Christ and the content of the gospel and can genuinely repent and embrace the truth of God.

Those who do baptize their infants do so for the following reasons. Even though they see some discontinuity between circumcision and baptism, continuity is predominant. Circumcision in the Old Testament was the sign of the old covenant, and baptism is the sign of the new covenant. We know for certain that God commanded the sign of the old covenant to be given both to adults and to their children. This is an important covenantal precedent, which suggests that the sign of the new covenant should also be given to the children of believers.

Another point of continuity is that whatever else circumcision indicated, it was a sign of faith, just as baptism is a sign of faith. The Old Testament clearly teaches that circumcision was to be given to a child before he had any capacity for faith. In the case of adults, faith must be present before the sign is applied; in the case of their children, the sign comes first and then the faith. The point is that the administering of the sign was not tied to the time when faith was exercised. If it is wrong to give the sign of faith to someone before he has faith, then it was wrong for the people in Israel to circumcise infants. But God explicitly commanded them to do so.

In the New Testament church, we see cases of repentance and faith preceding the sign of the covenant, which would have been the sequence for converts to the household of Israel. A gentile had to make a public profession of faith before he could be circumcised and become a Jew. In the Old Testament, we find both infant circumcision and adult circumcision. Similarly, every church that practices infant baptism also practices adult baptism, and adult baptism is reserved for those who are not already baptized. They are required to make a credible profession of faith before they can receive the sign of baptism. There is no dispute about that. What is in dispute is whether that is also a requirement for the children of believers.

We go to the examples of baptism in the New Testament. There is no reference to infants among them—or is there? It depends on the meaning of the Greek word *oikos*, which is the word for "household." Three of the twelve baptisms refer to adults and their household being baptized. In one-quarter of the recorded baptisms in the New Testament, we are told that not only did an adult receive the sacrament, but also the members of his or her household, which may have included infants. Oscar Cullmann, the Swiss New Testament scholar, has argued that the term *oikos* refers specifically to infants. If he is right about that, then the debate is over. That would be a clear indication that the New Testament church baptized infants. Even if he is not, however, the language of "household" at least suggests a concept of familial unity, of corporate solidarity. That same concept, while admittedly foreign to modern ears, is found throughout the Old Testament.

Each instance of adults being baptized in the New Testament involves first-generation converts. Even under the Old Testament's pattern for circumcision, they would have been required to make a profession of faith before receiving the sign of the covenant—yet their infant children would also have received the sign. If it could be shown that one of the people who was baptized as an adult was born to a believer, then there would be strong evidence against infant baptism. Since that can't be shown, the narratives of adult baptism in the New Testament have no relevance to the question of infant baptism. They have great relevance to the question of what is necessary for adults to be baptized, but they tell us nothing about what should be done with infants.

The question whether the infant children of believers are to be included in the new covenant is not so ambiguous. Paul teaches: "For the unbelieving husband is made holy because of his wife, and the unbelieving wife is made holy because of her husband. Otherwise your children would be unclean, but as it is, they are holy" (1 Cor. 7:14). The sanctification in view here is consecration—being set apart, being deemed holy. The unbelieving spouse is considered holy or set apart so that the believing spouse's children will not be "unclean." To the Jews, to be unclean meant to be a stranger to the covenant. Paul says that the infants of one believing parent, no less than those of two believing parents, are "holy"— members of the covenant community. If infants are members of the new covenant community, why would they not be given the sign of the covenant, just as God gave the sign of the covenant to infants in the old covenant community?

As mentioned above, there is not a single mention in extant literature of babies being baptized until the middle of the second century. However, very little Christian literature before that time has survived. Furthermore, the German scholar Joachim Jeremias has argued that infant baptism was the universal practice of the church by AD 200 (at least in North Africa). It is hard to believe that a major departure from Apostolic practice could have become so widespread without opposition, yet church history knows of no controversy over infant baptism in the ancient church. This historical evidence is best explained by the assumption that infant baptism was of Apostolic origin, as the learned church father Origen declared.

There is no clear mandate for infant baptism in the New Testament, but there is also no clear prohibition. For thousands of years before that, the sign of the covenant was always given to the infants of believers. If, under the new covenant, the practice of marking the children of believers with the sign of the covenant suddenly stopped, that would have been perplexing—and it would have called for explanation somewhere in the New Testament. But there is no such explanation. It would seem that the reason why the New Testament is silent with respect to infant baptism is that Christians assumed that the sign of the covenant would be placed on their children, just as it had been since the days of Abraham, the father of the faithful.

5. Although it be a great sin to contemn or neglect this ordinance, yet grace and salvation are not so inseparably annexed unto it, as

that no person can be regenerated, or saved, without it; or, that all that are baptized are undoubtedly regenerated.

There are certain truths that are essential to, or of the essence of, the Christian faith. To reject them or to deny them would be to repudiate Christianity. The church has argued historically that the doctrines of the Trinity and the deity of Christ are essential to Christianity. If a person denies the deity of Christ and yet claims to be a Christian, his claim would be invalid, according to orthodox Christianity.

For the most part, throughout church history, whether we sprinkle or dip or pour in baptism has not been considered an essential of the Christian faith. So, although we may differ on that question, we can remain in fellowship and recognize one another as Christians, realizing that the difference is nonessential. It may be important, but it is not essential to the Christian faith. All doctrine is important, but not everything is equally important.

We can distinguish between something that is necessary for salvation and something that is necessary for the health and well-being of the church. Some things may not be necessary for salvation but may be necessary for one's spiritual health. The confession here affirms that baptism is not essential for salvation. We do not have to be baptized in order to be saved. A few Christian denominations have insisted that baptism is essential for salvation, but, for the most part, Protestants have agreed that baptism is not essential for salvation. The thief on the cross, for example, was not baptized, yet Jesus promised him redemption (Luke 23:39–43).

We could infer that if baptism is not essential to salvation, then it is insignificant and unimportant. However, the confession teaches that even though baptism is not essential for salvation, it is nevertheless essential for the spiritual well-being of a Christian. If a Christian does not receive the sacrament of baptism, he is living in disobedience to Christ, who commands all Christians to be baptized. The confession says that it is not only a sin to refuse or neglect to be baptized, but a grievous sin.

In the Old Testament, the sign of the covenant was circumcision, and God required all males of the household of Israel to be circumcised.

When Moses neglected to have his own son circumcised, God was angry with him for failing to carry out this responsibility (Ex. 4:24–26).

We could say that since circumcision is not the same thing as baptism, we can't draw conclusions from that sign of the old covenant. However, the Bible describes the new covenant as a better covenant. It is not less inclusive but more inclusive. To neglect the means of grace in the new covenant economy is even more serious than to neglect them in the Old Testament economy. If God was so displeased with Moses for failing to circumcise his son, how much more displeased will He be if we neglect baptism today?

The confession is correct when it says that it is **a great sin to . . . neglect this ordinance**—not a sin that would exclude us from the kingdom of God, but one that would do great damage to the church and our own Christian growth. It is a serious matter, and we must pay close attention to our obligation at this point.

The confession continues: **Although it be a great sin to contemn or neglect this ordinance, yet grace and salvation are not so inseparably annexed unto it, as that no person can be regenerated, or saved, without it.** We do not have to be baptized in order to be regenerated and saved. (Conversely, even if we are baptized, there is no guarantee that we are regenerated or saved.) Baptism is a sign and seal of the works of God's grace, which are not dependent on baptism. Even though the confession is quick to point out that we can be regenerated and saved without baptism, it also insists that we are not to despise or neglect it.

> 6. The efficacy of baptism is not tied to that moment of time wherein it is administered; yet, notwithstanding, by the right use of this ordinance, the grace promised is not only offered, but really exhibited, and conferred, by the Holy Ghost, to such (whether of age or infants) as that grace belongeth unto, according to the counsel of God's own will, in his appointed time.

The efficacy or effectiveness of the sacrament is not tied to the time of its administration. The sacrament is the sign and seal of our ingrafting into Christ, our participation in His death and resurrection, our cleansing from original sin, our regeneration, and our baptism by the Holy Spirit.

What baptism signifies may never come to pass because these things are dependent upon faith, and we do not receive any of these benefits of salvation apart from faith. However, that which the sacrament signifies can happen truly in the life of a person, either before or after he or she receives the sign of the sacrament.

In the Old Testament, circumcision is a sign of faith. Abraham believed God as an adult, and then he was circumcised. But Isaac was circumcised as an infant, before he became a believer. Similarly, today, adults must make a profession of faith (and therefore be regenerate) before they receive the sacrament of baptism. The thing signified comes before the sign in the case of the adult. But when infants receive the sign, regeneration and faith come later, if at all. What baptism represents is not tied to the moment that it is administered.

Section 6 continues: Yet, notwithstanding, by the right use of this ordinance, the grace promised is not only offered, but really exhibited, and conferred, by the Holy Ghost. The authors of the Westminster Confession have already said that the grace of regeneration is not automatically conferred by the sacrament, and now they write about the grace of the sacrament being really conferred in and through the sacrament. But finish the sentence: to such (whether of age or infants) as that grace belongeth unto, according to the counsel of God's own will, in his appointed time. The grace promised by the sacrament of baptism is conferred by the Holy Spirit at whatever time God has decided to confer it. This is an oblique reference to the doctrine of election. Every person who is numbered among the elect will certainly receive the grace indicated by baptism, and he will do so in God's own time, according to His good pleasure. Most certainly, God will confer the grace and all the benefits of that grace on those who are baptized if they are numbered among the elect.

The Westminster divines are pointing out that this sacrament is no naked sign, empty of any significance. It is full of significance for the elect. God elects them not only to receive salvation but also to receive all the means to that end. God ordained from the beginning of time that all His elect would be brought to faith. He ensures that all the conditions for salvation are present through His grace and through the power and operation of the Holy Spirit. Baptism is one of the means of grace by which God brings salvation to His people.

The promised grace is really exhibited, and conferred, by the Holy Ghost, to such (whether of age or infants) as that grace belongeth unto. Note the mention of infants. Is it possible for an infant to meet the requirements of justification by faith alone? Saving faith involves a certain level of understanding that, presumably, young infants do not have. However, they can have the grace of regeneration, where their hearts' disposition is changed and they are redeemed from the power of original sin. The merit of Christ can also be imputed to them without expressed faith. Though infants are too young to process or articulate it, faith is in the heart of the regenerate at least in seminal form. If they are regenerated, they can have the merit of Christ imputed to them and be saved. Expressed faith is a requirement only for people who have the capacity for cognition. Reformed theologians have generally held that infants who die in infancy, being the children of believers, are numbered among the elect and are saved.

If and when a dying infant is saved, that infant is saved not because of innocence, but because of grace. That grace includes the application of the merit of Christ to the child, without which it would perish. If we believe that infants who die in infancy can be and are saved, we must believe that they receive the benefits of the work of Christ to meet the requirements of God for salvation, and that they are regenerated by the Holy Spirit. The Holy Spirit can certainly change the disposition of the soul of an infant. John the Baptist was presumably sanctified while he was still in the womb of his mother (Luke 1:39–45), and Jeremiah had a similar experience (Jer. 1:5).

Normally, we do not expect the regenerative work of the Holy Spirit to occur until we are older, but the Holy Spirit is not restricted to waiting for cognitive faculties to develop before He does His saving work within the human soul. That would apply not only to infants who die in infancy but also to people who with cognitive impairments or who do not have the ability to grasp all the content of the gospel. God can and does graciously impute the righteousness of Christ to those people and change the disposition of their hearts through the regeneration of the Holy Spirit. That is why there is a parenthesis in the confession's statement. It is possible for the Holy Spirit to confer everything that is signified by baptism to such (whether of age or infants). Grace is not only offered, but really exhibited and conferred by the Holy Spirit to infants as well as to those of age, if grace belongs to them, according to the counsel of God's own will, in his appointed time. God, in His sovereignty, can bestow the grace of salvation when and where and on whom He decides, because salvation is of the Lord. It is a divine and supernatural work, which is not restricted to geniuses or to the learned but can go to infants, to the infirm, to all sorts of people whom God in His grace so determines.

7. The sacrament of baptism is but once to be administered unto any person.

Many of us were probably baptized long before we actually came to faith. In those intervening years, the things of God meant nothing to us, and then we were converted to Christ, and we were raised from spiritual death. The things that were formerly repugnant to us then became matters of pure delight.

People say: "I wasn't a Christian when I was baptized. Now I understand, so I would like to experience that sacrament again from the perspective of someone who embraces what it signifies." It is understandable why people desire to do that, but what they fail to understand is that in baptism the Lord God has promised them eternal life and adoption into His family, and the privilege of being joint heirs with Christ and receiving the benefits poured out on Jesus, if they have faith and put their trust in Christ. He sealed that promise with the sacrament of baptism, which they received as infants. Now they have come to faith, have been adopted into the family of God, have had their sins remitted, have been empowered by the Holy Ghost for ministry, have received eternal life, and have been united with Christ. All the things that God promised at their baptism have now been actualized in their life.

There is a parallel illustration in the New Testament. People who were believers came to Paul, wanting to be circumcised. Early in his ministry, Paul said that people could be circumcised if they wanted to, but that it wasn't necessary anymore because everything circumcision signified in the Old Testament had been fulfilled.

Then came the Judaizers, who claimed that a person is required to be circumcised and can't be saved unless he is circumcised. The Apostle Paul wrote to the Galatians and chided them for foolishly entertaining such ideas. In Galatians 3, Paul asks, in effect: "What's the matter with you? You have begun in the faith, and now, so quickly, you want to return to the old ways. You're putting yourself again under the burden of the law and trying to fulfill all the requirements of the old covenant law that have been fulfilled for you by Jesus. If you are circumcised now, after coming to faith and having experienced what circumcision points to, you are, by implication, repudiating the work of Christ."

This is what the author is talking about in Hebrews 6, where he takes this question to its logical conclusion. He says that it would be impossible to restore a person again to salvation, if he repudiates Christ. Circumcision won't save a person. Paul spells out what the inference would be if a person knowingly and willfully submitted to circumcision after having embraced Christ. It would be, by implication, a repudiation of Christ. The same principle would apply to rebaptism. In effect, it would be a repudiation of the validity of the promise that God made in the first place. Certainly, that is not a true believer's intent when he requests rebaptism, but many have indeed been baptized more than once out of such motivations. So the divines affirm that baptism is **but once to be administered unto any person.**

Of the
Lord's Supper

1. Our Lord Jesus, in the night wherein he was betrayed, instituted the sacrament of his body and blood, called the Lord's Supper, to be observed in his church, unto the end of the world, for the perpetual remembrance of the sacrifice of himself in his death; the sealing all benefits thereof unto true believers, their spiritual nourishment and growth in him, their further engagement in and to all duties which they owe unto him; and, to be a bond and pledge of their communion with him, and with each other, as members of his mystical body.

2. In this sacrament, Christ is not offered up to his Father; nor any real sacrifice made at all, for remission of sins of the quick or dead; but only a commemoration of that one offering up of himself, by himself, upon the cross, once for all: and a spiritual oblation of all possible praise unto God, for the same: so that the popish sacrifice of the mass (as they call it) is most abominably injurious to Christ's one, only sacrifice, the alone propitiation for all the sins of his elect.

3. The Lord Jesus hath, in this ordinance, appointed his ministers to declare his word of institution to the people; to pray, and bless the elements of bread and wine, and thereby to set them apart from a common to an holy use; and to take and break the bread, to take the cup, and (they communicating also themselves) to give both to the communicants; but to none who are not then present in the congregation.

4. Private masses, or receiving this sacrament by a priest, or any other, alone; as likewise, the denial of the cup to the people, worshiping the elements, the lifting them up, or carrying them about, for adoration, and

the reserving them for any pretended religious use; are all contrary to the nature of this sacrament, and to the institution of Christ.

5. The outward elements in this sacrament, duly set apart to the uses ordained by Christ, have such relation to him crucified, as that, truly, yet sacramentally only, they are sometimes called by the name of the things they represent, to wit, the body and blood of Christ; albeit, in substance and nature, they still remain truly and only bread and wine, as they were before.

6. That doctrine which maintains a change of the substance of bread and wine, into the substance of Christ's body and blood (commonly called transubstantiation) by consecration of a priest, or by any other way, is repugnant, not to Scripture alone, but even to common sense, and reason; overthroweth the nature of the sacrament, and hath been, and is, the cause of manifold superstitions; yea, of gross idolatries.

7. Worthy receivers, outwardly partaking of the visible elements, in this sacrament, do then also, inwardly by faith, really and indeed, yet not carnally and corporally but spiritually, receive, and feed upon, Christ crucified, and all benefits of his death: the body and blood of Christ being then, not corporally or carnally, in, with, or under the bread and wine; yet, as really, but spiritually, present to the faith of believers in that ordinance, as the elements themselves are to their outward senses.

8. Although ignorant and wicked men receive the outward elements in this sacrament; yet, they receive not the thing signified thereby; but, by their unworthy coming thereunto, are guilty of the body and blood of the Lord, to their own damnation. Wherefore, all ignorant and ungodly persons, as they are unfit to enjoy communion with him, so are they unworthy of the Lord's table; and cannot, without great sin against Christ, while they remain such, partake of these holy mysteries, or be admitted thereunto.

The meaning of the Lord's Supper continues to be one of the most controversial issues in Christianity. The great tragedy of the sixteenth-century Protestant Reformation was that the Reformers could not maintain unity among themselves. The principal reason was their failure to come to an agreement on the doctrine of the Lord's Supper. The

Lutherans and the Calvinists were never able to resolve this issue, and, even within the Reformed community in Switzerland, there was significant disagreement between Huldrych Zwingli and John Calvin. These differences among Protestants, and the greater differences between Protestants and Roman Catholics, continue to this day.

One good thing about theological controversy is that it usually takes place when Christians are taking their faith seriously. People who don't believe anything don't usually argue about what they don't believe. It is when something is important to us that we engage in debate and controversy in order to avoid error or corruption. There has been controversy about the Lord's Supper throughout church history because it has been important to the church through the centuries. When we examine life in the first-century Christian community, even apart from the pages of the New Testament, it is clear that the celebration of the Lord's Supper was central to the worship of the people of God. It became, in many respects, their identity, because they celebrated the sacrament in direct obedience to the command of Christ to do so until He returned.

In chapter 29 of the confession, we find eight sections devoted to the exposition of the meaning and practice of the Lord's Supper. This shows its importance in the eyes of the Westminster divines.

1. Our Lord Jesus, in the night wherein he was betrayed, instituted the sacrament of his body and blood, called the Lord's Supper, to be observed in his church, unto the end of the world, for the perpetual remembrance of the sacrifice of himself in his death; the sealing all benefits thereof unto true believers, their spiritual nourishment and growth in him, their further engagement in and to all duties which they owe unto him; and, to be a bond and pledge of their communion with him, and with each other, as members of his mystical body.

Section 1 is both substantive and lengthy. It begins by reiterating the words of institution used in most churches at the celebration of the Lord's Supper. Beginning at 1 Corinthians 11:23, Paul speaks of the institution of the Lord's Supper in the upper room by Jesus, on the night in which He was betrayed. The first affirmation that is made is that the Lord's

Supper was indeed instituted by Christ. That is part of the definition of a sacrament. This affirmation reminds us that the Lord's Supper was not invented by the church but was instituted and observed in the first instance by Jesus Himself.

He was entering into His passion, and we are told in Luke 22:15 that He had a strong desire to celebrate the Passover one last time before His death. He gave specific instructions to His disciples to find a place where they could celebrate the Passover. Jesus had no place to lay His head, but He was concerned about having a place for worship, a place to celebrate the Passover with His disciples. There is nothing sacrosanct about a church building. The people of God can meet together outside or even in the catacombs of Rome, which was a terrible place. Persecution, especially in the early centuries, has forced the church to carry on its worship in strange places. The New Testament community, when it was very small, met in people's homes. As long as there has been a people of God, all the way back to Abel, they have needed a place to gather.

As we have previously seen, in the midst of celebrating the Passover, Jesus changed the centuries-old liturgy of the feast and gave it new meaning. Instead of the wine representing the blood on the doorposts on the night of the Passover, it would now represent His blood, which would be shed on the next day for the remission of sins. Jesus did not say, "It is My blood which the wine will represent now, instead of some animal's blood that was posted on the door centuries ago." The blood on the doorposts at the start of the exodus really represented the blood of Christ. In that sense, Jesus didn't change the meaning of the wine, except in terms of its redemptive-historical significance. That which had been foreshadowed and promised by the Passover was now about to reach its consummation. It was not the blood of the paschal lamb that grazed peacefully in the field, but the supreme Lamb of God, whose blood would be shed for the perfect sacrifice once and for all. All this Jesus did as He modified the liturgy of the Passover and instituted the new covenant. He commanded at that point that the Lord's Supper be observed in His church until the end of the world, for the perpetual remembrance of His sacrifice.

The first reason for the institution of the sacrament has to do with remembrance. Jesus spent three years as a peripatetic rabbi. A periscope is something that looks around, and a peripatetic is someone who walks around. Aristotle was known as a peripatetic philosopher because he walked through groves of trees with his students following behind him. Aristotle lectured while he walked, and his students followed him, trying to write down what the great teacher was saying. Most rabbis had a particular venue where their students came and sat at their feet to learn. As a rabbi, or teacher, Jesus called people to be His disciples, or learners—students in His school. He called them by saying, "Follow Me." He was speaking literally: "Follow behind Me, listen to what I am saying." His disciples were to pay close attention.

Memorization played a large role in ancient education, if only because writing materials were expensive. In some respects, that is superior to the method we have today. Our students busily scribble in their notebooks while the professor lectures, and then the notebooks are put on the shelf, where the information remains. Notebooks won't help when a pastor is called to the home of a grieving parent whose child has just died. The knowledge of God must be in the pastor's head. Learning doesn't actually occur until it becomes integral to one's thinking, in the mind. That is the way Jesus taught.

Jesus was the incarnation of truth, so He never made a desultory remark or an idle comment. When Jesus lectured and taught, there was no extraneous information. Every word that came from His mouth was supremely important. But even Jesus stopped on occasion to say to His disciples, "Amen, amen, I say unto you"—that is, "Truly, truly" or "Verily, verily." He was underlining a particular point. In this way, He called attention to something that was especially important, because He understood that students forget what they have been taught.

To the Jew, apostasy was closely related to forgetting. Apostasy is literally a falling away from the favor of God, from fellowship with God, and from communion with the people of God. The people of Israel sinned against God when they forgot who He was and what He had done for them. They had constant celebrations, festivals, and covenant renewal ceremonies to remind them of these things. God has a history with His people. In those days, just as today, people's spiritual vitality and commitment to the things of God tended to be only as strong as the memory of their latest blessing. Sometimes our attitude toward God is, "What have You done for me lately?" Forgetting is connected with apostasy. The psalmist declares, "Bless the LORD, O my soul, and forget not all his benefits" (Ps. 103:2).

When Jesus celebrated the Passover in the upper room, He redefined the liturgy and said, "This is My body, broken for you, and this is My blood, shed for you." He then commanded them, "Do this in remembrance of Me." In effect, Jesus said: "As I enter into My passion and fulfill the work of redemption promised in the garden of Eden when the curse was placed upon the serpent, I am going to crush the head of the serpent. While I crush the head of the serpent, My heel will be wounded and My blood will be poured out. I will not die to satisfy the penal code of the Roman Empire. I will die to satisfy the justice of God. I will shed My blood for the remission of your sins. Don't ever forget what you will see tomorrow. To make sure you don't forget it, you must repeat it—not once a year, like the Passover, but often. When the children ask about the Lord's Supper, the parents will say, 'We are remembering when the Lamb of God redeemed us from an oppressor far worse than Pharaoh. He redeemed us from the hands of the one who had enslaved our souls, from Satan himself. Jesus has reconciled us to God through His sacrifice on the cross.'"

But remembering what Christ did on the cross is not the full significance of the Lord's Supper. It has three dimensions to it with respect to time: past, present, and future. Our Lord commanded His disciples in the upper room not to forget the past (in which His death would soon be). When Scripture is read at the Lord's Supper, it is usually Isaiah 53, the crucifixion narratives from the Gospels, or the celebration of the Lamb who was slain in Revelation 5. The Word and the sacrament are used together, so that the Word calls our attention to what was accomplished by Christ. The Scripture readings focus our thinking as we commune, to make sure that we remember what Jesus did. There aren't too many churches that read Scripture during the distribution of the elements, but that is how John Calvin celebrated the Lord's Supper at his church in Geneva.

There is also a future reference in the Lord's Supper. Paul said of the supper, "For as often as you eat this bread and drink the cup, you proclaim the Lord's death until he comes" (1 Cor. 11:26), a reference to the future consummation of the kingdom. In the celebration of the Lord's Supper, we have a foretaste of the marriage feast of Christ with His bride in heaven. Remembering what He has done for us in the past, we also look ahead to what He has promised to do for us in the future.

The church also believes that Christ is truly present here and now, meeting with His people in a special way at the Lord's Table, so that we are not only looking to the past or foretasting the future. There is a present reality that we experience with Him and with each other when we celebrate the Lord's Supper.

Christ instituted the Lord's Supper **for the perpetual remembrance of the sacrifice of himself in his death.** Jesus, as our High Priest, did not sacrifice an animal but rather sacrificed Himself. He is our eternal High Priest and also the Lamb of God. In the celebration of the Lord's Supper, we remember the sacrifice that our High Priest made of Himself.

Only Christ could offer Himself as a sacrifice. Only He was worthy to offer that sacrifice, as He made very clear: "For this reason the Father loves me, because I lay down my life that I may take it up again. No one takes it from me, but I lay it down of my own accord" (John 10:17–18). People mocked Him when He was on the cross: "He saved others; he cannot save himself. . . . He trusts in God; let God deliver him now" (Matt. 27:42–43). At any moment, He could have stopped His own execution, for He had more authority and more power than the entire Roman army. He had myriads of angels at His disposal. He suffered voluntarily, so we call that the passive obedience of Christ. He was the Lamb who did not open His mouth, who was silent before His shearers, as Isaiah wrote, and He allowed it all to happen to Him (Isa. 53:7). There was no authority over Him except that which was given from above. The Romans merely helped Him carry out a mission that He chose to perform for us.

There was no priest there to put Him on an altar. It was a voluntary act. That was what Paul celebrated: "He humbled himself by becoming obedient to the point of death, even death on a cross" (Phil. 2:8). By the sacrifice of Himself in His death came **the sealing all benefits thereof unto true believers** in the Lord's Supper. Every time we celebrate the Lord's Supper, His death is impressed not just on our memories but on our souls.

The Lord's Supper is to be observed for the sealing all benefits thereof (i.e., of His death) unto true believers, their spiritual nourishment and growth in him, their further engagement in and to all duties which they owe unto him, and, to be a bond and pledge of their communion with him. We call this sacrament holy communion, because it is communion with him, and with each other, as members of his mystical body. People often think that Reformed theology is all cerebral, all intellectual, with nothing in the heart, nothing in the emotions. The more we understand it with our head, however, the more our heart pulsates with passion over these things. And the more emotional we get, the more we understand. The more we understand with our minds, the more the heart is inflamed in response to these things.

We come to the Lord's Supper to have communion with Him and with each other. That is the mystical element. When He is here and we enter this relationship with Him, there is a real communion with the real Jesus. It is not just that we are all partaking separately. Rather, when we commune with Christ, we also commune with everyone in His body. This is what binds us together.

> 2. In this sacrament, Christ is not offered up to his Father; nor any real sacrifice made at all, for remission of sins of the quick or dead; but only a commemoration of that one offering up of himself, by himself, upon the cross, once for all: and a spiritual oblation of all possible praise unto God, for the same: so that the popish sacrifice of the mass (as they call it) is most abominably injurious to Christ's one, only sacrifice, the alone propitiation for all the sins of his elect.

In the seventeenth century, when the confession was written, Reformed theology often defined itself vis-à-vis Roman Catholic theology. Section 2 has to do with one of the critical disagreements between Rome and Protestantism. That critical issue is how Rome understands the drama of the Mass.

The question is whether the Lord's Supper is an actual repetition of the sacrifice of Christ on the cross. The Roman Catholic Church teaches that every time the Mass is celebrated, Christ is offered up afresh to the

Father in a real sacrifice. Although this sacrifice is considered to be an "unbloody" sacrifice, it is nevertheless a real sacrifice and involves a real repetition. There is no question, historically and theologically, that the Roman Catholic Church teaches that Christ is sacrificed in the Mass. The priest offers Him up to remind the Father of the work that Christ accomplished in the past, as if the Father needed any reminder. The disagreement on this matter is irreconcilable unless Rome retreats from her teaching of the sacrificial character of the Mass. There is no hope of reconciliation between the Catholic and the Reformed churches because this is such a major point of controversy.

In this sacrament, Christ is not offered up to his Father; nor any real sacrifice made at all, for remission of sins of the quick or dead; but only a commemoration of that one offering up of himself, by himself, upon the cross, once for all. The word only here is unhelpful. The Lord's Supper is indeed a commemoration, but it is more than that. Of course, every member of the Westminster Assembly understood that. What is meant by only is that the Lord's Supper is a commemoration of that sacrifice that was made once for all, and that there is no actual repetition of the sacrifice that Christ made.

There was one offering up of himself, by himself, upon the cross, once for all. In the English language, we use three words, *once for all*, because we do not have a single word that captures this idea. The closest word we have is *unique*, but there is a difference between unique and once for all. In German, there is a word that captures this concept: *Einmaligkeit*. *Einmal* means "one time," and *-igkeit* on the end makes it "one-timeness." Christ offered Himself at one time for all time. There was no room for repetition of any kind. Because of the perfection of Christ's sacrifice, there is no need to repeat it in any way. Our Lord said on the cross, before He died, "It is finished" (John 19:30). Christ's work was finished; when He died, our debt was paid in full.

This is tied together with the person and work of Christ and how He has saved us in Himself. No priest offered Him up for us. He offered Himself up for us. When we remember His sacrifice in the Lord's Supper, we offer up a spiritual oblation of all possible praise unto God. Thus, the popish sacrifice of the mass (as they call it) is most abominably

618 • TRUTHS WE CONFESS

injurious to Christ's one, only sacrifice, the alone propitiation for all the sins of his elect. If a person commits mortal sin in the Roman Catholic scheme of things, he loses the grace of his justification and needs to be justified a second time, through the sacrament of penance. The sacrament of penance was objectionable to the Reformers, not because of confession or priestly absolution but because of the demand for works of satisfaction. The sinner has to do enough to satisfy the demands of God's justice that it would be fitting or congruous for God to restore him to a state of grace. But Christ's perfect sacrifice offered perfect propitiation once for all. God's righteousness and justice were satisfied by Christ for us, forever. We cannot add to the propitiatory value of the cross. Our works of satisfaction have neither condign nor congruous merit. God's demand for justice was satisfied once for all on the cross.

When we come to celebrate the Lord's Supper, we come rejoicing in the perfection of the atonement that Christ has already given. We must not try to repeat it or add to it. God says that He requires us to worship Him in spirit and in truth (John 4:23). The truth matters in worship, not just whether we feel good. There is good reason for, and content to, what we celebrate in the Lord's Supper.

The contemporary worship movement that has swept across America is riding the crest of bad theology. Worship is not an indifferent matter. As early as the sixteenth century, Calvin was concerned that worship had become married to the entertainment principles of the world. And now we are in the most entertainment-saturated age in human history, and people conclude that if the church is to compete, it must entertain.

There is a theology at work here. Our theology dictates that worship, above all else, involves the giving of honor, glory, and praise to the majesty of God. Everything that we do in our worship should serve that end. There should be a sense of transition from the world to the church, from the parking lot to the sanctuary. People should enter His courts with a sense of preparation of the soul. We come to honor God and His Son, who has won salvation for us once for all.

The Westminster divines say, in polemical language, "Here is not only what we believe, but also what we do not believe and why we do not believe it." When people say, "Doctrine doesn't matter," they are really saying that they are unconverted—if they really understand what they are saying and mean it. If doctrine doesn't matter, then it doesn't matter whether we worship Christ or the Antichrist, whether we're saved by grace or by works, whether we worship Buddha or Jesus. A person who says, "I am a Christian," and then adds, "Doctrine doesn't matter," publicly betrays Jesus Christ. Christians can do that unwittingly and still be Christians, but we need to realize that it does matter what we believe and how we worship God.

Even if it does not matter to us, it does matter to God. In Leviticus 10, we learn that the sons of Aaron were instantly killed by God for a transgression, when they offered strange fire on the altar, which God had not commanded. They were being innovative and experimental. When Aaron protested to Moses, Moses replied, "This is what the LORD has said: 'Among those who are near me I will be sanctified, and before all the people I will be glorified'" (Lev. 10:3). In our worship, the first thing we want to do is regard God as holy.

> 3. The Lord Jesus hath, in this ordinance, appointed his ministers to declare his word of institution to the people; to pray, and bless the elements of bread and wine, and thereby to set them apart from a common to an holy use; and to take and break the bread, to take the cup, and (they communicating also themselves) to give both to the communicants; but to none who are not then present in the congregation.

In this corporate celebration, all the people of God are involved. The confession requires that the words of institution be declared and that the prayer of consecration be said. We do not believe that the prayer of consecration changes the essential structure of the bread and the wine or that any miracle takes place. We do believe in a prayer of consecration, so that the elements, commonly used for daily nourishment, may now be set apart for a special, holy, and sacred activity. When we pray over the elements, we do not change them into the actual body and blood of Jesus; rather, we ask God, who instituted this sacrament, to "assign" special significance to the elements. There is nothing magical about the elements or the prayer of consecration, but we do ask God to set them apart from their common, everyday usage, to signify for us the atonement of Christ.

> 4. Private masses, or receiving this sacrament by a priest, or any other, alone; as likewise, the denial of the cup to the people, worshiping the elements, the lifting them up, or carrying them about, for adoration, and the reserving them for any pretended religious use; are all contrary to the nature of this sacrament, and to the institution of Christ.

Reformed confessions, such as the Westminster Confession, the Belgic Confession, the Heidelberg Catechism, and the Thirty-Nine Articles, characteristically set themselves over against the Roman Catholic Church in light of the controversies that arose in the sixteenth century. This is nowhere more evident than in this section on the Lord's Supper because of the serious differences between the Reformed view of the Lord's Supper and the Roman view of the Mass. We will look at this with respect to the Roman Catholic understanding of the presence of Christ in and through the sacraments.

Section 4 is a far-reaching condemnation of Roman Catholic practices: **Private masses, or receiving this sacrament by a priest, or any other, alone; as likewise, the denial of the cup to the people, worshiping the elements, the lifting them up, or carrying them about, for adoration, and the reserving them for any pretended religious use; are all contrary to the nature of this sacrament, and to the institution of Christ.** No polemical rhetoric is spared when the Westminster divines repudiate the Roman Catholic understanding of the Lord's Supper here in section 4—or in sections 5 and 6, where there are references to the Roman Catholic doctrine of transubstantiation.

Worshiping the elements is wrong. The elements are not to be adored. They are exalted and adored in Roman Catholic liturgy and ritual. In every Roman Catholic church, at the back of the altar, there is a so-called tabernacle. It is usually a gold box of sorts. The tabernacle contains the consecrated element, which means that Christ is truly present at all times in the tabernacle. A Roman Catholic, upon entering the church sanctuary, before being seated, genuflects. The priest, ministering in front of the altar, genuflects repeatedly during the service when he passes the tabernacle. They genuflect because they believe Christ is physically present in the tabernacle. It was in opposition to such a view that section 4 was written.

5. The outward elements in this sacrament, duly set apart to the uses ordained by Christ, have such relation to him crucified, as that, truly, yet sacramentally only, they are sometimes called by the name of the things they represent, to wit, the body and blood of Christ; albeit, in substance and nature, they still remain truly and only bread and wine, as they were before.

6. That doctrine which maintains a change of the substance of bread and wine, into the substance of Christ's body and blood (commonly called transubstantiation) by consecration of a priest, or by any other way, is repugnant, not to Scripture alone, but even to common sense, and reason; overthroweth the nature of the sacrament, and hath been, and is, the cause of manifold superstitions; yea, of gross idolatries.

The substance of bread and wine, according to Roman Catholic doctrine, is changed by priestly consecration into **the substance of Christ's body and blood.** This change is called transubstantiation, referring to an alleged change in substance. Ancient philosophers talked about the essence or substance by which something is truly and ultimately what it is. Aristotle distinguished between the substance of a thing and its *accidents*, or external, nonessential qualities. A duck, for example, can lose one of its external qualities but still remain a duck. If it gets laryngitis and doesn't quack anymore, one of its accidents is removed, but it is still a duck. Various outward manifestations may be changed without destroying the essence of the duck. It is important to understand Aristotle's view because Thomas Aquinas created a synthesis between Christian theology and Aristotelian philosophy. Since the Middle Ages, much of theology has been cast in the language of Aristotle.

For Aristotle, if an object has the accidents of an elephant, then it is certainly an elephant and not a daffodil. There is an inseparable unity

624 • TRUTHS WE CONFESS

between the substance of a thing and its accidents. Now when the priest says the prayer of consecration during the Mass, the bread and wine supposedly change into the body and blood of Jesus. However, they still look, taste, sound, feel, and smell like bread and wine. So Rome says that, in the miracle of transubstantiation, while the substance of the elements is transformed into the substance of the body and blood of Christ, the accidents remain unchanged. Before the miracle, we have the substance of bread and wine and the accidents of bread and wine. After the miracle, we have the substance of Christ's body and blood and still the accidents of bread and wine. There is a double miracle because the substance changes and the new substance does not have its accidents.

Martin Luther wrote a scathing critique of transubstantiation in *The Babylonian Captivity of the Church*. However, Luther still insisted on the corporeal presence of Christ in the Lord's Supper. He asserted that Christ's physical body and blood are truly present in the Lord's Supper. Because of that view, the Lutheran wing of the Reformation and the Reformed wing could not maintain doctrinal agreement. Luther's view is called consubstantiation, although Lutherans reject that designation. According to Luther, the miracle is that Christ, in His human body and blood, becomes present in, under, and through the bread and wine. There is not a change of elements, but an addition to them. Added to the bread and wine are the body and blood of Christ, though the latter are not visible.

Luther insisted on the physical presence of Christ's body and blood because he believed that Christ's words of institution ("This is My body; this is My blood") had to be interpreted literally. However, Jesus also said, "I am the door" and "I am the vine." He frequently used the verb *to be* in a metaphorical or representative sense. It is perfectly natural to interpret "This is My body" as "This represents My body."

Calvin and other Reformers rejected both transubstantiation and consubstantiation on Christological grounds. If the physical body of Christ is in heaven, they asked, how can it also be present wherever on earth the sacrament is being observed—and all at the same time? That would require the human nature of Christ to have the divine attribute of omnipresence.

At one of the most important ecumenical councils, the Council of Chalcedon in 451, the church defined her understanding of the mystery of the incarnation and the dual nature of Christ to stop the mouths of heretics, particularly Eutyches and Nestorius. Rome still holds to the declarations of Chalcedon, as do Protestants and all of Orthodox Christianity. Chalcedon represents the limit of where the minds of theologians can go in seeking to understand the mystery of the incarnation. Chalcedon said that Christ is *vere homo, vere Deus*—truly man, truly God. Chalcedon affirmed the dual nature of Christ, saying that He is one person with two natures, a divine nature and a human nature. The difficulty lies in understanding how the human nature and the divine nature relate to one another. In the fifth century, a heretical group called the Monophysites said that in Christ there is only one nature. That single nature was neither human nor divine, but rather a mixture of deity and humanity. Eutyches, the chief proponent of Monophysitism, said that Christ has a single, theanthropic (God-man) nature. That was either a deified humanity or, even worse, a humanized deity. The church responded to the Monophysites by declaring their belief to be heretical.

The church said that the two natures of Christ are united in such a way that they are not confused or mixed. By saying that they are not confused or mixed, the church repudiated the Monophysite heresy. The church also said that the two natures are united without separation or division. This repudiated the Nestorians, who separated the two natures almost to the point of saying that Jesus is two persons.

There are two natures in Christ, a divine nature and a human nature. To explain the connection of relationship between these two natures, the church fathers used the way of negation. They didn't tell us how the two natures are united. Rather, they told us how they are not united. They are united without mixture, without confusion, without separation, and without division. We cannot penetrate the mystery of the incarnation. We do not understand how the divine nature and the human nature are united, but we do know how they are not united. They are not to be understood in terms of confusion, mixture, separation, or division.

The Council of Chalcedon established the boundaries within which one must work to try to understand the person of Christ. To step over those boundaries in any direction is to enter into heresy. Whenever one compromises one of the negatives of Chalcedon, one ends up in some Christological heresy.

The Roman Catholic Church affirmed the Council of Chalcedon, as did Luther. But Calvin insisted that both of them failed to apply the message of Chalcedon when they developed their understanding of the Lord's Supper. After stating the four negatives—without confusion, without mixture, without separation, without division—Chalcedon added: each nature retains its own attributes. In the incarnation, the divine nature does not stop being divine. The second person of the Trinity did not give up His divine nature in the incarnation, nor did God die on the cross. If God had died on the cross, the universe would have disappeared. God not only created the universe, but He maintains its existence, moment to moment. In the incarnation, the divine nature did not lose any of its attributes, and the human nature of Christ retained its humanity after the resurrection and ascension. We must neither deify the human nature nor humanize the divine nature.

But the doctrines of transubstantiation and consubstantiation give a divine attribute to the human nature of Christ. In order for Christ's body and blood to be physically present whenever and wherever the Lord's Supper or the Mass is celebrated, His physical body must be ubiquitous or omnipresent—everywhere at the same time. But that is a divine attribute. In the Middle Ages, the Roman Catholic Church explained this as the communication of attributes from the divine to the human nature (*communicatio idiomatum*). In this view, the divine nature, in the incarnation, not only communicated information from the mind of God to the mind of the human nature of Christ but also communicated or transferred divine powers and attributes, such as omnipresence, to the human nature. This could explain how the physical body and blood of Christ are present in thousands of places at the same time, but it compromises the Chalcedonian view that each nature of Christ retains its own attributes. The divine nature of Christ can be here and there at the same time, but the human nature of Jesus is in heaven, at the right hand of God. This explains how Jesus could tell His disciples that He was departing from them, yet would still be present with them to the end. The Heidelberg

Catechism teaches, "In his human nature Christ is not now on earth; but in his divinity, majesty, grace, and Spirit he is never absent from us" (Q&A 47). Thus, we do not see the human nature of Jesus when we celebrate the Lord's Supper. Body and blood belong to His humanity, not to His deity.

Christ is present at the Lord's Supper, but He is made present to us by the divine nature. The people who were in Jesus' company when He was on earth in the flesh, and who communed with Him, were communing not only with a human being but also with God, because Christ has two natures. If they communed with the human nature, they communed at the same time with the divine nature, and vice versa. When we commune with the divine nature, we are thereby communing with the whole Christ, even though His human nature is in heaven. We commune with the human nature because wherever the divine nature is, He is. His divine nature is not separated from the human nature. The only difference is that He does not bring His human nature to communion; it remains in heaven. Unfortunately, Luther embraced the concept of the communication of attributes, and that is why Reformed theologians considered the Lutheran view of the Lord's Supper to be Monophysite. They placed Christ's human nature in different places at the same time. On the other hand, Lutheran theologians accuse Reformed theology of Nestorianism, saying that if Jesus is not present everywhere physically, then the two natures of Christ are divided. But Reformed theology is not Nestorian. It distinguishes between the two natures but never separates them.

In the sixteenth century, Calvin defended the Reformed view of the Lord's Supper on two fronts. On the one hand, he had to deal with the Roman Catholic and Lutheran views of Christ's physical presence. On the other hand, he had to deal with the so-called spiritualists, who argued that the Lord's Supper is a mere memorial service, where the elements symbolize a past event. They denied the real presence of Christ in any significant way in the Supper. But Calvin insisted that Christ was spiritually present in a special way.

The key word in these debates was *substance*. Calvin's Roman Catholic and Lutheran opponents used the word to refer to the physical or corporeal presence of Christ in the sacrament. But when Calvin debated with the spiritualists, he used the term differently, referring to the "real" presence of Christ in the sacrament, not just a symbolic or intellectual presence. Calvin taught the real presence of Christ, but not His physical presence.

To go further with the controversy, one of Calvin's principles was *Finitum non capax infinitum*, "The finite cannot contain (or grasp) the infinite." Expressions like this are useful because they have a precise meaning, which does not get muddied by overuse. Calvin used it to express the incomprehensibility of God. Our finite minds cannot comprehend the infinite God.

In the incarnation, God took to Himself a human nature, but the nature of God was not thereby confined to the geographical location of the body of Jesus. When Jesus, in His human nature, prayed to the Father, He was not talking to Himself. The divine nature was present far beyond the boundaries of His human nature. The fullness of the Godhead dwells in Jesus, but it is not limited by human finitude. The divine nature remained infinite after the incarnation, retaining all its attributes, including omniscience, omnipotence, eternality, and omnipresence.

The disciples once asked Jesus when He would return. He answered, "But concerning that day or that hour, no one knows, not even the angels in heaven, nor the Son, but only the Father" (Mark 13:32). We find that hard to believe. How could Jesus not know? Wasn't He God?

We know from Scripture that Jesus got tired, hungry, and thirsty. We don't generally ask, "How could Jesus get tired, hungry, or thirsty, since God doesn't need to sleep, eat, or drink?" We understand that those things refer to His human nature. He had both a divine nature and a human nature, which were perfectly united; nevertheless, we can and must distinguish them. Certain things that Jesus did were clear manifestations of His human nature rather than the divine nature. So we don't get upset when Jesus sleeps, eats, or drinks. But when He says, "I don't know," we think that cannot be. This is the Jesus who knew Nathaniel before meeting him (John 1:43–51). This is the Jesus who knew everything about the woman at the well before meeting her (John 4). He had supernatural knowledge and insight. He even knew what people were thinking. How could He not have known the day of His return?

Throughout Israel's history, God supernaturally revealed information to human beings like the prophets, who then declared the message to the world. We do not therefore conclude that Jeremiah or Isaiah knew everything. Similarly, the divine nature of Christ communicated information to the human nature of Christ. His divine nature had all the attributes of deity, including omniscience. The divine nature knew the day and the hour. But the divine nature did not communicate everything to the human nature, including that information, so His human knowledge was limited. Jesus, as a human being, could manifest supernatural knowledge only when His divine nature communicated it to His human nature.

Thomas Aquinas struggled with this and was perplexed by the mystery of the incarnation. He devised what he called an "accommodation" theory to explain Jesus' apparent lack of knowledge. He said that Jesus had to know the time of His return, since His human nature was perfectly united with the divine nature. Therefore, Jesus must have sidestepped His disciples' question by telling them that He did not know the answer, when in fact He did.

Such a theory rescues the omniscience of Christ, but at a very heavy price. Under this system, Jesus, who is the truth incarnate, speaks falsehood. If He ever told a lie, He would have disqualified Himself from being our Redeemer. We cannot accept that Jesus ever lied. We must reject the theory of accommodation.

Subsequently, the Roman Catholic Church developed a doctrine of the *communicatio idiomatum*—the communication of attributes. In this scenario, not only is information communicated from the divine nature to the human nature of Christ, but attributes are also communicated from the divine to the human nature. In this view, the divine nature empowers the human nature, making it possible for the human nature to be everywhere or to know everything. The divine attributes of omniscience and omnipresence are communicated to the human nature. It was at this point that Calvin vehemently disagreed.

When we try to understand the two natures of Jesus, heresy lurks on both sides. Liberals allow the deity of Christ to be swallowed up in His humanity, effectively denying His deity. Conservatives and evangelicals, on the other hand, are zealous to affirm and protect the deity of Christ, but sometimes His humanity is obscured and swallowed up by His deity. We must protect a true union of two natures, one that is truly divine and one that is truly human. Jesus has a true human nature and a true divine nature that exist in perfect unity.

> 7. Worthy receivers, outwardly partaking of the visible elements, in this sacrament, do then also, inwardly by faith, really and indeed, yet not carnally and corporally but spiritually, receive, and feed upon, Christ crucified, and all benefits of his death: the body and blood of Christ being then, not corporally or carnally, in, with, or under the bread and wine; yet, as really, but spiritually, present to the faith of believers in that ordinance, as the elements themselves are to their outward senses.

This section carefully articulates the Reformed view of the Lord's Supper. It is a summary of Calvin's position. Sometimes we say, "I can't be with you physically, but I will be with you in spirit." But the confession is not talking about Christ's being present in His thoughts. Nor is He present merely in our thoughts, as we remember Him so vividly that He seems to be with us.

In section 7, Christ's spiritual presence is twice qualified by the word **really**. He is not present just in our thinking or in our imagination, but really in a spiritual way. He is truly present in His divine nature, so that we really feed on the risen Christ. Christ's human nature is at the right hand of God in heaven; His divine nature is at the Lord's Table, where we meet Him. When we meet Him, we meet the One who still perfectly unites the human and divine natures. Through His divine nature, we commune with the whole Christ. We meet the whole person of Jesus at the Lord's Table, not because His human nature can be physically present here and all over the world, but because He comes to us according to His divine nature, which is perfectly united to His human nature. When He comes, He does so with the whole person.

That is mystical and difficult to grasp. Reformed people, Rome, Lutherans, and Episcopalians believe in the real presence of Christ in the Lord's Supper. But we disagree in how we understand that real presence. The difference has to do with the dual nature of Christ as it was set forth at the Council of Chalcedon.

8. Although ignorant and wicked men receive the outward elements in this sacrament; yet, they receive not the thing signified thereby; but, by their unworthy coming thereunto, are guilty of the body and blood of the Lord, to their own damnation. Wherefore, all ignorant and ungodly persons, as they are unfit to enjoy communion with him, so are they unworthy of the Lord's table; and cannot, without great sin against Christ, while they remain such, partake of these holy mysteries, or be admitted thereunto.

The reference here is to what is known as the *manducatio indigna*—the eating and drinking unworthily. In 1 Corinthians 11:28–29, Paul warns the people of Corinth to examine themselves before they come to the Lord's Supper, because they have been abusing it. He warns that it is not a neutral event to be approached with a casual, cavalier attitude. It is the table of Jesus Christ. Those who come into His presence with a haughty, arrogant, impenitent spirit or an unbelieving participant are trampling on holy ground. They are eating and drinking to their own damnation because this sacrament is given to those who believe. If those who receive it are not true believers, they mock the truth of what is signified. The cross is being handled in a blasphemous way.

Paul adds to his warning about eating and drinking unworthily: "That is why many of you are weak and ill, and some have died" (1 Cor. 11:30). We take our life into our hands when we come to the Lord's Table. We come to feed on His spiritual life, which wells up into everlasting life. To come hypocritically in unbelief while we are still at enmity with Christ is heaping up wrath against the day of judgment. That is why the table is fenced. The idea is not for us to be arrogantly exclusive but to protect people from the consequences and dangers of improperly participating in the celebration of the Lord's Supper. We believe that Christ is present in a special way to pour out His tender mercy on us, to condescend to our weakness, to restore the joy of our salvation, to assist us in our struggle for sanctification. We enter His house, come to His table, and commune with the risen Christ in a real way. We need to be discerning.

Of Church Censures

1. The Lord Jesus, as King and Head of his church, hath therein appointed a government, in the hand of church officers, distinct from the civil magistrate.

2. To these officers the keys of the kingdom of heaven are committed; by virtue whereof, they have power, respectively, to retain, and remit sins; to shut that kingdom against the impenitent, both by the Word, and censures; and to open it unto penitent sinners, by the ministry of the gospel; and by absolution from censures, as occasion shall require.

3. Church censures are necessary, for the reclaiming and gaining of offending brethren, for deterring of others from the like offenses, for purging out of that leaven which might infect the whole lump, for vindicating the honor of Christ, and the holy profession of the gospel, and for preventing the wrath of God, which might justly fall upon the church, if they should suffer his covenant, and the seals thereof, to be profaned by notorious and obstinate offenders.

4. For the better attaining of these ends, the officers of the church are to proceed by admonition; suspension from the sacrament of the Lord's Supper for a season; and by excommunication from the church; according to the nature of the crime, and demerit of the person.

---

1. The Lord Jesus, as King and Head of his church, hath therein appointed a government, in the hand of church officers, distinct from the civil magistrate.

One essential characteristic of the true church, according to the Westminster divines, is the presence of a duly established government. This government is designed to promote the purity and peace of the church and to enforce discipline when necessary. Section 1 declares that the government of the church has been established by the Head and King of the church, the Lord Jesus Himself. Just as God has appointed civil magistrates, who are given the power of the sword to protect, maintain, and defend life and liberty, so He has ordained the officers of the church to govern that holy institution. The church is not the state, nor is the state the church. The responsibility to preach the gospel, administer the sacraments, and provide for the spiritual well-being of the people is given to the church, not to the state.

2. To these officers the keys of the kingdom of heaven are committed; by virtue whereof, they have power, respectively, to retain, and remit sins; to shut that kingdom against the impenitent, both by the Word, and censures; and to open it unto penitent sinners, by the ministry of the gospel; and by absolution from censures, as occasion shall require.

Section 2 focuses on **the keys of the kingdom of heaven.** Christ declared in Matthew 16:19 that He would give the keys of the kingdom of heaven to His disciples, and church officers are seen as the heirs of those keys. The keys of the kingdom are central to the Roman Catholic Church's belief in the treasury of merit, the granting of indulgences, and the release from purgatory, which in large part provoked the Protestant Reformation. But in that provocation and protest, the Reformers, though they rejected the Roman view of the keys of the kingdom, did not repudiate them, but restored their proper, biblical function.

Here the keys of the kingdom are understood in terms of church discipline. The officers of the church are given the power and authority to retain and remit sins. That is, the church has the power to grant the assurance of pardon to those who repent and to impose censures and discipline on those who remain impenitent. The language of the confession is: **to shut that kingdom against the impenitent.** The shutting of the kingdom is done by removing people from that place where the means of grace are most intensely focused, namely, the church, where the Word of God is preached and the sacraments are celebrated. This follows Paul's injunction to the Corinthian church to impose discipline in the scandalous situation of a man who practiced incest openly but wasn't disciplined (1 Cor. 5). When the church finally disciplined the incestuous man, Paul required that he be fully restored to fellowship after he repented (2 Cor. 2). We see in that instance that the purpose of discipline is not merely to remove sinners from the church but also to rehabilitate and restore those who are repentant. Therefore, the language of the confession involves not only the shutting of the kingdom but also the opening of it. It is shut to the impenitent and open to the penitent. This is inseparably linked to the ministry of the gospel, which announces the forgiveness of sins for all who repent.

> 3. Church censures are necessary, for the reclaiming and gaining of offending brethren, for deterring of others from the like offenses, for purging out of that leaven which might infect the whole lump, for vindicating the honor of Christ, and the holy profession of the gospel, and for preventing the wrath of God, which might justly fall upon the church, if they should suffer his covenant, and the seals thereof, to be profaned by notorious and obstinate offenders.

Section 3 declares that church censures are not only permissible but are indeed necessary **for the reclaiming and gaining of offending brethren.** This means that the goal of church discipline is to bring sinful people to repentance, so that they may be restored to full, active participation in the church. Church discipline is also seen as a deterrent. When discipline is absent from the church, there may be rapid degeneration into worldly vices. Indeed, gross and heinous sin that goes unpunished becomes like that leaven of which Paul warns (1 Cor. 5:6), which may **infect the whole lump.** Another purpose for church censures is to vindicate the honor of Christ. The church is first and foremost the body of Christ, and that body is called to bear witness to its Head and King, Jesus Himself.

When scandalous sin is left unchecked, unbridled, and undisciplined in the visible church, it brings serious dishonor to Christ. It is the duty of Christians, individually and corporately, to make a holy profession of the gospel. Another purpose for church discipline is to prevent the wrath of God, which would justly fall upon the church if sins were left unchecked. But we seek to rescue individuals and the whole body from the corrective wrath of God. The whole of sacred Scripture makes it clear that though God is patient and long-suffering with His people, there comes a point when His church is so profaned by notorious and obstinate sinners that He will no longer permit His covenant community to be so profaned.

4. For the better attaining of these ends, the officers of the church are to proceed by admonition; suspension from the sacrament of the Lord's Supper for a season; and by excommunication from the church; according to the nature of the crime, and demerit of the person.

Section 4 makes it clear that church discipline is not to be carried out haphazardly in the Christian community, nor is it to be done in a vigilante fashion. The **officers of the church** are responsible to proceed with church discipline. They must use discretion, for church discipline should not be brought to bear for every transgression. Since "love covers a multitude of sins" (1 Peter 4:8), every peccadillo or minor slight is not legitimate grounds for bringing a complaint against our neighbor. Rather, church discipline is to be reserved for those sins that are gross and heinous, that are public and scandalous, that bring dishonor to Christ and to His church.

We are also cautioned in section 4 that the ends for which church discipline has been established are better achieved when it proceeds in an orderly and progressive manner. The church does not jump to the final stage of excommunication in the first instance of church discipline but rather proceeds by degrees, hoping that with each step of the discipline, the desired result of repentance will be achieved, without further discipline being needed. The first step mentioned in section 4 is **admonition**. When admonition does not cause the offender to repent, the next step is **suspension from the sacrament of the Lord's Supper for a season**. The length of that suspension is not specified by the confession and is therefore left to the prudence and discretion of the church.

The final step is **excommunication**, in which people are removed from membership and from fellowship within the visible body of Christ. The steps of church discipline to be taken depend on **the nature of the crime** and the level and severity of the **demerit of the person**. It should be noted, however, that in one sense, there is only one sin that leads to excommunication: contumacy, which is the willful refusal to repent. When a person is caught up in gross and heinous sin, is called to repentance throughout the process of church discipline, and still refuses to repent, he is contumacious, unwilling to repent. The elders then determine that such a person's profession of faith is no longer credible, and he is put out of the church, in the hope that this last step will lead him to repentance.

Of Synods and Councils

1. For the better government, and further edification of the church, there ought to be such assemblies as are commonly called synods or councils: and it belongeth to the overseers and other rulers of the particular churches, by virtue of their office, and the power which Christ hath given them for edification and not for destruction, to appoint such assemblies; and to convene together in them, as often as they shall judge it expedient for the good of the church.

2. It belongeth to synods and councils, ministerially to determine controversies of faith, and cases of conscience; to set down rules and directions for the better ordering of the public worship of God, and government of his church; to receive complaints in cases of maladministration, and authoritatively to determine the same: which decrees and determinations, if consonant to the Word of God, are to be received with reverence and submission; not only for their agreement with the Word, but also for the power whereby they are made, as being an ordinance of God appointed thereunto in his Word.

3. All synods or councils, since the Apostles' times, whether general or particular, may err; and many have erred. Therefore they are not to be made the rule of faith, or practice; but to be used as a help in both.

4. Synods and councils are to handle, or conclude nothing, but that which is ecclesiastical: and are not to intermeddle with civil affairs which concern the commonwealth, unless by way of humble petition in cases extraordinary; or, by way of advice, for satisfaction of conscience, if they be thereunto required by the civil magistrate.

1. For the better government, and further edification of the church, there ought to be such assemblies as are commonly called synods or councils: and it belongeth to the overseers and other rulers of the particular churches, by virtue of their office, and the power which Christ hath given them for edification and not for destruction, to appoint such assemblies; and to convene together in them, as often as they shall judge it expedient for the good of the church.

Churches should not exist in isolation or be unrelated to each other. Local congregations should be involved with other congregations in the broader church. In the New Testament, we see, for example, the Council of Jerusalem in Acts 15. Representatives from the Apostolic community met to deal with issues that related to all the churches. We also see how Paul appealed to the churches outside of Jerusalem to receive offerings for the saints in Jerusalem. There was an interaction and interrelatedness among the early churches. During church history, different forms of government have developed, each one appealing to the New Testament as the basis for its structure.

In the episcopal form of government, bishops rule the church. The bishop rules over the churches in a geographical area, usually called a diocese. Within the diocese, there may be fifty local churches, led by individual priests. There may be a consistory that governs the local church, but over the local church is the bishop. The bishops meet together regularly to determine policies that affect the entire church.

There is clear historical evidence that before the first century had ended, an episcopal form of government was in effect in many places. There were bishops in Smyrna, bishops in Rome, and bishops in Ephesus. Gradually, the idea developed that certain bishops are higher than others, and eventually the bishop of Rome became the supreme pontiff in the Western church.

When questions of wide interest needed to be settled, bishops and other delegates met together in ecumenical (churchwide) councils and regional synods. The decisions of the great ecumenical councils of the early church have been received and adopted by most branches of the church. The Trinitarian formulas were established at the Council of Nicaea in 325. Christological formulas, which affect the doctrine of the Lord's Supper, were devised at the Council of Chalcedon in 451. The Roman Catholic Church has had its own councils, particularly the Council of Trent in the sixteenth century. This council was summoned to respond to the Protestant Reformers, whose distinctive views were condemned as heretical. The next great council was the First Vatican Council in 1869–70, which defined the doctrine of papal infallibility. The Second Vatican Council was held in the 1960s to come to grips with the modern world.

In addition to episcopal church government, there is a representative form of church government, usually called presbyterian. Ministers and elders meet in regional assemblies, called presbyteries or classes (in the Dutch tradition), and representatives from those groups then meet in synods or general assemblies. The presbytery or classis has many of the responsibilities handled by the bishop in an episcopal system. Ecclesiastical and judicial authority is vested in the local church leaders (the session or consistory), subject to review by the higher representative bodies.

Another type of church government is called the congregational form. In this system, all authority is vested in the local congregation. Many congregational or independent churches belong to loose federations, giving them a connectional relationship to similar churches. They meet periodically in assemblies or conventions to share ideas and policies, and to make public statements that are not binding on particular congregations. But many other independent churches have no such connections. In an independent church, authority is usually vested either in the minister or in a board. In many congregational churches, the congregational meeting is the highest court.

The Westminster Confession favors a presbyterian form of government. Presbyterianism has its roots in Scotland and, to some degree, in the Swiss Reformation. Most of those who developed this form of church government saw it as established in the New Testament.

> 2. It belongeth to synods and councils, ministerially to determine controversies of faith, and cases of conscience; to set down rules

and directions for the better ordering of the public worship of God, and government of his church; to receive complaints in cases of maladministration, and authoritatively to determine the same: which decrees and determinations, if consonant to the Word of God, are to be received with reverence and submission; not only for their agreement with the Word, but also for the power whereby they are made, as being an ordinance of God appointed thereunto in his Word.

The Westminster Confession affirms that when decisions are made at the local church level with respect to doctrine, behavior, or matters of discipline, there is a court of appeal. If a person is convicted of something in the civil realm, he has the right to appeal to a higher court. Similarly, decisions made in a local congregation can be appealed to a higher court (the presbytery), and then to the highest court (the general assembly). People who are directly involved in a dispute often become so subjective that it helps to have a higher court rule on it.

It belongeth to synods and councils, ministerially to determine controversies of faith. There is a distinction between political power that is vested in the state and the authority that is vested in the church. The church's authority is ministerial, and it deals with controversies of faith, that is, matters of doctrine, cases of conscience, and the public worship of God. The church does not bear the sword or raise a standing army. Those are responsibilities that God has given to the civil magistrate. The arena of faith is a matter for the church, and it is a ministerial matter. In matters of faith, Christians are not to go to the civil magistrate to air their grievances with each other. Many Christians believe we are not supposed to go to the civil magistrate for anything. This is likely overstating things. But certainly, in a theological dispute with a brother, we do not go to the sheriff or to the civil magistrate to have him solve our problem. Likewise, we do not want the civil magistrate interfering in matters of the faith.

The ordering of the public worship of God is and should be under ecclesiastical control. Someone has to order the way in which worship takes place.

How God is to be worshiped is not a matter of personal preference, as we know from the Old Testament. Few things provoked the wrath of

God more than people's worshiping him in a manner contrary to His instructions. Throughout Israel's history, there was the problem of syncretism. After God established how He was to be worshiped, the people, the clergy, the priests, and the false prophets borrowed elements from their pagan neighbors. They incorporated those pagan or secular elements into the worship of God and provoked His judgment upon the nation.

That did not stop with the Old or New Testament. We can find examples throughout history where the church, to use the late James M. Boice's phrase, "was doing the Lord's work in the world's way." What works in the secular culture may not be legitimate in the house of God.

> 3. All synods or councils, since the Apostles' times, whether general or particular, may err; and many have erred. Therefore they are not to be made the rule of faith, or practice; but to be used as a help in both.

A principle that came out of the Reformation, called *sola Scriptura*, requires that our consciences be bound by the Word of God alone. Luther was shown to be out of line with decisions made by various councils and papal pronouncements, and he said, "My conscience is held captive by the Word of God. Unless you can show me where I am wrong by Scripture, I cannot recant."

While church councils are not infallible, they can be helpful. The Council of Chalcedon helps us understand Christology in a way that it faithful to the Bible, and so the church at large has historically valued its work. If the church fathers at Chalcedon were wrong, we must be able to demonstrate how they were wrong from Scripture. That is the point of *sola Scriptura*.

Synods and councils, according to section 3, **are not to be made the rule of faith, or practice; but to be used as a help in both.** When pastors preach from a text of Scripture, they consult commentaries and the historic wisdom of the church. God has gifted the church's great teachers with tremendous insights. To be diligent in studying the Scriptures, pastors have to examine them, not only from our own twenty-first-century perspective but from the perspective of the past. As C.S. Lewis once said, "It is helpful to have the winds of the ages blow through your head, lest you be guilty of carrying the contemporary cultural baggage to the text."

Consider, for example, the question of whether Paul in 1 Timothy 2:11–12 allows for the ordination of women. There is probably no commentator in the history of the church before 1960 who took the position that this passage was intended to be of local application only. It could be argued that the monolithic interpretation of this passage through the centuries was an expression of perpetual male chauvinism. Some may think that it wasn't until women's liberation came to the forefront that this error, repeated for two thousand years, was finally exposed. That is possible, but highly unlikely. That is why we look to what church leaders of the first century, the fifth century, and the sixteenth century said and did. It is important to see how the church down through the centuries has understood the Word of God. We don't want simply to depend on tradition, but we want to be helped by the tradition. It is highly unlikely that someone today is going to come up with an insight that will overthrow two thousand years of church history. We use assemblies, councils, and synods of the past as a help to understand the truths of God.

> 4. Synods and councils are to handle, or conclude nothing, but that which is ecclesiastical: and are not to intermeddle with civil affairs which concern the commonwealth, unless by way of humble petition in cases extraordinary; or, by way of advice, for satisfaction of conscience, if they be thereunto required by the civil magistrate.

This statement limits the scope of church councils to ecclesiastical matters. The church ought not to usurp authority that God has given to the civil magistrate. However, there is a debate, in Presbyterian circles, whether the church has the right or the responsibility to speak on civil matters. For instance, should the church have had anything to say about whether the American colonists should revolt against England?

Churches in the United States are not allowed by law, as tax-exempt organizations, to preach politics. This is outrageous, because in the Old Testament and in the New, the people of God were called to be engaged in prophetic criticism. When Ahab confiscated Naboth's vineyard, he abused his power as king, and the prophet of God rebuked him. Herod's marriage was against the law of God, and John the Baptist paid with his life for criticizing the king. When the civil government endorses abortion on demand, it is the duty of the church—not only as individuals, but in council—to speak out against those miscarriages of justice and the failure of the church to be what God has called it to be.

When the church speaks out, people say that Christians are trying to take over the government and force their views on others. But we are not calling the state to be the church. We are calling the state to be the state. We are reminding the state of why it was created in the first place and what its responsibility is under God. The state was ordained by God and its primary task is to maintain, protect, and sustain human life. The German church spoke out against Hitler with the Barmen Declaration.

There are divisions within Reformed communities on how section 4 should be applied. Does it mean that the church should never say anything except on ecclesiastical matters, or does the church have the responsibility to be the conscience of the nation? The church is supposed to be the conscience, not the government.

Of the State of Men after Death, and of the Resurrection of the Dead

1. The bodies of men, after death, return to dust, and see corruption: but their souls, which neither die nor sleep, having an immortal subsistence, immediately return to God who gave them: the souls of the righteous, being then made perfect in holiness, are received into the highest heavens, where they behold the face of God, in light and glory, waiting for the full redemption of their bodies. And the souls of the wicked are cast into hell, where they remain in torments and utter darkness, reserved to the judgment of the great day. Besides these two places, for souls separated from their bodies, the Scripture acknowledgeth none.

2. At the last day, such as are found alive shall not die, but be changed: and all the dead shall be raised up, with the selfsame bodies, and none other (although with different qualities), which shall be united again to their souls forever.

3. The bodies of the unjust shall, by the power of Christ, be raised to dishonor: the bodies of the just, by his Spirit, unto honor; and be made conformable to his own glorious body.

With chapter 32, we enter the subdivision of theology that is called "eschatology." Eschatology has to do with the future: the return of Jesus, the consummation of the kingdom of God, the state of our existence after death, and the final resurrection. Much information is given about our future state in sacred Scripture. However, there are still many questions about the state of our existence after we die. Will we be old in heaven? Will we be young? Will we show any kind of age? What will our bodies look like? We have hints from the glorified body of Christ, which is the model for us all, but questions remain for which we will not know the answer until we get there.

1. The bodies of men, after death, return to dust, and see corruption: but their souls, which neither die nor sleep, having an immortal subsistence, immediately return to God who gave them: the souls of the righteous, being then made perfect in holiness, are received into the highest heavens, where they behold the face of God, in light and glory, waiting for the full redemption of their bodies. And the souls of the wicked are cast into hell, where they remain in torments and utter darkness, reserved to the judgment of the great day. Besides these two places, for souls separated from their bodies, the Scripture acknowledgeth none.

Volumes of theological information about eschatology have been compacted and condensed in this short paragraph. It assumes that the human soul has an **immortal subsistence**. An immortal soul is not mortal and therefore cannot die or be destroyed. Thomas Aquinas gives a cogent argument for affirming the substantive immortality of the human soul because God made it a spiritual substance, not given to corruption. We must be careful with the word *immortal*, however, because of the baggage it carries from ancient Greek philosophy, in which the soul was seen as eternal. As Christians, we believe that human souls are created, not eternal. If we are created, our lives depend on the Creator in whom we live and move and have our being. Our souls are equally dependent on God for their sustenance and continuity of being. To the Greeks, souls have always been and always will be. The Greek notion of the immortality of the soul is that the human soul is inherently and intrinsically immortal. We do not believe that. A human soul cannot survive for five seconds without the sustaining power of God. God will preserve our souls and even the souls of the damned forever, but they are not inherently indestructible. They would perish if God withdrew His providential support from them. He preserves the soul, and in that sense it is immortal extrinsically but not intrinsically. The perpetual life of the soul rests in the power of God, not in its own power.

The bodies of men, after death, return to dust, and see corruption. In John 11, we read the story of Lazarus and his resurrection. Lazarus had been in the tomb for four days, and his body was already beginning to undergo the natural decomposition of the flesh. When we die, our bodies see corruption. Of course, the notable exception is that God refused to allow His Holy One to see corruption between His death and His resurrection (Ps. 16:10). But all other dead bodies of human beings decay and return to dust. At the funeral service, we say, "Ashes to ashes, dust to dust," but that is not the end of the story. The body that dies will be raised again. It is sown in corruption but raised in incorruption. It is sown in mortality but raised in immortality (1 Cor. 15:35–49). The curse of corruption that we experience in this body will not be associated with the new body that we will receive at the resurrection.

The bodies of men, after death, return to dust, and see corruption: but their souls . . . neither die nor sleep. There are two things that do not happen to us at death. First, our souls do not die. That means that we have the continuity of personal existence beyond the grave. Our personal life, which is currently housed in our physical bodies, does not stop at death. The interim between our birth and our death in this world is an infinitesimal drop in the ocean of the full extent of our life. Second, our souls do not sleep. We sing "Amazing Grace," and in that last verse we acknowledge:

When we've been there ten thousand years,
bright shining as the sun,
We've no less days to sing God's praise
than when we first begun.

When we join the saints in heaven, even if they died two thousand years ago, they still have as much time left to enjoy life as we do when we get to heaven. It is not that when we go to heaven we get an extra life, or an extra thousand or two thousand years; we live forever.

According to the confession, the soul does not die when the body dies, nor does it go to sleep. According to a popular error called "soul sleep," or *psychopannychia*, the soul goes to sleep when the body dies. It goes into a state of suspended animation until the great resurrection, at which time it will be awakened, so it will seem as if there has been no passage of time. This view is based on the Bible's sometimes speaking of death as sleep. For example, an Old Testament king is said to have "slept with his fathers" when he dies (e.g., 1 Kings 2:10). But this was a common Jewish figure of speech. It was not meant to describe an intermediate state of suspended animation.

The doctrine of soul sleep is thoroughly demolished in a volume titled *Psychopannychia*, which is one of the lesser-known works of John Calvin. The Bible teaches that we do not lose consciousness when we die. We will be in heaven, aware of Christ, aware of God, and aware of the other saints who are there. We will not be clothed with our resurrected bodies at that point, but we will be in an intermediate state, in which the soul exists without the body. According to the New Testament, life in this world is a good thing. It is a blessing to be able to live a long life. But the intermediate state is better. Paul said: "I am hard pressed between the two. My desire is to depart and be with Christ, for that is far better. But to remain in the flesh is more necessary on your account" (Phil. 1:23–24). Paul was not in conflict between the good and the bad. It was between the good and the better—and in this case, far better.

Life in the intermediate state is far better than life now, Paul said, because we are then in the immediate presence of Jesus. However, it is still not the best. The best will come at the final resurrection, when our souls will be united with our glorified bodies. We will live forever in that glorified state. The options for the believer are good, better, and best. But for the unbeliever, they are bad, worse, and unspeakably horrible.

The souls of the deceased immediately return to God who gave them: the souls of the righteous, being then made perfect in holiness. So, as soon as we die, we are perfected (Heb. 12:23). Our sanctification is completed. As we enter into glory, we enter into the state of sinlessness. There will be no sin there. Immediately, the souls of the righteous, being then made perfect in holiness, are received into the highest heavens, where they behold the face of God, in light and glory, waiting for the full redemption of their bodies. The Bible tells us a lot about life after death, but many questions are left unanswered. John wrote, "See what kind of love the Father has given to us, that we should be called children of God" (1 John 3:1). Then he says, "What we will be has not yet appeared; but we know that when he appears we shall be like him, because we shall see him as he is" (v. 2). The highest hope of the Christian is the beatific vision of God. We shall see Him, John says, as He is.

The promise to see God, in the Beatitudes, is given to the pure in heart: "Blessed are the pure in heart, for they shall see God" (Matt. 5:8). They will see Him. The vision is described graphically in the last two chapters of the Bible, in the book of Revelation. The saints will behold the unveiled glory of God. One of the hardest things about living the Christian life is that we serve a God whom we have never seen. The culture senses His absence, not His presence, but though we cannot see Him, we see the evidence of Him, of the work of His hands and His work in history. We have not seen Him because it is forbidden for sinners to see Him. There is nothing wrong with our eyes. Rather, there is something wrong with our hearts. When our hearts are totally sanctified, when we reach that state of glorification, when we will indeed be altogether pure in heart, then, at last, the beatific vision will flood our souls. We will see Him and will continue to see Him always.

The confession expresses the hope found in John's epistle. We will see the splendid glory unveiled, the majesty of God. John later described the New Jerusalem coming down from heaven: "There is no moon; there is no sun." There will be no artificial lights in the heavenly Jerusalem, because such modes of illumination will be completely unnecessary. There will be no night there, because the glory of God and of the Son will never be turned off. It radiates and shines forever, and we will live in the midst of that light.

We need to fill our minds with the promises of God and believe them. The martyrs of the first century died singing the praises of God and believing His promises. They believed, and they knew where they were going. They were eager to get there. We will all go in God's time, and we will be in the immediate presence of God.

They behold the face of God, in light and glory, waiting for the full redemption of their bodies. The beatific vision is the ultimate joy and delight for which we were created in the first place. The word beatitude comes from the same root as beatific. It is the vision that brings with it the supreme state of blessedness.

In the Old Testament, God's promise of blessing stood in stark contrast to the threat of His curse. The curse manifested God's judgment and wrath on disobedient people, whereas the blessing was His reward for His obedient people. The Mosaic covenant was set up with regard to those dual sanctions. In Deuteronomy 28, God promised the people manifold blessings if they obeyed Him, and all manner of curses if they disobeyed Him. To be cursed is not only to miss the blessing but to be cut off from all the benefits that God has promised to His people.

When Christ died, He took the place of those who were covenant breakers. He took upon Himself the curse of God on the cross. "Cursed is everyone who is hanged on a tree" (Gal. 3:13). Jesus took the punishment, the curse, that we deserved. Because His righteousness is applied to our account, He wins for us the blessing by His perfect obedience. The supreme level of blessedness that we can hope to experience is the beatific vision.

In the garden of Eden, Adam and Eve were in a state of pure delight, fellowshiping with God as He walked in the cool of the evening. When sin entered into the relationship, Adam and Eve hid from God. God admonished them for their sin and drove them out of the garden. He cursed the man, the woman, the serpent, and the earth. He prevented anyone from ever entering the garden again.

Because of this breach in intimate fellowship between the Creator and the creature, man could no longer behold the glory of God directly. God did, however, allow His people to come near Him. He pitched His tent in their midst but would not permit His face to be seen. He said to Moses, "You cannot see my face, for man shall not see me and live" (Ex. 33:20). The benediction in the Old Testament says, "The LORD bless you and keep you; the LORD make his face to shine upon you and be gracious to you; the LORD lift up his countenance upon you and give you peace" (Num. 6:24–26). To the Jew, the supreme state of blessedness was not only to experience the nearness of God but to see the brightness of His countenance.

When the glory of God is manifested in the Scriptures, it is usually accompanied by a cloud that shields people from directly perceiving the face of God. The shekinah cloud bursts forth with a heavenly radiance, the refulgence of which is so intense that it is blinding to those who see it. Throughout the Scriptures, there are images and metaphors of God as a consuming light. When the risen Christ appeared to Saul on the road to Damascus, he was blinded by a light more intense than the sun. The disciples, on the Mount of Transfiguration, saw the glory of Christ break through the veil of His humanity, and they fell on their faces, blinded by the brilliance. When the Jews prayed, "The LORD make his face to shine upon you," they wanted to see the unveiled glory of God.

In the fields outside Bethlehem one night, all heaven broke loose. The glory of God shone brilliantly and filled the shepherds in the fields with terror and fear. They realized they were in the holy presence of God, encountering the supernatural in a brilliant, blinding light. It was every Jew's dream: "Lord, show me Your glory." We will see God Himself in heaven. That is the beatific vision, to see God unveiled, not as He has been outwardly manifested in a cloud or in a burning bush, but as He really is.

How is it that we will be able to see God? After all, God is invisible—not only because of our sin, but also because He has no physical body. He is a spirit. We don't know the answer to that, and it can be dangerous to speculate. John Calvin commented that, where God closes His holy mouth, we ought to desist from inquiry. But Jonathan Edwards peeled away the layers of Scripture to come up with an idea of how the beatific vision may take place. God is not physical, but neither will we be physical in heaven. He said that we will no longer have a brain, optic nerves, or eyes. But Edwards said that we won't need them because our soul will have a direct and immediate view of the being of God. That goes beyond anything we can truly imagine. The perception that we will have of God in heaven, even without our eyes, will be far greater than anything we can perceive right now. If we want to know what is going on in someone's mind, we have to allow that person to tell us. But that person may not want to tell us much about himself. So imagine communication soul to soul, mind to mind, with no barriers. We were made for that kind of communication with the living God, and that is what awaits us in heaven.

Section 1 also describes the souls of the wicked. **The souls of the wicked are cast into hell, where they remain in torments and utter darkness, reserved to the judgment of the great day. Besides these two places, for souls separated from their bodies, the Scripture acknowledgeth none.** Mark 9:43–48 and Revelation 20:14 describe hell as a lake of fire where the worm never dies and the fire never goes out. These are likely images and symbols of hell, not to interpreted literally. Saying that does not mean denying the Bible, nor does it mean denying that there is a literal lake of fire. When Jesus uses an image, do we suppose that the reality is less intense or more intense than the image? The reason for using images and symbols is that we are not able to bear a more precise picture of reality. That Jesus would choose these terrifying symbols in describing hell indicates that the reality will be far worse. The sinner in hell will wish he could be in a lake of fire, rather than the reality to which it points.

Some define hell as the absence of God. But the Bible teaches that the most tormenting thing for the sinner in hell is not the absence of God but His presence. Psalm 139:7–8 says: "Where shall I go from your Spirit? Or where shall I flee from your presence? If I ascend to heaven, you are there! If I make my bed in Sheol, you are there!" There is no place where God is not. Therefore, the presence of God extends to the depths of hell.

It is not just His presence that is so troubling but what He is doing. He is manifesting His judgment. He is pouring out His wrath upon those who are in hell. The two great errors we hear about hell are that God is not there and that the sinner is not there.

> 2. At the last day, such as are found alive shall not die, but be changed: and all the dead shall be raised up, with the selfsame bodies, and none other (although with different qualities), which shall be united again to their souls forever.

All the dead shall be raised up. At the final trumpet, according to the New Testament, those who are still alive on this earth will not die, but will be instantly changed. At the same time, all the dead will be raised.

This refers to what we call the general resurrection. And those who are raised from the dead will be raised with the same bodies in which they perished. Their bodies will be transformed in the resurrection and will not be affected by the manner in which they died. Some people are concerned that those who have lost limbs or have had other physical harm to their body will somehow be lacking in the resurrection. By no means. When God, who has the power of life and the power of resurrection, gives to His people a resurrected body, His power to do so will hardly be limited by our physical condition at death. In the general resurrection, we will reach the final state, for our resurrected bodies will be united with our souls and will remain like that forever.

> 3. The bodies of the unjust shall, by the power of Christ, be raised to dishonor: the bodies of the just, by his Spirit, unto honor; and be made conformable to his own glorious body.

The bodies of the unjust shall . . . be raised to dishonor. Here is the affirmation that the resurrection of the body is not limited to the redeemed, but that the resurrection of the body applies to all who die. All people will have their bodies raised in the last judgment. The redeemed will have their bodies raised so that they may enjoy the glorious, honorable resurrection for all eternity. The bodies of the unjust will also be raised by Christ, but to dishonor.

In recent decades, annihilationism has gained some adherents in the evangelical world. The annihilation of the wicked has been the position of some sects and cults, but it has not been considered an orthodox view of hell over the centuries of church history. However, some evangelical leaders have taken an interest in it. John Stott, for example, took a position in which he at least held out the possibility of annihilation for the unjust. A similar position was taken by Philip Edgcumbe Hughes, a formidable New Testament scholar and theologian.

The Christian view of immortality differs from the Greek view of immortality. The Greek view teaches that the soul is by its very nature indestructible and eternal. Hughes argued that the idea of the eternal damnation and punishment of the soul was based on the Greek view of the soul's indestructibility. As we mentioned above, the proper Christian view is that the soul is extrinsically, not intrinsically, immortal. Souls continue after death because God preserves them. The souls of human beings are mortal in the sense that they could be destroyed, were it not for God, who sustains their ongoing existence.

According to the confession, Christ raises the bodies of the damned and preserves them to endure everlasting punishment. That is difficult to fathom or even to contemplate. One of the metaphors used in the New Testament is that hell is the place where the worm does not die. That suggests the possibility of a parasite that lives off the flesh of another creature. If the flesh is completely consumed, the parasite dies. The ghastly image is that in hell the worm always has more flesh to eat. That means that the body of the damned has to be preserved by the power of God in order to endure the punishment that it is to receive.

It is interesting to note that Jesus talked more about hell than about heaven. Almost everything that we know about hell comes from the lips of Jesus. Jesus warns that there will be a last judgment and that every human being will appear before the throne of God and be held accountable for his life. God will judge each one of us according to the standard of His own righteousness. Every idle word that we have spoken will be brought up.

We know of people who, no matter how godless their lives were, suddenly seem to become saints at their funerals. It is a dreadful thought, of course, that someone who has just died has gone to that awful place of judgment. But the Apostle Paul warns us that every sin of the impenitent will be judged by a holy and just God. "But because of your hard and impenitent heart you are storing up wrath for yourself on the day of wrath when God's righteous judgment will be revealed. He will render to each one according to his works" (Rom. 2:5–6).

The Evangelism Explosion program asks diagnostic questions. The first question is: Have you come to the place in your thinking that you know for sure that when you die you are going to heaven? Many people say they don't know. And then the second question is: If you were to die tonight, and stand before God, and God said to you, "Why should I let you into My heaven?" what would you say?" Ninety percent of the people answer that question by saying, "I tried to live a good life," or words to that effect, rather than fleeing to the gospel of Christ. Rare is the person who says, "I know that when I die I'm going to hell." Most unbelievers either do not believe in hell or think that they will be able to escape it.

The doctrine of evolution has sparked controversy and debate between scientists and theologians. Many people in our culture have happily embraced macroevolution. Why would they be happy to find out that they are a cosmic accident and that their final destiny is annihilation? There is really only one answer: evolution offers people an escape from accountability. When we die, it is over. We don't have to worry about facing a holy and righteous Creator. But if macroevolution is in fact true, we should be in utter despair. We would have to recognize that we are utterly insignificant and that our lives and labor are meaningless. People like Jean-Paul Sartre, the pessimistic existentialist, considered life to be a "useless passion." Even so, people would rather have their life be a useless passion than for death to bring them before a just and holy God. Perhaps that accounts for the great hostility that the world has toward the church. Christians are often accused of being "holier than thou." People assume that we think we will get to heaven because of our holiness. The hostility is there because people do not want to confront the thought that they will someday have to face God and His judgment.

Of the
Last Judgment

1. God hath appointed a day, wherein he will judge the world, in righteousness, by Jesus Christ, to whom all power and judgment is given of the Father. In which day, not only the apostate angels shall be judged, but likewise all persons that have lived upon earth shall appear before the tribunal of Christ, to give an account of their thoughts, words, and deeds; and to receive according to what they have done in the body, whether good or evil.

2. The end of God's appointing this day is for the manifestation of the glory of his mercy, in the eternal salvation of the elect; and of his justice, in the damnation of the reprobate, who are wicked and disobedient. For then shall the righteous go into everlasting life, and receive that fullness of joy and refreshing, which shall come from the presence of the Lord; but the wicked who know not God, and obey not the gospel of Jesus Christ, shall be cast into eternal torments, and be punished with everlasting destruction from the presence of the Lord, and from the glory of his power.

3. As Christ would have us to be certainly persuaded that there shall be a day of judgment, both to deter all men from sin; and for the greater consolation of the godly in their adversity: so will he have that day unknown to men, that they may shake off all carnal security, and be always watchful, because they know not at what hour the Lord will come; and may be ever prepared to say, Come Lord Jesus, come quickly, Amen.

1. God hath appointed a day, wherein he will judge the world, in righteousness, by Jesus Christ, to whom all power and judgment is given of the Father. In which day, not only the apostate angels shall be judged, but likewise all persons that have lived upon earth shall appear before the tribunal of Christ, to give an account of their thoughts, words, and deeds; and to receive according to what they have done in the body, whether good or evil.

The language in this section was taken directly from the pages of the New Testament. When the Apostle Paul was at Athens, he confronted the Stoic and Epicurean philosophers. Although the Stoics and the Epicureans differed sharply in their cosmology, they agreed that ultimate truth cannot really be known. They were the relativists of their day. They taught that since we cannot know ultimate truth, we should only be concerned with how we live out our days in this world. The Stoics faced the ultimate meaninglessness of their existence by trying to be imperturbable. Even today, we describe such people as being stoic, as having a stiff upper lip. Stoics recognize that they have no control over what happens and can control only their feelings about what happens to them. Stoicism was a philosophical escapism from the grim reality of a meaningless life.

The Epicureans developed a sophisticated philosophy of hedonism. They defined the good as the maximum enjoyment of pleasure and the minimum amount of pain. They sought their meaning through physical pleasure.

Paul met with the Greeks at the Areopagus and saw that they had an altar to an unknown god. "What therefore you worship as unknown, this I proclaim to you," Paul said (Acts 17:23). He explained that the God in whom they lived and moved and had their being was the God who had made them. He cautioned that the former days of ignorance, when God overlooked people's sins, were over, and that now all people everywhere are commanded to repent (v. 30). That is the universal mandate of God.

We soften the gospel in our day. In modern forms of mass evangelism, part of the strategy is called the invitation. People are "invited" to come to Christ. That was not how the Apostles did it. An invitation is something that can be politely declined with impunity. But a command cannot be declined with impunity. Paul said that God commands everyone, everywhere, to repent. We decline that command at our own peril.

Paul went on to say that God has appointed a day in which He will judge the world (v. 31). In God's calendar, there is already a fixed date for the day of judgment. Each one of us will be brought before God to be judged by Christ on that date. Those who are Christ's will have Him not only as their judge but also as their defense attorney. We will be garbed in His righteousness, which alone can meet the requirements of God. Those who are not in Christ will also appear before Him, standing there on their own, as their every idle word is judged. The description in the New Testament of the response of the unbeliever on that day is always the same. Their response will be silence. When God reads the indictment and makes the charge against them, it will be so clear, so irrefutable, that every mouth will be stopped. People will see the utter futility of arguing with God about the record.

Jesus says that the last judgment will be the end of secrets. Nothing will any longer be hidden. If the world knew everything we had ever done or thought, we would be ruined.

In the last judgment, there will be nowhere to flee. The things we have done in darkness will be brought to the light. People do not want to believe that there will, in fact, be a last judgment. But if Jesus of Nazareth taught anything as a teacher, He taught that there will be a final judgment. Paul echoed that teaching. There is a day coming that no one will be able to erase.

2. The end of God's appointing this day is for the manifestation of the glory of his mercy, in the eternal salvation of the elect; and of his justice, in the damnation of the reprobate, who are wicked and disobedient. For then shall the righteous go into everlasting life, and receive that fullness of joy and refreshing, which shall come from the presence of the Lord; but the wicked who know not God, and obey not the gospel of Jesus Christ, shall be cast into eternal torments, and be punished with everlasting

> destruction from the presence of the Lord, and from the glory of
> his power.

The opening phrase, **the end of,** means "the purpose of." The confession is stating the purpose for the last judgment. Both heaven and hell have the same ultimate purpose: to glorify God.

People argue for and against capital punishment. Those who argue against it insist it does no good and will not deter anyone. Nor will it bring back the one who was killed. The only real justification for capital punishment is to satisfy the demands of justice. God instituted capital punishment in the Old Testament because life is sacred. He taught in the Noahic covenant that because people are made in the image of God, they are so precious that if someone willfully takes another person's life, he forfeits his own (Gen. 9:6). God has placed His image on human beings, and He manifests the importance of that image by protecting individual lives. When the murderer is executed and justice prevails, the sanctity of human life is honored.

God created people who are in rebellion against Him and who daily disobey His law, insult His dignity, and deny His glory. Yet He graciously saves some of us through Jesus Christ, and He manifests the glory of His grace in the salvation of the saints. But He also displays the glory of His righteousness by condemning the unsaved for their wickedness. Heaven declares the glory of God's grace. Hell declares the glory of God's justice. In both cases, the glory of God is made manifest.

No one will be able to say, when God dispenses a verdict at the last judgment, "That is not fair." Jonathan Edwards, in his famous sermon "Sinners in the Hands of an Angry God," says that the only reason we do not fall into the fire is the grace of God. His hand has held us back. Edwards says, "Oh, sinner, you can give no reason why, since you got out of your bed this morning, God hasn't thrown you into that fire." His sermon is about grace, about the hand of God's mercy, which keeps His people from what they deserve.

Some people think that a good God would never actually punish anyone. But just the reverse is true. A judge who never punishes the wicked is not a good judge. And God is the perfect Judge, whose judgment is good.

3. As Christ would have us to be certainly persuaded that there shall be a day of judgment, both to deter all men from sin; and for the greater consolation of the godly in their adversity: so will he have that day unknown to men, that they may shake off all carnal security, and be always watchful, because they know not at what hour the Lord will come; and may be ever prepared to say, Come Lord Jesus, come quickly, Amen.

It is important that we understand the teaching of Christ with respect to the last judgment. This section tells us that **Christ would have us to be certainly persuaded that there shall be a day of judgment**. His reason is **both to deter all men from sin; and for the greater consolation of the godly in their adversity**. If people are convinced that they will be held accountable by God for their behavior, they will be restrained in their evil, if only out of fear and enlightened self-interest. Even if they never come to full repentance and faith in Christ, they can, to some degree, ameliorate their punishment in hell.

Scripture is clear that both in heaven and in hell there are degrees. There are degrees of blessedness in heaven, for each person will be rewarded according to his works. Their works are not meritorious, but God, in His grace, has determined to reward people according to their measure of service and obedience. There are at least twenty-five texts in the New Testament that speak of degrees of reward for godliness. We are encouraged to work out our salvation with fear and trembling (Phil. 2:12). That does not mean that we can earn our way into heaven, because even the obedience we offer to Christ is rendered in His strength and by His grace. We would still, by a strict standard of justice, be unprofitable servants, unable to claim any reward. Nevertheless, God graciously saves us on the grounds of Christ's righteousness, and also, in His grace, gives in heaven extra rewards to those who are obedient and diligent in serving Christ. We are given incentives to work for that reward, to store up for ourselves treasures in heaven. Augustine, in explaining the gracious aspect of God's rewards—not *because of* our works but *according to* them—said that God will simply be crowning His own works.

In like manner, Paul warns against heaping up wrath for the day of wrath because, at the final judgment, those who are not believers will have to give an account before God for every single sin. They will receive a just punishment for their transgressions. God will judge them according to His perfect standard of righteousness. Jonathan Edwards encouraged the people of Northampton, Mass., who were not certain of their salvation to be present at the preaching of the Word. Even if the gospel did not bring forth the fruit of salvation in their hearts, he said, at least they would have the benefit of restraint on their evil inclinations, making their punishment in hell less severe.

It is not just unbelievers who will face the judgment of God, but also believers. Many Christians seem to think that being saved means not having to stand before the judgment seat of Christ. It is true that we will not face condemnation, but we will still undergo an evaluation. Christ will examine our lives and determine our degree of obedience and sanctification. The knowledge that examination awaits us at the last judgment should motivate us to be more diligent in our obedience and desire to please Him, so that when we appear before Him, He will say to us, "Well done, good and faithful servant."

The second advantage to knowing that the last judgment is coming is that it provides **consolation of the godly in their adversity.** This was of great importance to the early church and is certainly important to any Christian today who has suffered persecution. Our Lord tells us that if we are faithful to Him in this life, we will encounter tribulation. The Christian can reasonably expect to be a victim of injustice in this world. Indeed, if we are not, it indicates that we have distanced ourselves from Christ. When we embrace Him fully, we are called to participate in His humiliation, as well as in His exaltation. Christians are often downcast but never bereft of hope. We need the comfort of God's promise that there will come a time when we will experience His vindication.

In His parable of the persistent widow, in Luke 18:1–8, Jesus describes a judge who has no regard either for people or for God. Luke tells us that Jesus taught this parable to encourage us always to pray and never to give up. In the parable, an importunate widow, a victim of injustice, goes before the judge for her vindication. The judge won't hear her case because he is corrupt and unjust. But the woman persists in her plea to the judge. Finally, to rid himself of this woman, he hears her case. The point of Jesus' parable is seen at the end: "And will not God give justice to his elect, who cry to him day and night? Will he delay long over them? I tell you, he will give justice to them speedily. Nevertheless, when the Son of Man comes, will he find faith on earth?" (vv. 7–8). If a corrupt, insensitive human judge will on some occasions administer justice, how much more will the Judge of heaven and earth, who is perfectly righteous, make sure that those who have suffered unjustly for the name of Christ are vindicated in the end?

But then Jesus asks, in effect, "When I come, will I find anyone who needs to be vindicated?" He is speaking to us. Though the world despises Christ's people, and though we may never receive vindication or justice in this world, we have the absolute promise of God that He will vindicate His people who cry unto Him day and night. Paul repeats the biblical teaching, "Vengeance is mine, I will repay, says the Lord" (Rom. 12:19). When God pays the debt, He does it justly. We may be so blinded by our pain that we inflict more damage on the person who hurts us than justice requires. Vengeance is to be God's own activity, and we are to take heart that He will repay. The last judgment is part of the consolation that God provides.

Jonathan Edwards served the people of Northampton for many years. A member of his congregation opposed him and spread false rumors that attacked his character. People fed on the rumors, and a major crisis developed at the church. The church elders begged Edwards to speak to the matters and defend himself. Edwards didn't want to respond publicly to the false charges. The elders inquired, "Dr. Edwards, don't you want to be vindicated?" He replied that he did, but he thought that if he defended himself, that would be the extent of his defense. He believed that if he suffered those things in silence, then God Himself would move heaven and earth to vindicate him, and Edwards preferred to have the vindication that God brings to bear rather than anything that Edwards could accomplish on his own.

As a direct result of the slander, Edwards was removed from his church's pulpit, and he became a missionary to the Indians in Stockbridge, where he wrote *Freedom of the Will*. About ten years later, the man who had falsely accused him was so guilt-stricken about what he had done that he confessed publicly that he had lied. Edwards was completely vindicated, but in the meantime he had suffered the slander in silence. We don't always need do that; there are times when we need to respond to slander. But we need to learn to expect it as part of the way of this world. When we are plunged into misery by unfair and unjust charges or other experiences, we are not to be as people without hope. We have God's promise that there will be a last judgment.

Edwards' final sermon at Northampton had no bitterness in it. He displayed his concern for his congregation. He told them that it wasn't the last time that they would meet together as pastor and congregation, because they would meet at least one more time—at the judgment throne of God. He commended the blessing of God on the people and left. When we feel that we have been wronged and that justice has not been served, we know that there will be the last judgment.

Section 3 continues: So will he have that day unknown to men, that they may shake off all carnal security, and be always watchful, because they know not at what hour the Lord will come. The Lord has told us that He will come. God has appointed a day. It is fixed. Nothing will cause it to be postponed.

The reason God doesn't reveal the day may be to keep us alert and ready. We are to flee from carnal security. The longer God delays judgment, the more people begin to assume that there will be no judgment. They think they will continue to get away with their sin with impunity. That is carnal security, the security of the flesh, the security of the hardened heart and of the stiff-necked person. It is a false security. We are to remind people that there will be a time of judgment, and that we do not know when it will be. It could be tonight; it could be tomorrow. It could be a thousand years from now.

There is a story about Dwight L. Moody, who preached an intense, fiery, evangelistic service one night in Chicago. At the close of the service, he told the people to go home and think about his admonition, and that the following week they would be called to make a decision. That very night, after the service, came the Great Chicago Fire. Many of those who had attended his service died. Moody said after that experience that he would never again postpone the calling of people to commit their lives to Christ. You never know if you have more time.

The confession ends with these words: That they may . . . be always watchful, because they know not at what hour the Lord will come; and may be ever prepared to say, Come Lord Jesus, come quickly, Amen. These are the same words with which the New Testament ends, praying that Jesus will return quickly.

Are we prepared to say, "Lord, come"? Augustine said, "Lord, change me, but not yet." We should be in such a state of reconciliation with Christ that we earnestly desire that He not delay another day but come right now. Do we instead say, "Lord, we want You to come, but give us a little bit of time to get our house in order or to take care of some things that we would like to accomplish." The prayer of the godly heart is "Lord come, and come quickly."

At the beginning of this book, we noted that the Westminster Confession of Faith is a creedal statement that was not written by divinely inspired men. The confession is not sacred Scripture. It is not absolutely binding on our conscience. It was designed in the seventeenth century by Puritan divines to set forth the system of doctrine that is found in sacred Scripture. There has never been written a more precise, more accurate, more thorough, and more comprehensive confession of faith. The Lord raised up bright and godly men to write this document. More than half of them were eventually excommunicated from the church by those who could not bear this doctrine. Those divines ended up saying, Come Lord Jesus, come quickly.

APPENDIX 1

The Westminster Larger Catechism

Q. 1. *What is the chief and highest end of man?*
A. Man's chief and highest end is to glorify God, and fully to enjoy him forever.

Q. 2. *How doth it appear that there is a God?*
A. The very light of nature in man, and the works of God, declare plainly that there is a God; but his word and Spirit only do sufficiently and effectually reveal him unto men for their salvation.

Q. 3. *What is the Word of God?*
A. The Holy Scriptures of the Old and New Testament are the Word of God, the only rule of faith and obedience.

Q. 4. *How doth it appear that the Scriptures are the Word of God?*
A. The Scriptures manifest themselves to be the Word of God, by their majesty and purity; by the consent of all the parts, and the scope of the whole, which is to give all glory to God; by their light and power to convince and convert sinners, to comfort and build up believers unto salvation: but the Spirit of God bearing witness by and with the Scriptures in the heart of man, is alone able fully to persuade it that they are the very Word of God.

Q. 5. *What do the Scriptures principally teach?*
A. The Scriptures principally teach what man is to believe concerning God, and what duty God requires of man.

WHAT MAN OUGHT TO BELIEVE CONCERNING GOD

Q. 6. *What do the Scriptures make known of God?*
A. The Scriptures make known what God is, the persons in the Godhead, his decrees, and the execution of his decrees.

Q. 7. *What is God?*
A. God is a Spirit, in and of himself infinite in being, glory, blessedness, and perfection; all-sufficient, eternal, unchangeable, incomprehensible, everywhere present, almighty, knowing all things, most wise, most holy, most just, most merciful and gracious, longsuffering, and abundant in goodness and truth.

Q. 8. *Are there more Gods than one?*
A. There is but one only, the living and true God.

Q. 9. *How many persons are there in the Godhead?*
A. There be three persons in the Godhead, the Father, the Son, and the Holy Ghost; and these three are one true, eternal God, the same in substance, equal in power and glory; although distinguished by their personal properties.

Q. 10. *What are the personal properties of the three persons in the Godhead?*
A. It is proper to the Father to beget the Son, and to the Son to be begotten of the Father, and to the Holy Ghost to proceed from the Father and the Son from all eternity.

Q. 11. *How doth it appear that the Son and the Holy Ghost are God equal with the Father?*
A. The Scriptures manifest that the Son and the Holy Ghost are God equal with the Father, ascribing unto them such names, attributes, works, and worship, as are proper to God only.

Q. 12. *What are the decrees of God?*
A. God's decrees are the wise, free, and holy acts of the counsel of his will, whereby, from all eternity, he hath, for his own glory, unchangeably foreordained whatsoever comes to pass in time, especially concerning angels and men.

Q. 13. *What hath God especially decreed concerning angels and men?*
A. God, by an eternal and immutable decree, out of his mere love, for the praise of his glorious grace, to be manifested in due time, hath elected some angels to glory; and in Christ hath chosen some men to eternal life, and the means thereof: and also, according to his sovereign power, and the unsearchable counsel of his own will (whereby he extendeth or withholdeth favor as he pleaseth), hath passed by and foreordained the rest to dishonor and wrath, to be for their sin inflicted, to the praise of the glory of his justice.

Q. 14. *How doth God execute his decrees?*
A. God executeth his decrees in the works of creation and providence, according to his infallible foreknowledge, and the free and immutable counsel of his own will.

Q. 15. *What is the work of creation?*
A. The work of creation is that wherein God did in the beginning, by the word of his power, make of nothing the world, and all things therein, for himself, within the space of six days, and all very good.

Q. 16. *How did God create angels?*
A. God created all the angels spirits, immortal, holy, excelling in knowledge, mighty in power, to execute his commandments, and to praise his name, yet subject to change.

Q. 17. *How did God create man?*
A. After God had made all other creatures, he created man male and female; formed the body of the man of the dust of the ground, and the woman of the rib of the man, endued them with living, reasonable, and immortal souls; made them after his own image, in knowledge, righteousness, and holiness; having the law of God written in their hearts, and power to fulfill it, and dominion over the creatures; yet subject to fall.

Q. 18. *What are God's works of providence?*
A. God's works of providence are his most holy, wise, and powerful preserving and governing all his creatures; ordering them, and all their actions, to his own glory.

Q. 19. *What is God's providence towards the angels?*
A. God by his providence permitted some of the angels, willfully and irrecoverably, to fall into sin and damnation, limiting and ordering that, and all their sins, to his own glory; and established the rest in holiness and happiness; employing them all, at his pleasure, in the administrations of his power, mercy, and justice.

Q. 20. *What was the providence of God toward man in the estate in which he was created?*
A. The providence of God toward man in the estate in which he was created, was the placing him in paradise, appointing him to dress it, giving him liberty to eat of the fruit of the earth; putting the creatures under his dominion, and ordaining marriage for his help; affording him communion with himself; instituting the Sabbath; entering into a covenant of life with him, upon condition of personal, perfect, and perpetual obedience, of which the tree of life was a pledge; and forbidding to eat of the tree of the knowledge of good and evil, upon the pain of death.

Q. 21. *Did man continue in that estate wherein God at first created him?*
A. Our first parents being left to the freedom of their own will, through the temptation of Satan, transgressed the commandment of God in eating the forbidden fruit; and thereby fell from the estate of innocency wherein they were created.

Q. 22. *Did all mankind fall in that first transgression?*
A. The covenant being made with Adam as a public person, not for himself only, but for his posterity, all mankind descending from him by ordinary generation, sinned in him, and fell with him in that first transgression.

Q. 23. *Into what estate did the fall bring mankind?*
A. The fall brought mankind into an estate of sin and misery.

Q. 24. *What is sin?*
A. Sin is any want of conformity unto, or transgression of, any law of God, given as a rule to the reasonable creature.

Q. 25. *Wherein consisteth the sinfulness of that estate whereinto man fell?*
A. The sinfulness of that estate whereinto man fell, consisteth in the guilt

of Adam's first sin, the want of that righteousness wherein he was created, and the corruption of his nature, whereby he is utterly indisposed, disabled, and made opposite unto all that is spiritually good, and wholly inclined to all evil, and that continually; which is commonly called original sin, and from which do proceed all actual transgressions.

Q. 26. *How is original sin conveyed from our first parents unto their posterity?*
A. Original sin is conveyed from our first parents unto their posterity by natural generation, so as all that proceed from them in that way are conceived and born in sin.

Q. 27. *What misery did the fall bring upon mankind?*
A. The fall brought upon mankind the loss of communion with God, his displeasure and curse; so as we are by nature children of wrath, bond slaves to Satan, and justly liable to all punishments in this world, and that which is to come.

Q. 28. *What are the punishments of sin in this world?*
A. The punishments of sin in this world are either inward, as blindness of mind, a reprobate sense, strong delusions, hardness of heart, horror of conscience, and vile affections; or outward, as the curse of God upon the creatures for our sakes, and all other evils that befall us in our bodies, names, estates, relations, and employments; together with death itself.

Q. 29. *What are the punishments of sin in the world to come?*
A. The punishments of sin in the world to come, are everlasting separation from the comfortable presence of God, and most grievous torments in soul and body, without intermission, in hell-fire forever.

Q. 30. *Doth God leave all mankind to perish in the estate of sin and misery?*
A. God doth not leave all men to perish in the estate of sin and misery, into which they fell by the breach of the first covenant, commonly called the covenant of works; but of his mere love and mercy delivereth his elect out of it, and bringeth them into an estate of salvation by the second covenant, commonly called the covenant of grace.

Q. 31. *With whom was the covenant of grace made?*
A. The covenant of grace was made with Christ as the second Adam, and in him with all the elect as his seed.

Q. 32. *How is the grace of God manifested in the second covenant?*
A. The grace of God is manifested in the second covenant, in that he freely provideth and offereth to sinners a mediator, and life and salvation by him; and requiring faith as the condition to interest them in him, promiseth and giveth his Holy Spirit to all his elect, to work in them that faith, with all other saving graces; and to enable them unto all holy obedience, as the evidence of the truth of their faith and thankfulness to God, and as the way which he hath appointed them to salvation.

Q. 33. *Was the covenant of grace always administered after one and the same manner?*
A. The covenant of grace was not always administered after the same manner, but the administrations of it under the Old Testament were different from those under the New.

Q. 34. *How was the covenant of grace administered under the Old Testament?*
A. The covenant of grace was administered under the Old Testament, by promises, prophecies, sacrifices, circumcision, the passover, and other types and ordinances, which did all foresignify Christ then to come, and were for that time sufficient to build up the elect in faith in the promised messiah, by whom they then had full remission of sin, and eternal salvation.

Q. 35. *How is the covenant of grace administered under the New Testament?*
A. Under the New Testament, when Christ the substance was exhibited, the same covenant of grace was and still is to be administered in the preaching of the word, and the administration of the sacraments of baptism and the Lord's supper; in which grace and salvation are held forth in more fullness, evidence, and efficacy, to all nations.

Q. 36. *Who is the mediator of the covenant of grace?*
A. The only mediator of the covenant of grace is the Lord Jesus Christ, who, being the eternal Son of God, of one substance and equal with the Father, in the fullness of time became man, and so was and continues to be God and man, in two entire distinct natures, and one person, forever.

Q. 37. *How did Christ, being the Son of God, become man?*
A. Christ the Son of God became man, by taking to himself a true body, and a reasonable soul, being conceived by the power of the Holy Ghost

in the womb of the virgin Mary, of her substance, and born of her, yet without sin.

Q. 38. *Why was it requisite that the mediator should be God?*
A. It was requisite that the mediator should be God, that he might sustain and keep the human nature from sinking under the infinite wrath of God, and the power of death; give worth and efficacy to his sufferings, obedience, and intercession; and to satisfy God's justice, procure his favor, purchase a peculiar people, give his Spirit to them, conquer all their enemies, and bring them to everlasting salvation.

Q. 39. *Why was it requisite that the mediator should be man?*
A. It was requisite that the mediator should be man, that he might advance our nature, perform obedience to the law, suffer and make intercession for us in our nature, have a fellow-feeling of our infirmities; that we might receive the adoption of sons, and have comfort and access with boldness unto the throne of grace.

Q. 40. *Why was it requisite that the mediator should be God and man in one person?*
A. It was requisite that the mediator, who was to reconcile God and man, should himself be both God and man, and this in one person, that the proper works of each nature might be accepted of God for us, and relied on by us, as the works of the whole person.

Q. 41. *Why was our mediator called Jesus?*
A. Our mediator was called Jesus, because he saveth his people from their sins.

Q. 42. *Why was our mediator called Christ?*
A. Our mediator was called Christ, because he was anointed with the Holy Ghost above measure; and so set apart, and fully furnished with all authority and ability, to execute the offices of prophet, priest, and king of his church, in the estate both of his humiliation and exaltation.

Q. 43. *How doth Christ execute the office of a prophet?*
A. Christ executeth the office of a prophet, in his revealing to the church, in all ages, by his Spirit and word, in divers ways of administration,

the whole will of God, in all things concerning their edification and salvation.

Q. 44. *How doth Christ execute the office of a priest?*
A. Christ executeth the office of a priest, in his once offering himself a sacrifice without spot to God, to be a reconciliation for the sins of the people; and in making continual intercession for them.

Q. 45. *How doth Christ execute the office of a king?*
A. Christ executeth the office of a king, in calling out of the world a people to himself, and giving them officers, laws, and censures, by which he visibly governs them; in bestowing saving grace upon his elect, rewarding their obedience, and correcting them for their sins, preserving and supporting them under all their temptations and sufferings, restraining and overcoming all their enemies, and powerfully ordering all things for his own glory, and their good; and also in taking vengeance on the rest, who know not God, and obey not the gospel.

Q. 46. *What was the estate of Christ's humiliation?*
A. The estate of Christ's humiliation was that low condition, wherein he for our sakes, emptying himself of his glory, took upon him the form of a servant, in his conception and birth, life, death, and after his death, until his resurrection.

Q. 47. *How did Christ humble himself in his conception and birth?*
A. Christ humbled himself in his conception and birth, in that, being from all eternity the Son of God, in the bosom of the Father, he was pleased in the fullness of time to become the son of man, made of a woman of low estate, and to be born of her; with divers circumstances of more than ordinary abasement.

Q. 48. *How did Christ humble himself in his life?*
A. Christ humbled himself in his life, by subjecting himself to the law, which he perfectly fulfilled; and by conflicting with the indignities of the world, temptations of Satan, and infirmities in his flesh, whether common to the nature of man, or particularly accompanying that his low condition.

Q. 49. *How did Christ humble himself in his death?*
A. Christ humbled himself in his death, in that having been betrayed by Judas, forsaken by his disciples, scorned and rejected by the world, condemned by Pilate, and tormented by his persecutors; having also conflicted with the terrors of death, and the powers of darkness, felt and borne the weight of God's wrath, he laid down his life an offering for sin, enduring the painful, shameful, and cursed death of the cross.

Q. 50. *Wherein consisted Christ's humiliation after his death?*
A. Christ's humiliation after his death consisted in his being buried, and continuing in the state of the dead, and under the power of death till the third day; which hath been otherwise expressed in these words, *He descended into hell.*

Q. 51. *What was the estate of Christ's exaltation?*
A. The estate of Christ's exaltation comprehendeth his resurrection, ascension, sitting at the right hand of the Father, and his coming again to judge the world.

Q. 52. *How was Christ exalted in his resurrection?*
A. Christ was exalted in his resurrection, in that, not having seen corruption in death (of which it was not possible for him to be held), and having the very same body in which he suffered, with the essential properties thereof (but without mortality, and other common infirmities belonging to this life), really united to his soul, he rose again from the dead the third day by his own power; whereby he declared himself to be the Son of God, to have satisfied divine justice, to have vanquished death, and him that had power of it, and to be Lord of quick and dead: all which he did as a public person, the head of his church, for their justification, quickening in grace, support against enemies, and to assure them of their resurrection from the dead at the last day.

Q. 53. *How was Christ exalted in his ascension?*
A. Christ was exalted in his ascension, in that having after his resurrection often appeared unto and conversed with his apostles, speaking to them of the things pertaining to the kingdom of God, and giving them commission to preach the gospel to all nations, forty days after his resurrection,

he, in our nature, and as our head, triumphing over enemies, visibly went up into the highest heavens, there to receive gifts for men, to raise up our affections thither, and to prepare a place for us, where himself is, and shall continue till his second coming at the end of the world.

Q. 54. *How is Christ exalted in his sitting at the right hand of God?*
A. Christ is exalted in his sitting at the right hand of God, in that as God-man he is advanced to the highest favor with God the Father, with all fullness of joy, glory, and power over all things in heaven and earth; and doth gather and defend his church, and subdue their enemies; furnisheth his ministers and people with gifts and graces, and maketh intercession for them.

Q. 55. *How doth Christ make intercession?*
A. Christ maketh intercession, by his appearing in our nature continually before the Father in heaven, in the merit of his obedience and sacrifice on earth, declaring his will to have it applied to all believers; answering all accusations against them, and procuring for them quiet of conscience, notwithstanding daily failings, access with boldness to the throne of grace, and acceptance of their persons and services.

Q. 56. *How is Christ to be exalted in his coming again to judge the world?*
A. Christ is to be exalted in his coming again to judge the world, in that he, who was unjustly judged and condemned by wicked men, shall come again at the last day in great power, and in the full manifestation of his own glory, and of his Father's, with all his holy angels, with a shout, with the voice of the archangel, and with the trumpet of God, to judge the world in righteousness.

Q. 57. *What benefits hath Christ procured by his mediation?*
A. Christ, by his mediation, hath procured redemption, with all other benefits of the covenant of grace.

Q. 58. *How do we come to be made partakers of the benefits which Christ hath procured?*
A. We are made partakers of the benefits which Christ hath procured, by the application of them unto us, which is the work especially of God the Holy Ghost.

Q. 59. *Who are made partakers of redemption through Christ?*
A. Redemption is certainly applied, and effectually communicated, to all those for whom Christ hath purchased it; who are in time by the Holy Ghost enabled to believe in Christ according to the gospel.

Q. 60. *Can they who have never heard the gospel, and so know not Jesus Christ, nor believe in him, be saved by their living according to the light of nature?*
A. They who, having never heard the gospel, know not Jesus Christ, and believe not in him, cannot be saved, be they never so diligent to frame their lives according to the light of nature, or the laws of that religion which they profess; neither is there salvation in any other, but in Christ alone, who is the Savior only of his body the church.

Q. 61. *Are all they saved who hear the gospel, and live in the church?*
A. All that hear the gospel, and live in the visible church, are not saved; but they only who are true members of the church invisible.

Q. 62. *What is the visible church?*
A. The visible church is a society made up of all such as in all ages and places of the world do profess the true religion, and of their children.

Q. 63. *What are the special privileges of the visible church?*
A. The visible church hath the privilege of being under God's special care and government; of being protected and preserved in all ages, notwithstanding the opposition of all enemies; and of enjoying the communion of saints, the ordinary means of salvation, and offers of grace by Christ to all the members of it in the ministry of the gospel, testifying, that whosoever believes in him shall be saved, and excluding none that will come unto him.

Q. 64. *What is the invisible church?*
A. The invisible church is the whole number of the elect, that have been, are, or shall be gathered into one under Christ the head.

Q. 65. *What special benefits do the members of the invisible church enjoy by Christ?*
A. The members of the invisible church by Christ enjoy union and communion with him in grace and glory.

Q. 66. *What is that union which the elect have with Christ?*
A. The union which the elect have with Christ is the work of God's grace, whereby they are spiritually and mystically, yet really and inseparably, joined to Christ as their head and husband; which is done in their effectual calling.

Q. 67. *What is effectual calling?*
A. Effectual calling is the work of God's almighty power and grace, whereby (out of his free and special love to his elect, and from nothing in them moving him thereunto) he doth, in his accepted time, invite and draw them to Jesus Christ, by his word and Spirit; savingly enlightening their minds, renewing and powerfully determining their wills, so as they (although in themselves dead in sin) are hereby made willing and able freely to answer his call, and to accept and embrace the grace offered and conveyed therein.

Q. 68. *Are the elect only effectually called?*
A. All the elect, and they only, are effectually called; although others may be, and often are, outwardly called by the ministry of the word, and have some common operations of the Spirit; who, for their willful neglect and contempt of the grace offered to them, being justly left in their unbelief, do never truly come to Jesus Christ.

Q. 69. *What is the communion in grace which the members of the invisible church have with Christ?*
A. The communion in grace which the members of the invisible church have with Christ, is their partaking of the virtue of his mediation, in their justification, adoption, sanctification, and whatever else, in this life, manifests their union with him.

Q. 70. *What is justification?*
A. Justification is an act of God's free grace unto sinners, in which he pardoneth all their sins, accepteth and accounteth their persons righteous in his sight; not for anything wrought in them, or done by them, but only for the perfect obedience and full satisfaction of Christ, by God imputed to them, and received by faith alone.

Q. 71. *How is justification an act of God's free grace?*
A. Although Christ, by his obedience and death, did make a proper, real, and full satisfaction to God's justice in the behalf of them that are

justified; yet inasmuch as God accepteth the satisfaction from a surety, which he might have demanded of them, and did provide this surety, his own only Son, imputing his righteousness to them, and requiring nothing of them for their justification but faith, which also is his gift, their justification is to them of free grace.

Q. 72. *What is justifying faith?*
A. Justifying faith is a saving grace, wrought in the heart of a sinner by the Spirit and Word of God, whereby he, being convinced of his sin and misery, and of the disability in himself and all other creatures to recover him out of his lost condition, not only assenteth to the truth of the promise of the gospel, but receiveth and resteth upon Christ and his righteousness, therein held forth, for pardon of sin, and for the accepting and accounting of his person righteous in the sight of God for salvation.

Q. 73. *How doth faith justify a sinner in the sight of God?*
A. Faith justifies a sinner in the sight of God, not because of those other graces which do always accompany it, or of good works that are the fruits of it, nor as if the grace of faith, or any act thereof, were imputed to him for his justification; but only as it is an instrument by which he receiveth and applieth Christ and his righteousness.

Q. 74. *What is adoption?*
A. Adoption is an act of the free grace of God, in and for his only Son Jesus Christ, whereby all those that are justified are received into the number of his children, have his name put upon them, the Spirit of his Son given to them, are under his fatherly care and dispensations, admitted to all the liberties and privileges of the sons of God, made heirs of all the promises, and fellow-heirs with Christ in glory.

Q. 75. *What is sanctification?*
A. Sanctification is a work of God's grace, whereby they whom God hath, before the foundation of the world, chosen to be holy, are in time, through the powerful operation of his Spirit applying the death and resurrection of Christ unto them, renewed in their whole man after the image of God; having the seeds of repentance unto life, and all other saving graces, put into their hearts, and those graces so stirred up, increased,

and strengthened, as that they more and more die unto sin, and rise unto newness of life.

Q. 76. *What is repentance unto life?*
A. Repentance unto life is a saving grace, wrought in the heart of a sinner by the Spirit and Word of God, whereby, out of the sight and sense, not only of the danger, but also of the filthiness and odiousness of his sins, and upon the apprehension of God's mercy in Christ to such as are penitent, he so grieves for and hates his sins, as that he turns from them all to God, purposing and endeavoring constantly to walk with him in all the ways of new obedience.

Q. 77. *Wherein do justification and sanctification differ?*
A. Although sanctification be inseparably joined with justification, yet they differ, in that God in justification imputeth the righteousness of Christ; in sanctification his Spirit infuseth grace, and enableth to the exercise thereof; in the former, sin is pardoned; in the other, it is subdued: the one doth equally free all believers from the revenging wrath of God, and that perfectly in this life, that they never fall into condemnation; the other is neither equal in all, nor in this life perfect in any, but growing up to perfection.

Q. 78. *Whence ariseth the imperfection of sanctification in believers?*
A. The imperfection of sanctification in believers ariseth from the remnants of sin abiding in every part of them, and the perpetual lustings of the flesh against the spirit; whereby they are often foiled with temptations, and fall into many sins, are hindered in all their spiritual services, and their best works are imperfect and defiled in the sight of God.

Q. 79. *May not true believers, by reason of their imperfections, and the many temptations and sins they are overtaken with, fall away from the state of grace?*
A. True believers, by reason of the unchangeable love of God, and his decree and covenant to give them perseverance, their inseparable union with Christ, his continual intercession for them, and the Spirit and seed of God abiding in them, can neither totally nor finally fall away from

the state of grace, but are kept by the power of God through faith unto salvation.

Q. 80. *Can true believers be infallibly assured that they are in the estate of grace, and that they shall persevere therein unto salvation?*
A. Such as truly believe in Christ, and endeavor to walk in all good conscience before him, may, without extraordinary revelation, by faith grounded upon the truth of God's promises, and by the Spirit enabling them to discern in themselves those graces to which the promises of life are made, and bearing witness with their spirits that they are the children of God, be infallibly assured that they are in the estate of grace, and shall persevere therein unto salvation.

Q. 81. *Are all true believers at all times assured of their present being in the estate of grace, and that they shall be saved?*
A. Assurance of grace and salvation not being of the essence of faith, true believers may wait long before they obtain it; and, after the enjoyment thereof, may have it weakened and intermitted, through manifold distempers, sins, temptations, and desertions; yet are they never left without such a presence and support of the Spirit of God as keeps them from sinking into utter despair.

Q. 82. *What is the communion in glory which the members of the invisible church have with Christ?*
A. The communion in glory which the members of the invisible church have with Christ, is in this life, immediately after death, and at last perfected at the resurrection and day of judgment.

Q. 83. *What is the communion in glory with Christ which the members of the invisible church enjoy in this life?*
A. The members of the invisible church have communicated to them in this life the firstfruits of glory with Christ, as they are members of him their head, and so in him are interested in that glory which he is fully possessed of; and, as an earnest thereof, enjoy the sense of God's love, peace of conscience, joy in the Holy Ghost, and hope of glory; as, on the contrary, sense of God's revenging wrath, horror of conscience, and a

fearful expectation of judgment, are to the wicked the beginning of their torments which they shall endure after death.

Q. 84. *Shall all men die?*
A. Death being threatened as the wages of sin, it is appointed unto all men once to die; for that all have sinned.

Q. 85. *Death being the wages of sin, why are not the righteous delivered from death, seeing all their sins are forgiven in Christ?*
A. The righteous shall be delivered from death itself at the last day, and even in death are delivered from the sting and curse of it; so that, although they die, yet it is out of God's love, to free them perfectly from sin and misery, and to make them capable of further communion with Christ in glory, which they then enter upon.

Q. 86. *What is the communion in glory with Christ which the members of the invisible church enjoy immediately after death?*
A. The communion in glory with Christ which the members of the invisible church enjoy immediately after death, is, in that their souls are then made perfect in holiness, and received into the highest heavens, where they behold the face of God in light and glory, waiting for the full redemption of their bodies, which even in death continue united to Christ, and rest in their graves as in their beds, till at the last day they be again united to their souls. Whereas the souls of the wicked are at their death cast into hell, where they remain in torments and utter darkness, and their bodies kept in their graves, as in their prisons, till the resurrection and judgment of the great day.

Q. 87. *What are we to believe concerning the resurrection?*
A. We are to believe that at the last day there shall be a general resurrection of the dead, both of the just and unjust: when they that are then found alive shall in a moment be changed; and the selfsame bodies of the dead which were laid in the grave, being then again united to their souls forever, shall be raised up by the power of Christ. The bodies of the just, by the Spirit of Christ, and by virtue of his resurrection as their head, shall be raised in power, spiritual, incorruptible, and made like to his glorious body; and the bodies of the wicked shall be raised up in dishonor by him, as an offended judge.

Q. 88. *What shall immediately follow after the resurrection?*
A. Immediately after the resurrection shall follow the general and final judgment of angels and men; the day and hour whereof no man knoweth, that all may watch and pray, and be ever ready for the coming of the Lord.

Q. 89. *What shall be done to the wicked at the day of judgment?*
A. At the day of judgment, the wicked shall be set on Christ's left hand, and, upon clear evidence, and full conviction of their own consciences, shall have the fearful but just sentence of condemnation pronounced against them; and thereupon shall be cast out from the favorable presence of God, and the glorious fellowship with Christ, his saints, and all his holy angels, into hell, to be punished with unspeakable torments, both of body and soul, with the devil and his angels forever.

Q. 90. *What shall be done to the righteous at the day of judgment?*
A. At the day of judgment, the righteous, being caught up to Christ in the clouds, shall be set on his right hand, and there openly acknowledged and acquitted, shall join with him in the judging of reprobate angels and men, and shall be received into heaven, where they shall be fully and forever freed from all sin and misery; filled with inconceivable joys, made perfectly holy and happy both in body and soul, in the company of innumerable saints and holy angels, but especially in the immediate vision and fruition of God the Father, of our Lord Jesus Christ, and of the Holy Spirit, to all eternity. And this is the perfect and full communion which the members of the invisible church shall enjoy with Christ in glory, at the resurrection and day of judgment.

HAVING SEEN WHAT THE SCRIPTURES PRINCIPALLY TEACH US TO BELIEVE CONCERNING GOD, IT FOLLOWS TO CONSIDER WHAT THEY REQUIRE AS THE DUTY OF MAN

Q. 91. *What is the duty which God requireth of man?*
A. The duty which God requireth of man, is obedience to his revealed will.

Q. 92. *What did God first reveal unto man as the rule of his obedience?*
A. The rule of obedience revealed to Adam in the estate of innocence, and

to all mankind in him, besides a special command not to eat of the fruit of the tree of the knowledge of good and evil, was the moral law.

Q. 93. *What is the moral law?*
A. The moral law is the declaration of the will of God to mankind, directing and binding every one to personal, perfect, and perpetual conformity and obedience thereunto, in the frame and disposition of the whole man, soul, and body, and in performance of all those duties of holiness and righteousness which he oweth to God and man: promising life upon the fulfilling, and threatening death upon the breach of it.

Q. 94. *Is there any use of the moral law since the fall?*
A. Although no man, since the fall, can attain to righteousness and life by the moral law; yet there is great use thereof, as well common to all men, as peculiar either to the unregenerate, or the regenerate.

Q. 95. *Of what use is the moral law to all men?*
A. The moral law is of use to all men, to inform them of the holy nature and will of God, and of their duty, binding them to walk accordingly; to convince them of their disability to keep it, and of the sinful pollution of their nature, hearts, and lives: to humble them in the sense of their sin and misery, and thereby help them to a clearer sight of the need they have of Christ, and of the perfection of his obedience.

Q. 96. *What particular use is there of the moral law to unregenerate men?*
A. The moral law is of use to unregenerate men, to awaken their consciences to flee from the wrath to come, and to drive them to Christ; or, upon the continuance in the estate and way of sin, to leave them inexcusable, and under the curse thereof.

Q. 97. *What special use is there of the moral law to the regenerate?*
A. Although they that are regenerate, and believe in Christ, be delivered from the moral law as a covenant of works, so as thereby they are neither justified nor condemned; yet besides the general uses thereof common to them with all men, it is of special use, to show them how much they are bound to Christ for his fulfilling it, and enduring the curse thereof in their stead, and for their good; and thereby to provoke them to more

thankfulness, and to express the same in their greater care to conform themselves thereunto as the rule of their obedience.

Q. 98. *Where is the moral law summarily comprehended?*
A. The moral law is summarily comprehended in the Ten Commandments, which were delivered by the voice of God upon mount Sinai, and written by him in two tables of stone; and are recorded in the twentieth chapter of Exodus; the four first commandments containing our duty to God, and the other six our duty to man.

Q. 99. *What rules are to be observed for the right understanding of the Ten Commandments?*
A. For the right understanding of the Ten Commandments, these rules are to be observed:

1. That the law is perfect, and bindeth every one to full conformity in the whole man unto the righteousness thereof, and unto entire obedience forever; so as to require the utmost perfection of every duty, and to forbid the least degree of every sin.

2. That it is spiritual, and so reacheth the understanding, will, affections, and all other powers of the soul; as well as words, works, and gestures.

3. That one and the same thing, in divers respects, is required or forbidden in several commandments.

4. That as, where a duty is commanded, the contrary sin is forbidden; and, where a sin is forbidden, the contrary duty is commanded: so, where a promise is annexed, the contrary threatening is included; and, where a threatening is annexed, the contrary promise is included.

5. That what God forbids, is at no time to be done; what he commands, is always our duty; and yet every particular duty is not to be done at all times.

6. That under one sin or duty, all of the same kind are forbidden or commanded; together with all the causes, means, occasions, and appearances thereof, and provocations thereunto.

7. That what is forbidden or commanded to ourselves, we are bound, according to our places, to endeavor that it may be

avoided or performed by others, according to the duty of their places.

8. That in what is commanded to others, we are bound, according to our places and callings, to be helpful to them; and to take heed of partaking with others in what is forbidden them.

Q. 100. *What special things are we to consider in the Ten Commandments?*
A. We are to consider, in the Ten Commandments, the preface, the substance of the commandments themselves, and several reasons annexed to some of them, the more to enforce them.

Q. 101. *What is the preface to the Ten Commandments?*
A. The preface to the Ten Commandments is contained in these words, *I am the LORD thy God, which have brought thee out of the land of Egypt, out of the house of bondage.* Wherein God manifesteth his sovereignty, as being JEHOVAH, the eternal, immutable, and almighty God; having his being in and of himself, and giving being to all his words and works: and that he is a God in covenant, as with Israel of old, so with all his people; who, as he brought them out of their bondage in Egypt, so he delivereth us from our spiritual thraldom; and that therefore we are bound to take him for our God alone, and to keep all his commandments.

Q. 102. *What is the sum of the four commandments which contain our duty to God?*
A. The sum of the four commandments containing our duty to God, is, to love the Lord our God with all our heart, and with all our soul, and with all our strength, and with all our mind.

Q. 103. *Which is the first commandment?*
A. The first commandment is, *Thou shalt have no other gods before me.*

Q. 104. *What are the duties required in the first commandment?*
A. The duties required in the first commandment are, the knowing and acknowledging of God to be the only true God, and our God; and to worship and glorify him accordingly, by thinking, meditating, remembering, highly esteeming, honoring, adoring, choosing, loving, desiring, fearing of him; believing him; trusting, hoping, delighting, rejoicing in him; being zealous for him; calling upon him, giving all praise and thanks,

and yielding all obedience and submission to him with the whole man; being careful in all things to please him, and sorrowful when in anything he is offended; and walking humbly with him.

Q. 105. *What are the sins forbidden in the first commandment?*
A. The sins forbidden in the first commandment, are, atheism, in denying or not having a God; idolatry, in having or worshiping more gods than one, or any with or instead of the true God; the not having and avouching him for God, and our God; the omission or neglect of anything due to him, required in this commandment; ignorance, forgetfulness, misapprehensions, false opinions, unworthy and wicked thoughts of him; bold and curious searching into his secrets; all profaneness, hatred of God; self-love, self-seeking, and all other inordinate and immoderate setting of our mind, will, or affections upon other things, and taking them off from him in whole or in part; vain credulity, unbelief, heresy, misbelief, distrust, despair, incorrigibleness, and insensibleness under judgments, hardness of heart, pride, presumption, carnal security, tempting of God; using unlawful means, and trusting in lawful means; carnal delights and joys; corrupt, blind, and indiscreet zeal; lukewarmness, and deadness in the things of God; estranging ourselves, and apostatizing from God; praying, or giving any religious worship, to saints, angels, or any other creatures; all compacts and consulting with the devil, and hearkening to his suggestions; making men the lords of our faith and conscience; slighting and despising God and his commands; resisting and grieving of his Spirit, discontent and impatience at his dispensations, charging him foolishly for the evils he inflicts on us; and ascribing the praise of any good we either are, have, or can do, to fortune, idols, ourselves, or any other creature.

Q. 106. *What are we specially taught by these words, before me, in the first commandment?*
A. These words, *before me*, or before my face, in the first commandment, teach us, that God, who seeth all things, taketh special notice of, and is much displeased with, the sin of having any other God: that so it may be an argument to dissuade from it, and to aggravate it as a most impudent provocation: as also to persuade us to do as in his sight, whatever we do in his service.

Q. 107. *Which is the second commandment?*

A. The second commandment is, *Thou shalt not make unto thee any graven image, or any likeness of anything that is in heaven above, or that is in the earth beneath, or that is in the water under the earth. Thou shalt not bow down thyself to them, nor serve them: for I the LORD thy God am a jealous God, visiting the iniquity of the fathers upon the children unto the third and fourth generation of them that hate me; and shewing mercy unto thousands of them that love me, and keep my commandments.*

Q. 108. *What are the duties required in the second commandment?*

A. The duties required in the second commandment are, the receiving, observing, and keeping pure and entire, all such religious worship and ordinances as God hath instituted in his word; particularly prayer and thanksgiving in the name of Christ; the reading, preaching, and hearing of the word; the administration and receiving of the sacraments; church government and discipline; the ministry and maintenance thereof; religious fasting; swearing by the name of God, and vowing unto him: as also the disapproving, detesting, opposing, all false worship; and, according to each one's place and calling, removing it, and all monuments of idolatry.

Q. 109. *What sins are forbidden in the second commandment?*

A. The sins forbidden in the second commandment are, all devising, counseling, commanding, using, and any wise approving, any religious worship not instituted by God himself; the making any representation of God, of all or of any of the three persons, either inwardly in our mind, or outwardly in any kind of image or likeness of any creature whatsoever; all worshiping of it, or God in it or by it; the making of any representation of feigned deities, and all worship of them, or service belonging to them; all superstitious devices, corrupting the worship of God, adding to it, or taking from it, whether invented and taken up of ourselves, or received by tradition from others, though under the title of antiquity, custom, devotion, good intent, or any other pretense whatsoever; simony; sacrilege; all neglect, contempt, hindering, and opposing the worship and ordinances which God hath appointed.

Q. 110. *What are the reasons annexed to the second commandment, the more to enforce it?*

A. The reasons annexed to the second commandment, the more to enforce it, contained in these words, *For I the LORD thy God am a jealous God, visiting the iniquity of the fathers upon the children unto the third and fourth generation of them that hate me; and shewing mercy unto thousands of them that love me, and keep my commandments;* are, besides God's sovereignty over us, and propriety in us, his fervent zeal for his own worship, and his revengeful indignation against all false worship, as being a spiritual whoredom; accounting the breakers of this commandment such as hate him, and threatening to punish them unto divers generations; and esteeming the observers of it such as love him and keep his commandments, and promising mercy to them unto many generations.

Q. 111. *Which is the third commandment?*
A. The third commandment is, *Thou shalt not take the name of the LORD thy God in vain: for the LORD will not hold him guiltless that taketh his name in vain.*

Q. 112. *What is required in the third commandment?*
A. The third commandment requires, that the name of God, his titles, attributes, ordinances, the word, sacraments, prayer, oaths, vows, lots, his works, and whatsoever else there is whereby he makes himself known, be holily and reverently used in thought, meditation, word, and writing; by an holy profession, and answerable conversation, to the glory of God, and the good of ourselves, and others.

Q. 113. *What are the sins forbidden in the third commandment?*
A. The sins forbidden in the third commandment are, the not using of God's name as is required; and the abuse of it in an ignorant, vain, irreverent, profane, superstitious, or wicked mentioning or otherwise using his titles, attributes, ordinances, or works, by blasphemy, perjury; all sinful cursings, oaths, vows, and lots; violating of our oaths and vows, if lawful; and fulfilling them, if of things unlawful; murmuring and quarreling at, curious prying into, and misapplying of God's decrees and providences; misinterpreting, misapplying, or any way perverting the word, or any part of it, to profane jests, curious or unprofitable questions, vain janglings, or the maintaining of false doctrines; abusing it, the creatures, or

anything contained under the name of God, to charms, or sinful lusts and practices; the maligning, scorning, reviling, or any wise opposing of God's truth, grace, and ways; making profession of religion in hypocrisy, or for sinister ends; being ashamed of it, or a shame to it, by unconformable, unwise, unfruitful, and offensive walking, or backsliding from it.

Q. 114. *What reasons are annexed to the third commandment?*
A. The reasons annexed to the third commandment, in these words, *The LORD thy God*, and, *For the LORD will not hold him guiltless that taketh his name in vain*, are, because he is the Lord and our God, therefore his name is not to be profaned, or any way abused by us; especially because he will be so far from acquitting and sparing the transgressors of this commandment, as that he will not suffer them to escape his righteous judgment, albeit many such escape the censures and punishments of men.

Q. 115. *Which is the fourth commandment?*
A. The fourth commandment is, *Remember the sabbath day, to keep it holy. Six days shalt thou labor, and do all thy work; but the seventh day is the sabbath of the LORD thy God: in it thou shalt not do any work, thou, nor thy son, nor thy daughter, thy manservant, nor thy maidservant, nor thy cattle, nor thy stranger that is within thy gates. For in six days the LORD made heaven and earth, the sea, and all that in them is, and rested the seventh day: wherefore the LORD blessed the sabbath day, and hallowed it.*

Q. 116. *What is required in the fourth commandment?*
A. The fourth commandment requireth of all men the sanctifying or keeping holy to God such set times as he hath appointed in his word, expressly one whole day in seven; which was the seventh from the beginning of the world to the resurrection of Christ, and the first day of the week ever since, and so to continue to the end of the world; which is the Christian sabbath, and in the New Testament called *The Lord's Day.*

Q. 117. *How is the sabbath or the Lord's day to be sanctified?*
A. The sabbath or Lord's day is to be sanctified by an holy resting all the day, not only from such works as are at all times sinful, but even from such worldly employments and recreations as are on other days lawful; and making it our delight to spend the whole time (except so much of it

as is to be taken up in works of necessity and mercy) in the public and private exercises of God's worship: and, to that end, we are to prepare our hearts, and with such foresight, diligence, and moderation, to dispose and seasonably dispatch our worldly business, that we may be the more free and fit for the duties of that day.

Q. 118. *Why is the charge of keeping the sabbath more specially directed to governors of families, and other superiors?*
A. The charge of keeping the sabbath is more specially directed to governors of families, and other superiors, because they are bound not only to keep it themselves, but to see that it be observed by all those that are under their charge; and because they are prone ofttimes to hinder them by employments of their own.

Q. 119. *What are the sins forbidden in the fourth commandment?*
A. The sins forbidden in the fourth commandment are, all omissions of the duties required, all careless, negligent, and unprofitable performing of them, and being weary of them; all profaning the day by idleness, and doing that which is in itself sinful; and by all needless works, words, and thoughts, about our worldly employments and recreations.

Q. 120. *What are the reasons annexed to the fourth commandment, the more to enforce it?*
A. The reasons annexed to the fourth commandment, the more to enforce it, are taken from the equity of it, God allowing us six days of seven for our own affairs, and reserving but one for himself, in these words, *Six days shalt thou labor, and do all thy work:* from God's challenging a special propriety in that day, *The seventh day is the sabbath of the LORD thy God:* from the example of God, who *in six days . . . made heaven and earth, the sea, and all that in them is, and rested the seventh day:* and from that blessing which God put upon that day, not only in sanctifying it to be a day for his service, but in ordaining it to be a means of blessing to us in our sanctifying it; *Wherefore the LORD blessed the sabbath day, and hallowed it.*

Q. 121. *Why is the word* Remember *set in the beginning of the fourth commandment?*

A. The word *Remember* is set in the beginning of the fourth commandment, partly, because of the great benefit of remembering it, we being thereby helped in our preparation to keep it, and, in keeping it, better to keep all the rest of the commandments, and to continue a thankful remembrance of the two great benefits of creation and redemption, which contain a short abridgment of religion; and partly, because we are very ready to forget it, for that there is less light of nature for it, and yet it restraineth our natural liberty in things at other times lawful; that it cometh but once in seven days, and many worldly businesses come between, and too often take off our minds from thinking of it, either to prepare for it, or to sanctify it; and that Satan with his instruments much labor to blot out the glory, and even the memory of it, to bring in all irreligion and impiety.

Q. 122. *What is the sum of the six commandments which contain our duty to man?*
A. The sum of the six commandments which contain our duty to man, is, to love our neighbor as ourselves, and to do to others what we would have them do to us.

Q. 123. *Which is the fifth commandment?*
A. The fifth commandment is, *Honour thy father and thy mother: that thy days may be long upon the land which the Lord thy God giveth thee.*

Q. 124. *Who are meant by* father *and* mother *in the fifth commandment?*
A. By *father* and *mother*, in the fifth commandment, are meant, not only natural parents, but all superiors in age and gifts; and especially such as, by God's ordinance, are over us in place of authority, whether in family, church, or commonwealth.

Q. 125. *Why are superiors styled* Father *and* Mother?
A. Superiors are styled *Father* and *Mother*, both to teach them in all duties toward their inferiors, like natural parents, to express love and tenderness to them, according to their several relations; and to work inferiors to a greater willingness and cheerfulness in performing their duties to their superiors, as to their parents.

Q. 126. *What is the general scope of the fifth commandment?*
A. The general scope of the fifth commandment is, the performance of those duties which we mutually owe in our several relations, as inferiors, superiors or equals.

Q. 127. *What is the honor that inferiors owe to their superiors?*
A. The honor which inferiors owe to their superiors is, all due reverence in heart, word, and behavior; prayer and thanksgiving for them; imitation of their virtues and graces; willing obedience to their lawful commands and counsels; due submission to their corrections; fidelity to, defense, and maintenance of their persons and authority, according to their several ranks, and the nature of their places; bearing with their infirmities, and covering them in love, that so they may be an honor to them and to their government.

Q. 128. *What are the sins of inferiors against their superiors?*
A. The sins of inferiors against their superiors are, all neglect of the duties required toward them; envying at, contempt of, and rebellion against their persons and places, in their lawful counsels, commands, and corrections; cursing, mocking, and all such refractory and scandalous carriage, as proves a shame and dishonor to them and their government.

Q. 129. *What is required of superiors towards their inferiors?*
A. It is required of superiors, according to that power they receive from God, and that relation wherein they stand, to love, pray for, and bless their inferiors; to instruct, counsel, and admonish them; countenancing, commending, and rewarding such as do well; and discountenancing, reproving, and chastising such as do ill; protecting, and providing for them all things necessary for soul and body: and by grave, wise, holy, and exemplary carriage, to procure glory to God, honor to themselves, and so to preserve that authority which God hath put upon them.

Q. 130. *What are the sins of superiors?*
A. The sins of superiors are, besides the neglect of the duties required of them, an inordinate seeking of themselves, their own glory, ease, profit, or pleasure; commanding things unlawful, or not in the power of inferiors

to perform; counseling, encouraging, or favoring them in that which is evil; dissuading, discouraging, or discountenancing them in that which is good; correcting them unduly; careless exposing, or leaving them to wrong, temptation, and danger; provoking them to wrath; or any way dishonoring themselves, or lessening their authority, by an unjust, indiscreet, rigorous, or remiss behavior.

Q. 131. *What are the duties of equals?*
A. The duties of equals are, to regard the dignity and worth of each other, in giving honor to go one before another; and to rejoice in each others' gifts and advancement, as their own.

Q. 132. *What are the sins of equals?*
A. The sins of equals are, besides the neglect of the duties required, the undervaluing of the worth, envying the gifts, grieving at the advancement or prosperity one of another; and usurping preeminence one over another.

Q. 133. *What is the reason annexed to the fifth commandment, the more to enforce it?*
A. The reason annexed to the fifth commandment, in these words, *That thy days may be long upon the land which the LORD thy God giveth thee*, is an express promise of long life and prosperity, as far as it shall serve for God's glory and their own good, to all such as keep this commandment.

Q. 134. *Which is the sixth commandment?*
A. The sixth commandment is, *Thou shalt not kill.*

Q. 135. *What are the duties required in the sixth commandment?*
A. The duties required in the sixth commandment are, all careful studies, and lawful endeavors, to preserve the life of ourselves and others by resisting all thoughts and purposes, subduing all passions, and avoiding all occasions, temptations, and practices, which tend to the unjust taking away the life of any; by just defense thereof against violence, patient bearing of the hand of God, quietness of mind, cheerfulness of spirit; a sober use of meat, drink, physic, sleep, labor, and recreations; by charitable thoughts, love, compassion, meekness, gentleness, kindness; peaceable, mild and courteous speeches and behavior; forbearance, readiness to be

reconciled, patient bearing and forgiving of injuries, and requiting good for evil; comforting and succoring the distressed, and protecting and defending the innocent.

Q. 136. *What are the sins forbidden in the sixth commandment?*
A. The sins forbidden in the sixth commandment are, all taking away the life of ourselves, or of others, except in case of public justice, lawful war, or necessary defense; the neglecting or withdrawing the lawful and necessary means of preservation of life; sinful anger, hatred, envy, desire of revenge; all excessive passions, distracting cares; immoderate use of meat, drink, labor, and recreations; provoking words, oppression, quarreling, striking, wounding, and whatsoever else tends to the destruction of the life of any.

Q. 137. *Which is the seventh commandment?*
A. The seventh commandment is, *Thou shalt not commit adultery.*

Q. 138. *What are the duties required in the seventh commandment?*
A. The duties required in the seventh commandment are, chastity in body, mind, affections, words, and behavior; and the preservation of it in ourselves and others; watchfulness over the eyes and all the senses; temperance, keeping of chaste company, modesty in apparel; marriage by those that have not the gift of continency, conjugal love, and cohabitation; diligent labor in our callings; shunning all occasions of uncleanness, and resisting temptations thereunto.

Q. 139. *What are the sins forbidden in the seventh commandment?*
A. The sins forbidden in the seventh commandment, besides the neglect of the duties required, are, adultery, fornication, rape, incest, sodomy, and all unnatural lusts; all unclean imaginations, thoughts, purposes, and affections; all corrupt or filthy communications, or listening thereunto; wanton looks, impudent or light behavior, immodest apparel; prohibiting of lawful, and dispensing with unlawful marriages; allowing, tolerating, keeping of stews, and resorting to them; entangling vows of single life, undue delay of marriage; having more wives or husbands than one at the same time; unjust divorce, or desertion; idleness, gluttony, drunkenness, unchaste company; lascivious songs, books, pictures, dancings,

stage plays; and all other provocations to, or acts of uncleanness, either in ourselves or others.

Q. 140. *Which is the eighth commandment?*
A. The eighth commandment is, *Thou shalt not steal.*

Q. 141. *What are the duties required in the eighth commandment?*
A. The duties required in the eighth commandment are, truth, faithfulness, and justice in contracts and commerce between man and man; rendering to every one his due; restitution of goods unlawfully detained from the right owners thereof; giving and lending freely, according to our abilities, and the necessities of others; moderation of our judgments, wills, and affections concerning worldly goods; a provident care and study to get, keep, use, and dispose these things which are necessary and convenient for the sustentation of our nature, and suitable to our condition; a lawful calling, and diligence in it; frugality; avoiding unnecessary lawsuits, and suretiship, or other like engagements; and an endeavor, by all just and lawful means, to procure, preserve, and further the wealth and outward estate of others, as well as our own.

Q. 142. *What are the sins forbidden in the eighth commandment?*
A. The sins forbidden in the eighth commandment, besides the neglect of the duties required, are, theft, robbery, man-stealing, and receiving anything that is stolen; fraudulent dealing, false weights and measures, removing landmarks, injustice and unfaithfulness in contracts between man and man, or in matters of trust; oppression, extortion, usury, bribery, vexatious lawsuits, unjust enclosures and depredation; engrossing commodities to enhance the price; unlawful callings, and all other unjust or sinful ways of taking or withholding from our neighbor what belongs to him, or of enriching ourselves; covetousness; inordinate prizing and affecting worldly goods; distrustful and distracting cares and studies in getting, keeping, and using them; envying at the prosperity of others; as likewise idleness, prodigality, wasteful gaming; and all other ways whereby we do unduly prejudice our own outward estate, and defrauding ourselves of the due use and comfort of that estate which God hath given us.

Q. 143. *Which is the ninth commandment?*
A. The ninth commandment is, *Thou shalt not bear false witness against thy neighbour.*

Q. 144. *What are the duties required in the ninth commandment?*
A. The duties required in the ninth commandment are, the preserving and promoting of truth between man and man, and the good name of our neighbor, as well as our own; appearing and standing for the truth; and from the heart, sincerely, freely, clearly, and fully, speaking the truth, and only the truth, in matters of judgment and justice, and in all other things whatsoever; a charitable esteem of our neighbors; loving, desiring, and rejoicing in their good name; sorrowing for and covering of their infirmities; freely acknowledging of their gifts and graces, defending their innocency; a ready receiving of a good report, and unwillingness to admit of an evil report, concerning them; discouraging talebearers, flatterers, and slanderers; love and care of our own good name, and defending it when need requireth; keeping of lawful promises; studying and practicing of whatsoever things are true, honest, lovely, and of good report.

Q. 145. *What are the sins forbidden in the ninth commandment?*
A. The sins forbidden in the ninth commandment are, all prejudicing the truth, and the good name of our neighbors, as well as our own, especially in public judicature; giving false evidence, suborning false witnesses, wittingly appearing and pleading for an evil cause, outfacing and over-bearing the truth; passing unjust sentence, calling evil good, and good evil; rewarding the wicked according to the work of the righteous, and the righteous according to the work of the wicked; forgery, concealing the truth, undue silence in a just cause, and holding our peace when iniquity calleth for either a reproof from ourselves, or complaint to others; speaking the truth unseasonably, or maliciously to a wrong end, or perverting it to a wrong meaning, or in doubtful or equivocal expressions, to the prejudice of the truth or justice; speaking untruth, lying, slandering, backbiting, detracting, talebearing, whispering, scoffing, reviling, rash, harsh, and partial censuring; misconstructing intentions, words, and actions; flattering, vainglorious boasting, thinking or speaking too highly or too meanly of ourselves or others; denying the gifts and graces of God;

694 • TRUTHS WE CONFESS

aggravating smaller faults; hiding, excusing, or extenuating of sins, when called to a free confession; unnecessary discovering of infirmities; raising false rumors, receiving and countenancing evil reports, and stopping our ears against just defense; evil suspicion; envying or grieving at the deserved credit of any; endeavoring or desiring to impair it, rejoicing in their disgrace and infamy; scornful contempt, fond admiration; breach of lawful promises; neglecting such things as are of good report, and practicing, or not avoiding ourselves, or not hindering what we can in others, such things as procure an ill name.

Q. 146. *Which is the tenth commandment?*
A. The tenth commandment is, *Thou shalt not covet thy neighbour's house, thou shalt not covet thy neighbor's wife, nor his manservant, nor his maidservant, nor his ox, nor his ass, nor anything that is thy neighbour's.*

Q. 147. *What are the duties required in the tenth commandment?*
A. The duties required in the tenth commandment are, such a full contentment with our own condition, and such a charitable frame of the whole soul toward our neighbor, as that all our inward motions and affections touching him, tend unto, and further all that good which is his.

Q. 148. *What are the sins forbidden in the tenth commandment?*
A. The sins forbidden in the tenth commandment are, discontentment with our own estate; envying and grieving at the good of our neighbor, together with all inordinate motions and affections to anything that is his.

Q. 149. *Is any man able perfectly to keep the commandments of God?*
A. No man is able, either of himself, or by any grace received in this life, perfectly to keep the commandments of God; but doth daily break them in thought, word, and deed.

Q. 150. *Are all transgressions of the law of God equally heinous in themselves, and in the sight of God?*
A. All transgressions of the law are not equally heinous; but some sins in themselves, and by reason of several aggravations, are more heinous in the sight of God than others.

Q. 151. *What are those aggravations that make some sins more heinous than others?*

A. Sins receive their aggravations,

1. From the persons offending; if they be of riper age, greater experience or grace, eminent for profession, gifts, place, office, guides to others, and whose example is likely to be followed by others.

2. From the parties offended: if immediately against God, his attributes, and worship; against Christ, and his grace; the Holy Spirit, his witness, and workings; against superiors, men of eminency, and such as we stand especially related and engaged unto; against any of the saints, particularly weak brethren, the souls of them, or any other, and the common good of all or many.

3. From the nature and quality of the offence: if it be against the express letter of the law, break many commandments, contain in it many sins: if not only conceived in the heart, but breaks forth in words and actions, scandalize others, and admit of no reparation: if against means, mercies, judgments, light of nature, conviction of conscience, public or private admonition, censures of the church, civil punishments; and our prayers, purposes, promises, vows, covenants, and engagements to God or men: if done deliberately, willfully, presumptuously, impudently, boastingly, maliciously, frequently, obstinately, with delight, continuance, or relapsing after repentance.

4. From circumstances of time, and place: if on the Lord's day, or other times of divine worship; or immediately before or after these, or other helps to prevent or remedy such miscarriages: if in public, or in the presence of others, who are thereby likely to be provoked or defiled.

Q. 152. *What doth every sin deserve at the hands of God?*

A. Every sin, even the least, being against the sovereignty, goodness, and holiness of God, and against his righteous law, deserveth his wrath and curse, both in this life, and that which is to come; and cannot be expiated but by the blood of Christ.

Q. 153. *What doth God require of us, that we may escape his wrath and curse due to us by reason of the transgression of the law?*
A. That we may escape the wrath and curse of God due to us by reason of the transgression of the law, he requireth of us repentance toward God, and faith toward our Lord Jesus Christ, and the diligent use of the outward means whereby Christ communicates to us the benefits of his mediation.

Q. 154. *What are the outward means whereby Christ communicates to us the benefits of his mediation?*
A. The outward and ordinary means whereby Christ communicates to his church the benefits of his mediation, are all his ordinances; especially the word, sacraments, and prayer; all which are made effectual to the elect for their salvation.

Q. 155. *How is the word made effectual to salvation?*
A. The Spirit of God maketh the reading, but especially the preaching of the word, an effectual means of enlightening, convincing, and humbling sinners; of driving them out of themselves, and drawing them unto Christ; of conforming them to his image, and subduing them to his will; of strengthening them against temptations and corruptions; of building them up in grace, and establishing their hearts in holiness and comfort through faith unto salvation.

Q. 156. *Is the Word of God to be read by all?*
A. Although all are not to be permitted to read the word publicly to the congregation, yet all sorts of people are bound to read it apart by themselves, and with their families: to which end, the holy Scriptures are to be translated out of the original into vulgar languages.

Q. 157. *How is the Word of God to be read?*
A. The holy Scriptures are to be read with an high and reverent esteem of them; with a firm persuasion that they are the very Word of God, and that he only can enable us to understand them; with desire to know, believe, and obey the will of God revealed in them; with diligence, and attention to the matter and scope of them; with meditation, application, self-denial, and prayer.

Q. 158. *By whom is the Word of God to be preached?*
A. The Word of God is to be preached only by such as are sufficiently gifted, and also duly approved and called to that office.

Q. 159. *How is the Word of God to be preached by those that are called thereunto?*
A. They that are called to labor in the ministry of the word, are to preach sound doctrine, diligently, in season and out of season; plainly, not in the enticing words of man's wisdom, but in demonstration of the Spirit, and of power; faithfully, making known the whole counsel of God; wisely, applying themselves to the necessities and capacities of the hearers; zealously, with fervent love to God and the souls of his people; sincerely, aiming at his glory, and their conversion, edification, and salvation.

Q. 160. *What is required of those that hear the word preached?*
A. It is required of those that hear the word preached, that they attend upon it with diligence, preparation, and prayer; examine what they hear by the Scriptures; receive the truth with faith, love, meekness, and readiness of mind, as the Word of God; meditate, and confer of it; hide it in their hearts, and bring forth the fruit of it in their lives.

Q. 161. *How do the sacraments become effectual means of salvation?*
A. The sacraments become effectual means of salvation, not by any power in themselves, or any virtue derived from the piety or intention of him by whom they are administered, but only by the working of the Holy Ghost, and the blessing of Christ, by whom they are instituted.

Q. 162. *What is a sacrament?*
A. A sacrament is an holy ordinance instituted by Christ in his church, to signify, seal, and exhibit unto those that are within the covenant of grace, the benefits of his mediation; to strengthen and increase their faith, and all other graces; to oblige them to obedience; to testify and cherish their love and communion one with another; and to distinguish them from those that are without.

Q. 163. *What are the parts of a sacrament?*
A. The parts of a sacrament are two; the one an outward and sensible sign, used according to Christ's own appointment; the other an inward and spiritual grace thereby signified.

Q. 164. *How many sacraments hath Christ instituted in his church under the New Testament?*
A. Under the New Testament Christ hath instituted in his church only two sacraments, baptism and the Lord's supper.

Q. 165. *What is baptism?*
A. Baptism is a sacrament of the New Testament, wherein Christ hath ordained the washing with water in the name of the Father, and of the Son, and of the Holy Ghost, to be a sign and seal of ingrafting into himself, of remission of sins by his blood, and regeneration by his Spirit; of adoption, and resurrection unto everlasting life; and whereby the parties baptized are solemnly admitted into the visible church, and enter into an open and professed engagement to be wholly and only the Lord's.

Q. 166. *Unto whom is baptism to be administered?*
A. Baptism is not to be administered to any that are out of the visible church, and so strangers from the covenant of promise, till they profess their faith in Christ, and obedience to him, but infants descending from parents, either both, or but one of them, professing faith in Christ, and obedience to him, are in that respect within the covenant, and to be baptized.

Q. 167. *How is baptism to be improved by us?*
A. The needful but much neglected duty of improving our baptism, is to be performed by us all our life long, especially in the time of temptation, and when we are present at the administration of it to others; by serious and thankful consideration of the nature of it, and of the ends for which Christ instituted it, the privileges and benefits conferred and sealed thereby, and our solemn vow made therein; by being humbled for our sinful defilement, our falling short of, and walking contrary to, the grace of baptism, and our engagements; by growing up to assurance of pardon of sin, and of all other blessings sealed to us in that sacrament; by drawing strength from the death and resurrection of Christ, into whom we are baptized, for the mortifying of sin, and quickening of grace; and by endeavoring to live by faith, to have our conversation in holiness and righteousness, as those that have therein given up their names to Christ; and to walk in brotherly love, as being baptized by the same Spirit into one body.

Q. 168. *What is the Lord's supper?*

A. The Lord's supper is a sacrament of the New Testament, wherein, by giving and receiving bread and wine according to the appointment of Jesus Christ, his death is showed forth; and they that worthily communicate feed upon his body and blood, to their spiritual nourishment and growth in grace; have their union and communion with him confirmed; testify and renew their thankfulness, and engagement to God, and their mutual love and fellowship each with other, as members of the same mystical body.

Q. 169. *How hath Christ appointed bread and wine to be given and received in the sacrament of the Lord's supper?*

A. Christ hath appointed the ministers of his word, in the administration of this sacrament of the Lord's supper, to set apart the bread and wine from common use, by the word of institution, thanksgiving, and prayer; to take and break the bread, and to give both the bread and the wine to the communicants: who are, by the same appointment, to take and eat the bread, and to drink the wine, in thankful remembrance that the body of Christ was broken and given, and his blood shed, for them.

Q. 170. *How do they that worthily communicate in the Lord's supper feed upon the body and blood of Christ therein?*

A. As the body and blood of Christ are not corporally or carnally present in, with, or under the bread and wine in the Lord's supper, and yet are spiritually present to the faith of the receiver, no less truly and really than the elements themselves are to their outward senses; so they that worthily communicate in the sacrament of the Lord's supper, do therein feed upon the body and blood of Christ, not after a corporal and carnal, but in a spiritual manner; yet truly and really, while by faith they receive and apply unto themselves Christ crucified, and all the benefits of his death.

Q. 171. *How are they that receive the sacrament of the Lord's supper to prepare themselves before they come unto it?*

A. They that receive the sacrament of the Lord's supper are, before they come, to prepare themselves thereunto, by examining themselves of their being in Christ, of their sins and wants; of the truth and measure of their knowledge, faith, repentance; love to God and the brethren, charity to all men, forgiving those that have done them wrong; of their desires after Christ, and of their new obedience; and by renewing the exercise of these graces, by serious meditation, and fervent prayer.

Q. 172. *May one who doubteth of his being in Christ, or of his due preparation, come to the Lord's supper?*

A. One who doubteth of his being in Christ, or of his due preparation to the sacrament of the Lord's supper, may have true interest in Christ, though he be not yet assured thereof; and in God's account hath it, if he be duly affected with the apprehension of the want of it, and unfeignedly desires to be found in Christ, and to depart from iniquity: in which case (because promises are made, and this sacrament is appointed, for the relief even of weak and doubting Christians) he is to bewail his unbelief, and labor to have his doubts resolved; and, so doing, he may and ought to come to the Lord's supper, that he may be further strengthened.

Q. 173. *May any who profess the faith, and desire to come to the Lord's supper, be kept from it?*

A. Such as are found to be ignorant or scandalous, notwithstanding their profession of the faith, and desire to come to the Lord's supper, may and ought to be kept from that sacrament, by the power which Christ hath left in his church, until they receive instruction, and manifest their reformation.

Q. 174. *What is required of them that receive the sacrament of the Lord's supper in the time of the administration of it?*

A. It is required of them that receive the sacrament of the Lord's supper, that, during the time of the administration of it, with all holy reverence and attention they wait upon God in that ordinance, diligently observe the sacramental elements and actions, heedfully discern the Lord's body, and affectionately meditate on his death and sufferings, and thereby stir up themselves to a vigorous exercise of their graces; in judging themselves, and sorrowing for sin; in earnest hungering and thirsting after Christ, feeding on him by faith, receiving of his fullness, trusting in his merits, rejoicing in his love, giving thanks for his grace; in renewing of their covenant with God, and love to all the saints.

Q. 175. *What is the duty of Christians, after they have received the sacrament of the Lord's supper?*
A. The duty of Christians, after they have received the sacrament of the Lord's supper, is seriously to consider how they have behaved themselves therein, and with what success; if they find quickening and comfort, to bless God for it, beg the continuance of it, watch against relapses, fulfill their vows, and encourage themselves to a frequent attendance on that ordinance: but if they find no present benefit, more exactly to review their preparation to, and carriage at, the sacrament; in both which, if they can approve themselves to God and their own consciences, they are to wait for the fruit of it in due time: but, if they see they have failed in either, they are to be humbled, and to attend upon it afterwards with more care and diligence.

Q. 176. *Wherein do the sacraments of baptism and the Lord's supper agree?*
A. The sacraments of baptism and the Lord's supper agree, in that the author of both is God; the spiritual part of both is Christ and his benefits; both are seals of the same covenant, are to be dispensed by ministers of the gospel, and by none other; and to be continued in the church of Christ until his second coming.

Q. 177. *Wherein do the sacraments of baptism and the Lord's supper differ?*
A. The sacraments of baptism and the Lord's supper differ, in that baptism is to be administered but once, with water, to be a sign and seal of our regeneration and ingrafting into Christ, and that even to infants; whereas the Lord's supper is to be administered often, in the elements of bread and wine, to represent and exhibit Christ as spiritual nourishment to the soul, and to confirm our continuance and growth in him, and that only to such as are of years and ability to examine themselves.

Q. 178. *What is prayer?*
A. Prayer is an offering up of our desires unto God, in the name of Christ, by the help of his Spirit; with confession of our sins, and thankful acknowledgement of his mercies.

Q. 179. *Are we to pray unto God only?*
A. God only being able to search the hearts, hear the requests, pardon the sins, and fulfill the desires of all; and only to be believed in, and

worshiped with religious worship; prayer, which is a special part thereof, is to be made by all to him alone, and to none other.

Q. 180. *What is it to pray in the name of Christ?*
A. To pray in the name of Christ is, in obedience to his command, and in confidence on his promises, to ask mercy for his sake; not by bare mentioning of his name, but by drawing our encouragement to pray, and our boldness, strength, and hope of acceptance in prayer, from Christ and his mediation.

Q. 181. *Why are we to pray in the name of Christ?*
A. The sinfulness of man, and his distance from God by reason thereof, being so great, as that we can have no access into his presence without a mediator; and there being none in heaven or earth appointed to, or fit for, that glorious work but Christ alone, we are to pray in no other name but his only.

Q. 182. *How doth the Spirit help us to pray?*
A. We not knowing what to pray for as we ought, the Spirit helpeth our infirmities, by enabling us to understand both for whom, and what, and how prayer is to be made; and by working and quickening in our hearts (although not in all persons, nor at all times, in the same measure) those apprehensions, affections, and graces which are requisite for the right performance of that duty.

Q. 183. *For whom are we to pray?*
A. We are to pray for the whole church of Christ upon earth; for magistrates, and ministers; for ourselves, our brethren, yea, our enemies; and for all sorts of men living, or that shall live hereafter; but not for the dead, nor for those that are known to have sinned the sin unto death.

Q. 184. *For what things are we to pray?*
A. We are to pray for all things tending to the glory of God, the welfare of the church, our own or others' good; but not for anything that is unlawful.

Q. 185. *How are we to pray?*
A. We are to pray with an awful apprehension of the majesty of God, and deep sense of our own unworthiness, necessities, and sins; with

penitent, thankful, and enlarged hearts; with understanding, faith, sincerity, fervency, love, and perseverance, waiting upon him, with humble submission to his will.

Q. 186. *What rule hath God given for our direction in the duty of prayer?*
A. The whole Word of God is of use to direct us in the duty of prayer; but the special rule of direction is that form of prayer which our Savior Christ taught his disciples, commonly called *The Lord's prayer.*

Q. 187. *How is the Lord's prayer to be used?*
A. The Lord's prayer is not only for direction, as a pattern, according to which we are to make other prayers; but may also be used as a prayer, so that it be done with understanding, faith, reverence, and other graces necessary to the right performance of the duty of prayer.

Q. 188. *Of how many parts doth the Lord's prayer consist?*
A. The Lord's prayer consists of three parts; a preface, petitions, and a conclusion.

Q. 189. *What doth the preface of the Lord's prayer teach us?*
A. The preface of the Lord's prayer (contained in these words, *Our Father which art in heaven*) teacheth us, when we pray, to draw near to God with confidence of his fatherly goodness, and our interest therein; with reverence, and all other childlike dispositions, heavenly affections, and due apprehensions of his sovereign power, majesty, and gracious condescension: as also, to pray with and for others.

Q. 190. *What do we pray for in the first petition?*
A. In the first petition (which is, *Hallowed be thy name*), acknowledging the utter inability and indisposition that is in ourselves and all men to honor God aright, we pray, that God would by his grace enable and incline us and others to know, to acknowledge, and highly to esteem him, his titles, attributes, ordinances, word, works, and whatsoever he is pleased to make himself known by; and to glorify him in thought, word, and deed: that he would prevent and remove atheism, ignorance, idolatry, profaneness, and whatsoever is dishonorable to him; and, by his overruling providence, direct and dispose of all things to his own glory.

Q. 191. *What do we pray for in the second petition?*

A. In the second petition (which is, *Thy kingdom come*), acknowledging ourselves and all mankind to be by nature under the dominion of sin and Satan, we pray, that the kingdom of sin and Satan may be destroyed, the gospel propagated throughout the world, the Jews called, the fullness of the Gentiles brought in; the church furnished with all gospel officers and ordinances, purged from corruption, countenanced and maintained by the civil magistrate; that the ordinances of Christ may be purely dispensed, and made effectual to the converting of those that are yet in their sins, and the confirming, comforting, and building up of those that are already converted: that Christ would rule in our hearts here, and hasten the time of his second coming, and our reigning with him forever: and that he would be pleased so to exercise the kingdom of his power in all the world, as may best conduce to these ends.

Q. 192. *What do we pray for in the third petition?*

A. In the third petition (which is, *Thy will be done in earth, as it is in heaven*), acknowledging that by nature we and all men are not only utterly unable and unwilling to know and to do the will of God, but prone to rebel against his word, to repine and murmur against his providence, and wholly inclined to do the will of the flesh, and of the devil: we pray, that God would by his Spirit take away from ourselves and others all blindness, weakness, indisposedness, and perverseness of heart; and by his grace make us able and willing to know, do, and submit to his will in all things, with the like humility, cheerfulness, faithfulness, diligence, zeal, sincerity, and constancy, as the angels do in heaven.

Q. 193. *What do we pray for in the fourth petition?*

A. In the fourth petition (which is, *Give us this day our daily bread*), acknowledging that in Adam, and by our own sin, we have forfeited our right to all the outward blessings of this life, and deserve to be wholly deprived of them by God, and to have them cursed to us in the use of them; and that neither they of themselves are able to sustain us, nor we to merit, or by our own industry to procure them; but prone to desire, get, and use them unlawfully: we pray for ourselves and others, that both they and we, waiting upon the providence of God from day to day in the use of lawful means, may, of his free gift, and as to his fatherly wisdom shall seem best, enjoy a competent portion of them; and have the same continued and blessed unto us in our holy and comfortable use of them, and contentment in them; and be kept from all things that are contrary to our temporal support and comfort.

Q. 194. *What do we pray for in the fifth petition?*
A. In the fifth petition (which is, *Forgive us our debts, as we forgive our debtors*), acknowledging that we and all others are guilty both of original and actual sin, and thereby become debtors to the justice of God; and that neither we, nor any other creature, can make the least satisfaction for that debt: we pray for ourselves and others, that God of his free grace would, through the obedience and satisfaction of Christ, apprehended and applied by faith, acquit us both from the guilt and punishment of sin, accept us in his Beloved; continue his favor and grace to us, pardon our daily failings, and fill us with peace and joy, in giving us daily more and more assurance of forgiveness; which we are the rather emboldened to ask, and encouraged to expect, when we have this testimony in ourselves, that we from the heart forgive others their offenses.

Q. 195. *What do we pray for in the sixth petition?*
A. In the sixth petition (which is, *And lead us not into temptation, but deliver us from evil*), acknowledging that the most wise, righteous, and gracious God, for divers holy and just ends, may so order things, that we may be assaulted, foiled, and for a time led captive by temptations; that Satan, the world, and the flesh, are ready powerfully to draw us aside, and ensnare us; and that we, even after the pardon of our sins, by reason of our corruption, weakness, and want of watchfulness, are not only subject to be tempted, and forward to expose ourselves unto temptations, but also of ourselves unable and unwilling to resist them, to recover out of them, and to improve them; and worthy to be left under the power of them; we pray, that God would so overrule the world and all in it, subdue the flesh, and restrain Satan, order all things, bestow and bless all means of grace, and quicken us to watchfulness in the use of them, that we and all his people may by his providence be kept from being tempted to sin; or, if tempted, that by his Spirit we may be powerfully supported

and enabled to stand in the hour of temptation; or when fallen, raised again and recovered out of it, and have a sanctified use and improvement thereof: that our sanctification and salvation may be perfected, Satan trodden under our feet, and we fully freed from sin, temptation, and all evil, forever.

Q. 196. *What doth the conclusion of the Lord's prayer teach us?*
A. The conclusion of the Lord's prayer (which is, *For thine is the kingdom, and the power, and the glory, forever. Amen.*) teacheth us to enforce our petitions with arguments, which are to be taken, not from any worthiness in ourselves, or in any other creature, but from God; and with our prayers to join praises, ascribing to God alone eternal sovereignty, omnipotency, and glorious excellency; in regard whereof, as he is able and willing to help us, so we by faith are emboldened to plead with him that he would, and quietly to rely upon him, that he will fulfill our requests. And, to testify this our desire and assurance, we say, *Amen.*

APPENDIX 2

The Westminster Shorter Catechism

Q. 1. *What is the chief end of man?*
A. Man's chief end is to glorify God, and to enjoy him forever.

Q. 2. *What rule hath God given to direct us how we may glorify and enjoy him?*
A. The Word of God, which is contained in the Scriptures of the Old and New Testaments, is the only rule to direct us how we may glorify and enjoy him.

Q. 3. *What do the Scriptures principally teach?*
A. The Scriptures principally teach what man is to believe concerning God, and what duty God requires of man.

Q. 4. *What is God?*
A. God is a spirit, infinite, eternal, and unchangeable, in his being, wisdom, power, holiness, justice, goodness and truth.

Q. 5. *Are there more Gods than one?*
A. There is but one only, the living and true God.

Q. 6. *How many persons are there in the godhead?*
A. There are three persons in the Godhead; the Father, the Son, and the Holy Ghost; and these three are one God, the same in substance, equal in power and glory.

Q. 7. *What are the decrees of God?*
A. The decrees of God are his eternal purpose, according to the counsel of his will, whereby, for his own glory, he hath foreordained whatsoever comes to pass.

Q. 8. *How doth God execute his decrees?*
A. God executeth his decrees in the works of creation and providence.

Q. 9. *What is the work of creation?*
A. The work of creation is God's making all things of nothing, by the word of his power, in the space of six days, and all very good.

Q. 10. *How did God create man?*
A. God created man male and female, after his own image, in knowledge, righteousness and holiness, with dominion over the creatures.

Q. 11. *What are God's works of providence?*
A. God's works of providence are his most holy, wise and powerful preserving and governing all his creatures, and all their actions.

Q. 12. *What special act of providence did God exercise toward man in the estate wherein he was created?*
A. When God had created man, he entered into a covenant of life with him, upon condition of perfect obedience; forbidding him to eat of the tree of the knowledge of good and evil, upon pain of death.

Q. 13. *Did our first parents continue in the estate wherein they were created?*
A. Our first parents, being left to the freedom of their own will, fell from the estate wherein they were created, by sinning against God.

Q. 14. *What is sin?*
A. Sin is any want of conformity unto, or transgression of, the law of God.

Q. 15. *What was the sin whereby our first parents fell from the estate wherein they were created?*
A. The sin whereby our first parents fell from the estate wherein they were created was their eating the forbidden fruit.

Q. 16. *Did all mankind fall in Adam's first transgression?*
A. The covenant being made with Adam, not only for himself, but for his posterity; all mankind, descending from him by ordinary generation, sinned in him, and fell with him, in his first transgression.

Q. 17. *Into what estate did the fall bring mankind?*
A. The fall brought mankind into an estate of sin and misery.

Q. 18. *Wherein consists the sinfulness of that estate whereinto man fell?*
A. The sinfulness of that estate whereinto man fell consists in the guilt of Adam's first sin, the want of original righteousness, and the corruption of his whole nature, which is commonly called original sin; together with all actual transgressions which proceed from it.

Q. 19. *What is the misery of that estate whereinto man fell?*
A. All mankind by their fall lost communion with God, are under his wrath and curse, and so made liable to all miseries in this life, to death itself, and to the pains of hell forever.

Q. 20. *Did God leave all mankind to perish in the estate of sin and misery?*
A. God having, out of his mere good pleasure, from all eternity, elected some to everlasting life, did enter into a covenant of grace, to deliver them out of the estate of sin and misery, and to bring them into an estate of salvation by a redeemer.

Q. 21. *Who is the redeemer of God's elect?*
A. The only redeemer of God's elect is the Lord Jesus Christ, who, being the eternal Son of God, became man, and so was, and continueth to be, God and man in two distinct natures, and one person, forever.

Q. 22. *How did Christ, being the Son of God, become man?*
A. Christ, the Son of God, became man, by taking to himself a true body and a reasonable soul, being conceived by the power of the Holy Ghost in the womb of the virgin Mary, and born of her, yet without sin.

Q. 23. *What offices doth Christ execute as our redeemer?*
A. Christ, as our redeemer, executeth the offices of a prophet, of a priest, and of a king, both in his estate of humiliation and exaltation.

Q. 24. *How doth Christ execute the office of a prophet?*
A. Christ executeth the office of a prophet, in revealing to us, by his word and Spirit, the will of God for our salvation.

Q. 25. *How doth Christ execute the office of a priest?*
A. Christ executeth the office of a priest, in his once offering up of himself a sacrifice to satisfy divine justice, and reconcile us to God; and in making continual intercession for us.

Q. 26. *How doth Christ execute the office of a king?*
A. Christ executeth the office of a king, in subduing us to himself, in ruling and defending us, and in restraining and conquering all his and our enemies.

Q. 27. *Wherein did Christ's humiliation consist?*
A. Christ's humiliation consisted in his being born, and that in a low condition, made under the law, undergoing the miseries of this life, the wrath of God, and the cursed death of the cross; in being buried, and continuing under the power of death for a time.

Q. 28. *Wherein consisteth Christ's exaltation?*
A. Christ's exaltation consisteth in his rising again from the dead on the third day, in ascending up into heaven, in sitting at the right hand of God the Father, and in coming to judge the world at the last day.

Q. 29. *How are we made partakers of the redemption purchased by Christ?*
A. We are made partakers of the redemption purchased by Christ, by the effectual application of it to us by his Holy Spirit.

Q. 30. *How doth the Spirit apply to us the redemption purchased by Christ?*
A. The Spirit applieth to us the redemption purchased by Christ, by working faith in us, and thereby uniting us to Christ in our effectual calling.

Q. 31. *What is effectual calling?*
A. Effectual calling is the work of God's Spirit, whereby, convincing us of our sin and misery, enlightening our minds in the knowledge of Christ, and renewing our wills, he doth persuade and enable us to embrace Jesus Christ, freely offered to us in the gospel.

Q. 32. *What benefits do they that are effectually called partake of in this life?*
A. They that are effectually called do in this life partake of justification, adoption and sanctification, and the several benefits which in this life do either accompany or flow from them.

Q. 33. *What is justification?*
A. Justification is an act of God's free grace, wherein he pardoneth all our sins, and accepteth us as righteous in his sight, only for the righteousness of Christ imputed to us, and received by faith alone.

Q. 34. *What is adoption?*
A. Adoption is an act of God's free grace, whereby we are received into the number, and have a right to all the privileges of, the sons of God.

Q. 35. *What is sanctification?*
A. Sanctification is the work of God's free grace, whereby we are renewed in the whole man after the image of God, and are enabled more and more to die unto sin, and live unto righteousness.

Q. 36. *What are the benefits which in this life do accompany or flow from justification, adoption and sanctification?*
A. The benefits which in this life do accompany or flow from justification, adoption and sanctification, are, assurance of God's love, peace of conscience, joy in the Holy Ghost, increase of grace, and perseverance therein to the end.

Q. 37. *What benefits do believers receive from Christ at death?*
A. The souls of believers are at their death made perfect in holiness, and do immediately pass into glory; and their bodies, being still united to Christ, do rest in their graves till the resurrection.

Q. 38. *What benefits do believers receive from Christ at the resurrection?*
A. At the resurrection, believers being raised up in glory, shall be openly acknowledged and acquitted in the day of judgment, and made perfectly blessed in the full enjoying of God to all eternity.

Q. 39. *What is the duty which God requireth of man?*
A. The duty which God requireth of man is obedience to his revealed will.

Q. 40. *What did God at first reveal to man for the rule of his obedience?*
A. The rule which God at first revealed to man for his obedience was the moral law.

Q. 41. *Where is the moral law summarily comprehended?*
A. The moral law is summarily comprehended in the ten commandments.

Q. 42. *What is the sum of the ten commandments?*
A. The sum of the ten commandments is to love the Lord our God with

all our heart, with all our soul, with all our strength, and with all our mind; and our neighbor as ourselves.

Q. 43. *What is the preface to the ten commandments?*
A. The preface to the ten commandments is in these words, I am the Lord thy God, which have brought thee out of the land of Egypt, out of the house of bondage.

Q. 44. *What doth the preface to the ten commandments teach us?*
A. The preface to the ten commandments teacheth us that because God is the Lord, and our God, and redeemer, therefore we are bound to keep all his commandments.

Q. 45. *Which is the first commandment?*
A. The first commandment is, Thou shalt have no other gods before me.

Q. 46. *What is required in the first commandment?*
A. The first commandment requireth us to know and acknowledge God to be the only true God, and our God; and to worship and glorify him accordingly.

Q. 47. *What is forbidden in the first commandment?*
A. The first commandment forbiddeth the denying, or not worshiping and glorifying the true God as God, and our God; and the giving of that worship and glory to any other, which is due to him alone.

Q. 48. *What are we specially taught by these words* before me *in the first commandment?*
A. These words before me in the first commandment teach us that God, who seeth all things, taketh notice of, and is much displeased with, the sin of having any other god.

Q. 49. *Which is the second commandment?*
A. The second commandment is, Thou shalt not make unto thee any graven image, or any likeness of anything that is in heaven above, or that is in the earth beneath, or that is in the water under the earth: thou shalt not bow down thyself to them, nor serve them: for I the Lord thy God am a jealous God, visiting the iniquity of the fathers upon the children unto

the third and fourth generation of them that hate me; and showing mercy unto thousands of them that love me, and keep my commandments.

Q. 50. *What is required in the second commandment?*
A. The second commandment requireth the receiving, observing, and keeping pure and entire, all such religious worship and ordinances as God hath appointed in his word.

Q. 51. *What is forbidden in the second commandment?*
A. The second commandment forbiddeth the worshiping of God by images, or any other way not appointed in his word.

Q. 52. *What are the reasons annexed to the second commandment?*
A. The reasons annexed to the second commandment are, God's sovereignty over us, his propriety in us, and the zeal he hath to his own worship.

Q. 53. *Which is the third commandment?*
A. The third commandment is, Thou shalt not take the name of the Lord thy God in vain: for the Lord will not hold him guiltless that taketh his name in vain.

Q. 54. *What is required in the third commandment?*
A. The third commandment requireth the holy and reverent use of God's names, titles, attributes, ordinances, word and works.

Q. 55. *What is forbidden in the third commandment?*
A. The third commandment forbiddeth all profaning or abusing of anything whereby God maketh himself known.

Q. 56. *What is the reason annexed to the third commandment?*
A. The reason annexed to the third commandment is that however the breakers of this commandment may escape punishment from men, yet the Lord our God will not suffer them to escape his righteous judgment.

Q. 57. *Which is the fourth commandment?*
A. The fourth commandment is, Remember the sabbath day, to keep it holy. Six days shalt thou labor, and do all thy work: but the seventh day is the sabbath of the Lord thy God: in it thou shalt not do any work, thou,

nor thy son, nor thy daughter, thy manservant, nor thy maidservant, nor thy cattle, nor thy stranger that is within thy gates: for in six days the Lord made heaven and earth, the sea, and all that in them is, and rested the seventh day: wherefore the Lord blessed the sabbath day, and hallowed it.

Q. 58. *What is required in the fourth commandment?*
A. The fourth commandment requireth the keeping holy to God such set times as he hath appointed in his word; expressly one whole day in seven, to be a holy sabbath to himself.

Q. 59. *Which day of the seven hath God appointed to be the weekly sabbath?*
A. From the beginning of the world to the resurrection of Christ, God appointed the seventh day of the week to be the weekly sabbath; and the first day of the week ever since, to continue to the end of the world, which is the Christian sabbath.

Q. 60. *How is the sabbath to be sanctified?*
A. The sabbath is to be sanctified by a holy resting all that day, even from such worldly employments and recreations as are lawful on other days; and spending the whole time in the public and private exercises of God's worship, except so much as is to be taken up in the works of necessity and mercy.

Q. 61. *What is forbidden in the fourth commandment?*
A. The fourth commandment forbiddeth the omission or careless performance of the duties required, and the profaning the day by idleness, or doing that which is in itself sinful, or by unnecessary thoughts, words or works, about our worldly employments or recreations.

Q. 62. *What are the reasons annexed to the fourth commandment?*
A. The reasons annexed to the fourth commandment are, God's allowing us six days of the week for our own employments, his challenging a special propriety in the seventh, his own example, and his blessing the sabbath day.

Q. 63. *Which is the fifth commandment?*
A. The fifth commandment is, Honor thy father and thy mother; that thy days may be long upon the land which the Lord thy God giveth thee.

Q. 64. *What is required in the fifth commandment?*
A. The fifth commandment requireth the preserving the honor, and performing the duties, belonging to every one in their several places and relations, as superiors, inferiors or equals.

Q. 65. *What is forbidden in the fifth commandment?*
A. The fifth commandment forbiddeth the neglecting of, or doing anything against, the honor and duty which belongeth to every one in their several places and relations.

Q. 66. *What is the reason annexed to the fifth commandment?*
A. The reason annexed to the fifth commandment is a promise of long life and prosperity (as far as it shall serve for God's glory and their own good) to all such as keep this commandment.

Q. 67. *Which is the sixth commandment?*
A. The sixth commandment is, Thou shalt not kill.

Q. 68. *What is required in the sixth commandment?*
A. The sixth commandment requireth all lawful endeavors to preserve our own life, and the life of others.

Q. 69. *What is forbidden in the sixth commandment?*
A. The sixth commandment forbiddeth the taking away of our own life, or the life of our neighbor unjustly, or whatsoever tendeth thereunto.

Q. 70. *Which is the seventh commandment?*
A. The seventh commandment is, Thou shalt not commit adultery.

Q. 71. *What is required in the seventh commandment?*
A. The seventh commandment requireth the preservation of our own and our neighbor's chastity, in heart, speech and behavior.

Q. 72. *What is forbidden in the seventh commandment?*
A. The seventh commandment forbiddeth all unchaste thoughts, words and actions.

Q. 73. *Which is the eighth commandment?*
A. The eighth commandment is, Thou shalt not steal.

Q. 74. *What is required in the eighth commandment?*
A. The eighth commandment requireth the lawful procuring and further-ing the wealth and outward estate of ourselves and others.

Q. 75. *What is forbidden in the eighth commandment?*
A. The eighth commandment forbiddeth whatsoever doth or may unjustly hinder our own or our neighbor's wealth or outward estate.

Q. 76. *Which is the ninth commandment?*
A. The ninth commandment is, Thou shalt not bear false witness against thy neighbor.

Q. 77. *What is required in the ninth commandment?*
A. The ninth commandment requireth the maintaining and promoting of truth between man and man, and of our own and our neighbor's good name, especially in witness-bearing.

Q. 78. *What is forbidden in the ninth commandment?*
A. The ninth commandment forbiddeth whatsoever is prejudicial to truth, or injurious to our own or our neighbor's good name.

Q. 79. *Which is the tenth commandment?*
A. The tenth commandment is, Thou shalt not covet thy neighbor's house, thou shalt not covet thy neighbor's wife, nor his manservant, nor his maidservant, nor his ox, nor his ass, nor anything that is thy neighbor's.

Q. 80. *What is required in the tenth commandment?*
A. The tenth commandment requireth full contentment with our own condition, with a right and charitable frame of spirit toward our neigh-bor, and all that is his.

Q. 81. *What is forbidden in the tenth commandment?*
A. The tenth commandment forbiddeth all discontentment with our own estate, envying or grieving at the good of our neighbor, and all inordinate motions and affections to anything that is his.

Q. 82. *Is any man able perfectly to keep the commandments of God?*
A. No mere man since the fall is able in this life perfectly to keep the

commandments of God, but doth daily break them in thought, word and deed.

Q. 83. *Are all transgressions of the law equally heinous?*
A. Some sins in themselves, and by reason of several aggravations, are more heinous in the sight of God than others.

Q. 84. *What doth every sin deserve?*
A. Every sin deserveth God's wrath and curse, both in this life, and that which is to come.

Q. 85. *What doth God require of us that we may escape his wrath and curse due to us for sin?*
A. To escape the wrath and curse of God due to us for sin, God requireth of us faith in Jesus Christ, repentance unto life, with the diligent use of all the outward means whereby Christ communicateth to us the benefits of redemption.

Q. 86. *What is faith in Jesus Christ?*
A. Faith in Jesus Christ is a saving grace, whereby we receive and rest upon him alone for salvation, as he is offered to us in the gospel.

Q. 87. *What is repentance unto life?*
A. Repentance unto life is a saving grace, whereby a sinner, out of a true sense of his sin, and apprehension of the mercy of God in Christ, doth, with grief and hatred of his sin, turn from it unto God, with full purpose of, and endeavor after, new obedience.

Q. 88. *What are the outward and ordinary means whereby Christ communicateth to us the benefits of redemption?*
A. The outward and ordinary means whereby Christ communicateth to us the benefits of redemption, are his ordinances, especially the word, sacraments, and prayer; all which are made effectual to the elect for salvation.

Q. 89. *How is the word made effectual to salvation?*
A. The Spirit of God maketh the reading, but especially the preaching, of the word, an effectual means of convincing and converting sinners, and of building them up in holiness and comfort, through faith, unto salvation.

Q. 90. *How is the word to be read and heard, that it may become effectual to salvation?*

A. That the word may become effectual to salvation, we must attend thereunto with diligence, preparation and prayer; receive it with faith and love, lay it up in our hearts, and practice it in our lives.

Q. 91. *How do the sacraments become effectual means of salvation?*

A. The sacraments become effectual means of salvation, not from any virtue in them, or in him that doth administer them; but only by the blessing of Christ, and the working of his Spirit in them that by faith receive them.

Q. 92. *What is a sacrament?*

A. A sacrament is an holy ordinance instituted by Christ; wherein, by sensible signs, Christ, and the benefits of the new covenant, are represented, sealed, and applied to believers.

Q. 93. *Which are the sacraments of the New Testament?*

A. The sacraments of the New Testament are baptism and the Lord's supper.

Q. 94. *What is baptism?*

A. Baptism is a sacrament, wherein the washing with water in the name of the Father, and of the Son, and of the Holy Ghost, doth signify and seal our ingrafting into Christ, and partaking of the benefits of the covenant of grace, and our engagement to be the Lord's.

Q. 95. *To whom is baptism to be administered?*

A. Baptism is not to be administered to any that are out of the visible church, till they profess their faith in Christ, and obedience to him; but the infants of such as are members of the visible church are to be baptized.

Q. 96. *What is the Lord's supper?*

A. The Lord's supper is a sacrament, wherein, by giving and receiving bread and wine according to Christ's appointment, his death is showed forth; and the worthy receivers are, not after a corporal and carnal manner, but by faith, made partakers of his body and blood, with all his benefits, to their spiritual nourishment and growth in grace.

Q. 97. *What is required to the worthy receiving of the Lord's supper?*
A. It is required of them that would worthily partake of the Lord's supper, that they examine themselves of their knowledge to discern the Lord's body, of their faith to feed upon him, of their repentance, love, and new obedience; lest, coming unworthily, they eat and drink judgment to themselves.

Q. 98. *What is prayer?*
A. Prayer is an offering up of our desires unto God, for things agreeable to his will, in the name of Christ, with confession of our sins, and thankful acknowledgment of his mercies.

Q. 99. *What rule hath God given for our direction in prayer?*
A. The whole word of God is of use to direct us in prayer; but the special rule of direction is that form of prayer which Christ taught his disciples, commonly called the Lord's prayer.

Q. 100. *What doth the preface of the Lord's prayer teach us?*
A. The preface of the Lord's prayer, which is, Our Father which art in heaven, teacheth us to draw near to God with all holy reverence and confidence, as children to a father able and ready to help us; and that we should pray with and for others.

Q. 101. *What do we pray for in the first petition?*
A. In the first petition, which is, Hallowed be thy name, we pray that God would enable us and others to glorify him in all that whereby he maketh himself known; and that he would dispose all things to his own glory.

Q. 102. *What do we pray for in the second petition?*
A. In the second petition, which is, Thy kingdom come, we pray that Satan's kingdom may be destroyed; and that the kingdom of grace may be advanced, ourselves and others brought into it, and kept in it; and that the kingdom of glory may be hastened.

Q. 103. *What do we pray for in the third petition?*
A. In the third petition, which is, Thy will be done in earth, as it is in heaven, we pray that God, by his grace, would make us able and willing to know, obey and submit to his will in all things, as the angels do in heaven.

Q. 104. *What do we pray for in the fourth petition?*

A. In the fourth petition, which is, Give us this day our daily bread, we pray that of God's free gift we may receive a competent portion of the good things of this life, and enjoy his blessing with them.

Q. 105. *What do we pray for in the fifth petition?*

A. In the fifth petition, which is, And forgive us our debts, as we forgive our debtors, we pray that God, for Christ's sake, would freely pardon all our sins; which we are the rather encouraged to ask, because by his grace we are enabled from the heart to forgive others.

Q. 106. *What do we pray for in the sixth petition?*

A. In the sixth petition, which is, And lead us not into temptation, but deliver us from evil, we pray that God would either keep us from being tempted to sin, or support and deliver us when we are tempted.

Q. 107. *What doth the conclusion of the Lord's prayer teach us?*

A. The conclusion of the Lord's prayer, which is, For thine is the kingdom, and the power, and the glory, forever, Amen, teacheth us to take our encouragement in prayer from God only, and in our prayers to praise him, ascribing kingdom, power and glory to him. And in testimony of our desire, and assurance to be heard, we say, Amen.

SCRIPTURE INDEX

SUBJECT INDEX

moral law, 423–27, 429–30, 483–84
Mormons, 404
mortality, 644
mortal sin, 262, 267, 341, 343, 345, 372, 581, 583, 618
Mosaic covenant, 174
Moses, 214, 222, 254, 328–29, 400
motivation, 162
Mount St. Helens, 109
Muhammad, 194, 254
murder, 341
music, 476–77
Muslims, 70, 467, 544
mystery, 17, 132, 152, 565, 586
mysticism, 43, 243, 398, 553, 554, 628
myth, 170

Nadab, 464
narcissism, 336
Nathan, 129, 337, 379, 445, 507
naturalism, 119
natural law, 23, 124, 424
natural liberty, 232
natural revelation, 482
natural theology, 8
Nebuchadnezzar, 509, 524
necessary condition, 236, 266
necessity, 487, 490–91
necromancy, 87
negation, way of, 201
neighbor, 284, 541
Neoorthodoxy, 14, 29–30
Neoplatonism, 112, 553
Nero, 509
Nestorianism, 203, 204, 625
new covenant, 176, 178, 183, 312, 413, 431, 591, 592
new revelation, 21
New Testament, 180, 183, 185, 594
Newton, Isaac, 124
Niceno-Constantinopolitan Creed, 199
Nicodemus, 399–400
Noah, 330
Noahic covenant, 413, 485, 656
nonbeing, 100

Nonconformists, 506
nonelect, 228–29, 230
normative science, 421
notitia, 274–75, 322, 325
nuda signa, 570
Nunc Dimittis of Simeon, 148–49, 477
Nuremberg trials, 516

oath, 177
oaths, 493–503
obedience
    and assurance, 365, 408–9, 410
    and blessing, 647, 657, 658
    of Christ, 186
    civil, 511, 522
    and motivation, 162, 362
    as perfect, 179–81, 215–16
    and sanctification, 291
    and saving faith, 323–24
    and sin, 153, 233
Obergefell v. Hodges, 528
objectivity, 164
obligation, 473
offerings, 375
officers, 633
oikonomia, 586
oikos, 601
old covenant, 183, 312, 463, 592
Old Testament, 180, 183, 185, 195–96
Old Testament saints, 220–21
omnipotence, 43–45
omnipresence, 35, 203–4, 624, 627
omniscience, 35, 46, 59, 223, 561, 627
only begotten, 199
ontological, 67
open theism, 36, 50, 59
opposition, 365–66
order of salvation, 90–91, 296–98
ordinances, 188
ordinary means, 407
ordination, 583, 587
ordo salutis, 90–91, 296–98
Origen, 602
original sin, 158, 163, 250, 261, 318, 341, 367, 573

ABOUT THE AUTHOR

Dr. R.C. Sproul was founder of Ligonier Ministries, first minister of preaching and teaching at Saint Andrew's Chapel in Sanford, Fla., first president of Reformation Bible College, and executive editor of *Tabletalk* magazine. His radio program, *Renewing Your Mind,* is still broadcast daily on hundreds of radio stations around the world and can also be heard online. He was author of more than one hundred books, including *The Holiness of God, Chosen by God,* and *Everyone's a Theologian.* He was recognized throughout the world for his articulate defense of the inerrancy of Scripture and the need for God's people to stand with conviction upon His Word.